Public Women, Public Words

VOLUME II: 1900 TO 1960

PUBLIC WOMEN, PUBLIC WORDS

A Documentary History of American Feminism

Edited by Dawn Keetley & John Pettegrew

A MADISON HOUSE BOOK
ROWMAN & LITTLEFIELD PUBLISHERS, INC.
Lanham • Boulder • New York • Oxford

ROWMAN & LITTLEFIELD PUBLISHERS, INC.

Published in the United States of America
by Rowman & Littlefield Publishers, Inc.
A Member of the Rowman & Littlefield Publishing Group
4720 Boston Way, Lanham, Maryland 20706
www.rowmanlittlefield.com

12 Hid's Copse Road, Cumnor Hill, Oxford OX2 9JJ, England

Copyright © 2002 by Rowman & Littlefield Publishers, Inc.

All rights reserved. No part of this publication may be reproduced, stored in a retrieval system, or transmitted in any form or by any means, electronic, mechanical, photocopying, recording, or otherwise, without the prior permission of the publisher.

British Library Cataloguing in Publication Information Available

Library of Congress Cataloging-in-Publication Data

Keetley, Dawn Elizabeth, 1965–
  Public women, public words : a documentary history of American feminism / edited by Dawn Elizabeth Keetley and John Charles Pettegrew
      p. cm.
  Includes bibliographical references and index.
  ISBN 0-7425-2224-5 (alk. paper)
  1. Feminism—United States—History—18th century—sources. 2. Feminism—United States—History—19th century—sources. I. Pettegrew, John Charles, 1959– .
HQ1410 .K444 2002
305.42'0973—dc21   97-3580

Printed in the United States of America

∞™ The paper used in this publication meets the minimum requirements of American National Standard for Information Sciences—Permanence of Paper for Printed Library Materials, ANSI/NISO Z39.48-1992.

Contents

Preface and Acknowledgments ... xi

Introduction
Splitting Differences: Conceiving of American Feminism ... xiii

Part I
Varieties of Modern Feminism ... 1

I. *What Is Feminism?* ... 3

[1] Elizabeth Cady Stanton, "The Solitude of Self" (1892) ... 7
[2] Sofia M. Loebinger, "Suffragism Not Feminism" (1909) ... 11
[3] Emma Goldman, "The Tragedy of Woman's Emancipation" (1910) ... 12
[4] Winnifred Harper Cooley, "The Younger Suffragists" (1913) ... 16
[5] Ellen Glasgow, "Feminism" (1913) ... 19
[6] Rose Young, "What Is Feminism?" (1914) ... 22
[7] "Feminist Mass Meeting" (1914) ... 26
[8] Marie Jenney Howe, Louise W. Kneeland, Maud Thompson, and Frances G. Richards, "A Feminist Symposium" (1914) ... 29
[9] Inez Milholland, "The Liberation of a Sex" (1913) ... 34
[10] Florence Tuttle, "The Psychic Side of Feminism" (1915) ... 37
[11] Gertrude Atherton, "What Is Feminism?" (1916) ... 41

II. *Early Feminist Scholarship* ... 47

[12] Marion Talbot, "Present-Day Problems in the Education of Women" (1897) ... 51
[13] M. Carey Thomas, "Present Tendencies in Women's College and University Education" (1908) ... 55
[14] Helen Bradford Thompson, "The Mental Traits of Sex" (1903) ... 64
[15] Charlotte Perkins Gilman, "Politics and Warfare" (1910) ... 66
[16] Mary Roberts Coolidge, "Why Women Are So" (1912) ... 71
[17] Elsie Clews Parsons, "Sex" (1915) ... 78
[18] Jessie Taft, "The Woman Movement and the Larger Social Situation" (1915) ... 81
[19] Leta Hollingworth and Robert Lowie, "Science and Feminism" (1916) ... 90

III. Public Housekeeping — 96

[20] JANE ADDAMS, "The Subjective Value of Social Settlements" (1892) — 105

[21] JANE ADDAMS, "A Function of the Social Settlement" (1899) — 113

[22] JANE ADDAMS, "Women and Public Housekeeping" (1910) — 116

[23] FANNIE BARRIER WILLIAMS, "An Extension of the Conference Spirit" (1904) — 117

[24] MARGARET MURRAY WASHINGTON (MRS. BOOKER T.), "Social Improvement of the Plantation Woman" (1904) — 119

[25] FLORENCE KELLEY, "Aims and Principles of the Consumers' League" (1899) — 121

[26] MABEL POTTER DAGGETT, "Women: The Larger Housekeeping" (1912) — 126

[27] CLARA CAHILL PARK, "Helping the Widowed Mother to Keep a Home" (1913) — 132

[28] CHARLOTTE PERKINS GILMAN, "Maternity Benefits and Reformers" (1916) — 136

[29] ELEANOR TAYLOR, "Wages for Mothers" (1920) — 137

IV. The Fight for Woman Suffrage — 141

[30] CARRIE CHAPMAN CATT, ANNA HOWARD SHAW, ALICE STONE BLACKWELL, AND IDA HUSTED HARPER, "NAWSA Declaration of Principles" (1904) — 152

[31] CATHARINE WAUGH MCCULLOCH, "The Protective Value of the Ballot" (1900) — 153

[32] BELLE KEARNEY, MARY WOOD SWIFT, CHARLOTTE PERKINS GILMAN, HALA HAMMOND BUTT, AND CARRIE CHAPMAN CATT, "The South, Suffrage, and the Educational Requirement" (1903) — 156

[33] ADELLA HUNT LOGAN, "Woman Suffrage" (1905) — 163

[34] VIRGINIA B. LE ROY, "A Woman's Argument against Woman Suffrage" (1908) — 165

[35] JOSEPHINE CONGER-KANEKO, "What Will Woman Suffrage Convention Do for the Working Woman?" (1908) — 169

[36] NATIONAL PROGRESSIVE WOMAN SUFFRAGE UNION, "Constitution" (1909) — 170

[37] SOFIA M. LOEBINGER, "Suffragist and Suffragette: A Sure Cure for Anti-Suffragitis" (1909) — 171

[38] HARRIET LAIDLAW, "Organizing to Win by the Political District Plan" (1914) — 172

[39] LUCY BURNS, ALICE PAUL, MRS. JOHN ROGERS, HARRIOT STANTON BLATCH, FLORENCE KELLEY, AND MRS. BAYARD HILLES, "Proposed Plan of the Congressional Union" (1914) — 179

[40] LUCY BURNS, "The Susan B. Anthony Amendment" (1916) — 183

[41] "National Suffrage and the Race Problem" (1914) — 185

[42] ALICE STONE BLACKWELL, "The Threefold Menace" (1913) — 186

[43] MRS. PAUL LAURENCE DUNBAR, MARY B. TALBERT, CORALIE FRANKLIN COOK, CARRIE W. CLIFFORD, MARY FITZBUTLER WARING, NANNIE H. BURROUGHS, M. E. JACKSON, JOSEPHINE ST. PIERRE RUFFIN, MRS. A. W. HUNTON, MARIA L. BALDWIN, ANNA H. JONES, MRS. B. K. BRUCE, ELIZABETH LINDSAY DAVIS, MARY CHURCH TERRELL, AND LILLIAN A. TURNER, "Votes for Women" (1915) — 189

[44]	CARRIE CHAPMAN CATT, "The Crisis" (1916)	197
[45]	ANNA HOWARD SHAW, "My Position on the Different Policies of the National Association and the Congressional Union" (1916)	203
[46]	"The NAWSA Faces World War I" (1917)	205
[47]	ALVA BELMONT (MRS. OLIVER H. P.), "Excuses for White House Picketing" (1917)	208
[48]	DORIS STEVENS, "The Militant Campaign" (1919)	209
[49]	INEZ HAYNES IRWIN AND AVA DAVENPORT KENDALL, "The Strange Ladies" (1921)	212
[50]	CHARLOTTE PERKINS GILMAN, "Women Are Free at Last in All the Land" (1920)	215
[51]	ALVA BELMONT (MRS. OLIVER H. P.), HARRIOT STANTON BLATCH, FLORENCE KELLEY, MARY AUSTIN, CRYSTAL EASTMAN, AND MARY WHITE OVINGTON, "What Next?" (1920)	216

PART II
Feminist Politics Beyond Suffrage — 225

I. *Political Mobilization* — 227

[52]	MARGERY CURREY AND CARRIE CHAPMAN CATT, "The Victory Convention" (1920)	235
[53]	CRYSTAL EASTMAN, "Now We Can Begin" (1920)	238
[54]	CRYSTAL EASTMAN, "Alice Paul's Convention" (1921)	240
[55]	FREDA KIRCHWEY, "Alice Paul Pulls the Strings" (1921)	242
[56]	BELLE CASE LA FOLLETTE, "National Convention of the National Woman's Party" (1921)	245
[57]	MARGARET SANGER, "Woman and the New Race" (1920)	247
[58]	THE NATION, "The White Woman's Burden" (1921)	250
[59]	ELLA RUSH MURRAY, "The Woman's Party and the Violation of the 19th Amendment" (1921)	254
[60]	MRS. ROBERT M. PATTERSON, "The Negro Woman in Politics" (1922)	256
[61]	AMY JACQUES GARVEY, "Women as Leaders Nationally and Racially" (1925)	258
[62]	ANNE MARTIN, "Woman's Vote and Woman's Chains" (1922)	259
[63]	CORINNE (ROOSEVELT) ROBINSON, MOLLY LIFSHITZ, GLORIA SWANSON, ROSE SCHNEIDERMAN, MRS. R. F. DECALLIES, ROSE PASTOR STOKES, MARY P. SCULLY, AND FLORENCE E. ALLEN, "Is Woman Suffrage Failing?" (1924)	262
[64]	MARY R. BEARD, "A Test for the Modern Woman" (1932)	267
[65]	GENEVIEVE PARKHURST, "Is Feminism Dead?" (1935)	271
[66]	ALMA LUTZ, "That Much-Maligned Feminism" (1935)	276
[67]	SUSAN B. ANTHONY II, "We Women Throw Our Votes Away" (1948)	279

II. *Equality versus Difference* — 284

[68]	CHARLOTTE PERKINS GILMAN AND ELLEN KEY, "The Conflict between 'Human' and 'Female' Feminism" (1914)	289

[69] ZONA GALE, "What Women Won in Wisconsin" (1922) ... 290
[70] INEZ HAYNES IRWIN, "The Equal Rights Amendment: Why the Woman's Party Is for It" (1924) ... 293
[71] FLORENCE KELLEY, "The Equal Rights Amendment: Why Other Women's Groups Oppose It" (1924) ... 295
[72] ETHEL M. SMITH, "Working Women's Case against Equal Rights" (1924) ... 298
[73] RHETA CHILDE DORR, "Should There Be Labor Laws for Women? *No*" (1925) ... 302
[74] MARY ANDERSON, "Should There Be Labor Laws for Women? *Yes*" (1925) ... 306
[75] MARGARET MEAD, "Sex and Achievement" (1935) ... 312
[76] "The Women's Charter" (1937) ... 315
[77] EDITH HOUGHTON HOOKER, "Beware of 'Women's Charter'" (1937) ... 317
[78] ALMA LUTZ, FRIEDA S. MILLER, OLLIE A. RANDALL, AND MARGARET CULKIN BANNING, "How Can We Raise Women's Status? A Symposium" (1938) ... 318
[79] ALICE PAUL, HATTIE W. CARAWAY, MARY T. NORTON, MARGARET C. SMITH, LENA MADESIN PHILLIPS, BURNITA SHELTON MATTHEWS, PEARL BUCK, KATHARINE HEPBURN, GLADYS SWARTHOUT, MOLLIE MALONEY, AND MIRIAM E. OATMAN, "Pro: Should Congress Approve the Proposed Equal Rights Amendment to the Constitution?" (1943) ... 323
[80] CARRIE CHAPMAN CATT; MARGUERITE M. WELLS; NATIONAL COUNCIL OF CATHOLIC WOMEN; MRS. J. AUSTIN STONE; AMERICAN ASSOCIATION OF UNIVERSITY WOMEN; THE WOMEN'S TRADE UNION LEAGUE, AND CONGRESS OF WOMEN'S AUXILIARIES, C.I.O., "Con: Should Congress Approve the Proposed Equal Rights Amendment to the Constitution?" (1943) ... 330
[81] ETHEL ERNEST MURRELL, "An Equal Rights Amendment" (1952) ... 336
[82] MIRRA KOMAROVSKY, "Women in the Modern World" (1953) ... 338

III. *Work, Labor, and Socialism* ... 345

[83] ANNA A. MALEY, "The New York Shop Girl" (1908) ... 351
[84] THERESA SERBER MALKIEL, "The Diary of a Shirtwaist Striker" (1910) ... 353
[85] ROSE SCHNEIDERMAN, "The Triangle Fire" (1911/1967) ... 361
[86] MARY WHITE OVINGTON, "Socialism and the Feminist Movement" (1914) ... 363
[87] PAULINE M. NEWMAN, "Low Wages and White Slavery" (1912) ... 366
[88] MARY CHURCH TERRELL, "My Experience as a Clerk in a Government Department" (1917–1918/1940) ... 367
[89] MARY E. JACKSON, "The Colored Woman in Industry" (1918) ... 373
[90] ELIZABETH ROSS HAYNES, "Two Million Negro Women at Work" (1922) ... 377
[91] MARY McLEOD BETHUNE, "Faith That Moved a Dump Heap" (1941) ... 380
[92] NATIONAL WOMEN'S TRADE UNION LEAGUE, "Post-War Program Proposal" (1919) ... 386
[93] KATHARINE FISHER, "Women Workers and the A. F. of L." (1921) ... 388
[94] THE WOMEN'S BUREAU, U.S. DEPARTMENT OF LABOR, "What the Women's Bureau Has Accomplished" (1930) ... 391

[95] MARY VAN KLEECK, "Women and Machines" (1921) — 394

[96] MOTHER JONES, "You Don't Need a Vote to Raise Hell" (1925) — 400

[97] MERIDEL LE SUEUR, "Women on the Breadlines" (1932) — 404

[98] SABINA MARTINEZ, "Negro Women in Organization—Labor" (1941) — 408

[99] GRACE HUTCHINS, "Women under Capitalism" (1934) — 409

[100] REBECCA PITTS, "Women and Communism" (1935) — 416

[101] BETTY MILLARD, "Woman against Myth" (1947–1948) — 425

[102] UNITED ELECTRICAL, RADIO, AND MACHINE WORKERS OF AMERICA, "UE Fights for Women Workers" (1952) — 433

[103] HYDE PARK CHAPTER, CHICAGO WOMEN'S LIBERATION UNION, "Socialist Feminism: A Strategy for the Women's Movement" (1972) — 445

IV. War and Peace — 452

[104] WOMAN'S PEACE PARTY, "Program for Constructive Peace" (1915) — 456

[105] JANE ADDAMS, "Women and War" (1915) — 457

[106] PEARL S. BUCK, "Women and War" (1940) — 459

[107] ELEANOR ROOSEVELT, "Defense and Girls" (1941) — 467

[108] MRS. J. BORDEN HARRIMAN, "Women Enlist Now!" (1941) — 469

[109] MINNIE L. MAFFETT, M.D., "We Too Must Fight This War" (1942) — 470

[110] DOROTHY THOMPSON, "A Woman's Manifesto" (1947) — 475

[111] CHARLOTTA A. BASS, "You Can Vote for Peace" (1952) — 480

[112] SOPHIA WYATT, "One Day Strike for Peace" (1962) — 482

[113] KAREN KOONAN AND BOBBI CIECIORKA, "Anti-Draft and Women's Rights" (1967) — 484

[114] JILL SEVERN, "Women and Draft Resistance: Revolution in the Revolution" (1968) — 486

[115] BELLA ABZUG, "Testimony before the 1968 Platform Committee of the Democratic National Convention on Behalf of Women Strike for Peace" (1968) — 487

[116] WOMEN STRIKE FOR PEACE, "A Woman's Declaration of Liberation from Military Domination" (1970) — 490

[117] SHIRLEY MARGOLIN, AMY SWERDLOW, AND IRMA ZIGAS, "The Longest Day of the Longest War!" (1971) — 491

[118] MAUDE, "Women and War" (1970) — 491

[119] BREAD AND ROSES, "Speech at the Women's Anti-Imperialist Rally" (1970) — 492

[120] LINDA ALBAND AND STEVE REES, "Women and the Volunteer Armed Forces: First Report on a Rocky Romance" (1977) — 494

INDEX — 505

ABOUT THE EDITORS — 525

Preface and Acknowledgments

VOLUMES II AND III OF *Public Women, Public Words,* released five years after volume I, are different in form and intent. The greater number of documents for much shorter periods of time offer material proof of the proliferation of U.S. feminism during the twentieth century. And because of the diffusion of feminist thought and activism over the last one hundred years, volumes II and III make no real claims to comprehensiveness: a great many canonical feminist texts can be found in the pages that follow, but others are missing—due to copyright law, permissions costs, their accessibility in other volumes, and the fact that we decided early on that it would be impossible to include all the period's major works in two volumes.

In continuing our focus on the relationship between feminist thought and action, volumes II and III present documents that locate different institutions through which women's movements for equality and liberation occurred. While public writing and speech-making remain paramount, we also looked into newer media such as Hollywood, television, and the Internet. The result is a somewhat impressionistic account of U.S. feminism, with some important topics such as pornography, women's health and medicine, abortion, and women in law and religion given relatively little attention. Late-twentieth and early-twenty-first-century American feminism has been a dispersed and uncertain undertaking: volume III contributes an early effort toward its historicization.

A note on the text: obvious typographical errors in the original documents have been corrected, as in a misspelled word or name; for some of the older documents, footnotes have been omitted when their content was deemed unnecessary to understanding or appreciating the document.

The better part of this project's work was done at the University of Wisconsin, Madison, and we therefore want to thank the staffs at the University of Wisconsin Memorial Library and especially at the State Historical Society of Wisconsin Library and Special Collections. Also helpful were the librarians at Stanford University's Green Library. The speedy work of Pat Ward and others in Lehigh University's Inter Library Loan office proved invaluable to the completion of volumes II and III.

The latter volumes also benefited from the work of a number of Lehigh research assistants: Jonathan Hagel, Robert Nill, and Suzanne Shriver—thanks to all. Janet Walters of Lehigh's history department also helped considerably in handling these volumes' seemingly endless printing and correspondence. And John Lennon, Chris Robe, and Lisa Vetere contributed timely proofreading for volume II.

Mary Fiorenza's copyediting and intelligently close reading made significant improvements to the section introductions to volumes II and III.

Over the past nine years of work on *Public Women, Public Words,* several friends, colleagues, and teachers have offered help, advice, and inspiration. Thank you Paul Boyer, Ellen DuBois, Susan Stanford Friedman, Linda Gordon, Daniel Horowitz, William Shade, and Landon Storrs.

We are indebted to Gregory Britton, John Kaminski, and Madison House Publishers for picking up this project when it was little more than an outline on a napkin; after Rowman & Littlefield took over production of the last two volumes, Mary Carpenter, Janice Braunstein, and Laura Roberts have seen it through with great patience, efficiency, and consideration.

We have made a good faith effort to contact those who have rights to the documents printed here. We would like to thank everyone who responded and who granted permission.

INTRODUCTION

Splitting Differences: Conceiving of American Feminism

THIS COLLECTION OF DOCUMENTS traces the development of feminist thought from colonial North America through U.S. political and popular culture of the late twentieth century. A primary goal of the book is to offer an intellectual history of American feminism: that is, to examine not only the *conceptual* composition of the subject, but also to study how women have used ideas *practically* to gain power within specific historical circumstances. We understand feminism as a process, an activity, a social movement that has flourished through the polypragmatic expression of women's needs in public-political discourses and institutions. Feminism describes *enactments* of thought meant to improve social-sexual relations.

Overview

Many of the following documents reflect our interest in revealing the confluence between thought and action in American feminism. For example, Frances Wright—a founding figure of the early-nineteenth-century women's rights movement—not only wrote and lectured throughout the 1820s but also established the utopian community of Nashoba in Tennessee. Maintaining that "mankind must reasonably hesitate to receive as truths, theories, however ingenious, if unsupported by experiment," Wright instituted greater freedom for women at Nashoba than any other American community of its time, nullifying all marriage laws and further declaring that no woman entering the community would "forfeit individual rights and her independent existence." Insisting on "liberty" and "equality" for every individual, Wright infused immediate substance into these ideals by founding Nashoba.

A second principal goal of this collection is to represent the diversity of American feminism. Rather than rendering feminism as the battle of a homogeneous group of women in the name of a single cause such as suffrage or equal rights with men, we discuss feminism specific to various races, ethnicities, classes, regions, and sexualities and seek to illuminate the distinct interests that have sprung from these social groups. We document, in other words, a history that has been varied, multiple, and far from unified. But even while concentrating on the contested nature of American feminism, we do not want to rule out the possibility of locating shared concerns and common actions among women of different orientations. Our selection of texts attempts to establish a middle ground between arguments for, on one side, the dispersion of an infinite number of feminisms and, on the other side, the overarching unanimity of American feminism.

This effort to represent both the diversity and the common purposes of feminism is reinforced by our use of an eclectic mix of published documents, including speeches and manifestos; fiction and poetry; articles in radical, popular, and middle-brow magazines; underground newspapers; professional and academic journals; and courtroom transcripts and records of other official proceedings. Such published texts may be used historically to connect ideas and actions to specific groups of people. Attention to the author of a feminist tract, for example, places that woman and her thoughts within a certain time and place and suggests further the identities and mind-sets and circumstances of the women for whom she wrote. Close examination of a document, then, may reveal not only textual meaning regarding specific principles of feminist thought but also crucial information about the context of its production. We have tried to include documents—the 1794 commencement oration to the Young Ladies Academy of Philadelphia, for instance, or the 1971 preamble to *Asian Women*, a feminist newspaper published at the University of California, Berkeley—that help locate and detail women's institutional organization and political activism.

It should be emphasized that this collection is meant to chronicle the activism of different groups of American women. We are concerned with the interrelationship between ideas and the circumstances of social change, between words and political action. We have a bias for documents that place women in specific public contexts. Some texts provide official record of feminist activism, as in the trial transcript of the U.S. government's case against Susan B. Anthony for voting in the congressional election of 1872. This account of Anthony's willful defiance of federal law, along with her impassioned and insistent courtroom defense of the "fundamental privilege" of female citizenship, offer dramatic evidence of how feminists have publicly opposed state-sanctioned subordination of women.

Feminist activism, of course, has not been limited to legal proceedings; public opposition to women's subordination can be found in every one of the texts in this collection. In fact, we see literature itself as a form of activism. Even though writing and reading are often understood as acts of private or personal dimension, literature should also be seen, ideally, as something that happens between people. We hope readers of this book will consider the following documents as types of public speech. American feminism has developed in the form of argument; it has been produced with the self-conscious intention of persuasion. This includes feminist fiction, autobiography, and poetry—work, which, in its own way, has been written to change minds.

In contrast to the battle for legal rights, undertaken in more formal arenas such as the courtroom or the political convention, "creative" writing demonstrates how feminism has also been concerned with the subjective development of diverse women. These forms of feminist literature attempt to displace fixed ideas of the female self, conceptions that support women's subordinate position in the workplace, the family, and, more generally, in relationships with men and male-dominated structures of power. Finally, feminist fiction, autobiography, and poetry are historically valuable because they allow the reader to compare subjectivities among different racial, ethnic, and class-based groups of American women, reminding one that a woman's identity is determined through a number of factors, not just sexuality and gender.

Competing Definitions of Feminism

Despite the fact that no common identity exists among American women, there is philosophical support for the idea that in some ways women have been united by historical circumstance. There has been a type of "synchronicity" involved in the female experience of living in cultures and societies similarly influenced by masculine interests: social institutions, relations, and practices have, as the theorist Iris Marion Young describes, situated women "serially," placing them within sexually determined "limits and restraints"; "enforced heterosexuality," for instance, and the "sexual division of labor," work to "collectivize" women's conceptions of how they have been individually constrained by male-based systems of power. Young is quick to point out that this shared history of women is not the same thing as *feminism*, which she defines as an explicit attempt to improve women's conditions. Feminism is "a particularly reflexive impulse of women grouping," Young emphasizes, "women grouping in order to change or eliminate the structures that serialize them."[1] This distinction is crucial to understanding the specific scope and purpose of this book. It explains the difference between the history of American women and the history of American feminism. Feminist thought and activism—the organizing theme of the following collection of documents—are only a small (albeit crucial) part of the history of women in colonial North America and the United States. Both women's history and feminism depend on female subjectivity: the felt experience of being a woman. But another, essential, element of feminism is the deliberate creation of solidarity among women: it is a self-conscious effort to connect with others for the express purpose of more effectively challenging sexual inequality.

One problem, though, with defining feminism through the idea of solidarity is that the history of feminism, at least among women in the United States, is anything but one of unity. In both its theory and practice, American feminism has embraced exclusion, in some ways matching the social divisiveness found in U.S. history at large. African American female thinkers have made clear how racial bias has been written into nonblack feminist politics. White feminist thought, as bell hooks explains, is often produced "from a standpoint that ignores black women's experiences and thus reinforces white supremacist thinking by viewing white women's experiences as the universal standard for evaluating gender status and identity."[2] By concentrating purely on issues of sexism, many white feminists extend the prejudices of a dominant race, failing to realize their own implication in and to some extent responsibility for the subjugation of other women.

Consider Charlotte Perkins Gilman, who—as author of "The Yellow Wallpaper" (1892); *Women and Economics* (1898); her own monthly journal, *The Forerunner* (1909–1916); and voluminous other writings of social science, literary criticism, utopian fiction, autobiography, and poetry—is rightfully considered to be one of the most intellectually productive feminists in U.S. history. Gilman also adopted, however, some of the most conservative racial views of her day—prejudices that necessarily "color" the value of her feminist thought. Gilman openly described blacks as an "inferior" race, adding that their current "degenerative" status caused a drag on "human evolution," inevitably slowing the social progress of white America. In typical fashion, Gilman offered a comprehensive answer to the "negro problem," suggesting that the least evolved blacks be separated out of society and placed in a compulsory state-run corps until they could pass out of that group. This class of black internees would include, of course, a large number of "women," the same group Gilman insisted, in other contexts, needed to "set ourselves free" and whose independence determined overall "human development."[3] This contradiction in Gilman's thought is an extreme example of racism within feminism—of course not all white feminists have believed these things—but the point should by now be clear: if feminism involves the coming together of women (a process of "grouping"), then it needs to be realized that the social dynamics of that process have brought diversity as well as consensus, exclusion as well as solidarity, and opposition as well as unity.

The intellectual history of feminism—how the movement developed conceptually and theoretically, as a body of political thought, as an "ism"—is also largely a story of conflict and schism. Consider, for instance, the origins of the word "feminism" in the United States. As Nancy Cott has explained, "feminism" did not appear regularly in print or public speech until the 1910s, with common usage beginning in 1913.[4] And yet by 1914 one could read in the popular magazine *Current Opinion* that, in addition to the immediate rise of antifeminist thought, "[n]ow it appears that there are two emergent forces in the feminist movement itself." The article goes on to cite Charlotte Perkins Gilman in *The Forerunner*, who distinguished between "female feminists"—those who believe fundamental differences exist between the sexes and that women need the opportunity for full expression of their distinct attributes—and "human feminists"—those who minimize sexual difference and emphasize that women should be allowed to develop themselves as people, free from preexistent notions of proper feminine identity and behavior.

Notice how these two strands of feminism are, as *Current Opinion* recognized, "not only distinct but opposed."[5] The prefixes "human" and "female" do not signify variations of a common definition of feminism; they are, rather, set against each other as opposites, involving wholly different formulations of female self-identity and suggesting competing agendas for political mobilization. American feminism—before and after the word entered the national lexicon—has had no true "essence," except perhaps this one of opposition and duality. This point, as paradoxical as it is, needs to be considered in any intellectual history of American feminism: American feminist thought has developed through the creation of a series of mutually exclusive categories, usually organized in a series of either–or choices, or what some theorists would call "binary oppositions."

Keep this point in mind while studying the documents. To recognize the binate nature of feminist thought is to gain critical distance on the intellectual limitations of American feminism. This distancing is not necessarily in order to transcend these dualisms, or even to try always to move past them. If we return to Gilman's delineation of "female" and "human" feminists we can see how this binary (and its many variations) is ingrained in generations of American feminist discourse. In 1855, for instance, we find Elizabeth Cady Stanton debating Antoinette Brown in the women's journal *The Una* about the existence of "natural" differences between the sexes. And this same core issue—whether women should deem themselves not only equal to but also fundamentally the same as men—still constitutes the most basic division in early-twenty-first-century feminist theory. What Gilman called "human" feminism is commonly known today as "equality" feminism: it urges the full integration of women into society, demanding women's equal rights, equal work, equal pay, and, generally, equal status and treatment in private and public relations; equality feminism bases itself on an ideal of the autonomous human individual, aiming ultimately to erase most if not all distinctions based on sex. And what Gilman labeled "female" feminism is now known as "difference" feminism: it values women's unique perspective and envisions a society in which women are not subject to male-dominated institutions, values, and individualist-based standards of self-identity; instead of pushing for a sexually integrated society, difference feminism envisions an autonomous female world, one that ultimately separates the concepts of femininity and masculinity.

Attention to this and other categories within feminist thought, then, is crucial to understanding the intellectual history of American feminism: dualisms help us reconstruct ideas as they were thought at the time under study; they also help locate continuities in feminism, giving it a visible and "usable past." We can see something of a tradition, for instance, running from Anne Hutchinsons's battle to realize equal status of men within the Puritan church, through Mary Gove Nichols's strong, wide-ranging assertions in the 1850s of women's sexual freedom, up to Naomi Wolf's problematic lifestyle feminism or "power feminism," in which individualist-minded women succeed in corporate America and simply have "fun." We can also recognize a countertradition, from Catharine Beecher's mid-nineteenth-century insistence that women's power to effect social reform, including abolition of slavery, lay exclusively in her private feminine influence, to Camille Paglia's assertion of absolute differences between active male sexuality and a passive female sex principle.

We want to urge readers here, though, to guard against accepting the equality-difference split as a complete accounting of American feminism. Dualisms, while historically edifying, have always been far too schematic. The categorization of feminism into sets of either–or decisions obscures the full range of ways women have formulated their opposition to male-based systems of power. To draw mutually exclusive lines of feminist thought is to overlook how individual feminists have mixed and matched categories, refusing the confines of neatly delineated binaries.

Once again, the expansive thought of Charlotte Perkins Gilman provides a good example. Even though she recognized (and thereby promoted) the equality-difference split—and even though she identified with the equality or "human" side of the equation—much of her thought advanced the difference or "female" tradition of feminism. Gilman recognized distinctive female characteristics, as in her utopian novel *Herland* (1915), which presents a separate society of women who have a strong commitment to mothering and who have banished "masculine" values of competition.

In general terms, dualisms work against appreciation of the multiplicity of feminist perspectives. To assert an either–or vision of feminism not only lessens the ability to recognize those women who choose both (or neither) poles, but it can finally narrow that vision until only one side of the equation is illuminated. Most dualistic accounts of feminism privilege one viewpoint or the other as the essence of feminism, representing it as the most productive for contemporary feminism and, in less than objective hindsight, the one that has predominated historically. This is a pivotal point at which unnecessary exclusion begins in feminist theorizing. The act of defining "true feminism" involves subordinating those outside of the fold. While categorical systems of thought have made it easier to tell who is a feminist, they have also made it easier to identify who is *not* a feminist—a concern, in some feminist discourses, that eclipses attention to the different ways women subvert male power. Indeed, this is another problem of dualist thinking: one's politics are determined by and, ultimately, confined to what one opposes; one is defined, in other words, in the negative—by what one is not rather than what one is.

In light of the dangers of essentializing feminism, some women's historians and other scholars have fashioned an explicitly inclusive and self-consciously antitheoretical formulation of the movement. This effort begins with finding an "unrestrictive definition of feminism" itself, as Nancy Cott has written, one that "dispense[s] with totalizing, either/or questions (was she a feminist or not?)." One definition that Cott favors is offered by Linda Gordon: "Feminism is a critique of male supremacy, formed and offered in the light of a will to change it, which in turn assumes a conviction that it is changeable."[6] Gordon's definition has been central to our project, as it values action over essence, circumventing rigid, dualistic tests of true feminism. Moreover, this conception of feminism not only eliminates the need to choose one side or another of a binary opposition, it goes one step further in suggesting the benefit of holding equality-difference, individualism-community, and other dualisms in creative and productive tension. The conceptual umbrella of feminism is broad enough to contain diverse and even contradictory elements, allowing women to choose the ideas that best apply to the political exigencies of the time; they are thus not always constrained by an overarching and predetermined agenda that dictates choices without regard to context and consequences.

"Feminism" or "Feminisms"?

This broad-based, nonexclusive conceptualization of feminism is pluralist in nature: it is most concerned with practical details of activism, focusing on specific strategies of political organization and local sites of resistance.

But does feminism comprise nothing more or less than a sequence of local acts of resistance? As suggested above, some feminists (Iris Marion Young and Nancy Cott, for example) believe that a necessary part of the movement has been the recognition of "women acting as women"—that is, a self-consciousness of womanhood and of one's connection to that community. Who, though, are the "women" who have self-consciously acted as women? With what women have they tried to connect? And in the name of which "women" has the feminist movement acted? Historically, mainstream feminist thought has too often relied uncritically on the concept of "women" as a legitimating and cohesive category, while in practice including only a few social groups and racial types within its rubric. The utopian female intersubjectivity—women acting as, with, and for women—that has undergirded so much feminist discourse has in fact been imperfect, excluding and omitting large numbers of American women.

As articulated by middle-class white women, feminism has more often than not served the needs and interests of those women alone, women who have often been unable to recognize that the "sisterhood" of women extended also to women of color. For instance, both before and after the Civil War some women's rights activists debated whether or not they should work for the abolition of slavery and for the rights of black women during the Reconstruction—about whether or not, in other words, the rights of African American women were "woman's rights." A century later, Betty Friedan's *The Feminine Mystique* centered its analysis on the plight of upper-middle-class housewives, women confined to the home and a life of mindless leisure. Clearly not accounting for variables of race and class, Friedan omitted the majority of women who had neither the money nor the ideological impetus to leave the paid workforce and stay at home. To the extent that African American women—to name just one marginalized group—have been less than supportive of mainstream or white American feminism, it is because, as Pauline Terrelonge Stone has argued, "[r]acism . . . is so entrenched among many white women, that black females have been reluctant to admit that anything affecting the white female could also affect them."[7] Women of all races have both perceived and construed the category of "women" as a bar to collective action as much as they have seen it as the foundation of feminist collectivity.

In addition to disagreeing over the identity of feminist subjects, marginalized groups of women have also pointed out the propensity of the movement to fix exclusively on issues of sexual inequality. Deborah King describes this single-minded agenda as "monist": it illuminates only one form of domination, insisting that "social relations can be reduced to one factor" of gender.[8] For an illustrative case of monism in practice, consider how the debate over the extension of suffrage after the Civil War routinely asserted that either black men or white women could gain the vote—but not both. Black women found themselves torn between former antislavery organizations, which sought to extend the franchise to blacks (i.e., black men), and the woman's rights movement, which sought the vote for women (i.e., white women). In such an either–or situation, black women fell into a middle ground of nonidentity; neither black men nor white women, they were asked to support causes that did not include them.

The liminal situation of African American women reveals how the subjugation of most women has arisen not simply from an ingrained sexism but also from intersecting forms of oppression such as racism, heterosexism, and class inequality. Women who are oppressed by other systems as well as the sex/gender system are necessarily oppressed *differently* by sexism: a poor, black woman does not experience sexual inequality in the same way that a wealthy white woman does. As a consequence, women who are not white, middle class, and heterosexual, while not denying the importance of fighting sexism, have refused to grant that it is paramount. Many black feminists, for instance, will not make a choice between race or gender as the predominant category that structures their resistance, insisting on the need to hold both within the same worldview.

The phenomenon of monism among American feminists results from a failure to conceptualize adequately the relation between sexism and forms of oppression based on categories other than gender. When they have theorized the relation between race and feminism at all, white feminists have traditionally done so mostly through analogy, claiming that oppression on the grounds of race is structurally equal to oppression on the grounds of sex and is experienced in the same way. When

Mary Gove Nichols argued in 1857 that white women are "enslaved" by marriage laws as inexorably as the African American is by slavery, she implied not only that institutionalized racism and sexism are analogous but also that racism is secondary, serving merely to illuminate the horrors of sexism. In fact, Nichols adds, slavery is only "*nearly* parallel in its evils" to marriage. This method of integrating race into theories of feminism works to subsume race into gender—making race invisible at the very moment it is ostensibly being rendered visible.

Recently, feminist theorists of color have moved beyond the confines of the race-sex analogy, employing first the concept of the "double jeopardy" of race and sex oppression and then of the "triple jeopardy" of racism, sexism, and classism. Deborah King has called for a move even beyond the "triple jeopardy" model, which, while it does recognize the different kinds of discrimination women of color face, does so in an additive way: the effects of race and class are simply appended to the effects of sex. The model of triple jeopardy presupposes that each variable—race, sex, and class—has a "single, direct, and independent effect on status." King, on the other hand, thinks that the effects are not independent of each other, proposing an "interactive model," which she calls "multiple jeopardy." The term "multiple" incorporates "not only . . . several, simultaneous oppressions" but also the "multiplicative relationships among them as well. In other words," she continues, "the equivalent formulation is racism multiplied by sexism multiplied by classism."[9] This model recognizes the multiple linkages between different forms of structural inequality and also the "multiplicative"—as opposed to additive—oppressive effect that such linkages bring to bear on an individual.

Our collection—our historical vision of American feminism, as it were—is fundamentally shaped by the theorizing of women of color in terms of the multiple ways in which women have been oppressed and by the similarly multiple and contextualized positions from which women have acted to challenge their oppression. These positions are always gendered somehow—or they could not be considered "feminism"—but gender is not the only or even always the principal point of critique or site of resistance. For women of all races—including white—those disempowering systems that support male privilege often also support class privilege, heterosexual privilege, or white privilege. When one subverts a certain racist practice, then, one may also be subverting sexism at the same time. For instance, when Harriet Jacobs exposed in her autobiography the evils of slavery, she also exposed the sexual and economic power that white men had over both white and black women.

In light of the wholesale critique of the category "women" as it has historically been employed by the mainstream feminist movement, the word has lost its status as a unified concept fixed in a simple binary opposition to "men." It can best be understood, instead, as a dispersed, fluid, and contested category. This is not to say, however, that a woman's self-conscious belief that she is a part of the collective group "women" is no longer important to a definition of feminism. Philosopher Judith Butler has argued that it is precisely "the rifts among women over the content of the term ["women"] that ought to be affirmed as the ungrounded ground of feminist theory."[10] While continuing to act for "women," feminists should constantly question their own internal preconceptions and biases about what that entails.

This collection of documents demonstrates that there has indeed been a history of such self-questioning; it reveals both a lack of and a struggle toward consensus about who the "women" are in whose name feminism has spoken, written, and acted. These rifts need not be wholly divisive but can be, rather, the basis of a self-aware, flexible, and contingent community of feminist interests.

Women and the Public

Our conception of the public nature of American feminism is influenced by two key points. The first is the imbrication of public spheres of feminist activism with the private realm of women's lives. "The personal is political"—a stock phrase of mid- to late-twentieth-century feminism—still provides an important reminder that, in contrast to the traditionally masculine world of electoral politics, feminist politics has always concerned itself with so-called private issues of domestic labor, sexuality, family, and the like. Feminists have strived continually to transform personal power relations between men and women into the stuff of politics, taking what often occurs "behind closed doors" and exposing it to the vicissitudes of public analysis and opinion making. Integral to this understanding of a feminist public, as Sara Evans has pointed out, is the history of American women's voluntary associations.[11] Organizations such as moral reform and temperance societies have provided an essential link between the lived daily experience of women and opportunities for political change, collapsing the border between public and private worlds.

A second critical idea concerning women's public sphere involves the political value of those feminist institutions, discourses, and strategies that are separate from and opposed to dominant social and cultural forces. Women's integration into masculine sources of power and prestige—from labor unions to elite social clubs, from schools and colleges to the U.S. Congress—is certainly a central component of American feminism; but we also mean to emphasize the "contestatory function" of what Nancy Fraser calls "subaltern counterpublics"—"parallel discursive arenas where members of subordinated social groups invent and circulate counterdiscourses, which in turn permit them to formulate oppositional interpretations of their identities, interests, and needs." Counterpublics, as Fraser points out, have a dual purpose: they provide "spaces of withdrawal and regroupment" for those already located outside of the fold of power; at the same time, though, they "function as bases and training ground for agitational activities directed towards wider publics."[12] In as much as feminist counterpublics are separate enclaves, then, they also foster communication for the purpose of disseminating their oppositional message. Many of the feminist words and deeds represented in this collection originated from such public associations of activism and subversion—counterpublics of women created both to provide a separate source of strength and purity of feminist purpose but also meant to connect with and change the institutional powers that be.

This documentary history does not pretend to provide the impossible—a coherent, comprehensive narrative of integrative and "counterpublic" American feminism; but we do, however, want to close by tracing the various key institutions, both separatist and integrated, into which women have entered at specific historical periods.

Women's voices were first heard within the church, as they intermittently challenged traditional religious practices in the colonies. In particular, women questioned their place within the Puritan establishment, drawing for their dissent on more marginal religions, such as Quakerism, or on their own material experiences as women.

In the post-Revolutionary period, some women not only had available, for the first time, some kind of systematic formal education, but they also started to found separate female academies. The subsequent rise in women's literacy rates led at the end of the eighteenth century to the creation of a distinctly feminine literary culture, which included the first women's magazines and the first popular women's fiction—novels of seduction and sentiment.

Beginning in the late 1830s and 1840s, American women became active in a variety of reform movements, notably antislavery, from which the nineteenth-century women's rights movement grew. Central to this key development were woman's rights conventions, which proliferated in the middle of the century; while not formal institutions, the conventions established networks and communities of activist women and inculcated strategies of organization building—not the least of which was the art of public speaking. Drawing on organizational skills acquired in the early years of the women's rights movement, feminists in the second half of the nineteenth century created a number of women's institutions—from middle-class women's clubs to trade unions and suffrage associations.

While women had first gained entry into the medical profession, as physicians, in the 1840s, it was not until the 1870s and 1880s that women's encroachment into the previously male bastions of the elite professions such as the law and higher education became discernable.

With the dramatic increase in immigration and the rapid growth of an urban industrial social environment at the turn of the twentieth century, American feminism became markedly more diverse and complex. Along with mass immigration to the United States, a more regionally, racially, and ethnically diverse group of American women started to challenge forms of masculine dominance. This variegated feminist consciousness shaped itself during and in conjunction with the rise of modern mass culture and media, including widely circulated popular magazines and newspapers, many of which represented the interests of specific populations such as Chinese Americans in California or Jews in New York. White middle-class women made still greater inroads within the university, gaining a foothold in both white-collar professions and academia itself, hence adding to the burgeoning intellectual class in New York and other large cities.

While many historians continue to characterize the period between the passage of the Nineteenth Amendment (which, in 1920, gave all women the vote) and the 1960s as a time in which feminism remained dormant, we trace the continued activity of women within already established institutions such as trade unions, voluntary clubs, and professional associations. These four decades were a particularly active period for those women interested in women's labor rights, in part because of women's massive entry into the paid labor force during two world wars. The period is also marked by heightened socialist consciousness, and some feminists even attempted a union between feminist activism and communism.

The late 1960s saw what has been called the "second wave" of American feminism, a reemergent, broad-based, and coherent movement for women's "liberation" akin to that of the 1850s. Just as the "first wave" of American feminism had grown from the antislavery movement, the "second-wave" was historically interwoven with African Americans' struggle for civil rights. Along with the founding of mainstream organizations such as the National Organization for Women (NOW), the 1960s and 1970s also saw the large-scale emergence of women's small groups and collectives, each centered on experiences of oppression and communal responses including radical plans for liberation.

In the late twentieth and early twenty-first centuries, during a time of a "backlash" against feminism and a retrenchment of the movement, women continued to assert themselves in public life, attaining increasingly influential positions in business, the university, and in the government. Perhaps in part as a result of the success of some highly visible women, some heralded a "postfeminist" age, claiming that feminism is obsolete and should be either abandoned or radically revised. Feminism has thus become still more fragmented and contentious, producing internally conflicted and opposing views of itself and its potential role in women's lives. While the rhetoric of the 1990s put feminism in an unprecedented state of crisis, our book aims to show that such contention has not only always been present but is, perhaps, feminism's grounding premise. In other words, American feminism continues.

Notes

1. Iris Marion Young, "Gender as Seriality: Thinking about Women as a Social Collective," *Signs* 19 (Spring 1994), 728, 736.

2. bell hooks, "Black Students Who Reject Feminism," *The Chronicle of Higher Education*, July 13, 1994, A44.

3. Charlotte Perkins Gilman, "A Suggestion on the Negro Problem," originally published in *The American Journal of Sociology* 14 (July 1908), 78–85, reprinted in *Charlotte Perkins Gilman: A Nonfiction Reader*, ed. Larry Ceplair (New York: Columbia University Press, 1991), 176–83; Charlotte Perkins Gilman, "Our Androcentric Culture; or the Man-Made World," *The Forerunner* 1 (June 1910), 20.

4. Nancy F. Cott, *The Grounding of Modern Feminism* (New Haven: Yale University Press, 1987), 13.

5. "The Conflict between 'Human' and 'Female' Feminism," *Current Opinion* 56 (1914), 9.

6. Nancy F. Cott, "What's in a Name? The Limits of 'Social Feminism': or, Expanding the Vocabulary of Women's History," *Journal of American History* 76 (1989), 826; Linda Gordon, "What's New in Women's History," in *Feminist Studies/Critical Studies*, ed. Teresa De Lauretis (Bloomington: Indiana University Press, 1986), 29.

7. Pauline Terrelonge Stone, "Feminist Consciousness and Black Women," in *Women: A Feminist Perspective*, ed. Jo Freeman (Palo Alto: Mayfield, 1979), 583.

8. Deborah K. King, "Multiple Jeopardy, Multiple Consciousness: The Context of a Black Feminist Ideology," *Signs* 14 (1988), 51.

9. King, "Multiple Jeopardy," 46–47.

10. Judith Butler, "Contingent Foundations: Feminism and the Question of 'Postmodernism,'" in *Feminists Theorize the Political*, ed. Judith Butler and Joan Scott (New York: Routledge, 1992), 16.

11. Sara M. Evans, "Women's History and Political Theory: Toward a Feminist Approach to Public Life," in *Visible Women: New Essays On American Activism*, ed. Nancy A. Hewitt and Suzanne Lebstock (Urbana: University of Illinois Press, 1993), 119–39; also important is Mary P. Ryan, *Women in Public: Between Banners and Ballots, 1825–1880* (Baltimore: Johns Hopkins University Press, 1990).

12. Nancy Fraser, "Rethinking the Public Sphere: A Contribution to the Critique of Actually Existing Democracy," in *Between Borders: Pedagogy and the Politics of Cultural Studies*, ed. Henry A. Giroux and Peter McLaren (New York: Routledge, 1994), 84–85.

PART I

Varieties of Modern Feminism

I. What Is Feminism?

SOCIAL MOVEMENTS CAN BE ENERGIZED BY THE introduction of a new word or phrase. And so it was with the American women's movement when the word *feminism* came into common use around 1910. The second decade of the twentieth century saw a new intensity of activism for sexual equality, culminating in the ratification of the Nineteenth Amendment to the U.S. Constitution, which recognized women's right to vote. Far from creating unity of purpose, however, the emergence of the word *feminism* ushered in a multiplicity of definitions, creating a vogue in magazines and other publications to explain exactly what it meant. The origin of the term *feminism* lies in New York literary culture and among the young intellectuals of Greenwich Village, where sexual liberation and general opposition to middle-class convention injected a radical bohemian quality into the women's movement.

In addition to its powerful countercultural appeal to radicalism and newness, the twentieth-century feminist effort to define an independent sense of female self drew support from the earlier natural rights tradition so crucial to the mid-nineteenth-century women's conventions and the initial push for the ballot. As historian Ellen Carol DuBois has pointed out, Elizabeth Cady Stanton and her monumental speech "The Solitude of Self" (1892) can be seen as a bridge between the political philosophy of individual rights and the more modern feminist interest in the psychology of the inner existential self. Although possessive individualism had always been a white male ideal, stemming from claims to autonomy in the workplace and the privilege of citizenship, Stanton goes farther and insists on the "birthright of self-sovereignty" for women. Since external structures and relations are contingent, undependable, and to be shared, Stanton argues not only for the necessity of woman's political independence, but also for the independence of her core self. While suffrage and economic independence are rudimentary, true evolution of the self also means freedom to throw off the feminine roles of wife and mother and to draw from inner spiritual resources. Stanton delivered one of her last major speeches, "The Solitude of Self," at a suffrage convention and before the U.S. House and Senate Judiciary Committees. It remains among the most poignant and eloquent affirmations of individual autonomy in modern American letters.

Throughout the twentieth century the word *feminism* has been used in the negative, as an all-inclusive label for what is wrong with women's activism. Aggressive demands for sexual equality and female independence have galvanized modern American conservatism and its promotion of social order and tradition. The essay "Suffragism Not Feminism" (1909) provides an early example of this dynamic. Sofia M. Loebinger employs the word *feminism* to mark what is beyond the pale of reasonable, productive changes in the balance of power between women and men. In ostensibly responding to the excesses of feminism, Loebinger actually stakes out her own interest in maintaining sexual differences, including the recognition of male superiority.

Russian-born Emma Goldman—pacifist, anarchist, free love and birth control advocate, and one of the most dynamic thinkers in early-twentieth-century America—summarizes her views on feminism in "The Tragedy of Woman's Emancipation" (1910). Unlike Loebinger, Goldman is unimpressed with suffragism: as an anarchist, she does not put much stock in conventional processes of representative government. In addition, she criticizes young women's narrow-minded self-involved detachment from the rewards of heterosexual romantic love and childbirth. Goldman is not alone, however, in urging the balancing of individual and society. The overall goal, as she puts it, is "to be one's self and yet in oneness with others." In 1917 the U.S. government deported Goldman for her outspoken opposition to military conscription.

The word *feminism* has also been used to mark a generational break among activists in the women's movement. In "The Younger Suffragists" (1913), Winnifred Harper Cooley offers a classic formulation of this generationalism by distinguishing herself and the "younger feminists" from the "older suffragists" and their idea that gaining the ballot will change the world for women. For the younger, more radical feminists, suffrage is only a means to the end of "complete social revolution" and the realization of women's economic independence and full civic participation; sexual freedom is also central to feminism, as Cooley calls for eradicating the double standard that holds women to an unrealistic ideal of constraint and virtue while men follow their more natural impulses. Woman's rights activists criticized the sexual double standard throughout the nineteenth century, but their interest was in holding men to the same degree of virtue to which women were supposed to adhere. Cooley epitomizes the modern revolution in sexual norms, casting rules that mandate purity as artificial and unrealistic for either sex. Invoking a new generation of feminists became an invaluable rhetorical strategy. It helped create unity out of disparate interests; it raised consciousness of a collective destiny and a common historical role—crucial elements in any successful social movement.

The intellectual history of feminism includes increasing attention to the artificiality of traditional roles and identities for women and analyzing how ideals of femininity are ideologically constructed as natural and unchanging. A leading facet of this analysis has been delineation of the ways that male-authored fiction and poetry manipulate femininity into something that serves masculine interests. In her book review "Feminism" (1913), Southern-born best-selling novelist, essayist, and short-story writer Ellen Glasgow warns that a woman's conventional reading habits produce "false thinking about herself." She urges resistance through the cultivation of "personality"—to her mind the primary goal of feminism. In the early twentieth century the word *personality* was without its latter-day connotation of superficiality, the product of a commercially driven therapeutic culture; rather, *personality* connoted the flowering of the self, the full development of subjectivity, free from institutional constraints and all preexistent psychological forms and social expectations. *Personality* became a watchword for pre–World War I cultural radicalism.

The importance of the concept of personality to women's independence is elaborated in Rose Young's article "What Is Feminism?" (1914), one of the most thorough and accomplished discussions of feminist theory during these early years. Like many of her fellow feminists, Young stresses the pleasures of a highly differentiated subjectivity, adding that the very act of self-definition could be the most liberating process for women. What makes this text so valuable, though, is its clear equation between the individual and society, the crucial link between self-development and the advancement of women as a social group. Young never separates woman from community. She balances her imperative "know yourself" with a basic concern that women maintain engagement with larger social spheres, and she goes on to contrast this integrated understanding of feminism to male countercultural rebellion that involves the "flaunting" of things social—what amounts to a type of narcissism served by a formulaic split between self-exploration and political commitment. The appearance of this essay in the popular women's magazine *Good Housekeeping* belies the notion that feminism was only discussed among radical bohemians. Indeed, Young begins the essay with the impression that interest in feminism is spreading throughout the country.

As Young's article illustrates, feminism extended itself via the ever-widening circulation of middlebrow literature—a channel that reached hundreds of thousands of women in a single publication. Another key medium for advancing feminist messages was the large public meeting, a leading example of which is the two-night gathering in February of 1914 at the People's Institute in Greenwich Village's Cooper Union. This "Feminist Mass Meeting" was organized by Marie Jenney Howe, who founded in 1912 the Heterodoxy Club, a women's group devoted (as its name suggests) to feminism by way of counterculture, the self-conscious opposition to convention. Many of the speakers at Cooper Union were members of the Heterodoxy Club, including Rose Young, Charlotte Perkins Gilman, Crystal Eastman Benedict, and Frances Perkins. Men also participated in the first meeting. These included Floyd Dell and Max Eastman (Crystal's older brother), both editors of the radical journal *The Masses,* which was quite effective in disseminating feminist ideas. The fact that *The New York Times* paid attention to these gatherings (in its articles "Talk on Feminism Stirs a Great Crowd" and "Feminists Ask for an Equal Chance") suggests a broad-based interest in the meaning of feminism.

"A Feminist Symposium" (1914) in *The New Review* adds political dimension to the early-twentieth-century definition of this social movement. In addition to Marie Jenney Howe's emphasis on psychological freedom and Frances Richards's trenchant critique of the antifeminist man, Louise Kneeland examines feminism's imbrication with socialism and how women need to work against capitalism as well as other institutions of male dominance. Maud Thompson contributes to this formulation of socialist feminism by replying to the common male socialist claim that the movement for sex equality is a distraction to the real goal of freeing the working class: empowerment of the working class can never be fully realized, Thompson suggests, until women achieve equality, since they make up half of that social group. In response to the point that socialist activism can only counter sociological (as opposed to biological) sources of power, Thompson argues that innate sexual differences are minimal, while women are greatly hindered by man-made systems of subjugation.

The socialist-feminist Inez Milholland's article "The Liberation of a Sex" (1913) combines many preeminent components found in the emerging constitution of feminism: after appealing for unity among her younger generation of women, Milholland insists that feminism's future lies beyond gaining the vote and in disrupting the institutions of marriage and family, which consign women to a form of property: after assuring the readership that the matter is already being talked about openly, she insists that women must free themselves from the sexual double standard, which underlies female subservience to men; and finally, as in many other contemporary discussions of the topic, she assures men that, rather than inhibiting them, feminism will mean greater freedom for everyone. Before dying in 1916 at the age of thirty, Milholland enjoyed a very high profile among New York feminists. A lawyer, journalist, labor activist, suffragist, and member of the Heterodoxy Club, Milholland edited a new "Department for Women" for *McLure's Magazine* early in 1913 and then oversaw another series on feminism for which "The Liberation of a Sex" is an opening statement.

Many white American feminists of this period argued that expansion of woman's personal capacity and social responsibility would benefit the race as a whole. This appeal to the good of the race—that is, the Anglo-Saxon race—is based on the hierarchical polygynist schema of human progress, a conservative comparative view of social evolution that has each race passing through the stages of savagery, barbarism, and civilization. As used in Florence Tuttle's "The Psychic Side of Feminism" (1915), the success of the woman's movement is one way to assure the continued advancement and supremacy of white Anglo-Saxons—a growing concern in the face of increased immigration from southern and eastern Europe and Asia. Tuttle's writing is also significant in its great attention to cultivating women's "creative imagination" and "life of the spirit"; other feminist theory of the time focuses on women's psychological development, but Tuttle—influenced by a World War I–era vogue of Nietzschean aestheticism—takes it a step further by portending female evolution through culture and artistry.

Most American reform movements did an about-face with the beginning of World War I (1914–1918) and U.S. entrance in 1917. True, the country finally decided to add universal suffrage to the Constitution during and immediately after the war years. Overall, though, the war effort drained political attention and, more crucially, human and material resources away from what had been a high point in domestic reform—what historians call the Progressive Era. In short, as popular novelist Gertrude Atherton points out in "What Is Feminism?" (1916), the demands of World War I took women activists from their expanded goals of full equality and self-development. It brought a new conservatism in social relations between women and men, with the sexes encouraged to revert back to type during a time of national crisis. In this broad-ranging essay, Atherton is very suggestive in her use of theories of Darwinian evolution and sexual difference. Most compelling is her critique of masculinity, the castigation of the male sex for getting the world into war just at the height of Euro-American civilization. She sees men in wartime as little more than devolved beasts. And, while fearing that women will be further distracted from their goals by the drama and martial heroism of war, Atherton ends on a positive, almost utopian, note, anticipating women's ascension to a position of leadership, excelling in politics and the arts, with men taking up traditional roles of female subservience.

1
ELIZABETH CADY STANTON
The Solitude of Self (1892)

The point I wish plainly to bring before you on this occasion is the individuality of each human soul; our Protestant idea, the right of individual conscience and judgment; our republican idea, individual citizenship. In discussing the rights of woman, we are to consider, first, what belongs to her as an individual, in a world of her own, the arbiter of her own destiny, an imaginary Robinson Crusoe, with her woman Friday on a solitary island. Her rights under such circumstances are to use all her faculties for her own safety and happiness.

Secondly, if we consider her as a citizen, as a member of a great nation, she must have the same rights as all other members, according to the fundamental principles of our government.

Thirdly, viewed as a woman, an equal factor in civilization, her rights and duties are still the same; individual happiness and development.

Fourthly, it is only the incidental relations of life, such as mother, wife, sister, daughter, that may involve some special duties and training. In the usual discussion in regard to women's sphere, such men as Herbert Spencer, Frederic Harrison and Grant Allen, uniformly subordinate her rights and duties as an individual, as a citizen, as a woman, to the necessities of these incidental relations, neither of which a large class of women may ever assume. In discussing the sphere of man, we do not decide his rights as an individual, as a citizen, as a man, by his duties as a father, a husband, a brother or a son, relations he may never fill. Moreover, he would be better fitted for these very relations, and whatever special work he might choose to do to earn his bread, by the complete development of all his faculties as an individual.

Just so with woman. The education that will fit her to discharge the duties in the largest sphere of human usefulness will best fit her for whatever special work she may be compelled to do.

The isolation of every human soul, and the necessity of self-dependence, must give each individual the right to choose his own surroundings.

The strongest reason for giving woman all the opportunities for higher education, for the full development of her faculties, forces of mind and body; for giving her the most enlarged freedom of thought and action; a complete emancipation from all forms of bondage, of custom, dependence, superstition; from all the crippling influences of fear—is the solitude and personal responsibility of her own individual life. The strongest reason why we ask for woman a voice in the government under which she lives; in the religion she is asked to believe; equality in social life, where she is the chief factor; a place in the trades and professions, where she may earn her bread, is because of her birthright to self-sovereignty; because, as an individual, she must rely on herself. No matter how much women prefer to lean, to be protected and supported, nor how much men desire to have them do so, they must make the voyage of life alone, and for safety in an emergency, they must know something of the laws of navigation. To guide our own craft, we must be captain, pilot, engineer; with chart and compass to stand at the wheel; to watch the winds and waves, and know when to take in the sail, and to read the signs in the firmament over all. It matters not whether the solitary voyager is man or woman; nature, having endowed them equally, leaves them to their own skill and judgment in the hour of danger, and, if not equal to the occasion, alike they perish.

To appreciate the importance of fitting every human soul for independent action, think for a moment of the immeasurable solitude of self. We come into the world alone, unlike all who have gone before us; we leave it alone, under circumstances peculiar to ourselves. No mortal ever has been, no mortal ever will be like the soul just launched on the sea of life.

From *Woman's Journal,* January 23, 1892.

There can never again be just such a combination of prenatal influences; never again just such environments as make up the infancy, youth and manhood of this one. Nature never repeats herself, and the possibilities of one human soul will never be found in another. No one has ever found two blades of ribbon grass alike, and no one will ever find two human beings alike. Seeing, then, what must be the infinite diversity in human character, we can in a measure appreciate the loss to a nation when any large class of the people is uneducated and unrepresented in the government.

We ask for the complete development of every individual, first, for his own benefit and happiness. In fitting out an army, we give each soldier his own knapsack, arms, powder, his blanket, cup, knife, fork and spoon. We provide alike for all their individual necessities; then each man bears his own burden.

Again, we ask complete individual development for the general good; for the consensus of the competent on the whole round of human interests, on all questions of national life; and here each man must bear his share of the general burden. It is sad to see how soon friendless children are left to bear their own burdens, before they can analyze their feelings; before they can even tell their joys and sorrows, they are thrown on their own resources. The great lesson that nature seems to teach us at all ages is self-dependence, self-protection, self-support. What a touching instance of a child's solitude, of that hunger of the heart for love and recognition, in the case of the little girl who helped to dress a Christmas tree for the children of the family in which she served. On finding there was no present for herself, she slipped away in the darkness and spent the night in an open field sitting on a stone, and when found in the morning was weeping as if her heart would break. No mortal will ever know the thoughts that passed through the mind of that friendless child in the long hours of that cold night, with only the silent stars to keep her company. The mention of her case in the daily papers moved many generous hearts to send her presents, but in the hours of her keenest suffering she was thrown wholly on herself for consolation.

In youth our most bitter disappointments, our brightest hopes and ambitions, are known only to ourselves. Even our friendship and love we never fully share with another; there is something of every passion, in every situation, we conceal. Even so in our triumphs and our defeats. The successful candidate for the presidency, and his opponent, each has a solitude peculiarly his own, and good form forbids either to speak of his pleasure or regret. The solitude of the king on his throne and the prisoner in his cell differs in character and degree, but it is solitude, nevertheless.

. . . Seeing, then, that life must ever be a march and a battle, that each soldier must be equipped for his own protection, it is the height of cruelty to rob the individual of a single natural right.

To throw obstacles in the way of a complete education is like putting out the eyes; to deny the rights of property, like cutting off the hands. To deny political equality is to rob the ostracized of all self-respect; of credit in the market place; of recompense in the world of work; of a voice in those who make and administer the law; a choice in the jury before whom they are tried, and in the judge who decides their punishment. Shakespeare's play of "Titus Andronicus" contains a terrible satire on woman's position in the 19th century. Rude men (the play tells us) seized the king's daughter, cut out her tongue, cut off her hands, and then bade her go call for water and wash her hands. What a picture of woman's position! Robbed of her natural rights, handicapped by law and custom at every turn, yet compelled to fight her own battles, and in the emergencies of life to fall back on herself for protection.

The girl of sixteen, thrown on the world to support herself, to make her own place in society, to resist the temptations that surround her and maintain a spotless integrity, must do all this by native force or superior education. She does not acquire this power by being trained to trust others and distrust herself. If she wearies of the struggle, finding it hard work to swim up stream, and allows herself to drift with the current, she will find plenty of company, but not one to share her misery in the hour of her deepest humiliation. If she tries to retrieve her position, to conceal the past, her life is hedged about with fears lest willing hands should tear the veil from what she fain would hide. Young and friendless, *she* knows the bitter solitude of self.

How little courtesies of life on the surface of society, deemed so important from man towards woman, fade into utter insignificance in view of the deeper tragedies in which she must play her part alone, where no human aid is possible!

The young wife and mother, at the head of some establishment, with a kind husband to shield her from the adverse winds of life, with wealth, fortune and position, has a certain harbor of safety, secure against the ordinary ills of life. But to manage a household, have a desirable influence in society, keep her friends and the affections of her husband, train her children and servants well, she must have rare common sense, wisdom, diplomacy, and a knowledge of human nature. To do all this, she needs the cardinal virtues and the strong points of character that the most successful statesman possesses. An uneducated woman trained to dependence, with no resources in herself, must make a failure of any position in life. But society says women do not need a knowledge of the world; the liberal training that experience in public life must give, all the advantages of collegiate education; but when for the lack of all this, the woman's happiness is wrecked, alone she bears her humiliation; and the solitude of the weak and the ignorant is indeed pitiable. In the wild chase for the prizes of life, they are ground to powder.

In age, when the pleasures of youth are passed, children grown up, married and gone, the hurry and bustle of life in a measure over, when the hands are weary of active service, when the old arm chair and the fireside are the chosen resorts, then men and women alike must fall back on their own resources. If they cannot find companionship in books, if they have no interest in the vital questions of the hour, no interest in watching the consummation of reforms with which they might have been identified, they soon pass into their dotage. The more fully the faculties of the mind are developed and kept in use, the longer the period of vigor and active interest in all around us continues. If, from a life-long participation in public affairs a woman feels responsible for the laws regulating our system of education, the discipline of our jails and prisons, the sanitary condition of our private homes, public buildings and thoroughfares, an interest in commerce, finance, our foreign relations, in any or all these questions, her solitude will at least be respectable, and she will not be driven to gossip or scandal for entertainment.

The chief reason for opening to every soul the doors to the whole round of human duties and pleasures is the individual development thus attained, the resources thus provided under all circumstances to mitigate the solitude that at times must come to every one. I once asked Prince Krapotkin, a Russian Nihilist, how he endured his long years in prison, deprived of books, pen, ink and paper. "Ah!" said he, "I thought out many questions in which I had a deep interest. In the pursuit of an idea, I took no note of time. When tired of solving knotty problems, I recited all the beautiful passages in prose and verse I had ever learned. I became acquainted with myself, and my own resources. I had a world of my own, a vast empire, that no Russian jailer or Czar could invade." Such is the value of liberal thought and broad culture, when shut off from all human companionship, bringing comfort and sunshine within even the four walls of a prison cell.

As women ofttimes share a similar fate, should they not have all the consolation that the most liberal education can give? Their suffering in the prisons of St. Petersburg; in the long weary marches to Siberia; and in the mines, working side by side with men, surely call for all the self-support that the most exalted sentiments of heroism can give. When suddenly roused at midnight, with the startling cry of "Fire! Fire!" to find the house over their heads in flames, do women wait for men to point the way to safety? And are the men, equally bewildered, and half suffocated with smoke, in a position to more than try to save themselves? At such times the most timid women have shown a courage and heroism, in saving their husbands and children, that has surprised everybody. Inasmuch, then, as woman shares equally the joys and sorrows of time and eternity, is it not the height of presumption in man to propose to represent her at the ballot box and the throne of grace, to do her voting in the State, her praying in the church, and to assume the position of High Priest at the family altar?

Nothing strengthens the judgment and quickens the conscience like individual responsibility; nothing adds such dignity to character as the recognition of one's self-sovereignty; the right to an equal place, everywhere conceded; a place earned by personal merit, not an artificial attainment by inheritance, wealth, family and position. Seeing, then, that the responsibilities of life rest equally on man and woman, that their destiny is the same, they need the same preparation for time and eternity. The talk of sheltering woman from the fierce storms of life is the sheerest mockery, for they beat on her from every point of the compass, just as they do on man, and with more fatal results, for he has been trained to protect himself, to resist, and to conquer. Such are the facts in human experience, the responsibilities of individual sovereignty. Rich and poor, intelligent and ignorant, wise and foolish, virtuous and vicious, man and woman; it is ever the same, each soul must depend wholly on itself....

But when all artificial trammels are removed, and women are recognized as individuals, responsible for their own environments, thoroughly educated for all positions in life they may be called to fill; with all the resources in themselves that liberal thought and broad culture can give; guided by their own conscience and judgment, trained to self-protection, by a healthy development of the muscular system, and skill in the use of weapons of defence; and stimulated to self-support by a knowledge of the business world and the pleasure that pecuniary independence must ever give; when women are trained in this way, they will in a measure be fitted for those hours of solitude that come alike to all, whether prepared or otherwise. As in our extremity we must depend on ourselves, the dictates of wisdom point to complete individual development.

In talking of education, how shallow the argument that each class must be educated for the special work it proposes to do, and that all those faculties not needed in this special walk must lie dormant and utterly wither for want of use, when, perhaps, these will be the very faculties needed in life's greatest emergencies! Some say, Where is the use of drilling girls in the languages, the sciences, in law, medicine, theology? As wives, mothers, housekeepers, cooks, they need a different curriculum from boys who are to fill all positions. The chief cooks in our great hotels and ocean steamers are men. In our large cities, men run the bakeries; they make our bread, cake and pies. They manage the laundries; they are now considered our best milliners and dressmakers. Because some men fill these departments of usefulness, shall we regulate the curriculum in Harvard and Yale to their present necessities? If not, why this talk in our best colleges of a curriculum for girls who are crowding into the trades and professions, teachers in all our public schools, rapidly filling many lucrative and honorable positions in life?

... Women are already the equals of men in the whole realm of thought, in art, science, literature and government. With telescopic vision they explore the starry firmament and bring back the history of the planetary spheres. With chart and compass they pilot ships across the mighty deep, and with skillful fingers send electric messages around the world. In galleries of art the beauties of nature and the virtues of humanity are immortalized by them on canvas, and by their inspired touch dull blocks of marble are transformed into angels of light. In music they speak again the language of Mendelssohn, Beethoven, Chopin, Schumann, and are worthy interpreters of their great thoughts. The poetry and novels of the century are theirs, and they have touched the keynote of reform, in religion, politics and social life. They fill the editor's and professor's chair, and plead at the bar of justice; walk the wards of the hospital, and speak from the pulpit and the platform. Such is the type of womanhood that an enlightened public sentiment welcomes today, and such the triumph of the facts of life over the false theories of the past.

Is it, then, consistent to hold the developed woman of this day within the same narrow political limits as the dame with the spinning-wheel and knitting-needle occupied in the past? No! no! Machinery has taken the labors of woman, as well as man, on its tireless shoulders; the loom and the spinning-wheel are but dreams of the past; the pen, the brush, the easel, the chisel, have taken their places, while the hopes and ambitions of women are essentially changed.

We see reason sufficient in the outer conditions of human beings for individual liberty and development, but when we consider the self-dependence of every human soul we see the need of courage, judgment and the exercise of every faculty of mind and body, strengthened and developed by use, in woman as well as man.

Whatever may be said of man's protecting power in ordinary conditions, amid all the terrible disasters by land and sea, in the supreme moments of danger, alone woman must ever meet the horrors of the situation. The Angel of Death even makes no royal pathway for her. Man's love and sympathy enter only into the sunshine of our lives. In that solemn solitude of self, that links us with the immeasurable and the eternal, each soul lives alone forever. A recent writer says: "I remember once, in crossing the Atlantic, to have gone upon the deck of the ship at midnight, when a dense black cloud enveloped the sky, and the great deep was roaring madly under the lashes of demoniac winds. My feeling was not of danger or fear (which is a base surrender of the immortal soul) but of utter desolation and loneliness; a little speck of life shut in by a tremendous darkness. Again I remember to have climbed the slopes of the Swiss Alps, up beyond the point where vegetation ceases, and the stunted conifers no longer struggle against the unfeeling blasts. Around me lay a huge confusion of rocks, out of which the gigantic ice peaks shot into the measureless blue of the heavens; and again my only feeling was the awful solitude!"

And yet, there is a solitude which each and every one of us has always carried with him, more inaccessible than the ice-cold mountains, more profound than the midnight sea; the solitude of self. Our inner being which we call ourself, no eye nor touch of man or angel has ever pierced. It is more hidden than the caves of the gnome; the sacred adytum of the oracle; the hidden chamber of Eleusinian mystery, for to it only Omniscience is permitted to enter.

Such is individual life. Who, I ask you, can take, dare take on himself the rights, the duties, the responsibilities of another human soul?

2

SOFIA M. LOEBINGER

Suffragism Not Feminism (1909)

The right to vote is not based on contrasts between the sexes nor on animosity of one sex against the other, nor do we take refuge to any perverse theories, but the demand for the suffrage is based upon sound reasoning within the realm of logic and nature, and needs, in accordance with history, individual organization and human society.

Each sex has its own characteristics and peculiarities. Women do not want to ape men, but

From *The American Suffragette,* December 1909.

wish to remain true women, good daughters, sisters, mothers, and we claim emphatically that none of the attributes of ideal womanhood will be sacrificed to the ballot. Quite the contrary, they will be enhanced and refined.

Endowed with such true feminine attributes the woman will retain her position in the family and in society and yet become a factor in public life, using her best efforts towards evolution of mankind in general, and the propagation and progression of human civilization.

The women who want the suffrage wish to remain the companions of men and to work with them harmoniously. They do not deny the superiority of men in certain directions, but they claim for themselves superiority in other directions. Men make good warriors, good prize-fighters and perhaps also good statesmen, street-laborers, masons, iron-workers, Wall Street brokers, boot-blacks, etc., while women make better educators, clerks, accountants, writers, nurses, milliners, dressmakers, and both make good politicians, good cooks, physicians, lawyers, etc.

In contrast to this sound demand for the suffrage stand the eccentric theories of the "feminists"—men and women who reach out to the other extreme and wish to force womanly attributes on the man.

Such extravagant ideas as are occasionally expressed by over-zealous individuals are eagerly grasped by the *Antis* of both sexes and used as arguments against woman suffrage.

There is no fear that when women get the vote, the world will be feminized or that society will be debased, or that the man will be forced out of his sphere, that manly strength will be emasculated, or dainty womanhood will be coarsened.

We want no animosity between the sexes, but willing cooperation on the common ground—the *"Public Welfare."*

Let both sexes take to heart the watchword of Roman history which led to unparalleled success—*"Videant Consules ne quid detrimenti respublica capiat!"* i.e.—"See to it that no detriment comes to the public welfare."

To accomplish this end both sexes must co-operate harmoniously. Woman cannot be ignored, or civilization will suffer!

3

Emma Goldman
The Tragedy of Woman's Emancipation (1910)

I begin with an admission: Regardless of all political and economic theories, treating of the fundamental differences between various groups within the human race, regardless of class and race distinctions, regardless of all artificial boundary lines between woman's rights and man's rights, I hold that there is a point where these differentiations may meet and grow into one perfect whole.

With this I do not mean to propose a peace treaty. The general social antagonism which has taken hold of our entire public life today, brought about through the force of opposing and contradictory interest, will crumble to pieces when the reorganization of our social life, based upon the principles of economic justice, shall have become a reality.

Peace or harmony between the sexes and individuals does not necessarily depend on a superficial equalization of human beings; nor does it call for the elimination of individual traits and peculiarities. The problem that confronts us today, and which the nearest future is to solve, is how to be one's self and yet in oneness with others, to feel deeply with all human beings and still retain one's own characteristic qualities. This seems to me to be the basis upon which the mass and the individual, the true democrat and the true individual, man and woman, can meet without antagonism and opposition. The motto should not be: Forgive one another; rather, Understand one another. The oft-quoted sentence of Maame de Staël: "To un-

From Emma Goldman, *Anarchism and Other Essays* (New York: Mother Earth Publishing, 1910), 219–31.

derstand everything means to forgive everything," has never particularly appealed to me; it has the odor of the confessional; to forgive one's fellow-being conveys the idea of pharisaical superiority. To understand one's fellow-being suffices. The admission partly represents the fundamental aspect of my views on the emancipation of woman and its effect upon the entire sex.

Emancipation should make it possible for woman to be human in the truest sense. Everything within her that craves assertion and activity should reach its fullest expression; all artificial barriers should be broken, and the road towards greater freedom cleared of every trace of centuries of submission and slavery.

This was the original aim of the movement for woman's emancipation. But the results so far achieved have isolated woman and have robbed her of the fountain springs of that happiness which is so essential to her. Merely external emancipation has made of the modern woman an artificial being, who reminds one of the products of French arboriculture with its arabesque trees and shrubs, pyramids, wheels, and wreaths; anything, except the forms which would be reached by the expression of her own inner qualities. Such artificially grown plants of the female sex are to be found in large numbers, especially in the so-called intellectual sphere of our life.

Liberty and equality for woman! What hopes and aspirations these words awakened when they were first uttered by some of the noblest and bravest souls of those days. The sun in all his light and glory was to rise upon a new world; in this world woman was to be free to direct her own destiny—an aim certainly worthy of the great enthusiasm, courage, perseverance, and ceaseless effort of the tremendous host of pioneer men and women, who staked everything against a world of prejudice and ignorance.

My hopes also move towards that goal, but I hold that the emancipation of woman, as interpreted and practically applied today, has failed to reach that great end. Now, woman is confronted with the necessity of emancipating herself from emancipation, if she really desires to be free. This may sound paradoxical, but is, nevertheless, only too true.

What has she achieved through her emancipation? Equal suffrage in a few States. Has that purified our political life, as many well-meaning advocates predicted? Certainly not. Incidentally, it is really time that persons with plain, sound judgment should cease to talk about corruption in politics in a boarding-school tone. Corruption of politics has nothing to do with the morals, or the laxity of morals, of various political personalities. Its cause is altogether a material one. Politics is the reflex of the business and industrial world, the mottos of which are: "To take is more blessed than to give"; "buy cheap and sell dear"; "one soiled hand washes the other." There is no hope even that woman, with her right to vote, will ever purify politics.

Emancipation has brought woman economic equality with man; that is, she can choose her own profession and trade; but as her past and present physical training has not equipped her with the necessary strength to compete with man, she is often compelled to exhaust all her energy, use up her vitality, and strain every nerve in order to reach the market value. Very few ever succeed, for it is a fact that women teachers, doctors, lawyers, architects, and engineers are neither met with the same confidence as their male colleagues, nor receive equal remuneration. And those that do reach that enticing equality, generally do so at the expense of their physical and psychical well-being. As to the great mass of working girls and women, how much independence is gained if the narrowness and lack of freedom of the home is exchanged for the narrowness and lack of freedom of the factory, sweat-shop, department store, or office? In addition is the burden which is laid on many women of looking after a "home, sweet home"—cold, dreary, disorderly, uninviting—after a day's hard work. Glorious independence! No wonder that hundreds of girls are so willing to accept the first offer of marriage, sick and tired of their "independence" behind the counter, at the sewing or typewriting machine. They are just as ready to marry as girls of the middle class, who long to throw off the yoke of parental supremacy. A so-called independence which leads only to earning the merest subsistence is not so enticing, not so ideal, that one could expect woman to sacrifice everything for it. Our highly praised independence is, after all, but a slow process of dulling and stifling woman's nature, her love instinct, and her mother instinct.

Nevertheless, the position of the working girl is far more natural and human than that of her seemingly more fortunate sister in the more cultured professional walks of life—teachers, physicians, lawyers, engineers, etc., who have to make a dignified, proper appearance, while the inner life is growing empty and dead.

The narrowness of the existing conception of woman's independence and emancipation; the dread of love for a man who is not her social equal; the fear that love will rob her of her freedom and independence; the horror that love or the joy of motherhood will only hinder her in the full exercise of her profession—all these together make of the emancipated modern woman a compulsory vestal, before whom life, with its great clarifying sorrows and its deep, entrenching joys, rolls on without touching or gripping her soul.

Emancipation, as understood by the majority of its adherents and exponents, is of too narrow a scope to permit the boundless love and ecstasy contained in the deep emotion of the true woman, sweetheart, mother, in freedom.

The tragedy of the self-supporting or economically free woman does not lie in too many, but in too few experiences. True, she surpasses her sister of past generations in knowledge of the world and human nature; it is just because of this that she feels deeply the lack of life's essence, which alone can enrich the human soul, and without which the majority of women have become mere professional automatons.

That such a state of affairs was bound to come was foreseen by those who realized that, in the domain of ethics, there still remained many decaying ruins of the time of the undisputed superiority of man; ruins that are still considered useful. And, what is more important, a goodly number of the emancipated are unable to get along without them. Every movement that aims at the destruction of existing institutions and the replacement thereof with something more advanced, more perfect, has followers who in theory stand for the most radical ideas, but who, nevertheless, in their every-day practice, are like the average Philistine, feigning respectability and clamoring for the good opinion of their opponents. There are, for example, Socialists, and even Anarchists, who stand for the idea that property is robbery, yet who will grow indignant if anyone owe them the value of a half-dozen pins.

The same Philistine can be found in the movement for woman's emancipation. Yellow journalists and milk-and-water litterateurs have painted pictures of the emancipated woman that make the hair of the good citizen and his dull companion stand up on end. Every member of the woman's rights movement was pictured as a George Sand in her absolute disregard of morality. Nothing was sacred to her. She had no respect for the ideal relation between man and woman. In short, emancipation stood only for a reckless life of lust and sin; regardless of society, religion, and morality. The exponents of woman's rights were highly indignant at such misrepresentation, and, lacking humor, they exerted all their energy to prove that they were not at all as bad as they were painted, but the very reverse. Of course, as long as woman was the slave of man, she could not be good and pure, but now that she was free and independent she would prove how good she could be and that her influence would have a purifying effect on all institutions in society. True, the movement for woman's rights has broken many old fetters, but it has also forged new ones. The great movement of *true* emancipation has not met with a great race of women who could look liberty in the face. Their narrow, Puritanical vision banished man, as a disturber and doubtful character, out of their emotional life. Man was not to be tolerated at any price, except perhaps as the father of a child, since a child could not very well come to life without a father. Fortunately, the most rigid Puritans never will be strong enough to kill the innate craving for motherhood. But woman's freedom is closely allied with man's freedom, and many of my so-called emancipated sisters seem to overlook the fact that a child born in freedom needs the love and devotion of each human being about him, man as well as woman. Unfortunately, it is this narrow conception of human relations that has brought about a great tragedy in the lives of the modern man and woman....

A rich intellect and a fine soul are usually considered necessary attributes of a deep and beautiful personality. In the case of the modern woman, these attributes serve as a hindrance to the complete assertion of her being. For over a hundred years the old form of marriage, based on the Bible, "till death doth part," has been denounced as an institution that stands for the sovereignty of the man over the woman, of her complete submission to his whims and commands, and absolute dependence on his name and support. Time and again it has been conclusively proved that the old matrimonial relation restricted woman to the function of man's servant and the bearer of his children. And yet we find many emancipated women who prefer marriage, with all its deficiencies, to the narrowness of an unmarried life; narrow and unendurable because of the chains of moral and social prejudice that cramp and bind her nature.

The explanation of such inconsistency on the part of many advanced women is to be found in the fact that they never truly understood the meaning of emancipation. They thought that all that was needed was independence from external tyrannies; the internal tyrants, far more harmful to life and growth—ethical and social conventions—were left to take care of themselves; and they have taken care of themselves. They seem to get along as beautifully in the heads and hearts of the most active exponents of woman's emancipation, as in the heads and hearts of our grandmothers.

These internal tyrants, whether they be in the form of public opinion or what will mother say, or brother, father, aunt, or relative of any sort; what will Mrs. Grundy, Mr. Comstock, the employer, the Board of Education say? All these busybodies, moral detectives, jailers of the human spirit, what will they say? Until woman has learned to defy them all, to stand firmly on her own ground and to insist upon her own unrestricted freedom, to listen to the voice of her nature, whether it call for life's greatest treasure, love for a man, or her most glorious privilege, the right to give birth to a child, she cannot call herself emancipated. How many emancipated women are brave enough to acknowledge that the voice of love is calling, wildly beating against their breasts, demanding to be heard, to be satisfied....

The greatest shortcoming of the emancipation of the present day lies in its artificial stiffness and its narrow respectabilities, which produce an emptiness in woman's soul that will not let her drink from the fountain of life. I once remarked that there seemed to be a deeper relationship between the old-fashioned mother and hostess, ever on the alert for the happiness of her little ones and the comfort of those she loved, and the truly new woman, than between the latter and her average emancipated sister. The disciples of emancipation pure and simple declared me a heathen, fit only for the stake. Their blind zeal did not let them see that my comparison between the old and the new was merely to prove that a goodly number of our grandmothers had more blood in their veins, far more humor and wit, and certainly a greater amount of naturalness, kind-heartedness, and simplicity, than the majority of our emancipated professional women who fill the colleges, halls of learning, and various offices. This does not mean a wish to return to the past, nor does it condemn woman to her old sphere, the kitchen and the nursery.

Salvation lies in an energetic march onward towards a brighter and clearer future. We are in need of unhampered growth out of old traditions and habits. The movement for woman's emancipation has so far made but the first step in that direction. It is to be hoped that it will gather strength to make another. The right to vote, or equal civil rights, may be good demands, but true emancipation begins neither at the polls nor in courts. It begins in woman's soul. History tells us that every oppressed class gained true liberation from its masters through its own efforts. It is necessary that woman learn that lesson, that she realize that her freedom will reach as far as her power to achieve her freedom reaches. It is, therefore, far more important for her to begin with her inner regeneration, to cut loose from the weight of prejudices, traditions, and customs. The demand for equal rights in every vocation of life is just and fair; but, after all, the most vital right is the right to love and be loved. Indeed, if partial emancipation is to become a complete and true emancipation of woman, it will have to do away with the ridiculous notion that to be loved, to be sweetheart and mother, is synonymous with being slave or subordinate. It will have to do away with the absurd notion of the dualism of the sexes, or that man and woman represent two antagonistic worlds.

Pettiness separates; breadth unites. Let us be broad and big. Let us not overlook vital things because of the bulk of trifles confronting us. A true conception of the relation of the sexes will not admit of conqueror and conquered; it knows of but one great thing: to give of one's self boundlessly, in order to find one's self richer, deeper, better. That alone can fill the emptiness, and transform the tragedy of woman's emancipation into joy, limitless joy.

4

Winnifred Harper Cooley
The Younger Suffragists (1913)

Middle-aged reformers are tremendously excited over the radical utterances of some of the younger generation. Woman suffragists of a

From *Harper's Weekly*, September 27, 1913.

past decade, seeing the cherished goal of emancipation in sight, tremble lest the work of the pioneers be undone by revolutionary utterances of a few "hot-headed young women."

To these I would commend the following truth: *The radicalism of to-day becomes the conservatism of to-morrow.* Even in the memory of the youngest of us, the public once considered a woman suffragist a female outlaw, and the press pictured her invariably with short hair and trousers. Within a decade the entire attitude of the public has changed, until it is allowed that suffragists may be beautiful and fashionable, and only in rare instances is a little good-natured fun poked at them. I myself have witnessed the evolution of woman suffrage from a revolutionary measure to a conservative one!

The articles signed by Mrs. Belmont in a contemporary magazine, which so passionately denies that the women leaders of the suffrage movement demand anything other than the vote, has a grain of truth, in that many of these women are of a past generation, and, while once radical, are now conservative. They have not kept ahead of the times. To them the vote is a fetish—a magician's wand to conjure with. Having once obtained it, all human problems are to be solved easily and expeditiously. Many of them, in fact, scarcely think ahead toward the solving of problems at all, but merely want the vote to prove their equality with man, and to demonstrate democracy.

The younger generation has no quarrel with this attitude, for it is absolutely necessary for any democracy to enfranchise all of its adult population; but there are within the fold of modern franchise-seekers a number of women who consider the vote the merest tool, a means to an end—that end being a complete social revolution.

Any reformer is apt to be frightened for the success of his cause when others seek to couple with it still more unpopular measures. We have a deep sympathy with those older women who have borne the brunt and ignominy of the jeers and social ostracism of past public opinion. They are in terror lest the old unjust terms of opprobrium—"free love," "destruction of the family," and such—will drag the vigorous present cause back a few paces.

The younger feminists, however, do not look with any alarm upon temporary setbacks that might conceivably be given to woman's enfranchisement. So certain are they that evolution is necessitating changes in social and economic conditions, which may on the surface appear revolutionary, that they smile contentedly, knowing that no human agency can stem the tide.

What, then, are the demands of the younger radicals who are so agitating the elders within the fold?

1. *The abolition of all arbitrary handicaps calculated to prevent woman's economic independence.* This applies to spiritual as well as to material stumbling-blocks, for public opinion forms quite as impassable a barrier as rules and regulations. The woman of the future—married or single—must be absolutely free to earn her livelihood, and must receive equal pay for equal service. The younger feminists consider that the day is rapidly approaching when to be supported by a man in return for sexual privileges, or mere general housekeeping, or to be paid for motherhood, will be morally revolting to every self-respecting wife. They claim that as soon as men and women elevate their standards to the conception of a free womanhood, choosing its mate from deliberate affection, rather than in a wild scramble to be "taken care of" in idleness, they will look with horror on the old days when women "married to get a home."

2. *The opportunity for women to serve in all civic capacities*—on municipal, educational, institutional, and reform boards, on juries, and in every function by which they can be of service to their own sex and to children. This is coming about gradually, through women probation officers, attendants at Juvenile Courts, police matrons, "policewomen," physicians in insane asylums, in children's institutions, etc. It is only surprising that there yet is a violent struggle every time a woman runs for membership on a local school board.

3. *A demand for single standard of morality.* This is not to be interpreted arbitrarily as meaning either a strictly puritanical standard or an objectionably loose standard. It merely means that there shall be no unjust and persecuting *discrimination* against the woman offender, when both man and woman offend.

There is a violent altercation going on continually, within the ranks of feminists in all countries, regarding this question. Every woman in her right senses bitterly resents the injustices of the man-made world, which has for centuries branded the scarlet letter on the woman's breast, and let the man go scot-free. But the conservative women reformers think the solution is in hauling men up to the standard of virginal purity that has always been set for women. The other branch, claiming to have a broader knowledge of human nature, asserts that it is impossible and perhaps undesirable to expect ascetisicm from all men and women. Naturally, the former group of women are horrified that the latter are willing to face facts as they are, and constantly say to them: "In advocating a single standard of morality, instead of elevating men to the plane of women, you are dragging women down to the plane of man!"

Now, this is not a moral treatise. I am quite willing to let the future citizens work out their own salvation, with a fair certainty that they will attain considerably more fairness, and a generally higher standard, than ever before in any century. The all-important contention is that men and women as human beings, frail or strong as the case may be, must be judged from the broad human standpoint, and, legally and socially, receive fair play. The old-line suffragist who seeks the vote in order to gain laws by which the mother has an equal guardianship with the father of her children, an equal ownership of property, etc., and yet who condones the ostracism of a woman and the adulation of a man, when both have broken a law of conventionality, is absurdly inconsistent.

4. *The abolition of white slavery and prostitution.* This is only one form of the age-long insistence of man's ownership of woman. Its manifestations are quite as real in the harem, and in some phases of marriage, as in the poor creature who is sequestered, an absolute prisoner, in "houses" in our cities. The radical feminists consider it the highest moral duty of educated woman to instruct the young so that they may accomplish their own protection; and we resent the insinuation of the writer of the aforesaid article that women who wish to investigate and abolish the social evil are "morbid and discontented" and "discuss the subject from the housetops, dragging young women and children into it." White slavery is due very largely to the ignorance of young girls—in many cases regarded as highly desirable on the part of their parents. The trend of many modern dramas has been to awaken woman's responsibility for her sisters, and to impress upon her the actual criminality of ignorance. . . .

5. *The right to activity of expression and of creating social ideals, quite unhampered by old superstitions.* For centuries women, like cows, have been over-sexed. No wonder that they are often self-conscious and hysterical. They are regarded as "*the* sex," and are seldom allowed self-expression as individuals. Thus it is that, in discussing all questions of divorce, of marriage, of the home, of children, people eternally drivel and become effusive regarding women. They are never referred to except in their relation to men. It is always "the wife and mother," "the sweetheart and sister," not simply "the woman." As a matter of fact, public opinion in the future will regard men as quite as essential to the home as are women; and women as quite as essential to the world as are men.

If the above claims of certain advanced feminine thinkers in all countries seem revolutionary and shocking, let me hasten to assert that they are not the claims of suffragists, *in toto.* All feminists are suffragists, but all suffragists are not feminists. As I suggested in the beginning, the suffragists who only a decade ago were regarded as wild radicals are now considered quite conservative. They claim the vote as "wives and mothers," as "home-makers," as "helpmeets." They urge the rights of the child—the fact that pure food and milk and gas and water are municipal problems as well as housekeeping ones as reasons for women entering municipal housekeeping. The public and press, now educated up to this point, applaud this attitude which seems to them agreeably housewifely.

It is a well established fact that women suffrage in itself does not bring about a revolution. Wyoming, which has had women citizens for forty-three years, has a remarkable record for few divorces. Colorado and the other States where women are enfranchised show a praiseworthy list of laws relating to women and children, factory inspection, protection and reform, introduced as bills by women legislators. The feminists applaud all these things, but go much further in their demands. They are glad that suffrage has not disrupted homes; but they are quite willing to inquire frankly into monogamy, studying it with open mind, not churchly terror, and to see homes disrupted which rest on an immoral foundation, believing that divorce is far preferable to "legal prostitution."

They regard as somewhat absurd the statement of the writer previously alluded to, that the record of women's political rights "shows beyond all controversy that the effect of equal suffrage has been to raise the standards of domestic life, to make wives happier, to increase the number of marriages; and it is a literal fact that there is far less of the abnormal discussion of the sex question where women have the suffrage!" Just why wives should be happier, *as wives,* because they vote, is difficult to see. I am a born suffragist, dyed in the wool; but I certainly base my happiness as a wife on the excellent traits of my husband, not on the fact that I have gone to the polls several times in my lifetime. . . .

Woman suffrage to-day rests on a "safe," conservative basis. It does not abolish monogamy.

Now, the younger generation are quite curious to see the experiment of monogamy tried in some country! The majority of women have always been constrained to a monogamous existence; but no sane person would assert that monogamy actually exists anywhere, except in rare cases. If it does, how can we account for the curious fact—claimed by investigating sociologists—that the great majority of the patrons of houses of prostitution are married men?

These may be "indiscreet utterances of young women who deny the necessity of a proper regard for the conventionalities, and claim for themselves a liberty of speech and an independence of action that are wholly indifferent to the effect on a critical public." And it may be true that "it is most unfortunate for any reform to be championed by this class of enthusiasts." However, it is not my belief that any reform ever really prospered through moral cowardice. However persecuted the pioneers who express what they believe to be the truth, the world has a way of justifying them in the end. A terror of public opinion is not a part of the mental equipment of the world's great leaders.

If the kind public will but exercise a little thinking power, and try to realize the mental concepts of those who present a new viewpoint, they frequently will find it to be *intensely moral*. Invariably, the feminists of the world, in seeking woman's social freedom, her economic independence, and her responsibility toward all activities, are actuated by the highest moral purpose; and their newly constructed world will be one of greater civic and personal morality, far greater kindness, charity, and justice, and considerably greater happiness per person. . . .

There is something rather noble and lofty in women who might be lazy and live by their sex, as their ancestors for centuries have done, deliberately putting themselves to work. There is a growing feeling among sensible women that alimony is absurd and unfair to men. Most people are fairly greedy, and it would seem natural that a disgruntled woman who obtained a divorce because her husband was at fault might be glad to secure all the "financial reparation" the court would allow her. Many women believe, however, that it is sufficiently absurd for an able-bodied woman to be supported by a man while living with him, but doubly so during long years after they have ceased to be on speaking terms!

The support of children is another matter. Of course, there is a grain of justice in the alimony idea, founded on the fact that if a woman has lived with a man for twenty years she probably has fallen behind in the race for a livelihood, and can not make a place for herself in the economic struggle, and so, as marriage has deprived her of her earning capacity, some restitution should be made. In the future, when women continue to make money after marriage, they will not be a drag (should they become divorced) on an ex-husband!

Such are a few of the claims and beliefs and hopes of a surprising number of women all over the world. They are not always brave enough to speak them openly. Many a man would be amazed if he could turn an X-ray on the brain of his demure little helpmeet! I hasten to say that suffrage is not responsible for these radical opinions. It might, and probably would, repudiate many of them. But I will tell you a little secret: Although woman suffrage does not know it, it is a part of the social revolution that is surely sweeping every civilized country, and is the prophecy of the dawn of a to-morrow far brighter and better than yesterday or to-day.

5

ELLEN GLASGOW

Feminism (1913)

When the most popular of men's heroines, after being blighted by love, went to the undertaker's

From *The New York Times,* November 30, 1913.

to select her coffin, ordered that a broken lily should be engraved on the lid, and had it sent home to use as a writing table during her decline, an admiring eighteenth century public exclaimed that this touching episode had immortalized the womanly woman. No other heroine in fiction has been so passionately eulogized or so widely mourned, and even to-day she remains the most convincing of the feminine prigs with which the imagination of man has enriched the pages of literature. For Clarissa belongs not only to the evolving novel, but to the evolving masculine ideal of woman.

. . . When woman herself has shown such eagerness to conform to man's ideal of her that she has cheerfully defied nature and reshaped both her soul and body after the model he put before her, one can hardly demand of a man novelist that he should write of her as she is and not as he desires that she should be. Ages of false thinking about her on the part of others have bred in woman the dangerous habit of false thinking about herself, and she has denied her own humanity so long and so earnestly that she has come at last almost to believe in the truth of her denial.

So it is not surprising that, until the day of George Meredith, English novelists, though they often wrote of men and things as they were, invariably treated woman as if she were the solitary exception to natural law, and particularly to the law of development. Fielding, Thackeray, Dickens, and a host of others prepared their womanly woman after the same recipe—modesty, goodness, self-sacrifice, an inordinate capacity for forgiveness, "about as much religion as my William likes," and, now and then, a little vivacity—all sufficiently diluted to make the mixture palatable to the opposite sex. And in time, after the manner of mankind, this formula received the sanction of custom. . . .

For before Meredith's splendid heroines appeared, when English novelists portrayed woman in heroic dimensions, it was invariably in dimensions of sex. She lived for man, and failing this, she died for man, and at long intervals she even disguised her sex and wore man's clothes for man but the beginning, middle, and end of her existence was simply man. Without the prop of man she was as helplessly ineffectual as the "tender parasite" to which Thackeray compared her. And with the sacred inconsistency possible only to tradition, she was represented as passive even in the single activity to which her energies were directed—for in love, as in all else, she was supposed to sit with smiling patience and wait on the convenience of man. When she grew restless it proved merely that she was not the womanly woman—since to grow restless in the opinion of most novelists is the exclusive prerogative of man. And so deeply rooted in the masculine mind is this inherited belief in the right of the male to want to rove, if not actually to pack up and go, that we find so essentially modern a writer as Mr. Galsworthy speaking of "the aching for the wild, the passionate, the new, that never quite dies in a man's heart" implying, one gathers from the context, that this aching has either never been born in the heart of a woman or has died there in its infancy. Yet Mr. Galsworthy possesses an understanding of woman's nature—of her strength, her weakness, her blindness to the virtue of expediency, her tragic wastefulness in love—that is not equaled—that is not even approached by any other of our younger novelists. In his perfect novel "The Dark Flower"—for it is impossible for one who is by temperament a novelist, not a reviewer, to speak in measured terms of praise of work so rare, so delicately wrought as this—he has painted the portraits of four women that stand out as softly glowing, as mysteriously lovely, as the figures in Titian's Sacred and Profane Love. About them one and all, ardently as they are imagined, there is a certain wistfulness—a pathos that seems inherent in sex—as if Mr. Galsworthy were oppressed by the feeling that woman could never really be happy—that Nature had, from the beginning, ordained her for suffering. These four women are but exquisite variations for the indestructible type of man's womanly woman—the woman who lives by love alone—the woman for whom Goldsmith wrote his famous advice on the simplest and most satisfactory way of wringing her lover's bosom. These women exist only in their relation to man; and, despite a feverish energy that love gives them, one feels that they could never become free women, that they are doomed to remain the slaves of passion or of memory. Only in self-sacrifice have they power, and it is not often that the beauty of self-sacrifice in woman is denied by one of the opposite sex. But it is Mr. Galsworthy's peculiar distinction that in his masculine insistence upon the beauty of self-sacrifice in women, he should understand the full cost of it to women themselves, the tragic waste of useless renunciation, the bitter loss to the world of that joy which is the crown and heritage of fulfillment, never of crucifixion.

Now, it is only by perfectly realizing this tradition of the womanly woman, it is only by completely understanding how deeply it has colored almost all that man has written about woman from the wisdom of Solomon to the folly of Sir Almroth Wright, that we shall begin to grasp the profound significance of the woman's movement. For what we call the woman's movement is a revolt from a pretense of being—it is at its best and worst a struggle for the liberation of personality. After centuries of silence or of idle chatter on the part of woman about their own natures, there has come, within the present decade, a rather startling burst of world confidences. Women novelists are still content, with some honorable exceptions to copy the models as well as the methods of men: but in the brilliant and fearless books of Ellen Kay, of Rosa Mayreder, of Olive Schreiner, of C. Gasquoine Hartley (Mrs. Walter Gallichan), woman has become at last not only human, but articulate. Mrs. Gallichan's "The Truth About Woman" is an honest and courageous attempt to view woman, not through man's colored spectacles of tradition and sentiment, but by the clear, searching light of reality. It is not a book for babes, nor, for the matter of that, is it a book for octogenarians, unless they have abandoned most of the opinions held by the octogenarians of my acquaintance. She destroys much that the world has long valued, and particularly does she destroy the image worship of the womanly woman of fiction. One may not always agree with her conclusions; but she has admirably succeeded in freeing herself from sex prejudices and superstitions, and she brings to the familiar facts of biology and history an entirely fresh point of view and a remarkable keenness of insight. In preaching the gospel of freedom to women, however, it is well to remember—and it is not fair to imply that Mrs. Gallichan wholly forgets this—that the best use man has made of his liberty in the past has been to place restrictions upon it. For love, which would be so easy a solution of life's problems if it existed as a pure essence, may become sometimes, through its strange interminglings, as morally destructive as hatred.

But Mrs. Gallichan writes with conviction, fairness, and sincerity, and she appears splendidly above that feminine priggishness, the irritating assumption of woman's moral superiority to man, which to the present writer at least sounds out of place, though not without humor, on a woman's lips. For virtue, after all, is not biological, but spiritual, and is of an infinite complexity....

... There is a song of joy in her pages—a song so different from the many mournful hymns with which men have celebrated the fact of sex, that one is tempted to ask if, after all the sorrows of woman have existed chiefly in the imagination of men. She rejoices in womanhood, but it is a womanhood so free, so active, so conquering, that the word takes a new meaning from her interpretation, and she strikes her deepest note when she adds: "that from which woman must be freed is herself—the unsocial self that has been created by a restricted environment.... Woman is what she is because she has lived as she has. And no estimate of her character, no effort to fix the limit of her activities, can carry weight that ignores the totally different relations toward society that have artificially grown up, dividing so sharply the life of woman from that of man."

. . . To her clear vision man appears, not as a conscious tyrant, but, equally with woman, as a victim to the conditions of social evolution. Beneath the historic fact of man's dominance, she discerns the invincible purpose of nature without which man's efforts to dominate would have been as useless as a child's cries for the moon. If the balance of power passed from the matriarch to the patriarch, this was possible only because the growing race needed to cradle itself in the fatherage before it could gather its strength. Not male tyranny, but the selective agency of life decided the issue. While the race needed woman's subjection, she was condemned to remain subject; when it needs her freedom, she is inevitably ordained to become free. It is as useless for men to fight progress as it is for women to fight men—"For to go on with man, not to get from man, this is the goal of woman's freedom. Just in measure as the sexes fall away from love and understanding of each other do they fall away from life into the futility of personal ends." In the harmonious adjustment of the future she sees:

"Neither mother-right alone, nor father-right alone, can satisfy the new ideals of the true relationship of the sexes. The spiritual force, slowly unfolding, that has uplifted, and is still uplifting, womanhood, is the foundation of woman's claim that the further progress of humanity is bound up with her restoration to a position of freedom and human equality. But this position she must not take from man—that, indeed, would be a step backward. No, she is to share it with him, and this for her own sake and for his, and, more than all, for the sake of their children and all the children of the race. This replacement of the mother side by side with the father in the home and in the larger home of the State is the true work of the Woman's Movement."

But where this very modern interpretation diverges most widely from the traditional ideal of the sexes is in the writer's rejection of the belief in woman's natural passivity, and by this single point, small as it may appear to some thinkers, will probably be decided the future success or failure of the movement we know as Feminism. If, as man has so confidently asserted in the past, woman exists, not as an active agent of life, but merely as the passive guardian of the life force, then, indeed, is her revolt doomed to fall and her struggle to bear fruit in her sorrow. If her fight is a fight against law, if it is nature's purpose that woman shall sit and watch, then, as surely as night follows day, she will continue to sit and watch until the end of time. To Mrs. Gallichan, of course, as to all feminists, this apparent passivity is not inherent, but acquired, and is obliged, therefore, to disappear in the higher development of the race. By an appeal to history, indeed, she shows how often it has vanished in the past when it ceased to be one of the necessary conditions of woman's relation to man. "Woman," she repeats, "is what she is because she has lived as she has." It is foolish to talk of a revolt against nature as if, by taking thought, one could change the principle of one's being; and it is not without deep significance that woman's long endeavor to exist artificially, instead of naturally, should result in the violent reaction of the present. For this hunger for freedom that is driving women to-day into strange countries, as it drove the pioneers of old across oceans to the wilderness of new continents, is bound up with the imperative striving of life.

6

ROSE YOUNG

What Is Feminism? (1914)

Has the question reached your home town yet? If it has not, it soon will. And if the people in your home town are like the people in mine, the answers will be various and sundry—as many different answers probably as there are people.

From *Good Housekeeping,* May 1914.

"Femi-what?" your average citizen will venture. "Feminism? Something about women, isn't it?"

"It's the woman's movement"—"It's the furthering of the interests of women"—"It's the revolt of the women"—"It's the assertion of woman's right to individual development"—"It's the doctrine of freedom for women"—"It's woman's struggle for the liberation of her personality"—

The suggestions have crowded one on the heels of the other so rapidly, and so dogmatically, during this early part of the twentieth century, that the onlooker may be forgiven for deciding that there are as many definitions of feminism as there are feminists. Yet what distinguishes the contribution of the times on the subject is the really synthetic effort back of all the definitions, the effort to get "the woman question" assembled on a broader base than any from which it has as yet been projected. Higher education for women, economic opportunity for women, rights of person and property for women, political enfranchisement for women—all begin to be placed as parts of something greater, vaster. And for this something we seek the larger term.

Whether or not we have found it in feminism is still an open question. Some draw back because, they say, it means too much. Some don't like it because, they say, it doesn't mean enough. Some want the woman question to stay concentrated upon suffrage. Some fear to have the woman question fitted with a name, however expansive, seeing in any name impending organization, a creed to swear by, hard-and-fast rules to go by, when what is desired is the open mind, ready and willing to abide by the individual's development.

It is perhaps as well to note at the outset the current confusion as to the relation between woman suffrage and feminism. To feminists suffrage may, or may not, be one of the many fences which must come down as woman pushes upward and onward in individual development. Being an anti-suffragist by no means opposes one to far-reaching feministic conviction as to the individual development of women. Some of the ablest workers for the cause of women that I have ever met in this country are anti-suffragists. One of the men who was working hardest yesterday to secure higher education for women is working hardest today to keep them away from the ballot-box. Dora Marsden, the most professedly individualistic woman in England today, the most relentless in her jeers and jibes at the spiritual subjection of women, is harshly, sneeringly anti-suffrage. So is individualistic Emma Goldman in this country. On the other hand, being a suffragist by no means implies being a feminist. Being a suffragist may mean being only enough of a woman to keep up with only that part of the woman question which concerns itself only with woman's political enfranchisement.

One fact that stands out above all vagaries of conviction and all quibbles of language, however, is the feministic insistence upon the development of the individual. To be sure, this insistence is by no means limited to the woman question; it manifests itself in association with the man question, the question of education, the children question. Routineism is falling into general disrepute. In art, in philosophy, in business, the twentieth-century demand is for the man who "thinks for himself." Even in pedagogy, most encumbered of all departments of progress, there is a sleep-heavy effort to unwind the red tape that binds the minds of the teachers. And, thanks in huge part to Montessori, the very little children are no longer so universally required to duplicate and reduplicate a set pattern of childhood, but are allowed to flower up into *themselves.*

But men as individuals, children as individuals, individualistic art and philosophy and pedagogy, seem not half so staggering to tradition as the idea of women as individuals. "Woman for the sake of man," "woman for the sake of the children," "woman for the sake of the community," yes; but woman for her own sake seems even yet not only too much of a luxury, but too much of a menace to a civilization long used to regard woman not as herself, but only in relation to somebody else—as somebody's mother, wife, sister, daughter.

That explains why, as feminism is put forward as the doctrine of the self-development of woman, you may be met by the insistence that this self-development must be shown to mean racial development. Quite frequently this insistence makes the rigorous pronouncement, "Racial, or nothing!" Now, isn't that a little like telling the poet that he must not write poetry unless his poems are to serve the cause of prohibition, or child-welfare, or some other cause fine in itself, but hardly the be-all and end-all of poetry?

Again, still advocating feminism for its potency in the self-development of women, you may be met with the other insistence: "Why, it's perfectly plain that feminism is headed toward the good of the race. All the women have got to come to it, whether they want to or not."

Feminism can show justification for taking issue with both insistences. At no other angle of attack on the preconceived idea does the new faith more urgently hurl itself than at that historic regard of woman as mere race-agent. Now, it just so happens that in no other way does it more automatically assert its own racial import, for never was there so unracial a tenet as that which held women as consecrate, not to living, but to passing on life. It is only by living that one is fit to pass on life.

To the other insistence, that if feminism can be proved racially benign women must bow to it, willy-nilly, feminists may oppose the argument that every woman who knows much knows that the matter of developing herself, as an individual is mainly an inside matter, a spiritual introduction to herself. The social hope must rest with the individual development being self-sought with each and every woman. To attempt to herd women into a woman's movement for the race's sake, a movement bounded and defined by set purpose from the very start-off, would be to keep on treating women like sheep—and the race like a stepchild.

Does not feminism's call to women ring the clearer for the surer faith? "Know yourselves! Be yourselves! Use yourselves!" comes the call. And if there is in it not a tremor of doubt but that the knowing, the being, and the using will add to life's complement in the large, there is in it, too, not a shadow of prejudgment of the impending discoveries.

As for that question of seeming conflict between feminism, woman's cause, and the cause of society and the race, it is entitled to—and it gets from all the feminists I know—the most earnest consideration. But again, it is not exclusively a woman question. Ever since human beings began to be human beings their minds and their consciences have been engaged with that same question. And though today's crisis is unusually sharp, because of woman's active involvement in it, it is not to be forgotten that never before were there so many men stirred to their inmost being, frayed and frazzled in their inmost souls, between the compulsion toward individualistic expression and their so-named "social sense."

It is unfair to accuse the times of any lack of faith and conscience on this score. More ardently than ever before both men and women cry for the truth. More intelligently than ever before they insist upon the best. Less stupidly than ever before they reject what does not promise growth; and more indefatigably than ever before they seek, in growth, the right answer to that seeming irreconcilability between individual right and social right.

"Seeming," because there is no such irreconcilability. There can be none, in the ultimate. There can be, for instance, no social efficiency without individual efficiency, no harm to the individual without harm to society, the group. If by social compulsions—precedent, law, opinion, rule—we suppress in a person something that would enrich his living capacity, we suppress something that would enrich the group by just so much. Harm the mothers, and you harm the children; harm the present, and you harm the future.

All this is so axiomatic that your "race-minded" person will admit it off-handedly, will say, "Yes, that's so"—and turn around in his tracks to argue that the "race question must always have precedence over the woman question."

Meantime, from the other horn of the dilemma, the individualist may be shouting that woman's individual development must go on "at whatever cost to society." Why fiddle on a chimerical contingency? Cost to society is cost to the individual. You can't develop your muscles at a cost to your constitutional well-being without sequential cost to your muscles.

The individualist may be motivated by an intense sense of individualistic right, which he recognizes as stopping with the bare fact that he is an individual. He won't let you call him "social-minded." He flies out at the term. He fights every foot of the way to keep you from reading social ends into individual being, doing, growing. He flaunts society. He calls society harsh names—"Liar! Hypocrite!"—and, in his turbulence, may overlook the fact that the individual's relations to society—his need of others, their dependence and love, their help, the convenience of being able to buy butter and eggs from them, the stimulus of trying to impose ideas upon them—is a demandant, irresistible *part of the individual:* in a word, that social relations are implicit in individuality.

It is to accommodate the pull between the individual and "the others" that society is "organized" and social relations are established. And what will bear special scrutiny is the contention that when we organize society we don't detach, break off, something from our individuality to turn over to the group. On the contrary we play out into the group some of our thought, some of our power of control, some of our aspiration, some of our love, some of our fear; and back from the group plays the effect of the thought, power of control, aspiration, love, and fear of the others into us. The bond is no dead thing. It is vibrantly alive, alive for its contact with us, alive for its contact with the group. As individuals we don't really want to escape it. To escape it would be to escape part of our individuality. What, as individuals, we may try to escape from in organized society is not the inherently social part, but the organization part, the rules that we make in the effort to get good team work. Rules don't grow. But thought grows, and aspiration grows, and love and power of control grow, and fear lessens, with individual growth. And to get room for their growth the individual may have to war with the outgrown rule, a "social custom," "the established precedent"; may have to get under the crust of conventional thought and shove, until some of "the others" join him, the crust cracks, and society en masse shoulders on through. . . .

Perhaps the most short-sighted of all interferences with life's possibilities is consequent upon the assumption that a human being's social impulses, his hang-together-with-the-others impulses, are not a part of his individuality. It would not matter so much if attitude of mind were not so surely reflected in both individual and social efficiency. But for the individual woman to work under the conviction that she is "sacrificed to the others," or that her claims as an individual are forcefully subordinated to those of "the others," instead of with a clear vision of her own dual involvement and elective powers, is for her to restrict her own spirit's freedom at the expense of the social. Spiritual freedom evolves out of *consciousness of powers possessed,* sense of self and opportunity, and it is only out of spiritual freedom that the whole individual evolves, bringing the social along with him.

Most conclusive of all arguments that the individual does carry the social within him is that found in the inter-association of the dominant characteristics of the times. Never was there so individualistic a day; never so many people, women like men, bent on self-expression, bent on arriving at truth in their own way—and never was the individual so deeply and humanely concerned for his growth; never was there so general a recognition of the interdependence and coming amalgamation of "the masses" and "the classes"; never such sturdy growth, and blossoming beauty of the social.

So, not to have faith in the benignity of individual development is not to have faith in life itself. And that is why, from the viewpoint of many feminists, any detachment of the woman question from the communal question, in order to voice that well-known reminder of woman's well-known duty to the well-known human race, is not merely meddlesome but illogical. What is an integral part of woman can be trusted to give an account of itself in the self-development of woman. Is it not, in fact, continuously giving an account of itself, with woman on every hand today, both as home-mother and as world-mother, showing that she takes her racial and social involvement along with herself; that she can't help so taking it, can't do well by herself without doing well by the whole world?

Is not that a law of her individuality?

7
Feminist Mass Meeting (1914)

TALK ON FEMINISM STIRS GREAT CROWD

What is Feminism? Twelve speakers, six men and six women, attempted to answer the question in Cooper Union last night in what was called the first feminist mass meeting ever held. The People's Institute made the arrangements for the discussion. The auditorium was filled almost to capacity, and it was remarked that there were more men than women in the audience. The applause was frequent and hearty. Many definitions of feminism were given, differing in details, but agreeing in the essential fact that the movement sought freedom for women.

There was Rose Young, who said that feminism to her was "some fight, some fate, and some fun," and there was Edwin Bjorkman, who said that feminism meant "that woman shall have the same right as man to be different." Henrietta Rodman said that when feminism was the vogue women would lose such privileges as "the right to alimony and the right

From *The New York Times*, February 18 and 21, 1914.

to be supported all of her life," and Will Irwin added that feminism would "disprove all of the bunk talked about the home and fireside."

George Middleton considered the subject of feminism from several points of view. He said in part:

"Feminism means trouble; trouble means agitation; agitation means movement; movement means life; life means adjustment and readjustment—so does feminism. Feminism is not a female with fewer petticoats; it does not seek to crinoline men. It asks a new fashion in the social garments of each. Feminism is a spiritual attitude; it recognizes that men and women are made of the same soul stuff. It places this above biological bosh.

"In another aspect, feminism is an educational ideal. It asks that children be educated according to temperament and not according to maleness and femaleness. It asks that a girl be educated for work and not for sex. Feminism seeks to change social opinion toward the sex relation, not to advocate license, but to recognize liberty."

Rose Young, when her turn to speak came, said:

"To me feminism means that woman wants to develop her own womanhood. It means that she wants to push on to the finest, fullest, freest expression of herself. She wants to be an individual. When you mention individualism to some people they immediately see a picture of original sin; but the freeing of the individuality of women does not mean original sin; it means the finding of her own soul.

"The first thing that we have to overcome is custom and convention and the common attitude of mind, and then this fear of individuality will pass away. We have to compel conviction that woman is a human being."

This idea of the assertion of individuality by woman was dwelt upon by Edwin Bjorkman. He said that feminism meant that woman should have the right to be a full-fledged personality and not merely a social unit.

"We want woman to have the same right as man to experiment with her life," he said. Mr.

Bjorkman also attacked what he called the "now infamous article of Prof. Sedgwick," saying that Prof. Sedgwick's idea of a woman was that she was merely a hen. "If she's a hen," Mr. Bjorkman said, "then man is a rooster; and you know what a rooster is. He is a vain, strutting, supercilious polygamist who crows about his own glory. Economically the hen is the more valuable of the two."

"Feminism means revolution, and I am a revolutionist," said Frances Perkins. "I believe in revolution as a principle. It does good to everybody."

Max Eastman, as his contribution to the discussion, said:

"Feminism is the name for the newly discovered and highly surprising fact that it is just as important for a woman to be happy as a man. And one woman will be happy by going out and seeking adventures of her own and another will be happy staying at home and thinking about babies and baked beans. Both should be allowed to do what they want to do. There'll be a great deal more fun for everybody when women are universally active and free and independent."

Marie Jenney Howe, who was the Chairman of the meeting, said that feminism was "the entire woman movement," and she added that "while men were held in a prison by convention, custom, and tradition, women were confined to one room in the prison and had to watch the men walk about in the corridors in comparative freedom."

"Feminism is simply part of the great world fight for freedom and justice and equality, and might better be called humanism," said George Creel.

"The basis of feminism, the basis of suffragism, the basis of all of the modern movements for progress, lies in the labor movement," said Mrs. Frank Cothren, the only speaker who used her husband's name.

FEMINISTS ASK FOR EQUAL CHANCE

Six of the country's leading feminists spoke on "Breaking Into the Human Race," under the auspices of the People's Institute last night at Cooper Union.

Mary Jenney Howe, Chairman of the meeting, introduced each speaker as "a practical liver of her own feminist theories." The world, she said, was human, and women wanted to be human, not merely emotional, personal, feminine creatures.

"We're sick of being specialized to sex," she cried. "We intend simply to be ourselves, not just our little female selves, but our whole, big, human selves. We have no intention of interfering with men, or telling them what they may do and what they may not do. We do not put any fence around men, but we insist that they shall not put any fence around us, either. We want to remove the fence they have put around us and which is crumbling and decaying. But they object, because we might destroy the vines that have clambered over that rotten old fence, and the flowers and poems that grow on that vine. They do not see the human lives behind that fence."

Rheta Childe Dorr spoke on "The Right to Work." She admitted that no one had ever questioned woman's right to work—to drudge without pay. But she said it was conceded nowhere that woman had a right to work with equal pay for equal work with men, and with equal chances of promotion. She herself, she said, had run into a veritable hullabaloo when at the age of 17—twenty-five years ago—she first decided to work for a living despite the wishes of her family. Three years after she got a job, she got a husband, and six years later she found herself with a baby she had to support.

"I tried to get work on a newspaper," she said, "but they said I could only write such stuff as 'Advice to the Lovelorn.' I wouldn't. Finally in three years, I got a $25 a week job; and I never got a raise in four years thereafter. That's what I mean when I say women haven't got the same right as men to work for promotion."

Rose Schneiderman, the shirt waist strike leader, discussed woman's "Right to Organize." She pointed out that among the women of the real working class there was not and never had been any question as to their right to work, which Mrs. Dorr had so insisted upon. Most of them, she said, had never been denied that privilege, and they wished they could stay at home a bit.

"We are learning that as we must work the same as our brothers and sweethearts, it behooves us to organize the same as they for higher wages and better conditions," she said. "Last week there were women of the unemployed here. Some of them could not get work because they had gray hair. We used to be told that gray hair meant a person had reached that stage when he or she deserved a rest, and that there should be reverence shown to the gray head. But these women were thrown on the scrap heap because of their gray hair.

"The working woman not only faces the sex question but the question of exploitation as well. Only when industrial solidarity has been achieved can she gain industrial freedom and with it sex freedom."

"The Right of a Woman to Keep Her Own Name" was discussed by Miss Fola La Follette.

"Should a man keep his own name?" asked Miss La Follette, adding that the question was no more absurd than the one that formed her subject. "If a woman is to change her name simply as an acknowledgment that she loves a man and has married him, why should not the same sacrifice be made by him toward her? The ready acceptance of the custom of a woman's retaining her maiden name plus the name of her husband may be taken as a token of how in a very few years we may expect to see women in marriage keeping their own maiden name intact.

"What about the children? Let them combine the name of their father and of their mother, thus linking them more closely to each; or let that matter be settled by each individual father and mother."

Miss La Follette urged the abandonment also of the title "Mrs.," saying it was unnecessary to label spinster and matron: that if a woman was single or married or had children or none, husband or none, was her concern and no one else's. Society didn't ask a man first of all whether he was married and had children or not; and what was good for the gander was good for the goose, she asserted.

"If Miss is the form of address for women before marriage," she said, "let it be so after marriage, too. Let the term acquire a larger social significance. When women keep their own name, a woman will not have to explain her children by wearing the name of a perfectly good legitimate husband who's at home."

Feminists, she said, lived their theories out in practice; and then it came out why Mrs. Howe was introduced as Marie Jenney Howe; she explained that she liked Frederick C., but not his name compared to hers.

Beatrice Forbes-Robertson Hale spoke on the "Right of the Mother to Her Profession." Mrs. Howe had introduced her as qualified to speak on that subject by reason of her twins. Mrs. Hale insisted, however, that the breaking into the human race of those much praised twins was "due to no particular ability or prowess on my part, but merely showed that I always accomplish what I set out to do."

She insisted that every married woman if she wished had a right to pursue her profession as well as be a mother, adding that it could be done.

"There is a round dozen of women in my village working at their profession to help papa, and still having babies from time to time; and the census of families there shows those babies to be just as numerous as in the homes of the mothers who stay at home and read Vogue," she said.

Mrs. Hale said that girls ought to be brought up with serious aims and with the intention of helping their husbands feather and keep the nest, as the best check to race suicide, in which she hadn't any faith, anyway.

"As for mothers' pensions," she said, "I don't care if you have the State pay them or individual husbands and bachelors. But why, just because I'm a woman, should I expect to be supported all my life by a man—first by a father, then by a husband, and ultimately by a son? I've no objection myself to letting my husband help. Let him make himself useful at these critical times, by all means. But let him know always that there's another capable working partner at his side, ready and able to do her share."

And then Nina Wilcox Putnam spoke on "The Right to Ignore Fashion." She wore a flowing yellow kimono, with many other startling effects, including a string of big green, red, white, and yellow beads around her neck and a wide silver hairband around her forehead. Mrs. Charlotte Perkins Gilman was the last speaker. She discussed "The Right of Women to Specialize in Home Industries."

8
Marie Jenney Howe, Louise W. Kneeland, Maud Thompson, and Frances G. Richards
A Feminist Symposium (1914)

MARIE JENNEY HOWE

Feminism

No one doubts that women are changing. We need an appropriate word which will register this fact. The term feminism has been foisted upon us. It will do as well as any other word to express woman's effort toward development.

No one movement is feminism. No one organization is feminism. All woman movements and organizations taken together form a part of feminism. But feminism means more than these. It means woman's struggle for freedom. Its political phase is woman's will to vote. Its economic phase is woman's effort to pay her own way. Its social phase is woman's revaluation of outgrown customs and standards. Feminism includes the misdirected as much as the well directed efforts of women.

Anti-Suffrage is a phase of feminism. It is the struggle of conservative women to defend their temperament. For the sake of conviction they enter public life. They are impelled to study, speak, write, publish and organize. Anti-Suffrage is the effort of a group of women to express themselves. The effort is developing. It redeems them from inertia and makes them part of that process of growth which is feminism.

English militancy is equally a phase of feminism. It is the same struggle on the part of a different group to defend a different temperament.

Feminism is not limited to any one cause or reform. It strives for equal rights, equal laws, equal opportunity, equal wages, equal standards, and a whole new world of human equality.

But feminism means more than a changed world. It means a changed psychology, the creation of a new consciousness in women.

The essence of this new consciousness is woman's refusal to be specialized to sex. The evolved feminist does not find all of life in a love affair. She knows that any normal woman can recover from an unrequited passion. She is able to be happy though unmarried.

She does not adjust her life according to the masculine standard of what is womanly. She decides for herself what is womanly and what is natural. She thinks for herself. She lives according to her own convictions. If married, she retains her own identity. Underneath her wifehood and motherhood she knows herself a human being with human capacities for work, service and impersonal ideals.

Woman's effort toward freedom cannot be won without man's willingness. The awakening of women involves an adjustment on the part of men. Feminism strive to put right whatever is wrong in the changing relation between men and women. Many leading feminists are men. Men are helping woman to evolve. In so doing they are helping their own evolution. The feminist evolution is the evolution of women and men. In so far as woman is behind man, it means catching up to man. And where woman is ahead of man, it means holding her own until man shall catch up to her.

Feminism is woman's part of the struggle toward humanism.

After feminism,—humanism.

From *The New Review*, August 1914.

LOUISE W. KNEELAND

Feminism and Socialism

The Socialist who is not a Feminist lacks breadth. The Feminist who is not a Socialist is lacking in strategy. To the narrow-minded Socialist who says: "Socialism is a working class movement for the freedom of the working class, with woman as woman we have nothing to do," the far-sighted Feminist will reply: "The Socialist movement is the only means whereby woman as woman can obtain real freedom. Therefore I must work for it." Granted the Socialist is not necessarily a Feminist, nevertheless the bona fide Feminist must be, or become, a Socialist, as an analysis of the conditions will prove.

Feminism has been called a middle class movement. And so it is, in its origin. The reason is not far to seek. The machine that binds the working class woman and her children to its wheels sets the middle class woman free from the drudgery of the old-time home and gives her unwonted leisure. A leisure hers, not in the sterile, enervating environment of an Eastern harem, but in the complex, stimulating surroundings of modern civilization. But this of itself would be of no value to her without the ability to profit by these advantages. That this ability is hers woman's place in the larger social life of to-day gives sufficient testimony. The home no longer absorbs all her energies. She reaches out after a broader life. She struggles for what she wants, develops her capabilities, becomes ever more conscious of her power and desirous of wider fields for this exercise, at the same time arousing in her working class sister an uneasy consciousness of like demands.

Feminism is the result of human energy set free by machinery to find new outlets in a rapidly developing civilization. That its most striking manifestation takes the form of a Votes for Women campaign is but natural, considering that the movement itself is a middle class product and that political power is the most effective weapon the middle class possesses for the attainment of its ends. The ends in this case are the enlargement of individual opportunity for middle class women and an influential voice in matters that affect the general status of women as well as in the enactment and administration of humanitarian reforms. And in conjunction with this we must not forget that political power offers many opportunities for efficient self-support, which a constantly increasing economic pressure makes desirable to some of these rebels in a class accustomed to comfortable incomes.

This middle class origin and character it is that accounts for much of that antagonism to the Feminist movement among timid and cautious Socialists in and out of the Party. We should expect, of course, that a working class movement would be more or less hostile to middle class activity of any kind, especially when that activity seeks an extension of political power. And if middle class men fear and dislike the incursion of women of their own class into what has hitherto been considered their own peculiar province, politics—how much more must working men resent the intrusion of the increasingly capable and dominant middle class women into the working class movement. A few such women, it is true, are a valuable asset, because of their energy and ability. But the acquisition of any considerable number of them must be regarded with even more apprehension than an infusion of middle class men. The latter give to the Party, as is well known, a reformist cast that weakens and confuses it, and this tendency would be still further complicated and aggravated by Feminist activities which would tend to divide the movement on sex lines. Not until the Socialist movement has reached such a degree of maturity as renders it stable enough to absorb, or co-operate with, this by-product of capitalism without danger to itself, can Feminism expect a friendly, helping hand from Socialist organizations. In Germany that degree of maturity seems to have been reached, and in several of the smaller European countries as well. Where this stage of development has not yet been attained, Feminism is apt to become violent, as in England, although there these conditions are aggravated by the outnumbering of the men by the women and the consequent fear on the part of some of the men of a reversal of the present sex domination.

The question now arises how in spite of all the opposition and antagonism to their movement, Feminists proceed to obtain the political power they must have, and what the ultimate outcome will be. Their main lines of attack are four. First, the appeal to woman as woman, that is, practically, to woman as a class in the sense that she as a mother performs certain special work for society which has resulted in her being treated as different from, if not inferior to, men. It is on the ground of freeing her from such discriminations and also of enabling her to protect herself and her children that this appeal is made. Second, the appeal to all those who are susceptible to the influence of a high social ideal. Third, the appeal to those to whose advantage on the political field the influence and activity of the movement can be used. Fourth, the appeal through terrorism to those who are obdurate to every other argument or influence. Who can doubt the success of efforts as varied and appeals as powerful as these when made by determined and capable women growing ever more skilful in the use of their tools?

Say, then, the vote is won. What next? The application of political power to the enlargement of opportunities for women of the middle class; the removal of all sex discriminations against woman as woman; and the carrying out of such social reforms as are possible under capitalism. And then? Then the true condition of affairs is made clear. Then it is plainly seen that the working class woman is still a working class woman who has but helped her more favored middle class sister to obtain still greater advantages, but remains herself, together with her children, in spite of all middle class reforms and the removal of sex discriminations, a slave to the capitalist machine. From this slavery there is but one thing that can set her free—Socialism, the common ownership of the means of production and distribution. And further, as the ever increasing economic pressure forces numerous members of the middle class down into the working class and accentuates competition among the remaining members of the middle class, Feminists will come to see that in spite of all the freedom they have won, and the development of their ability, middle class women have become nothing more than upper class servants of capitalism into whose hands is confided largely (but under strict supervision) the care of the health, morals, education and recreation of the rising generation, and to a considerable extent of the public in general. A sorry task that of keeping slaves in good condition so that they may be all the more thoroughly plundered by capitalist parasites! What, considering all the circumstances, can the bona fide Feminist do but turn to Socialism?

And the narrow-minded Socialist? Oh, he has been working hard all this time to perfect those Socialist organizations that are to give woman the very freedom he doesn't want her to have.

MAUD THOMPSON

Socialism and Feminism: A Reply to Belfort Bax

It need not surprise us to find over the signature of one who calls himself a Socialist the same arguments used by the advocates of chattel slavery, the opponents of popular government, and the critics of Socialism. For every social movement, especially after it is in full swing, draws to itself those who see of it only the segment which suits their temperament. They conceive of a social revolution as altering a single political or economic system without transforming those social, moral and intellectual conditions that adhere to our economic system as the flesh to the bones of the living creature. So we have in the Socialist movement some who do not believe in political democracy, some who cling to their race prejudices, and some who oppose sex equality....

The argument of Mr. Bax's article is that feminism is not an essential part of Socialism, because Socialism implies economic and political equality between classes and nations, not between sexes. As proof of his argument, he refers (1) to the contrast between the way class differences and sex differences have arisen; (2) to the difference in goal between the movement for sex equality and the movement for class equality.

Differences between classes, he says, were "created by economic conditions and social environment"; between the sexes "we are concerned not with a sociological but with a biological difference." The difficulty here is merely a lack of definition. Sex differences which are biological are differences of sex function. Sex differences which are sociological are "created by economic conditions and social environment."

The only important difference in sexual function is that the woman bears and nurses the child. It is recognized now that the physiological differences which accompany this function are in healthy women of slight import as far as their effect on the physical or mental powers goes. Such physiological differences may, therefore, be disregarded in considering woman's social or political functions. There remains the one supreme difference of biological function, the power to bear and nurse a child. Whatever difference in social function there is between the two sexes must connect with this.

Sex privileges doubtless arose in a savage and warlike society from the unequal ability of the two sexes (due to this one difference in sex function) to adapt themselves to that form of society. Unequal physical strength can scarcely have determined the difference in the social functions of the sexes, for there are tales enough of warrior women to show that woman was not regarded as incapable of defense or even of attack. But better proof of her physical endurance is found in the heavy burden of labor which she bore throughout the ages and still bears.

Nevertheless, her sexual function did, in primitive society, limit her social functions. She who bore and nursed the children had to stay within reach of nest or lair or home. No hunt far afield for her, no long trails after the foe. To her fell naturally the agricultural and industrial duties close to home.

But among primitive people community service and the power that springs from opportunity for service was largely that of the hunt and the chase. It was with later civilization that agriculture, industry and the home became community affairs. Government has not only come home now from the battlefield and the hunt, it *is* in part the home. So complex have our civic duties become, so efficient our means of communication, that every citizen, whether kept at home by a baby or at the shop by business, can do her or his full duty through some of the many channels of community life.

Yet the old alignment persists. And it will persist, like the alignment of economic class, until a social revolution casts society anew. It is the business of Feminism to adapt law and convention to the new community life and community service. And this is the business of Socialism too.

But the goal of Socialism is not merely equal opportunity, not merely the abolition of classes. So that if the abolition of classes still left any group of people deprived of social opportunity, the goal of Socialism would not be attained. But a group of people who are deprived of the same social opportunities through exclusion from the same social privileges do constitute a subject class. In the case of woman, the dependent position of woman in the family has relegated the various members of their class to the different economic classes to which the heads of their families belonged. These cross-currents of family and social organization have separated women from each other by barriers of differing economic conditions, but brought them together again in a common economic dependence on men. This is their economic class, the class whose common economic status is a dependence within the family. To deny the possibility of more than one kind of economic class, or of a double economic dependency, is to construct a paper society on lines of theoretical simplicity instead of analyzing society as it really exists. Only by abolishing special privilege in all classes, not merely between two classes, can Socialism reach the goal of equal opportunity.

Mr. Bax's argument as to goal is as follows: Socialism aims at the extinction of classes, feminism does not aim at the extinction of sex; therefore they are not identical in goal. If goals are to be used as tests of identity, it does not seem logical to compare what one goal is with what another goal is not. The goal of feminism is not a negative. It aims at the abolition of sex privilege. The aim of Socialism is to abolish all class privilege. Feminism aims at removing one barrier to equal opportunity, Socialism at removing all. Feminism is, then, a part of Socialism, though Socialism is more than Feminism. And as Feminism means much more than the enfranchisement of women, draws in its train, in fact, all the liberty that frees the woman socially, sexually, intellectually, as well as politically and economically; so Socialism means not merely the removing of political and economic barriers that now keep men from their true opportunity, but the opening of the gates of individual opportunity to all humanity.

FRANCES G. RICHARDS

Some Anti-feminist Vagaries

Many persons regard the woman movement as an emergence from passivity to activity on the part of half the human race. However, except in a technical biological sense (and Lester F. Ward assails the validity of the exception) woman's passivity has been a delusion—and, sometimes at least, a snare. This is well shown in the Evelina type of eighteenth century novel, in which the author, the heroine, and the reader chase a man through three to five hundred pages of incident pre-ordained to end in his capitulation.

Heroines are different from Evelina to-day, and the immediate cause of woman's unrest (second, of course, to the economic urge), is her changing attitude toward man. She has done what Lassalle exhorted workingmen to do: she has increased her wants, or rather, education has increased them for her. And it is this change in attitude toward the matter of sex that irks the anti-Feminist man. He likes to be woman's "favorite phantom," and who can blame him? His ambition to be the leading figure in the pageant is commendable, perhaps; yet the Feminist has a case against him in that, in times past, this same anti-Feminist man has accorded woman second place and then regarded her with more or less friendly contempt because she was secondary. Thus it has been that an element of condescension, repugnant to the Feminist mind, has always been traceable in chivalry and in the sentimental arguments adduced to oppose every step in woman's advancement. And thus it has been, too, that in estimating human excellence a masculine standard has been established and those who have failed to measure up to it have been pronounced "inferior." Occasionally a world-weary pessimist has referred to the "eternal duel" between the sexes, whereupon some sentimental anti-Feminist has amended the phrase by substituting *duet* for *duel,* but usually with the subtle implication that the bass was too strong for the soprano and the soprano was inferior, anyway, because it was not bass.

The invidious masculine criterion has been employed in estimating woman physically, mentally, and morally; and your confirmed anti-Feminist never concedes that the sexes are equal in any respect, though he (or she) may darken counsel with honeyed words of compliment. Thus, in the days when Grant Allen, Goldwin Smith, and other gentlemen of the old school, by their discussion of the woman question rendered the *North American Review,* the *Popular Science Monthly* and other American and English magazines anything but polite literature, we heard much—oh, so painfully much!—of "women's smaller head and brains," "women's inferior nervous organization," "the futility of women's beating their little heads against the solid wall of male supremacy," and other distressing feminine disabilities. Methodists may recall, too, that when Frances Willard and another woman went to take their seats as the first women delegates to the governing body of the church, their physical disqualifications were discussed by very wise men, seriously sometimes, flippantly at others, and, I am sorry to say, indelicately upon more than one occasion.

Owing to our strictly masculine standard of human worth, the poets, from times remote, have attested to woman's mental and moral inferiority. Occasionally, it is true, an Orlando has hung his chivalric effusions upon the trees. However, some sagacious European has declared that no man should write about the fair sex until he is too old to be interested in the subject; and the veriest tyro in literary criticism can see that the sonnet indited by a youth to his sweetheart's dimples is less expressive of the poet's lasting conviction than the utterances of a Dante or a Milton. Now, old Hesiod probably meant to sum up woman's mental vacuity and moral turpitude in one sound, water-tight dictum suitable as a "starter" for all future anti-Feminist argument, when he said, with admirable candor, be it admitted: "Woman is an accursed brute." And one may be sure there were in Greece gentle dames who concurred in his opinion. Again, Virgil's "*Varium et mutabile semper femina*" sounds convincing, but loses weight when one recalls that it was Æneas, not Dido, whose vows were "writ in water." But perhaps Milton ought to be regarded as the anti-Feminist laureate. The masculine standard was always present to his mind, as for example when he sang:

". . . God set thee above her, made of thee
And for thee, whose perfection far excelled
Hers in all real dignity."

In this Puritan press pearl we have a permanent contribution to anti-Feminist literature. Even the mild and lovely Tennyson played into the hands of the enemy, as when he thought it desirable that woman should grow more and more fit to be man's helpmeet,

"Till at last she set herself to man
Like perfect music unto noble words."

Why the poet did not suggest that man set himself to woman we can only conjecture. Goethe, too, seems to have entertained the set-herself-to-man idea. To be sure, he credits the Woman Soul with leading us upward and on, but he also says, "A wife is a convenient loaf of brown bread." One might pursue the upward way on a diet of brown bread, but we have reason to believe that the great Johann Wolfgang preferred white bread and cake.

Sidney Lanier is said to have left the following pathetic memorandum in a note-book: "I have been in Boston. I have written a poem. It is not like the poetry of Longfellow. I am damned." Woman might make a similarly touching confession of failure: I have lived in a world of endeavor; I have made my little effort; it is not like the efforts of man; I am condemned. But before long our time-honored masculine standard will be relegated to the limbo of outworn ideas, and whereas we have known the blessed relations of mother and son, father and daughter, brother and sister, lover and sweetheart, husband and wife, with clear vision will come mutual respect and we shall achieve this also—to be friends. In other words, our love will ripen into friendship.

9

INEZ MILHOLLAND

The Liberation of a Sex (1913)

Roughly, some three million women in California, Oregon, Kansas, Arizona, Idaho, Wyoming, Colorado, Utah, and Washington now have the vote. From the rapidity with which the suffragist movement and its deeper parent, the feminist movement, are traveling, it seems reasonable to assume that within the next five or ten years there will be many more States and a good many million more voters added to the list. The women, then, for the first time in our history, are to have some-

From *McClure's Magazine*, February 1913.

thing approaching an equal voice in the administration of human affairs. They are to sit on juries, to administer public offices, to confer in the high councils of the nation. They are to bring directly to the problems of government and of civilization those qualities, in certain respects different from man's, which they have hitherto been permitted to employ only indirectly, in the private influence of the individual woman on the man who has acted for himself and her in the world of government and affairs. In the course of this great advance they are to be educated in a manner and to a degree different from any experience in the history of the sex.

Is this new freedom of woman to mean merely a large numerical addition to the voting list, or something more? If more, what?

What are the conditions of bondage or restraint from which women are so determined to work free? Can they work free without, consciously or unconsciously, bringing about immense changes in certain of our existing human institutions?

Is this sudden liberation of an entire sex going to mean a revolution of a new and bewildering kind, touching and changing life at every point?

No thoughtful observer can look on at what is taking place before his eyes without coming face to face with some such questions as these. They are so important as to demand some attempt, however inadequate, at an answer.

At the moment, of course, the situation is confused by the fact that a large proportion of the new voters are women of the old types, bred to another standard, not equipped to comprehend the power that has been placed in their hands. Many are of the parasitic sort that Olive Schreiner has so clearly defined in "Woman and Labor." These are naturally conservative, clinging to the conditions that maintain them in idleness or in partial idleness. But it will certainly not be long before the steady influx to the voting ranks of those millions of younger women whose impressions are being formed in the more alert, stirring air of to-day, adding their clearer vision and greater independence of spirit to the hard-headedness of several million workingwomen, will bring the real issues more sharply before us.

We may assume that a sex, with certain bonds of common interest among its members, that are as distinct even to the casual observer as the common interest among a group of bankers or the members of a court or a profession or a political party, will inevitably, like these struggle and press to extend ever more widely its freedom and power. This will follow as surely as a court always tends to increase its jurisdiction. It may be further assumed that this pressure toward a constantly growing freedom and power on the part of the sex means that, in the long run, the institutions most certain to be touched and changed are the institutions in which the sex, as a sex, is most peculiarly and vitally interested. And these institutions, it is hardly necessary to point out, are the home, and marriage itself.

In later issues of the magazine an attempt will be made, in the light of the new attitude toward hitherto forbidden topics, to discuss the coming problems of the home and marriage, leading up to the last and greatest mystery to be illuminated by the modern spirit of inquiry, the baffling riddle of the ages—sex itself as a basis of human relations.

Needless to say, no attempt will be be made to offer solutions to these puzzles. The time is not here for conclusions. The time is distinctly here, however, for discussion to begin. So long as what John Stuart Mill termed "The Subjection of Women," continued, certain ugly facts of life in man's world could be kept from her.

Those unthinking ones who expect the old submission and silence from the free woman of to-day and to-morrow are certainly in for some exceedingly rude shocks. They may lament as they will the passing of what they consider beautiful, innocent womanhood; they are certain to be confronted with a new, alert woman who has discovered that her "home" has, in the complex social life of our time, become entangled in a thousand ways with the outside life of the community and the nation, and who insists, therefore, on her right to inquire into every phase of life, and to act with some authority regarding it.

In the present article it is enough to point out the magnitude of the change that is to-day actually taking place in the mind of woman. This change is, of course, a part and a result of the widespread social stir that is beginning to remake civilization on a new basis of thought.

Study what the women are printing and saying, in the light of the underlying body of modern thought from which they are clearly drawing their ideas and their inspiration, and you will arrive at certain rather obvious conclusions. The most inescapable of these conclusions will be that the new spirit of inquiry is penetrating into the remotest, obscurest corners of life, searching boldly under the premises of everything profane and sacred, and publishing its discoveries broadcast. The most serious mistake we can make is to underrate the pervasive strength of this new leaven in human life. The old reticences are destroyed forever. The myriad army of new thoughts is sapping and mining its way into human minds everywhere in the world. And, as the minds change and grow, civilization and all its institutions will change and grow.

This change and growth is already taking certain observable directions, all apparently converging into a new morality.

The first step was, learning to be frank. Only a few years ago, when certain publications began a discussion of the need of telling children the secrets of sex and life, "good" people everywhere were outraged. The great majority, ignorant and apathetic, clearly preferred that their children should gather this information furtively and perversely from the street. But the discussion grew and gathered force until now we talk the problems of prostitution, and its terribly complex and devastating consequences, in public forums, in suffrage conventions, in our general magazines, even in our pulpits.

We have about dropped the leering furtiveness that formerly characterized all talk about sex. We are openly reading Bernard Shaw's keen and witty but powerful utterances on the forbidden topic, Havelock Ellis on sex psychology and social hygiene, Reginald Wright Kaufman on the terribly tragic life of the prostitute. The plays of Brieux dealing bluntly with topics that have hitherto lain far beneath the plane of public discussion, are lying on center tables in thousands of homes. We read in Ellen Key's "Love and Marriage" that the monogamy to which we attribute so much of our virtue does not exist and never has existed, and there are those who accept it as a fact. A stupid and backward post-office department closes the mails to the exceedingly plain-spoken report of the Chicago Vice Committee, and is promptly put to shame (and to a reversal of its ruling) by the indignant voices of thoughtful, respectable women demanding that the book be circulated as widely as possible.

And through all this frankness runs a definite tendency toward an assault on the dual standard of morality and an assertion of sex rights on the part of woman.

There is a play, "Hindle Wakes," which is arousing interest in London, New York, and Chicago. A girl has slipped away for a weekend with the son of her father's employer. The fact is discovered. The boy is persuaded to marry her, "to save her honor." The girl flatly refuses; she can not see how it will save her honor to spend her life in a degrading alliance with a man she does not love.

"But you *did* love me," he insists. "You must have loved me!"

She turns on him and asks: "Did you love me?"

"No," he replies, falling back on the old dual standard. "But I'm a man. It was just my fancy of the moment."

"Well," she replies uncompromisingly, "I'm a woman. It was just my fancy of the moment."

There you have the new issue stated flatly and boldly. It was a challenge, and it was applauded.

To deny that such thoughts are stirring in women's minds is to deny an overwhelmingly obvious fact. To keep quiet about it any longer is a useless deference to the reticence of yesterday—the reticence that is passing with the secluded, the parasitic woman. Nothing has been mentioned here that is not already actually a commonplace of open discussion. To be sure, there are many thoughtful and distinctly modern women who will disclaim some of the above statements. But, as was said near the beginning of this article, woman's new freedom and power will inevitably tend to increase. And it does seem reasonable, even necessary, to believe that they are bound to find themselves ultimately fighting for freedom from the domination of man and property in their lives. And it is further difficult to see how they can change that condition without changing, at the same time, the terms on which woman has until now bestowed her sex, without, indeed, changing the institutions that we have until now regarded as basic to civilization itself.

To those who find themselves unable to trust to the immensely complex adaptive ingenuity of the race in following out the processes of evolution and in creating new conditions of life to meet new needs, the prospect is bound to be deeply alarming. We are releasing a full half of our people from a sex-property enslavement that has endured, through various modifications, from the dim background of history until the present time. There is no use in blinking the fact that we can not liberate woman without ultimately finding ourselves facing radical changes in her relations with man as regards the two vital matters of property and sex. For, acting from a deep-lying sense of injustice, guided by minds that study deeper and see further, the mass of women are fighting to change these very things. Many of them, naturally, shrink from such radical thoughts. But to expect that they can change these vital relations, and still leave them as they were, is to expect too much.

The old social doctrines insisted on submission. In the new, submission is the last quality desired. The quality of the age is a flat refusal to submit to anything on faith, but to insist on testing and examining life at every point. And, as is well known, women, when they are thoroughly aroused, can ask a good many questions.

10

Florence Tuttle
The Psychic Side of Feminism (1915)

The European war instead of relegating the woman question to the background in reality forces it to the front. The work of Europe today is to a large degree being done by women. While the war is making widows and orphans it is also creating feminists of an advanced type.

A feminist we assume to be a woman with an awakened sense of individual responsibility toward life, expressing this responsibility in action. Feminism becomes thus a matter of spiritual initiative and impulse.

The woman's movement has been viewed from many angles. It has been seen as a sex problem, a domestic problem, an industrial problem, and a political problem, according to the insight, or the bewilderment, of the spectator. But the psychic awakening—the real cause of feminism—has been relatively overlooked.

These chapters are an effort to trace to their mental and spiritual sources the growing activities of women, and to indicate that the freeing of woman's creative energies, instead of being inimical to human progress, is in reality necessary to it. . . .

It is hardly an exaggeration to say that no other question of modern times has been so much discussed, and so befogged and obscured in the discussion, as the omnipresent woman question. And the reason is not far to seek: we are still in its throes. An object viewed too near

From Florence Guertin Tuttle, *The Awakening of Woman: Suggestions from the Psychic Side of Feminism* (New York: The Abingdon Press, 1915), 7–8, 11–21, 23–28.

is likely to be thrown out of focus. Also the very magnitude of the question alarms and confuses us. One half the race, and all posterity, seem threatened by the new activities of women. The business of life is to preserve racial integrity. Small wonder, then, that the world regards obliquely and with suspicion the apparent revolt of so large a proportion of its component parts.

But is there any occasion for real alarm? May we not, by a process of elimination, arrive at the source of misunderstanding? We may not comprehend the woman question, for instance, if we regard merely the woman of to-day. It is necessary to take the long look down the ages and visualize the woman of all time. And one must focus this woman in her relation to the march of human events. To isolate the question is to see woman under the shadow of an eclipse, an attenuated crescent, not a fully rounded orb.

When woman is placed, thus, in her historic setting, the question of feminism becomes not a woman's problem but a race problem. For the woman question is the child question, and the child question is, or should be, the subject of paramount importance to both men and women. The woman question becomes, therefore, of supreme interest to humanity, ranking first in those problems that loom largest on the twentieth century horizon.

Nor may this vital subject be comprehended while it is still regarded in the light of sex, only. In the great changes of modern life the position of woman has become not a sex but a social question—a question of how best to utilize to social advantage woman's liberated energies. He who still considers woman as an individual in her relationship to man alone—after the manner of certain novelists upon whose sensitive souls the undigested woman question lies heavily—must necessarily regard her with sex predominant. Scientific sociology forbids this exclusive view. To comprehend the woman question fully one must also consider woman in her relationship to society, with its multifarious, complex demands.

The true banner bearers of the woman's movement are women who, for the most part, have fulfilled themselves as wives and mothers and who are now fulfilling themselves still further in some form of socially productive work. Such women embody the true meaning of feminism: mental and spiritual advancement. They do not decry sex. They are too sane and too human. Neither do they unnecessarily extol it nor acknowledge its so-called "limitations." If women in the past, they would argue, when families were large, could still fulfill themselves as industrial workers, when the labor of the world was cruelly manual, and woman bore the lion's share—surely woman to-day can fulfill herself as mother and world worker, when the family is reduced and work has become largely mechanical or clerical. The woman's movement includes sex but is not limited by it.

Above all, the woman question is not one of sex antagonism, as a few ultrafeminists charge. No movement in history has ever made for so profound sex unity, since the aim of feminism is to place humanity on a more equitable and unifying plane. The interests of men and women are equal and indissoluble: race guardianship and preservation. The opportunities must also be equal. One might as well talk of antagonism between wave and tide, or moon and star. Fortunately the deep-seated law of attraction between men and women is potent enough to offset any antagonism, fancied or real.

How do we judge this subject of primary racial importance? Do we view it in the light of pure reason and applied science? The very strength of our interest forbids. It is not an exaggeration to say that two thirds of the world consider the woman question, not according to reason and logic, but from the mists of individual prejudice and an inherited bias.

Yet because of its very gravity no other problem so challenges the impersonal, scientific mind. No question is regarded seriously, to-day, that will not survive the scientific test. Scientific formula is applied in every direction, from the efficiency of the brick-layer to the method of the college professor, but not to the woman question. A womanhood evolving, according to well-established laws, from the lower to the higher, from the simple to the complex, from the homogeneous to the heterogeneous, is not yet considered, except in rare instances, a normal, scientific growth.

In the average mind, wherein lies the supposed menace of feminism? Analyzed, would it not read thus: if woman be allowed unlimited freedom to expand and to enter all channels of creative activity, will she not neglect the most fundamental part of her nature, motherhood, or at least disregard the more than precious blood of her blood and bone of her bone?

This view of the question is supremely important. But it is a material view and as such only partial. For herein lies the crux of the misunderstood woman question: it is usually regarded in its material aspect, whereas the woman's movement, in its original essence, is spiritual. It is an inner revolution before it is an outer revolt, subjective before objective. All the recent unprecedented activities of women have been but manifestations of this inner quickening. Arising from interior necessity, they are but symbols of a spiritual revolution sweeping the sisterhood of the earth. They are the result of cause and effect, of action and reaction on a psychic plane. Any view less comprehensive than this spiritually inclusive view is superficial, and therefore imperfect. . . .

Admitting that the woman's movement has arisen from the compulsion of newly awakened powers, what do the terms mental and spiritual expansion for women imply? Do they embrace qualities of practical race value? Or do they signify the mystical, the visionary, and the unreal?

Considering mental enlargement for women—does feminism aim to make an intellectual Amazon of the future woman? Freedom of mental opportunity has not thus abnormally transformed man. All that can be claimed for man is that widespread educational opportunity—long confined to the nobility and the clergy—has raised the mental average. Can we not endure a like elevation of the sex whose average mentality has been the joke of the ages? . . .

Mental expansion for women, then, implies a higher average of trained intelligence unfolding normally into all lines of human activity, not only where a certain accuracy of thought is required, but also where success depends absolutely upon the efficiency and initiative there attained.

To define spiritual expansion becomes far more difficult since we find ourselves in the realm of the abstract rather than the concrete. Perhaps no phrase in the English language is more misinterpreted than the phrase, "The life of the spirit." Belonging to the unseen, we do not yet recognize its relationship to the seen. Itself immaterial, we do not yet grasp its value materially. Invested almost entirely with the idea of religion, of the mystic and supernatural, the life of the spirit has been dismissed by the practical as good, possibly, for priests, for dreamers, for women, but not for strong human beings with coursing red corpuscles. Yet modern metaphysicians tell us that the life of the spirit is as real as flesh and blood and doubly important since it dominates the physical.

It is true that the life of the spirit is the God-life. To worship, however, is but one of its functions. The life of the spirit is also the life of the imagination, without which there could be no conception of Deity. To originate is its high mission. Consciously or unconsciously it becomes the motive power of character, of vocation, of destiny. The life of the spirit must, therefore, be widened to include the life of the imagination, of creative gifts and capacities. No invention, no work of art, no great business enterprise, but must first have its spiritual, imaginative prototype. The cultivation of the imagination becomes, thus, of the highest practicality since upon its recognition depend all kinds and all degrees of success. The life of the spirit, instead of being supernatural, becomes, in reality, the supreme expression of the natural—not yet understood.

The term, "the spiritual awakening of woman," then, does not denote the religious awakening of woman, though a higher form of religion is necessarily a part of it. It signifies a womanhood moving irresistibly toward this highest realm of existence—the exercise of creative imagination—a movement absolutely essential for symmetrical racial development if humanity is to utilize all its creative possibilities.

From this spiritually creative realm women, by the necessity of past material obligations, have been almost entirely debarred. No sex is responsible for this inhibition. Evolution is responsible. In the establishment of civilization it was imperative that material foundations should be laid first. And women have been the pile drivers of the race. . . .

Comprehended, then, as the liberation of woman's mental and spiritual energies for racial advantage—is the woman's movement scientific? That is, does it run counter or parallel to established ideas of human growth?

To do any logical thinking we are told that we must think in terms of the controlling scientific thought of the age. As is well known, the scientific principle of to-day is the one of evolutionary development—that the species, acted upon by heredity and environment, is constantly passing through certain organic variations and adaptations. Without knowledge of this widespread law, human crafts have little perception of whence they came or whither they are going. Evolution becomes thus more than a compass. It is a mariner's chart for life.

Comparatively recently this principle has taught us that nothing is fixed and stationary, as we once amazingly believed, but that all things are moving, dynamic, being constantly acted upon by attractions from within and without.

Darwin traced the law patiently through the tireless formation of species. Herbert Spencer applied it to government, to education, to marriage, and to religion, showing that human institutions, too, are not fixed and final, but are fluid, plastic, still in the making. Karl Marx fitted the development theory to the evolution of industry, foretelling, as only the man of science who deals with law may foretell, the great industrial combinations of to-day. And Buckle, in his monumental fragment of generalization, successfully applied the idea to the growth of English civilization.

We are generously willing to admit the working of this universal law in all these directions. Only over the heads of women do our affections, ever blinding our interests, inscribe, "Thou, and thou only, must not change." The habit of ages is against our possessing sufficient elasticity to allow even natural law to work, without protest, in the mothers of men.

But is natural law unnatural only where women are concerned? Is science not science in conjunction with mothers only? Is evolution going off at a tangent in women? We may answer only by learning what direction it has taken in man. Women are the other half of the same species.

We know that the variety of man's experiences has been the instigator of his progress. He has grown in proportion as he has exercised new functions, new abilities, daring to enter new fields. To the privilege of unrestricted range man owes his supremacy as world builder and master.

The history of woman reveals a creature specialized almost entirely to one set of interests. From such specialization we should not expect versatility nor complete expression.

In point of developed mentality and exercise of the imagination, woman is far behind man. With woman, evolution has only just begun the conscious unfolding of the psychic. But it has begun. The same law is at work. Conditions at last permit. Racial advance demands it. The barque of womanhood, bearing the sacred freight of the children of the future, is turned in the same general direction of creative evolution as that of man. Together they sail on the same seas, moving toward the same goal—the port of a spiritually perfected race.

The woman's movement, running thus parallel with accepted laws of human growth, and not counter to them, is distinctively scientific. Viewed in the light of human evolution, with its steady push from the physical to the mental, from the mental to the spiritual, the feminist movement takes its place logically in the sequence of the development of the human family. In cosmic history it is of all events the most significant and far-reaching.

To those of us who sit at the feet of science and still retain the old faith in expanded form, this spiritual development of the race seems a not impossible ideal. In fact any lesser goal is insufficient. Life on the material side, merely, fails to satisfy. We are born for spiritual adventure, true sailors, not of the wave but of the soul.

Considered thus in its spiritual interpretation, alone, may the misunderstood woman question be comprehended. It is then recognized as constructive, not destructive, in character. To recapitulate: the woman question is not an isolated question, but a related question. It is not a woman problem; it is a race problem. It is not a sex question only—it is social. Above all it is not material; it is spiritual—a loosening of the psychically creative forces of women for race advancement. As such it follows the general trend of all human development on the three planes of being: body, mind, and spirit, and becomes scientific. It is not making for sex antagonism, but for deeper sex unity. Its influence is, therefore, not baneful but beneficent. Its object is not race confusion but race completion. With far higher aspirations than women were capable of fulfilling in the past, it is developing a far higher type of motherhood than the world has ever known. It is Nature's own movement. To misunderstand and try to check it is not only to retard the cause of woman, but also to retard the spiritual advancement of mankind.

11

GERTRUDE ATHERTON

What Is Feminism? (1916)

...These are not to be suffrage papers. There is no doubt in my mind that the women of all nations will have the franchise eventually, if

From *The Delineator*, October and November 1916.

only because it is ridiculous that they should be permitted to work like men (often supporting men) and not be permitted all the privileges of men. Man, who grows more enlightened every year—often sorely against his will—will appreciate this anomaly in due course, and will almost automatically give the franchise as freely to women as they have given it to negroes and imbeciles. When women have received the vote for which they have fought and bled, they will use it with just about the same proportion of conscientiousness and enthusiasm that busy men do.

But while Suffrage and Feminism are related, they are far from identical. Suffrage is but a milestone in Feminism, which may be described as the more or less concerted sweep of women from the backwaters into the broad central stream of life. Several times before in the history of the world comparatively large numbers of women have made themselves felt, claiming certain equal rights with men. But their ambitions were generally confined to founding religious orders, obtaining admission to the universities, or to playing the intellectual game in the social preserves. In the wonderful Thirteenth Century women rivaled the men in learning and accomplishments, but this is the first time that millions of them have been out in the world "on their own," and have invaded almost every field of work, for centuries sacrosanct to man. There is even a boilermaker in the United States who worked her way up in poor-boy fashion and now attends conventions of boilermakers on equal terms. In tens of thousands of cases women have made good, in the arts, professions, trades, businesses, clerical positions, and even in agriculture, ranching, and cattle-raising. Whether this success is to be permanent, whether they have done wisely in invading man's domain so generally, are questions to be attacked later, when considering the biological differences between man and woman. The most interesting problem relating to woman that confronts us at present is the effect of the European war on the whole status of woman.

If we of the United States are able to remain at peace, we shall at least keep our men, and the males of this country are already so far in excess of the females that it is odd so many American women should be driven to work. In Great Britain the women have long outnumbered the men; it was estimated before the war that there were some three hundred thousand women for whom no husbands were available. After the war there will be at best something like a proportion of one whole man to ten women, and the other afflicted countries, with the possible exception of Russia, will show a similar dislocation of the normal balance. The acute question will be repopulation—with a view to another trial of military strength a generation later!—and all sorts of expedients are being suggested, from polygamy to artificial fertilization. Now, the whole future of woman, after this war is over, depends upon whether she concludes to serve the state or herself.

There is hardly any doubt that a year or two hence, possibly a few months hence, women for the first time in the history of civilization will have it in their power to seize the reins of the world; that they can, if they will, compel man to share with them on equal terms.

But will the women do it? It is to be supposed that all the men who are fighting in this great war are heroes in the eyes of the women over there, and those that survive are likely to be regarded with awe and passionate admiration. The traditional weakness of woman where men are concerned (which, after all, is but a cunning device of Nature) may swamp their great opportunity. They may fight over the surviving males like dogs over a bone, marry with sensations of profound gratitude any old wreck that does them the honor to propose, and drop forever out of the ranks of Woman as differentiated from the ranks of mere women. The blind, the halt, the disfigured, may seem nine times more desirable than no man at all; for one thing that has hampered the cause of woman in Europe is that the women are so generally man-crazy. This is partly temperamental, but is even more deeply rooted in centuries of man's persistence in proclaiming and maintaining his superiority. Circumstances helped him for centuries, and he has been taken at his own valuation. It is difficult for American women to realize this almost servile attitude of even British women toward the male animal. One of the finest things about the militant woman, one by which she scored most heavily, was her flinging off of this tradition and displaying a shining armor of indifference toward man as man. This startled the men almost as much as window-smashing, and made other women, living out their little lives under the smiles and frowns of the all-powerful sex, think and ponder, wonder if their small rewards amounted to half as much as the untasted pleasures of power and independence.

It is doubtful if even the militants can revert to their former singleness of purpose; after many months, possibly years, of devotion to duty, serving others, forgetfulness of self, appreciation of the naked fact that the integrity of their country matters more than anything else on earth, they may be quite unable to rebound to their old fanatical attitude toward suffrage as the one important issue of the Twentieth Century. Even the very considerable number of these women who have reached an age and appearance which would eliminate them from the contest over such men as are left may be so softened by the horrible sufferings they have witnessed, so moved by the astounding endurance and the grim valor of men, that they will have lost the disposition to tear from men the few compensations the end of the war will leave them. If that is the case, if women at the end of the war are soft, completely restored to the femininity, the femaleness, which was their original endowment from Nature, the whole great movement, will subside, and the work will all have to be begun over again by women and their accumulated grievances, some fifty years hence.

Nothing is more sure than that Nature will take advantage of the lull to make a desperate attempt to recover her lost ground. Progressive women—and they are numbered by the hundreds of thousands—their ranks before the war recruited daily, were one of the most momentous results of the forces of the higher civilization, an evolution that in Nature's eyes represented a lamentable divergence from type. Here is woman, with all her physical disabilities, become man's rival in all of the arts and nearly all of the productive walks of life, as well as in a large percentage of the professional and executive; intellectually the equal, if not the superior, of the average man—who in these days, poor devil, is born a specialist,—and making a bold bid for political equality.

BRAIN WORK VERSUS BRUTE WORK

It was a magnificent accomplishment, in spite of its limitations, and it marked one of the most brilliant and picturesque milestones in human progress. It seems incredible that woman, in spite of the tremendous pressure Nature will put upon her, may weakly revert to type. The most powerful of all the forces working for Nature and against Feminism will be the quite brutal and obscene naturalness of war, and the gross familiarity of Civilization with it throughout so long a period. There is reversion to type with a vengeance! The ablest of the men inheritors of the accumulated wisdom and experiences and civilizing influences of the centuries were in power during the month of July, 1914, and not one of them, nor all combined, could think of a better way of settling their jealousies and imaginary grievances than by brute fighting! Combined with the more powerful and ingenious engines of destruction evolved by the modern scientific mind is a singular reaction to certain of the weapons and resources of the dark ages. There has been some brain-work during the war, so far, but a long sight more brute-work. And the women, giving every waking hour to ameliorating the lot of the fighters or tending them in hospital, have been stark up against the physical side; whether making bombs in factories, bandages and uniforms, washing gaping wounds, or listening to the hideous tales of the soldiers home on leave.

WOMAN BRED TO SERVE

The European woman, in spite of her exalted pitch, is living more or less of a mechanical life at present. And she is automatically performing those duties of women for which Nature so elaborately equipped her, ministering to man exclusively, even when temporarily filling his place in the factory or the tram-car. *Dienen! Dienen!* is the motto of one and all of these Kundrys, whether they realize it or not, and it is on the cards that they may never again wish to somersault back to that mental attitude where they would dominate, not serve.

On the other hand, Civilization may for once be stronger than Nature. Thinking women—and millions of women have been thinking these last ten or fifteen years, whether they were suffragettes, feminists, or merely household women—may emerge from this hideous reversion of Europe to barbarism with an utter contempt for man. They may despise the men of affairs—for muddling Europe into the most terrible war in history, in the very midst of the greatest civilization of which there is any record. They may experience a secret but profound revulsion from the men wallowing in blood and living to kill for so many months, returning home for an interval of peace like beasts from the jungle, with bloody chops, but sleepy and satiated for the moment. Women have grown very fastidious. I heard a cultivated European woman say last Summer that it was unthinkable that any decent women would ever live again with the men who had lived so long like filthy beasts in the trenches.

The end of this war may mark a conclusive revulsion of European women from men, a revulsion that will last until they have passed the productive age. Instead of softening, disintegrating back to type, they may be insensibly hardening in a mold that will eventually cast them forth a more definite third sex than any that threatened before the war. . . .

Now, this may sound fantastic, but it is absolutely probable. And it is to be remembered that woman has in her subconscious brain-cells ancestral memories of the Matriarchate. It is interesting to quote in this connection what Patrick Geddes and G. Arthur Thompson have to say on the mooted question of the Mother-Age.

"Prehistoric history" is hazardous, but there is a good case to be made out for the reality of a "Mother-Age." This has been reconstructed from fossils of the folk-lore of agriculture and housewifery, in old customs, ceremonies, festivals, games; in myths and fairy-tales and age-worn words. . . .

In the Mother-Age the inheritance of property passed through the mother; the woman gave her children her own name; husband and father were in the background—often far from individualized; the brother and uncle were much more important; the woman was the depository of custom, lore and religious tradition; she was, at least the nominal head of the family; and she had a large influence in tribal affairs.

WHAT NAME FOR THE CHILDREN?

For some years past certain progressive women have shown signs of a reversion to the matriarchal state. In marrying, for instance, they have retained their own name, even not being addressed as Mrs. In fact, the custom is growing prevalent. Then there is the hyphen marriage, more common still, in which the woman retains her own name, but condescends to annex the man's. Once in a way a man will prefix his wife's name to his own, and there is one on record who prefixed his own to his wife's. But we may have our opinions of him!

So far as I have been able to ascertain, these marriages are quite as successful as the average; and if the woman has a career on hand—and she generally has—she pursues it unhampered. The grandmother or aunt takes care of the children, if there are any, while she is at her duties without the home, and, so far, the husband has been permitted the compensation of endowing his children with his name.

The reversion to the prehistoric Matriarchate can hardly be complete in these days, but there are many significant straws that indicate the rising of a new wind directed by ancient instinct. To look upon them as shockingly advanced or abnormal is a mistake.

A still more significant sign of the times (the linking of past to present) is the ever-increasing number of women doctors and their enormous success. Men for the most part have ceased to sneer or even to be more than humanly jealous, often speaking in terms of the warmest admiration not only of their skill, but of their conscientiousness and power of endurance. . . .

. . . It would seem that the biological differences between the male and the female, which are so often the causes of women's failure in so many spheres preempted throughout long centuries by man, is in her case counteracted not only by her ancestral inheritance, but by the high moral element without which no doctor or surgeon can long stand the terrible exactions and strain of his profession. No woman goes blithely into surgery or medicine merely to have a career or to make a living, although ten thousand girls to her one will try to write or paint or clerk or cultivate her bit of a voice, without a thought of her peculiar fitness or of any obligations it may evolve. But the woman who enters deliberately the profession of healing has, almost invariably, a certain nobility of mind, a lack of personal selfishness, and a power of devotion to the race quite unknown to the average woman, even the woman of genius, when seeking a career. . . .

. . . Are women the equal of men in all things? Their emancipation from mere marriage, and successful invasion of so many remunerative walks of life, have made so much noise in the world since woman really took the bit between her teeth, that the feministic pæan of triumph has almost smothered an occasional protest from those concerned with biology; but, as a matter of fact, statistics regarding the staying power of woman in what for all the centuries have been avocations especially suited to the mental and physical equipment of man are too misleading to be of any value. . . .

Now, why has no one ever thought of employing men as "maids" of all work? On ocean liners it is the stewards that take care of the staterooms, and they keep them like wax, and make the best bed known to civilization. The stewardesses in heavy weather attend to the prostrate of their own sex, but otherwise do nothing but arrange the baths, hook up, and receive tips. Men wait in the dining-room and look out for the passengers on deck. There isn't the most militant suffragist who would not be surprised and annoyed to see stewardesses scurrying round on deck with the morning broth and rugs, or dancing attendance in a nauseous sea.

I can conceive of a household where a well-trained man, cooking, doing the "wash," waiting on the table, sweeping, and, if the mistress has a young child, or is indolent and given to the rocking-chair and a novel-a-day, making the beds without a wrinkle. I will venture to say that a man thus employed would finish his work before eight o'clock, and spend two hours with his girl or at his club. Many a Jap in California does the amount of work I have described and absorbs knowledge in and out of books during his hours of leisure. Indeed, I have talked with Japs in San Francisco who make a hundred dollars a month by getting up at five in the morning to wash a certain number of front steps and sweep sidewalks, cook a breakfast, and wash up the dinner dishes in one servantless household, the lunch in another, clean up generally in another, cook the dinner, wait on the table, and clean up in another. As white men are stronger, they could do even more, and support some girl in an intensive little flat where her work would be both light and spiritually remunerative. As thousands of men really have no brains or real fitness for the great struggle with life, the domestic service not only would solve the problem for them, but release as many thousand young women from the factory, the counter, and the exhausting misery of a home that can never be theirs. At night he could feel like a householder and that he lived to some purpose. Certainly such an innovation would thin the ranks of the most ancient of all industries, if, according to the statisticians, they are recruited by the lonely servant, the tired shop-girl, and the despairing factory hand.

For it is all a question of muscle and biology.

I have stated before that I believe in equal suffrage, if only because women are the mothers of men, and therefore their equals. But I think there are several times more reasons why women should not overwork their bodies and brains and wear themselves out trying to be men, than why it is quite right and fitting that they should walk up to the polls and cast a vote for men who more or less control their destinies.

When it comes to the arts, it is another matter. If a woman finds herself with a talent (I'll refrain from such a big word as genius, as only posterity should presume to apply that term to any one's differentiation from his fellows), by all means let her work like a man, and make every necessary sacrifice to develop this blessed gift, not only because it is a duty, but because the rewards are adequate. The artistic career, where the impulse is genuine, furnishes, both in its rewards and in the exercise of the gift itself, far more happiness and even more satisfaction than husband, children, or home. The chief reason is that it is the supreme form of self-expression, the ego's apotheosis, the power to indulge in the highest form of spiritual pride, differentiation from the mass. These are brutal truths, and another truth is that happiness is what we are all after, whatever form our hypocrisy takes; only civilization has taught us not to sacrifice others too much in its pursuit. In fact, entirely selfish people rarely are happy, unless they happen to be fools.

To create, to feel something spinning out of your brain, which you hardly realize is there until formulated on paper, the adventurous life involved in the exercise of any art, with its uncertainties, its varieties, its disappointments, its supreme satisfactions after recognition, the mistakes, and the fight, and the exaltations, the highly developed appreciation of beauty and art—all this is the very best that life has to offer. And as art is as impartial as a microbous disease, women often achieve, individually, as much as men; sometimes more. If their bulk has not in the past been as great, the original handicaps, which women in general, aided by science and a more educated public, are fast shedding, alone were to blame. Certainly as many women as men, in this country, at least, are engaged in artistic careers, and more, if one judged by the proportion in the magazines. . . .

But when it comes to working like men for the sake of independence, of avoiding marriage, of "doing something," that is another matter. To my mind it is abominable that society is so constituted that women are forced to work for their bread at tasks that are far too hard for them, and that extract the sweetness from youth, and unfit them physically for what the vast majority of women want more than anything else in life—children. That is why the outcry against giving women the vote, *i.e.,* an entering wedge into politics, is so stupid; nine-tenths of all the women any one can meet in a year's investigation, or in a lifetime's, for that matter, want children. The trouble is that they do not realize it early in youth, and are often worn out in body and nerves before they awaken to the fact that the independent life *per se* is a delusion, and that their completion, as well as happiness and economic security, lies in a brood and a husband to support it.

There used to be volumes of indignation expended upon the American mother toiling in the household, at the washtub for hire, or trudging daily to some other remunerative task, while her daughters, after a fairly good education, idly flirted, and danced, and read, and finally married. Now, although that *modus operandi* sounds vulgar and ungrateful, it is, biologically speaking, quite as it should be. Girls of that age should be tended as carefully as house-plants, and, indeed women until they are at least thirty-five (when they will have completed their families, if they married young) should be protected as much as possible from severe physical and mental strain. If women ever are to compete with men on anything like an equal basis, it is when they are in their middle years, when Nature's handicaps are fairly outgrown, child-bearing and its years of intervening lassitude are over, as well as the recurrent carboniferous waste and relaxations. . . .

. . . But I hope I have made it clear that any woman who wastes her precarious early vitality in self-support, when the choice lies with herself, is a fool. Nature designed and equipped men to take care of women during the years of maximum femaleness, and to deprive them of this privilege is unjust to both sexes.

II. Early Feminist Scholarship

AS DOCUMENTED IN VOLUME I OF *PUBLIC WOMEN, PUBLIC WORDS,* post–Civil War America saw higher education become a crucial site of feminist contention over access to male institutions. A college or university degree meant an education, self-definition, and new experiences relatively free from family supervision, while opening doors to the increasingly comfortable middle class. For women, college was a way to economic independence and social mobility, a way that didn't require marriage but (for better or worse) provided a personal route into corporate America, the professoriate, and the professions of law and medicine. By the turn of the twentieth century, American women could count on greater access to various institutions of higher learning. More and more liberal arts colleges became coeducational, while a number of private women's colleges in the Northeast flourished and gained national prominence. State land-grant universities in the Midwest and the West—among them California, Illinois, Iowa, Kansas, Michigan, Minnesota, Missouri, Nebraska, Ohio, Washington, and Wisconsin—enrolled an equal number of men and women as incoming undergraduates by 1900. And new, private, richly endowed institutions such as the University of Chicago and Stanford University were explicitly founded as coeducational. Nevertheless, assumptions regarding women's comparative physical and intellectual inability in higher education proved difficult to overcome. They were rooted in elaborate pre-twentieth-century social-cultural prescriptions of women's domestic role and bolstered by conservative applications of Darwinian science. Leading male educators—such as Edward Clarke, M.D., author of the highly influential book *Sex and Education* (1873), and psychologist G. Stanley Hall, early-twentieth-century president of Clark University—continued to maintain, among other things, that women were constitutionally unsuited for the rigors of study and that social evolution required an all-male environment of learning. Thus, the struggle for equality in American higher education is a long story that continues into and throughout the twentieth century.

One of the central figures in turn-of-the-twentieth-century coeducation was sociologist Marion Talbot, author of "Present-Day Problems in the Education of Women" (1897). The first dean of women at the University of Chicago, Talbot fought throughout her career for "greater freedom" for female students and faculty. In 1881–1882 Talbot cofounded the Association of Collegiate Alumnae (precursor to the American Association of University Women), designed to define, unify, and support the interests of women in college and graduate school. She served as the organization's president from 1895 to 1897. Among the "present-day problems" Talbot identifies is overspecialization of curriculum. Critical of the encroaching utilitarian ethic of education, Talbot stresses the value of broad learning for its own sake. Paradoxically, Talbot convinced University of Chicago President William Rainey Harper in 1904 to establish and appoint her director of a department of household administration. Thus, Talbot's legacy is mixed: while striving for coeducational equality, her interest in domestic science appears to support sexual segregation in college curricula.

M. Carey Thomas's essay "Present Tendencies in Women's College and University Education" (1908) was originally given as a 1907 speech commemorating the twenty-fifth anniversary of the Association of Collegiate Alumnae. Thomas used the occasion to recall the grave doubt that she and her generation of women had about their place in higher education; seemingly everything she read as a girl during the 1860s and 1870s—from the Bible, to Shakespeare, to Edward Clarke's *Sex and Education* ("that gloomy little specter")—assumed female frailty and intellectual inferiority. This speech, then, celebrates women's success in partially breaking down these views. As Thomas points out, few in 1907 challenged the propriety of coeducation itself. Thomas enjoyed unusual authority on the subject of women in higher education. One of the first female graduates of Cornell University, she earned a Ph.D. in classics in 1882 from the University of Zurich and then went on to serve as president from 1894 to 1922 of Bryn Mawr College, where she tried to maintain standards equal to or higher than those of the most elite men's institutions.

Despite the growing acceptance of women into institutions of higher education, women's ability to think at a level equal to men continued to be questioned. Evolutionary theory provided a major source and rationale for this doubt, mixing popular cultural views on women's developmental differences from men with the rigid system of sexual dimorphism found in the writings of Charles Darwin himself. After his monumental treatise *Origin of the Species* (1859), which identifies the mechanism of natural selection as determinative of all organic evolution, Darwin focused on human history in *The Descent of Man* (1871). Like most other discourse in mid-nineteenth-century Euro-American thought, Darwin's writings in natural science assumed that the word *man* covered all humans, with males being prototypical of the species and females consigned to a secondary almost inconsequential status. Even when *man* was used in a way superficially gender neutral, its contextual meaning applied specifically if not always exclusively to the male sex. Thus, when Darwin stated that through his theory of natural selection "much light will be thrown on the origin of man and his history," he referred to *both* humans in general and men in particular. *Descent of Man* minimizes the definition and activity of women. In diametric contrast to the highly metabolic and variable males of the species, human females are conceived in Darwinism as low level, low energy, and indistinct: they are smaller and weaker in size and, perhaps more important to modern understanding of sexual difference, less productive intellectually—women's minds are less analytical, less resistant to emotion. From these Darwinian tenets, then, came new support for cultural assumptions about man's proper place being in the public spheres of politics and business and woman's place being in the family and other "less demanding" private realms.

The Darwinian biases against women's intelligence, along with their devastating cultural implications, prompted young feminist scholars to challenge the objective scientific bases of such positions. This early-twentieth-century scholarship came primarily in psychology, sociology, and anthropology—relatively new disciplines in the human sciences that, compared to history and political science for instance, more easily opened themselves up to women and feminist-based research. Helen Bradford Thompson's study "The Mental Traits of Sex" (1903) (a section from her University of Chicago Ph.D. dissertation of the same title) is representative of this pioneering effort in psychology. Setting out to test the biological origins of psychological differences between the sexes, Thompson chose twenty-five male and twenty-five female undergraduates from the University of Chicago and proceeded to examine their motor skills and sensory abilities. The results did not prove innate traits based on sex, only random patterns of differences between the women and the men. Thus, Thompson conjectures that such differences as physical strength, motor skills, and ingenuity are determined environmentally—that is, by the greatly divergent expectations society has for women and men.

While Darwin's belief in natural male primacy could be used for conservative purposes, the broader Darwinian evolutionary framework of adaptation and natural selection supported feminist revisions of historical relations between the sexes. No one contributed more to this project than Charlotte Perkins Gilman, author of *Women and Economics* (1898) and one of the most respected and well-known feminist intellectuals of early-twentieth-century America. Between 1909 and 1916, Gilman single-handedly published *The Forerunner,* a monthly journal of feminist literary and cultural criticism, social science, fiction, and poetry that included the long series "The Man-Made World: or, Our Androcentric Culture." In these articles (published as a book of the same title in 1911), Gilman draws from the evolutionary sociology of Lester Ward to trace the growth of male dominance over women's lives. For Gilman, sexual history is largely a story of patriarchy, or what she calls *androcentricism:* the broad-based set of social practices, relationships, and institutions that systematically subordinates women well after any original reasons for sexual distinctions have been eliminated. As

Gilman sees it, an overemphasis on sexuality and motherhood retarded women's development. In the chapter "Politics and Warfare," which appeared in *The Forerunner* in 1910, she argues that the modern state is prepossessed by war because it has not overcome an "ultra male" instinct toward group aggression—an impulse stemming from early heterosexuality, since (as she points out) the first raids were for women, not land. Gilman also has a keen eye for how the state translates this primitive masculine urge into a modern ideology of martial heroism and the archetype of the soldier. Writing just a few years before World War I, Gilman anticipates the highly successful use of propaganda to persuade men to fight.

Although American women in the early twentieth century had, at best, a marginal place in the history profession—of the approximately one hundred history Ph.D.s in 1905, only eight were women, and none of them worked on women's history—the use of historical perspective and scholarship served as a key feminist method of exposing masculine assumptions about power. The prevailing Darwinian view of human evolution provided a historical template for understanding the constructed rather than permanent quality of women's identities and relationships between the sexes. Thus, women's contemporary roles could be exposed as archaic, the product of "coercive social habits of past times," as described by Mary Roberts Coolidge in "Why Women Are So" (1912), an excerpt from her book by the same title. Coolidge's examination of American women's history focuses on how the drudgery of nineteenth-century household labor slowed the growth of female intelligence and physical capacity, and, even though the modern home demands less work, she writes, women are still bound by the old ideal of domesticity. Typical of feminist intellectuals of the time, Coolidge used her grasp of history to make meliorative prescriptions: she saw sex roles becoming malleable, somewhat interchangeable, as women and men began to empathize with each other's condition. Coolidge enjoyed a long scholarly career. Making her name as one of the first Americans to conduct scientific research on human sexuality, she went on to do graduate work in history at Stanford University, where she eventually taught in the sociology department.

Perhaps the most prominent feminist sociologist of the early twentieth century was Elsie Clews Parsons, author of "Sex" (1915), a chapter from her book *Social Freedom: A Study of the Conflicts between Social Classifications and Personality*. After graduating from Barnard College and teaching high school history, Parsons earned her Ph.D. from Columbia University, which included extensive historical training. Her background in history is evident in her early scholarship—including the books *The Family* (1906), *The Old-Fashioned Woman; Primitive Fancies about the Sex* (1913), and *Fear and Conventionality* (1914)—all of which challenged contemporary standards of sexual difference by linking them to formulations of the distant (and even primitive) past. Like Coolidge, Gilman, and many other feminist intellectuals of the day, Parsons hoped to free American women from the routines and customs governing relations between the sexes by describing from whence they came, by arguing that their "truth" and thus their cultural force came not from their status as natural or universal but from their persistent repetition within history. Parsons later turned to anthropology and the study of Native American folklore under the influence of Franz Boas, thus beginning a long line of Columbia University feminist anthropologists, which later included Ruth Benedict and Margaret Mead.

Jessie Taft's essay "The Woman Movement and the Larger Social Situation" (1915) is another broadly gauged, historically based study that examines modern capitalism and its alienating effects on women. Men are also limited by American corporatism, but they are better off overall, as Taft points out, through their control of politics and other key institutions. Taft's view that the transformation of women from producers to consumers has left them bereft of any social control should be contrasted with the conviction of municipal reformers (especially the National Consumers' League) that it is precisely as consumers that women can influence business and industry. Taft's delineation of the distinct female conflict in pursuing a professional career and fulfilling the social expectations of marriage and family is telling in its solution of turning to other single women for loving companionship and making a "real home." (Taft followed this course herself in a long-standing relationship.) After teaching high school, Taft received a Ph.D. in sociology from the University of Chicago in 1915—"The Woman Movement and the Larger Social Situation" is a short published excerpt of her dissertation. She devoted the better part of her career to social work and clinical psychology.

Leta Hollingworth's coauthored essay "Science and Feminism" (1916) clearly illustrates how early-twentieth-century feminist scholars—having gained access to Ph.D. programs in certain disciplines in the human sciences—used their professional expertise and authority to challenge deeply rooted assumptions concerning biological sources of sexual difference. Born and raised in rural Nebraska, Hollingworth earned a Ph.D. in psychology from Columbia University in 1916, writing her dissertation on women's mental and motor abilities during menstruation. She went on to teach at Columbia for the rest of her career, while also staying active in the Heterodoxy Club and other New York City feminist organizations. In "Science and Feminism," Hollingworth relies on her own study of newborn infants to oppose the Darwinian view that human males are more intellectually variable; she also cites new research to debunk the notion that men's large brain size makes them more intelligent. She ends this piece on an amusing note that sums up the impetus underlying the work of all these early-twentieth-century scholars: she questions the objectivity of male social scientists and their determination to twist research findings into proof of female inferiority.

12
Marion Talbot
Present-Day Problems in the Education of Women (1897)

The collegiate training of women has an assured place in the educational activities of the present age, in spite of the reluctance with which in some quarters it has been accepted. This movement, whose aim is systematic intellectual training of a high order, presents problems which are of vital interest not only to educators but to all students of social progress.

The intellectual education of women has always been closely related on the one hand to their general status in society, and on the other to the condition of intellectual acquirement among men. In most countries the position of women has not, until recent times, been such as to demand any training of their intellectual powers. Their education has been extremely limited, and this is equally true whether the term education is used in its broadest sense or in the erroneously restricted sense of merely mental training. It has been the part of women in the past to be unlettered, and they have been content to be so. . . .

. . . There is another fact which must be noted before it is possible to understand the problems of to-day. As intellectual training has gradually come within the reach of a larger number of men, and has been extended to women, the methods of training which to each age seemed wisest and best for men have been sought and followed by women. Long before any college or university was open to women, college professors gave private instructions to girls, teaching them just as they taught the boys in the classroom. Since the time when formal recognition was first given to women in institutions of learning, in colleges and schools alike, attempts to differentiate the sexes in matter and mode of teaching have not prospered. Efforts in that direction have, on the contrary, tended to bring undeserved ridicule on the whole movement in behalf of women. It is now generally admitted, except by the newspaper humorist, that there is no such thing as *feminine* logic or discernment, or accuracy of power of observation or of analysis, any more than there is sex in language or mathematics or science. If education is considered as a matter of intellectual training, the means proved best for one sex are equally good for the other.

If, then, it is granted that women are to share with men the best that the world affords in the realm of mental training, we are brought to a consideration of the problems which confront the movement to-day. These problems are not what they were a generation ago. When collegiate education for women began to make notable progress and to attract the attention of thoughtful observers, the cry was that women were incapable of strenuous mental effort; that they were not fitted by nature to receive the same intellectual training as men; that their mental powers were feeble and limited. In spite of predictions of failure, women made the venture and succeeded. Experience proved that theory was at fault. The minds of women were shown to be worthy of the new opportunities for their development. Surrender on the part of objectors was complete at this point.

The contest was next waged in another battlefield. It was vehemently and persistently asserted that the physical powers of women would prove unequal to the strain, even if their mental powers were sufficient. For years the arguments pro and con were bandied, with the evidence constantly growing from experience that systematic mental occupation tended rather to improve than to destroy the physical health of women. The final answer came through the efforts of the Association of Collegiate Alumnæ, whose statistics and data, collated by the Massachusetts Bureau of Statistics of Labor, practically settled forever this long-mooted point and gave all women reason to be thankful that one more form of opposition had been removed from their path.

From *Educational Review,* October 1897.

It would be a serious error if the adherents of this movement should be content with the steps which have been gained and overlook the difficulties which now confront them. The problems which face all who are interested in the education of women were never more serious, never more perplexing, never more worthy of careful study and incessant effort than they are to-day. The first of these problems which demands attention is the proper correlation of the physical powers with the mental. We are still seriously handicapped by the notion, which prevailed widely not more than a generation ago, that physical vigor is incompatible with mental strength or intellectual achievement. The scholar was supposed to be characterized inevitably by drooping shoulders, pale countenance, and all the marks of physical deterioration. Fortunately we are outgrowing that conception. A good many people are now convinced that "a sound mind in a sound body" is not a mere oratorical phrase generally impossible of realization in actual life, and they are being greatly helped in demonstrating their belief by the increasing favor shown to physical vigor independent of mental activity. It is now no longer the fashion, as it once was, for a girl, any more than a boy, to be feeble physically. The popular sports which have taken such a hold on the American people of late years are playing a great part in giving us, as a nation, the strength which we need in coping with our duties and responsibilities. This favorable attitude of the public mind will do much to lessen the difficulty by solving this special problem. The investigation of the condition of physical education among girls in colleges and universities, made by the Association of Collegiate Alumnæ thirteen years ago, showed how nearly hopeless was the state of affairs. Much of the strength of the Association was straightway put into efforts to promote an interest in physical education among girls and women, and the outcome is most encouraging. There is reason to be glad that so much has been done; yet how much remains to be done! Well-appointed gymnasiums and expert teachers in physical culture are not enough, though their value cannot be overestimated. We need more definite instruction in the laws of health, we need more attention to the quality of food supplied to students and to the sanitary condition of their homes; we need a better understanding of the physical disaster which follows a wanton misuse of the hours of sleep or of social diversion, and we need most of all a still stronger conscience in our college communities, whose voice shall be raised in constant condemnation of the student who violates the welfare of her physical nature.

Certainly of no less importance is the problem of the correlation of the moral and spiritual natures with the intellectual. This is a burning question, and one which needs courage as well as wisdom. It would seem as if there never could have been a time when the demand was greater than it is now for the true interpretation of the principles of right and honor. The nation should be able to look confidently to its educated youth as leaders in this time of need; yet they fail all too frequently. It is true that they know the principles; but they lack the courage to voice them. Every college student knows in her own college experience how hard it is to stand for the right, when popular sentiment among her associates is tending the other way. Is it not possible to contrive a course for the development of a moral backbone which shall be worthy of the brain power it has to carry? Should not there be more open recognition of the truth all feel that the ethical nature of youth deserves and demands training?

Almost the same thing is to be said of the spiritual nature. It is claimed now and again that colleges are hotbeds of atheism. The accusation is false. The condition which is thus characterized is the same spirit of unrest and of dissatisfaction with old forms which prevails in society at large. Underneath it is a deep yearning for an expression of all that man holds most sacred. There are many signs that this is true. The eagerness with which people are reading books which deal with the vital truths of the higher life, or are listening to great preachers of God's word, shows this. Far from being the enemies of spiritual uplifting, student bodies in reality are quick to respond to real leadership in the higher life. How this immense power for good can be best developed is the problem.

Experience and investigation have demonstrated very clearly another problem in college training for women. Over and over again the four years of college work have utterly failed in effective results because of the lack of an adequate basis of early training. Any consideration, therefore, of the college movement must take into account the home and school training of childhood. The two periods are closely dependent—they are, in fact, one and the same, and any attempt to dissociate them is doomed to failure. The modern movements in primary and secondary education are destined to bear fruit, and their ultimate value will depend largely on the readiness of university educators to profit by them. On the other hand, the spirit of the university must be felt through all the lower grades of schools. What serves one serves the other, and constant watchfulness and power of adaptation is necessary for both. . . .

A problem which comes more strictly within the narrower limits of our theme is the choice of subjects which properly belong to the collegiate years. Everybody knows how great a field for controversy this presents. There are a few general points which should be considered. In the first place, our heritage of university courses has come from the Church. The subject-matter of the university curriculum has been largely determined by the needs of the priesthood. The present generation has seen an immense revolution whose results are full of promise, but whose tendencies also present points of danger. The radical revolt of modern times against mediæval scholasticism has done a noble work, but there is a possibility that in our enthusiastic devotion to the results of modern research and scholarship we may hold in too light esteem the treasures of ancient thought and experience.

In the second place, education is not merely intellectual training, though that may perhaps be its first function. It should also seek to widen the range of knowledge. As Professor Earl Barnes nobly says: "The curriculum of any grade of school to-day aims to bring before the student through types an epitome of all that man has thought and felt, and a vision of all that God has built into his infinite universe." But here too lurks a danger. The spirit of our age and land is such that the utilitarian aspect of education has an immense hold on popular opinion, and there is a constant effort to place acquisition before training. Superficial knowledge which can immediately be made use of in breadwinning is too generally prized. Moreover there is the demand for specialization, and it is made to begin more and more early. The truth is overlooked that the specialist needs a broad, general education of the higher sort; otherwise he will fail in much of his power as a specialist through his inability to relate his own piece of work to the rest of the universe, even if he is able to grasp it in more than a limited and sectional way. On all sides we feel the pressure of an age of haste, an age of utilitarianism. The problem of the college is to maintain through the repose of true scholarship the ideals of genuine learning. . . .

Closely allied with this theme of the curriculum in general is the question of choice of subjects by women for their best development as women. It is not as easy to lay down the law for all on this point as some would assert. Any attempt to do this rests on the assumption, in the first place, that emphasis must be given to acquisition rather than to training; and, in the second place, that all women have need of the same kind of information. In reply it must be said that the work which women are now more and more called on to do in the world demands, first of all, the best intellectual discipline. For instance, there are few forms of activity among men which require more carefully trained powers than housekeeping,—an occupation which is supposed to be women's peculiar sphere. Soundness of judgment, keenness of perception, quickness of decision, promptness of execution, all the higher powers are needed at their best to meet the manifold responsibilities and emergencies which arise. Failure to recognize this fact and the assumption that housekeeping comes by nature to women undoubtedly lie at the root of the disasters which are but too common in household administration, and which would be still more frequent were it not for the quick wit and ready adaptability which generally characterize women. It is manifestly true that in general, when men undertake such cares, they meet with a larger measure of success than women do. The administration of household affairs on a large scale, as in clubs, hotels or public institutions, is almost entirely carried on in this country by men. The explanation undoubtedly is that the ordinary training and experience of the boy are much more likely to fit him to estimate properly the relation of one fact to another. Girls are not usually brought in such contact with the affairs of the world as to learn how to see things in their right proportions, and consequently, unless they are given special training, are harassed and discouraged by non-essentials.

Again, if it is granted that union of training and of acquisition is practicable, the fact must be acknowledged that the kind of acquisition to be chosen is a matter for the individual rather than for the sex. This is recognized in the case of men. The facts studied by a lawyer are totally different from those studied by a physician. The difference between lawyer and physician is far greater than that between physician and housekeeper. The woman in charge of a family would have more need of the kind of information a physician uses than a lawyer would have. It is evident that there are many phases of this problem, that it should be soberly and wisely studied, and that women—and educated women—should be most competent to study it.

Another problem which faces the advocates of collegiate education for women is how best to bring the college training in touch with the world and its work. The old idea has not yet been given up that the life of a scholar is something apart from the common interests of mankind. The charge is made that the college woman often considers that her special training sets her quite apart from the rest of the world. If this is true, as may be the case sometimes, the result is farcical, for the one conception that a woman should certainly gain from collegiate study is that these few years of effort can after all merely open her mental vision to the vast stores which are yet beyond her reach, and train her to use them as time and opportunity come hand in hand. Her friends and acquaintances may sometimes be to blame. It frequently happens that a girl feels herself placed in an entirely false position by the adulation of her immediate circle of friends. She longs to be taken simply, as her brother is, and freed from the artificial expectations which surround her. Moreover, she feels more helpless as to her real place and value in the world than she would if the college had done its whole duty. Here again there are on the one hand tradition and conventionality, on the other the newly awakened soul ready and eager for its task; the question is how the chasm shall be bridged.

Finally, the best results cannot be obtained from collegiate training until an atmosphere of greater freedom prevails. Lucy Larcom once said that genuine liberty was essential for a poet. Women can never be great lyric singers as long as they have any sense of oppression or restraint. This is true also of the best intellectual expression, and is undoubtedly the reason why so little creative work of a high order has been done by women. Fortunately many of the conventional aspects of the woman's college are disappearing, and greater freedom in social life is everywhere accorded to women. How to maintain the restraint essential to a period of development and at the same time the spirit of independence, sincerity, and frankness,—in other words, the sacredness of individuality,—is the problem.

It may be claimed that the questions suggested are not peculiar to the education of women. Many of them belong as well to the education of men. This must be true in so far as the individual is regarded as a human being rather than as a member of one sex or the other. It must be granted that the collegiate education of women is now an integral part of the whole system of education. The young of the race are all to be trained as citizens whose ideals of honor, of right, of justice, of truth, shall be the same whether they are men or women. Certain fundamental principles which are common to both sexes must be established. Moreover, whatever a woman's specific work in life is to be, she should be given in the college the scientific training on which she can build her professional learning. This foundation is the same whether she is to be a physician, housewife, philanthropist, or mother.

True progress in education can be made only by constant study and vigilant effort. Every thoughtful and interested student should be ready to contribute from experience and investigation of the solution of the problem which to-day confront the education of women and which to-morrow will give place to others. Every college woman especially has a great responsibility, as well as opportunity, in standing as the sympathetic critic and loyal supporter of the men and institutions whose efforts in behalf of women are one of the wonders in a century of wonders.

13
M. Carey Thomas
Present Tendencies in Women's College and University Education (1908)

Anniversaries like this which compel us to pause for a moment and review our progress come with peculiar significance to women of my generation. I doubt if the most imaginative and sympathetic young women in this audience can form any conception of what it means to women of the old advance guard, among whom you will perhaps allow me to include myself, to be able to say to each other without fear of con-

From *Educational Review,* January 1908. This address was delivered at the Quarter-Centennial Meeting of the Association of Collegiate Alumnae, Boston, November 6, 1907.

tradiction that in the twenty-five years covered by the work of the Association of Collegiate Alumnæ the battle for the higher education of women has been gloriously, and forever, won.

The passionate desire of women of my generation for higher education was accompanied thruout its course by the awful doubt, felt by women themselves as well as by men, as to whether women as a sex were physically and mentally fit for it. I think I can best make this clear to you if I refer briefly to my own experience. I cannot remember the time when I was not sure that studying and going to college were the things above all others which I wished to do. I was always wondering whether it could be really true, as every one thought, that boys were cleverer than girls. Indeed, I cared so much that I never dared to ask any grown-up person the direct question, not even my father or mother, because I feared to hear the reply. I remember often praying about it, and begging God that if it were true that because I was a girl I could not successfully master Greek and go to college and understand things to kill me at once, as I could not bear to live in such an unjust world. When I was a little older I read the Bible entirely thru with passionate eagerness because I had heard it said that it proved that women were inferior to men. Those were not the days of the higher criticism. I can remember weeping over the account of Adam and Eve because it seemed to me that the curse pronounced on Eve might imperil girls' going to college; and to this day I can never read many parts of the Pauline epistles without feeling again the sinking of the heart with which I used to hurry over the verses referring to women's keeping silence in the churches and asking their husbands at home. I searched not only the Bible, but all other books I could get for light on the woman question. I read Milton with rage and indignation. Even as a child I knew him for the woman hater he was. The splendor of Shakespere was obscured to me than by the lack of intellectual power in his greatest women characters. Even now it seems to me that only Isabella in *Measure for Measure* thinks greatly, and weighs her actions greatly, like a Hamlet or a Brutus. . . .

It was not to be wondered at that we were uncertain in those old days as to the ultimate result of women's education. Before I myself went to college I had never seen but one college woman. I had heard that such a woman was staying at the house of an acquaintance. I went to see her with fear. Even if she had appeared in hoofs and horns I was determined to go to college all the same. But it was a relief to find this Vassar graduate tall and handsome and dressed like other women. When, five years later, I went to Leipzig to study after I had been graduated from Cornell, my mother used to write me that my name was never mentioned to her by the women of her acquaintance. I was thought by them to be as much of a disgrace to my family as if I had eloped with the coachman. Now, women who have been to college are as plentiful as blackberries on summer hedges. Even my native city of Baltimore is full of them, and women who have in addition studied in Germany are regarded with becoming deference by the very Baltimore women who disapproved of me.

During the quarter of the century of the existence of the Association of Collegiate Alumnæ two generations of college women have reached mature life, and the older generation is now just passing off the stage. We are therefore better prepared than ever before to give an account of what has been definitely accomplished, and to predict what will be the tendencies of women's college and university education in the future.

I think I can best tell you in a concrete way what has been accomplished in women's education by describing to you the condition of affairs which I found in 1884, when I returned from Germany, and set about planning the academic organization of Bryn Mawr. The outlook was discouraging except for the delight women were beginning to show in going to college. No one knew at all how things were going to turn out. The present achievement was small; the students were immature and badly trained; the scientific attainments of the professors teaching in colleges for women, with a few shining exceptions, were practically *nil*. Women were teaching in Wellesley, Mount Holyoke, and Smith without even the elementary training of a college course behind them. Men in general, including highly intelligent presidents of colleges for women, as well as highly intelligent presidents of colleges for men, held in good faith absurd opinions on women's education. When I protested to the president of the most advanced college for women in regard to this lack of training, he told me that we could never run Bryn Mawr if we insisted on the same scholarly attainments in women professors. He—and I think he will forgive me for quoting his opinion in those early days, because I am sure that he has since changed it—and the president of perhaps the greatest university for men in the United States, both told me that there was an intuitive something in ladies of birth and position, which enabled them to do without college training, and to make on the whole better professors for women college students than if they had themselves been to college.

Every one I consulted prophesied disaster if we carried out our plan of appointing to our professorships young unmarried men of high scientific promise. They said: in the first place such men will not consent to teach women in a woman's college; in the second place, if they should consent, their unmarried students will distract their minds; and in the third place, if by chance they should be able to teach coherently, then surely such will be the charm of their bachelor estate that their girl students will compete with each other for proposals out of the classroom rather than for marks in the classroom.

The president of Harvard College, when he visited Bryn Mawr a few years after its opening and found that our students were governing themselves and going away for the night, or for the week-end, as they saw fit, said to me: "If this continues, I will give you two years, and no more, in which to close Bryn Mawr College." From that day to this Bryn

Mawr College students have had free and unrestricted self-government, and have proved that women of the age our mothers were when we were born are old enough to govern themselves. Student self-government is now working well in thirteen eastern colleges where women study, and is, I believe, destined to spread to all other colleges for women.

And so it has been with many other questions in women's college education which were experiments only five and twenty years ago. Our highest hopes are all coming gloriously true. It is like reading a page of one of Grimm's fairy tales. The fearsome toads of those early prophecies are turning into pearls of purest radiance before our very eyes.

The curriculum of our women's colleges has steadily stiffened. Women, both in separate, and in coeducational colleges, seem to prefer the old-fashioned, so-called disciplinary studies. They disregard the so-called accomplishments. I believe that to-day more women than men are receiving a thoro college education, even altho in most cases they are receiving it sitting side by side with men in the same college lecture rooms.

The old type of untrained woman teacher has practically disappeared from women's colleges. Her place is being taken by ardent young women scholars who have qualified themselves by long years of graduate study for advanced teaching. Even the old-fashioned untrained matron, or house-mother, is swiftly being replaced in girls' schools, as well as in women's colleges by the college-bred warden or director.

Unmarried men are now teaching in all colleges for women. The experience of Bryn Mawr has proved that men of the highest scholarly reputation are not only willing to accept positions in a college for women, but that they decline to resign them except for the most tempting posts in colleges for men. This year, after respectively twenty-one and eighteen years of service, we are losing to the Johns Hopkins University, which creates special chairs for them, our senior professors of teutonic philology and history. No college for men and women, as slenderly endowed as are all our women's colleges, can hold for a lifetime the few productive scholars in any given science. Such men are entitled to the highest salaries and the best positions their country can bestow. Bryn Mawr has also proved that a faculty composed of such men has no hesitation in working under a woman president, or under women scholars as heads of departments when they too are eminent. In the world of intellect eminence is so rare, and excellence of any kind so difficult to attain, that when we are dealing with intellectual values, or genuine scholarly, literary, or artistic excellence, the question of sex tends to become as unimportant to men as to women.

We did not know when we began whether women's health could stand the strain of college education. We were haunted in those early days by the clanging chains of that gloomy little specter, Dr. Edward H. Clarke's *Sex in Education*. With trepidation of spirit I made my mother read it, and was much cheered by her remark that, as neither she, nor any of the women she knew, had ever seen girls or women of the kind described in Dr. Clarke's book, we might as well act as if they did not exist. Still, we did not *know* whether colleges might not produce a crop of just such invalids. Doctors insisted that they would. We women could not be sure until we had tried the experiment. Now we have tried it, and tried it for more than a generation and we know that college women are not only not invalids, but that they are better physically than other women in their own class of life. We know that girls are growing stronger and more athletic. Girls enter college each year in better physical condition. For the past four years I have myself questioned closely all our entering classes, and often their mothers as well. I find that an average of sixty per cent. enter college absolutely and in every respect well, and that less than thirty per cent. make, or need to make, any periodic difference whatever in exercise, or study, from year's end to year's end. This result is very different from that obtained by physicians and others writing in recent magazines and medical journals. These alarmists give grewsome statistics from high schools and women's colleges, which they are very careful not to name. Probably they are investigating girls whose general hygienic conditions are bad. The brothers of such girls would undoubtedly make as poor a showing physically when compared to Harvard and Yale men, or the boys of Groton or St. Paul's, as their sisters make when compared to Bryn Mawr students. Certainly their sisters who have not been to high school or college would in all probability be even more invalided and abnormal. Seventy per cent. of the Bryn Mawr students come from private schools and from homes where the nutrition and sanitary conditions are excellent. They have undoubtedly been subjected up to the age of nearly nineteen to strenuous and prolonged college preparation, yet their physical condition is far above that of the girls of these other investigations. One investigation yields the shocking result that sixty-six per cent. of college freshmen are practically invalids during certain times in each month, and another that seventy-three per cent. of high school girls are in similar condition. If such results are to be credited, the explanation must be found, as I have said, in the general mal-nutrition and unsanitary life of such girls. Here, as so often when women are investigated, causes which would produce ill-health in boys are not excluded. Surely the Bryn Mawr students approach much more nearly to the normal type. Those other girls are horribly abnormal.

We did not really know anything about even the ordinary everyday intellectual capacity of women when we began to educate them. We were not even sure that they inherited their intellects from their fathers as well as from their mothers. We were told that their brains were too light, their foreheads too small, their reasoning powers too defective, their emotions too easily worked upon to make good students. None of these things have proved true. Perhaps the most wonderful thing of all to have come true is the wholly unexpected, but altogether delightful, mental ability shown by women college students. We should have been satisfied if they had been proved to be only a little less good than men college students, but, tested by every known test of examination or classroom recitation, women have proved themselves equal to men, even slightly superior. It is more like a fairy story than ever to discover that they are not only as good, but even a little better. When this came to be clearly recognized, as was the case early in the movement, we were asked to remember that those first women students were a picked class, and could not fairly be compared to average men students. But now in many colleges, such as Chicago, the numbers of men and women are practically equal, and many of the women who attend college to-day have not the bread and butter incentive of men to do well in their classes, yet the slight superiority continues. Year after year, for example, Chicago reports fewer absences and fewer conditions incurred by women than by men in the same classes. This success of women in college work is producing a curious situation in men's education which is beginning to make itself felt in coeducational colleges.

We are now living in the midst of great and, I believe on the whole beneficent, social changes which are preparing the way for the coming economic independence of women. Like the closely allied diminishing birth rate, but unlike the higher education of women, this great change in opinion and practise seems to have come about almost without our knowledge, certainly without our conscious coöperation. The passionate desire of the women of my generation for a college education seems, as we study it now in the light of coming events, to have been a part of this greater movement.

In order to prepare for this economic independence, we should expect to see what is now taking place. Colleges for women and college departments of coeducational universities are attended by ever-increasing numbers of women students. In seven of the largest western universities women already outnumber men in the college departments.

A liberal college course prepares women for their great profession of teaching. College women have proved to be such admirably efficient teachers that they are driving other women out of the field. Until other means of self-support are as easy for women as teaching, more and more women who intend to teach will go to college. Such women will elect first of all the subjects taught by women in the high schools, such as Latin, history, and the languages. They will avoid chemistry, physics, and other sciences which are usually taught by men. Until all women become self-supporting, more women than men will go to college for culture, especially in the west, and such women will tend to elect the great disciplinary studies which men neglect because they are intrinsically more difficult and seem at first sight less practical. For these obvious reasons certain college courses are therefore already crowded by women and almost deserted by men in many of the coeducational universities.

Certain college presidents and professors are busily at work drawing conclusions as to the primary difference between men's and women's minds because different electives are chosen by men and women in coeducational colleges. But, if we compare the electives of men and women in the best separate colleges in the east, where more men are studying for culture, we find that the same electives are chosen by men at Harvard, Yale and Princeton, and by women at Vassar, Wellesley and Bryn Mawr. I was greatly struck by this similarity as illustrated by the elective charts of men's colleges at the St. Louis Exposition in 1904. If we exclude all required work, and examine the group studies chosen by all the women who have been graduated from Bryn Mawr, up to and including June, 1906, we find that each of the 783 graduates had the option of two group studies to be pursued five hours a week each for two years after election. Thus there were open to the 783 graduates 1566 possible group choices. Of these, Latin has obtained 35 per cent., economics 29 per cent., history 26 per cent., Greek 19 per cent., English 16.73, French 16.34, German 13, chemistry 12, biology 10, and so on. These choices, and others like them, should suffice to refute the often-repeated statement that women desert economics, chemistry, mathematics, and such supposedly masculine subjects, and crowd into English literature and foreign language courses because they are women. As so frequently happens in women's education, external circumstances have been mistaken for *a priori* causes. In western state universities, where it has been observed that women do not as a rule elect economics and science, such subjects are said by women students—at least if I may credit what has been repeatedly told me by many of our western graduate students—to be taught very differently from the way in which they are taught at Bryn Mawr, or, of course, at any eastern college for men, or women, where theoretical knowledge and intellectual training are the chief aim of a liberal college course. I am told that economics in many western colleges is simply applied economics and deals almost exclusively with banking, railroad rates, etc., and is therefore, of course, not elected by women who are at present unable to use it practically, whereas in the eastern colleges for women theoretical economics is perhaps their favorite study. In the same way, chemistry, which is a close second at Bryn Mawr to German as an elective study, is taught in the college departments of many western universities, as it is taught in many industrial or trade schools in the east, as a preparation for pharmacy or dyeing industries, and equally of course is not elected by women, who cannot as yet make practical use of such training. Surely this is a more reasonable explanation for the different choices of electives by women in the east and west than what seems to me the improbable one that women will not elect certain subjects, even if they would otherwise desire them, because they dislike to work in classes with men. Still more improbable seems the statement that men, who are eager to study literature and French and German, deny themselves because there are too many women in the classroom. The fact seems to me to be that women and men in the west and east elect what suits their needs best. If the present practical tendency in teaching certain large and important groups of studies continues in state universities, I believe that not only western women but all western men who wish a liberal college education in science, economics, mathematics, and other subjects must seek it in eastern colleges.

These three developments in women's college education have brought about a situation which is much misunderstood and yet is perfectly natural. Women are beginning, as I have said, to outnumber men in college departments. Women elect in larger numbers than men, for the reasons I have already given, certain very important disciplinary studies, and many such courses contain almost no men. Women do slightly better than men in daily recitations in spite of their supposedly less good health, they are absent less often from their college classes; and they get an average of higher marks in the examinations. None of this is very pleasing to men students, especially in the east, where young men have been taught to look down on women. Men are said in consequence—with some truth, I think—to show a tendency to prefer separate colleges. It would be only human if they did—annoying as it is. Men teaching in eastern colleges undoubtedly sympathize with, and sometimes encourage this feeling. Women students also resent this attitude on the part of professors and students, and seem to prefer women's college, where they feel that they have rights, and where they are the chief, instead of only the secondary, interest of their professors. Every now and then we hear mutterings of discontent from one or another coeducational college. Usually it is some eastern man, called to teach in a western coeducational college, thrown off his balance by the shock, running amuck through the pages of some eastern magazine. . . .

There is, however, one grave peril which must be averted from women's education at all hazards. Most of the universities of the west and many eastern universities, like Cornell, Columbia, and Pennsylvania, are boring thru their academic college course at a hundred places with professional courses. In many colleges everything that is desirable for a human being to learn to do counts towards the bachelor's degree—ladder work in the gymnasium (why not going upstairs?), swimming in the tank (why not one's morning bath?), cataloging in the library (why not one's letter home?).

People who used to believe in the free elective system used to believe also that all studies one could elect were equally good for purposes of mental training and discipline. Indeed, the free elective system could not have existed for a moment on any other hypothesis. There never was any real reason given for this belief. The presidents of Harvard and of other free elective colleges just said so, and said so over and over again, until every one came to think that it must be so.

Now, however, we have been trying the experiment of acting as if it were so in our men's colleges for over a generation, and we know that it is *not* so. No one can read the educational articles and addresses based on practical experience with college students which have appeared, say since 1900, and not become convinced of this.

Indeed, I personally have come to regard this vitally important question in education as now settled by this very costly method of practical experience for most truly intelligent and open-minded people. I am in consequence astounded to see the efforts which have been made within the past few years, and perhaps never more persistently than during the past year, to persuade, I might almost say to compel, those in charge of women's education to riddle the college curriculum of women with hygiene and sanitary drainage and domestic science and child-study, and all the rest of the so-called practical studies.

The argument is a specious one at first sight and seems reasonable. It is urged that college courses for women should be less varied than for men and should fit them primarily for the two great vocations of women, marriage, or teaching, the training of children in the home, or in the schoolroom. Nothing more disastrous for women, or for men, can be conceived of than this specialized education of women as sex. It has been wholly overlooked that any form of specialized education which differs from men's education, will tend to unfit women in less than a generation to teach their own boys at home, as well as, of course, other boys in the schoolroom. Women so educated will eventually be driven out of the teaching profession, or confined wholly to the teaching of girls. But there is a more far-reaching answer to this shortsighted demand for specialized women's courses. If fifty per cent. of college women are to marry, and nearly forty per cent. are to bear and rear children, such women cannot conceivably be given an education too broad, too high, or too deep, to fit them to become the educated mothers of the future race of men and women to be born of educated parents. Somehow or other such mothers must be made familiar with the great mass of inherited knowledge which is handed on from generation to generation of civilized educated men. They must think straight, judge wisely, and reverence truth; and they must teach such clear and wise and reverent thinking to their children. And we have only the four years of the college course to impart such knowledge to women who are to be mothers. If it is true—and it is absolutely true—that all subjects do not train the mind and heart and intellect equally well, it is unalterably true that sanitary and domestic science are not among the great disciplinary race studies. The place for such studies, and they undoubtedly have an important place, is *after* the college course, not during it. They belong with law, medicine, dentistry, engineering, architecture, agriculture in the professional school, not in the college. If they are introduced into the college course of liberal training in any fashion whatsoever, our present efficient college woman, like the old-fashioned type of efficient college man, will become a tradition of the past.

And for college women who may be teachers as well as for those who may be mothers, any form of special education is also highly objectionable. If the education of women is directed mainly, or exclusively, towards the profession of teaching, their specialized training will drive women who must support themselves into the teaching profession without regard to their special qualifications for teaching, which will be an overwhelming misfortune for the women themselves as well as for the children they teach. If women are to support themselves even as generally as they do now (and there will undoubtedly be many more self-supporting women in the immediate future) they must find entrance into the professions and into various kinds of business activity. Their education must be at least as varied and open to modification as men's education.

But the indications of successive editions of the census in all civilized countries and many other signs of the times make us sure that in two or three generations practically all women will either support themselves, or engage in some form of civic activity. I have said that about fifty per cent. of college women will marry. We know now that college women marry in about the same proportion, and have about the same number of children as their sisters and cousins who have not been to college. We know also that no one nowadays has more than about two children per marriage—neither college men, nor college women, nor the brothers or sisters of college men and women who have not been to college, nor native white American families, nor American immigrant families in the second generation. This great diminution in the birth rate has taken place notably in the United States, France, Great Britain, and Australia, and is manifesting itself in lesser, but ever increasing degrees, in all other civilized countries. In bringing about this great social change college women have borne no appreciable part. Indeed, only one-half a college woman in every 1000 women is married, the ratio of college women to other women being as 1 to 1000. Although this diminishing birth rate is wholly independent of women's college education, it can not fail to effect it greatly. If it is true, as it seems to be, that college women who marry will have on an average only two children apiece, they could not, if they wished, spend all their time in caring for these two rapidly growing up children, who, moreover, after ten years will be at school, unless they perform also the actual manual labor of their households. In such cases women will presumably prefer to do other work in order to be able to pay wages to have this manual labor done for them. No college-bred man would be willing day after day to shovel coal in his cellar, or to curry and harness his horses, if by more intellectual and interesting labor he could earn enough to pay to have it done for him. Nor will college women be willing to do household drudgery if it can be avoided. Such married women must, therefore, also be prepared for self-support. Likewise the increasingly small proportion of the married fifty per cent. who will marry men able to support them and their two children in comfort will not wish to be idle. They too must be prepared for some form of public service. Of course, the fifty per cent. of college women who do not marry, that is, all except the very few who will inherit fortunes large enough to live on thruout life, must be prepared for self-support.

It seems, therefore, self-evident that practically all women, like practically all men, must look forward after leaving college to some form of public service, whether paid, as it will be for the great majority of both men and women, or unpaid, does not matter. Why should not women, like liberally educated men, fit themselves after college for their special work? When their life-work is more or less determined, let those women who expect to marry and keep their own houses (after all, the women householders will be only about half even of those who marry, say twenty-five per cent. of all college women) study domestic and sanitary science. But it is as unreasonable to compel all women to study it irrespective of their future work as it would be to compel all men to study dentistry or medicine. It is the same with child-study and all other specialized studies. They belong, one and all, in the graduate professional school.

How do these economic conditions affect women's entrance into the professional schools already in existence for men? Everything seems to indicate, as I have pointed out, that women will not only make their way into all except a few of the trades and professions, but that they will be compelled by economic causes beyond their control to stay in them after marriage. Already in teaching, nursing, library work, typewriting, bookkeeping, telephoning, telegraphing, they are steadily taking possession and driving men before them. It is already clear that all professional and trade schools must admit women. No separate schools will be founded for them. The few university professional schools of law, medicine, theology, and architecture now closed will open, probably within the next decade. Separate professional schools for women are an anachronism. The expense of maintaining them is too vast. Indeed, women's medical schools were only brought into existence by the savage prejudices of many men physicians. They are now almost extinct....

This brings us squarely face to face with a vitally important question in women's education. Shall our colleges for women maintain graduate schools of philosophy and confer Ph.D. degrees? The experience of Bryn Mawr has shown that women will choose to pursue graduate work in such schools if they come into existence, and it has also shown that a Ph.D. from a women's college has a commercial value equal to that given by the oldest and most richly endowed men's universities. I regard the question as to all other professional schools as settled. It would be unwise and harmful to women's professional standing for women's colleges to maintain them. They must be coeducational. Is this the case also with schools of philosophy? I think not. The conditions are wholly different. From one-third to one-half of all the students studying in our women's colleges expect to teach. They must be prepared by advanced work in their special subjects beyond the A.B. degree. Only one-seventh of the men and women studying in graduate schools take the doctor's degree. The remaining six-sevenths are studying only for a year or two to prepare for teaching. Many more women will go on with advanced work if they can go on at the college where they have taken their undergraduate work. The experience of men's colleges has proved this. Far more women are now taking college courses in Smith, Wellesley, Vassar, Mount Holyoke, Bryn Mawr, Radcliffe, and Barnard than anywhere else in the east. In only three of the seven, Bryn Mawr, Radcliffe, and Barnard, can women really fit themselves for teaching. It seems to me inevitable that the other four colleges for women will provide these opportunities.

But it is not only for the graduate students that the graduate school is needed. It is needed most of all for the undergraduate students. I do not believe that the best undergraduate teaching is ever given in a college where the professors do not also conduct research and investigation courses. In no other way, I believe, can a faculty of enthusiastic scholars abreast of modern scientific methods be maintained. Such scholars make infinitely better teachers for college students, and even for children in a kindergarten, if they were attainable. It is impossible for a teacher of any kind to know too much. Also, a progressive graduate school weeds out non-productive scholars from a college as nothing else will. Already there are signs of the great colleges for women taking on this true university function. Vassar, Wellesley, Smith, and Mount Holyoke have already created a few resident graduate scholarships and fellowships. . . .

But have women ability of this highest kind to be developed? Can they compete successfully with men in the field of original and productive scholarship? Before this pertinent question even our dearest friends among college presidents and professors who are generously educating women balk and shy and lose themselves in a maze of platitudes about women's receptive and unoriginative minds. But what do we ourselves, what do we women, think? I for one am sure that women possess this ability. My opinion has been greatly strengthened by the scientific and sociological investigations of the past few years. Recent studies in heredity, including the work on Mendel's law, seem to me to show conclusively that boys and girls inherit equally from both mothers and fathers in mathematical proportion, that a woman's place in the inheritance and transmission of physical, mental and moral qualities is precisely the same as a man's, that she is discriminated against in no way. Sociological investigations such as Professor Odin's exhaustive study of 6382 French men and women of talent, Mr. Havelock Ellis's study of 902 British men and women of genius, Professor Cattell's statistical study of 1000 American scientific men, and other studies show us for the first time that favorable conditions of intellectual life are immensely important factors in the manifestation of men's genius and talent. In many parts of our own country a man of great intellectual ability has scarcely any chance at all of emerging. Massachusetts, for example, has 108.8 eminent men of science for every million of its population, while my own adopted state of Pennsylvania has only 22.7 per million; in Georgia the proportion dwindles to 2.8 and in Mississippi to only 1.3 per million.

But only women know how true it is that in the development of the highest scientific and scholarly qualifications women have today far less favorable conditions than even men in Mississippi.

Mr. Havelock Ellis found that in Great Britain women of genius formed only one-twentieth of the whole number. Professor Odin found that in France women of talent were in precisely the same proportion, only one-twentieth of the whole number, but that women furnished 29 per cent. of eminent actors, and 20 per cent. of all prose writers of distinction. In Great Britain likewise 53 per cent. of all women of genius were authors, and 30 per cent. actors. The explanation is clear. Women of genius and talent had more opportunity to come to the surface in these two professions. In all probability the same proportion of women of genius and talent were born with aptitude for scientific research, but were crushed by their unfavorable environment.

It seems to me then to rest with us, the college women of this generation, to see to it that the girls of the next generation are given favorable conditions for this higher kind of scholarly development. To advance the bounds of human knowledge, however little, is to exercise our highest human faculty. There is no more altruistic satisfaction, no purer delight. I am convinced that we can do no more useful work than this—to make it possible of the few women of creative and constructive genius born in any generation to join the few men of genius in their generation in the service of their common race.

14

HELEN BRADFORD THOMPSON

The Mental Traits of Sex (1903)

...The suggestion that the observed psychological differences of sex may be due to difference in environment has often been met with derision, but it seems at least worthy of unbiased consideration. The fact that very genuine and important differences of environment do exist can be denied only by the most superficial observer. Even in our own country, where boys and girls are allowed to go to the same schools and to play together to some extent, the social atmosphere is different, from the cradle. Different toys are given them, different occupations and tames are taught them, different ideals of conduct are held up before them. The question for the moment is not at all whether or not these differences in education are right and proper and necessary, but merely whether or not, as a matter of fact, they exist, and if so, what effect they have on the individuals who are subjected to them.

From Helen Bradford Thompson, *The Mental Traits of Sex* (Chicago: Univ. of Chicago Press, 1903), 177–82.

The difference in physical training is very evident. Boys are encouraged in all forms of exercise and in out-of-door life, while girls are restricted in physical exercise at a very early age. Only a few forms of exercise are considered lady-like. Rough games and violent exercise of all sorts are discouraged. Girls are kept in the house and taught household occupations. The development of physical strength is not held up to girls as an ideal, while it is made one of the chief ambitions of boys.

While it is improbable that *all* the difference of the sexes with regard to physical strength can be attributed to persistent difference in training, it is certain that a large part of the difference is explicable on this ground. The great strength of savage women and the rapid increase in strength in civilized women, wherever systematic physical training has been introduced, both show the importance of this factor. When we consider the other forms of motor ability than mere muscular force, such as quickness of reaction and accuracy of co-ordination, it seems very probable that mere differences of physical training are ample to account for these differences of sex. While it seems to be true that slower rates of movement and decreased accuracy of co-ordination do result from greatly inferior physical strength it is not true that the correlation is quantitatively a close one. Even with wide differences in muscular force, the difference in motor ability is comparatively slight. Where the differences in strength are slight, we have no reason to expect differences in motor ability on that ground.

When we consider the other important respect in which men are supposed to be superior to women—ingenuity or inventiveness—we find equally important differences in social surroundings which would tend to bring about this result. Boys are encouraged to individuality. They are trained to be independent in thought and action. This is the ideal of manliness held up before them. They are expected to understand the use of tools and machinery, and encouraged to experiment and make things for themselves. Girls are taught obedience, dependence, and deference. They are made to feel that too much independence of opinion or action is a drawback to them—not becoming or womanly. A boy is made to feel that his success in life, his place in the world, will depend upon his ability to go ahead with his chosen occupation on his own responsibility, and to accomplish something new and valuable. No such social spur is applied to girls. Royce (73) in his article on the psychology of invention says:

"Only heredity can account for the very wide differences between clever men and stupid men, or explain why men of genius exist at all. But the minor and still important inventiveness of the men of talent, the men of the second grade, is somehow due to a social stimulation which sets their habits varying in different directions. And this stimulation is of the type which abounds in periods of individualism. . . . For once more, the primary character of the social influences to which we are exposed is that, within limits, they set us to imitating models; they tend to make us creatures of social routine, slaves of the mob, or obedient servants of the world about us. . . . Inventions thus seem to be the results of the encouragement of individuality."

If one applies these words to the question of the relative inventiveness of the sexes, and realizes the wide differences in social influence which still exist even in a community where women have more freedom and more education than anywhere else in the world, it seems rash to assume that the observed difference in inventiveness represents a genuine and fundamental sexual difference of mind. The fact that the difference revealed by experiment is so slight in men and women whose educations have been as nearly alike as those of students in a co-educational university, tends to throw further doubt on the fundamental importance of this distinction. The very brief period in which women have been given any systematic education, or any freedom of choice in occupation makes it impossible to decide the question on the basis of previous achievement.

The same social influences which have tended to retard the development of motor ability and of inventiveness in women would tend to develop keenness of sense and the more reproductive mental processes, such as memory. The question is largely one of the distribution of attention. A large part of a boy's attention goes toward his activities—the learning of new movements, the manipulating of tools, the making of contrivances of various sorts. A girl's less active existence must be filled with some other sort of conscious process. The only possibility is that sensory and perceptual processes should be more prominent. In some cases the special training of girls tends directly toward the development of a special sense. This is notably true in color, and perhaps has some influence in taste. On the more purely intellectual level, it is only natural that in the absence of a sufficient social spur toward originality and inventiveness, they should depend more upon memory for their supply of ideas. It is easier for any individual to learn some one else's ideas than to think out his own. Every teacher has to struggle against the tendency to memorize merely, and to endeavor in every way to stimulate original thought and help pupils to form the habit of doing their own thinking. It is no great matter for surprise that in the absence of social stimulus toward originality of thought, women should have tended, from inertia, to stay in the realm of reproductive thinking.

It will probably be said that this view of the case put the cart before the horse—that the training and social surroundings of the sexes are different because their natural characteristics are different. It will be said that a boy is encouraged to activity because he is naturally active—that he is given tools instead of a doll because he is naturally more interested in tools than in dolls. But there are many indications that these very interests are socially stimulated. A small boy with an older sister and no brothers is very sure to display an ambition to have dolls. It is in most cases quenched early by ridicule, but it is evident that a boy must be taught what occupations are suited to boys. The sorrows of a small girl with brothers because she is not allowed to run and race with the boys and take part in their sports and games have frequently been recounted. If it were really a fundamental difference of instincts and characteristics which determined the difference of training to which the sexes are subjected, it would not be necessary to spend so much effort in making boys and girls follow the lines of conduct proper to their sex. The more probable interpretation of the facts is that the necessities of social organization have in the past brought about a division of labor between the sexes, the usefulness of which is evident. Social ideals have been developed in connection with this economic necessity, and still persist.

This is not the place to discuss the question whether or not the conditions of social organization still demand the same division of labor, and make the preservation of the traditional ideals for the sexes necessary to the good of society. If such is the case, there is no doubt that the present state of affairs will persist. There are, as everyone must recognize, signs of a radical change in the social ideals of sex. The point to be emphasized as the outcome of this study is that, according to our present light, the psychological differences of sex seem to be largely due, not to difference of average capacity, nor to difference in type of mental activity, but to differences in the social influences brought to bear on the developing individual from early infancy to adult years. The question of the future development of the intellectual life of women is one of social necessities and ideals,rather than of the inborn psychological characteristics of sex.

15
Charlotte Perkins Gilman
Politics and Warfare (1910)

I go to my old dictionary, and find: "Politics, 1. The science of government; that part of ethics

From *The Forerunner,* October 1910; reprinted in Charlotte Perkins Gilman, *The Man-Made World* (New York: Charlton, 1911), 208–26.

which has to do with the regulation and government of a nation or state; the preservation of its safety, peace and prosperity; the defence of its existence and rights against foreign control or conquest; the augmentation of its strength and resources, and the protection of its citizens in their rights; with the preservation and improvement of their morals. 2. The management of political parties; the advancement of candidates to office; in a bad sense, artful or dishonest management to secure the success of political measures or party schemes, political trickery."

From present day experience we might add, 3. Politics, practical; The art of organizing and handling men in large numbers, manipulating votes, and, in especial, appropriating public wealth.

We can easily see that the "science of government may be divided into "pure" and "applied" like other sciences, but that it is "a part of ethics" will be news to many minds.

Yet why not? Ethics is the science of conduct, and politics is merely one field of conduct; a very common one. Its connection with warfare in this chapter is perfectly legitimate in view of the history of politics on the one hand, and the imperative modern issues which are to-day opposed to this established combination.

There are many to-day who hold that politics need not be at all connected with warfare; and others who hold that politics is warfare from start to finish.

In order to dissociate the two ideas completely, let us give a paragraph of the above definition, applying it to domestic management— that part of ethics which has to do with the regulation and government of a family; the preservation of its safety, peace and prosperity; the defense of its existence and rights against any stranger's interference or control; the augmentation of its strength and resources, and the protection of its members in their rights; with the preservation and improvement of their morals.

All this is simple enough, and in no way masculine; neither is it feminine, save in this;

that the tendency to care for, defend and manage a group, is in its origin maternal.

In every human sense, however, politics has left its maternal base fare in the background; and as a field of study and action is as well adapted to men as to women. There is no reason whatever why men should not develop great ability in this department of ethics, and gradually learn how to preserve the safety, peace and prosperity of their nation; together with those other services as to resources, protection of citizens, and improvements of morals.

Men, as human beings, are capable of the noblest devotion and efficiency in these matters, and have often shown them; but their devotion and efficiency have been marred in this, as in so many other fields, by the constant obtrusion of an ultra-masculine tendency.

In warfare *per se*, we find maleness in its absurdist extremes. Here is to be studied the whole gamut of basic masculinity, from the initial instinct of combat, through every form of glorious ostentation, with the loudest possible accompaniment of noise.

Primitive warfare had for its climax the possession of the primitive prize, the female. Without dogmatising on so remote a period, it may be suggested as a fair hypothesis that this was the very origin of our organized raids. We certainly find war before there was property in land, or any other property to tempt aggressors. Women, however, there were always, and when a specially androcentric tribe had reduced its supply of women by cruel treatment, or they were not born in sufficient numbers, owing to hard conditions, men must needs go farther afield after other women. Then, since the men of the other tribes naturally objected to losing their main labor supply and comfort, there was war.

Thus based on the sex impulse, it gave full range to the combative instinct, and further to that thirst for vocal exultation so exquisitely male. The proud bellowings of the conquering stag, as he trampled on his prostrate rival, found higher expression in the "triumphs" of the old days, when the conquering warrior returned to his home, with victims chained to his chariot wheels, and trumpets braying.

When property became an appreciable factor in life, warfare took on a new significance. What was at first mere destruction, in the effort to defend or obtain some hunting ground or pasture; and, always, to secure the female; now coalesced with the acquisitive instinct, and the long black ages of predatory warfare closed in upon the world.

Where the earliest form exterminated, the later enslaved, and took tribute; and for century upon century the "gentleman adventurer," i.e., the primitive male, greatly preferred to acquire wealth by the simple old process of taking it, to any form of productive industry.

We have been much misled as to warfare by our androcentric literature. With a history which recorded nothing else; a literature which praised and an art which exalted it; a religion which called its central power "the God of Battles"—never the God of Workshops, mind you!—with a whole complex social structure man-prejudiced from center to circumference, and giving highest praise and honor to the Soldier; it is still hard for us to see what warfare really is in human life.

Some day we shall have new histories written, histories of world progress, showing the slow uprising, the development, the interservice of the nations; showing the faint beautiful dawn of the larger spirit of world-consciousness, and all its benefitting growth.

We shall see people softening, learning, rising; see life lengthen with the possession of herds, and widen in rich prosperity with agriculture. Then industry, blossoming, fruiting, spreading wide; art, giving light and joy; the intellect developing with companionship and human intercourse; the whole spreading tree of social progress, the trunk of which is specialized industry, and the branches of which comprise every least and greatest line of human activity and enjoyment. This growing tree, springing up wherever conditions of peace and prosperity gave it a chance, we shall see continually hewed down to the very root by war.

To the later historian will appear throughout the ages, like some Hideous Fate, some Curse, some predetermined check, to drag down all our hope and joy and set life forever at its first steps over again, this Red Plague of War.

The instinct of combat, between males, worked advantageously so as it did not injure the female or the young. It is a perfectly natural instinct, and therefore perfectly right, in its place; but its place is in a pre-patriarchal era. So long as the animal mother was free and competent to care for herself and her young; then it was an advantage to have "the best man win": that is the best stag or lion; and to have the vanquished die, or live in sulky celibacy, was no disadvantage to any one but himself.

Humanity is on a stage above this plan. The best man in the social structure is not always the huskiest. When a fresh horde of ultra-male savages swarmed down upon a prosperous young civilization, killed off the more civilized males and appropriated the more civilized females; they did, no doubt, bring in a fresh physical impulse to the race; but they destroyed the civilization.

The reproduction of perfectly good savages is not the main business of humanity. Its business is to grow, socially; to develop, to improve; and warfare, at its best, retards human progress; at its worst, obliterates it.

Combat is not a social process at all; it is a physical process, a subsidiary sex process, purely masculine, intended to improve the species by the elimination of the unfit. Amusingly enough, or absurdly enough; when applied to society, it eliminates the fit, and leaves the unfit to perpetuate the race!

We require, to do our organized fighting, a picked lot of vigorous young males, the fittest we can find. The too old or too young; the sick, crippled, defective; are all left behind, to marry and be fathers; while the pick of the country; physically, is sent off to oppose the pick of another country, and kill—kill—kill!

Observe the result on the population! In the first place the balance is broken—there are not enough men to go around, at home; many women are left unmated. In primitive warfare, where women were promptly enslaved, or, at the best, polygamously married, this did not greatly matter—to the population; but as civilization advances and monogamy obtains, whatever eugenic benefits may once have sprung from warfare are completely lost, and all its injuries remain.

In what we innocently call "civilized warfare" (we might as well speak of "civilized cannibalism!"), this steady elimination of the fit leaves an ever lowering standard of parenting at home. It makes a widening margin of what we call "surplus women," meaning more than enough to be monogamously married; and these women, not being economically independent, drag steadily upon the remaining men, postponing marriage, and increasing its burdens.

The birth rate is lowered in quantity by the lack of husbands, and lowered in quality both by the destruction of superior stock, and by the wide dissemination of those diseases which invariably accompany the wifelessness of the segregated males who are sold off to perform our military functions.

The external horrors and wastes of warfare we are all familiar with: A. It arrests industry and all progress. B. It destroys the fruits of industry and progress. C. It weakens, hurts and kills the combatants. D. It lowers the standard of the non-combatants. Even the conquering nation is heavily injured; the conquered sometimes exterminated, or at least absorbed by the victor.

This masculine selective process, when applied to nations, does not produce the same result as when applied to single opposing animals. When little Greece was overcome it did not prove that the victors were superior, nor promote human interests in any way; it injured them.

The "stern arbitrament of war" may prove which of two peoples is the better fighter, but it does not prove it therefore the fittest to survive.

Beyond all these more or less obvious evils, comes a further result, not enough recognized; the psychic effects of [the] military standard of thought and feeling.

Remember that an androcentric culture has always exempted its own essential activities from the restraints of ethics,—"All's fair in love and war!" Deceit, trickery, lying, every kind of skulking underhand effort to get information; ceaseless endeavor to outwit and overcome "the enemy"; these, with cruelty and destruction are characteristic of the military process; as well as the much prized virtues of courage, endurance and loyalty, personal and public.

Also classed as virtue, and unquestionably such from the military point of view, is that prime factor in making and keeping an army, obedience.

See how the effect of this artificial maintenance of early mental attitudes acts on later development. True human progress requires elements quite other than these. If successful warfare made one nation unquestionably master of the earth, its social progress would not be promoted by that event. The rude hordes of Genghis Khan [1162?–1227] swarmed over Asia and into Europe, but remained rude hordes; conquest is not civilization, nor any part of it.

When the northern tribes-men overwhelmed the Roman culture they paralyzed progress for a thousand years or so; set back the clock by that much. So long as all Europe was at war, so long the arts and sciences sat still, or struggled in hid corners to keep their light alive.

When warfare itself ceases, the physical, social and psychic results do not cease. Our whole culture is still hag-ridden by military ideals.

Peace congresses have begun to meet, peace societies write and talk, but the monuments to soldiers and sailors (naval sailors of course), still go up, and the tin soldier remains a popular toy. We do not see boxes of tin carpenters by any chance; tin farmers, weavers, shoemakers; we do not write our "boys' books" about the real benefactors and servers of society; the adventurer and destroyer remains the idol of an androcentric culture.

In politics the military ideal, the military processes, are so predominant as to almost monopolize "that part of ethics."

The science of government, the plain wholesome business of managing a community for its own good; doing its work, advancing its prosperity, improving its morals—this is frankly understood and accepted as A Fight from start to finish. Marshall [sic] your forces and try to get in, this is the political campaign. When you are in, fight to stay in, and to keep the other fellow out. Fight for your own hand, like an animal; fight for your master like any hired bravo; fight always for some desired "victory"—and "to the victors belong the spoils."

This is not by any means the true nature of politics. It is not even a fair picture of politics to-day; in which, the human being, is doing noble work for humanity; but it is the effect of man, the male, on politics.

Life, to the "male mind" (we have heard enough of the "female mind" to use the analogue!) *is* a fight, and his ancient military institutions and processes keep up the delusion.

As a matter of fact life is growth. Growth comes naturally, by multiplication of cells, and requires three factors to promote it; nourishment, use, rest. Combat is a minor incident of life; belonging to low levels, and not of a developing influence socially.

The science of politics, in a civilized community, should have by this time a fine accumulation of simplified knowledge for diffusion in public schools; a store of practical experience in how to promote social advancement most rapidly, a progressive economy and ease of administration, a simplicity in theory and visible benefit in practice, such as should make every child an eager and serviceable citizen.

What do we find, here in America, in the field of "politics"?

We find first a party system which is the technical arrangement to carry on a fight. It is perfectly conceivable that a flourishing democratic government [could] be carried on *without any parties at all*; public functionaries being elected on their merits, and each proposed measure judged on its merits; though this sounds impossible to the androcentric mind.

"There has never been a democracy without factions and parties!" is protested.

There has never been a democracy, so far,—only an androcracy.

A group composed of males alone, naturally divides, opposes, fights; even a male church, under the most rigid rule, has its secret undercurrents of antagonism.

"It is the human heart!" is again protested. No, not essentially the human heart, but the male heart. This is so well recognized by men in general, that, to their minds, in this mingled field of politics and warfare, women have no place.

In "civilized warfare" they are, it is true, allowed to trail along and practice their feminine function of nursing; but this is no part of war proper, it is rather the beginning of the end of war. Sometime it will strike our "funny spot," these strenuous efforts to hurt and destroy, and these accompanying efforts to heal and save.

But in our politics there is not even provision for a nursing corps; women are absolutely excluded.

"They cannot play the game!" cries the practical politician. There is loud talk of the defilement, the "dirty pool" and its resultant darkening of fair reputations, the total unfitness of lovely woman to take part in "the rough and tumble of politics."

In other words men have made a human institution into an ultra-masculine performance; and, quite rightly, feel that women could not take part in politics *as men do*. That it is not necessary to fulfill this human custom in so masculine a way does not occur to them. Few men can overlook the limitations of their sex and see the truth; that this business of taking care of our common affairs is not only equally open to women and men, but that women are distinctly needed in it.

Anyone will admit that a government wholly in the hands of women would be helped by the assistance of men; that a gynaecocracy must, of its own nature, be one-sided. Yet it is hard to win reluctant admission of the opposite fact; that an androcracy must of its own nature be one-sided also, and would be greatly improved by the participation of the other sex.

The inextricable confusion of politics and warfare is part of the stumbling block in the minds of men. As they see it, a nation is primarily a fighting organization; and its principal business is offensive and defensive warfare; there the ultimatum with which they oppose the demand for political equality—"women cannot fight, therefore they cannot vote."

Fighting, when all is said, is to them the real business of life; not to be able to fight is to be quite out of the running; and ability to solve our growing mass of public problems; questions of health, of education, of morals, of economics; weighs naught against the ability to kill.

This naive assumption of supreme value in a process never of the first importance[,] and increasingly injurious as society progresses, would be laughable if it were not for its evil effects. It acts and reacts upon us to our hurt. Positively, we see the ill effects already touched on; the evils not only of active war; but of the spirit and methods of war; idealized, inculcated and practiced in other social processes. It tends to make each man-managed nation an actual or potential fighting organization, and to give us, instead of civilized peace, that "balance of power" which is like the counted time in the prize ring—only a rest between combats.

It leaves the weaker nations to be "conquered" and "annexed" just as they to be; with "preferential tariffs" instead of tribute. It forces upon each the burden of armament; upon many the dreaded conscription; and continually lowers the world's resources in money and in life.

Similarly in politics, it adds to the legitimate expenses of governing the illegitimate expenses of fighting; and must needs have a "spoils system" by which to pay its mercenaries.

In carrying out the public policies the wheels of state are continually clogged by the "opposition"; always an opposition on one side or the other; and this slow wiggling uneven progress, through shorn victories and haggling concessions, is held to be the proper and only political method.

"Women do not understand politics," we are told; "Women do not care for politics"; "Women are unfitted for politics."

It is frankly inconceivable, from the androcentric view-point, that nations can live in peace together, and be friendly and serviceable as persons are. It is inconceivable also, that, in the management of a nation, honesty, efficiency, wisdom, experience and love could work out good results without any element of combat.

The "ultimate resort" is still to arms. "The will of the majority" is only respected on account of the guns of the majority. We have but a partial civilization, heavily modified to sex—the male sex.

16

Mary Roberts Coolidge
Why Women Are So (1912)

These chapters are neither a defense nor an arraignment of womankind; they are, rather, a first-hand study of the ordinary, orthodox, middle-class women who have constituted the domestic type for more than a century; the exotic great lady and the morbid woman with a grievance have alike been omitted. They try to answer the query: why are women so? Is the characteristic behavior which is called feminine an inalienable quality or merely an attitude of mind produced by the coercive social habits of past times?

As a working hypothesis it is assumed that the women of the nineteenth century in America were for the most part what men expected them to be; modified only by the disintegrating, and at the same time reconstructive, forces of modern society. In other words, sex traditions rather than innate sex character have produced what is called "feminine" as distinguished from womanly behavior. . . .

In the making of a human being there are three variables—what he was when he came into the world, what he found there, and what he made of it and of himself when he grew up. Boys and girls, if not precisely alike in the beginning, were probably substantially equal, the advantage of greater size in the one being made up in the other by finer nervous organization and endurance. What each sex found in our American world in the nineteenth century was, however, very different; for social tradition ordained a wide differentiation in nurture and habit, which was justified in theory by the sex-specialization of females. Neither the education nor the duties of girls, in spite of their special function, prepared them in any direct fashion for motherhood; rather, they were consciously designed to fit them to be domestic servers and housekeepers.

There had been a time in history not long past, when the choice of a vocation was confined to certain occupations open to the class in which men happened to be born, but in the new democracy every field was at least nominally open to any man. Women, meanwhile, whether married or not, whether likely to be mothers or not, were still limited to the group of occupations which could be carried on under the home roof. At the beginning of the last century these comprised a variety of crafts and manufacturers, but in the course of fifty years the sphere of the domestic countrywoman was coming to be limited to a few miscellaneous and belated trades, which were still assigned to women merely because they were performed within the household.

Although it continued to be assumed that the static and limited condition of women was due chiefly to their primary function as mothers and nurses, an analysis of these purely domestic lives will show that a relatively small portion of women's time and energy was spent in actual mothering. Less than half the fifty years of her adult life were so consumed by the

From Mary Roberts Coolidge, *Why Women Are So* (New York: Henry Holt, 1912), v, 65–86.

average woman; and in all but the largest families the wife actually occupied more hours per day in washing and laundry work than in the care of children. If the capacity to bear children had in fact incapacitated women for other physical exertion to the extent that it was always assumed it did whenever women wished to do anything outside the home, most families would have lacked food, clothing, and comfort for long periods of time.

From six to twelve children were born during twenty years to the average wife, and during those years she did most of the labor of the household, including a good deal of manufacturing now done in factories, with only such help as the older children could give. The life of my own grandmother was typical of that of many another well-to-do farmer's wife between 1825 and 1875, and an almost exact counterpart of that of Lucy Read Anthony, as described by her daughter.

"Lucy Anthony soon became acquainted with the stern realities of life. Her third baby was born when the first was three years and two months old. That summer she boarded eleven factory hands who roomed in her house, and she did all the cooking, washing, and ironing, with no help except that of a thirteen-year-old girl, who went to school, and did chores night and morning. The cooking for a family of sixteen was done on the hearth in front of the fireplace, and in a brick oven at the side. Daniel Anthony was a generous man, loved his wife, and was well able to hire help, but such a thing was not thought of at that time. No matter how heavy the work, the woman of the household was expected to do it, and probably would have been the first to resent the idea that assistance was needed."

Domesticity is here used for convenience to designate all the duties which a married woman of the past century was expected to perform. It consisted first of the physiological functions of wifehood and motherhood; second, of the handicrafts of a civilized household—cooking, sewing, washing, cleaning, and household decoration; and third, the social duties of hospitality and the cultivation of good manners. In the earlier part of the century it involved also the manufacture of nearly all the raw products of the farm into the necessary food, clothing, and bedding for a family of six to twelve persons. The household was then not merely a shelter and a boarding-house, but a miniature factory, to which the men-folk furnished the raw products, and over which the wife presided as the working boss.

The amount of labor, skill, and knowledge necessary to the successful performance of such a variety of duties may be imagined when one remembers that from this family-factor have already been differentiated the separate vocations of nursing, dressmaking, tailoring, knitting, laundering, and baking, every kind of cloth manufacture, and almost all the primary preparation of foods. If a woman really mastered to the point of competence the essentials of most of these handicrafts, she was necessarily strong, intelligent, and skilful. Under such circumstances the vocation of domesticity was an immense and stimulating field of action, and likely, therefore, to produce a high quality of mind and character.

In the attempt to measure the effect of domestic occupations upon women's capacity and character, it is difficult to find any perfect analogy with men's industries. Most of the occupations assigned to men had long ago been specialized into separate trades; while there remained to women, even after a considerable portion of the domestic processes had been transferred to factories, several miscellaneous vocations which had no inherent connection except that they were undertaken under a single family roof. In this respect domesticity was heterogeneous in much the same sense that general farming was, and still is. Agriculture, as practised in America before the War, comprised several branches, which had no necessary relation except that all of them required the use of land. The raising of grain and hay, of livestock of the several kinds; the production of butter, milk, and cheese; the growing and marketing of vegetables and fruit; all required a vast amount and variety of technique and knowledge, but the farmer's education, like the housewife's, consisted in acquiring the traditional methods of several, if not all of these specialties. Although they involved such difficult scientific subjects as the chemistry of soils, the effects of tillage and moisture, the laws of heredity and breeding, the chemistry of milk and its products, the growth and fertilization of plants; there was no available fund of information and no opportunity for systematic education on these points. Each farmer started with his father's traditional ideas and methods; if he learned to think for himself, he varied them, made some experiments on his own account, and, if he were successful, was imitated by a few of his neighbors, thus promoting the progress of science. If he failed he paid a penalty in a loss of profits and reaped the scorn of the neighborhood.

Housewifery, though as heterogeneous in character and traditional in method as farming, differed from it in several other ways. Though the farmer's work was from "sun to sun," the woman's work was never done. During all the years of child-bearing the mother added to the twelve- or fourteen-hour day of housework the nightly tending of children; and, in case of illness in the family, nursing as well. Toward the latter part of the century, the agitation by workingmen for a shorter day in other occupations reacted to shorten the farmer's day; and, coincidently, the removal of manufacturers from the home lessened the amount of labor in the house. It did not, however, perceptibly alter the intermittent character of domestic occupations and, as a rule, it tended to make them less and less educative.

The domestic sphere was gradually being narrowed in much the same way as the shoemaker's. He had once been a highly skilled workman, whose trade demanded a knowledge of a number of skilful processes, from the tanning of leather to the designing of lasts. If he followed his trade into the factory he was reduced to performing a few monotonous operations requiring little intelligence; if he remained outside he became a handy repairer of half-worn footwear. Like the housewife, he was left with only the fragmentary processes of his trade, and those the least interesting, and gradually lost the stimulus to originality and skill which had been in itself an education.

Cooking, which was the most varied of the crafts left in the home, became more and more elaborate as women expended more time and thought upon it. Every housewife tried to vie with her neighbor in concocting some new combination of eggs, milk, sugar, and flour, et cetera; recipes became more complicated and laborious—though the food did not become more nutritious and digestible—until the principal literature of the self-educated woman consisted of cookbooks filled with hundreds of formulæ. Such meager schooling as she received had no relation either to housewifery or motherhood. It was inevitable that when she had mastered the technique of ordinary homekeeping, whatever originality and ambition she might possess would have to be exercised within the limits of her sphere, and would, therefore, develop in the direction of elaboration of living. As we shall see in the chapters on dress, personal adornment and clothes became almost an occupation in themselves, engaging more and more time and attention. Like a squirrel in a cage, she must exercise herself by running around in the wheel contrived for her, instead of roaming freely at large to gather nuts against the winter's need.

Another simple difference between domesticity and farming—the difference between indoor and outdoor life—has produced effects upon women so far-reaching as to be incalculable. The farmer, as general agriculture began to be subdivided into special lines, concentrated his energy and technique on those to which his taste and his land were adapted. He was not shut up in the barn to devote himself solely to milking cows and currying horses and feeding the animals three times a day. Merely from a hygienic standpoint, housekeeping, as it became more narrow and more elaborate, became less healthful. Thousands of steps—patter, patter from one end of the house to the other, upstairs and down cellar; hundreds of mechanical operations—sweeping, dusting, beating of eggs, kneading of bread, washing, ironing, and scrubbing; millions of stitches in sewing, mending, knitting, quilting—these and similar petty labors, varied by three meals a day and three piles of dishes to wash, and, mayhap, the care of a baby or two, made up the vocation of domesticity. It was a monotony of heterogeneous drudgery, comparable only to farming, and as much more enervating as four walls and a roof are than the blue sky, the brown furrow, and the live and growing world outside.

A few years ago two college women tested the ordinary household operations by the criteria of hygienic gymnastics. Beginning with the customary assumption that "gravity is the enemy of woman," they found that all the work of the housewife except scrubbing kept her on her feet excessively, that most of the arm and back movements were in a cramped and strained position; and that she walked from five to eight miles a day in dead, if not altogether bad, air—in short, that housekeeping was hard manual labor. Though every housewife knew this without scientific demonstration, it has not been sufficiently recognized that housework of the old-fashioned kind lacked fresh air, variety, and exhilaration precisely as factory labor does, and to a much greater degree than farming.

The mental element of joy in the product, which is the highest compensation one can have for any labor, was to a great extent lost in the *repetition* involved in domestic production. No doubt the woman who made the first chocolate cake or the first pumpkin pie got lots of fun out of it, and so long as she kept her reputation as the superior and original maker, she was stimulated to further skill. But no woman could keep up her enthusiasm for preparing potatoes three times a day, much less for washing the tri-daily dishes, any more than the ditchdigger could develop his mind and continue to lift with zest so many hundred shovelfuls of dirt during three hundred days in a year.

Work is, undoubtedly, the chief means by which human capacity is increased and moral perceptions lifted to a higher level; but drudgery—that is, the indefinite repetition of operations requiring the minimum of technique and intelligence—deadens the mind, and if pursued in the midst of filth and darkness, brutalizes the worker. In our day it is being recognized that in proportion as drudgery is done under healthful conditions and for the attainment of an interesting and worthy goal, it may become a means of self-development. Professor Lillien J. Martin made more than seventy-five thousand observations, extending over a period of three years, on one subject, in order to determine a certain fact in experimental psychology; in point of repetition it was as wearisome as if she had washed dishes three times a day for a lifetime; but in point of mental interest it had the zest of working in a new field, and for its goal the greatest intellectual joy in life, the making of a scientific discovery.

One further parallel may be drawn between domesticity as a vocation and the occupations of men. At the beginning of the nineteenth century the American family was still an industrial unit. All of its members were producers according to their age, sex, and ability, and all pooled their products and shared the results. Very little ready money was in circulation, and the male head of the family had relatively small chance to rob his dependents while living, although he might distribute his estate very unjustly after he was dead. When the family gradually ceased to be an industrial unit, the minor children began to control their own earnings as soon as they left home, and the husband sold the products of the farm or the business for money. But the women of the household, no longer economically important as manufacturers of raw material, were not in a position to sell their services in the public market. They were still producers, but only secondary producers, so to speak, by so much as a cooked egg is better than a raw one, and a clean sheet than a dirty one; and they were in consequence reduced to a position of quasi-peonage. Just as the serf of medieval times was at the mercy of his master-employer because he could not leave the land for another and better-paid job, so mothers and daughters became dependent upon the goodwill of the master of their household.

Nor did the fact that, unlike the peon, many a woman might receive more than the value of her service, alter her economic dependence. Greedy, idle, seductive females practised the arts of their kind to wring from industrious men a luxurious living to which they were not entitled; while the majority of hardworking, devoted wives were left without recourse against their particular supporter's notion of what they had earned.

How this situation worked out occasionally is illustrated by the following story, told by a lawyer about an old farmer's wife down on Cape Cod. The farmer died without a will, and his greedy heirs, grudging her the life-use of one-third of the estate, which the law gave her, managed to prove that the farmer had imposed upon her by an illegal ceremony of marriage, and that she, therefore, was not entitled to any of the estate. The Judge, thereupon, advised the old woman to bring in a bill for her services, for if she had not been his wife, the farmer was not entitled to have her do his housework for nothing. Accordingly, she brought in a bill at the current rate of wage of a domestic servant, which the Court allowed, and it took the whole of the estate to pay it. Of course, she had been "supported" all that time, but with the discovery that she was not the man's wife, it was also discovered that her support alone was not a full equivalent for her labor. . . .

The economic disintegration of the Puritan-Colonial family in the last century resulted in taking away from the housewife one of the chief incentives of any labor, *i.e.,* definite money compensation. Marriage, though nominally a partnership, left the second partner in the position of putting in her property and her labor, and then being obliged to trust the first partner to give her as much or as little of the increase as he chose. Stripped of its sentimental aspects, such a bargain was a much greater risk for the woman than for the man, and equally unjust, whether wife got more or less.

The reaction of an occupation pursued through a lifetime is so tremendous upon the physique and the mental and moral development of men, that its effects are easily recognized everywhere. But in a country where a man is comparatively free to choose or to drift into the occupation to which he is suited, the affinity between a man and his calling would naturally reinforce his stronger characteristics, and become an element of general social progress. Men do better that which they are fitted for, and they are apt to like what they can do well. Now, the peculiar misfortune of women has been that, while the original field of domestic production was rapidly narrowed, social convention, during at least two generations, prevented them from engaging in any substitute for it outside the home. Although their primitive sphere was constantly shrinking they were not yet freed to find another. The theory of mankind and of the Church was still: all women must be domestic, whether married or single; whether by temperament maternal or celibate; whether adapted to domestic detail or not. The vocation manacled the woman, the woman could not choose what she liked, or what she was fitted to do.

The effect of this social coercion was to suppress initiative and originality to a degree beyond imagination. For it was inevitably the women of most active minds and of largest administrative capacity who found the limitations of housekeeping most irksome. Suppose every man in the world had to be a farmer, and could never break away into law or science or art or engineering or even literature, without paying a penalty in social ostracism, and—worst of all—in the sacrifice of a family and a home; suppose that he never received any wages directly, but was just "supported," and now and then accepted what his senior partner chose to give. Indeed, we need not suppose, for this was the state of a large class of men in the Middle Ages. But the historian calls them the "dark ages," and explains carefully that under such limitations the development of great men and great ideas was not to be expected. No more was it probable that domesticated women, inheriting an environment and a tradition of smallness, would show, even when the doors of opportunity were opened a little way, a high degree of talent in untried fields. It is only by some such analogy as this that we can realize the effect of housewifery in stunting women of exceptional ability who, conscientiously pinching themselves to fit their sphere, were unhappy or ill-tempered; or, if they had the courage to break through that domestic inclosure, found themselves pariahs, doomed to isolation, if not to failure, in the unfriendly *métier* for which they had no preparation.

When, toward the end of the last century, women first began to organize themselves into clubs for self-culture and social activity, they were ridiculed for their lack of ability to do teamwork. Their critics seemed to have forgotten that there had never been incentive or opportunity for coöperation toward larger ends, except in the sewing-bee and the Ladies' Aid Society. Miss Tarbell has clearly shown that the Civil War was the first occasion in which any large number of women came together outside the home to work for the public good. That excessive devotion to the need of her own family which was the glory of her womanhood prevented her from taking an interest in larger affairs. Just as the lawyer instinctively measured everything by the law, so the specialized domestic woman limited her thinking within the periphery of those matters which it was necessary for a woman to know. She took the personal view, because she had to—her happiness and comfort depended not on town government and trade, not on political theories and international quarrels, but on the will of the person nearest to her. In other words, her vocation was to wait upon and please a small circle of people, and therefore her intuitions in respect to personality were extraordinarily developed.

Many of the minor characteristics set down as peculiarly feminine are, in fact, the product of the universal domestic employment of women in past times; as, for instance, the proficiency in the observation and memory of details. Women remember certain personal details of indoor life for the same reason that the ornithologist sees and remembers the markings of every bird. This same man, however, would probably not remember the pattern of the wallpaper in his bed-chamber, nor be capable of choosing a tasteful necktie; while his equally capable wife could not tell a robin from a peewee, and yet could describe accurately the dress of all her guests at a tea party.

Women are precisely like men in that they follow the line of least resistance, and of greatest apparent self-interest. Since successful domesticity required the mastery of an immense number of petty details inside the house, and the attainment of order, cleanliness, and comfort therein, the mind of the homekeeping woman dealt incessantly not alone upon these affairs, but also upon the persons whom they concerned. Formerly women could recall the marriage relationship of the whole family connection, and the number of the children; while many a man could not tell how old his wife was, nor whether the first baby was born in the old house or the new one. It is, indeed, no more masculine for men to be oblivious of domestic details than it is feminine to be master of them—it is merely human to be what one has to be in the station to which one was born and reared.

It is a natural corollary to this principle that the purely domestic woman of the end of the nineteenth century should have been quite as "eager in the pursuit of trifles" as the lady of leisure whom Mercy Warren complained of a hundred years earlier. Given a vocation which demanded incessant attention to a thousand small matters, even when the number of those affairs was diminished so as to greatly release the housewife, the average woman would still inevitably pursue trifles until there was both a chance and an incentive to follow larger things. Only a very exceptional girl would make a new path for herself because the cost of any departure from the sanctified conventions of women's lives was so tremendous. It cost a man something to refuse to treat other men to liquor in a country where that was the universal custom, but it did not make him a by-word or prevent him from marrying and having a home. And it is not exaggeration to say that nothing less than this was the penalty for any women who broke through the appointed sphere and offered opinions on those larger questions relegated to men.

There were thus both negative and positive reasons for woman to become small-minded. On the one hand, the sole occupation of her life consisted of exacting, repetitious, and ephemeral things; on the other, until there was an imperative call to other vocations outside, she could not develop the larger mind and become convinced of the futility of the conventional methods of housekeeping. The more conscientious the housewife was, the more petty she surely became, devoting herself to the elaboration of food, clothes, decoration, and needlework in the effort to be the perfectly correct feminine creature.

Curiously enough, it was not purely domestic women who revolutionized domestic science in the last quarter of the century and relieved it of its terrible drudgery and picayune monotony, but rather *thinking*, educated women, who, having escaped into a larger world of scientific, sanitary, and economic progress, looked back and, out of pity, began to rescue their sisters from the bog of household tradition. One woman, Ellen H. Richards, devoting herself to chemistry and hygiene, did more to make the home a livable place than a thousand other conscientious, devoted homekeepers, who remained imprisoned in the woman's sphere of her generation, and that without the sacrifice of any truly feminine quality. The "model domestic woman" is now generally the one whose methods are belated; who cannot keep her servants, and does not yet dream that this is the day of employé; who does her tasks in the old-fashioned way; who still thinks it shiftless to leave any of the laundry unironed; who balks at a patent dishwasher and a fireless cooker and who has not yet found out that there is a whole library of household science with which she might educate herself and mitigate the endless pettiness of living.

It was inevitable, as soon as women in any numbers understood work outside the home for wages, that they should begin to compare domesticity disadvantageously with other vocations. The first effect of this was that the American girl would no longer work out as a servant, and, when she married, would have as her social ambition the employment of some immigrant to do the more laborious and tedious things. The next and logical result was that a good many young women declined to keep house even for their husbands, and went to boarding; and that indulgent husbands, who preferred good-temper and dainty, agreeable companionship in a wife, encouraged wives to rid themselves of every form of drudgery. Whenever the wife had earned money before marriage she could not help measuring her wifehood in financial terms—whether she did any household labor or not—for she had been brought up on the theory that because of her potential motherhood she was "entitled to support." At the beginning of the present century not a few such women have become intelligent enough to question the tradition of economic dependence, and cannot keep their self-respect unless they give a full return for what they receive.

The "strictly domestic" woman is a rapidly vanishing type, eliminated by world-changes in social and industrial conditions, but it will be several generations probably before the effects of domesticity upon the character and mentality of women will disappear. Women of the more belated kind will continue to be petty, devoted to unnecessary details of dress and household affairs, timid, and unoriginal—the sport of hereditary and conventional forces which they do not comprehend. Of necessity, being out of touch both with the old and the new order, they will be discontented and will make the homes of which they are the mistresses as unsatisfactory as themselves. But in proportion as domesticity is remodeled and made tolerable by scientific administration, women, even domestic women, will cease to be petty, gossipy, unthinking servants of the household. There will be as great a revolution in the characteristics of the homemaking woman as there has been in the qualities of the farmer since the spread of agricultural science. It is significant that, as the traditional household labors are modified or vanish altogether from the home, wifehood and motherhood are seen to have no essential connection with sewing, cooking, or laundry-work under the conditions of modern life, and stand out as true vocational functions in themselves.

17
Elsie Clews Parsons
Sex (1915)

To us and probably to all peoples sex is quite as definite and dominant a category as age. It is quite as ambitious, our sense of it as imperative, so imperative that, as in our treatment of age, every detail of life (and of death) becomes an opportunity for formalized expression— ornament and dress, food and drink, occupations, gait, posture and gesticulation, cries and language, laughter and tears, innumerable particulars of manners and morals.

Like age, too, sex makes for social segregation. The sexes, like the age-classes, are seclusive or exclusive. In endless ways men will have nothing to do with women or women, with men. Each sex has always kept a great deal to itself, avoiding the other, shy, apprehensive. In general the separation has been practically contrived by the rule that woman's place is in the home, or a subdivision of it, and man's place, outside, in the world, in interests and occupations not open to women. In public places the presence of women has been forbidden or unwelcome, covert or ignored. Of course the circumstances vary. In certain New Guinea tribes during times of religious excitement the village is deserted by the women; they have to take to the woods. With us it is the woods, sometimes men say, which are no place for women. The streets of Seoul were once taboo to women by day; there are streets in New York once taboo to them at night. Once in England ladies went to the play wearing masks, today they sit in the House of Commons behind a grill. "Through a lattice made of bamboo and a sort of silken net, they see and hear all that passes without being seen themselves," writes a traveler of the accommodation made for ladies at Chinese banquets two or more centuries ago.[1]

The opinion of these Chinese ladies is not available, but Englishwomen will tell you that they find the arrangement of the ladies' gallery a grateful protection.

Their satisfaction with it, their feeling that it is a safeguard against the men below them, is in part an expression, I take it, of that sex antagonism not uncommonly manifest in more direct ways in primitive society. In Australia, for example, in tribes where each sex has its own totem, men and women will fight together, men with their clubs, women with their digging sticks, whenever their totem bird or bat has been killed by one of the other sex.[2] The creature may have been attacked in a spirit of mischief or malice, in much the same spirit boys shy stones at an old maid's cat.

Now and again one sex or the other frankly avows that its exclusiveness or seclusiveness is a matter of discrimination in its own favour. We remember how Livy puts in the mouth of Cato the Elder a caution against letting women have their own way. "Suffer them once to arrive at an equality with you," he warns, "and they will from that moment become your superiors." American housewives are given to saying that

From Elsie Clews Parsons, *Social Freedom: A Study of the Conflicts Between Social Classifications and Personality* (New York: G. P. Putnam's Sons, The Knickerbocker Press, 1915), 24–37.

1. Astley, Th., *Voyages and Travels,* vol. iv., p. 83. London, 1747.
2. Howitt, A. W., *The Native Tribes of South-East Australia,* pp. 148–51. London and New York, 1904.

they for their part do not like to have men hanging all day about the house. It upsets their housekeeping. The Ainu of Japan admits that women are kept ignorant of sacred things lest they turn their prayers against the men.[3] Less than a century ago it was at times thought rather unsafe in the Episcopalian hierarchy to permit women to hold separate missionary meetings. "You can never tell," said one clergyman who attended every session of the women of his church, "You never can tell what these women will take it into their heads to pray for next."[4]

But in these expressions of sex antagonism we must see mere suspicion and apprehensiveness, the feelings which readily arise between any segregated groups. There is here nothing but a desire to keep the sex boundaries undisturbed, no sign at all of a desire to cross them. For that one must turn to the fabled Amazons or to those buoyant spirits of the Renaissance by whom more than one aphorism of sex was questioned.

Renaissance challenges of sex distinctions bore fruit in the nineteenth century in that struggle for sex mobility Huxley and fellow "philogynists" called emancipation and we of a later period feminism. In its most obvious aspect this great sex adventure is an agitation against the exclusiveness of men. In regard to the exclusiveness of women the movement has as yet taken no destructive position, rather has it from time to time countenanced or even encouraged that invidious spirit, the very spirit most characteristic of the ardent woman hater. "As women," declares the Woman's Peace Party in the preamble of its platform, "as women, we feel a peculiar moral passion of revolt against both the cruelty and the waste of war." Seldom have men been more exclusive.

There has been no concerted protest of feminists against sex segregation, but individual voices have been raised—sometimes because the very admission of women into men's fields necessitates association with men, an association in itself regarded as an indifferent or even an unfortunate circumstance; sometimes because of the theory that co-operation is truly desirable, the sexes through their differences supplementing one another; sometimes contrariwise, because sex, it is believed, does not enter into the co-operation at all—only personality. Let men and women associate as personalities, it is urged, not merely as sexes. It is just because their intercourse has been surcharged with sex in the past that feministic propaganda is needed.

Very pregnant is this charge by the feminist of oversexing, and highly significant the analysis it prompts. Freedom from the domination of personality by sex is the gift *par excellence* of feminism, a gift it brings to men as well as women, and not only to men as men but to men in their relation to women. As long as women are *the sex,* preoccupation with sex being to such a degree undisturbed, personality has little chance to enter into sex relations. A woman, a man too,[5] is a personification of sex,[6] not a personality in whose nature sex plays but a part. Towards him or her as a personification, set duties are owing; over him or her, set rights are enforcible. In so far as he or she is husband or lover, wife or mistress, the collective, institutional attitude is easy, the line of least resistance, involving an adjustment once and for all, certain, reassuring. He or she has but to be considered as a member of a class, a class towards which a given attitude is assumed or presupposed.

---

3. Batchelor, J., *The Ainu and their Folk-lore,* pp. 550–51. London, 1901.

4. *The Woman's Journal,* May 29, 1915.

5. The plea against treating men merely as men has certainly been less vociferous and persistent than that against treating women merely as women, but it was made earlier. Years before the publication of *The Doll House,* an American writer recommended to young ladies "always, when conversing with gentlemen, to endeavor to think of them as human beings, and to forget other distinctions." (Coxe, Margaret, *The Young Lady's Companion,* p. 53. Columbus, 1846.)

6. I cannot forbear giving the illustration at this moment under my eye. "The nearer you approach to the masculine in your apparel," writes the Rev. John Bennet, "the further you will recede from the appropriate graces and softness of your sex. . . . We forget that you are woman in such a garb, and we forget to love." (*Letters to a Young Lady,* p. 142.)

Any shirking of this attitude or violation of the standardized feelings or ideas it implies is condemned or penalized by society as an offence against itself, or, from a modern standpoint, against those prescriptions it established for the sexes at a period of culture when only an economic or a sexual relation between them was ever considered. Offences between men and women as personalities, offences or obligations, are not taken into account in the primitive institution of marriage or, in that institution of the less primitive cultures, prostitution. Relations other than economic or sexual do not figure. If ever they compel attention, if personal relations enter into marriage or prostitution, anti-institutional conduct is imminent, and if such conduct is not entirely suppressed by the group, "sex problems," as we call them, arise.

At first these problems appear not as questions of personality but as conflicts in the status of the sexes. The sex problems of the nineteenth century were concerned with the property rights of married women, the double standard of sex morals, the rehabilitation of the old maid, all changes in status, or with the difficulties of passing from one sex status to another,— the trials of the woman with a past, of the divorcée,—or with the propriety even of separate social compartments for the unmarried and the married, for the married and the prostitute. The contrast for lifelong support was compared, and sometimes even unfavourably, with the contract for shorter periods.

In this century the orientation of the problems of sex relationship is changing. In mating, responsiveness or reciprocity takes the place of proprietorship. Since mating and parenthood are seen to be theoretically[7] distinguishable, is not any relation of sex, we are asking, to be self-determining, rising and developing according to the nature of the lovers themselves, not to be determined by or in the interests of others, the only test of the relationship, the effect of the one personality upon the other?

Other questions, profound and subtle, are arising from this shifting of interest in sex relations. Sympathy and insight are called upon in measure undreamed of by the antique moralist whose sole anxiety is to preserve his reassuring social categories intact. The marriage law and custom he finds so satisfactory, divorce law, laws about seduction or adultery or bigamy, estimates of prostitution, the law of parental consent to marriage, all are matters certain to demand readjustment when mating comes to be considered for itself. Parental consent, one may forecast, will disappear, the age of consent at marriage becoming the legal age at majority, maturity the only age-criterion for mating. Prostitution will be thought of as a sin against sex on the part of men as well as women, a greater sex sin in men in fact than in women, the part of women in it being economic rather than sexual, and the discrimination against women prostitutes being in reality a caste discrimination.[8] As for single-heartedness in mating, under free circumstances the single-hearted will seek his or her like, as will he or she of polygamic tendency. One foresees an increase of monogamous unions. One foresees too in mating a far larger measure of candour and frankness. With reciprocity as the paramount principle in sex relationships, many of the reasons for covertness will disappear. Seduction will be redefined as deception on the part of either man or woman as to what he or she asks or the other offers.

There will be more sincerity, less sentimentality. Change as it comes will be met, not lied about or shirked. Life is change and any live personal relation is a changing relation. And so the principle of permanence will cease to be the final criterion of virtue in mating. It will lose its very egregious place. Lasting love will be esteemed a good, like lasting health or

---

7. Practically, the increase of lifelong celibacy, of later marriage, of childless marriage, has led up to the making of this distinction. The introduction of contraceptives has made its acceptance inevitable. (See Parsons, Elsie Clews, "Marriage and Parenthood—a Distinction," *The International Journal of Ethics,* July, 1915.)

8. *Cp.* Parsons, Elsie Clews, *The Family,* pp. 347–48. New York and London, 1906.

energy or happiness. But, as in health or happiness, the enduring character of passionate love will not be considered solely of itself, will not be its justification, as it were, for existing. The surcease of love will be accounted a disaster, a tragedy, not an offence; a misfortune society should regret or pity, not condemn or revile.

Whatever fresh measure of sympathy given sex relations, however, the new sex questions are answered, it will be realized that relations between personalities, whether sex enters into them or not, run the risk, given publicity, of becoming impersonal and monopolistic, that personal relations cannot be standardized, that each relationship, if considered at all, will have to be considered in itself. But would such a task be possible, we may well ask, for collective thought or action? Recognizing its limitations, will not society begin to regard sex relations as purely private relations, no more its business than friendships? In early culture, friendship, we are to see, is itself an affair of covenant and ceremonial, a public relationship. With us it is not a community concern. Time will be, one ventures to predict, when the sex relationship likewise will come into its rights to privacy, to freedom from direct community control.

Again standing in the circles of status and of personality, standing in their common segment of sex, as we face towards status, we see sex differences a cause of apprehension and alarm, a reason for separating the sexes as completely as possible—physically and psychically. All intrusions of one sex upon the other sex are fearful and hateful, to be precluded by the utmost ingenuity, by social devices of all kinds, by supernatural, moral, and legal sanctions. Sex consciousness is encouraged to spread out over non-sexual things or circumstances; it expresses itself in quite irrelevant habits, it is given all manner of fanciful associations. When the sexes do meet, the conditions are carefully planned, planned for the most part by the Elders and planned to suit their convenience. Feeling but little the impulses of sex, the Elders deprecate them, belittle and degrade them. Courtship and marriage custom, the practice of periodic license or of prostitution are determined by the Elders to suit themselves, or at most, as compromises with the cravings of youth. The "good of society" in sex relationships generally means the good of the Elders, of those to whom the intimacies of sex are distasteful and change in sex relations, vexatious.[9]

Facing towards personality, the aspects of sex are very different. Sex becomes a factor in the enrichment of personality and of contacts between personalities. It is a factor, not an obsession. It counts only where it really exists, but there it is free to really count. No longer a source of distress or annoyance, it is not kept separate from life nor repressed into the obscene. It is free to express itself, developing its own tests, standards, ideals. According to these ideals, relations between men and women will be primarily personal relations, secondarily sexual. The standards set them will be standards of frankness, sincerity, single-heartedness, and above all of reciprocity. That these standards can be lived up to best in a private, anti-monopolistic relationship will be realized or realized enough to free sex relations from compulsory advertisement or from the necessity of furtiveness. Then at last, assured of privacy and of freedom, passionate love will forget its shameful centuries of degradation to spread its wings into those spaces whereof its poets sing.

18

JESSIE TAFT

The Woman Movement and the Larger Social Situation (1915)

Women find themselves as a matter of hard fact in the equivocal position of being neither one thing nor the other, neither in the home nor

From *International Journal of Ethics,* April 1915.

9. *Cp.* Parsons, Elsie Clews, "Sex and the Elders," *New Review,* May 1, 1915.

out of it, neither wholly mediæval nor wholly modern. The world to which women have been accustomed for centuries and to whose patterns their minds have been shaped is not for the most part the world of the modern man. His world is not only different, it is even hostile and antagonistic in many respects to the world of the woman; so much so that women who attempt to conform to both worlds, as many are compelled to do, find themselves face to face with conflicts so serious and apparently irreconcilable that satisfactory adjustment is often quite impossible on the part of the individual woman. The world outside the home has proved itself so ill-suited to women and children, even to the extent of being positively injurious, and the home in its present form has seemed to be so little adapted to the larger world's ideals of trained motherhood, scientific domestic economy, and socialized ethics, that the problems arising from the clashing of the two spheres have grown into great social questions to be handled by society as a whole.

An unprejudiced examination of the actual conditions which the average middle class woman has to meet in adjusting her life to the home and to the man's world gives sufficient evidence of the reality of the problems which are back of the so-called "woman question" and reveals their intimate connection with every other great social movement of our day. The cry of the uneasy woman is not merely the reprehensible expression of her own personal restlessness. Consciously or unconsciously it voices her share in the protest of the age against the impossible situation in which humanity finds itself today, and her struggles, even though they seem to be but a vain beating against the righteous and inevitable order of things, are a real part of that larger conflict which society as a whole is waging in its effort to combine modern industry and modern individualism.

I.

It is not necessary to review in detail the problems which justify the woman movement. They fall under the two aspects of personal difficulties which the individual woman must face in shaping her own life, and public questions which threaten the welfare of society. Those of the first class are very real to the young woman and the young woman's parents. Shall she prepare for marriage—or for wage-earning, for neither or for both? In view of the contingencies of non-marriage or widowhood, if for no other reasons, self-support and preparation for it appears to be part of prudence and good judgment. But having entered upon training for work in the world rather than for homemaking, the desire of a normal woman for a husband, children, and a home inevitably clashes with other desires developed in connection with her work in the world or in her preparation for such work. Economic freedom, regular hours, specialized, standardized work, the dignity of a trade or profession, resist the heterogeneous unsystematized tasks, the infinite detail of housekeeping.

Ethical conflicts between the standards of the sexes are another aspect of the practical problem. A standard of absolute physical chastity for the woman is confronted by a world where almost unlimited license is taken for granted. This fact, reinforced by the ordinary training of the home to the effect that sex, especially in all its physical manifestations, is inherently and mysteriously evil and is allowable only when the evil is counteracted by the charm of the marriage ceremony, that the flesh and the devil are one, may lead the woman to revolt in disgust against sex in general to such an extent that the natural impulse to marry is actually checked by her intense horror of the physical relationship involved and by her belief that all men are brutes in so far as they seek sex satisfaction.[1] The antagonism between her bringing up in the home and the world of sex as she finds it beyond the home, makes for every thinking woman a problem that may last over years of her life—the task of building up an idea of sex that is consistent with the facts and yet leaves a

1. Havelock Ellis, *Sex in Relation to Society,* II, p. 77.

universe in which she can live comfortably, of escaping from her own barren chastity while avoiding the man's meaningless license, of creating a new appreciation and expression of the most fundamental human instinct.

From the standpoint of society as a whole the same problems emerge which disturb the individual woman. Women are the consumers, but they are untrained and society is carrying the burden of their ignorance of food, clothing, sanitation, and hygiene. Women in occupations, unskilled and unorganized, render labor problems more acute. On the other hand, the invasion of women into the regions beyond the home has very naturally forced into prominence the interests for which women stand and has brought into sharp relief the incompatibility of business for money only and municipal government for politicians, with the ends which women hold essential—the welfare of children and the health and happiness of human beings. Prostitution offers yet another aspect of the dualism between the older ideas and the newer conditions. Defectives furnish a large number of the victims but the presence of such a number of defectives in the population is itself evidence of lack of social knowledge and control. The conditions under which women work the barbarous state of domestic service, unsanitary surroundings, low wages, postponement of marriage are contributing agencies. Another agency which nonetheless brings out the interaction between the home side and the changed social conditions, is the tendency of the unmarried woman to turn to other women, to build up with them a real home, finding in them the sympathy and understanding, the bond of similar standards and values, as well as the same æsthetic and intellectual interests, that are often difficult of realization in a husband, especially here in America, where business so frequently crowds out culture. One has only to know professional women, teachers, social workers, doctors, nurses, and librarians to realize how common and how satisfactory is this substitute for marriage. They have worked out a partial solution to their problem in that they have contrived to combine a real home based on love and community of interests with work in the world, but they have solved it at the expense of men and children.[2]

What is the root of the conflicts—and I have noted but a few of the more obvious—which perplex the individual woman, challenge the social reformer, and furnish conspicuous motives to drama, fiction and essay? The simplest solution is that of a well-known tradition of psychology, recently presented as an induction by Heymans: Woman is emotional; hence is inferior in science, reasoning, and every kind of theory—in art also, for she is too narrowly personal. Women excel only in morality and in the use of intuition, and their activities should be limited to the home, the church, the sickbed, and practical philanthropy. But modern psychology is not content with such blanket terms as emotional; even if women are emotional, it asks "Why?" for emotion is not according to present analysis a water-tight compartment of the mind. Nor is it to be either valued or depreciated apart from its connection with the whole process of life and thought. The great man is not the man of no emotion but the man in whom emotion sensitizes and kindles intellect, or stirs to great achievement in action. Emotion appears in any field when there is an obstructed interest, and when it functions properly, far from being a hindrance, it is a stimulus to the analyzing and abstracting that follow. The charge that fairly might be made is that women have failed to develop the reflective process and that emotion with them seems too often to be just emotion which does not lead to any rationalized expression. Certain ends are emotionally evaluated and the thought of them as already obtained is set up in a vague abstract way as something highly desirable and something which may come to pass somewhere, somehow, but there is no actual attempt to work out concrete means for obtaining the ends in question. With men, on the contrary,

2. Edward Carpenter, *The Intermediate Sex*.

the emotion is much more frequently counterbalanced by the attempt to do something. The rational part of the process is given its innings. The whole matter might be put this way: Emotion appears to be functioning more normally in men than in women. The history of women offers reason enough for this condition so that there is no need to assume an inherent abnormality in women with regard to the ordinary course of mental process.

Four solutions of the problem by women themselves have at least the merit of still farther bringing out the dual factors of home and work in the world.

Olive Schreiner emphasizes the importance of useful labor for health, life, and individual development. The traditional field of woman's labor has contracted; compensation must be found in other socially useful labor or woman degenerates and becomes unfit even for matrimony. Miss Tarbell finds the root of the trouble in the fact that women have become consumers instead of producers and have not realized the new task involved. Having failed to see or develop their own field, they have gone over to the men's and find it impossible to combine men's work successfully with their feminine temperaments and maternal functions. But personal ambition and the joys of individual freedom and independence have too often overcome their sense of duty to the nation and they have not infrequently decided for the men's field against a marriage and motherhood. Mrs. Gilman and Ellen Key are at one on the necessity of economic independence at all times; they coincide in regarding the child as the supreme end of all social activities; but they differ fundamentally in what they regard as the essential relation of effective maternity to the occupations of the mother and in their general attitude towards the meaning of sex for life. Mrs. Gilman tends to minimize sex, to limit it to the bare field of reproduction, and to leave all the rest of life to that which is common, social, higher than sex. She also maintains that if domestic work is to be put on a modern business basis, the system which allows each woman to manage all the various forms of it for her own individual household will have to be replaced by co-operation and specialization. Ellen Key insists on the final worth and importance of sex in its highly developed forms and on the necessity of maintaining sex distinction. While she still believes that the mother should retain economic independence through the state, she also thinks that the greatest opportunity for a woman to develop all the possibilities of her personality, especially those qualities which are peculiarly hers, lies in her work within the home; that if she is to function most effectively she must not try to combine any profession or outside occupation with motherhood.

Every position here noted indicates a conviction either of a lack in woman's personality or a lack of harmony between the nature of woman and the modern world, which is unfavorable to the development of her personality. Mr. Heymans unintentionally tries to prove that the woman is quite unfit for any share in a civilization that has reached the stage of reflective consciousness. Miss Tarbell emphasizes the difference between the greater unity and restfulness of the personality of the woman of the past as compared with the uneasy split-up consciousness of the modern woman. Both Miss Tarbell and Ellen Key point out the tendency of the world outside the home to crush the essential womanliness of the woman, yet admit a certain amount of sacrifice of personal development as necessary to the woman in the home. Ellen Key recognizes this so keenly that she advocates minimizing the sacrifice by such means as the vote, economic independence through motherhood pensions and work at the end of the child-bearing period. Mrs. Gilman lays greatest stress on the individualistic narrowness of the woman who is confined to the isolated home life and the bad effects on society of the unscientific methods of feeding, clothing, training a family and keeping a house clean under the régime of the woman who is not on a par with modern society intellectually, while

Olive Schreiner gives a general picture of the dwarfing of the woman's personality in terms of her diminishing usefulness as a worker.

II.

The case is not different with the modern man. The woman has no monopoly on conflict and disharmony. He, too, is swamped by the system in which he finds himself. He, too, is being made, willy-nilly, by the relations in which modern business and industry are involving him; yet he is not expressing himself consciously through these relations. One has only to recall the struggle between capital and labor, the way in which life with its ideal interests is being crowded out by the pressure of the economic machinery not only on the laborer but on the man who is chained down to money-making, the frequent incompatibility of home and family with the work for which the man is fitted by nature, the alienation of the father from his home responsibilities through lack of leisure, to realize that the unsatisfactory character of the woman's life is but a conspicuous part of a wider and more basic situation which involves men as well.

Industry and trade, as carried on in the Middle Ages within a single family, a small community, or even in the craft and merchant guild of the larger towns, was a social institution controlled to a large extent from within by natural social impulses. A man had no business relations which did not involve relations of an immediate personal character. He was in direct contact with the people for whom he worked or who worked for him and he had a self, a personality, formed by these relationships and adequate to them.

Modern business and finance, on the other hand, has become so complex, so impersonal and abstract in its organization that it seems to involve only economic values. In form it is purely economic, in content it is still as social as ever it was in the Middle Ages. The changes that have brought all this about have been so tremendous and so sudden, the introduction of machinery and the consequent centralization and systematization of industry have so depersonalized it that the human beings involved in it have not yet had time to develop personalities that are equal to the complexity of the system.

The world to-day is confronted by this kind of a problem: Men are being forced to act under enormously widened social conditions in which their relationships to their fellows have multiplied increasingly while becoming correspondingly difficult to perceive as social, because of the growing abstractness of the business medium. Yet they bring to this enlarged social activity only the selves that are formed on the feudal patten—neighborhood, family selves too narrow to respond socially beyond a limited and obviously social circle. In the narrower personal connections, natural conflict of egoistic and social impulses furnish a rough control; in the new and unrecognized social relations there is nothing to call up social tendencies. Egoistic motives easily predominate. A man who would as soon lose his own life as injure a child he knew personally, can, without ever being conscious of the fact, injure hundreds of children and indirectly an entire community by feeling no responsibility for their employment in his factory through his superintendents. The man in the world of business, therefore, is not constituted a self, a person, a moral and social agent, by the individuals at the other end of the system. He does not make their motives and attitudes a part of his consciousness, thus bringing all the elements of the situation within his grasp. He uses his connections with people for his own benefit while remaining oblivious to their social character. The maxim for this procedure is "business is business." The results are social as well as economic, but only the economic factor is recognized and consciously intended. Hence we have these unlooked for social elements actually altering our civilization but absolutely uncontrolled because external to the consciousness of the individual or group of individuals that is responsible for them. This means the loosing of a great stream of social activities which *as social* are without rational guidance. No control of modern life is to be hoped for short of a complete consciousness of the social character of business and industry, and the development of a self large enough to answer to the new environment with the substitution of thoughtful control for the instinctive controls of personal contact....

Just what, then, is to be expected in the case of the average woman whose only recognized environment is the home? Logically, she must be the kind of self that answers to the form of the family. Just in so far as society has been able to preserve the feudal family, it has also succeeded in preserving the feudal woman and until within the last few years all women have been theoretically of the feudal type. The feudal lady was the center of activity in her household which included a small community. She was the great producer and knew personally every handmaid, farmer, herd boy, or retainer who assisted her in keeping her family clothed, housed and fed. Her personality was organized on the basis of all these relationships, none of which were abstract or impersonal, even though they were not yet reflectively conscious. So far as they went these connections were all real and effective. Woman responded actively to all of them just because they lay within her control. She was mistress of the situation, a working part of the social scheme in which she found herself.

How does she compare with the modern woman in the home? There is supposed to be no difference except that producing is replaced by consuming. But just this change makes the fundamental difference of connecting the modern woman with a new world of production, increasing her relationship to outside institutions infinitely, and at the same time depriving her of any effective control over her own actions. How can an individual woman exert any essential control over consumption, while production is in the power of a huge system managed collectively?[3] It is useless to ask women to try to express themselves through their work as consumers as long as they stand alone outside the system in which production takes place, and without the technique through which it is controlled.

It is the same with all of the woman's interests. She may satisfy the emotional side in love for her family, but that love will not find any complete, active and intelligent expression except as she is enabled to exert an influence through organized society. Just the fact that she loves her husband and children will give her as an individual no measure of control over the environment that surrounds them. The home is no longer individualistic and the control over its interests is no longer within the power of the individualistic woman. Unless she becomes an active member of the larger social order and adopts its socialized technique, she must be content to be battered this way and that by social forces which are external to her.

In terms of self-consciousness, the woman, like the man, is not as large as the situation in which she acts, or exists passively. The relations of the family to the larger social institutions are accepted in a perfectly abstract way. No work that she could take up outside the home would be more impersonal as far as recognized social content is concerned than her occupation as consumer. She treats it as purely economic, oblivious of the part played by human beings at the other end of the transaction. She is buying for her family and in that sense what she does has meaning for her, but she is quite unaware that her act is social also in its effect on the producer, the middleman, and other consumers. Even so the factory girl finds her work social in the sense that it helps to keep her family together in comfort. She works for them but she has no idea that her work has any other social value. It is just business.

The woman in the home, then, as well as the man in the world, has not a conscious self built up with reference to all the social relations by which she is affected and through which she in turn affects society. The chief difference is that the man does have some control

---

3. Walter Lippmann, *Drift and Mastery*, Chap. IV.

since he has learned the power of organization and co-operation and can express himself through the ballot, whereas the woman, even if she were to become socially conscious, would be at the mercy of the machine until she had acquired modern methods of expression.

It is this last point which shows us why the modern woman is in worse straits than the modern man. The woman because she is allowed to remain passive, because she has no part in the system through which some control is possible, develops no sense of responsibility for any of the results which accrue. She takes good and bad with the same absence of any positive grip on the situation. She may avail herself in a small selfish way of any advantages which the system brings but she makes no attempt to exploit these seemingly abstract relations on a large scale for her own gain as men do. Passivity is the keynote of her existence because society has striven to keep the form of the home and the woman in it as they were in the Middle Ages even after the transformation that came with the industrial revolution.

The woman can never become a full-fledged, rational human being nor can she be held responsible for any of the conditions in modern life until society ceases to consider it essential to womanliness that she receive passively the impact of all the currents of present day organized existence. As long as woman has no part in directing the forces which determine the family, herself, the least detail of her domestic life, society is retaining the lady of chivalry at the expense of conscious motherhood and is encouraging the immediate impulsive reactions of the simple situation at the price of deliberate reflection and social consciousness which alone are effective under the complex conditions of to-day. Just as the great labor movement is trying to bring the laborer to consciousness of his needs and possibilities, and society to awareness of the advantage of conscious labor, so the woman movement has before it a two-fold task; first, to make women conscious of their relations to a social order, second, to show society its need of conscious womanhood.

III.

The woman movement, viewed not as an isolated phenomenon but as an integral part of the vaster social evolution is thus seen to be only the woman's side of what from the man's angle is called the labor movement. It is a reaction against the same conditions and a demand for changes in the social order such that life will once more become harmonious. The accident of modern civilization has brought about inevitable conflict in the fundamental human impulses for both men and women. It has apparently allowed for complete, almost over expression of one set of impulses, at the expense of a partial or sometimes complete repression of the other. This has meant of course that the set of impulses which was allowed to develop unchecked by the other set was as abnormal and as far from a well-balanced rounded fulfilment as were the unexpressed impulses. The industrial and economic system of to-day, which has come into being more or less unconsciously and accidentally, has so divorced the economic and the social that it is only with a tremendous struggle for more inclusive forms of consciousness that we shall be able to recognize that the split is only apparent and that a system which not only believes in, but insists on, such a separation results in irreconcilable dualism in the lives of the men and women involved, persisting to the point of gigantic social problems, agitations and movements. Thus the labor movement symbolizes the impossibility of choosing between the fulfillment of the economic impulse and the fulfillment of the impulse to live. Men are granted unlimited opportunities to work, but no provision is made by the system for intelligent parenthood, for good citizenship, for a thoughtful development and use of the sex impulses. A man's parental expression is limited to caring for the economic welfare of his family. His own growth as a person must be sacrificed to the necessity of supporting himself and family. Work must be combined with life but our system makes little provision for such a combination hence forcing into opposition fundamental impulses clamoring for expression. The labor movement demands a new society in which creative, sexual, parental, and other social impulses will have an unquestioned right to fulfilment.

With women, on the other hand, social impulses are the only ones which are overtly recognized. Women are constantly forced into the economic world but the system ignores that fact and provides in no way for combining the peculiar social function of women with any economic function which they may find desirable or necessary. Such economic expression as has been conceded to them is confined to the home. Likewise, the other impulses, even the maternal, have no recognized place outside the limits of the individual home. For the woman, the system has no avenues of fulfillment foreseen and provided beforehand for any impulse whatsoever outside the home itself. Everything which has opened up has been at best, even after long and patient effort, only makeshift and haphazard. Society is always emphasizing the obligation of the woman to carry out the sex and maternal impulses at all costs and minimizing the need for value of the economic as far as she is concerned. In the conditions of living which are forced upon her, she is compelled to make the sorry choice of a limited sex and maternal expression or a doubtful and hazardous attempt on the economic side. In either case, she loses as far so society's aid or provision is concerned. Only by the extraordinary force of a powerful personality will she make a signal success at either venture. Society no more makes a thoughtful attempt to give the maternal interests the most complete development and employment possible than it makes any pretense at all of using intelligently the natural impulse of the woman to be of economic value in the world. Much less does it offer a rational scheme for combining both motives within a possible form of living for the average normal woman. Thus the woman, even more than the man, faces a perfectly hopeless alternative. Neither side at the present moment is overwhelmingly attractive in itself even aside from the sacrifice of other impulses which its choice involves. What woman would willingly abandon love and children? What normal woman would accept a life in which she gave up all effort at serious work of genuine economic value to society? What woman would attempt without shrinking the almost impossible task of combining the two as affairs stand to-day? Above all, what woman would undertake wifehood and motherhood with the limitations placed on it by our present social system and feel that those two fundamental parts of herself could ever reach a satisfactory and adequate fulfilment?

That the peculiarly unhappy position of the woman is a reality and not an illusion can be detected in the arguments used to convince woman of her obligation to bear and rear. The element of sacrifice is so obvious that it is even seized upon and treated as a virtue, an added glory for the crown of the wife and mother. Moreover, this notion of necessary sacrifice on the part of the woman and the bare fact of motherhood itself have grown into a sort of fetish. The experiences of motherhood are exalted to the point where they are assumed to be a sufficient compensation for any and all sacrifices. To silence our own doubts and justify our procedure, we have come to believe in the inherent and absolute value to the woman of the mere fact of giving birth to a child, even though the emotions and purposes thus originated are never carried past the instinctive or intuitive level to a rationalized and socialized expression. We are afraid to face the fact that the home in its present unrelated, individual form does demand of woman, and men too for that matter, a sacrifice so great as to have lost a great part of its value for spiritual growth, an overwhelming and crushing sacrifice of the possibilities of motherhood and fatherhood that defeats its own end.

All of this hopeless conflict among impulses which the woman feels she has legitimate right, even a moral obligation, to express, all of the rebellion against stupid, meaningless sacrifice of powers that ought to be used by society, constitutes the force, conscious or unconscious, which motivates the woman movement and will continue to vitalize it until some adjustment is made.

The labor movement and the woman movement do not understand always how close is their relationship nor do they see clearly that the reason why the obviously stupid and unsuitable social conditions which they combat are so difficult to alter is because human beings have not yet arrived at the stage where they know how to attack and solve social problems. The real goal of both movements is a society whose consciousness shall have reached the social stage and hence is capable of dealing scientifically with social as well as physical problems, a society which no longer leaves the social forms and relationships whereby human impulses are expressed to chance or physical force but subjects them to rational control.

In the physical world we have at last become conscious of our method and hence have acquired a control over physical conditions which promises to become more and more complete. If the desire arises in a community to do something for which present physical conditions make no allowance it becomes instantly a problem for the experts and it is only a question of time when a way will be found for the gratification of the felt need. The very basis of the physical problem is the thwarted desire of human beings to do something, and the method of obtaining the end is of course a full and free admission of the inherent right and value of the desire, a deliberate searching for every element involved in the physical conditions of the problem, and a careful experimental attempt to find the combination which will satisfy all the conditions. We should not consider our problem solved if the scientist said to us, "You do not really want this thing, you only imagine it, and in any case it would be bad for you to have it. You have managed to live all these years without it, why complain now?" Imagine such an answer to the determination to fly in the air. But, supposing, if we persisted in our wish to fly and began to talk about it and clamor for a way to be opened, the authorities were to turn on us, demand silence on pain of arrest and imprisonment, label us socialists or anarchists, and tell us we were rebelling against the fixed and righteous order of things as they are. Should we consider that any attempt had been made at solving our problem of how to make a machine that would fly in the air? Yet, impossible as it may seem, that is thus far the favorite method of dealing with any unsatisfied, insufficiently expressed set of human wants, whose fulfilment would mean change of the social order. First, deny the existence of the want; second, call it wicked, foolish, or injurious to individual and society; third, suppress it by force—and you have dealt with it adequately.[4]

The chief task of all social movements, then, must be at first to impress upon the rest of society the right of unsatisfied and unexpressed human impulses to constitute a real problem worthy of the same amount of expert attention whether they demand a new way of crossing the Atlantic Ocean or a new combination of work and social expression in the lives of men and women. This they will never bring about until there is a sufficient number of people who are so socially sensitive and adaptable that they feel within themselves as their own the impulses and points of view of all classes and both sexes. Such individuals will be the social scientists who will offer solutions to our social problems because they are able to place themselves at the very heart of these problems and thus to comprehend the conditions, the unsatisfied, conflicting impulses, upon the harmonization and fulfillment of which any solution that has the right to the name must be based. The fundamental purpose of the woman movement, therefore, as of any great social movement, is bound to be the producing of social scientists who will be capable of offering hypotheses that are based on the actual data constituting the problems, and the bringing about of an increasing social consciousness among all

---

4. For a complete presentation of this failure of our civilization to handle its social problems see Mr. Walter Lippman's *Preface to Politics*.

19
Leta Hollingworth and Robert Lowie
Science and Feminism (1916)

Feminism demands the removal of restrictions imposed on woman's activity. Opponents of feminism seek to justify these restrictions on two grounds: (1) because of undesirable social and ethical consequences that are believed to be the necessary outcome of their removal; (2) because of the alleged unfitness of women to undertake certain forms of activity. The considerations that come under the first head lie wholly outside the field of science; for what is socially or ethically desirable depends on the individual point of view assumed, and has nothing to do with the objective determination of fact that constitutes scientific judgment. At best social science might establish what consequences would actually flow from a removal of restrictions; but social science is at present far from being able to predict future events within its domain. Science, then, can deal only with the arguments of the second order, the question whether woman is by nature debarred from successfully following pursuits open to man, and the present paper is confined exclusively to this problem. It is true that some scientists have categorically affirmed woman's inferior equipment, notably Professor Sedgwick in a much-advertised statement in the *New York Times*. In so doing they have voiced folk-lore and folk-ethics rather than science. On the other hand, avowedly feminist literature has not been free from misrepresentation of the facts. The following pages are designed to fill the long-felt want of a concise popular summary of the present state of knowledge in regard to the question of woman's supposedly natural disabilities.

The widespread conviction of a woman's inability in certain directions is in large measure due to the fact that, to the knowledge of those disqualifying her, she never works and never has worked in these directions; hence the desire on her part to perform such work appears "unnatural." This point of view, is, of course, not a strictly logical one; for even if woman had been uniformly debarred from work along certain lines, this might have been due to special historical causes and not at all to her native endowment. The occupation of typist-stenographer is at present practically monopolized by women, while a few decades ago the corresponding secretarial positions were uniformly filled by men. Yet we do not attribute this fact to a change in the natural fitness of the sexes to perform the required work. Nevertheless, while the argument from universal exclusion would not be rigorously demonstrative, it must be admitted that if women were *everywhere* shut out from a number of occupations open to men, regardless of racial and social differences, this would be fair *presumptive* evidence that woman is naturally less fit to undertake the tasks in question. Before making a direct comparison of the biological and psychological status of the sexes, we will therefore try to determine woman's sphere in different forms of society.

Woman's Sphere in Different Cultures.—Unfortunately this particular problem has been obscured by feminists as much as by any of their opponents. Among many adherents of woman's cause, there is a firm belief that all mankind at one time passed through a stage of society called "the matriarchate," in which women ruled supreme and men played the second fiddle. Only at a later period men are supposed to have risen to the ascendancy, hence, it is argued, the inferior position of woman in modern times is not rooted in sexual differences, but results from man's social position of vantage.

From *Scientific Monthly*, September 1916.

A correct conclusion should never be bolstered up by erroneous reasoning; and in the present instance the argument is scientifically worthless, because no satisfactory evidence of a general matriarchate condition has ever been advanced. The following are the facts: A great many primitive peoples of the world reckon kinship either exclusively through the mother or exclusively through the father; the matrilineal kin group being commonly called (by American ethnologists) a "clan," the patrilineal kin group a "gens." However, there are also not a few tribes without either clans or gentes; and in many cases there is not a shred of evidence for the view that the gentes were ever preceded by a clan system. Thus, it can not be regarded as a fact that the matrilineal clan represents a once universal stage of social development. But, even if it did, this would be very different from asserting a matriarchal state. To trace descent through the mother is one thing; to yield social prerogatives to woman is a very different thing. Thus, we find a well-developed system of maternal descent among the coastal tribes of British Columbia, but though a man inherits his mother's clan name and his maternal uncle's property, women play an altogether subordinate part in the tribal life. It is true that instances may be cited on the other side: among the Iroquois, in particular, there is not only descent through the mother, but something approaching a matriarchate, *i.e.,* a far-reaching influence of women on the conduct of social and political affairs. Such examples, however, are decidedly rare; as a rule, whether in North America, Australia or other areas, the matrilineal system is *not* coupled with matriarchal privileges.

The really important question is, what has been the field of woman's activity in different times and regions? The care of the children devolves on her from biological necessity. This task and her inferior muscular powers would keep her from war and the chase. Are there any further restrictions which the consensus of human societies has declared as inherent in sex? The answer of ethnology seems to be a clearly negative one. In every tribe there is indeed a division of labor between the sexes over and above what seems determined by the demands of infants and the differences in physical strength. But the types of activity associated with woman and man differ from tribe to tribe. Among the Hopi all the weaving was done by men, while among the Navajo, who are supposed to have learned the art from the Hopi, its practise fell to the woman's share. In North America the shaping of earthenware vessels seems to be a feminine pursuit; but in some sections of Africa men function as potters. It is not *a priori* obvious why the tanning of skins should be executed by women among the Redskins; why agriculture is the work of men among the Pueblo and of women among the Iroquois Indians; why the realistic painting of Plains Indian robes should be done by men; while the geometrical painting of rawhide bags is a prerogative of woman.

Without going into further detail, we may safely state that almost everywhere woman's contribution to culture is an important one. So far from being confined to the activities currently associated with the household, she often plays a most important part in the economic life, and practises indispensable tribal arts and industries. It is indeed true that these activities do not involve so sharp a separation from the household work as would result in modern conditions. An African agriculturist can ply her hoe with a child on her back; an Indian tanner may scrape and smoke hides, plait baskets and embroider quillwork in the intervals of domestic duties. But for our present purpose this fact is irrelevant. We are concerned with determining whether there are fields of work that woman should be debarred from for reasons of natural unfitness. What we actually find is that the work assigned to woman (beyond the obvious biological duties) is a matter of social custom, due doubtless in each particular case to specific historical causes. Ethnological evidence does not permit us to say that it is natural for women to exercise political functions as among the Iroquois, or to be rigidly excluded from tribal activity as in Melanesia and Australia; it does not prove that women are naturally more or less fit to be potters, weavers, tanners, gardeners, artists, poets or what not. It merely indicates in different communities considerable differences in the apportionment of modes of employment between the sexes. It does not justify the theory that the apportionment that had developed in our own civilization until the most recent times represents the one natural division of labor. If that conventional restriction of feminine activity is a natural one, proof must be given on other than ethnological grounds.

Biological Status.—Let us then turn to a direct comparison of woman's and man's biological and psychological status. Is woman by virtue of her organization anatomically and mentally in any way an inferior being?

As late as 1884, Paul Albrechts attempted to establish the "greater bestiality of woman from an anatomical point of view" by showing that in no less than nine points she approached more nearly to "our wild ancestors." In the tenth edition of Ploss and Bartels's "Das Weib"[1] Professor Paul Bartels exposes the absurdity of this view (p. 6). Of Albrechts's nine propositions, four are either erroneous or doubtful, one irrelevant, the remainder of no importance for the problem at issue. "The entire question," concludes Professor Bartels, "is wrongly put; it is, in my opinion, ideal to debate, which of the two sexes of a single class of mammals is of 'lower' rank; moreover, we could, if we so desired, urge the more powerful masticatory apparatus of man, or, following O. Schultze, his larger face in proof of the contrary assertion." Professor Schultze, who emphasizes the relatively childlike character of woman, is indeed careful to refrain from drawing the inference that for this reason man is anatomically superior. It is true that woman, like the new-born infant, has a relatively long trunk, short legs and a rather large head, but, as Schultze points out, any argument for inferiority on such grounds proves a two-edged sword: for, by virtue of his longer extremities and smaller head, man approaches the ape type in greater measure than does his mate.[2] Schultze, who is by no means an adherent of feminism, arrives at the general conclusion that man and woman are fundamentally different organisms, but of equal biological perfection. This is likewise Bartels's summing up of the situation.[3] The fact that these authors nevertheless contend for a differentiation of function because of the anatomical differences need not concern us in this connection.

One point that continues to be urged with much insistency and much lack of intelligence is the inferior size of woman's brain, for in the popular mind intellect and brain weight are closely associated. It is therefore worth while to consider this subject at somewhat greater length.

It is true that the *absolute* weight of man's brain is greater than woman's in every people among whom the comparison has been made. Thus, a large series of English brains shows an average of 1325 g. for the males and of 1,183 for the females; while in a Saxon series male and female brains average 1,355 and 1,223, respectively. A corresponding result is obtained when the brains are compared for cubic capacity rather than for weight: a Bavarian series of 100 male, and an equal number of female, brains yielded average capacities of 1,503 and 1,335 c.c., respectively. In short, the *absolute* size of man's brain does exceed that of woman.[4]

However, it is equally true that the absolute size of an elephant's or whale's brain considerably exceeds that of the male human brain, the weight of the elephant's being from 4,100 to 4,800 g., and that of the whale from 1,900 to 2,800 g. Hence it would seem rash to attach much importance to absolute brain size in comparing male and female intelligence. This skepticism is supported by the individual

---

1. Leipzig, 1913.

2. "Das Weib in anthropologischer Betrachtung," Würzburg, 1906, p. 20 f.
3. *Op. cit.,* p. 55.
4. See Bartels, *op. cit.,* pp. 34–35.

differences in the brain weight of men as compared with concomitant individual differences in intellect. While it is true that distinguished men often have a brain of more than average size, this is by no means uniformly the case. Noted scientists have been known to fall appreciably below the mean, while persons of moderate ability have turned out to possess enormous brains. In Waldeyer's series the two extremes, 900 and 2,000 g., were found to belong to two mentally quite normal men.

Abandoning the comparison on this basis, we may investigate the *relative* brain weights, *i.e.*, the weight of the brain in relation to the total weight of the body. But here we get the result that woman has a relatively larger brain than man. While the ratio of male and female body weight is as 100:83, the brain weights stand in the ratio of 100:90. Schultze has calculated the proportion of brain and body weight in man and woman according to the determination of various scholars, and finds a uniform difference in favor of woman. Thus, Schwalbe sets man's average brain weight at 1,375 g., woman's at 1,245 g.; and man's total weight at 65,000 g., and woman's at 55,000 g. This yields a proportion of 1:47.47 for man and of 1:44.17 for woman.

Can we legitimately infer from these undoubted facts that woman is intellectually superior to man? Hardly, if we draw upon corresponding data from the animal kingdom at large. For then we discover that the human species as a whole is surpassed by the rat, that the mole occupies an intermediate position between man and woman, and that the elephant has a very small relative brain weight. The comparison on this basis is not wholly worthless, for we find that of equally heavy animals the biologically higher type has a relatively heavier brain, and that of two closely related and presumably equally intelligent animals (such as the lion and the cat) the smaller invariably has a greater relative brain weight. It has been suggested with some plausibility that woman's superior relative brain weight is an illustration of the general rule last-mentioned.

What conclusion, then, can be drawn from the facts of brain weight as to the superior mental organization of either sex? Obviously, the only sane inference is that such superiority on either side is quite unproved. Some correlation between brain and intelligence undoubtedly exists; but not in the sense that the size of the brain fully determines intelligence. Bartels's summing up of the situation seems the only warrantable one: so far as we can infer anything from the brain weight of man and woman there is presumably equality of mental ability.[5]

The Psychological Data.—Let us now turn to the argument from psychology. Formerly it was held by men of science and laymen alike that women were mentally inferior to men, on the average; that if the mental abilities of all men and of all women could be averaged separately the result would show a great advantage in favor of men. Exact experiment and class-room experience, however, have led many men of science to abandon the hypothesis that women are on the average mentally inferior to men.

It should be noted that the laboratory experiments purporting to establish sex differences are frequently without bearing on the question of differences in the higher mental processes, and that perfect correlation between efficiency in laboratory tests and efficiency in normal pursuits has not been established. Indeed, Heymans, a careful and conscientious thinker, in his monograph on feminine psychology[6] falls back almost entirely on the direct estimates of university professors as to their men and women students. To be sure, his informants, on the whole, support the time-honored view that women are more industrious, but lack creative power and independence of thought, yet, as Heymans himself recognizes, these judgments may have been largely affected by the judges' initial bias. That this is indeed so is suggested by a comparison of equally offhand judgments by various scholars not cited by

---

5. Plotz-Bartels, *op. cit.*, p. 48.
6. "Die Psychologie der Frau."

Heymans. Thus, Paul Bartels[7] is convinced that the average woman is as competent as the average man, whether at the chessboard or in politics, in science or at the stock exchange, or wherever else in life activity depends predominantly on the intellect. Her great inferiority appears, according to this writer, where efficiency is the result of a well-developed personality: she fails as a leader of crowds or captain of a ship, in poetry, as a physician, as a teacher and leader of boys, etc. In striking contrast to this view stands that of Forel, who considers women and men on a par emotionally, men superior intellectually, and women superior in point of volition. In the face of such disagreement, we may well doubt whether the time has come for a definite statement as to the psychological equipment of woman as compared to man. To revert to the method employed by Heymans, it is interesting to note that a number of American professors who have answered Professor Sedgwick's article in the *New York Times* find no inferiority on the part of their female students. The general change of attitude noticeable on this subject in academic circles gives at least presumptive evidence to the effect that the older opinion was a doctrine of more or less rationalized folk-belief without adequate foundation in fact.

Nevertheless, it is true that woman's intellectual achievement as recorded in history has been inferior, and even scholars who admit the equality of man's and woman's intellectual endowment now seek to explain this fact on the score of alleged greater male variability.

About a century ago the anatomist Meckel in his "Manual of Descriptive and Pathological Anatomy" concluded on pathological grounds that the human female was more variable than the human male; and he thought that, "since woman is the inferior animal, and variation a sign of inferiority, the conclusion is justified." Later, when variability came to be regarded as a sign of superiority and as a trait affording the greatest hope for progress, anatomists and naturalists arrived at the conclusion that the male is more variable. Men of science who had gone so far as to take the stand that women are *on the average* equally able with men, now inferred from the alleged greater anatomical variability of males that males must also be mentally more variable, and declared women's failure in intellectual achievement to be due to this fact.

Unfortunately for this theory of inherently greater male variability, however, there appears to be no support for it in precise data. Karl Pearson, in his "Variation in Man and Woman" (1897), showed that when anatomical measurements of adults are treated with proper statistical precision, "there is no evidence of greater male variability, but rather of a slightly greater female variability." More recently Montague and Hollingworth[8] have shown from a study of 2,000 newborn infants that there is no demonstrable difference in variability between the sexes at birth. As for mental variability, the precise data at present available have been summed up by Leta S. Hollingworth[9] in a critique recently published. No proof of greater male variability in mental traits can be found in the scant and inconclusive data available on the subject. The theory exists, but the evidence does not.

Yet it is possible to admit equal endowment and equal variability and still to regard as impossible equal achievement on the part of woman. The traditions and tales of savages are replete with the primitive superstitions that center round the functional periodicity of women. And the literature of the nineteenth and twentieth centuries is replete with dogmatic assertions respecting the same subject. A long and patient search through this literature brings to light a veritable mass of conflicting statements by men of science, misogynists, practitioners, and general writers as to the dire effects of periodicity on the mental and physical life of women; but the search reveals

---

7. *L. c.,* p. 48.

8. Helen Montague and Leta S. Hollingworth, "The Comparative Variability of the Sexes at Birth," *Amer. Jour. of Sociology,* 1914.

9. Leta S. Hollingworth, "Variability as Related to Sex Differences in Achievement," *Amer. Jour. of Sociology,* 1914.

scarcely a single fact upon which the earnest, but critical, seeker after truth can lay his hand and say, "Here is a point established." Men eminent in their professions are found announcing the most dogmatic and contradictory notions. Unfortunately for the scientifically minded, they fail, for the most part, to give any hint of the methods by which they arrive at their conclusions, usually prefacing their remarks merely with the convenient phrase, "It is very well known." It is certain, at all events, that they did not arrive at their conclusions by introspection; and it scarcely seems likely that much trustworthy information will be accessible on this subject till women have prosecuted their own researches into it. As in the case of variability, the most recent and thorough study, in fact the only precise study, made as to the effects of school work on the periodic function fails utterly to confirm theory. A. E. Arnold,[10] who made the study, announces as his conclusion, after closely following up the records of over 1,000 women over eighteen years of age during two years of college work, that "all effects thus far observed have been in the direction of improvement."

It is amusing to note how every sex difference that has been discovered or alleged has been interpreted to show the superiority of males. When students of institutional statistics discovered that there are more males among inmates of idiot asylums, and supposed this to mean that there must be more males than females among the feeble-minded, this apparently unfavorable fact was at once interpreted as confirmatory evidence of greater male variability; and as such it became immediately favorable to the theory of male superiority. Had it been found that there were more females among inmates of idiot asylums, how easily it could have been used as evidence of the general inferior quality of female mind.

Conclusion.—We may now sum up the argument as follows: The restrictions of woman's sphere on the ground that certain occupations are not *natural* for woman because they are not customary feminine occupations in modern civilization, rests on sheer ignorance of history and ethnology, which reveal a very considerable range of activity under varying social conditions. Anatomically, it may definitely be stated that both sexes occupy the same level. A comparison of male and female brains fails to establish the superiority of either sex. With the removal of folk-psychological prejudices, and with the advance of psychological experiment, a corresponding conclusion is gaining ground as to the average mental equipment. And while the scarcity of female geniuses, and corresponding infrequency of epoch-making achievement, has been attributed to greater male variability, a sex difference in variability has never been scientifically demonstrated. Finally, the hackneyed objection, that women are unable to perform work with male efficiency because of their catamenial function, appears as pure dogma. The verdict of present-day science is thus an uncompromisingly negative one: no rational grounds have yet been established that should lead to artificial limitation of woman's activity on the ground of inferior efficiency.

---

10. "The Effects of School Work on Menstruation," *Amer. Phys. Ed. Rev.*, 1914.

III. Public Housekeeping

EARLY-TWENTIETH-CENTURY WOMEN ACTIVISTS INHERITED a thriving tradition of social reform from their nineteenth-century foremothers, a tradition deeply entwined with feminism itself. Beginning with the abolitionist movement and ending with the immensely powerful Women's Christian Temperance Union, Victorian women learned how to enter and increasingly shape pubic debate while still drawing on, and to all appearances adhering to, traditional expectations for feminine behavior, notably: purity, piety, submissiveness, and domesticity. These ideals have typically been cast by later commentators as constraining in that they relegated women to the private sphere—the home and family—and subjected them to public institutions that were controlled by men. Both purity and piety in particular were often irreconcilable with such subjection, however, and women used their claims to the moral high ground to launch various movements for the reform of corrupt social and political practices. This kind of social reform is part of the broader philosophy that has been dubbed after the fact *difference feminism* in that it is based on views of women as distinct from men. Difference feminism is often seen as conflicting with other forms of female activism in the early twentieth century, in particular with that of women who were among the first to call themselves feminists—demanding that women develop individuality and personal style—and with suffragists' pervasive arguments about women's equality with men.

In the first two decades of the twentieth century, feminist activists received broad cultural support from Progressivism—a widespread reform movement that looked to local, state, and federal governments to mediate, through legislation and bureaucratic initiatives, the increasing inequalities generated by monopoly capitalism, a thriving industrialism, urbanization, and an unprecedented level of immigration. The Progressive Era followed hard on the heels of the excesses of the Gilded Age, the era of robber barons, laissez-faire capitalism, conspicuous consumption, and the introduction of social Darwinism. As the inevitable workings of the unfettered competition at the heart of industrial capitalism created a wealthy elite, it also created mass poverty. Increasingly influential social Darwinists did not believe in doling out state aid to those crushed by the progress of civilization, for such intervention could impede the "natural" growth of society. The Progressives and other social reformers in the early twentieth century challenged this view and relentlessly argued for a less vicious conception of society—one in which every citizen is seen as interconnected and where one's own best interests lie in the best interests of others; they argued, furthermore, for the preeminent responsibility of government to ensure that the social body was not rent asunder by intolerable inequalities.

The feminist reformers of the Progressive Era who fall into the "difference feminism" camp have been labeled "maternalist," and historian Linda Gordon explains three tenets that characterized their gendered activism: first, they regarded family responsibilities as essential, both to women themselves and to the social order; second, they imagined themselves in a motherly relation to the poor; and third, they believed that their own socialization to be mothers made them uniquely able to care for and change society. Maternalist reformers in the early twentieth century, then, explicitly politicized and broadened the role of the mother so that it no longer connoted a solitary figure confined within the walls of an individual home. Indeed, some women's reform efforts were not only maternalist in philosophy but also in practice, as much of their labor focused on the practical problems facing dependent children and women *as mothers*. The impoverishment of women and the exploitation of both women (especially working mothers) and children by sweatshop labor—characterized by poor pay, long hours, and terrible conditions—were some of the most compelling areas of reform in the first two decades of the twentieth century. Settlement houses, African American women's clubs, and the National Consumers' League all worked for the betterment of mothers and their children, and some of the most widely supported legislative reforms of the period created "maternal pensions," which subsidized poor mothers and enabled them to support their dependent children.

Another useful way to conceive of the agenda of these social reformers is summed up in a phrase coined by the writers we include here—"public housekeeping," as Jane Addams puts it, and "the larger housekeeping," according to Mabel Potter Daggett. Similar to the idea of maternalist activism, public housekeeping extended the borders of the single family and home and exposed the entire terrain of the social sphere not only as the purview of the national mother but also as an appropriate arena for women's work as housekeepers.

A crucial aspect of early-twentieth-century social reform was its creation of new female-dominated institutions that provided an independent base for women's political action. The settlement house was the earliest and most influential such institution. The settlement house movement in the United States essentially began in 1889 when Jane Addams and Ellen Gates Starr established Hull House in a poor immigrant area of Chicago. The ideal of the settlement house was not only to reform poverty-stricken neighborhoods but also to promote understanding across the classes and connect the educated elite with meaningful work. The notion of reform inherent in the settlement movement was not that of a descent from above or a gracious bestowing of charity but rested on a belief that the reformer must live among the poor and needy as a cooperative neighbor. The settlement movement particularly attracted upper-middle-class, college-educated women looking for a way to contribute something of significance to society.

Jane Addams was the daughter of a wealthy Illinois state senator who believed, fortunately, in female education. Addams attended the Rockford Female Seminary and planned to be a doctor but recast her dreams after an attempt at medical school and a subsequent illness. On a trip to Europe, Addams and her two close friends, Ellen Gates Starr and Sara Anderson, visited the first settlement house, Toynbee Hall, which was founded by Samuel A. Barnett in London in 1884. While Toynbee Hall was populated by "university men," the settlement movement in the United States would be predominantly female: by 1911, 53 percent of the 215 settlements reporting to investigators housed women only; less than 2 percent only men; the rest accommodated both sexes. It was women, according to Addams, who suffered most from enforced inaction and scarcity of meaningful labor once their education was complete—and it was mostly women whom Addams recruited for Hull House.

Two pivotal essays defining the settlement movement are Jane Addams's "The Subjective Value of Social Settlements" (1892) and "A Function of the Social Settlement" (1899). The former is a pamphlet that extends a speech Addams first delivered at the Ethical Culture Societies' summer school in Plymouth, Massachusetts, in 1892; the speech was also reprinted in her autobiography, *Twenty Years at Hull House* (1910). The latter was published as a pamphlet by the prestigious American Academy of Political and Social Science. Both documents make clear that the foundational principle of the settlement movement in the United States was the recognition that politics alone, including political freedoms and rights, did not make a true democracy. A true democracy must encompass the *social* existence of citizens; it is not just an aggregate of free representative political institutions. A democracy is, to quote the influential early-twentieth-century pragmatist philosopher John Dewey (in a speech influenced by what he saw at Hull House), "a way of living together and working together." As Jane Addams puts it in the first sentence of her 1892 pamphlet, a social settlement "may be defined as an attempt to make *social intercourse* express the growing sense of the economic unity of society and as an effort to add the *social function* to democracy" (italics added). Black men and immigrants have the vote, Addams adds as an exemplifying note, but they are socially ostracized and heaped with abuse—denied a meaningful social existence. An underlying belief in Addams's essay is that merely enfranchising a person, making him or her a citizen in name only, is a sham if the living dimensions of a democracy are denied.

Of the three motives that Addams outlines in "The Subjective Value of Social Settlements" as constituting the "subjective necessity for a social settlement," the need to make "the entire social organism democratic, to extend democracy beyond its political expression" is the most central. She describes all the ways in which the social sphere has been eviscerated by a desperately narrow conception of politics: the devastating poverty throughout large districts of U.S. cities, political corruption, segregation of the wealthy and "cultivated" from the poor and uneducated, and the absence of a cohesive community among the poor (one wonders though whether Addams was simply unable to see the indigenous communities immigrants brought with them, whether she looked only for the kind of intellectual community—including libraries and clubhouses—that existed among the middle class). Addams notes a breakdown in the social existence of wealthy young people, especially women, who are shut off from common labor and who see the decay around them but are unable to find a path to reverse it. She envisions the settlement movement as a solution for both wealthy and poor, educated and uneducated. In Addams's view, the settlement workers, as they move into the poor neighborhoods of cities and take on whatever work is most needed, are moving toward nothing less than a true social democracy, developing elaborate social networks, typically composed of women, that cross lines of class, education, race, and ethnicity.

A second fundamental tenet that informs Addams's description of the creation of settlement houses is the belief that thought and knowledge are only efficacious to the extent that they are transformed into *action*; in fact, knowledge becomes a type of action as the traditional distinction between them is dissolved. Educated people, especially women, Addams argues, feel "a lack of co-ordination between thought and action." In "A Function of the Social Settlement," Addams crystallizes this precept, contributing to the pragmatist philosophy of John Dewey and William James. The "dominating interest in knowledge," Addams says, "has become its use, the conditions under which, and ways in which it may be most effectively employed in human conduct." Knowledge becomes a kind of hypothesis that must consistently be subjected to the rigors of experiment and experience in different situations, its usefulness in any of those situations serving as the marker of its validity and its proximity to truth. In fact, in this particular essay, Addams locates the necessity of putting thought into action as *the* defining characteristic of a settlement house: the settlement, she writes, "is an attempt to express the meaning of life in terms of life itself, in forms of activity."

Related to her emphasis on putting knowledge to work, Addams identifies two further interwoven tenets that inform the settlement movement: the settlement, she argues, should propagate *no* agenda, *no* fixed set of ideological principles, although it should always welcome the potential efficacy of any *part* of any agenda or ideology. A knowledge system should not, in other words, be embraced fully and unconditionally, but only to the extent that elements of it serve to solve the problems at hand. As Addams puts it in "The Subjective Value of Social Settlements": "From its very nature [the Settlement] can stand for no political or social *propaganda*. It must, in a sense, give the warm welcome of an inn to all such propaganda, if perchance one of them be found an angel. The one thing to be dreaded in the Settlement is that it lose its flexibility, its power of quick adaptation, its readiness to change its methods as its environment may demand." Implicit in this notion of adapting only constituent parts of philosophies is the fourth principle underlying the settlement movement: its goals, tenets, and practices are all contingent on local vicissitudes. The settlement aims, Addams writes, "to lead whatever of social life its neighborhood may afford."

A fifth and final aspect of the settlement movement, according to Addams, is its conviction that reform occurs through communal, not individual, action; through solidarity, not separation. The settlement houses, moreover, tried to foster diverse communities, including people of different nationalities, classes, races, and ethnicities—reaching out to local immigrant communities. As one Hull House worker, Mary McDowell, put it: "Here was something I had been looking for all my life, a chance to work with the least skilled workers in our great industry; not *for* them as a missionary, but *with* them as a neighbor and seeker after truth."[1] The distinction McDowell made between working *with* the needy rather than working *for* them was crucial to the ideal of the settlement house. The settlement workers tried to imaginatively put themselves in another's shoes. As Addams says in "A Function of the Social Settlement," the notion of collectivity is crucial—making "experience continuous beyond the individual." The collective spirit was finally probably strongest among the settlement workers themselves, however, and strong private relationships were forged that often lasted a lifetime and gave these women the strength to create often unconventional careers for themselves.

Given the underlying philosophy of the settlement movement, it is not surprising that the residents of Hull House resisted setting an a priori agenda, and instead responded to the immediate needs of the neighborhood. Realizing, for instance, that many mothers worked outside the home, Addams and Starr started a day nursery along with a free labor bureau for both men and women. They also invited labor unions to meet at the settlement, built a cooperative living club for working women, and experimented with a public kitchen. In "A Function of the Social Settlement," Addams offers a specific example of the settlement's responsiveness. She describes how the residents of Hull House recognized that local Italian residents needed help keeping their children clean and healthy. Instead of lecturing to these immigrant mothers, the Hull House women invited them over for informal communal breakfasts, where they learned to "feed their children oatmeal instead of tea-soaked bread."

Jane Addams most directly addresses the gendered nature of social reform in her later essay, "Women and Public Housekeeping" (1910)—from which we derive the title of this section. Addams articulates again her persistent concern that all interest in the social good has been bleached from democracy. In this essay she explicitly argues that women are the answer to the impoverishment of the modern political system. Addams defines the modern city as an environment in need of an "enlarged housekeeping." She asserts that cities are slipping into poverty and desolation because men run them by means of political systems that emulate predatory and competitive corporate tactics. Women, politically disenfranchised, are excluded from the life of the city—but the ability to participate in politics (narrowly defined) has virtually nothing, Addams insists, to do with running the "household" of city life. Addams urges women to let go of a narrow conception of their responsibility, to recognize that what goes on beyond the strict limits of their home crucially impinges on that home, and to accept that it is their business to set in order the entire municipality.

The settlement house movement in the United States was preceded by a flourishing women's club movement. Among the most active were African American women's clubs, most of which—although conceived in the 1880s—began forming into more cohesive and powerful national organizations at the turn into the twentieth century (notably the National Federation of Afro-American Women and the National Association of Colored Women). At this time, black leaders sought to address the needs of both southern and northern African American women, and of farming and industrial women alike. As with primarily white women's reform organizations and settlement houses, the newly formed national associations of African American women focused, in the early 1900s, on the problems generated by industrial capitalism, mass organization, and the exploitation of working women; and they tended to address such issues from the perspective of woman's moral influence as homemaker—even as women of both races defined home and housekeeping more and more broadly.

Fannie Barrier Williams, daughter of a middle-class family in Brockport, New York, and graduate of the New England Conservatory of Music, was one of the few black members of the Chicago

---

1. Quoted in Allen F. Davis, *Spearheads for Reform: The Social Settlements and the Progressive Movement, 1890–1914* (New York: Oxford Univ. Press, 1967), 113.

Women's Club, and in "An Extension of the Conference Spirit" (1904) she describes a conference promoted by the Chicago Women's Club that addressed the question of "Women in Modern Industrialism." For Williams, this conference was an extension of the conferences held by black women's clubs—and she points out the similar problems facing both white and black working-class women. Williams focuses on the issue of domestic service, which the conference concluded was one of the "healthiest" industrial professions a woman could choose. Indeed, Williams may have focused on this issue because the majority of working black women were in domestic service, and the calls at the conference for respect and appropriate pay for this trade echoed calls at numerous conferences held by the National Association of Colored Women. Williams's essay is an optimistic call for women to unite across the divide of race and class, but her optimism is belied by the severe racial segregation of women's reform organizations—and by the fact that Williams was likely the only African American woman at the conference (at least she mentions no black speakers).

In her "Social Improvement of the Plantation Woman" (1904), Margaret Murray Washington, Booker T. Washington's third wife, addresses a different kind of work undertaken by African American women, mostly in the South—that is, farming. Using the familiar strategy, Washington addresses the reformation of economic and working conditions, largely through the home, as she focuses on the intrinsic value of women's moving their families from one-room cabins to four-room houses and urges the improvement of morality as a means to effect a greater economic productivity. Washington talks about the good work that Farmers' Institutes have done throughout the South. A kind of social settlement that modeled a principled family life and good child-rearing practices, Farmers' Institutes also exemplified productive farming techniques and helped families buy their own farms. In her emphasis on farmwork, Margaret Murray Washington was clearly influenced by the philosophy of her husband, Booker T. Washington. Founder and president of the renowned Tuskegee Institute, Booker T. dominated black politics until his death in 1915, as did his controversial philosophy of industrial education—a philosophy that encouraged African Americans to train for (and satisfy themselves with) essentially blue-collar work and farming (not everyone could be a middle-class professional, he believed). This view of how the race could "lift" itself was starkly at odds with that of Washington's political rival, W. E. B. DuBois, who focused on creating what he called the "talented tenth," an elite and well-educated group of men and women to lead the race.

A very important split in the reform efforts of all races in the twentieth century separated those who pushed to form direct coalitions with government from those who advocated a relatively diffuse moral influence, as women's clubs had done in the nineteenth century. The former path in particular partook of the spirit of Progressivism, which galvanized millions of Americans who organized to pass legislation to address the growing problems of urban life. In the settlement movement, Florence Kelley served as a crucial link to local, state, and federal government. A graduate of Cornell and a socialist who believed in state intervention to ameliorate the inequalities and physical hardships promoted by industrial capitalism, Kelley brought a thoroughgoing knowledge of Marxism to Hull House: while studying law and government at the University of Zurich (after the Graduate School at the University of Pennsylvania refused to admit her), Kelley not only converted to socialism but also translated into English Friedrich Engels's classic *The Condition of the Working Class in England in 1844*. More than anyone else, Kelley made Hull House a center for social research and reform, infusing the work of the settlement with her socialist philosophy. She arrived at Hull House in 1891, a mother of three, and stayed for eight years. One of her first acts was to persuade the Illinois Department of Labor Statistics to hire her to study the sweatshop system in Chicago's garment industry. She moved from this position to becoming the first chief factory inspector of Illinois.

Kelley is perhaps best known for her leadership of the National Consumers' League (NCL)—just one of the means through which she engaged in her career-long battle with shameful working conditions. The NCL, though, may have been the first organization to recognize that such conditions could be improved not only by putting pressure on *manufacturers* but also by using the new power of the *consumers,* especially the power that accrued to women consumers. Formed in the early 1890s, the NCL educated consumers about manufacturing conditions and urged them to buy only those goods produced in a clean and humane workplace. Florence Kelley, who was appointed executive secretary of the NCL in 1899, explains its philosophy in "Aims and Principles of the Consumers' League" (1899). The NCL, she writes, "acts upon the proposition that the consumer ultimately determines all production, since any given article must cease to be produced if all consumers ceased to purchase it." However, Kelley adds, it is not enough for *individual* consumers to educate themselves; they also need to organize and put *collective* pressure on producers. The intention of the NCL is to help coalesce consumers, she explains. For instance, it recognizes, through a "white label," certain types of clothing that are made in factories with healthy surroundings and fair pay. Kelley particularly appeals to women, who, as she notes, have taken on the industrial function of purchaser since the "exodus of manufacture from the home"—a process that began during the Revolutionary War years. The end of the nineteenth century saw the culmination of that transformation of women from producers into consumers, and this process has frequently been viewed by feminist thinkers as a sign of women's declining efficacy in the public sphere. But women's new power of consumption could also, as Kelley recognized, become a means by which they could shape the very conditions of production. As a leader of the NCL, Kelley thus encouraged women to concern themselves not only with the products they bought but also, more broadly, with the conditions from which those products emerged, and she urged local consumers' leagues to support legislation limiting child labor and establishing minimum-wage and maximum-hour laws.

Like the settlement house, the National Consumers' League epitomized "public housekeeping" as a philosophy: it articulated the integral connection between women's work in the home, civic reform, and governmental regulation of the workplace. This philosophy also underwrites Mabel Potter Daggett's "Women: The Larger Housekeeping" (1912). Daggett's opening sentence, "The housekeeper is abroad in her city," encapsulates the mapping of the concerns of the home onto the entire city. While summarizing the progress that has been made in improving social conditions throughout her hometown of Boston, Daggett insists that every city dweller, from the poorest to the wealthiest, is connected under the conditions of modern industrialism. Years before, she points out, all a middle-class housekeeper had to mind was that *her* cook washed her hands; now she has to ask: "Did the *Superfine Baking Company* wash its hands?" Unhealthy conditions in a tailor shop affect the woman who wears lingerie produced there; dirt in one person's backyard affects all those who live nearby. In other words, Daggett uses the interconnectedness of city inhabitants to effect a bond that traverses those lines of economic class, geography, and race which appear to separate Bostonians. Daggett writes about the efficacy of the Consumers' League in Boston, which has given the seal of approval to certain bakeries and tailors. And she talks about a local, grassroots variant of the NCL called the "Market Tens," a way in which poor women who live in the tenement districts exercise the kind of influence over dealers that wealthy women and the power and prestige of the NCL exert more easily. The Market Tens are groups of ten women each, drawn from a poor often immigrant neighborhood, and pledged to supervise the sanitary condition of the stores in their vicinity. Any insufficiencies they find are reported to the Board of Health, as well as disseminated to other women in the area. Asserting her identity as one of the Market Tens, a poorer woman can have the same salutary effect on a store's treatment of both herself and its own produce that a rich woman can exact.

Daggett spends most of her time, however, describing the Woman's Municipal League of Boston, which uses private donations to launch major reform efforts (reforms that should, Daggett pointedly comments, be carried on by local government). For instance, the first action of the league was to launch a city-cleaning crusade, educating people about dangerous and unsanitary practices and urging everyone to clean up. The league then paid a salaried inspector to ensure that the city remained clean and to continue the campaign of educating people, especially new immigrants. The Municipal League's practice of raising private donations to pay social workers was like that of the settlement houses, with their institution of "fellowships" paid by wealthy patrons to allow needy women to take on careers in public service. This increasingly pervasive practice reinforced how women social reformers recognized their lack of direct influence (especially before suffrage) on the political process, as well as their well-founded distrust of the partisanship and corruption of politics. It demonstrates that, even given a generally progressive government, they were not willing to wait for local, state, and federal governments to act.

One of the most influential reform campaigns of the early twentieth century (and one that *did* manage to forge an effective bond between reformers and government) was the fight to gain pensions for mothers and dependent children. The success of this campaign underlines the centrality of maternalism to early-twentieth-century feminist reform: the mother, according to reformers, was uniquely victimized by industrialism and also (somewhat paradoxically) uniquely necessary, in her production of new workers, to the continuation of unprecedented industrial progress in the United States. Around the figure of the mother, which some historians have deemed an inherently conservative rallying point, developed some of the most radical arguments of modern social reformers, a handful of whom asserted the need for a cultural and economic recognition of the importance of motherhood that was still lacking in the late twentieth century.

The type of maternal pension to win most public visibility and governmental support was the widow's pension. In "Helping the Widowed Mother to Keep a Home" (1913), Clara Cahill Park, a member of the Massachusetts commission on widows' pensions, argues that it costs the state less to help single mothers support their children in their own home than it does to institutionalize those children—and, by preserving the family structure, such a pension benefits society as well as the individual mother and children. The first widow's pension law was passed in Missouri in 1911. It allowed mothers of minor dependent children ten dollars per month for the first child, until the child turned fourteen, and five dollars for each subsequent child. This type of legislation was so popular that forty-six states passed similar laws in the ensuing twenty years.

Although the legislation that Park supports is for the support of widowed mothers and their children, she is at times ambiguous about the necessity of the mother's bereaved state, labeling the object of assistance at one point "the woman who has to be father and mother"—in other words, any single mother. At other times she alternates between calling the reform the "Widows's Pension Law" and the "Mother's Pension Law." (In fact, as Linda Gordon points out, the mothers' aid programs passed in most states after 1911 were interchangeably called "mothers' pensions" and "widows' pensions."[2]) This lack of clarity and consistency may have been purposeful, since many reformers wanted to help all single mothers, including those who were unwed and those who had been deserted. There was, however, on the part of some reformers, legislators, and the general public an ambivalence about the appearance of promoting "immorality," that is, seeming to encourage out-of-wedlock pregnancies and desertions. The widow was a "pure" image around which to galvanize support and sympathy, and she did not risk becoming implicated in the cause of her own singleness. As we have witnessed in the late twentieth century, the symbolism of welfare—the ways in which its recipients are characterized

---

2. Linda Gordon, *Pitied But Not Entitled: Single Mothers and the History of Welfare* (New York: Free Press, 1994), 28.

in the public mind regardless of reality—is crucial to the maintenance of that welfare system. Indeed, as a consequence of the public need for the recipients of governmental subsidies to be "worthy"—notably pure and hardworking—early-twentieth-century pensions came along with rigorous scrutiny and social controls: mothers who received support had to maintain an eminently "respectable" household, including avoiding any suggestion of sexual "impropriety." In fact, some of the middle-class support for maternal pensions emerged from anxieties about how immigrant families were raising their children, along with, of course, less sinister concerns about abusive child labor.

The argument for state support of widowed mothers contained within it a more radical notion, which Park's essay veers toward as she quotes a supporter of widows' pensions who describes how to conceive of those pensions: "We treat it as a payment for a civic service, and the condition that we are inclined to make is precisely that she should not endeavor to add to it by earning wages, but rather that she should keep her home respectable and bring up her children in health and happiness." The idea informing this claim is that a mother performs a public function, akin to other workers—*and that she should be paid for her work.* After all, what other job, so vital to our nation, goes utterly unremunerated? This is exactly the claim made by Charlotte Perkins Gilman in "Maternity Benefits and Reformers" (1916) and by Eleanor Taylor in "Wages for Mothers" (1920). Gilman and Taylor represent much more radical voices in the debate over maternal pensions, and unlike the widely popular widows' pensions, their proposals were not enacted into legislation. The clear difference between the popular and the marginal calls for reform is that the widows' pensions kept mothers in a dependent role: the recipients were constructed as the hapless victims of circumstances beyond their control and in receiving aid they simply replaced reliance on a husband with reliance on the state. Both Gilman and Taylor, however, call for motherhood to be acknowledged as a legitimate and necessary social function, even profession, that should be recognized as such with a paycheck—and a paycheck (rather than a handout) would render women *independent* rather than keeping them *dependent.*

Writing in her journal *The Forerunner,* Gilman argues for a system of aid akin to what we know today as maternity leave (superseded in 1993 by the Family and Medical Leave Act, which allows fathers as well as mothers time off from work after the birth of a child—something Gilman, with her insistence that the sex difference was dangerously exaggerated, would have approved of but would hardly have been able to imagine in 1916). Gilman proposes that women who work outside the home should be granted leave *with pay* for eight weeks upon delivering a child. She argues that there could be only three objections to her proposal: "a desire to prevent maternity, to penalize maternity, or to prevent mothers from taking gainful occupations." Since the first two objections are inconceivable (both in her cultural climate and ours), Gilman points out that the resistance to supporting working mothers must stem from the deep-seated societal desire that women not work outside the home. Such a desire, she claims, works against the progress of civilization as women increasingly assert their right to take up whatever occupation appeals to them as individuals. The unfortunate fact that women remain unpaid when they, of necessity, take time off work to give birth would have been recognized by Gilman as a sign, first, that motherhood is still unrecognized as an important "social service," and second, that women are still not supported in their efforts to offer other kinds of social services through paid labor.

Taylor's "Wages for Mothers" most directly advocates that mothers receive fair pay for their work and most directly attacks the concept of the "family wage." The ideology of the family wage bolsters and is in turn bolstered by the traditional division and inequality between the sexes in that it promotes the conviction that earning is the sole responsibility of the husband and that his *dependent* wife should perform the *unpaid* labor within the home, including the work of reproduction. Taylor's essay was published in *The Suffragist,* the official organ of the more radical of the two major women's suffrage groups, the National Woman's Party—like Gilman's essay, it was confined to a marginal rather than a mainstream publication. One of Taylor's more incisive points unveils the persistent double standard surrounding motherhood in American culture: the "great service" that mothers perform, she claims, is sung by poets and mouthed by even those legislators who block all reforms concerning the welfare of mothers and their children—but at the same time there is no "proper recognition of the value of her work." Taylor goes on to endorse the kind of "national endowment of motherhood" that was at the time being seriously considered by lawmakers in Great Britain, and she sets out a concrete plan to compensate mothers for their service. Foreshadowing current liberal arguments for state spending on the good of the social body, Taylor points out that her proposed program would be just a fraction of what the government spends on "organized killing, that is, for recent and past wars. . . . Women are not wanting who will heretically maintain that these proportions might be reversed with benefit to the nation." Taylor's suggestion that more government money be spent on social welfare than on the military would most likely have won the consent of all the early-twentieth-century feminist reformers. Unfortunately, it was not to be, as massive government spending for U.S. intervention in World War I brought an untimely end to the Progressive Era.

20
Jane Addams
The Subjective Value of Social Settlements (1892)

A Social Settlement may be defined as an attempt to make social intercourse express the growing sense of the economic unity of society and as an effort to add the social function to democracy. It is based on the theory that the dependence of classes on each other is reciprocal; and that as the social relation is essentially a reciprocal relation, it gives a form of expression that has peculiar value. A Settlement is established in the belief that the mere foothold of a house, easily accessible, ample in space, hospitable and tolerant in spirit, situated in the very midst of the industrial quarters of large cities, is in itself a serviceable thing, and that, given a starting point, many educated young people can find various outlets for a certain sort of unexpressed activity.

I attempt in this paper to treat the subjective necessity for a Social Settlement, to analyze, as nearly as I can, the motives that underlie a movement which I believe to be based not only on conviction, but on genuine emotion. I have divided the motives which constitute the subjective pressure toward Social Settlements into three great lines: the first contains the desire to make the entire social organism, democratic, to extend democracy beyond its political expression; the second is the impulse to share the race life, to bring as much as possible of social energy and the accumulation of civilization to those portions of the race which have little; the third springs from a certain *renaissance* of Christianity, a movement toward its early humanitarian aspects.

It is not difficult to see that although America is pledged to the democratic ideal, the view of democracy has been partial, and that its best achievement thus far has been pushed along the line of the franchise. Democracy has made little attempt to assert itself in social affairs. We have refused to move beyond the position of its eighteenth-century leaders, who believed that political equality alone would secure all good to all men. We conscientiously followed the gift of the ballot hard upon the gift of freedom to the Negro, but we are quite unmoved by the fact that he lives among us in a practical social ostracism. We hasten to give the franchise to the immigrant from a sense of justice, from a tradition that he ought to have it, while we dub him with epithets deriding his past life or present occupation and feel no duty to invite him to our houses. We are forced to acknowledge that [it] is only in our local and national politics that we try very hard for the ideal so dear to those who were enthusiasts when the century was young. We have almost given it up as our ideal in social intercourse. In many a city ward the majority of the votes are openly sold for drinks and dollars; still there is a remote pretense, at least a fiction current, that a man's vote is his own. The judgment of the voter is consulted and an opportunity for remedy given. There is not even a theory in the social order, not a shadow answering to the polls in politics. The time may come when the politician who sells one by one to the highest bidder all the offices in his grasp will not be considered more base in his code of morals, more hardened in his practice, than the woman who constantly invites to her receptions those alone who bring her an equal social return, who shares her beautiful surroundings only with those who minister to a liking she has for successful social events. In doing this she is just as unmindful of the common weal, as unscrupulous in her use of power, as is any city "boss" who consults only the interests of the "ring."

In politics "bossism" arouses a scandal. It goes on in society constantly and is only beginning to be challenged. Our consciences are becoming tender in regard to the lack of democracy in social affairs. We are perhaps entering upon the second phase of democracy, as the

From *History of Women* microfilm series (New Haven: Research Publications, 1977), reel 942, no. 8457.

French philosophers entered upon the first, somewhat bewildered by its logical conclusions. The social organism has broken down through large districts of our great cities. Many of the people living there are very poor, the majority of them without leisure or energy for anything but the gain of subsistence. They move often from one wretched lodging to another. They live for the moment side by side, many of them without knowledge of each other, without fellowship, without local tradition or public spirit, without social organization of any kind. Practically nothing is done to remedy this. The people who might do it, who have the social tact and training, the large houses, and the traditions and customs of hospitality, live in other parts of the city. The club-houses, libraries, galleries, and semi-public conveniences for social life are also blocks away. We find workingmen organized into armies of producers because men of executive ability and business sagacity have found it to their interests thus to organize them. But these workingmen are not organized socially; although living in crowded tenement-houses, they are living without a corresponding social contact. The chaos is as great as it would be were they working in huge factories without foreman or superintendent. Their ideas and resources are cramped. The desire for higher social pleasure is extinct. They have no share in the traditions and social energy which make for progress. Too often their only place of meeting is a saloon, their only host a bartender; a local demagogue forms their public opinion. Men of ability and refinement, of social power and university cultivation, stay away from them. Personally, I believe the men who lose most are those who thus stay away. But the paradox is here: when cultivated people do stay away from a certain portion of the population, when all social advantages are persistently withheld, it may be for years, the result itself is pointed at as a reason, is used as an argument, for the continued withholding.

It is constantly said that because the masses have never had social advantages they do not want them, that they are heavy and dull, and that it will take political or philanthropic machinery to change them. This divides a city into rich and poor; into the favored, who express their sense of the social obligation by gifts of money, and into the unfavored, who express it by clamoring for a "share"—both of them actuated by a vague sense of justice. This division of the city would be the more justifiable, however, if the people who thus isolated themselves on certain streets and used their social ability for each other gained enough thereby and added sufficient to the sum total of social progress to justify the withholding of the pleasures and results of that progress from so many people who ought to have them. But they cannot accomplish this. The social spirit discharges itself in many forms, and no one form is adequate to its total expression. We are all uncomfortable in regard to the insincerity of our best phrases, because we hesitate to translate our philosophy into the deed.

It is inevitable that those who feel most keenly this insincerity and partial living should be our young people, our so-called educated young people who accomplish little toward the solution of this social problem, and who bear the brunt of being cultivated into unnourished, over-sensitive lives. They have been shut off from the common labor by which they live and which is a great source of moral and physical health. They feel a fatal want of harmony between their theory and their lives, a lack of co-ordination between thought and action. I think it is hard for us to realize how seriously many of them are taking to the notion of human brotherhood, how eagerly they long to give tangible expression to the democratic ideal. These young men and women, longing to socialize their democracy, are animated by certain hopes. These hopes may be loosely formulated thus: that if in a democratic country nothing can be permanently achieved save through the masses of the people, it will be impossible to establish a higher political life than the people themselves crave; that it is difficult to see how the notion of a higher civic life can be fostered save through common intercourse.

The blessings which we associate with a life of refinement and cultivation can be made universal and must be made universal if they are to be permanent. The good we secure for ourselves is precarious and uncertain, is floating in mid-air, until it is secured for all of us and incorporated into our common life. These hopes are responsible for results in various directions, pre-eminently in the extension of educational advantages. We find that all educational matters are more democratic in their political than in their social aspects. The public schools in the poorest and most crowded wards of the city are inadequate to the number of children, and many of the teachers are ill-prepared and overworked; but in each ward there is an effort to secure public education. The schoolhouse itself stands as a pledge that the city recognizes and endeavors to fulfill the duty of educating its children. But what becomes of these children when they are no longer in public schools? Many of them never come under the influence of a professional teacher after they are twelve. Society at large does little for their intellectual development. The dreams of transcendentalists that each New England village would be a university, that every child taken from the common school would be put into definite lines of study and mental development, had its unfulfilled beginning in the village lyceum and lecture courses, and has its feeble representative now in the multitude of clubs for study which are so sadly restricted to educators, to the leisure class, or only to the advanced and progressive workers.

The University Extension movement—certainly when it is closely identified with Settlements—would not confine learning to those who already want it, or to those who, by making an effort, can gain it, or to those among whom professional educators are already at work, but would take it to the tailors of East London and the dock-laborers of the Thames. It requires tact and training, love of learning, and the conviction of the justice of its diffusion to give it to people whose intellectual faculties are untrained and disused. But men in England are found who do it successfully, and it is believed there are men and women in America who can do it. I also believe that the best work in University Extension can be done in Settlements, where the teaching will be further socialized, where the teacher will grapple his students, not only by formal lectures, but by every hook possible to the fuller intellectual life which he represents. This teaching requires distinct methods, for it is true of people who have been allowed to remain undeveloped and whose faculties are inert and sterile, that they cannot take their learning heavily. It has to be diffused in a social atmosphere. Information held in solution, a medium of fellowship and good-will can be assimilated by the dullest.

If education is, as Froebel defined it, "deliverance," deliverance of the forces of the body and mind, then the untrained must first be delivered from all constraint and rigidity before their faculties can be used. Possibly one of the most pitiful periods in the drama of the much-praised young American who attempts to rise in life is the time when his educational requirements seem to have locked him up and made him rigid. He fancies himself shut off from his uneducated family and misunderstood by his friends. He is bowed down by his mental accumulations and often gets no farther than to carry them through life as a great burden. Not once has he had a glimpse of the delights of knowledge. Intellectual life requires for its expansion and manifestation the influence and assimilation of the interests and affections of others. Mazzini, that greatest of all democrats, who broke his heart over the condition of the South European peasantry, said: "Education is not merely a necessity of true life by which the individual renews his vital force in the vital force of humanity; it is a Holy Communion with generations dead and living, by which he fecundates all his faculties. When he is withheld from this Communion for generations, as the Italian peasant has been, we point our finger at him and say, 'He is like a beast of the field; he must be controlled by force.'" Even to this it is sometimes added that it is absurd to educate him, immoral to disturb his content. We stupidly use again the effect as an argument for a continuance of the cause. It is needless to say that a Settlement is a protest against a restricted view of education, and makes it possible for every educated man or woman with a teaching faculty to find out those who are ready to be taught. The social and educational activities of a Settlement are but differing manifestations of the attempt to socialize democracy, as is the existence of the Settlement itself.

I find it somewhat difficult to formulate the second line of motives which I believe to constitute the trend of the subjective pressure toward the Settlement. There is something primordial about these motives, but I am perhaps over-bold in designating them as a great desire to share the race life. We all bear traces of the starvation struggle which for so long made up the life of the race. Our very organism holds memories and glimpses of that long life of our ancestors which still goes on among so many of our contemporaries. Nothing so deadens the sympathies and shrivels the power of enjoyment as the persistent keeping away from the great opportunities for helpfulness and a continual ignoring of the starvation struggle which makes up the life of at least half the race. To shut one's self away from that half of the race life is to shut one's self away from the most vital part of it; it is to live out but half the humanity which we have been born heir to, and to use but half our faculties. We have all had longings for a fuller life which should include the use of these faculties. These longings are the physical complement of the "Intimations of Immortality" on which no ode has yet been written. To portray these would be the work of a poet, and it is hazardous for any but a poet to attempt it.

You may remember the forlorn feeling which occasionally seizes you when you arrive early in the morning a stranger in a great city. The stream of laboring people goes past you as you gaze through the plate-glass window of your hotel. You see hard-working men lifting great burdens; you hear the driving and jostling of huge carts. Your heart sinks with a sudden sense of futility. The door opens behind you and you turn to the man who brings you in your breakfast with a quick sense of human fellowship. You find yourself praying that you may never lose your hold on it all. A more poetic prayer would be that the great mother breasts of our common humanity, with its labor and suffering and its homely comforts, may never be withheld from you. You turn helplessly to the waiter. You feel that it would be almost grotesque to claim from him the sympathy you crave. Civilization has placed you far apart, but you resent your position with a sudden sense of snobbery. Literature is full of portrayals of these glimpses. They come to shipwrecked men on rafts; they overcome the differences of an incongruous multitude when in the presence of a great danger or when moved by a common enthusiasm. They are not, however, confined to such moments, and if we were in the habit of telling them to each other, the recital would be as long as the tales of children are when they sit down on the green grass and confide to each other how many times they have remembered that they lived once before. If that is the stirring of inherited impressions, just so surely is the other the stirring of inherited power.

There is nothing after disease, indigence, and a sense of guilt so fatal to health and to life itself as the want of a proper outlet for active faculties. I have seen young girls suffer and grow sensibly lowered in vitality in the first years after they leave school. In our attempt then to give a girl pleasure and freedom from care we succeed, for the most part, in making her pitifully miserable. She finds "life" so different from what she expected it to be. She is besotted with innocent little ambitions and does not understand this apparent waste of herself, this elaborate preparation, if no work is provided for her. There is a heritage of noble obligation which young people accept and long to perpetuate. The desire for action, the wish to right wrong and alleviate suffering, haunts them daily. Society smiles at it indulgently instead of making it of value to itself. The wrong to them begins even farther back when we restrain the first childish desires for "doing good" and tell them that they must wait until they are older and better fitted. We intimate that social obligation begins at a fixed date, forgetting that it begins with birth itself. We treat them as we would children who, with strong-growing limbs, are allowed to use their legs but not their arms, or whose legs are daily carefully exercised that after awhile their arms may be put to high use. We do this in spite of the protest of the best educators, Locke and Pestalozzi. We are fortunate in the meantime if their unused members do not weaken and disappear. They do sometimes. There are a few girls who, by the time they are "educated," forget their old childish desires to help the world and to play with poor little girls "who haven't playthings." Parents are often curious about this. They deliberately expose their daughters to the knowledge of the distress in the world. They send them to hear missionary addresses on famines in India and China; they accompany them to lectures on the suffering in Siberia; they agitate together over the forgotten region of East London. In addition to this, from babyhood the altruistic tendencies of these daughters are persistently cultivated. They are taught to be self-forgetting and self-sacrificing, to consider the good of the Whole before the good of the Ego. But when all this information and culture begins to show results, when the daughter comes back from college and begins to recognize her social claim to the "submerged tenth" and to evince a disposition to fulfill it, the family claim is strenuously asserted; she is told that she is unjustified, ill-advised in her efforts. If she persists the family too often are injured and unhappy, unless the efforts are called missionary, and the religious zeal of the family carry them over their sense of abuse.

We have in America a fast-growing number of cultivated young people who have no recognized outlet for their active families. They hear constantly of the great social maladjustment, but no way is provided for them to change it and their uselessness hangs about them heavily. Huxley declares that the sense of uselessness is the severest shock which the human system can sustain, and, if persistently sustained, it results in atrophy of function. These young people have had advantages of college, of European travel and economic study, but they are sustaining this shock of inaction. They have pet phrases, and they tell you that the things that make us all alike are stronger than the things that make us different. They say that all men are united by needs and sympathies far more permanent and radical than anything that temporarily divides them and sets them in opposition to each other. If they affect art, they say that the decay in artistic expression is due to the decay in ethics, that art when shut away from the human interests and from the great mass of humanity is self-destructive. They tell their elders with all the bitterness of youth that if they expect success from them in business, or politics, or whatever lines their ambition for them has run, they must let them consult all of humanity; that they must let them find out what the people want and how they want it. It is only the stronger young people, however, who formulate this. Many of them dissipate their energies in so-called enjoyment. Others, not content with that, go on studying and come back to college for their second degrees, not that they are especially fond of study, but they want something definite to do, and their powers have been trained in the direction of mental accumulation. Many are buried beneath mere mental accumulation with lowered vitality and discontent. Walter Besant says they have had the vision that Peter had when he saw the great sheet let down from heaven, wherein was neither clean nor unclean. He calls it the sense of humanity. It is not philanthropy nor benevolence. It is a thing fuller and wider than either of these. This young life, so sincere in its emotion and good phrases and yet so undirected, seems to me as pitiful as the other great mass of destitute lives. One is supplementary to the other, and some method of communication can surely be devised. Mr. Barnett, who urged the first Settlement—Toynbee Hall, in East London—recognized this need of outlet for the young men of Oxford and Cambridge, and hoped that the Settlement would supply the communication. It is easy to see why the Settlement movement originated in England, where the years of education are more constrained and definite than they are here, where class distinctions are more rigid. The necessity of it were greater there, but we are fast feeling the pressure of the need and reaching the necessity for Settlements in America. Our young people feel nervously the need of putting theory into action, and respond quickly to the Settlement form of activity.

The third division of motives which I believe make toward the Settlement is the result of a certain *renaissance* going forward in Christianity. The impulse to share the lives of the poor, the desire to make social service, irrespective of propaganda, express the spirit of Christ, is as old as Christianity itself. We have no proof from the records themselves that the early Roman Christians, who strained their simple art to the point of grotesqueness in their eagerness to record a "good news" on the walls of the catacombs, considered this "good news" a religion. Jesus had imposed no cult or rites. He had no set of truths labelled "Religious." On the contrary, his doctrine was that all truth was one, that the appropriation of it was freedom. His teaching had no dogma of its own to mark it off from truth and action in general. The very universality of it precluded its being a religion. He himself called it a revelation—a life. These early Roman Christians received the Gospel message, a command to love all men, with a certain joyous simplicity. The image of the Good Shepherd is blithe and gay beyond the gentlest shepherd of Greek mythology; the heart no longer pants, but rushes to the water brooks. The Christians looked for the continuous revelation, but believed what Jesus said, that this revelation to be held and made manifest must be put into terms of action; that action is the only organ man has for receiving and appropriating truth. "If any man will do His will, he shall know of the doctrine."

That Christianity would have to be revealed and embodied in the line of social progress is a corollary to the simple proposition that man's action is found in his social relationships in the way in which he connects with his fellows, that his motives for action are the zeal and affection with which he regards his fellows. By this simple process was created a deep enthusiasm for humanity, which regarded man as at once the organ and object of revelation; and by this process came about that wonderful fellowship, that true democracy of the early Church, that so captivates the imagination. The early Christians were pre-eminently non-resistant. They believed in love as a cosmic force. There was no iconoclasm during the minor peace of the Church. They did not yet denounce, nor tear down temples, nor preach the end of the world. They grew to a mighty number, but it never occurred to them, either in their weakness or their strength, to regard other men for an instant as their foes or aliens. The spectacle of the Christians loving all men was the most astounding Rome had ever seen. They were eager to sacrifice themselves for the weak, for children and the aged. They identified themselves with slaves and did not avoid the plague. They longed to share the common lot that they might receive the constant revelation. It was a new treasure which the early Christians added to the sum of all treasures, a joy hitherto unknown in the world—the joy of finding the Christ which lieth in each man, but which no man can unfold save in fellowship. A happiness ranging from the heroic to the pastoral enveloped them. They were to possess a revelation as long as life had a new meaning to unfold, new action to propose.

I believe that there is a distinct turning among many young men and women toward this simple acceptance of Christ's message. They resent the assumption that Christianity is a set of ideas which belong to the religious consciousness, whatever that may be, that it is a thing to be proclaimed and instituted apart from the social life of the community. They insist that it shall seek a simple and natural expression in the social organism itself. The Settlement movement is only one manifestation of that wider humanitarian movement which throughout Christendom, but pre-eminently in England, is endeavoring to embody itself, not in a sect, but in society itself. Tolstoi has reminded us all very forcibly of Christ's principle of non-resistance. His formulation has been startling, and his expression has deviated from the general movement, but there is little doubt that he has many adherents, men and women who are philosophically convinced of the futility of opposition, who believe that evil can be overcome only with good, and cannot be opposed by evil. If love is the creative force of the universe, the principle which binds men together, and by their interdependence on each other makes them human, just so surely is anger the destructive principle of the universe, that which tears down, thrusts men apart, and makes them isolated and brutal.

I cannot of course speak for other Settlements, but it would, I think, be unfair to Hull House not to emphasize the conviction with which the first residents went there, that it would simply be a foolish and an unwarrantable expenditure of force to oppose and to antagonize any individual or set of people in the neighborhood; that whatever of good the House had to offer should be put into positive terms; that its residents should live with opposition to no man, with recognition of the good in every man, even the meanest. I believe that this turning, this *renaissance* of the early Christian humanitarianism, is going on in America, in Chicago, if you please, without leaders who write or philosophize, without speaking, but with a bent to express in social service, in terms of action, the spirit of Christ. Certain it is that spiritual force is found in the Settlement movement, and it is also true that this force must be evoked and must be called into play before the success of any Settlement is assured. There must be the overwhelming belief that all that is noblest in life is common to men as men, in order to accentuate the likenesses and ignore the differences which are found among the people the Settlement constantly brings into juxtaposition. It may be true, as Frederic Harrison insists, that the very religious fervor of man can be turned into love for his race, and his desire for a future life into contempt to live in the echo of his deeds.

If you have heard a thousand voices singing in the Hallelujah Chorus in Handel's "Messiah," you have found that the leading voices could still be distinguished, but that the differences of training and cultivation between them and the voices of the chorus were lost in the unity of purpose and the fact that they were all human voices lifted by a high motive. This is a weak illustration of what a Settlement attempts to do. It aims, in a measure, to lead whatever of social life its neighborhood may afford, to focus and give form to that life, to bring to bear upon it the results of cultivation and training; but it receives in exchange for the music of isolated voices the volume and strength of the chorus. It is quite impossible for me to say in what proportion or degree the subjective necessity which led to the opening of Hull House combined the three trends: first, the desire to interpret democracy in social terms; secondly, the impulse beating at the very source of our lives urging us to aid the race progress; and thirdly, the Christian movement toward Humanitarianism. It is difficult to analyze a living thing; the analysis is at best imperfect. Many more motives may blend with the three trends; possibly the desire for a new form of social success due to the nicety of imagination, which refuses worldly pleasures unmixed with the joys of self-sacrifice; possibly a love of approbation so vast that it is not content with the treble clapping of delicate hands, but wishes also to hear the bass notes from toughened palms, may mingle with these.

The Settlement, then, is an experimental effort to aid in the solution of the social and industrial problems which are engendered by the modern conditions of life in a great city. It insists that these problems are not confined to any one portion of a city. It is an attempt to relieve, at the same time, the over-accumulation at one end of society and the destitution at the other; but it assumes that this over-accumulation and destitution is most sorely felt in the things that pertain to social and educational advantage. From its very nature it can stand for no political or social *propaganda*. It must, in a sense, give the warm welcome of an inn to all such *propaganda*, if perchance one of them be found an angel. The one thing to be dreaded in the Settlement is that it lose its flexibility, its power of quick adaptation, its readiness to change its methods as its environment may demand. It must be open to conviction, and must have a deep and abiding sense of tolerance. It must be hospitable and ready for experiment. It should demand from its residents a scientific patience in the accumulation of facts and the steady holding of their sympathies as one of the best instruments for that accumulation. It must be grounded in a philosophy whose foundation is on the solidarity of the human race, a philosophy which will not waver when the race happens to be represented by a drunken woman or an idiot boy. Its residents must be emptied of all conceit of opinion and all self-assertion, and ready to arouse and interpret the public opinion of their neighborhood. They must be content to live quietly side by side with their neighbors until they grow into a sense of relationship and mutual interests. Their neighbors are held apart by differences of race and language which the residents can more easily overcome. They are bound to see the needs of their neighborhood as a whole, to furnish data for legislation, and use their influence to secure it. In short, residents are pledged to devote themselves to the duties of good citizenship and to the arousing of the social energies which too largely lie dormant in every neighborhood given over to industrialism. They are bound to regard the entire life of their city as organic, to make an effort to unify it and to protest against its over-differentiation.

Our philanthropies of all sorts are growing so expensive and institutional that it is to be hoped the Settlement movement will keep itself facile and unencumbered. We have always been perfectly frank with our neighbors. I have never tried so earnestly to set forth the gist of the Settlement movement, to make clear its reciprocity, as I have to them. At first we were often asked why we came to live there when we could afford to live somewhere else. I remember one man who used to shake his head and say it was "the strangest thing he had met in his experience," but who was finally convinced that it was not strange, but natural. There was another who was quite sure that the "prayer-meeting snap" would come in somewhere, that it was "only a question of time." I trust that now it seems natural to all of us that the Settlement should be there. If it is natural to feed the hungry and care for the sick, it is certainly natural to give pleasure to the young and to minister to the deep-seated craving for social intercourse all men feel. Whoever does it is rewarded by something which, if not gratitude, is at least spontaneous and vital and lacks that irksome sense of obligation with which a substantial benefit is too often acknowledged. The man who looks back to the person who first put him in the way of good literature has no alloy in his gratitude.

I remember when the statement seemed to me very radical that the salvation of East London was the destruction of West London; but I believe now that there will be no wretched quarters in our cities at all when the conscience of each man is so touched that he prefers to live with the poorest of his brethren, and not with the richest of them that his income will allow. It is to be hoped that this moving and living will at length be universal and need no name. The Settlement movement is from its nature a provisional one. It is easy in writing a paper to make all philosophy point one particular moral and all history adorn one particular tale; but I hope you forgive me for reminding you that the best speculative philosophy sets forth the solidarity of the human race, that the highest moralists have taught that without the advance and improvement of the whole no man can hope for any lasting improvement in his own moral or material individual condition. The subjective necessity for Social Settlements is identical with that necessity which urges us on toward social and individual salvation.

21
JANE ADDAMS
A Function of the Social Settlement (1899)

The word "settlement," which we have borrowed from London, is apt to grate a little upon American ears. It is not, after all, so long ago that Americans who settled were those who had adventured into a new country, where they were pioneers in the midst of difficult surroundings. The word still implies migrating from one condition of life to another totally unlike it, and against this implication the resident of an American settlement takes alarm.

We do not like to acknowledge that Americans are divided into "two nations," as her prime minister once admitted of England. We are not willing, openly and professedly, to assume that American citizens are broken up into classes, even if we make that assumption the preface to a plea that the superior class has duties to the inferior. Our democracy is still our most precious possession, and we do well to resent any inroads upon it, even although they may be made in the name of philanthropy.

And yet because of this very democracy, superior privileges carry with them a certain sense of embarrassment, founded on the suspicion that intellectual and moral superiority too often rest upon economic props which are, after all, matters of accident, and that for an increasing number of young people the only possible way to be comfortable in the possession of those privileges, which result from educational advantages, is in an effort to make common that which was special and aristocratic. Added

From Jane Addams, *A Function of the Social Settlement* (Philadelphia: American Academy of Political and Social Science, 1899).

to this altruistic compunction one may easily discover a selfish suspicion that advantages thus held apart slowly crumble in their napkins, and are not worth having.

The American settlement, perhaps, has represented not so much a sense of duty of the privileged toward the unprivileged, of the "haves" to the "have nots," to borrow Canon Barnett's phrase, as a desire to equalize through social effort those results which superior opportunity may have given the possessor.

The settlement, however, certainly represents more than compunctions. Otherwise it would be but "the monastery of the nineteenth century," as it is indeed sometimes called, substituting the anodyne of work for that of contemplation, but still the old attempt to seek individual escape from the common misery through the solace of healing.

If this were the basis of the settlement, there would no longer be need of it when society had become reconstructed to the point of affording equal opportunity for all, and it would still be at the bottom a philanthropy, although expressed in social and democratic terms. There is, however, a sterner and more enduring aspect of the settlement which this paper would attempt to present.

It is frequently stated that the most pressing problem of modern life is that of a reconstruction and a reorganization of the knowledge which we possess; that we are at last struggling to realize in terms of life all that has been discovered and absorbed, to make it over into healthy and direct expressions of free living. Dr. John Dewey, of the University of Chicago, has written: "Knowledge is no longer its own justification, the interest in it has at last transferred itself from accumulation and verification to its application to life." And he adds: "When a theory of knowledge forgets that its value rests in solving the problem out of which it has arisen, that of securing a method of action, knowledge begins to cumber the ground. It is a luxury, and becomes a social nuisance and disturber."

We may quote further from Professor James, of Harvard University, who recently said in an address before the Philosophical Union of the University of California: "Beliefs, in short, are really rules of action, and the whole function of thinking is but one step in the production of habits of action," or "the ultimate test for us of what a truth means is indeed the conduct it dictates or inspires."

Having thus the support of two philosophers, let us assume that the dominating interest in knowledge has become its use, the conditions under which, and ways in which it may be most effectively employed in human conduct; and that at last certain people have consciously formed themselves into groups for the express purpose of effective application. These groups which are called settlements have naturally sought the spots where the dearth of this applied knowledge was most obvious, the depressed quarters of great cities. They gravitate to these spots, not with the object of finding clinical material, not to found "sociological laboratories," not, indeed, with the analytical motive at all, but rather in a reaction from that motive, with a desire to use synthetically and directly whatever knowledge they, as a group, may possess, to test its validity and to discover the conditions under which this knowledge may be employed.

That, just as groups of men, for hundreds of years, have organized themselves into colleges, for the purpose of handing on and disseminating knowledge already accumulated, and as other groups have been organized into seminars and universities, for the purpose of research and the extension of the bounds of knowledge, so at last groups have been consciously formed for the purpose of the application of knowledge to life. This third attempt also would claim for itself the enthusiasm and advantage of collective living. It has come to be a group of people who share their methods, and who mean to make experience continuous beyond the individual. It may be urged that this function of application has always been undertaken by individuals and unconscious groups. This is doubtless true, just as much classic learning has always been disseminated outside of the colleges, and just as some of the most notable discoveries of pure science have been made outside of the universities. Still both these institutions do in the main accomplish the bulk of the disseminating, and the discovering; and it is upon the same basis that the third group may establish its value.

The ideal and developed settlement would attempt to test the value of human knowledge by action, and realization, quite as the complete and ideal university would concern itself with the discovery of knowledge in all branches. The settlement stands for application as opposed to research; for emotion as opposed to abstraction, for universal interest as opposed to specialization. This certainly claims too much, absurdly too much, for a settlement, in the light of its achievements, but perhaps not in the light of its possibilities.

This, then, will be my definition of the settlement: that it is an attempt to express the meaning of life in terms of life itself, in forms of activity. There is no doubt that the deed often reveals when the idea does not, just as art makes us understand and feel what might be incomprehensible and inexpressible in the form of an argument. And as the artist tests the success of his art when the recipient feels that he knew the thing before, but had not been able to express it, so the settlement, when it attempts to reveal and apply knowledge, deems its results practicable, when it has made knowledge available which before was abstract, when through use, it has made common that knowledge which was partial before, because it could only be apprehended by the intellect.

The chief characteristic of art lies in freeing the individual from a sense of separation and isolation in his emotional experience, and has usually been accomplished through painting, writing and singing; but this does not make it in the least impossible that it is now being tried, self-consciously and most bunglingly we will all admit, in terms of life itself. . . .

. . . The experience of the resident who teaches the history of art, of the good friend who is ashamed of the lack of democracy and interpretive power among modern artists, added to many other bits of experience and emotion has resulted in the establishment of a Chicago Arts and Crafts Society, which was founded at Hull House more than a year ago. This society has developed an amazing vitality of its own. And perhaps a quotation from its constitution will show its trend:

"To consider the present state of the factories and the workmen therein, and to devise lines of development which shall retain the machine in so far as it relieves the workmen from drudgery, and tends to perfect his product but which shall insist that the machine be no longer allowed to dominate the workman and reduce his production into a mechanical distortion."

The Chicago Arts and Crafts Society has challenged the present condition and motive of art. Its protest is certainly feeble and may be ineffective, but it is at least genuine and vital. Under the direction of several of its enthusiastic members a shop has been opened at Hull House where articles are designed and made. It is not merely a school where people are taught and then sent forth to use their teaching in art according to their individual initiative and opportunity, but where those who have been carefully trained and taught may remain, to express the best they may in wood or metal. A settlement would avoid the always getting ready for life which seems to dog the school, and would begin with however small a group to really accomplish and to live. . . .

So far as my experience goes a settlement finds itself curiously more companionable with the state and national bureaus in their efforts in collecting information and analyzing the situation, than it does with university efforts. This may possibly be traced to the fact that the data is accumulated by the bureaus on the assumption that it will finally become the basis for legislation, and is thus in the line of applicability. The settlements from the first have done more or less work under the direction of the bureaus. The head of a federal department quite recently begged a settlement to transform into readable matter a certain mass of material which had been carefully collected into tables and statistics. He hoped to make a connection between the information concerning diet and sanitary conditions, and the tenement house people who sadly needed this information. The head of the bureau said quite simply that he hoped that the settlements could accomplish this, not realizing that to put information into readable form is not nearly enough. It is to confuse a simple statement of knowledge with its application.

Permit me to illustrate from a group of Italian women who bring their underdeveloped children several times a week to Hull House for sanitary treatment, under the direction of a physician. It has been possible to teach some of these women to feed their children oatmeal instead of tea-soaked bread, but it has been done, not by statement at all but by a series of gay little Sunday morning breakfasts given to a group of them in the Hull House nursery. A nutritious diet was thus substituted for an inferior one by a social method. At the same time it was found that certain of the women hung bags of salt about their children's necks, to keep off the evil eye, which was supposed to give the children crooked legs at first, and in the end to cause them to waste away. The salt bags gradually disappeared under the influence of baths and cod liver oil. In short, rachitis was skillfully arrested, and without mention that disease was caused not by evil eye but by lack of cleanliness and nutrition, and without passing through the intermediate belief that disease was sent by Providence, the women form a little centre for the intelligent care of children, which is making itself felt in the Italian colony. Knowledge was applied in both cases, but scarcely as the statistician would have applied it. . . .

A settlement in its attempt to apply the larger knowledge of life to industrial problems makes its appeal upon the assumption that the industrial problem is a social one, and the effort of a settlement in securing labor legislation is valuable largely in proportion as it can make both the working men and the rest of the community conscious of solidarity, and insists upon similarities rather than differences. A settlement constantly endeavors to make its neighborhood realize that it belongs to the city as a whole, and can only improve as the city improves. We, at Hull House, have undertaken to pave the streets of our ward only to find that we must agitate for an ordinance, that repaving shall be done from a general fund before we can hope to have our streets properly paved. We have attempted to compel by law, that the manufacturer provide proper work rooms for his sweater's victims, and were surprised to find ourselves holding a mass meeting in order to urge a federal measure upon Congress.

One of the residents at Hull House for three years faithfully inspected the alleys of our ward, but all her faithful service was set at naught because civil service has been but a farce in Chicago and to insist upon its administration, and the abolition of the contract system is the shortest method of cleaning the alleys.

22

JANE ADDAMS

Women and Public Housekeeping (1910)

A city is in many respects a great business corporation, but in other respects it is enlarged housekeeping. If American cities have failed in the first, partly because officeholders have carried with them the predatory instinct learned in competitive business, and cannot help "working a good thing" when they have an opportunity, may we not say that city housekeeping has failed partly because women, the traditional housekeepers, have not been consulted as to its multiform activities? The men of the city have been carelessly indifferent to much of its civic housekeeping, as they have always been

From Jane Addams, *Women and Public Housekeeping* (New York: National Woman Suffrage Publishing Co., 1910).

indifferent to the details of the household. They have totally disregarded a candidate's capacity to keep the streets clean, preferring to consider him in relation to the national tariff or to the necessity for increasing the national navy, in a pure spirit of reversion to the traditional type of government, which had to do only with enemies and outsiders.

It is difficult to see what military prowess has to do with the multiform duties which, in a modern city, include the care of parks and libraries, superintendence of markets, sewers and bridges, the inspection of provisions and boilers, and the proper disposal of garbage. It has nothing to do with the building department, which the city maintains that it may see to it that the basements are dry, that the bedrooms are large enough to afford the required cubic feet of air, that the plumbing is sanitary, that the gas pipes do not leak, that the tenement house court is large enough to afford light and ventilation, that the stairways are fireproof. The ability to carry arms has nothing to do with the health department maintained by the city, which provides that children are vaccinated, that contagious diseases are isolated and placarded, that the spread of tuberculosis is curbed, that the water is free from typhoid infection. Certainly the military conception of society is remote from the functions of the school boards, whose concern it is that children are educated, that they are supplied with kindergartens, and are given a decent place in which to play. The very multifariousness and complexity of a city government demand the help of minds accustomed to detail and variety of work, to a sense of obligation for the health and welfare of young children, and to a responsibility for the cleanliness and comfort of other people.

Because all these things have traditionally been in the hands of women, if they take no part in them now they are not only missing the education which the natural participation in civic life would bring to them, but they are losing what they have always had. From the beginning of tribal life, they have been held responsible for the health of the community, a function which is now represented by the health department. From the days of the cave dwellers, so far as the home was clean and wholesome, it was due to their efforts, which are now represented by the Bureau of Tenement House Inspection. From the period of the primitive village, the only public sweeping which was performed was what they undertook in their diverse dooryards, that which is now represented by the Bureau of Street Cleaning. Most of the departments in a modern city can be traced to woman's traditional activity; but, in spite of this, so soon as these old affairs were turned over to the city they slipped from woman's hands, apparently because they then became matters for collective action and implied the use of the franchise—because the franchise had in the first instance been given to the man who could fight, because in the beginning he alone could vote who could carry a weapon, it was considered an improper thing for a woman to possess it.

Is it quite public spirited for woman to say, "We will take care of these affairs so long as they stay in our own houses, but if they go outside and concern so many people that they cannot be carried on without the mechanism of the vote, we will drop them; it is true that these activities which women have always had are not at present being carried on very well by the men in most of the great American cities, but because we do not consider it 'lady-like' to vote, we will let them alone?"

23
FANNIE BARRIER WILLIAMS
An Extension of the Conference Spirit (1904)

During the month of April last, The Chicago Woman's Club inaugurated and successfully carried through, a three day's conference for

From *Voice of the Negro,* July 1904.

the purpose of studying "Women in Modern Industrialism."

This comprehensive subject led out into so many different interests that touch the economic and social life of all people, and the high character of the men and women who participated in the discussion, as well as the advanced ideas formulated and the deep interest manifested by the people on all sides, have given the work of the conference more than a local interest and significance.

To any one who has had the privilege of attending the annual conferences held at Tuskegee, Hampton and the Atlanta University, this Chicago Woman's Conference seemed to be an extension of the same anxiety and sincere purpose to get at the heart of the ills and perplexities that constitute the social problems that enter into our national life.

Among the men and women who spoke and urged a more inclusive sympathy and a more courageous stand for what is just and true in economic affairs may be mentioned, Mrs. Charles Henrotin, a former president of the National Woman's Federation, and president of the Chicago Woman's Club and the originator and leading spirit of the conference; Jane Addams, of Hull House; Graham Taylor, of the Chicago Commons; Miss Mary McDowal, of the University Settlement; Mr. Cooley, Superintendent of the Chicago Public schools; Mrs. Celia Parker Woolley, the well-known author and club woman, and many others of national reputation. These people may be fairly regarded as experts in the various lines of endeavor to bring about a better relationship between the educated and uneducated, the rich and the poor, the weak and the strong. They are not interested in one class of people as against another class, but every day of their lives is spent in behalf of all the people, including white and black, who through no fault of their own, are compelled to live short of their deserving in the struggle "for life, liberty and the pursuit of happiness."

The programme of the conference embraced the following subjects:

"The Home as a Financial Institution."

"Special Modifications in Education Needed to meet the Requirements of Good Housekeeping."

"The Status of Women in Literary and Artistic Professions."

"What Can the Public Schools do to Meet the Needs of Women for Industrial Training?"

"The Family and Financial Burdens Borne by Women."

"The Health of Women as Affected by Industrialism."

"Future Offered to Women in the Arts and Crafts."

"Women in the Professions."

"Status of Women Employed in Manufacturing, as Employers and Employees, as Clerks and Government Employees."

"The Political and Legal Disabilities of Women in Industry and Women in Trades Unions."

It will be readily admitted that these are all vital questions and too broad to admit of any line of color or caste.

By way of better understanding the spirit as well as the utterances of the speakers in this conference, it might be well to quote some of the more salient things said.

One speaker decried the present discrimination against women in remunerative occupations, and said, "You cannot get the good work that woman is capable of doing unless you give her ample compensation."—In speaking of the value of trades for young women, another speaker said, "No girl, no matter in what financial circumstances she may have been reared, ought to marry unless she has some trade or profession at her finger tips lest the death of her husband bring her face to face with adversity."

In discussing the question of the rights of women to receive the same pay for the same work that men receive, the following objections were urged:

First, "that, as a general rule, women are not constructive in the larger enterprises of business."

Second. "Men do not like to be subordinate to women."

Third. "Until women prove that they can be constructive, until they can compel men, by their superiority, to recognize them as efficient leaders in any line of work they undertake, they will certainly remain on the lowest round of the ladder."

Under the topic, "The Health of Women Effected by Industrialism," the discussion revealed the fact that when a woman is successful in a large undertaking, her work usually acts as a tonic, and the successful women are generally both healthy and happy. But when she attempts to do a man's work, at the office or shop, and a woman's work in the home, she fails miserably. The woman in industrialism does not spend enough time in recreation, in sleep and is careless in the matter of her food.

The women generally agreed that no portion of the working class of women is so well off, as to health, as those engaged in domestic service.

In the discussion of this question of Domestic Service, the whole conference was aroused to a high pitch of interest. One of the speakers, on this topic, was on the Hampton Conference program last summer. It was rather gratifying to see that the conclusions that were so heartily approved at Hampton, were as cordially endorsed at this conference. The sentiment here adopted was to the effect "that there is no reason why a woman of character, graciousness and skill should not change the whole current of public opinion in regard to the respectability of domestic service."

As a further evidence of the interest taken in this subject, prominent sociologists throughout the country were asked to answer the following question: "How can the servant girl problem be solved?" The following are some of the answers given:

   1st. Recognize that they are working at a trade.

   2nd. Pay experts by the hour.

   3d. Let them share the family life.

   4th. Give her the very best labor-saving inventions.

5th. Clearly define their duties and don't order suppers after the hired girl has completed her day's work.

6th. Eliminate the talk about social superiority, and recognize a servant as a human being worthy of consideration.

7th. Teach ignorant mistresses that caprice is not popular with the women who sell their time for specific duties.

The subject, "Home and Society," brought out many wholesome and helpful suggestions. One great need was declared to be education in domestic economy and raising the ideals of the home.

One woman of extensive experience and knowledge, said: "The large attendance at academies and industrial schools show that one-half of the world is trying to gain in the ability to think, and the other half in the ability to do." There is urgent need for a direct study of the problem of home, so much so that the establishment of a State School of Home Economics, where young women may be taught how to conduct a home, with social and financial economy, should be urged. It is just as much a disgrace for a girl to marry who does not understand the economic management of a home, as it is for a man to marry who is unable to support a family."

Another speaker on the same subject, fully echoed the philosophy of the Southern conferences, in the following words:

"The ideal of scholarly leisure and the life of the student recluse is very attractive, but in the days to come, the true education will not be that which is devoted to pure academic work, but rather that which prepares for service. The parents of a girl in college know, that even if they are not compelled to, their children should be able to take care of themselves, which shows, as fathers and mothers, that they have a high degree of intelligence."

The very interesting and involved question with reference to trades unions received a large and intelligent consideration by those competent to speak as experts. In this particular discussion, men and women of the highest intelligence in all the walks of Amercan life participated, and there was revealed in it all such sincerity and generousness of interest, as to show a new consciousness of sympathy in the every day life of the people.

Those of us of the colored race, persuade ourselves, at times, that ours is the only and the greatest problem in our civilization. The fact is that the spirit of injustice that we contend against is the same spirit of injustice that millions of white men, women and children are everywhere struggling against in the form of oppressive hours of labor, inadequate wages, unsanitary conditions of employment and the many inequalities that are crystallized into law and custom. The strong language used in this conference by those who are oppressed in various ways and compelled to live below their rights as citizens, sounded at times like the lamentations we so often indulge in. The interest taken in these high and perplexing questions, by women of wealth and position, and the sympathy revealed for those who are without the power to protect themselves, happily show that the forces that are to solve both the black and white problems, are in course of preparation. The largeness of soul and breadth of conception that are now enlisted in these economic problems, must certainly include within the range of their corrective influence, the wrongs under which we smart and suffer and justly complain.

24
MARGARET MURRAY WASHINGTON
(MRS. BOOKER T.)

Social Improvement of the Plantation Woman (1904)

The time is not so far remote as not to be remembered by the generation of yesterday when custom, growing out of conditions, fixed the

From *Voice of the Negro,* July 1904.

status of woman as "something better than a dog, a little dearer than a horse." In spite of Biblical mandate, the clamor of certain wide-awake women opened the way to unmistakable rights, not to political we grant, but to social rights, and the end is not yet. Woman was enslaved. She has come out into the freedom of this New Republic. She is making a way.

It is impossible to picture the social condition of the plantation colored woman forty years ago, for she had no status except commodity. Mind, soul, body were fettered. For her, there was no light. There was no fellowship; there was no home; there were no material ties. True there were exceptions in the case of the mansion house servants, who from contact absorbed something either good or bad from the lives of their owners, but in the main the masses of the race to-day are the descendants of the plantation field hands, who assisted without "the light within the brain."

A sound judgment of our own character is essential to moral improvement. There is no such advance without social improvement. How necessary, then, were the advantages of education when those millions of untrained slaves were set free without the first vestige of knowledge of correct living. And that was a tremendous responsibility of setting in motion those educative forces that unfolded a new life to an unlettered people which was shouldered by a few zealous missionaries! Home and marriage ties were established in the lives of those who had been victims of unchastity. Schools were opened to advance the cause, and light broke upon the untutored mind.

Just as the condition of the white races of women has been ripening under favorable circumstances, just so has the condition of the plantation colored woman been growing better as the years have come and gone since Providence opened a way for her to receive a knowledge of true living.

Of late years nothing has been more conducive in raising the social standards of life on plantations than the farmers' conferences. The ideas advanced of buying land, of getting away from the one-room cabin, of being producers rather than consumers, have had their effect. Today there are one hundred and fifty thousand plantations owned by colored farmers. There are over one hundred and twenty-five thousand homes containing on an average four rooms. That means an appreciation of the environments of social conditions that make for the welfare of this generation.

Four years since a woman in one of these conferences told of her first attempt to get money to buy a home. She traded a dog for a hog, and finally effected a sale that resulted in putting by the first sum for her purpose. The incident told in conference was noted by a reporter, and not long since the same woman now a property holder, wrote to us of reading of her conference statement in a Sunday-school quarterly. She has now gathered her neighbor women to hold weekly councils that will tend to better home life, and especially to promote the welfare of the children of their community.

In the Monthly Farmers' Institute in one of the counties of Alabama, another plantation woman recently testified as to the productivity of her poultry industry, that had enabled her to pay for a small truck farm, and to erect a three-room cottage in place of the one-room cabin that had been her home for fifteen years.

Numerous instances could be given of women who have been awakened to the possibility of bettering their condition by the practical knowledge gained first in the farmers' conferences, and again in the school for their farmers, that have been organized under the name of Farmers' Institutes all over the Black Belt. Special women's meetings are fraught with tangible good, and the weekly conferences, followed by careful visiting, have raised the plane of home and the standard of life on plantations that were once notorious for their "quarters of vice." Within a radius of fifty miles there are no less than four social settlements where the workers have entered into the heart of the family life around them, and disseminated principles that tend to mark an epoch in the history of the race.

One settlement of Calhoun, Alabama, has been the means of forty or fifty families purchasing homes principally through the economy of the mothers who have at heart the interest of their children. Another, organized by an association in New York, has an agent who is instructed to aid in the purchase of homes for only those whose lives are upright. Virtue is not at a discount in any of these settlements, and thus higher ideals are maintained in all families.

One settlement at Mount Meigs, Alabama, is especially devoted in training mothers to measure up to the duties devolved upon them in rearing their children.

Another social settlement work situated on a large plantation far away from the light, has worked along different lines. While others, with more means at command, have been holding out inducements to buy homes and better the family conditions by helpful environments, this smaller work has placed models before the mothers and children. Where there had been an indifferent attitude in respect to unmarried mothers, or to loose marital relations, there was a gradual awakening in the first instance that soon made itself felt. Constant pressure brought to bear on the latter breach has resulted in respect for the marriage ties, and if a new-comer in the settlement has dared to evade the law of common decency, he either soon marries or is banished.

The three-room cottage has been a mode for the mothers after the day's duties are over, and a training school for their young sons and daughters by day. The energy that produced a variety of vegetable and grains from the ten-acre lot has been the means of inducing others in the settlement neighborhood to concentrate on their forty-acre farms, and just as soon as the mind has become awakened to the possibilities of a small acreage, just so soon has there been a corresponding development of the social status of woman on the plantation and a consequent betterment of the family relations.

As a natural result of perverted souls, some may not be able to conceive of an ideal standard of morality existing among our plantation colored women. As a matter of fact, there are purer, truer minds that glory in the truth that can proclaim a knowledge of the virtue and constancy of thousands of these women whose souls are as white and clean as their fairer sisters who can boast of a line of ancestry that may have descended from the savagery of the Britons.

Like all subservient people, the colored race followed in the trend of their owners. They were the victims of a system that tended to demoralize, even from the old regime of the tribal life of the African forefathers. Like all freed objects, there was a rebound from enslavement, and when the race had placed before them the light, they followed after and found what they sought.

These educational forces that have accomplished so much in the social improvement of the plantation colored woman are vital. "As the woman, so the man is," and we firmly believe that this plantation colored woman will prove not "a menace" to the race, but a deliverer, for through her will come the earnest, faithful service for the highest development of home and family that will result in the solution of the so-called race problem.

25

Florence Kelley

Aims and Principles of the Consumers' League (1899)

The underlying principles of the Consumers' League are few and simple. They are partly economic and partly moral.

The first principle of the league is universality. It recognizes the fact that in a civilized community every person is a consumer. From the cradle (which may be of wood or of metal, with rockers or without them) to the grave (to

From *The American Journal of Sociology,* November 1899.

which an urn may be preferred), throughout our lives we are choosing, or choice is made for us, as to the disposal of money. From the newsboy who fosters the cigarette and chewing-gum trades, and is himself fostered by our failure to give the preference to some one-armed father of a family in the purchase of our papers, to the self-conscious patrons of the Kelmscott sheets, we all make daily and hourly choice as to the bestowal of our means. As we do so, we help to decide, however unconsciously, how our fellow-men shall spend their time in making what we buy. Few of us can give much in charity; giving a tithe is, perhaps, beyond the usual custom. But whatever our gifts may be, they are less decisive for the weal or woe of our fellows than are our habitual expenditures. For a man is largely what his work makes him—an artist, an artisan, a handicraftsman, a drudge, a sweater's victim, or, scarcely less to be pitied, a sweater. All these and many more classes of workers exist to supply the demand that is incarnate in us and our friends and fellow-citizens.

Those of us who enjoy the privilege of voting may help, once or twice in a year, to decide how the tariff, or the currency, or the local tax rate shall be adjusted to our industries. But all of us, all the time, are deciding by our expenditures what industries shall survive at all, and under what conditions. Broadly stated, it is *the* aim of the National Consumers' League to moralize this decision, to gather and make available information which may enable all to decide in the light of knowledge, and to appeal to the conscience, so that the decision when made shall be a righteous one.

The Consumers' League, then, acts upon the proposition that the consumer ultimately determines all production, since any given article must cease to be produced if all consumers ceased to purchase it, as in the case of the horsehair furniture of the early part of the century, which has now virtually ceased to be manufactured; while, on the other hand, any article, however injurious to human life and health the conditions of its production may be, or with whatsoever risk they may be attended, continues to be placed on the market so long as there is an effective demand for it; *e.g.*, nitroglycerine, phosphorus, matches, and mine products of all kinds.

While, however, the whole body of consumers determine, in this large way and in the long run, what shall be produced, the individual consumer has, at the present time, for want of organization and technical knowledge, no adequate means of making his wishes felt, of making his demand an effective demand. Illustrations of the truth of this proposition are plentiful in the experience of everyone.

A painful type of the ineffectual consumer may be found in the colony of Italian immigrants in any one of our great cities. These support at least one store for the sale of imported maccaroni, vermicelli, sausage (Bologna and other sorts), olive oil, Chianti wine, and Italian cheese and chestnuts. These articles are all excessively costly, by reason of transportation charges and the import duties involved; but the immigrants are accustomed to using them, and they prefer a less quantity of these kinds of foods rather than a greater abundance of the cheaper and more accessible supplies by which they are surrounded. The pitiful result is that the importer buys the least quantity of the real Italian product requisite for the purpose of admixture with American adulterants. The most flagrant example of this is, perhaps, the use of Italian olive oil, of which virtually none, really pure, is placed upon the market, for sale at retail. What the Italian immigrants really get is the familiar Italian label, the well-known package with contents tasting more or less as they used to taste at home in Italy. What the actual ingredients may be they know as little as we know when we place our so-called maple syrup, or our so-called butter, or honey, on our hot cakes at a hotel in the city. The demand of the Italians in America for Italian products, although large, persistent, and maintained at a heavy sacrifice on the part of the purchasers, is not an effective demand, because the immigrants have neither the knowledge nor the organization wherewith to enforce it.

That knowledge alone, without organization, is not sufficient to create an effective demand is well illustrated by the experience of a conscientious shopper of my acquaintance in Chicago. Deeply stirred by an eloquent appeal in behalf of the sweaters' victims and their sufferings, she determined to free her own conscience by buying only goods made in factories. She began her search for such goods in the great leading department store in which she had always fitted out her boys for school. The salesman assured her that "All our goods are made in our own factory; we handle no sweatshop goods." She, being a canny person and well-instructed, asked for the written assurance of that fact, signed by a member of the firm, to be sent home with the goods. They were never sent, though this was an excellent customer whom the firm was in the habit of obliging if possible. This process she repeated in several stores and outfitting establishments, until it became clear to her mind that she could not free her conscience alone and unaided. Her plight well illustrates the case of the individual consumer, enlightened but unorganized and, therefore, ineffectual. . . .

The National Consumers' League acts upon the proposition that, to constitute an effective demand for goods made under right conditions, there must be numbers of consumers sufficiently large to assure purchases steady and considerable enough to compensate for the expense incurred by humane employers. For this purpose the National Consumers' League has established a permanent office in New York city, and has entered upon a systematic work of organization of state leagues in addition to those of New York, Pennsylvania, Massachusetts, and Illinois which were in existence before it, and themselves constitute it. The National Consumers' League undertakes for the present year to investigate a single sharply defined branch of industry, as an experiment to determine the power of the purchaser when organized for a definite purpose. To manufacturers in that branch—women's white muslin underwear—the National Consumers' League offers the use of its label and the standard on which this rests, and pledges itself to advertise widely and persistently the humane conditions existing in the factories approved by it. The standard adopted for the present embraces four requirements, viz.: that all goods must be manufactured by the manufacturer on his own premises; that all the requirements of the state factory law must be complied with; that no children under sixteen years of age shall be employed; that no overtime shall be worked. It is hoped that within a reasonable time it may be possible to include a requirement as to minimal wages; the four which have been adopted are already realized in the best factories which have been found in the branch of manufacture under consideration.

Since the exodus of manufacture from the home, the one great industrial function of women has been that of the purchaser. Not only all the foods used in private families, but a very large proportion of the furniture and books, as well as the clothing for men, women, and children, is prepared with the direct object in view of being sold to women. It is, therefore, very natural that the first effort to educate the great body of miscellaneous purchasers concerning the power of the purchaser should have been undertaken by women, among women, on behalf of women and children. Having proved successful, within moderate limits, in that field, it is now extending among people irrespective of age and sex; and is asking the co-operation of the institutions of learning, and of learned societies.

The first effort in this country was made by two ladies, Mrs. Frederick Nathan and Mrs. Charles Russell Lowell, in New York city, in 1890. They selected two stores in which the treatment of the employés seemed to them more than usually humane; and, setting forth the good points of those stores as their standard, they wrote to 1,400 storekeepers on Manhattan Island inquiring whether they wished to arrange the work in their stores in conformity with the standard and have their establishments included in a proposed White

List. Out of the 1,400 *two* responded favorably; and from that modest beginning has grown the present "White List" of the Consumers' League of New York city, embracing nearly forty leading stores. For the two ladies proceeded to organize their friends; to bring their growing constituency to the attention of the retail merchant; to circulate their White List, and the Standard upon which it is founded; and to educate public opinion as to the power of purchasers to determine the conditions of labor in retail stores. The present principles, object, and Standard of the Consumers' League of New York city are as follows:

THE CONSUMERS' LEAGUE OF THE CITY OF NEW YORK

Principles.

I. That the interest of the community demands that all workers should receive, not the lowest wages, but fair living wages.

II. That the responsibility for some of the worst evils from which wage-earners suffer rests with the consumers who persist in buying in the cheapest market, regardless of how cheapness is brought about.

III. That it is, therefore, the duty of consumers to find out under what conditions the articles which they purchase are produced, and to insist that these conditions shall be at least decent and consistent with a respectable existence on the part of the workers.

IV. That this duty is especially incumbent upon consumers in relation to the products of woman's work, since there is no limit beyond which the wages of women may not be pressed down, unless artifically maintained at a living rate by combinations, either of the workers themselves or of consumers.

Object.

Recognizing the fact that the majority of employers are virtually helpless to improve conditions as to hours and wages, unless sustained by public opinion, by law, and by the action of consumers, the Consumers' League declares its object to be to ameliorate the conditions of the women and children employed in New York city, by helping to form a public opinion which shall lead consumers to recognize their responsibilities, and by other methods.

STANDARD OF A FAIR HOUSE

Wages.

A fair house is one in which equal pay is given for work of equal value, irrespective of sex. In the departments where women only are employed, in which the minimum wages are six dollars per week for experienced adult workers, and fall in few instances below eight dollars.

In which wages are paid by the week.

In which fines, if imposed, are paid into a fund for the benefit of the employees.

In which the minimum wages of cash girls are two dollars per week, with the same conditions regarding weekly payments and fines.

Hours.

A fair house is one in which the hours from 8 A.M. to 6 P.M. (with three-quarters of an hour for lunch) constitute the working day, and a general half-holiday is given on one day of each week during at least two summer months.

In which a vacation of not less than one week is given with pay during the summer sessions.

In which all overtime is compensated for.

Physical Conditions.

A fair house is one in which work, lunch, and retiring rooms are apart from each other, and conform in all respects to the present sanitary laws.

In which the present law regarding the providing of seats for saleswomen is observed, and the use of seats permitted.

Other Conditions.

A fair house is one in which humane and considerate behavior toward employees is the rule.

In which fidelity and length of service meet with the consideration which is their due.

In which no children under fourteen years of age are employed.

The Consumers' League of New York city, dealing exclusively with the stores on Manhattan Island, made its appeal exclusively to the conscience of the purchasers. Asking them to give the preference to the stores in the White List, it stated its purpose of encouraging humane employers to continue in their course, and of inducing others to imitate them. The success attending that appeal has encouraged the league to enter upon its more extended field of action; and, incidentally, to broaden the scope of its appeal. The National Consumers' League asks that purchasers, by insisting upon buying goods bearing its label, will discriminate in favor of those manufacturers who treat their employés humanely, so far as that is possible under the conditions of the competitive system; and that they will do so both for the sake of the employés and also for the sake of promoting that form of manufacture which is most wholesome for the whole community, in preference to conditions in which danger of spreading infection is constant and considerable. The appeal is still, as before, on behalf of the employé; but it is, also, on behalf of a far larger constituency— the whole purchasing public.

For, clearly, it is also a social duty to promote that form of manufacture which tends toward wholesome products, made under right conditions, rather than the sweatshop with its dangers to the family in which the work is done, and to the purchaser who may buy all the diseases to which reference has been made, despite the glib assurance of the salesman: "All our goods are produced in our own factory."

The present appeal of the National Consumers' League promises to be of increasing value to those employers who care to meet their employés as self-respecting people employed under reasonable conditions, and paid wages in proportion to the value of their work. Many such employers have greeted the league with cordial welcome. One proprietor of a factory, known for forty years as having most carefully selected employés, unusually intelligent, and in surroundings rarely desirable, on being visited by a representative of the National Consumers' League, stated that these were aspects of his factory in which the public had not seemed to be interested. The proprietors of such factories sustain constant intense pressure of competition of others who have a lower standard; and they need and welcome the offered support of an organized body of purchasers. One practical demonstration of this may be found in the offer of several such employers to use the label of the Consumers' League, bearing the expense of printing the labels and attaching them to the product; another is the help given by a manufacturer of wide experience in drafting the form of contract to be used, and many various designs for the label, from among which the one now in use was selected. As the league grows in numbers and in influence, this moral and financial support to the humane employer may be expected to stimulate the spirit of emulation in others who have hitherto been guided by the desire for cheapness rather than for goodness in the arrangement of their factories. This has been noticeably the effect in New York city, the most enlightened employers having been the first to comply with the requirements of the local league, and others hesitating, some of them for years, but finally coming to the point of making the required concessions....

In general, the power and usefulness of the Consumers' League will depend largely upon the intelligence and active work of the local organizations, and the degree of cooperation which these succeed in enlisting on the part of the general public. At present the league points out that consumers, even when unorganized, have power to put an end to the production of any given goods by refraining from purchasing them; to promote the production of others by demanding them. When organized, even very partially, consumers can decide, within certain limits, the conditions under which the desired goods shall be produced. Consumers have, however, done none of these things in an orderly and enlightened way, except so far as cooperative buying has been practiced and the adulteration of foods limited by legislation procured through the efforts of purchasers. The power of the purchaser, which is potentially unlimited, becomes great, in practice, just in proportion as purchasers become organized and enlightened, place themselves in direct communication with the producers, inform themselves exactly concerning the conditions of production and distribution, and are able thus to enforce their own will instead of submitting to the enticement and stimulus of the unscrupulous advertising seller.

Briefly stated, by the way of résumé, the aim of the National Consumers' League is to organize an effective demand for goods made under right conditions. As means to this end it endeavors:

1. To investigate existing conditions of production, and publish the results of its investigations.

2. To guarantee to the public goods found to have been made under conditions satisfactory to it, by attaching to them its label.

3. To appeal to the conscience of the purchaser as an offset to the continual appeal of advertisers to the credulity and cupidity of the public.

4. To coöperate with and encourage in every legitimate way those employers whose work is done under humane and enlightened conditions.

5. To procure further legislation for the protection of purchasers and employés.

6. To coöperate with the officials whose duty it is to investigate the conditions of production and distribution, or to enforce laws and ordinances dealing with those conditions.

7. To form organizations of purchasers for the purposes above set forth.

26
MABEL POTTER DAGGETT
Women: The Larger Housekeeping (1912)

The housekeeper is abroad in her city. There isn't so much to do at home as once there was. The spinning wheel had long been silent, the sewing machine was beginning to gather dust, the architects were drawing kitchenettes in their blue-print plans, when, in the dawn of the twentieth century, the more well-to-do women of Boston arose in their drawing rooms and, with skirts gathered in one hand, stepped firmly over their thresholds to find new duties.

The streets were filled with working-people on whom they looked with awakened interest. For science had recently confirmed our democracy by the revelation that, when Boston had 1,200 deaths a year from tuberculosis and 1,600 cases of typhoid, the Back Bay would have to have some of them. Beacon Street and Commonwealth Avenue might no longer live to themselves alone. Through this moving throng they were close linked to all the "ends" of Boston. Here were the tailors who fashioned the suits for the most exclusive Colonial Dame. Here were the seamstresses who sewed her lingerie. Here were the bakers who baked her bread.

The housewifely mind paused to ponder. Mary, the cook, who used to bake the bread in the kitchen, had to be carefully watched to see that she always wore a clean apron and washed her hands. Did the Superfine Baking Company wash its hands?

The committee a few years ago sent out to see, and came back with a shocked note in their report: "My dears, my dears," they said, "there are flies in the molasses and rats in the flour and there are weary, perspiring men who drop on the very moulding boards to sleep."

From *World's Work*, May–October 1912.

So the Consumers' League went to the legislature to ask for a law that should forbid the Superfine and other bakeries to make bread in a cellar and that should require medical inspection for employees as a guarantee against disease mixed in the dough. It is a woman's notion that has not yet been dignified by legal enactment.

But lacking a law, feminine ingenuity is using a "white list." It directs a discriminating purchaser to about twenty bakeries in Boston that have been investigated and found clean enough to meet the housewifely standard. There is likewise an "approved list" of fifty-six tailor shops that are light enough and airy enough so that the workers are not liable to disease. And once a month in two of the leading newspapers there is published the "Shopping Guide" to such department stores as are selling "white label" lingerie of sanitary manufacture to insure that it is not a menace alike to those who make it and to those who wear it.

Four years ago, in the season when the feminine mind turns energetically to thoughts of spring cleaning, the woman who cares looked across Boston Common with a friendly nod to Everywoman: "Come," she said, "let us join hands in a Woman's Municipal League." A platform of wide welcome was arranged to include alike Gentile and Jew, Syrian and Greek and Italian. This ideal was being explained at a parlor meeting in one of the ends of Boston. The wife of Guiseppe Bacigalupo, a prosperous Italian contractor, was present in the front row. Complacently stroking her velvet dress, she looked up in a sudden glow of comprehension: "Why, after all," she exclaimed, "we're all of us just foreigners together, aren't we? For, really, one never sees any red Indian natives about."

Madame Back Bay, in the chair, caught her breath. Then she smiled bravely back, "foreigners together," with the wife of Guiseppe Bacigalupo. And the Italian woman went out to bring one hundred of her neighbors into the League that now has a membership list of nearly two thousand.

These are a council of City Mothers of which Mrs. T. J. Bowlker is president. It is true that they are without the power of political action. But they have woman's influence organized to work for what they want. Within the League have been set up departments corresponding to every phase of the city's activities that affect the home. The office headquarters, at 79 Chandler Street, serves as the clearing house through which the Boston housewives' complaints or suggestions reach the City Hall. The officers of the League are working in cordial coöperation with the city officers.

The Department of Streets and Alleys first awakened Boston to the League's existence. They started a city cleaning crusade that swept from Jamaica Plain to East Boston, and from the Charles River Bank to South Bay. Committees were sent out to hang in Boston kitchens a neatly printed "Notice to Housekeepers," that cited city ordinances for the disposal of refuse and the penalty for throwing it into the street. They pasted the alleys with stickers that said, "Help keep the city clean!" They put advertising placards in the street cars that read: "Warning! The Health Laws demand that your premises shall be kept free from rubbish. Dirty air is death! You have no more right to poison the air that your neighbor breathes than the water he drinks!" Then they held meetings in every section of the city to urge that every housewife see how it was with her own back yard.

"What is all this fuss about?" demanded a Commonwealth Avenue matron. "I'm sure I haven't looked into my back yard in thirty years."

"Your neighbors have!" was the significant retort in a Beacon Street drawing room that sent her home for a private domestic survey. She found out the truth of what Genevieve Johnson, a little colored girl at the South Boston school, said in an essay on "Clean Back Yards": "Some of us live in houses that are like paper dolls with all fronts and no backs."

WOMEN SANITARY INSPECTORS

Boston was set in order. Then the League employed a salaried inspector to keep it so. She is a Wellesley College graduate, Miss Mabel Frost, and she daily patrols the streets and the alleys, especially the alleys. A garbage can uncovered or an alley littered with debris, brings from her a prompt notification to the householder that it is a violation of city ordinances. If anybody doubts the authority of this fashionably attired feminine person to speak her mind about garbage, she has only to flash the neat little nickel badge that is concealed beneath her coat lapel, and he realizes that what she says will go with the law. Not only private householders are thus regulated, some of the leading Tremont Street store keepers have come out into their alleys with shovels and hoes when she called. The North Station tidied up when she pointed out the debris that littered the pavement before it. The city increased its collections of refuse to three times a week and placed two hundred of the red metal "rubbish" boxes through the business district when the League laid her report of these needs before the Board of Health. . . .

The League's Department of Housing sent a second inspector, Miss M. E. Clarke, to the tenements where, day by day, she patiently interprets American civilization to the ignorant housekeepers who do not understand: for example, why they must not throw their ashes into the hopper that connects with the drain. They are usually quick to respond with "Scuzee! Scuzee!" It is harder to make them understand that dirt is dangerous. But by pointing to the little white hearses that are always going up and down their street, the "Clean Lady" at length makes them comprehend a connection between dirt and death that sends them to their knees, scrubbing brush in hand. The landlord is more difficult to deal with. Mr. Murphy in the West End was compelled to cut a window in a dark room, to whitewash the dirty walls, to put in a new sink, and to repair a dangerous stairway. When he had finished his labors, he announced: "I've lived in the West End twenty-five years, an' it's only lately these wimmin been nosin' 'roun'. Now a man inspector just puts his head in the door an' says, 'Board uv Health,' an' goes out again. But these wimmin, they know too much an' they see too much. No, sir, I don't believe in the idea uv wimmin inspectors."

The League does. The woman inspector is one of its "demonstrations." It hopes that some time the city fathers will take her on their own pay roll. For the present the city fathers only lend her the little nickel badge of the real man inspector, while the city mothers find her salary. And as fast as the treasury permits, the League adds another inspector to its staff. The Market Department inspector, Miss Therese Nortin, is a Radcliffe college graduate. Regularly she makes her morning trip through Faneuil Hall and Quincy markets, where a long line of dealers, bowing in white aprons beside polished glass show cases, are ready for her critical survey. In lesser districts, among poorer shops, the proprietor who sees her coming hastily shoos his flies and pulls a bit of mosquito netting over his meat or fish. Perhaps he even has time to raise a crate of vegetables to the top of an empty cracker box.

To get food stuff raised out of reach of dogs and covered out of range of typhoid flies has been the long persistent campaign of the League. After much effort they got a city ordinance, but it wobbled and wouldn't work when a shrewd dealer carried his case to court. Then they sent the market inspector out to make a map of three hundred provision stores, with red tacks put in to indicate the clean stores and black tacks to indicate the dirty stores. This map, laid before the last legislature, secured the law the women wanted. But while they waited for it, they had managed to get matters pretty well regulated in their own way.

League members all over Boston simply refused to buy of market men who did not meet their standards. One groceryman on Boylston Street, when he was requested by the market inspector "to raise and cover," answered that he was "just tired of having women come around telling him what to do," and he wouldn't. Immediately thereafter, twenty of his wealthy Back Bay clientele notified him that he need not serve them any longer. He used some strong language to the clerk who was weighing sugar. But he also got out a neat little printed circular and mailed it to every customer with the announcement that "Jones and Co. have 'raised and covered,' and will be glad of your continued patronage."

Nor are the Back Bay dealers the only dealers who have felt the force of feminine public opinion. Housewives in the tenement districts the League have organized in "Market Tens." The Market Ten is a neighborhood group of ten women pledged to exercise watchful supervision over the sanitary condition of the stores in which they make their daily household purchases. Is the food protected from dust and flies? Would the floor soil your dress? are some of the questions answered on the report cards they turn in to Chandler Street. When the record indicates that a store is persistently violating hygienic requirements, the market inspector visits it. She tells the proprietor why he ought to have screens. She gets his ice box cleaned. She puts the covers on his garbage pails. She is not even above handling a broom to show how it should be done. But if then he does not profit by the instruction, she makes a formal complaint to the Board of Health and they proceed against the shop as a menace to the health of the community.

HOW THE "MARKET TENS" WORK

The Market Ten, however, exercises a salutary influence all its own. One of its especial functions is to look sharply after those thrifty storekeepers in the poorer quarters who economize on wrapping paper by using old newspapers purchased from the rag men at a cent a hundred. Mrs. Levinsky in Salem Street opens a neat brown paper parcel to show her new neighbor a fish just purchased from Silverstein on the corner. "Such a nice fish," both women agree. And the new neighbor goes out to get one too. Lo, when it is done up and passed to her, it is wrapped in an old newspaper! With the withering glance of the woman who knows what she can do, when all the city statutes can't, she spurns the package.

"The Market Ten," murmurs Silverstein as one might mention the Mafia. "But I did not know you belonged! Pardon! Pardon!" And he would have wasted a dozen brown papers to rewrap the package. But already his customer has departed for the Model Market down the street.

What will the Market Ten do to him for his delinquency? Awful thought! Suppose they put him in the moving picture show. On Saturday night he is here at North and Blackstone Streets, where the Woman's Municipal League is displaying stereopticon pictures that are thrown against a building to instruct the moving throngs that are making Sunday purchases in the open market. How the typhoid fly carries disease germs from filth to food is told in pictures that take the fly from the stable to the baby's milk bottle. The clean alley and the dirty alley appear in succession; the clean street and the dirty street; and then the clean market and the dirty market flash into view. And Silverstein breathes easier. It is not his store that is labelled, for the city to see, "Dirty market! Don't buy here!"

CHILDREN AS GUARDIANS OF HEALTH

By such novel means the League is educating the public that grasps truth most readily when it is graphically presented. A drama, "The Play Shop," written and acted in the settlements by the children of the Junior Municipal League, is another potent hygienic influence. The stage "properties" of this play are a toy screen store, five feet square, with a window and a real awning that moves up and down, detachable shelves, and a complete equipment of flyless, dustless food packages. The principles of a sanitary shop are earnestly impressed on the audience by the play actors. Scornfully the leading lady comments on the store on which the first curtain rises, "All these flies, they spread so much germs, they give me the headache." And the dirty store is driven out of business while the neighborhood patronage makes prosperous the proprietor of the germ-proof store of the last act. . . .

The woman who cares is interested in this factory girl. She believes that she ought to have some preparation for the business of conducting the home with the plush parlor set. The League has talked over the possibility of sex instruction in the public schools. The question is being gradually approached. Meanwhile this year for the first time a new subject is to be introduced in the curriculum—the girls of the seventh and eighth grades of the Boston grammar schools are to be given lectures on "How to Care for a Baby."

TEACHING CHILDREN SKILL AND JOY

But before the factory girl reaches her home-making task, industry claims her for a time. For this, too, she must be made ready. Boston has 56,000 girls and boys between fourteen and eighteen years of age who work for a living. Many of them have been going out untrained to struggle for a foothold in the great army of labor, where more and more the battle is to be to the skilled. So the League's Department of Education, under the leadership of Mrs. Richard C. Cabot and later Mrs. B. B. Glenny, set out to make a complete survey of the opportunities for vocational training in Boston. Students from Wellesley and Radcliffe have volunteered as assistants. And the work has attained such proportions that the department is now permanently installed in an office of its own at No. 6 Beacon Street. The exhaustive information which it has compiled has been listed in the seven charts that have thus far been completed. The results are so highly esteemed that the Department of Commerce and Labor at Washington has incorporated in its 25th Annual Report an account of the chart plan and system of construction. And the seven charts, with all the facts as to location, length of the course, free tuition, etc., of several hundred classes and unsteadiness, hang in every public school of Boston to direct pupils to training for a vocation.

But girls and boys are looking for more than work. They are looking also for the joy of life. At night they stream through the city streets in search of it, and the bright lights of the saloon and the dance hall beckon, "It is here."

"Hang beacon lights in the school houses of Boston," the city mothers cried, "and we shall be able to lead them from temptation." But the city fathers thought that they could not afford it. So the League Committee on the Extended Use of School Buildings, with Miss Mary P. Follett as chairman, last year financed the $5,000 experiment of opening one high school in East Boston for evening social centre purposes. There are games and dancing and basket ball and the "Opportunity Clubs." The lighted school house had gathered 700 young people within two weeks after it was opened. The Mayor and the City Council of Boston, hearing of it, came up to see about it. And this year the Board of Education has taken over the work and will expand it by opening four schools as social centres.

The League Committee on Open Air Schools, under the direction of Miss Rose Lamb, presents another object lesson in the Castle Island School, an industry in citizenship that the city is almost ready to adopt. Throughout the summer, 250 anemic children from the crowded districts were taken daily to Castle Island to eat and sleep and play in the sunshine. At the end of the season they had gained an average of two and a half pounds, which is one and a half pounds more than is recorded for children of the same group remaining in the city slums. Incidentally, they were lined up at Castle Island for instruction in Clean Clubs. And Angelina Ristorini's mother reports: "That girl, now, she wanta mek a bath evera day, an' she have to have a clean shirt evera week."

PRENATAL CARE OF INFANTS

You cannot begin too early about the health of a child, the League agreed as they sat in council. Let us begin before it is born, urged the Committee on Social Welfare from the Department of Public Improvement. And what the League calls another "initiatory experiment of civic interest" was launched. Any expectant mother in Boston may have expert guidance through the nine months of preparation that lead to her travail and triumph. A trained nurse takes her under supervision and, at any variation from a normal condition, the services of a physician are promptly secured. Though the nurse's visits are made regularly every ten days, three dollars covers the cost of the entire period. The patient who is able may pay this nominal fee, but it is never required. All over Boston are humble homes where this professional care has averted disaster that hovered near. The nurse's route has been extended even out into the suburbs. In the little front parlors, where New England thrift has turned the Brussels rug right side down not to fade, and where a pink flowered china lamp on the centre table keeps sentinel guard in the best room, she sits down with the woman in a gingham apron and draws from a satchel all the appliances for scientific tests that a woman with a million of money might buy. There is advice about diet and rest and a warning nod toward the wash on the line, with a last injunction, "Don't work too hard."

The League shows the results of this Department of Public Improvement in statistics. Prenatal care has so lessened the dangers of pregnancy that, with 1,111 cases in three years, not a death has occurred, only one case of Bright's disease has developed, and the average weight of the babies is from eight to fifteen ounces more than that which is cited by the medical books. When the city fathers were presented with these figures, they went out to hire a city nurse. And Boston is now undertaking prenatal care as a regular part of its Board of Health programme.

Three thousand children are dying in Massachusetts every year because the law requiring that milk be clean is delayed. With this fact held up to the public, Mrs. William Lowell Putnam, the chairman of the committee on Milk from the Woman's Municipal League, has gone out and formed the Milk Consumers' League, of 2,000 members. And there are 2,000 men with a ballot behind them, whose enlistment is giving the politicians pause. But No. 49 Beacon Street, Mrs. Putnam's private residence, is the office address printed on their stationery. And this year, as last, when the milk bill reaches the senate, it will be she, sitting high in the woman's gallery, note book in hand and an attorney at her elbow, who will be giving the instructions that direct its progress on the floor below.

BUILDING BULWARKS OF THE HOME

A housekeeper, you see, shall lead them. Massachusetts does not yet seat her with its citizens elect. Nevertheless, she has followed the housekeeping that has gone from the kitchen to the legislative hall. And the woman behind the bill is a familiar figure at the Capitol. Up at the State House now is the representative sent by the Massachusetts Congress of Mothers, who believe that, with all the civic care-taking today, the home needs one more bulwark. Mrs. Clara Cahill Park is a member of the state commission that was appointed by the Governor to consider the question of motherhood pensions. House Bill No. 478, in regard to such state support for homes that need it, bears her name as the petitioner. "But you are neither a scientist nor a sociologist," objected a learned child specialist who is opposing her. "I am a mother," she rejoined quietly, little flames leaping in her bright brown eyes. "And he never will be," laughed several senators, turning the tide in favor of the one specialist in motherhood whom the Legislature of Massachusetts is disposed to recognize.

It is this same brooding motherhood, that knows so well how to take a little child to its breast, that is enfolding the city. The work that God specialized a woman for cannot well be done without her. And the home-making sex, with a capacity for detail that is the inheritance of generations, is at last solving the knotty problems that man alone may only fumble at. So the old occupation that was lost is found again.

I sat in a Beacon Street drawing room that is rich in ancestral mahogany. A woman who underwrites the work of the Boston Woman's Municipal League in checks of four figures was saying: "there is no more a woman of leisure in Boston. We have all been draughted for civic service."

And I thought, might not even Solomon praise her along with his historic housekeeper: "She eateth not the bread of idleness; she looketh well to the ways of her city."

Whether she be the old woman of limited sphere or the new woman of larger vision, it is the same world force that works within her and will not be stayed. City keeping is only the wider housekeeping that calls to-day for the hands that best know how. And civilization, responding to that transforming touch, commits its cities to the safe keeping of the woman who cares.

For all the fragrance of life flowers in the heart of her!

27
CLARA CAHILL PARK
Helping the Widowed Mother to Keep a Home (1913)

Living on a hill-top, tending my flock in peace, in the quiet, pastoral way that mothers often do, the thought has often come to me, as it has to other safeguarded mothers, "What does the mother do, who is left with nothing but children? What becomes of the Widow's Mite, if it happens to be a baby?" Visions of the terrific struggles that must ensue, to give the children a roof, food, clothing and other necessities stayed by me; for only a mother of growing children can know how imperative are the needs of childhood, and with what ill-success they can beset aside.

When I was a child I used to be taken, occasionally, in the Middle-Western town in which I lived, to political meetings, to hear some great man talk. But of all those speeches, heard so long ago, only one phrase can I remember, shouted in various tones of emphasis and conviction: "Take, for instance, the subject of Bessemer steel rails!" Everything used to be proved by them, as I remember; and they always proved that something should be done, whoever brought them out. So, in talking about this subject of mothers with young children, who must for one reason or another gain all, alone, I am always tempted to wish I were an orator, who could cry, in a wholly eloquent and convincing manner: "Take, for instance, the subject of children's rubbers! They cost twice as much as they used to! They wear half as long! And yet children have to have them,—to protect the shoes from wet, and the wearer from colds; and what are you to do about it, if there is no money for rubbers in your pocket?"

Rubbers are only an elastic example of the things that children need; and the point does not have to be stretched at all to show that, without some of the things which are not regarded as absolutely essential, children cannot be kept well, or in the "respectable element"; for without rubbers they cannot go to school in bad weather, there can be no Sunday school, and very little play out-of-doors. A cold is an expensive luxury; and so, without proper clothing, one must stop at home. If at home, there must be a fire; so, when the mother leaves for her day's work, she must face this problem: how to get along on too little, when each want foregone means an added care or danger. She is between necessity, and the surprising cost of things; and she has only her two hands with which to do both father and mother work. Recently I heard a prominent charity-worker tell of having visited a tenement where the mother was a sweat-shop worker. The mother had brought home her work, and

From *Home Progress*, April 1913.

around the table sat six small children, the oldest under the working age, pulling basting-threads. The speaker said that he, of course, had to warn the mother that if she persisted in that course, he would be obliged to take her children away from her; and left, shaking his head over the depravity of mothers. The woman who has to be father and mother both faces a question which often has to be answered by the law, charity, or some state institution.

Did you ever stop to think how your state answers that question? I have made a business of finding out, for I wanted to know. Do you know that, now, six states in the Union help the mother by keeping the children with her, and giving her the right to care for her own? But only three cities have a Widow's Pension Law: Kansas City, Chicago, and Milwaukee.

The reason why it made such a sensation when Jackson County, in Missouri (which county contains Kansas City), passed a bill, a year ago, in April, 1911, to allow mothers of minor dependent children ten dollars per month for the first child, until fourteen years old, and five dollars for each ensuing child, till fourteen, was that such a thing had never been done before. The habit of all states had been to relieve the mother by offering to take her children away from her; if she objected, why, then she was a very thankless woman, and might do as she thought best, until she grew ill, or failed in other ways, and then the state *could* take her children, and did.

The majority of the states board them in some institution, which costs, irrespective of the cost of buildings, about ten dollars a month per child. If they are very advanced in good works, like Massachusetts, they board them in country homes, but the mother must, even then, say farewell to her children. The idea is not to subsidize the mother of the children but only some other woman,—or institution. It is better to think of your children well cared for in another home than hungry and cold in your own, so many mothers have had to come to this; but most of them, let me tell you, after having put up a good fight, depending for its duration and success on the physical, mental and moral strength of the fighter.

No one seems to think, somehow, of the moral stress of such a struggle for existence; with little, hungry children depending on one, *actually* hungry, and cold, the temptation to get money, in any, the quickest way becomes "something fierce," as they put it. It reminds me of something that Myra Kelley heard one of her little East Side children say, explaining the children's side of it: "O' course youse can't *work,* fer de Cop will see youse, but de Cop don't never see youse when you swipe. How you goin' ter get things? De teacher is all right, but she don't *know.*"

I have talked to the state officials of the State Board of Charities, in Massachusetts; and I find, from their statements, that most of the mothers of the children cared for by this state, are sick; or their children have been taken from them because they are insane, or immoral, or have broken the child-labor laws. These officials claim that the only thing they can do is to take the children away from such mothers; and they may be right. These mothers have succumbed, that is all there is to it.

So, when the children are gathered to the marble bosom of the state, it generally means that the mother is also gathered in, ticketed, and put in some institution,—for the tuberculous, the insane, or the unfit. And so the state gets the whole family. But, on the other hand, I am told that when a *good capable mother* comes to the state for help, it passes her on to some private charity, its business being only with the derelict class! I talked with one young woman, in the State's Minor Wards Department, who said that if a mother did not drink, have fits, abuse her children, or was not feeble-minded or sick, she was not properly a ward of the state!

Kansas was the first state to have the so-called Mother's Pension Law; Illinois was the second. In Cook County, the measure was passed in June, 1911. It became a law in July. The bill was "an Act to amend an Act" of the Juvenile Court; and reads, "If the parent, or parents, of such dependent child are poor and unable properly to care for the said child, but are otherwise proper guardians, and it is for the welfare of such child to remain at home, the court may enter an order finding such facts, and fixing the amount of money necessary to enable the parent, or parents, to care properly for such child, and thereupon it shall be the duty of the county board through its county agent, or otherwise, to pay to such parent, or parents, at such times as said order may designate, the amount specified for the care of such dependent or neglected child until the further order of the court."

They have had to amend some of that, for the specification, "or parents," had to be, practically, abandoned. It seemed to put a sort of premium on the inefficient father, and they had to go back to the main proposition, the impossibility of being father and mother both, except under favorable conditions.

Mr. Sherman C. Kingsley, who is the chairman of the Citizen's Advisory Committee, which meets with Judge Pinckney, of the Juvenile Court, Chicago, to decide on such cases as may require pensions under this law, began to help solve this problem when the very newness of it, and its tremendous possibilities, made what to do first a puzzling matter, especially as the law had not been well safeguarded, and a tremendous number of applicants appeared. The Citizens' Advisory Committee was formed, consisting of presidents or representatives of the United Charities of Chicago, the Jewish Aid Society, the Catholic Charities, the Saint Vincent de Paul Society, the Visiting Nurse Association, the Woman's City Club, the Men's City Club, the Federation of Settlements, the Industrial Club of Chicago, the Immigrant Protective League, the Juvenile Protective Association, the Children's Day Association, the Elizabeth McCormick Memorial Fund, the Jewish Home Finding Association, the Bureau of Personal Service, and Hull House; and order soon ensued out of chaos. Mr. Kingsley tells me that as soon as the law was properly administered it began to be seen that it was of great constructive value, and agrees with Jacob Billikop of Kansas City, a member of the Public Welfare Board, that—but I will quote from him:—

"Those of us who have helped to institute the plan and have watched it with a great deal of interest, are convinced that, aside from the purely ethical and moral considerations involved, it is economically cheaper to keep the mother and children together than to commit the children to institutions.

"Considering the fact that the per capita expense in the average orphanage ranges from $150 to $200 a year, society can afford to grant the widow a subsidy of ten dollars a month per child to enable her to care for her children in a manner which would ensure their happiness and future development—in such a way as not to rob the children, in the words of Dr. Hirsch, of their personality, and the mother of her maternity.

"Thus, we no longer consider it desirable to force the mother into the shop or the factory with a view of eking out a miserable existence, nor do we consider her degraded by receiving public money.

"We cease, in fact, to regard the public money as a dole. We treat it as a payment for a civic service, and the condition that we are inclined to make is precisely that she should not endeavor to add to it by earning wages, but rather that she should keep her home respectable and bring up her children in health and happiness."

Help that a self-respecting mother can accept, that is what is needed, and even if it does not allow her complete freedom from outside work,—for as Jane Addams says, "the widow's pension is a crutch, not a wheeled chair,"—still, she can make terms with life. She is not forced to surrender by every untoward thing that comes along, sickness, and accidents and loss of work. Of course she cannot live without thrift, just as she must have the reputation for being capable before she is given the pension. And, in this connection, let me add that perhaps the friend that goes with the pension, to see that the mother knows how to administer her budget, may not be the least of her blessings, though one that she may be inclined to look at a little shrewdly before welcoming it. With tact on the part of the friendly visitor, this may be a wonderful chance for the scientific manager.

This care for the mother in her need, correcting, as it does, the greatest waste in our country,—worse than the waste of our forests, worse than the waste of game and fish,—the waste of health, of life and possibilities in childhood, has gone like a wave over our country. It is a wave of the great Child Welfare movement, which seeks to conserve the race by a kind of scientific management of the parts which are usually dumped into institutions. For the mother seems to be the best nurse for the child, unless she is a mistake altogether. A mother will do for nothing what some one else must be paid to do. No one else hears so quickly that child's cry in the night. No one else seems to see the possibilities of that child. No one else can so well direct the child's growing personality and develop the child's latent power.

A probation officer who has had twenty years' experience tells me that the hardest class of truants that he had to deal with were the children of poor widows who had to leave them alone, day after day; and added that the bravest persons he knew of had been the mothers who had succeeded in keeping their children's names off the dreaded pauper list, bringing their children up at last to be good citizens. To my mind, no one has ever honored them enough. Without the blare of the trumpet, or the sound of the drum, such a mother has carried her burden. Through the heat of the summer and the cold of winter she has stuck by her job; and nothing has discouraged her. With her babies, sick or well, with bad nights or good she has done her part. God grant that she receives her reward in this world or the next!

But all women, just because they are mothers, are not geniuses. It takes a genius to be away all day, hard at work, and still at home, in the thoughts of the children; to eat little, wear anything, and still manage, somehow, to go out into the world and keep a roof over those that must be sheltered and warmed and fed,—and never to forget the penny for Sunday school!

Now, California has followed Illinois's example; and here in Massachusetts a great movement is going on, to investigate all the facts which bear on this subject. We want to put our bill on the strongest possible basis; and, especially, to keep in mind the widow who will not ask charity. A list of the petitioners for the bill would be interesting reading. Labor leaders are there; the presidents of the Browning Society,—and of the Twentieth Century Club. Leaders in the prevention of tuberculosis, a Harvard professor, and a famous author,—all these and more decorate the white page of the petition, and show the varied interest aroused. The State Federation of Woman's Clubs has endorsed it, the W. C. T. U. have declared their interest, and the suffrage leaders have lent a hand; while, from the first, the National Congress of Mothers has mothered the idea, and has declared that until every state in the Union considers the widowed mother and the orphan in their need, they will not cease from making it their common cause.

There have been some objections. One is, that this rule will stimulate larger families! This, in Massachusetts, where only about one-third, less than 38 per cent, marry at all, and where small families are the rule! Another, is that we have had enough of pensions; and that the pension privilege of soldiers has been abused. But because of a few rascals, among veterans, would we have had our honored old soldiers die in almshouses, dependent on the whims of charity? Charity, you know, suffereth long, and is kind,—but not organized charity! You are expected to have so many virtues, when you are poor! You can't afford eccentricities, or failings. "If the mothers are worthy!" they cry, "and capable!" Well, a mother is a little more capable if she has enough to eat, if she has her rest at night, if she is not tempted to break the moral, and the child-labor law! Let us help her to be more worthy and capable. That is what all the Mother's Clubs are for, and the Parent-Teacher circles.

The labor leaders of the world are crying out against conditions of industrial slavery which keep men struggling for the bare right to live. Now, in the times of black slavery, little children were torn from their mothers for no crime but that of being slaves. I have heard witnesses this winter, at the hearings of this measure, tell of scenes when little white children were being torn away from their mothers for the bare crime of being poor. That makes us see that the words "industrial slavery" are not mere words, but a description of the bondage to conditions which still obtains, even in our land of social work and social ideals.

Only in the days of tyranny were the people compelled to make bricks without straw. Back of all these measures for pulling people out of ditches should be an appropriation for filling up the ditch.

28
Charlotte Perkins Gilman
Maternity Benefits and Reformers (1916)

One of the saddest obstacles in the way of legitimate social progress is seen when some of the noblest workers in one line oppose a movement of advance in others.

The American Association for Labor Legislation, through its committee on Social Insurance, has prepared the tentative draft of an act on Health Insurance, carefully drawn, and largely in accordance with the best measures now advocated and used in so many other countries, as England, Germany, Hungary, Italy, France, Switzerland and Russia.

In this act there was recognition of the great need of maternity benefits, and Section 15 provides as follows: "Maternity Benefits shall consist of:

From *The Forerunner*, March 1916.

All necessary medical, surgical and obstetrical aid, materials and appliances, which shall be given insured women and the wives of insured men.

A weekly maternity benefit, payable to insured women, equal to the regular sick benefit, of the insured, for a period of eight weeks, of which at least six shall be subsequent to delivery, on condition that the beneficiary abstain from gainful employment during period of payment."

In the remarks preparatory to the act, we are told that in our country we have a standing sick list of three million persons at any one time; that each of our thirty million wage earners loses on an average about nine days a year from sickness, with a total wage loss of $500,000,000, and a cost for medical treatment of $180,000,000. This is a total cost of $680,000,000, well for half a billion, coming out of the class which can least afford to lose it, as well as the interruption of industry that affects us all; and it is found that in some 75 per cent. of applications for aid, made to the New York Charity Organization Society, sickness was responsible for the distress. Few reasonable persons will object to the general plan of health insurance; why should anyone object to it for women? And if they do not object to it for other forms of temporary disability in women, why should the maternity benefit be objected to? It would seem as if there could be but three possible reasons: a desire to prevent maternity, to penalize maternity, or to prevent mothers from undertaking gainful occupations.

As the really good and in many ways wise people who are so valiantly opposing the maternity benefit cannot be suspected of the first two, it appears that their one desire is to prevent mothers from working; that is, from working at anything for which they are paid.

A more pitiful misconception of the best lines of social advance by those apparently well qualified to judge has seldom been offered. It is on a par with the opposition to "teacher mothers"—which frankly admits its object to be to prevent mothers from holding their positions as teachers.

All this foolish and wasted effort ignores one of the largest and most vitally important movements of the day—the specialization of women. Women are irresistibly pushing forward into all manner of "gainful occupations," first unprovided for spinsters and widows who "had to work"; then the growing multitude of young girls who worked to help their families and for their own freedom; then married women, to meet family wants and to preserve their own integrity; then, more and more, mothers.

This is the most important feature of the whole movement. Young girls are not women. Spinsters and widows are more or less unfortunate exceptions. The term "woman" should connote wifehood and motherhood. Until "mothers" earn their livings "women" will not.

The first steps of working motherhood, usually enforced by extreme poverty, bring the woman and the child in contact with some of our worst conditions; and we, in our dull social conscience, seeing evil fall upon mother and baby, seek only to push them back where they came from—instead of striving to make conditions fit for them.

What we must recognize is this:

Women; wives and mothers; are becoming a permanent half of the world workers. In their interest we shall inevitably change the brutal and foolish hardships now surrounding labor into such decent and healthful conditions as shall be no injury to any one. That children should be forced to work for their livings is an unnatural outrage, wholly injurious. That adult women should do it, is in no way harmful, if the hours and conditions of labor are suitable; and they never will be made suitable until overwhelming numbers of working women compel them.

Now since maternity is not "a preventable illness"—unless we wish the race to die out, but merely a temporary disability in which the woman discontinues one form of social service to practice another; there is even more reason for providing for it than for the "occupational diseases," which can largely be prevented; or the general diseases which attack us indiscriminately.

The efforts of any army to nurse back to health its fighting units, and to keep them in health—until they are killed!—should be paralleled by the efforts of a peaceful state to preserve the health of its workers, and to nurse them when disabled.

The theory that women must at all costs be kept in the home grows feebler daily. They will not stay there—they have definitely come out. By coming out, by bringing the mothers of the world into industry, we shall at last make the conditions of our workers what they ought to be. When these conditions are right, in hours of labor, in surroundings, in payment, then we shall have less sickness, and less need of health insurance; but with things as they are now, such insurance is wise and right, and most assuredly so for mothers.

29

ELEANOR TAYLOR

Wages for Mothers (1920)

A woman's movement which ignores the woman in the home, particularly the mother, proclaims itself short-sighted and invites failure.

Most women are and will be mothers. A majority of them will always, probably, take care of their children themselves. How incongruous, and how futile, the attempt to free woman merely by factory legislation or by new access to the professions.

Chained within four walls by the demands of the kitchen and the nursery, dependent for support and for her children's life upon the capacity and unselfishness of one man, the mother, lower economically than the wage slave, herself handicapped in the

From *The Suffragist,* November 1920.

expression of her personality, passes on her handicap to society, her children and to other women.

MUST MOTHERS BE KITCHEN MAIDS?

Society is deprived of the great contributions possible from women freed from the continued round of household drudgery which forms the daily life of some 19,000,000 women in this country. Children fail to get from their mothers the companionship and mental stimulus so vital to real growth. (How many mothers have time to play with their children?) Children of large families may fail to get even proper food and clothing, though the mother works her hands off. Women in industry struggling for a decent living wage find their work measured in terms of the unpaid never-ending toil of the woman in the household. Rebelling against the prevalent lower wage scale for women as compared with men, they are confronted by the fact that men need more money because some have large families to support.

The weak spot in the whole situation is the failure of the mother, through misguided sentiment and self-effacement, to secure proper recognition of the value of her work.

It is true that the importance of the mother and the great service which she renders to the state is sung by poets and mouthed even by the men who ignore the timid requests of the Children's Bureau. But too often this praise cloaks indifference to the real needs of the mother and her babies.

MOTHERS ARE TOO MODEST

Mothers, woman-like, have asked too little.

Requests for grants of money to teach rules which the mother has no money to carry out are futile. Much more than that will have to be gained before the mother takes her place beside her self-supporting sister, a complete and self-respecting personality.

Neither are the mothers' pension systems established in this country of any great value. These pensions, really widows' pensions, and a form of poor relief, prevail in one form or another in 39 states of the United States and in a few foreign countries. The earliest of the laws was that of Missouri, approved in 1911, which typically provided an allowance for mothers "whose husbands are dead or prisoners, when such mothers are poor and have a child or children under the age of 14 years." . . .

THE PROPOSAL FOR MOTHERHOOD ENDOWMENT

This plan, now being seriously debated in European counties, particularly Great Britain, proceeds from the assumption that all mothers bearing and caring for children are rendering a service to the state and should receive from the state maintenance for themselves during the time of their incapacitation for other work, and for their children during the latter's dependence.

Backing for some form of motherhood endowment has come in Great Britain from prominent men and women, from the national federation of women workers, and from the Scotish Trade Union Congress. The subject was discussed at the international woman's suffrage congress at Geneva last June, but no resolutions were passed. A resolution of the International Council of Women calls for endowment of needy mothers.

The most extensive investigation[1] of the whole subject so far made is that by a private committee in England of which Kathleen D. Courtney, formerly secretary of the British National Union of Women's Suffrage Societies, was chairman.

Their investigation covered the philosophy of the subject, answers to opposing arguments, and the administration and estimated cost of such a system for Great Britain.

---

1. Just published in this country by B. W. Huebsch, New York. Edited by Katharine Anthony.

THE CASE FOR THE MOTHER

The introduction to this committee's report states the case for motherhood endowment:

"Foremost among the barriers to equality for women is the system which ignores the mother's service to Society in making a home and rearing children. The mother is still the unchartered servant of the future, who receives from her husband at his discretion, a share in his wages. The system may work, on the average, fairly well. But even if, as is probable, the husband behaves well and 'brings home' the bulk of his earnings, these earnings do not vary with his family needs, and are subject to the arbitrary chances of unemployment and ill-health. And at its best the system leaves the woman with less self-respect and independence than she ought to have. At its worst it results in neglected homes and ill-nourished children.

"Even in the most fortunate cases, the system recognizes neither the personality of the woman nor her contribution to society. There can be no real independence, whether for man or woman, without economic independence. Few of us realize how constantly and subtly this half-conscious, but ever present sense of the economic dependence of the woman upon the man corrodes her personality, checks her development, and stunts her mind, even while she is still a girl, with marriage only as yet in prospect.

"National endowment of motherhood promises a measure of economic independence to the mother, and recognizes by a direct payment her services to society. It recognizes the varying needs of the family with an exactness impossible to wages. It recognizes the re-adjustment of the organization of society which the irresistible demand of 'equal pay for equal work' will involve. In its full application, the scheme will make it easy to decrease juvenile employment, and to raise the school age, since the child's wage will no longer be a supplement to the father's. It means, in short, an approach to the humane maxim, 'To each according to his need'; the abolition of hunger for the child; the economic and social emancipation of women; the safeguarding of men from the perils of low-paid competition; and such a leveling up of opportunities as our race has never known in all its history. It makes a ringing call to the ambition and vision of both men and women voters."

OBJECTIONS TO ENDOWMENT ANSWERED

Opposing arguments are met by the report. Against the prophesy that lower wages will result the committee cites the benefit to the worker of a system which increases his bargaining power by securing his wife and children from utter starvation during strikes. At the same time the committee recommends as an additional safeguard the establishment of a national minimum wage. As far as women are concerned, the effect on wages would no longer have their one plausible excuse for paying them less than men, namely, that the man's wages must allow for a possible large family; and since mothers would in most cases withdraw from the labor market.

In answer to the argument that such endowment would increase the birth rate, especially among the least desirable citizens, the report points out that the birth rate falls as the income rises, and that "the very hopelessness of a proper discharge of parental obligations breeds a recklessness in incurring them." Endowment would, the report predicts, increase the birth rate in the middle classes and probably not in the "hopeless" class in which there would now be the possibility of decently caring for a moderately large family.

THE CONCRETE PLAN

The form of endowment proposed is an allowance to every mother, regardless of income level, equivalent to the difference between the cost of maintaining a family and the cost of living for a man without children. This allowance would represent a certain sum for the mother, a lower sum for the first child and a still lower sum for other children. Such an endowment should, according to the committee, be extended to all children until school leaving age and to mothers during the period when child caring is or should be a full-time occupation.

As a compromise, however, the scheme worked out proposes the following scale of payments:

MOTHERS—Eight weeks before confinement, and as long as they have one or more children under five years old—12s. 6d. ($3.12) per week.

CHILDREN—Until they reach the age of five (as a first measure only to be extended later until school leaving age) 5s. ($1.25) a week for the first child under five, with 3s. 6d. (87 cents) a week for each child under five beyond the first.

That is to say, the total weekly allowance drawn by a mother with one child under five would be 17s. 6d. ($4.37), a mother with two children under five would be 21s. ($5.25), a mother with three children under five would be 24s. 6d. ($6.12), and so on.

HOW MUCH WILL ENDOWMENT COST?

The cost of such endowment is estimated for the 2,655,000 mothers and children under five and for their 4,670,000 children, at about £144,000,000 annually, or $720,000,000.

Such figures seem low compared with American standard. They are low. The cost for the United States, with its higher standards and its larger population, would be much greater than that for England. Compared with Great Britain's five million children under five years, we had in 1910 more than ten million, and no statistician here would consider the cost of a baby adequately met—no matter how thrifty his parents—at $1.25 a week. (With milk at 17 to 20 cents a quart!)

The United States can well afford to invest the needed billions in the establishment of motherhood upon a sound basis. At present less than one per cent of the nation's public funds is devoted to work for women and children, education, research and public health. More than five billion is spent yearly in connection with organized killing, that is, for recent and past wars, for the navy and war departments. Women are not wanting who will heretically maintain that these proportions might be reversed with benefit to the nation.

ADMINISTRATION

The administration of such a system would not be difficult. It should be combined, according to the English report, with existing schemes for child welfare under such an agency as a ministry of health. Necessary supervision of the mothers might be conveniently combined with the work of babies' welfare stations, the mothers being required to report there with their children at certain intervals. The condition of the child should be the only evidence required of the wise expenditure of the endowment on the part of the mother, and inspection of the home necessary only in cases of evident neglect.

One of the most significant results of endowment—barely mentioned by the report—will be a real advance in the efficient care of young children.

Mothers, with time and a little money in their hands, will begin to specialize. Cooperative undertakings, now limited to the middle class, will spring up. Neighborhood groups in which a mother or another trained woman qualified for child care, will relieve several mothers for work in occupations to which their talents attract them, will organize. The nursery school may be hoped for and childhood may no longer suffer the handicap of a neglected age.

Probably no more fundamental, and certainly no more appealing a measure could be fought for by women of all classes than some such scheme as this for the emancipation of the mothers of our country.

IV. The Fight for Woman Suffrage

AT THE OPENING OF THE TWENTIETH CENTURY women could vote in Wyoming (since 1890), Colorado (since 1893), Utah (since 1896), and Idaho (also 1896). After 1896, however, there were no victories for the women's suffrage movement until 1910 when the state of Washington's constitutional amendment passed. The next couple of years saw more successes in the West: California enfranchised women in 1911; Oregon, Kansas, and Arizona in 1912. In a major victory that broke the solidly antisuffrage East, Illinois granted women the right to vote in presidential elections in 1913. This list may seem impressive, but between 1870 and 1910, four hundred and eighty campaigns produced only seventeen state referenda and only two of those ended in victory. Since the major suffrage organizations put most of their effort into amending state constitutions, the number of losses they endured was daunting. It was not until 1917, when militancy among suffragists reached its height and a war for democracy consumed the world, that New York voters finally approved a full-suffrage constitutional amendment in referendum, in the process assuring victory throughout the nation. A national amendment was secured by Congress in 1919 and ratified by the thirty-sixth state, Tennessee, in 1920. All American women had at last won the right to vote.

The story of how women won this most basic of rights is a long one, beginning in 1848 at the first woman's rights convention in Seneca Falls, where the only controversial resolution was the demand for suffrage. Relatively unified until the Civil War, the nascent suffrage movement split in the 1860s over whether or not to support the Fifteenth Amendment, which gave African American men the vote. Elizabeth Cady Stanton and Susan B. Anthony, who opposed the Fifteenth Amendment because it excluded women, founded the National Woman Suffrage Association (NWSA), which demanded immediate suffrage for women. Lucy Stone and Henry Blackwell founded the more moderate American Woman Suffrage Association (AWSA), which worked for the Fifteenth Amendment as well as more gradual suffrage for all women. As a new generation of activists grew up, however, the old animosities that had divided their mothers grew less prevalent (most of them were rooted in the often uneasy alliance, in the antebellum years, between woman's rights activists and abolitionists). In 1890, as a result of the initiative of Alice Stone Blackwell (daughter of Lucy Stone and Henry Blackwell), the two organizations were joined and the National American Woman Suffrage Association (NAWSA) was founded. Its first two leaders were Stanton and Anthony, but by 1900 both had retired, and the twentieth century ushered in a suffrage movement that was, for the first time in more than half a century, without the guiding inspiration of its two founders.

One of the most striking differences of the suffrage movement in the twentieth century was its coalescence around the idea that the vote was *expedient*. In the nineteenth century, activists argued that *justice* and the ideal of *natural rights* demanded that women realize equality with men. While justice, in historian Aileen Kraditor's words, assumes "the natural equality of all human beings, and other ways of setting forth the belief that women ought to have political equality because justice required it," expediency denotes arguments that "woman suffrage would benefit society."[1] The justice argument was not discarded entirely, as is evident in the "NAWSA Declaration of Principles" adopted at its 1904 convention. In this declaration, the key figures in the NAWSA—Carrie Chapman Catt, Anna Howard Shaw (then chair), Alice Stone Blackwell, and Ida Husted Harper—drew upon the principles embedded in the U.S. Constitution, the reigning strategy throughout the nineteenth century (the "Declaration of Sentiments" created at Seneca Falls in 1848 literally echoed the Declaration of

---

1. For Kraditor's discussion of the difference between arguments based on justice and arguments based on expediency, see Aileen S. Kraditor, *The Ideas of the Woman Suffrage Movement, 1890–1920* (New York: Columbia Univ. Press, 1965), 49–55.

Independence): "we demand that the immortal principles established by the War of the Revolution shall be applied equally to women and men citizens." There was a dawning sense, however, of the inefficacy of such arguments, as much as most suffragists still believed in them. And in truth there was an increasing sense that the NAWSA was out of touch—in the doldrums. This sense was only heightened by the inability of the movement to make any substantial progress in enfranchising women during the second decade of the twentieth century. Historians generally agree, in fact, that under Shaw's leadership from 1902 to 1915, the NAWSA was disorganized, aimless, and backward-looking, a charge substantiated by the very familiar arguments—arguments rooted in Revolutionary rhetoric—expressed in this document.

Assertions about the expediency of the vote were not peculiar to the twentieth century, but their eventual predominance over other reasons for giving women the vote was unprecedented. In 1900 Catharine Waugh McCulloch gave a speech that epitomized the expediency argument. A pioneering lawyer from Chicago, McCulloch was instrumental in ushering in the victory for the suffrage movement in Illinois. Recognizing the difficulty of amending the state constitution, McCulloch drew up a bill providing for women to vote in presidential and certain local elections. For twenty years, beginning in 1893, this bill was regularly introduced into the legislature until it finally passed in 1913. McCulloch served as legal advisor to the NAWSA from 1904 to 1911 and as vice president from 1910 to 1911, but concerned about its eastern orientation, she helped found the Mississippi Valley Conference in 1912 for midwestern suffragists. Catharine Waugh McCulloch's address "The Protective Value of the Ballot" (1900) was delivered at a hearing of the House Judiciary Committee in Washington, D.C., and reprinted in *Woman's Journal,* the organ of the NAWSA. Women need the ballot, McCulloch argues, for self-protection—particularly from discriminatory laws, which prevent them from achieving liberty, justice, and equal education and remunerative employment. McCulloch raises the hypothetical charge that her argument is selfish, that women should fight for liberty for everyone, but she answers, "the protection of women themselves is of considerable importance."

The charge of selfishness that McCulloch imagines being directed at her call that women demand the vote simply *for themselves* was not imaginary. Perhaps the greatest problem with the expediency argument was that it could be used to legitimate the racism of the almost overwhelmingly white membership of mainstream suffragism. The primary way in which women's vote could serve as a tool for the betterment of society, the argument went, would be to augment white supremacy. This agenda is not even disguised but is reiterated in document after document published in the official journals of those same suffrage organizations that were fighting, in theory at least, for the realization of democratic ideals for "all citizens." Southern white women were not very active in the suffrage cause before the Civil War, in large part because of the movement's ties to abolitionism, but also because ideals of femininity that excluded women from a visible public life were more entrenched in the South than in other regions. When white southern women did begin organizing for the vote in the post–Civil War years, their principal argument dovetailed with the overall trajectory of southern white politics: it attempted to disenfranchise African Americans. Increasingly, the NAWSA supported what it called "states' rights"—which signified acquiescence to the demands of most southern suffrage organizations that constraints be imposed on any state constitutional amendment, limits that recognized local attitudes about race, immigration, and other issues and that thus ensured African American women would remain as disenfranchised in the South as African American men had become by the turn of the century. Even as the NAWSA turned from trying to amend state constitutions to focus almost exclusively on the federal amendment, its leaders recognized that they could never get the necessary backing of the southern states' representatives in Congress unless they temporized on the issue of racial equality.

In 1903 in New Orleans at the first NAWSA annual convention to be held in the South, the organization's leaders articulated their policy of "states' rights" for the first time. In the selection of speeches from this convention, "The South, Suffrage, and the Educational Requirement" (1903), Carrie Chapman Catt, who had just a year before retired as leader of the NAWSA, reassures southern suffragists that the NAWSA recognizes "State rights" and thus it "is perfectly safe for you to come in on that basis." The speech by Mississippian leader Belle Kearney clearly elucidates the position of most southern suffragists: "Just as surely as the North will be forced to turn to the South for the nation's salvation, just so surely will the South be compelled to look to its Anglo-Saxon women as the medium through which to retain the supremacy of the white race over the African." Kearney supports the means that were then being used to rob African American men of their vote and get around the Fifteenth Amendment: education and property requirements. (Less legitimate but just as pervasive means to the same end were bribing, coercing, and even threats and violence directed at black men at the poll booth.) Another Mississippi suffrage leader, Hala Hammond Butt, goes still further than Kearney, asserting that the desire for supremacy is the universal "ruling passion" and "inborn desire" of all Anglo-Saxons. Granting the vote to intelligent southern women, she claims, would happily lay to rest the Fourteenth and Fifteen Amendments (what she calls "the monstrous offspring of Frankenstein's unwise and impious ambition"). By such a strategy, "white domination [is] assured."

Northern suffragists not only turned a blind eye to southern racism, they had their own "race problem"—namely, mass immigration (mostly from eastern Europe). Mary Wood Swift argues in her address at the 1903 New Orleans NAWSA Convention that immigration rates are increasing in dizzying proportions and that the most "dangerous" part of this tide of new Americans is the mostly illiterate and uneducated men who "march almost directly from the steerage to the polls." American-born women, Swift points out, outnumber foreign-born men and women combined and would thus presumably lift the electorate to a more patriotic, temperate, moral, and intelligent level. Even in the foundational "Declaration of Principles" from the NAWSA convention of 1904, one of the main arguments is that white women are degraded by "being held not so competent to exercise the suffrage as a Filipino, a Hawaiian or a Porto Rican [sic] man." This comment makes it clear that suffragists were not above harnessing imperialist impulses (what the "Declaration" calls the extension of the U.S. government "over alien races in foreign countries") to support their own domestic agenda. Why colonize other nations abroad, the argument goes, when immigrants are allowed free rein at home?

Among the few African American women who belonged to mainstream suffrage organizations were Ida Wells-Barnett, who was also waging a war against lynching in the South, and Adella Hunt Logan, a life member of the NAWSA and the leading suffragist of the Tuskegee Woman's Club. Her "Woman Suffrage" (1905) was published in the *Colored American Magazine,* a periodical founded in 1900 in Boston notable for its appeal to African Americans from many and varied social spheres; in its early years it had a circulation of almost eighteen thousand. At the opening and closing of the essays, Logan embraces the Constitution, the Declaration of Independence, and the sovereignty of the self—all the tropes of justice and equal rights that women activists had traditionally used to claim the vote. She notably de-emphasizes the expediency argument, and it is clear that Logan, who invokes the Fourteenth Amendment and its erosion in the post–Civil War South, is indirectly rebuking the racism inherent in some arguments about the immediate political benefits of granting women the vote. She too, though, points out the abuses to which women are subject when they are denied the rights of citizenry. Suffrage is a right "protective of all other rights," Logan insists, and African Americans, both male and female, need it still more than Anglo-Saxons do "to help secure their right to life, liberty, and the pursuit of happiness."

Besides fitting unfortunately with the heightened racist, nativist, and imperialist sentiments that characterized the turn into the twentieth century—and from which suffragists were not immune—the expediency argument eroded claims that women as citizens and humans *necessarily* warranted the right to vote. The turn toward expediency, in fact, allowed some thinkers in favor of women's progress in general to argue that the vote was *in*expedient. In a forum called "Should Women Vote?" published in *The World To-Day* (one of the new, lower-middle-class "muckraking" magazines), the editors presented arguments for and against the vote because, they claimed, suffrage leaders would allow no discussion of this basic question. Virginia Le Roy's "A Woman's Argument against Woman Suffrage" (1908) epitomizes the expediency argument and what she calls the "fallacy of abstract rights." She insists that the vote "should not be based on an abstraction"—on, that is, suffrage as a natural right; much of her essay, in fact, debunks the very notion of essential, a priori rights. Le Roy takes a "pragmatist" view. For her, rights are contingent, "man-made," not universal; they grow out of social necessity. Thus, she insists that "it is up to the proponents of woman's suffrage to show that [the vote] will work practical good in some tangible way." She does not believe that it will, due to the corruption of political power and "the crass materialism of our sordid age." Ringing a change on the nineteenth-century private-public split, Le Roy argues for the salience of a social-political split instead. It is in the realm of "social spirit" that all the beneficial activities are being performed, all the great ideals of the United States aspired to, and all the great work being done—and it is being done by women, she says. Instead of the eighteenth-century "Republican mother" or the nineteenth-century moral mother, both of whom influenced the larger social realm *only* through exerting their influence in the private sphere, Le Roy describes a "great municipal housekeeper," who "diffus[es] maternal tenderness for all motherless children." For Le Roy, women are and should be active within the *public* (or social) sphere, but not in the degraded *political* sphere. Mainstream suffragists shared with Le Roy a deep skepticism about the machinery of party politics, both state and national, and hence they had a strong commitment to nonpartisanship; it would become a point of great contention when parts of the suffrage movement decided to enter directly into partisan politics.

Another particular problem with the NAWSA at the beginning of the twentieth century was its entrenched middle-class bias. Its prior battles and victories tended to favor the interests of middle-class women (marital property acts, for instance), and both its membership and purview remained relatively limited to that class. Some of the greatest changes to the suffrage movement between 1910 and 1919 came about because of increasing numbers of women entering the workforce, trade unionism growing among working-class women, and professionalism growing among middle-class women. (The number of married women in the labor force, for instance, rose from 14 percent in 1890 to 23 percent by 1920; and by far the most visible workers were the escalating numbers of young, single, immigrant women, working mostly in bad conditions in factories.) Along with Harriot Stanton Blatch, Josephine Conger-Kaneko, a leader of the socialist women's movement, was one of the most vocal critics of the NAWSA's "genteel" membership, policies, and strategies. Trained as a journalist, Conger-Kaneko wrote for a while for the *Appeal to Reason,* a major socialist paper, and much of her work involved reporting to her readers on the activities of the NAWSA. She recruited women for the Socialist Party and insisted that women's emancipation be part of its program. Conger-Kaneko published "What Will Woman Suffrage Convention Do for the Working Woman" (1908) in a magazine she founded herself in 1907, *The Socialist Woman,* which urged women in the socialist movement to assert their independent interests. She also challenged the NAWSA, as this article makes clear, to recognize the interests of working women and by doing so to recuperate its old militant spirit: "[T]he suffrage movement has lost its militant spirit, and has become lady-like and respectful in the last decade." Women are increasingly competing with men in the workplace, she states, and they are being paid only half what men are; surely any organization that agitates for women should recognize these two fundamental facts. The ballot could be a crucial tool to help women achieve a vital economic equity with men in the labor force.

Conger-Kaneko also points to the NAWSA's methods as a significant problem, a censure connected to her class critique in that the NAWSA's methods fit its middle-class constituency. The organization is "requesting" change, according to Conger-Kaneko, not demanding it. Its tactics, which are education, "genteel" and decorous meetings, and attempts to influence politicians through petitions, are increasingly ineffective. By the end of the first decade of the twentieth century, several alternative organizations to the NAWSA began to spring up—in large part in response to its inefficacy and its "genteel" methods. The new organizations were influenced by the English suffrage movement and its increasing militancy after 1903 under the direction of Emmeline Pankhurst and her daughters Christabel and Sylvia. They held marches and mass meetings and heckled British politicians whenever they could. After 1910 British suffragists intensified their strategies still further to include violence, riots, and even arson; many were jailed, went on hunger strikes, and were force-fed by prison guards.

American suffragists generally admired their militant and martyred sisters and welcomed leaders of the British suffrage movement to the United States. The first American group to employ the new tactics were the American Suffragettes, who organized unprecedented open-air meetings and all-woman parades in New York in 1907. The group, and the meetings, were galvanized by the visit of one of the British "prisoners," Anne Cobden-Sanderson, and another prominent British leader, Bettina Borrman Wells. Many of the American Suffragettes, a New York organization, came from the Equal Rights League, a group of mostly working women begun in 1904 by Harriot Stanton Blatch. The American Suffragettes also included actresses, artists, writers, teachers, and social welfare workers. Its official organ was *The American Suffragette,* which began publication in 1909. It believed in shaking up what it saw as widespread indifference to issues of public welfare and women's suffrage in particular, and it wanted to reach beyond the self-selected middle-class women who attended the NAWSA annual conventions. Members went out into the streets of New York and distributed "Votes for Women" badges, played "Votes for Women" on a hurdy-gurdy in the street, and drove around in a taxi shouting slogans through a megaphone.

The "Constitution" (1909) of the National Progressive Woman Suffrage Union, published in *The American Suffragette,* is notable for advocating "vigorous, forceful, aggressive agitation" and for its construction of women as an "outlaw" group—reinstating women's marginal, outsider status and disrupting the complacency of the middle-class NAWSA ethos. It also articulates the American Suffragettes' policy of reaching as many people as possible by the most direct means. Sofia Loebinger's "Suffragist and Suffragette" (1909) defines the ideal member of the new group self-constituted as "suffragettes," distinguishing her tactics from the "ineffectiveness of tea-table and drawing-room chat" practiced by traditional suffragists. This political group, while it drew its tactics from British suffragettes, was also clearly connected to the young New York intellectuals who were coining the term *feminist* to describe a woman who threw off the baggage of the past—all that was stifling and old in ideals of womanhood. (Ironically, however, in the article "Suffragism Not Feminism" Loebinger herself repudiated feminism as a disruption of natural differences between the sexes, a repudiation that left intact her conviction not only that women should vote but also that they would make good politicians.) The new strategies certainly worked; press coverage of the Suffragettes' activity precipitated the issue of women's vote into the spotlight.

Along with the American Suffragettes, numerous other suffrage groups sprang up around and after 1910, many of them local and all of them in response to the NAWSA's inadequate representation and tactics. One group was founded in 1909 by the erstwhile leader of the NAWSA, Carrie Chapman Catt: the New York City Woman Suffrage Party (WSP). The WSP set out to convert as many voters as possible, hoping for a mass demand on legislators (as opposed to the NAWSA's strategy of aiming its efforts directly at lawmakers through petitions). Although more overtly political in recognizing and appealing to an enfranchised citizenry, the WSP still retained the noncoercive approach of the NAWSA along with its nonpartisanship. The WSP, however, made a concerted effort to reach beyond the middle classes, with strategies similar to those of the American Suffragettes—speaking campaigns, leaflet distributions, and outdoor meetings. Many of its pamphlets were published in Italian, Yiddish, Bohemian, and other languages in order to reach new immigrants.

"Organizing to Win by the Political District Plan" (1914), compiled by Harriet Laidlaw (active in the WSP from its beginning), develops the plan adopted by the Woman Suffrage Party and other similar organizations throughout the country. It is a highly systematic handbook on working at the state level, targeting candidates for and members of the state legislature to ensure that the suffrage amendment is offered to the voters as a referendum. The plan involves close work with legislators but also a massive campaign of propaganda at the grassroots level—ensuring, as Laidlaw puts it, that politicians in every assembly district "should be fully conscious that [votes for women] is the most agitated, the most vital question that they will hear from during the legislative session." Laidlaw's pamphlet includes a call for suffragists themselves to take courses in parliamentary law—and the document is interesting in its assumption that its readers know virtually nothing of the local political process (she outlines, for instance, the division of state legislatures into a senate or upper house and an assembly or lower house). Laidlaw's pamphlet illustrates, on every page, how women know little about politics, lawmaking, campaigning, and raising money; it also insists on the vital necessity that they learn. Laidlaw's handbook delineates what Conger-Kaneko had recognized—the need for suffragists to join with the cause of workers, especially working women. Although Laidlaw is wary of deflecting too much energy away from the vote, she sees it as inevitable that as women commit themselves to the kind of local activism she calls for, they will respond to the needs of the suffering women and children whom they meet.

Perhaps the most significant institutional development in the early-twentieth-century fight for the vote was the 1914 founding of the Congressional Union (CU). Two members of the NAWSA, Alice Paul and Lucy Burns, revived the NAWSA Congressional Committee and obtained permission to organize a suffrage parade to disrupt (successfully, it turned out) Woodrow Wilson's inauguration. The NAWSA leadership was unwilling to support what it considered to be objectionable partisan and militant tactics, so Paul and Burns established the CU as a separate organization, with *The Suffragist* as its official publication. In 1917 the CU became the National Woman's Party (NWP), but under both names it continued on a trajectory very different from that of the NAWSA. Unlike the latter organization, the CU/NWP de-emphasized educational strategies and did not believe in simply adding often inactive members to its roll. It saw itself as a small, disciplined army, each member of which engaged in very strict and defined tactics. The greatest strategic difference between the two groups was that the CU/NWP worked to pressure Congress to pass a federal amendment, while the NAWSA focused on securing amendments to state constitutions. Another dramatic point of divergence between these two central groups concerned their relation to party politics. The NAWSA was fervently nonpartisan, in large part because of a belief around the turn of the century that party politics were corrupt; the organization thus did not think of using the votes of enfranchised women as a weapon against any particularly uncooperative party. The CU/NWP, on the other hand, worked to defeat any candidates for political office who opposed suffrage. For instance, it opposed Democratic candidates for Congress in the 1914 elections and Woodrow Wilson's candidacy in the 1916 presidential election. Like the NAWSA, the CU/NWP did not support a certain party. It was simply intent on demonstrating to lawmakers and politicians that inaction on woman suffrage would cost them votes and elections—and since the Democrats were in power, it was the Democrats to whom the CU/NWP taught this lesson. A final distinct strategy of the CU/NWP was its decision to beg no longer for votes but to rely on the votes women already had to enfranchise other women. Its leader, Alice Paul, reasoned that since four million women in the western states would be voting in the 1916 presidential election, an effective strategy for gaining suffrage would be to influence the women's vote in such a way as to affect the outcome of that election. This was a profound step away from the long-standing practice of supplicating men for the vote.

"Proposed Plan of the Congressional Union" (1914) includes addresses from the new group's first convention, which was held in Newport. In her key speech, Alice Paul identifies the Democratic Party as "the enemy" and announces that the meetings at the conference will be geared specifically toward detailing the CU's plan of attack against this "enemy." She asks the press to leave and imposes silence on her members until September when the plan is to be set in motion: going to the nine states in which women already have the vote and appealing to them to use their combined four million votes to defeat Democratic candidates in the congressional elections. The rest of this document gives the responses of other CU members to this revolutionary proposal. Harriot Stanton Blatch, who had only just agreed to join the advisory council of the CU, gives her wholehearted support, saying she has finally realized that work for an amendment to the New York state constitution is not enough—that women need, as Paul urges, to work toward a federal suffrage amendment. She had resisted taking part in national affairs and regrets having to do it now, but sees that it is necessary. There is some initial hesitation by Florence Kelley and Mrs. Bayard Hilles ("a member of an old Democratic family"), who suggest that there may be places where Democratic candidates are friends to suffrage, or where they might support other issues important to women, but both are ultimately convinced by the clarity of Paul's call to arms. The conclusion is unavoidable, they admit: the Democratic Party is responsible for quashing the suffrage question in Congress. Showing the persistence of the CU's strategy, two years later when the presidential elections were looming, *The Suffragist,* edited by Lucy Burns, published an important argument for the Susan B. Anthony federal suffrage amendment. "The Susan B. Anthony Amendment" (1916) insists upon the practical difficulties involved in amending the constitution of each state and reiterates the unprecedented opportunity presented by the four million women who would be able to vote in the presidential elections. As in 1914, the CU/NWP called for the defeat of the Democratic Party (in this case Woodrow Wilson), as it was still preventing the suffrage amendment from reaching voters.

Among the ways in which the CU diverged from the NAWSA, its willingness to temporize in terms of racial equality was *not* one of them. In "National Suffrage and the Race Problem" (1914), the official publication of the newly formed CU printed an essay arguing for the federal suffrage amendment solely on the grounds that it would bolster white supremacy. A table carefully tabulates how the preponderance of white women in the South, who exceeded in numbers all African Americans, would ensure that whites could continue to control national and regional politics. It is clearly designed to allay fears that enfranchising women will "complicate" the "race problem" in the South by enfranchising more African Americans.

Suffrage leaders never faltered in their practice of racial segregation. In fact, women of color at suffrage conventions were less visible in the twentieth century than they had been in the nineteenth, when Sojourner Truth and many other prominent African American abolitionists spoke regularly at woman's rights conventions. When groups of African American suffragists petitioned for delegate status at national conventions, their requests were relentlessly denied. A telling incident occurred in 1917 when Ida Wells-Barnett tried to march with the Chicago contingent at a suffrage parade in Washington. She was told that white southern women would not agree to march in an integrated line and that she must walk with the other women of color. Wells-Barnett refused to be deprived of her rightful place and slipped in with the Chicago paraders from the sidewalk as they passed her by. In 1919 Carrie Chapman Catt would not grant the request of the Northeast Federation of Women's Clubs (a black organization) to become affiliated with the NAWSA because she felt the federal amendment could only pass with the support of southern states. Through its racism, the mainstream suffrage movement lost a valuable ally—as can be seen by the number of women who were among those participating in the forum on women's suffrage "Votes for Women" (1915) in the *Crisis,* a powerful black publication. The fact that such discussions among African Americans only took place in explicitly black media demonstrates the extent to which blacks were shut out of the pages of white journals (another example is Adella Hunt Logan's 1905 essay, which appeared in *Colored American Magazine*). The forum includes women who represent numerous professions, from teachers to housewives, along with most of the prominent black women's organizations, notably the powerful National Association of Colored Women. They give, of course, many of the same reasons for demanding the vote as white women—but also some that are specific to the situation of African American women: preserving racial purity (African and Anglo-Saxon), "ransoming" the vote that has been so misused by black men (under coercion from white men), and preserving their chastity against assaults by white men.

The new visibility of the emerging militant "suffragette" organizations, along with the movement's increasingly prominent alliances with working and immigrant women, spurred a correspondingly visible critique of the suffrage movement. In "The Threefold Menace" (1913), Alice Stone Blackwell, the recording secretary for the NAWSA for two decades, highlights—and dismisses—the three most common charges leveled at the movement: militancy, feminism, and socialism. In a way, there was truth to these "accusations"; all three do represent ways in which the suffrage movement had changed and revitalized in the early twentieth century. But there is not, Blackwell argues, truth to the unfavorable animus behind the charges. Blackwell relativizes the new "militancy" of the suffrage movement (which consisted primarily of aggressively distributing badges and stump speaking in public places) by talking about the very real violence directed at women by antisuffragists, including cans of explosives hurled into a meeting in Tennessee. Blackwell also discusses how "feminism" has been perverted by its critics into a strain of thought and practice purportedly interested in abolishing marriage, destroying the home, and bringing on a reign of immorality (sadly, this concerted misunderstanding of the meaning of feminism persisted throughout the twentieth century). In terms of the suffrage movement's supposed alliance with socialism—an allegation that contained some truth since most socialist political candidates supported votes for women—Blackwell makes the insightful point that most women were finally conservative (advocates of temperance, for instance), and in those states in which women were able to vote, the Socialist Party did not fare well. When women demand equal rights with men, Blackwell's defense makes it depressingly clear that they become allied in the public imagination with *any* ideas or movements that appear, to the majority of citizens, to augur the degradation of social order and morality.

Dissension about suffrage was not only external to the movement, of course, as the CU's break with the NAWSA in 1913 had proved. In 1916, however, shortly after Carrie Chapman Catt took over leadership of the NAWSA from Anna Howard Shaw, the organization redefined its policies and tactics, reconstituting itself nearer to the CU and the other more militant groups that had emerged in recent years. At a landmark NAWSA convention in Atlantic City in 1916, Carrie Chapman Catt told her listeners that "The Crisis" was at hand: the organization had become too complacent, too willing to wait for the inevitable day of suffrage rather than fighting for it. It is time, Catt announces, for the NAWSA to stop simply signing up members and educating the public; there are, she says, enough people who already believe in votes for women—but they are not *acting* on that belief, in part because the NAWSA itself has become disorganized, has lost cohesion, and is no longer providing a clear sense of mission for its members and other converts. Catt's sense of crisis was accurate. Not only had the NAWSA been challenged by Alice Paul and her followers but in 1915 the suffrage amendment had been defeated in referenda in four eastern states (New York, Pennsylvania, Massachusetts, and New Jersey). In the face of these defeats the NAWSA finally changed its tactics and its primary goal. Sounding just like Paul two years earlier, Catt said she wanted to redefine the NAWSA as an "army" that would no longer politely "request" the vote but would "DEMAND THE VOTE!" She also switched the trajectory of the NAWSA's priorities, which had from its inception focused more on amending state constitutions and which had recently insisted on "states' rights" to define the terms of women suffrage. Catt now declared that the organization would channel most of its effort into seeking a federal amendment.

Although there was after 1916 some rapprochement between the NAWSA and the CU/NWP, there was not complete agreement. In "My Position on the Different Policies of the National Association and the Congressional Union" (1916), former head of the NAWSA Anna Howard Shaw reiterates its long-standing refusal to countenance political partisanship. Among other questions she raises about the NWP's principal strategy, Shaw asks why it should work to defeat individual Democrats who may actually advocate woman suffrage simply because the Democratic Party as a whole has blocked the reform. And despite Catt's new rhetoric defining the NAWSA as an "army," Shaw, at least, still forswears "militant" strategies, arguing that being jailed and going on hunger strikes have done nothing to advance the cause of suffrage in England and would do nothing in the United States.

Despite the apparent convergence of the two most powerful suffrage organizations, their differences became dramatically apparent once again in 1917 when the United States entered World War I. In the long tradition of women's organizations during the Revolutionary War and the Civil War, the NAWSA put to one side its work for the vote and helped the government in the war effort. As described in "The NAWSA Faces World War I" (1917), Anna Howard Shaw became the chair of the Woman's Committee of the Council of National Defense, which was created by the government to direct the patriotic labors of women. Revealing the persistent class bias of the NAWSA, this document conveys and endorses the government's request that women express their patriotism not by working in war industries (which one million women did) but by knitting, conserving food and clothes, and providing "the enthusiasm, inspiration and patriotism to make men want to fight." Some irony does seem to seep into Shaw's instructions to NAWSA members, however, as she details how mothers must smile and keep a perfect calm even while sending their sons to war. Indeed, many key members of the NAWSA had been opposed to U.S. entry into the conflict. Catt, for instance, was one of the organizers of the Woman's Peace Party in 1915. In the end, though, faced with the fait accompli in 1917, most members of the NAWSA laid aside their reservations and put their wholehearted support behind the war. They followed the originators of their organization, Susan B. Anthony and Elizabeth Cady Stanton, who in 1863 had suspended annual woman's rights conventions during the Civil War and formed the Loyal League to support the Union army. While their support of Wilson's policies brought the NAWSA little power, it did, as historian Sara Evans puts it, allow them to claim "the mantle of patriotic citizenship."[2]

Even the NAWSA, though, did not lose the opportunity to point out the hypocrisy of the U.S. government's going to war, encouraging American men to face death for an ideal of democracy it was at the same time denying to half its citizens. Members of the more radical NWP, headed by Quaker Alice Paul, devoted the war years to pointing this out to President Woodrow Wilson by picketing the White House—even chaining themselves to its gates. NWP suffragists refused to take their place quietly and knit comfort bags for soldiers, and they were widely and vehemently attacked for their perceived lack of support for U.S. troops, creating a national scandal—a scandal that won the Nineteenth Amendment, at least according to the NWP. Reasons for suffrage militancy during the war are laid out in both "Excuses for White House Picketing" (1917) by Alva E. Vanderbilt Belmont

---

2. Sara Evans, *Born for Liberty: A History of Women in America* (New York: Free Press, 1989), 172.

(Mrs. O. H. P. Belmont) and "The Militant Campaign" (1919) by Doris Stevens. More than two decades earlier Belmont, the author of the earlier document, had received a large divorce settlement from her first husband, a Vanderbilt heir, and after her interests turned toward feminism she used a good share of her fortune to support militant suffragism. In her letter to the editor of *The New York Times,* Belmont implicitly criticizes the NAWSA's wartime policy: any woman should be ashamed if she gives up the demand for the vote when "the whole world is dying to possess this precious political freedom," she writes. In "The Militant Campaign," which appeared in both the *Omaha Daily News* and *The Suffragist,* Stevens for her part argues that women are just pursuing a typical military strategy in attacking their opponent's weakest point. She observes that the Democratic Party is most vulnerable in the hypocrisy of its "boasted crusade for world democracy"; she and other women are intent on demonstrating the error, even absurdity of this claim. During World War I, American suffragists began using for the first time the most militant of tactics imported from the English suffragettes; they not only waved banners outside the White House, they were jailed for it—and, once in jail, many went on hunger strikes and were force-fed. According to Stevens this escalation of militancy was neither planned nor willful, and she remarks how shocked the demonstrators were that the government actually jailed them simply for organizing peaceful protests outside the White House. Inez Haynes Irwin and Ada Davenport Kendall describe the terrible conditions they suffered in jail and at Occoquan Workhouse in "The Strange Ladies" (1921), taken from Irwin's book *The Story of the Woman's Party.* Publication of such accounts, describing the workhouse as "a place of chicanery, sinister horror, brutality, and dread," caused Woodrow Wilson's administration some unease—panic, says Stevens—as it was faced with around two hundred middle-class white women being viciously treated and starving in jail. According to Stevens, the embarrassed government tried to coerce the jailed suffragists, offering to release them on the condition of passing the federal amendment through one house, but not the other. The suffragists refused and were finally released unconditionally.

Despite the militants' cries of victory, the federal suffrage amendment that passed the House of Representatives in 1918 was defeated in the Senate. A year later a national amendment was finally secured by Congress, and it was ratified by the thirty-sixth state, Tennessee, in 1920. On August 26, 1920, the Nineteenth Amendment became part of the U.S. Constitution. As Charlotte Perkins Gilman puts it in her celebratory poem: "Women Are Free at Last in All the Land" (1920). Although there was certainly reason to celebrate—women *had* indeed won a crucial victory, arguably the most crucial single victory in the history of women's activism—Gilman's poem contains the recognition that there is still much to be done to turn lines now added to the Constitution into a practical reality (the rights granted African American men by the Fifteenth Amendment had, after all, been successfully stolen in the South). Gilman's poem indicates, for instance, that the victory is potentially only a symbolic one, as she imagines woman "crowned" with "full freedom," "Queen of her soul and body," standing beside her "brother." At the same time, Gilman raises in the poem the specter of women's unpaid labor in the home and poorly paid labor in the marketplace—oppressions that will not disappear just because women have been "crowned" as citizens.

Politically active women did not sit on their laurels for long. In 1920 the official journal of the NWP, *The Suffragist,* organized a forum entitled "What Next?" to which most of the prominent members of the organization contributed. At stake, among other things, was the very existence of the NWP: would it have a role now that its primary aim, its coalescing mandate, had been won? The answer is a resounding yes—as each woman, perhaps somewhat wearily, comes to recognize what still needs to be accomplished. Harriot Stanton Blatch perfectly frames it: "In winning the vote all was not won. Indeed the ballot is but a tool in the hands of women for the winning of realities." The contributors almost unanimously agree that the NWP must remain, to provide a separate, nonpartisan organization devoted to promoting women candidates for office and issues of vital importance to women: among those issues are the worldwide enfranchisement of women, equality in industry and the professions, and (in Mary White Ovington's lone voice) the practical enfranchisement of black as well as white women. The forum anticipates what has generally been considered the splintering of women's activism after 1920, as it reveals the divergent paths former suffragists would take: agitating for the demise of industrial capitalism, for the rights of African Americans, for the election of women to political office, for powerful labor interests and trade unions, for international freedom for women, and for legal and social reform in the United States. This country would never again see women activists rallying in such a united way around a lone cause as it did in the first two decades of the twentieth century. Although coherence and singleness of purpose were lost, women's activism did not die (as is commonly concluded): it simply dispersed.

30
Carrie Chapman Catt, Anna Howard Shaw, Alice Stone Blackwell, and Ida Husted Harper
NAWSA Declaration of Principles (1904)

When our forefathers gained the victory in a seven years' war to establish the principle that representation should go hand in hand with taxation, they marked a new epoch in the history of man; but though our foremothers bore an equal part in that long conflict its triumph brought to them no added rights and through all the following century and a quarter, taxation without representation has been continuously imposed on women by as great tyranny as King George exercised over the American colonists.

So long as no married woman was permitted to own property and all women were barred from the money-making occupations this discrimination did not seem so invidious; but to-day the situation is without a parallel. The women of the United States now pay taxes on real and personal estate valued at billions of dollars. In a number of individual States their holdings amount to many millions. Everywhere they are accumulating property. In hundreds of places they form one-third of the taxpayers, with the number constantly increasing, and yet they are absolutely without representation in the affairs of the nation, of the State, even of the community in which they live and pay taxes. We enter our protest against this injustice and we demand that the immortal principles established by the War of the Revolution shall be applied equally to women and men citizens.

As our new republic passed into a higher stage of development the gross inequality became apparent of giving representation to capital and denying it to labor; therefore the right of suffrage was extended to the workingman. Now we demand for the 4,000,000 wage-earning women of our country the same protection of the ballot as is possessed by the wage-earning men.

The founders took an even broader view of human rights when they declared that government could justly derive its powers only from the consent of the governed, and for 125 years this grand assertion was regarded as a cornerstone of the republic, with scarcely a recognition of the fact that one-half of the citizens were as completely governed without their consent as were the people of any absolute monarchy in existence. It was only when our government was extended over alien races in foreign countries that our people awoke to the meaning of the principles of the Declaration of Independence. In response to its provisions, the Congress of the United States hastened to invest with the power of consent the men of this new territory, but committed the flagrant injustice of withholding it from the women. We demand that the ballot shall be extended to the women of our foreign possessions on the same terms as to the men. Furthermore, we demand that the women of the United States shall no longer suffer the degradation of being held not so competent to exercise the suffrage as a Filipino, a Hawaiian or a Porto Rican man.

The remaining Territories within the United States are insisting upon admission into the Union on the ground that their citizens desire "the right to select their own governing officials, choose their own judges, name those who are to make their laws and levy, collect, and disburse their taxes." These are just and commendable desires but we demand that their women shall have full recognition as citizens when these Territories are admitted and that their constitutions shall secure to women precisely the same rights as to men.

When our government was founded the rudiments of education were thought suffi-

From Ida Husted Harper, ed., *History of Woman Suffrage*, vol. 5 (New York: J. J. Little and Ives, 1922), 742–43.

cient for women, since their entire time was absorbed in the multitude of household duties. Now the number of girls graduated by the high schools greatly exceeds the number of boys in every State and the percentage of women students in the colleges is vastly larger than that of men. Meantime most of the domestic industries have been taken from the home to the factory and hundreds of thousands of women have followed them there, while the more highly trained have entered the professions and other avenues of skilled labor. We demand that under this new régime, and in view of these changed conditions in which she is so important a factor woman shall have a voice and a vote in the solution of their innumerable problems.

The laws of practically every State provide that the husband shall select the place of residence for the family, and if the wife refuses to abide by his choice she forfeits her right to support and her refusal shall be regarded as desertion. We protest against the recent decision of the courts which has added to this injustice by requiring the wife also to accept for herself the citizenship preferred by her husband, thus compelling a woman born in the United States to lose her nationality if her husband choose to declare his allegiance to a foreign country.

As women form two-thirds of the church membership of the entire nation; as they constitute but one-eleventh of the convicted criminals; as they are rapidly becoming the educated class and as the salvation of our government depends upon a moral, law-abiding, educated electorate, we demand for the sake of its integrity and permanence that women be made a part of its voting body.

In brief, we demand that all constitutional and legal barriers shall be removed which deny to women any individual right or personal freedom which is granted to man. This we ask in the name of a democratic and a republican government, which, its constitution declares, was formed "to establish justice and secure the blessings of liberty."

31
CATHARINE WAUGH McCULLOCH
The Protective Value of the Ballot (1900)

What do the people and nations of the age seek? Why do individuals labor and strive? For what do nations battle and seize territory and seek spheres of influence? The savage Filipino, the desperate Slav, the rough Boer, the strenuous Anglo-Saxon, for what do they all struggle? Freedom, opportunity, power.

To-day none is too degraded, savage or mean to feel within his breast the desire for liberty, independence, and improved conditions. Life itself is sacrificed in the struggle. Many precious lives are counted none too great a price for the people's liberty. Even against the greatest odds, sometimes in face of almost certain defeat, goes on the struggle for independence and equality. To the one vanquished in such a fight we give the laurel wreath. Far nobler to have struggled and died opposing tyranny than to have lived at ease a dependent, a subject.

The spirit of struggle against oppression and dependence is in the air, and all have breathed it in, women as well as men. The red corpuscles of the blood have been transmitted to daughters as well as sons. If women to-day did not feel this spirit of ambition, this thrill of aspiration, they would prove themselves untrue members of the race, of some other blood unrelated to humanity. But women are human. They are not only wives, mothers, sisters, and daughters, but are a portion of humanity. They, too, feel the desire for freedom, opportunity, progress; the wish for liberty, a share in government, emancipation.

The practical method by which these aspirations can be realized is through the ballot. The ballot to-day represents all for which this

From *Woman's Journal*, February 24, 1900.

great world-struggle is being carried on. It is the insignia of power. The Outlander wants it, so does the Filipino, the Slav, the Cuban. So do women.

Women need the ballot, not only for the honor of being esteemed free women among their peers, but for the practical value it will be to them in protecting them in the exercise of a citizen's prerogatives. This is perhaps a selfish view. It might be more lofty and unselfish to desire to benefit others, the nation, the world, through women's ballots, but still the protection of women themselves is of considerable importance. Women need protection of life, liberty, property. They want protection in securing educational advantages, in entering remunerative employments, in obtaining fair wages for work, protection for the safety of their persons from assault and disease, protection for their property from unjust seizure, unfair taxation, and outside encroachments. They want protection in the discharge of wifely duties and motherly cares. They want protection for the home and for the little ones for whose sakes they have imperiled their own lives.

But, it is asked, have not women had some sort of protection, without the ballot? Yes, but it has been only such protection as the caprice or affection of the voting class has given,—mere gratuities, revocable at will. The man of wealth or power defended his wife, daughter, or sweetheart because she was his, just as he would have defended his property. His own opinions, not her views, decided him concerning the things from which she should be protected. Should she ever have needed protection against her "protector," there was no one to give it. She had as much protection as other non-voting classes, who must always acquiesce and never demand. . . .

In seeking punishment of such crimes, which are always of a man against a woman, we may see the disadvantage under which women labor when they want legal protection. When a woman resorts to the court, the judge, the jury, the clerks, the bailiffs, are all men, elected by men or appointed by men, liable to look at each point from the man side. If she receives justice, great and lofty must be the spirit of those law enforcers, for it would not be unnatural if they should have been prejudiced against her, and not improbable that the side of the voters who were in the case would have been the more powerful. But should a judge continue to be fair to women, parties in actions, it would not be an impossible thing for his supporters, the voters, to serve notice on him that he was elected by them and should not decide against them. Of course, one or two isolated cases might make no great difference, but suppose all the women had a good cause of action against all the men, and a judge elected by men voters only, with a jury selected from these same men, tried the case. Even if the women were right, they would not win. The full influence of the ballot in securing protection would there appear. In the case of one woman against one man, as would generally be the fact in such legal procedure, a proportionate amount of influence would be felt. The power of the ballot to influence the judiciary must be admitted, especially where judges are elected.

As to women's personal liberty, it is protected in a general way, and yet not always from a woman's husband. There are decisions on the records sustaining a husband in restraining a wife's liberty, if he desired her not to go visiting, or if he wanted to prevent her from spending money, or going to church. But few husbands would need such harsh measures to keep them from church.

The husband's right to choose the family home, whither the wife must follow or be left out in the cold and be adjudged guilty of deserting him, is another violation of the wife's personal liberty.

But the ownership by the husband of the family pocket-book is a certain method of restraining a wife's liberty of movement, for street cars and railroad trains carry no passengers without fares. So, unless the wife is a good pedestrian, the withholding from her of money restrains her liberty. She who gives her life and strength to family cares should be protected in her right to use some portion of family money. If women voted, they would certainly be assured of some share in family funds.

Women need protection from disease, and yet that is largely a matter of enforcement of law. Women generally desire this protection. A recent instance of women's interest in warding off disease occurred in New Orleans, where many women came forward to vote for a better system of sewers. The women property owners were generally for the new method of sanitation, and with the men voters of similar views, they made a majority. Women rejoiced and thought they had succeeded. But at the election of councilmen, for whom women had no votes, members were elected who had no sympathy with the new plans, and so the women's great efforts in behalf of sanitation were almost useless. Without the ballot for officers, their wishes were not mandatory and had no influence.

Women's education is not receiving attention in many public and private schools. But the majority of our schools are public schools, regulated by the voters, through elected officials. The great common school system of this country rests on voters. The increasingly valuable State University and Normal schools rest also on voters. Admission to these schools is regulated by laws framed by people elected by voters. The money to run these schools is collected and expended by other officials elected by voters. The subjects taught are decided by the representatives of voters. Women have now no assurance of continued entrance to these schools, desirable curricula or wise expenditure of the tax money except through man's gratuity. To protect women in their aspiration for school privileges, nothing but the ballot is sufficient.

Concerning entrance into remunerative employments, that in many instances has been denied women. In many of the States the professions of law, medicine, dentistry and all elective offices were closed by law. Even appointive positions, which women might legally hold, were practically closed to women because of their lack of the ballot. The appointing power, president, governor, mayor, judge, or commissioner, all owed their own positions to voters, who expected some minor appointment in acknowledgment of service. Sometimes the appointing power found himself with less places at hand than he had given promises. His task then was to invent new places, or evade civil service laws to supply all his supporters, or else he must forget his promises. It can scarcely be expected, then, if he desired reëlection, that he would give any of these places to women who could not vote for him. . . .

At a caucus, a street parade, and on election day, the 500, or 10,000, or 100,000 persons employed in a certain industry make a considerable political showing, if they are all voters. In a street parade, it is not the floats filled with pretty girls, but the rows of sturdy men, trudging steadily forward, even without flowers or tarleton or smiles or frizzes, who count. We look on them, remembering their voting power, and feel that they are *the* procession. On such occasions women employees are of little value.

When some pretty factory girls once went to Washington beseeching increased tariffs, their influence was infinitesimal. Their visit was of no value except to make a news item. A similar delegation of men might not have looked as sweet, but they, being voters, could have accomplished more. So when a great corporation considers its occasional need of votes, it employs few women.

Women refused employment in such enterprises are injured not in their feelings, their pride, but in the matter of bread and butter. Women are not protected in their right to earn bread and butter.

But there are many different kinds of employment which do not debar women, and in these, women need protection in securing a fair return for their labor. This is no more than men workers ask, and it should be granted. But one peculiar thing appears in examining the schedules of wages for men and women,—men's wages are higher. For instance, in Massachusetts 78 per cent. of the females employed received less than $1.00 per day, while only 30 per cent. of the males received such low wages. This would not be unjust if men always did harder work or better work. But men as a rule receive higher wages, even in cases where their work is not more difficult and not more carefully done.

In an investigation conducted by the United States Department of Labor, concerning the wages received by men, women, and children, it appeared that in 75 per cent. of the 782 instances investigated, men received 50 per cent. higher wages than did women laboring with the same degree of efficiency on the same sort of work. This is not an isolated case of inequality, but averages of all; and it is a question of serious importance to women why their wages are so low. It is a question of even greater importance how these wages can be made higher. Dollars mean more than pride in good service. They mean relief from hunger, thirst, cold; they mean freedom to be good.

Women need special and peculiar factory legislation for their protection from long hours and insanitary conditions. Women inspectors are needed; but only six States recognize this necessity, for women do not vote. Women wage-workers need the ballot to secure proper protection. . . .

But, while the wage-earning women need protection, the nineteen millions of home women who work for their own families need even more legal attention for they have no wages. Wages, even low wages, are somewhat of a protection. Some plan would speedily be devised whereby home workers would be justly recompensed, if women voted. . . .

Should carpenters, engineers, lawyers, want protection for such varied purposes, or for any one purpose, on what would they depend? Upon their right to vote; and this right to vote would often cause their needs to be anticipated, and their requests granted even before spoken. They would never trust their own protection to those whose interests were different and possibly antagonistic. They would prefer the ballot to protect themselves.

The thousands of illiterate and degraded, who are seen crowding about the judges, seeking naturalization, are they anxious whether the party of Thomas Jefferson or Abraham Lincoln wins? Do they worry about the gold standard, or single tax? Are they naturalized for the purpose of saving the nation? They seek this honor because they want the nation to save them from ignorance, poverty, misery. They want to protect themselves by the governmental weapon of protection—the ballot.

A king, a leisure class cannot or will not plan for them the best government. This is the governmental question of the ages, and in this country it has been decided that no man should rule another. One class cannot, will not legislate better for all than all for all. So men alone cannot legislate better for women and men than can men and women together for men and women both.

Women need the ballot to protect themselves and all that they hold dear.

32
Belle Kearney, Mary Wood Swift, Charlotte Perkins Gilman, Hala Hammond Butt, and Carrie Chapman Catt
The South, Suffrage, and the Educational Requirement (1903)

MISS BELLE KEARNEY

. . . To-day one third of the population of the South is of the negro race, and there are more negroes in the United States than there are inhabitants in "Mexico, the third Republic of the world." In some Southern States the negroes far outnumber the whites, and are so nu-

From *Woman's Journal,* April 4, 1903. (Excerpts from speeches presented at the 1903 NAWSA Convention in New Orleans.)

merous in all of them as to constitute what is called a "problem." Until the present generation, they have always lived here as slaves.

The race question is national in its bearing. Still, as the South has the bulk of the negro population, the burden of the responsibility for the negro problem rests here.

The world is scarcely beginning to realize the enormity of the situation that faces the South in its grapple with the race question which was thrust upon it at the close of the Civil War, when 4,500,000 ex-slaves, illiterate and semi-barbarous, were enfranchised. Such a situation has no parallel in history. In forging a path out of the darkness, there were no precedents to lead the way. All that has been and is being accomplished is pioneer statecraft. The South has struggled under its death-weight for nearly forty years, bravely and magnanimously.

The Southern States are making a desperate effort to maintain the political supremacy of Anglo-Saxonism by amendments to their constitutions limiting the right to vote by a property and educational qualification. If the United States government had been wise enough to enact such a law when the negro was first enfranchised, it would have saved years of bloodshed in the South, and such experiences of suffering and horror among the white people here as no other were ever subjected to in an enlightened nation.

The present suffrage laws in the different Southern States can be only temporary measures for protection. Those who are wise enough to look beneath the surface will be compelled to realize the fact that they act as a stimulus to the black man to acquire both education and property, but no incentive is given to the poor whites; for it is understood, in a general way, that any man whose skin is fair enough to let the blue veins show through, may be allowed the right of franchise.

The industrial education that the negro is receiving at Tuskegee and other schools is only fitting him for power, and when the black man becomes necessary to a community by reason of his skill and acquired wealth, and the poor white man, embittered by his poverty and humiliated by his inferiority, finds no place for himself or his children, then will come the grapple between the races.

To avoid this unspeakable culmination, the enfranchisement of women will have to be effected, and an educational and property qualification for the ballot be made to apply, without discrimination, to both sexes and to both races. It will spur the poor white to keep up with the march of progression, and enable him to hold his own. The class that is not willing to measure its strength with that of an inferior is not fit to survive.

The enfranchisement of women would insure immediate and durable white supremacy, honestly attained; for, upon unquestionable authority, it is stated that "In every Southern State but one, there are more educated women than all the illiterate voters, white and black, native and foreign, combined." As you probably know, of all the women in the South who can read and write, ten out of every eleven are white. When it comes to the proportion of property between the races, that of the white outweighs that of the black immeasurably. The South is slow to grasp the great fact that the enfranchisement of women would settle the race question in politics.

The civilization of the North is threatened by the influx of foreigners with their imported customs; by the greed of monopolistic wealth, and the unrest among the working classes; by the strength of the liquor traffic, and by encroachments upon religious belief.

Some day the North will be compelled to look to the South for redemption from these evils, on account of the the purity of its Anglo-Saxon blood, the simplicity of its social and economic structure, the great advance in prohibitory law, and the maintenance of the sanctity of its faith, which has been kept inviolate. Just as surely as the North will be forced to turn to the South for the nation's salvation, just so surely will the South be compelled to look to its Anglo-Saxon women as the medium through which to retain the supremacy of the white race over the African.

I have heard it said in the South, "Oh, well, suffrage may be a very good thing for women in other sections of the United States, but not here. Our women are different." How are they unlike those of their own sex elsewhere? They are certainly as intelligent as any upon the face of the earth; they have the same deep love for the home, the same devotion to their country.

"Oh, yes; but, you see, if the white women were allowed to vote, the negro women would have the same privilege, and that would mean the humiliation of having to meet them at the polls on a basis of equality."

That difficulty would be settled by having separate polling places. When the ballot is given to the women of the South, you will find that these distinct voting precincts for the two races will be quickly established.

It is useless for me to attempt, at this late day, to refute the objections raised against woman suffrage, for every obstacle to its progress has been met years ago, and every argument for its existence justified. It is no longer a question of right with the people, for that old battle has been fought; it is now only one of expediency, and opposition by prejudice. . . .

The South, which has wrought so splendidly in the past, surely will measure up to its responsibility in taking the forward step of woman's enfranchisement in order to render justice to its own firesides and to fix the status of the white race for future years.

Anglo Saxonism is the standard of the ages to come. It is, above all else, the granite foundation of the South. Upon that its civilization will mount; upon that it will stand unshaken.

The white people of the North and South are children of the same heroic souls who laid the foundations of civil and religious liberty in this new world, and built thereon this great Republic. We call to you, men and women, across that invisible line that divides the sections, across the passage of deathless years, to unite with us in holding this mighty country safe for the habitation of the Anglo-Saxon.

Thank God the black man was freed! I wish for him all possible happiness and all possible progress, but not in encroachments upon the holy of holies of the Anglo-Saxon race.

The Old South, with its romantic ideals, its grace, its sorrow, has passed into history. Upon the ashes of its desolation has arisen a New South, strong and beautiful, full of majesty and of power. The ambition of the Old was for States' rights, for local supremacy; that of the New is for a limitless sweep of vision, and with the elixir in its veins of an intense patriotic enthusiasm. The destiny of the South is the destiny of the Republic. It will eventually become totally merged in the being of our imperial nation.

Even now, as dearly as I love my people, sacred as I hold their traditions, loyal as I am to their interests, I say with infinitely less pride that I am a Southern woman than that I am an American.

Our sectionalism must broaden without reservation into nationalism that means sovereignty, and that points to immortality.

One of the most interesting features of the recent National Suffrage Convention at New Orleans was the symposium on the last afternoon on the question, "Would an educational qualification for all voters tend to the growth of civilization and facilitate good government?"

Mrs. Pricilla D. Hackstaff made the opening address. It was published last week. Mrs. Eleanor C. Stockman of Iowa spoke on "Suffrage a human right, not a privilege," and Mrs. Mary Wood Swift of California on "Abolishment of illiteracy, its ultimate influence."

MRS. SWIFT'S ADDRESS

There will not be opportunity, in the ten minutes allotted, to set forth the advantages of education. Indeed, these are so universally recognized that this would be superfluous. There is no nation of the world that can even approximate the United States in the general education of the masses of its people, and it is not necessary to seek further for the reason why this comparatively new country has distanced all others in its achievements. . . .

And yet, with all this splendid showing, there were at the last national election 2,800,000 voters who could not read their ballots! At first thought this seems a most discouraging result of an immense expenditure of time and money, but the root of the matter is not far to seek. It lies in immigration. If this tremendous tide were checked, we might hope in time for an educated people, at least in most sections of the country; but with the pouring in of over half a million persons every year, all of whom are totally ignorant of our language, and a majority of whom can not read and write their own, the prospect is hopeless. Last year, the immigration was 20 per cent. higher than the year before, 648,743. More than one-third of it came from the lower classes of Italy, and over four-fifths from those of Turkey, Austria, Roumania, Russia, Bulgaria, Greece, Spain and Portugal. Of the Syrians, 62 per cent., and of the Italians, 55 per cent. of the adults, could not read their own language. Yet in spite of this terrible showing, the Congress just adjourned struck out the educational clause in its act to further regulate immigration.

The most dangerous feature of the situation is that these male immigrants, who comprise nearly two-thirds of the whole number, march almost directly from the steerage to the polls. Although the laws of the United States require a residence of five years before a naturalized citizen shall become a voter, these are directly nullified by the statutes of various States, which allow a man to vote on his "first papers," after a residence of from six months to a year. In order still further to protect him in his ignorance, many States provide that where a voter cannot mark his ballot, an "assistant" may go with him into the booth. Thus, where a vote has been bought, the agent can see the goods delivered.

To add further to the ignorant vote, the Government enfranchises every Indian who can be persuaded to abandon his blanket and moccasins, and many who cannot. We had the testimony of a Government agent just before the last presidential election that, after expending months of labor and hundreds of thousands of dollars, the vast majority of the Indians who would vote in November had scarcely a conception of what a ballot meant.

All this great mass of ignorance goes into the electoral hopper, and the marvel is that no worse quality of grist is turned out. It is true that the chief political schemers are by no means illiterate, but it is upon illiteracy in the mass that they must depend, to carry out their plans. An ignorant voter may be an honest one, but unless he is intelligent enough to study public questions for himself, he is an easy prey for the political sharper. It is beyond the power of the pen to portray what a magnificent government would be possible with an educated electorate. The idea can be approximated only when we consider how much we have been able to accomplish, even with all the inefficiency, vice and ignorance which are permitted to express their will at the polls.

It is because we have a noble ideal for the future of our government that we make our demand for women suffrage. We point to the official statistics for proof that there are more white women in the United States than colored men and women together; that there are more American-born women than foreign-born men and women combined; that women form only one-eleventh of the criminals in the jails and penitentiaries; that they compose more than two-thirds of the church membership; and that the percentage of illiteracy is very much less among women than among men. Therefore we urge that this large proportion of patriotism, temperance, morality, religion and intelligence may be allowed to impress itself upon the government through the medium of the ballot box.

MRS. GILMAN'S SPEECH

Mrs. Charlotte Perkins Gilman said in part:
"I think I stand almost alone in this convention in my disbelief in an educational qualification. We look upon government as something above us, a dominating power, and we naturally dislike to put above us those whom

we regard as below us. It is against this view of government that I wish to speak.

"The illiterate English sailors shipwrecked on uninhabited Norfolk Island had to organize some sort of a government for themselves. Would it have been best for them to revert to outworn forms, and set up a despotism—a patriarchate, or a matriarchate? Would they not have been better off for adopting the most improved modern kind of government?

"I speak as a resident of New York City, where the people to whose voting objection is made are mostly the foreigners. In California it was the Chinese, and here I suppose it is the colored folk. We have a great dread of being ruled by an alien or illiterate vote. But when did poor and illiterate people ever introduce a bad law? The people who manipulate the ignorant vote are very smart, and it is they who are dangerous. 'Yes,' you may say, 'but the harm that they do is done by means of the venal vote.' It is a mistake to think that the venal vote is all foreign or illiterate. The Connecticut farmer, the Massachusetts man, the church member, who ought to know better, sell votes. The question is, is it good to have this large, undigested mass in our midst? Contact makes the effect of one soul on another inexorable. If you have among you a mass of ignorant, superstitious, immoral people, it is sure to injure you. To prevent it, you must raise all your people. Will exclusion from suffrage educate them more quickly than the use of it? We shall educate them faster if we value and dread their votes. Whenever you speak of suffrage as a privilege and also as a duty, remember that this is our common work and not some heavenly blessing sifted down on us from above. I think it is true of every alien and ignorant class, and also of the disfranchised class to which I and most of those present belong."

MRS. BUTT'S ADDRESS

Mrs. Hala Hammond Butt, president of Mississippi, spoke on "Restricted suffrage from a Southern point of view." She said in part: . . .

"Did women not share with men this craving for freedom, then would they justly be reckoned as unnatural and unworthy members of the human family. But the same red blood pulses in our veins as in yours, fathers, sons, brothers; we are alive to the same impulses, our souls are kindled by the same aspirations as are yours. Why should this, our ambition, be held in leash by the same bond that binds the ignorant, the illiterate, the vicious, the irresponsible, in the human economy? What does the idea of government imply? The crystallized sentiments of an intelligent people? Then do we meet it with but half a truth. No stream ever rises higher than its source; no people is loftier than its ideal, either in statesmanship, literature, science, arts or government. The strength of the concrete body is commensurate with the value of its individual entities. This is one of the strongest arguments that can be advanced in behalf of an educated suffrage. If the ballot means power—and who will gainsay it?—an intelligent ballot means a power intensified by all those forces tending to conserve, to unify, to amplify, and to create. If government means the voice of the people, a government created by intelligent suffrage means the voice of reason, the voice of wisdom, the voice of justice. The various forms of suffrage of which we know to-day have but the one element in common, and that the idea that the functions of the ballot are exclusively masculine. The modifications that suffrage has undergone in various sections, while tending toward a broader conception of government, but emphasize the truth of this assertion. In its original state, even the constitutional conception is of masculine construction; the logical outcome of the prevalent masculine authority, and fortified by the primitive theory of physical superiority.

"But as a nation, we have cast off our swaddling clothes. The milk of babes is no longer our sufficient nourishment—we demand the meat of maturity. We are no longer governmentally, in an experimental stage. We are no longer confronted with the tomahawk, the scalping knife, or a savage horde of untried theories—we are men and women in a world of actual conditions, and conditions that in their equal insistence demand our equal and united consideration.

"We of the South occupy a unique position in the consideration of this question of an educated suffrage, by reason of conditions that do not exist in any other section of country. To the uninitiated, this condition as a whole is the logical fruit of broken faith and violated principle. To us who recognize, as can no other, its baleful and far-reaching influence in the illimitable evils that it has fathered in our social and political economy, it is as the monstrous offspring of Frankenstein's unwise and impious ambition—this product of the fourteenth and fifteenth amendments. But the organic principles embodied in these amendments cannot here and now be considered. It is only in relation to our Southern policies that we shall touch them in passing.

"Anglo-Saxon blood has about the same characteristics, happily, in all climates. The desire for supremacy seems from time immemorial to have been its ruling passion. As the wish is father to the thought, so thought, other things being equal, precedes action. A restricted or qualified suffrage is the South's practical expression of this inborn desire for white supremacy.

"By the restrictive educational qualifications now so generally adopted in our Southern States, the spirit of these amendments has practically been set at naught, and white domination assured. It is well to note in this connection that, as a vehicle for the furtherance of political policies antagonistic to its spirit and undreamt of by its authors, this fifteenth amendment is without a parallel. It has been wheedled, coaxed and cajoled into more inconsistencies, into more paradoxical constructions, than any other legislative enactment that the world has ever known. This 'educational qualification' that obtains with us, however, was born of the instinct of self-preservation. Yet to say that it, too, is an avenue for fraud and political chicanery; that it is the most pliable and elastic of tools in the hands of the self seeker and unscrupulous politician, is to enunciate no new truth to those of you who have followed the political fortunes of the South for the past few years. While not violative of the letter of the law, it clearly lynches it in spirit; and out of its inconsistency is evolved an endless train of race conflicts, labor problems, political intrigues, force bills, Crumpacker resolutions and sectional animosities, intensified by the consciousness of wrong and injustice on either side. Just so long, then, as this so-called restrictive 'educational qualification' prevails, a qualification so sadly disproportionate in its results to the intelligence of the South, so long will there rise up to vex and disquiet the ominous specter of a reduced representation, of a force bill, of post offices arbitrarily suspended, of race riots incited by the fanaticism of Northern political leaders, and all the endless category of imbroglios incident to stubborn passion and irreconcilable conviction, 'To test the constitutionality of such restriction' was the battle cry of a recent New York gathering; nor will there be lacking those to supply the sinews of war.

"Oh, men and women of the South, is this the honorable solution of this question? Must white supremacy be assured only by such questionable methods as these, inciting and intensifying the evils most to be avoided? Is sex so mean a setting for intelligence that intelligence itself is thereby set at naught? That there is a consciousness in the minds of our law makers, not only of injustice to the intelligent womanhood of the South, but of the inadequacy, from a moral point of view, the inexpediency, from a practical standpoint, of the present method of eliminating an objectionable factor from politics, is apparent to the most casual observer. Like an accusing conscience, this question of the enfranchisement of women, in some form or other persistently obtrudes itself.

"Thirteen years ago it was seriously considered in Mississippi, in connection with the race question, not as a matter of abstract justice, but as an expedient. Tennessee, Alabama, Virginia, and your own State of Louisiana have each been brought face to face with it in its various modifications—and withal it does seem that it is a question susceptible of more modifications in reluctant and unwilling minds than even the fifteenth amendment. There is an undercurrent of thought that recognizes in its true proportions, however, the value of an educated suffrage to the South; a restriction based not upon color, race, or previous condition of servitude, not upon sex, not upon the question of taxable property, but its sole requirement—the ability to perform worthily the functions of citizenship. This is the only honorable solution of those questions that are vexing not only the body political, but the body social of this Southern country. Give us the power of organized intelligence, and we will put to rout the scarecrows of partisan threats and intimidation. We will add our strength to your strength, our patriotism to yours, until the makeshifts and subterfuges that characterize our methods of attaining the ends desired are supplanted by the consciousness of an impregnable position gained, not at a sacrifice of truth and honor, but by a recognition of the just demands of a cultured and capable womanhood. Too long already have we of the South—beloved South—compromised with right. We deceive neither ourselves nor the outside world. There is not a man of conscience, of reasoning ability, or even of ordinary political acumen, who does not believe that with the growth of intelligence grows the demand for its embodiment in governmental function. The recognition of the woman-citizen in such functions is the logical fruit of the race's progress. This denied, Nature herself is thwarted, and humanity pays the penalty.

"To see 'the good and the beautiful,' with no power to live it; to glimpse the larger liberty that comes with unhindered growth; to feel the strength that springs from knowledge, the sympathy that springs from strength, and yet, with Moses on the Mountain of Nebo, to know it only as the 'unattainable,' the land at your feet and no power to enter—this is the logic of the woman question to-day."

MRS. CATT'S ADDRESS

Since Miss Kearney has said so many good things about her section, I hope I shall be excused for boasting a little about mine. We admit the early preëminence of the South in the history of our country; but I as a Western woman shall not admit its preëminence now, until Southern men take the same advance step that the men of Colorado and Wyoming have taken, and give the ballot to their women.

We are all of us apt to be arrogant on the score of our Anglo-Saxon blood; but we must remember that ages ago the ancestors of the Anglo-Saxons were regarded as so low and embruted that the Romans refused to have them for slaves. The Anglo-Saxon is the dominant race to-day, but things may change. The race that will be dominant through the ages will be the one that proves itself the most worthy.

Almost every day questions are sent up here as to our position on the race question. The woman question, as such, has nothing to do with the Negro question. Here is a letter just sent up by a New Orleans woman: "We are afraid, if we come into your Association, that colored clubs may some day be let in, and that we shall find ourselves obliged to meet colored women on a footing of equality." I think I have heard that the South believes in State rights. The National American W. S. A. recognizes them. Louisiana has the right to regulate the conditions of membership for Louisiana; it has not the right to regulate them for Massachusetts, nor has Massachusetts for Louisiana. It is perfectly safe for you to come in on that basis.

Miss Kearney is right in saying that the race problem is the problem of the whole country, and not that of the South alone. The responsibility for it is partly ours. But if the North shipped slaves to the south and sold them, remember that the North has sent some money since then into the South to help undo part of the wrong that we did to you and to them. Let us try to get nearer together, and to understand each other's ideas on the race question, and let us try to solve it together.

33
ADELLA HUNT LOGAN
Woman Suffrage (1905)

LIFE MEMBER NATIONAL AMERICAN WOMAN SUFFRAGE ASSOCIATION

After more than thirty years of trial some statesmen, real and pseudo, have concluded that the Fourteenth Amendment to the National Constitution was a mistake. It is not the purpose of this brief paper to discuss that opinion nor to pass judgment on the validity or wisdom of any of the new state constitutions which have in their own ways restricted manhood suffrage. It is the purpose of this article to direct thought to the justice and desirability of placing the ballot in the hands of the other half of the American people, their women citizens. Government of the people, for the people and by the people is but partially realized so long as woman has no vote.

"All persons born or naturalized in the United States and subject to the jurisdiction thereof, are citizens of the United States and of the states in which they reside." In the ordinary affairs of life women are regarded as persons. Why not treat them as such in questions of government? No, they are classed with minors, idiots and paupers.

It is a good plan to read the Declaration of Independence and the National Constitution at least once a year. It is helpful to one's political thought and strengthening to one's patriotism. In the Declaration of Independence we read, "All governments derive their just powers from the consent of the governed. Taxation without representation is tyranny." Men generally still accept these teachings as fundamental principles of republican government. Do they in practice live out such theories? Not all of them. Let a woman violate the law, her sex in no measure annuls the law's grip on her or stays the sentence of punishment for her crime. She is punished by man-made laws. She is governed by laws to which her consent has not been asked, much less given. The doctrine is not wrong; the classification is correct. Woman is a governed being. It must be there is abuse of the doctrine, "All governments derive their just powers from the consent of the governed." The power that coerces, that controls without consent, is unjust. Such is the status of most American women. "Taxation without representation is tyranny," is a principle sufficiently strong to have called into being one of the most powerful nations on the globe. In the cool light of justice, as they then viewed it, the oppression of taxation without representation justified the Revolutionary War and its outcome was welcomed by liberty loving men the world over. Strange to say, it seems exceedingly difficult for this liberty-loving people to apply their love of fair play to women.

Women are assessed and required by male officers to appear and pay their taxes, but when any question of appropriation of tax monies comes to a vote, they are told in most places by these same officers and other good men, that it is immodest for women to be seen in public places and bent on helping to run the government. Every man who thinks knows that every woman who thinks just a little sees through this screen to her modesty.

In Colorado, Wyoming, Idaho and Utah women have for years had full suffrage, and none of the evils that the hysterical anti-suffragists predict have come upon those vigorous Western commonwealths. On the contrary, their schools are better, their prisons less full, and civic affairs generally are in a more satisfactory condition than in many of those states where the women have no vote.

Judge Beau Lindsey of the Denver Juvenile Court says that Colorado has the best laws for the protection of women, children and the home, of any state in the Union; and that in his opinion this is due to woman suffrage.

In many other states women have exercised partial suffrage for years, and there are

From *Colored American Magazine,* September 1905.

few or no such states or municipalities in which there have been any backward steps taken. The school vote and the saloon vote have been immensely bettered by reason of enfranchising women on these two issues.

It is claimed by some that women do not want to vote. Many do not. A great many do. The elective franchise has not been made compulsory for men, neither should it be for women. Now, because some men do not want to vote—and so do not—should all men be deprived of the right? It is further charged that women do not know civics and are not interested in politics. The charge is measurably true, and small wonder. Create a demand for this kind of knowledge and woman will speedily qualify. The book-sellers of Denver say they sold more books on government in six months after woman suffrage was introduced than in ten years before.

The fear is expressed by the sympathetic (?) opponents that should woman go forth to vote the baby would be neglected. It would be taken care of by the same one who cares for it while she goes out to earn a dollar or to visit a friend, or to rescue a drunkard's neglected child, or to mail a letter, or even sallies forth in a public office or to pay her taxes.

They tell us, too, that the Australian system of voting is complicated. A few women once mastered as difficult problems! Again, it is claimed that women do not need the ballot, as they are represented by their husbands. How about those women who have no husbands? What of those whose views and lives are so different from their husbands'?

In some states the law allows a man to spend as he pleases the money his wife brings to him as a bride, the money he earns—if he earns any—the money she earns, if any. Should he choose to spend all on wine and women—and they sometimes choose to spend all—the wife has no redress before the law. This same husband may go to the polling booth and vote for open saloons and the licensed brothel. And thus he represents his wife! She meanwhile stays at home to cry, to swear or to suicide—as she chooses—or more probably to earn more money for her liege lord who represents her. The native born Chinaman can vote in California but the late Mrs. Stanford could not. She might direct the great university and her heathen servant might direct the government behind the great founder of the university. Oh, the accident of sex! One humiliating feature of the case is that the right of suffrage is withheld from women largely by ignorant and vicious men. A large proportion of the best educated men are ardently in favor of the reform, albeit not all find it expedient to express their sentiments.

England and her provinces have gained greatly by the limited or full suffrage for women that obtains almost everywhere in His Majesty's dominions. The United States has liberalized greatly in these matters, and the time is probably not distant when Charles Sumner's prediction will come to pass. More than a quarter of a century ago Sumner said, "In the progress of civilization woman suffrage is sure to come." And come it has in part, and it will doubtless come more fully with the evolution of the higher civic life on which the United States is now well entered.

If white American women, with all their natural and acquired advantages, need the ballot, that right protective of all other rights; if Anglo Saxons have been helped by it—and they have—how much more do black Americans, male and female, need the strong defense of a vote to help secure their right to life, liberty and the pursuit of happiness? And neither do the colored citizens of the Republic lag behind in the fundamental duties of tax-paying and using the elective franchise. The price of their freedom, as far as that freedom has progressed, was too dear a price to be treated lightly. Every morsel of political right and duty should be cherished; and in the opinions of many wise and eminent men, as well as women, these privileges and duties should be extended even to women. Susan B. Anthony stands to-day easily among the foremost ranks of the world's greatest women and men. Her message to civilization has been a beautiful plea for political justice to the weaker members of the human family, whether the black man or all women.

Many objections growing out of prejudice are given to woman's enfranchisement, but reasons against it are few. It is in process of evolution, and when worked out to its logical conclusion the world will wonder why it came so tardily.

Lord Blackstone said: "The elements of sovereignty are three—wisdom, goodness, power." In the United States of America the greatest power is exercised at the polls. Does the reader know any woman, any colored woman, who measures up to Blackstone's test for sovereignty? The writer knows women, some colored women, who claim and crave the sovereignty of full citizenship.

34
Virginia B. Le Roy
A Woman's Argument against Woman Suffrage (1908)

This age is developing an acute consciousness of the symptoms of our social disorders. Masterly and brilliant are the arraignments of our public corruptions; the pitiless searchlight of publicity illumines our most subtle perversities. We are, through the exercise of this awakened social consciousness, becoming experts in the diagnosis of our social diseases, and in our new-found zeal are prone to overlook the fact that this capacity, however valuable for some purposes, does not of itself qualify us as social healers, or inspire us with knowledge of adequate remedies. It is one thing to recognize the symptoms described on the label of a bottle of patent medicine, and quite another to confide in the contents of the bottle as a cure for the disease. There is no necessary connection between the diagnosis and the proposed remedy, but many social reformers make the mistake of assuming such to be the case.

THE FALLACY OF ABSTRACT RIGHTS

All social reform movements to-day seem to focus on some conception of "rights." Somewhere, somehow, there seem to be things out there that we call "rights," and we feel that if we could once grasp them and hold tight, their possession would insure our social machinery a smoother running. These "rights" seem to be independent and preëxistent principles, foreordained fiats, absolute verities, which to discover and possess promise us a short cut to an earthly paradise.

For example, there are the "rights of labor" ever seeming to taunt us with their challenge: if all men had their bellies full of food and the right kind of rags to cover them, democracy, that other glorious right and privilege, would be attained. Then there are those "inalienable rights of freedom," which can not be downed, but come frothing and sizzling from the word-intoxicated orator as he hypnotizes his emotionally receptive audience. These "rights" we have always with us. Our children begin to imbibe them with Patrick Henry, and we continue to absorb them till the last campaign gun is fired. True, they are becoming somewhat overworked, but under the wiles of the spellbinder they are often potent to galvanize into spasmodic semblance of activity the sluggish wills of the people.

Then there are those blessed rights called "woman's rights," that sound the clarion call to the recently emancipated industrial slave who fondly fancies because she has relegated the making of soap to the factories and the world's medicine to the chemist, she may with profit employ her leisure in legislating world politics. This is perhaps the most interesting, as it is the most recent, example of the "rights" fallacy.

From *The World To-Day,* October 15, 1908.

WOMEN'S REASONS FOR WOMAN'S RIGHTS

I have interviewed many prominent women, putting to them the question: "Why do you want to vote?"

Most of them replied: "It is our right. We have been deprived of our rights by man long enough. We must assert ourselves and demand the ballot." It requires no prophet's eye to see that these pseudo-individualists urged into politics by their personal longings for political prerogatives would speedily come to grief in the maelstrom of party politics, where the male politicians have the first innings in the game.

Again, a large number of women make the reply: "We have property interests to protect, and if we pay taxes we should vote on municipal questions. Our property rights are violated."

"Taxation without representation" is another one of those embalmed traditions, to gainsay which is to the average American like shaking the proverbial red rag at a bull.

AN INTERVIEW WITH SUSAN B. ANTHONY

I well remember one winter's afternoon several years ago, sitting with Susan B. Anthony in her cozy study in Rochester. Outdoors the frozen snow gleamed like crystal, the wind howled through the specter-like elms, but inside round the big fireplace the huge logs slowly smoldering sent out intermittently rose-colored flames, dispelling at rare intervals the twilight shadows, and softly lighting up the noble face of one great woman. As we sat there in the comfort and cheer of the firelight, reminiscing on "the woman question," the little maid brought in the evening paper. Instantly the quiet atmosphere was disturbed and the spell broken. The lights were turned on, and in indignant voice the priestess of woman suffrage read a certain city ordinance just passed which would mean the payment of a considerable tax by her.

"Now are you convinced?" she asked with confident directness. "Here am I obliged to pay this money, and I am allowed no voice in the direction of these civic affairs. Isn't this a rank injustice? Am I not deprived of my legitimate rights as a property-holder and taxpayer?"

I could fully understand her indignation but I could not assent to the inferences she drew, so I replied:

"But, Miss Anthony, do you think the suffrage should depend on property? If so, how much property? And should it vote if held by minors, imbeciles, or aliens? And if property is to be the test, should not the one who owns most vote most? In which case, wouldn't you be worse off than you are now? Isn't it rather doubtful after all whether representation should not depend on something other than taxation?"

A caller interrupted, and I never got Miss Anthony's response.

HOBBES AND ROUSSEAU STILL RULE US

The fallacy of absolute and *a priori* "rights" seems to vitiate the reasoning of most of our reformers and especially of our suffrage reformers, who accept it with a child-like naiveté that is touching. As it appears fundamental to the discussion I would like to turn the calcium on this whole question of "rights." I want to show that the idea itself is a mere verbal abstraction concocted in the intellectual laboratories of medieval Europe; that it is a sawdust idol fit to-day only for the circus ring, bloodless, lifeless, hopelessly grotesque and inadequate to form the backbone of any practical social purpose.

Our modern brand of "rights" runs way back to the sixteenth century when Hobbes manufactured the first batch of them to serve as a mediator between the leaders of the Long Parliament and the King. Hobbes declared the state was like a large man in whom was vested supreme rights, and that as the King personified the state, his sovereignty could not be impugned. Later came Rousseau, who let out a whole brood of rights, called "natural rights." The French Revolution scattered these rights as burning brands over the then civilized world, until every state smoldered with sympathetic conflagrations. This country, already aflame, gave generous recognition to them, supplemented the list with several varieties of its own, until to-day it is difficult to keep tab on all the different kinds of rights, more or less inalienable and independent.

THE PRAGMATIST DECLARATION OF INDEPENDENCE

The old-world doctrine of abstract rights has so permeated the structure of our social thinking that hardly a step can be taken in our reasoning processes without stumbling over its catch phrases. It holds us so tight that nothing short of a new declaration of independence can free us—and a few of the bolder spirits have already celebrated their new Fourth of July. These radicals are asking the old doctrinaires to make good, to turn their abstract "rights" into cash values, to test them by their power to do work. What will these "rights" do for us? Will they bake bread? Will they build schoolhouses? No. Then away with them, for they hinder the coming of ideas that are dynamic, that have the power to turn the wheels of social progress.

To the modern radical your communist, socialist, or anarchist, who prates about the rights of man and rants loudly about the principles of liberty, fraternity and equality, is as hopelessly conservative and reactionary as the most hide-bound Tory. For to the real radical all social rights are man-made. They are made by him for his own purposes, and can be unmade when his purposes change. To him all the rights of the individual are rights which he holds not as a unit apart from, but as an integral element in the social organism. These rights are not foreordained, not preëxistent, not independent, not things in themselves. They are called into being through the harmonious intercourse of rational beings, are man-wrought transformations in the social process, facilitating the interchange of human relations, elastic in their nature, their values relative and immediate.

NEW TEST FOR SUFFRAGE WANTED

Now it is evident that this new conception of human rights must have an important bearing on the question of suffrage. If the ballot is not a natural or abstract right but simply a question of social expediency, an instrument to effect a desired end, the whole question may be considered from a new viewpoint.

The fact that we made the mistake of thinking in our callow youth that giving the ballot was giving equality and freedom is no reason for continuing the mistake now that we have arrived at the years of discretion. Because we gave the ballot to hundreds of thousands who are unfit; because to-day we are suffering the full penalty of our mistaken zeal for freedom, and are trying to unbungle the whole miserable business by illegally disfranchising as many as possible, will it further the solution of our problem to add several million more votes from generally ignorant and unqualified voters?

If, following this reasoning, we are to discard the old criteria of suffrage, we ought to be able to apply some more adequate test before we can intelligently discuss the question. What should the test be? It does not fall within my purpose to define it, but it is at any rate clear that it should not be based on an abstraction. It should result in some concrete good to the voter, to the state, or to society at large, and it is up to the proponents of woman's suffrage to show that it will work practical good in some tangible way. If they can prove it can accomplish useful social results, as a good pragmatist I am bound to be with them. Up to the present time the arguments have not been forthcoming.

HOW WOULD SUFFRAGE AFFECT WOMAN?

What, for example, will the influence of suffrage be on woman herself? This is an old question, and it has been treated in a too trifling, too supercilious tone by men. I do not intend to rehash the old bosh about the defeminization of women, or the lowering of the sanctities of the home, etc. That sort of talk is puerile. Participation in public work need not of itself make a woman unwomanly, and I score no point on that ground. What damage, then, is to come to woman from voting? How are we to forecast the effect of suffrage on woman nature?

Obviously, by examining the influence of political activities on those who have had the suffrage—on the men. . . .

. . . What do men fight for to-day in the political arena? The most casual observer must be struck with the juggling of our political machinery which is making it possible for this huge organized political appetite to devour the public spoils. Men are playing the game for material prizes, not for principles. They join forces, play off great issues, toss the destinies of the nations lightly to and fro, all for the glittering bait of political advancement. The political conscience has become so atrophied, the public standard of morality so low, the premium on undiscovered chicanery so high, that the best brains of the century can find no more inspiring task than to haul over the political grab-bag and fight for such baubles as it may contain.

Would women play the game more wisely? There is nothing in my experience as a twentieth-century club woman that would warrant me in supposing them superior to the spoils of office or political preferment. The promise of a "merry-widow hat" or a "directoire gown" might as easily turn a nation's destiny as any form of a more masculine graft. . . .

. . . The point I here emphasize is that the suffrage would divert woman from her real social purpose. As between the two sexes to-day woman has practically a monopoly of the social spirit. Were she to become a competitor for political prizes on the same terms as men, there is little reason for believing she could preserve her social spirit any better than men have done. Her motives would tend to become personal and selfish instead of public and patriotic, and society can not afford to lose her as a generator of pure social spirit unpolluted by lust of political gain.

I am more and more convinced that women are particularly fortunate in being exempt from the temptations of political activity. Just because woman may not participate in the political scramble, just because she is free, unhampered to let her generous impulses have full sway, just because she, and she alone, has heart-to-heart contact with the great ideals and problems of human destiny, unbiased by political expediencies, is she the potent power to-day in the direction of the great spiritual forces that are slowly but surely undermining the crass materialism of our sordid age. She it is to-day who is really influencing great public issues, accomplishing great humanitarian reforms, devising expedient measures of public sanitation, becoming in a word a great municipal housekeeper. She it is who is royally diffusing maternal tenderness for all motherless children, who is battling for a militant idealism that shall rescue us from the gross complacency of our idols of clay and reveal to us the shining gods of beauty, order and love.

WHAT WOMEN ARE DOING WITHOUT VOTES

Women are doing the great work of the world to-day. They are doing it without votes. Who knows but what their unselfish capacity to work for ideals is due to their freedom from the venalities of petty politics? Men have degenerated, and lost their grip on the great realities, but women with only ideals to strive for have gloriously risen to the heights, have developed the power to strive for ideals, are not diverted by immediate results, and are alive to the call of the larger social consciousness.

It is to women we owe what measure of public service we have to-day; without her unselfish work we should be ignominiously bound by material and selfish expediencies. It is women who are the initiatory sources of much of the creative work of the world, who are inspiring men to nobler service, who are creating a finer atmosphere of national sentiment that will get itself expressed in great deeds of unselfish heroism. . . .

THE REAL SOCIAL PROBLEM

If in the course of our social evolution it ever comes to pass that our governmental mechanism becomes so adjusted that the lines of political power will run parallel with those of the public good, it may be found in that golden age that sex lines will have been obliterated. It may be found that the fit woman equally with the fit man will be vested with political power, not because she is a woman, but because she is capable of efficient public service. But that day will not be hastened, in my opinion, by now letting down the bars and further diluting the average voting intelligence by adding several millions more of incompetent voters.

After all, our main problem lies deeper than any question of political privilege. Our real problem is how to change our social values. How can we change our dispositions so that we shall care for the things that are socially worthy? What can women do to create a change of attitude? Are women of influence and opportunity now doing all they can to encourage the growth of true social values? Are their smiles and favors given for manly deeds, or do they honor most the man who can make the most money and buy the most exalted social position?

Woman molds the standard to which society conforms. Man is largely what woman makes him. What she admires, that man strives to be. She is the arbiter of social rewards, the dispenser of social dignities. She is the creator of the society of to-day; we will create the society of to-morrow. Will she create it in the interest of a truer social order, or will she perpetuate the false distinctions and sham aristocracies of the present régime? She will do well to remember that so long as social uniqueness consists in owning things, rather than in personal worth; so long as the aristocracy held up for emulation is of a purely fictitious character, its fruits vulgarity and sensuousness; so long as the keenest intellects of the day degrade their sovereign capacities in frenzied finance; so long as the mass of the people vainly strive to imitate the gorgeous spectacle of the passing show, we may look in vain for the coinage of real spiritual values.

WOMAN MUST CREATE NEW VALUES

How do we create new values? By the will to believe in them, the arraying of them in matchless splendor of dignity and beauty that they may win people into incorporating them in daily life. It takes an open mind, a clear vision, a large purpose to recognize the larger truth; it means generous surrender, splendid loyalties; it means sacrifice of lesser things, a brave forecasting of future victories; it means keeping intact the vision on the heights, that gleams of it may penetrate the daily levels of existence.

35
JOSEPHINE CONGER-KANEKO
What Will Woman Suffrage Convention Do for the Working Woman? (1908)

The Fortieth Convention of the National American Woman Suffrage Association will celebrate the 60th anniversary of the historic convention of Seneca Falls, N.Y., which first took a stand against the arbitrary limitations of the rights and privileges of women under the law.

It is not likely that the Fortieth Convention will greatly resemble the first convention of woman suffragists of America. The first convention, held at Seneca Falls, and attended by women of world-wide fame—Susan B. Anthony, Lucretia Mott, Lucy Stone, Elizabeth Cady Stanton, Martha C. Wright, Mary Ann McClintock and others—was a militant convention. There was hostility without, and determination within. Ugly, insulting newspaper

From *The Socialist Woman,* October 1908.

editorials, disgraceful conduct of audiences, disapproval everywhere without. Women with rare minds, set jaws, and grim determination of purpose within. It was a tense moment in the life of the woman's movement—so young, so frail, but not for a moment uncertain of itself.

The women of the first convention had a fight on their hands. They recognized that they were not only politically, but were also economically oppressed, and from these limitations grew every conceivable wrong. . . .

. . . During the long interval between the years of the first suffrage struggles, and the present, the ballot has been given to women in its fullest sense, in four states in the Union. Not a very great gain, to be sure. But the fact remains that the suffrage movement has lost its militant spirit, and has become lady-like and respectful in the last decade. This, because the main bone of the contention has been granted, even if the vote has not.

The women of the suffrage movement have been largely middle-class women. Women tax-payers, and those who desired to control their own property. In most of the states they have been gradually granted this latter desire. The "profitable employments," law, medicine, theology, have been opened to educated women. Practically all of the demands made in the first constitution have been granted, save the right to vote.

The middle-class suffragist therefore has ceased to fight; she has lost her militant spirit, her conventions are quiet, genteel gatherings, with but one demand—one request, it were better to say—that for the ballot.

There is another class of women, however, who, when they have captured the suffrage movement—and they must eventually capture it—will give to it the earnest, intense, interesting aspect it bore at its inception. This is the wage-earning woman. The wage-earning woman has an economic axe to grind. She is competing with man in the labor market, and for the same work in many cases, efficiency being equal, she is receiving fifty per cent less wages than he receives. Given the vote, she would have an equal chance with man in this struggle. Given the ballot she would not tend to pull down the whole wage scale as she does today, but her political power would tend to raise it to a higher average than it has ever been.

When you women of the suffrage movement recognize this need of your poorly paid, wage-earning sisters—of which there are more than five million in this country—when you are ready to take up their burden, to help force their demands; when you are willing to say that the woman toiler must receive the full product of her labor, minus the cost of machinery and the government tax, you will again be a militant movement, throbbing with the life of a divine purpose—worthy of your great and fearless predecessors. Of those who said, Man has taken from woman all right in property, even the wages she earns. The situation is not very different today with the working woman. Man has taken from her all property, and allows her but an insignificant portion of what she earns.

The whole nation is watching your convention, and it awaits your attitude on this question. What will it be?

36
NATIONAL PROGRESSIVE WOMAN SUFFRAGE UNION
Constitution (1909)

NAME

National Progressive Woman Suffrage Union, American Suffragettes.

OBJECTS

To secure the complete political enfranchisement of women and an equality of rights and opportunities between the sexes.

METHODS

This Union shall seek to obtain its objects by:

From *The American Suffragette*, June 1909.

1. Action entirely independent of all political parties.

2. Vigorous, forceful, aggressive agitation on lines justified by the position of outlawry to which women are at present condemned.

3. The organizing of women all over the country to give adequate expression to their desire for political freedom.

4. Education of public opinion by all methods which appear to be advisable, such as public meetings, debates, distribution of literature, newspaper correspondence and deputations to public representations.

Membership

Women and men of all shades of political opinion, and in particular, all women, whether of the home, the shop, or the office, are eligible to membership.

The annual membership fee shall not be less than twenty-five cents.

We believe that there is *no better way to reach the people* than by *going to them direct.* Hence our open-air meetings, Monday evenings, 125th Street and 7th Avenue; Wednesday evenings, 116th Street and Lenox Avenue, and during the week at other points. This method of addressing the people as we meet them in the street is *educational,* oftimes with spectacular effect, and it does the *effective work.*

Thursday evenings are devoted to discussions at headquarters. The rooms are open to all....

37
Sofia M. Loebinger

Suffragist and Suffragette: A Sure Cure for Anti-Suffragitis (1909)

In response to repeated and numerous inquiries as to what may be the distinction between the Suffragist and Suffragette, it may be apropos to define the difference, if such there is, for both are working for the cause at issue—each in her own way.

While the Suffragist plods along in the beaten track made by the great pioneers of the movement and contents herself with methods conservative, the Suffragette is the production of the modern period, and up-to-date in manner and method.

The Suffragette is militant; she is awake to present conditions and employs methods which are in keeping with these conditions, realizing the helplessness of that important though outclassed part of the people of the country, the women.

The Suffragette further realizes that ineffectiveness of tea-table and drawing-room chat, of indoor meetings where the participants are mainly those who are believers in suffrage.

And furthermore, the Suffragette is conscious of the necessity of converting the masses—all the people, and therefore goes to the people direct, in the streets, on the highways and byways, and holds open-air gatherings with able speakers to address the crowds. So does the Suffragette spread the gospel of Woman Suffrage, indiscriminately and effectively.

And still further does she recognize the necessity for recruiting and enlisting the men—the present voters! They alone can make Woman Suffrage possible. The voters must bring pressure upon their political bosses, who in turn, instruct the legislators whom they have placed in office! It is love's labor lost to send large delegations of women to Albany each year.

The Suffragette is unwilling to wait for the ballot another sixty years. She wants it *now* and she wants it *quick!* She needs it! It is her just right, her natural right and her constitutional right.

She is too sensible to be stung by any criticism, whatever may be the source, and simply follows along the path of duty, in her own way.

Woman Suffrage to-day is too serious an issue to be treated sentimentally or theoretically. *Practical treatment is needed!*

From *The American Suffragette,* June 1909.

The Suffragette is an expert in her treatment of the disease known as Anti-Suffragitis! And she uses her Anti-Toxine in such treatment with wonderful effect. Result—strong, healthy branches springing up in every direction! For a liberal supply of this propagating and strength-bringing Anti-Toxine, apply to the AMERICAN SUFFRAGETTE. An able staff of inoculating experts always on hand.

There is room for Suffragists and Suffragettes, with one common goal for all —the "Get the Ballot" goal.

38
Harriet Laidlaw
Organizing to Win by the Political District Plan (1914)

The following plan of organization was worked out and first applied by the Woman Suffrage Party of New York City, and while the term "Woman Suffrage Party" is used throughout this pamphlet, it can be equally well adopted by any association under its existing name or under any new name. This form of organization has spread all over the United States.

As long as we are endeavoring to attain suffrage state by state, through amendments to the constitutions of the various states, and as long as the members of the State Legislature alone have the power to place the amendment definitely before the whole body of the voters, just so long must those political units which send men to the Legislatures be our primary concern. In work for the Federal amendment the congressional units are important. But ever the assembly district stands pre-eminent in the life of the state.

These political units are the "Senatorial District" from which the members of the Senate or the Upper House of the State Legislatures are drawn, and the "Assembly" or "Legislative District" or "Ward," from which are drawn the members of the Lower House of the State Legislatures. This Lower House and its members are variously named in the different states. For convenience, we shall use the name "Assembly" and "Assembly district" through this pamphlet.

The basis of the Woman Suffrage Party organization is the Assembly District. We do not deal especially with the Senatorial District, for the reason that the several Assembly Districts (generally three) which make up a Senatorial District can always combine to bring pressure to bear upon the State Senator through every Woman Suffrage Party agency that is employed in the case of the Assemblyman.

The aim of the Woman Suffrage Party is to focus all the existing suffrage work directly upon these political representatives of the people to the end that they may be induced to work for the suffrage bill once it has been introduced into the Legislature.

In structure, the Party is like a great pyramid tapering upward from the enrolled membership throughout the entire city, which forms its base, through the Captains and the Leaders of the various Assembly Districts, to the Chairman of the city or state organization at the apex.

This plan of work did not originate with suffragists. It was merely appropriated by them. It is a plan which voters have evolved after a century of political experience. Under test, it has been found to be the most effective possible organization, and should, therefore, prove correspondingly effective to suffragists in their work of preparation for a suffrage campaign.

Collectively the Party can undertake as bold and picturesque work as any organization, but, in addition, this careful, undeviating, systematic political organization work must be constantly carried on by the central Chairmen, the Leaders of the Assembly Districts and the Captains of the various Election Precincts within the Assembly Districts.

The Party work not only intensifies the suffrage comradeship, but gives a pride in local

From *Organizing to Win by the Political District Plan: A Handbook for Working Suffragists* (New York: National Woman Suffrage Publishing Co., 1914), 2–12.

achievement and a strong neighborhood feeling that, in a great city, is most salutary. It is accompanied inevitably by an awakening of civic pride, and a wholesome breaking down of class distinctions, as women, of the same neighborhood but of widely different training and mode of life, are thus brought together for a common cause. . . .

THE ACTIVITIES OF THE WOMAN SUFFRAGE PARTY

For quick reference as a practical guide, the activities of the Woman Suffrage Party are here set forth from five different sides:

1. Political.
2. Legislative.
3. Propaganda.
4. Education for civic life.
5. Reform.

POLITICAL WORK

First and foremost, as its form indicates, the work of the Woman Suffrage Party is Political. It endeavors to walk step by step parallel with the legitimate activities of the dominant political parties. At every political meeting, and in every political committee, the Woman Suffrage Party's voice must be heard in undeviating demand for the submission of the woman suffrage amendment to the voters.

It must be impressed upon the minds of all citizens in political life that the members of the Woman Suffrage Party intend to pursue an unswerving course side by side with the men of the dominant parties from whom their enfranchisement in any State must come. Wherever the men are meeting, making platforms, considering candidates for the State Legislature, passing resolutions, or holding primaries or conventions, the Woman Suffrage Party officers and members should be with the insistent and persistent demand that they express themselves in some way upon the suffrage question, that they shall send men to the State Legislature who are pledged to submit the suffrage amendment to the voters of the State, whether the Legislator believes in suffrage or not.

It is necessary to follow the political routine from designation meetings and primaries to State Conventions.

1. Party officers should find the headquarters of the County and State committees for dominant parties. A friendly acquaintance, if possible, should be established between officers and members of these political committees and officers and members of the Woman Suffrage Party.

Much important information can be obtained at these headquarters during the summer. Get from the State headquarters the political calendar for the year. This is generally a printed folder. Supply Assembly District Leaders with copies of the political calendar. Also locate the board of elections. There one may get complete lists, names and addresses of all candidates for the Legislature. Leaders get these names, of course, in their own districts, but a complete list should be on hand at headquarters.

2. Party officers should in every possible way acquaint themselves with the State and local political situation.

3. The Woman Suffrage Party Assembly District Leader should become acquainted with the political party leaders of her District. She should know the location and the officers of all political clubs, and get admission to the clubs for suffrage speakers.

4. The Leader should learn as far as possible her district politics.

5. The Election District Captain should become acquainted with the political captains of her Election District.

6. Suffrage Leader, Captains and all District officers should become acquainted with their Senator and Assemblyman, follow his legislative activities closely and let him be keenly aware of their activities for suffrage. It is a part of district routine to send notices of meetings, invitations to speak, subscriptions to suffrage magazines, to all district men of prominence. The suffrage sentiment of his District must be impressed upon him at its highest value. No suffrage influence should be lost to the Legislators and politicians of an Assembly District.

They should be fully conscious that it is the most agitated, the most vital question that they will hear from during the legislative session.

7. On the day of the primary or designation meetings, a delegation of two to four women from every Assembly District should seek a hearing, if only for five minutes, asking: (a) For the nomination or designation of a candidate who believes in the submission of the Woman Suffrage amendment; and (b) For the passage of a result in favoring the submission of the Woman Suffrage amendment.

8. Before nominating conventions the same course should be pursued.

If suffrage representatives cannot get a hearing, they can distribute appeals within the hall. This being denied, they can stand outside and distribute the appeals. . . . This applies to the Senatorial conventions. The Leaders of the Districts that make up a Senatorial District should unite on this.

9. The year of the general State elections the Party should follow out the routine for State conventions and a hearing before the Resolutions Committee asking for a suffrage plank in their platform. . . . In a presidential year the same action should be taken with reference to delegates to the State convention asking them to advocate a plank in the National platform as a recommendation from their State. . . .

10. Immediately after the candidates for Senate and Assembly (or House of Representatives) have been nominated, begin a systematic interviewing and if possible a pledging of the candidates on the suffrage question. . . .

11. If the organization decides to campaign against a particularly refractory candidate, they should consider: (a) Whether the District is a close one or whether there is a chance of success; (b) Whether the opposing candidate is sincerely for the submission of the question; and (c) The past legislative record of the candidate to be fought. (Methods and plans for an aggressive campaign are treated in another leaflet.)

12. The Woman Suffrage Party should never work for a candidate nor ally itself with any political party or organization.

13. After election, one of the first things the new Senator and the new Assemblyman or Representative should hear is the Woman Suffrage question. By simultaneous onslaught upon the conventions or designation meetings of every Assembly District, the undeviating presence of the suffrage advocates at every step in the political routine, he should already have realized that he cannot escape the suffrage demand.

Between election and the convening of the Legislature, each Legislator for the State should be tabulated as to his position on submitting the amendment.

Nothing should satisfy suffrage workers as a culmination to their Political work short of a Legislature, a majority of whose members are pledged to the submission of the Woman Suffrage Amendment.

LEGISLATIVE WORK

In every case, except through a constitutional revision or an initiative petition, an amendment must pass the State Legislature (or sometimes two successive Legislatures), before it can be referred to the voters. Therefore, in nearly every case one of the great fights in our war is to get the bill safely through and out of the Legislature.

1. Form a co-operating legislative committee, composed of heads of all organizations in the State, of which the Woman Suffrage Party Chairman or the State President is Chairman. This committee should meet immediately after election, and thereafter once a week or once in two weeks throughout the winter.

2. Decide upon the form of amendment or suffrage bill.

3. Select a Senator to introduce the bill in the State Senate and an Assemblyman or Representative to introduce it into the Assembly or House of Representatives. If necessary, do some work in the man's own District to show him that there is a strong enough sentiment among his constituents to warrant his championship of the bill. If there is a Men's

League in the state, district the members and ask them to call upon, write to and petition their legislators. . . .

4. Have a legislative agent, some earnest woman, continually at the State Capitol in friendly relations with the introducers of the bill. She should be a student of the political combinations and of the whole legislative procedure, ever pushing the claims of the suffragists, interviewing Assemblymen, sending timely word to Suffrage Party leaders in this and that Assembly District regarding work that needs to be done in a legislative crisis. Here is where the strength of a Woman Suffrage Party organization is shown. Word is sent into a District, "Your Assemblyman says he does not believe there is much demand in his District." Forthwith he receives a list of the enrolled members, he is showered with letters and telegrams from his own constituents. Many may come to the State Capitol to see him.

5. Urge an early and timely introduction of the bill.

6. After the first reading of the bill, it is referred to a committee. Since this is, in so many States called the Judiciary Committee, we will use that name here. This is where in most instances the suffrage bills quietly die. The Suffrage Party proposes the bill shall not so die, and that if it does, it shall not die quietly. At this step in the legislative routine, there is one clear-cut piece of work:—To get the suffrage bill out of the committee.

(a) To this end get a hearing before the Judiciary Committees, joint or separate.

(b) Try to get a vote open or soon after the hearing.

(c) Demand a report favorable or unfavorable. The latter at least gets it before the House for a discussion and gets that vote, so important to the suffragists of a State, which enables them to see where the Legislators stand.

(d) If the bill is not reported out in reasonable time, interview the members of the Committee.

(e) Begin an aggressive campaign through the press by street meetings, by the rolling up of a petition signed preferably by the voters of the Committeeman's district asking that he vote to report the bill out of Committee. Here, Assembly District organization is invaluable. Canvas the District from the voters' lists obtained from the Board of Elections. Hold mass meetings in the District and always pass resolutions on the submission of the Woman Suffrage amendment and mail them immediately to the Legislator. . . . Have prominent people in the district write to him. . . . The Woman Suffrage Party Leader should keep in touch with the political party leaders of her District during this time. The courtesy of the political headquarters for suffrage meetings may often be obtained at this time and such meetings are very effective.

7. If the Committee remains obdurate, get the introducer of the bill "To move the discharge of the Committee from further consideration of the Woman Suffrage bill." This means a close and careful polling of the members of the Legislature to get votes for the discharge.

8. Where the bill is triumphantly out of Committee, let the Party or Co-operative Committee workers realize that "Eternal vigilance is the price of liberty!" See that it is advantageously placed upon the calendar for its second reading. Poll the Legislature again. Be as active as possible in the men's districts. This is the height of the season's work. Hold a chain of legislative mass meetings. In many cases have the Legislators themselves speak. When the day comes for the second reading have deputations from throughout the State, ideally from each Assembly District, the Leader, and two or three Captains on the floor of the House or in their gallery. A parade in the Capitol City is a good idea. Demonstrations at this time need be limited by nothing but money and workers. A whirlwind suffrage week in the Capitol City is effective. Never forget work at home in the Assembly Districts of doubtful or adverse men.

9. When the bill has been passed through the second reading, dilatory tactics are often used by those corrupt politicians who are opposing the passage of the Woman Suffrage bill

with that desperate eagerness that constitutes the highest tribute to and the best argument for Woman Suffrage.

10. The next step is for placing the bill on the calendar for the final reading and successful passage. One political trick to block the suffragists is to refer the bill at last to a Committee, often the Committee on Rules. Then the suffragists must fight strenuously to the last ditch. Again they must begin the routine, send out circulars, hold meetings, and besiege the members of this Committee to report the bill out for final passage. . . .

11. In the meanwhile on the eve of success, the Governor and his signature should be assured. (Not in all States.)

12. In some States this entire program must be carried out in two successive Legislatures.

We do not in this pamphlet attempt to cover the procedure of the final campaign in the State where the amendment has been submitted; but from past experience and by evident deduction any suffrage worker can see that in proportion as the State is covered by a Woman Suffrage Party district organization, in that proportion a successful campaign is certain.

PROPAGANDA

All our technical, political and legislative work will profit us little unless we are at the same time preparing the minds of the people for this great reform.

The means by which the Suffrage message can be conveyed are innumerable, from toy "Votes for Women" balloons to magnificent banners; from Suffrage Party enrollment blanks and brown paper grocery bags to artistic booklets; from street meetings to parades. The resourceful worker, the Publicity and Public Demonstration and Entertainment Committees of a district will devise a thousand ways of appealing locally and generally to the heart and mind of the unconvinced, and of getting the message of equal suffrage to those who would never come to us in a regular suffrage meeting.

1. The hard but fruitful way is through the work of the Election District Captain in her house to house canvassing. She will speak to and leave literature with all the tradespeople, all the apartment house janitors. She will call, call, call on all the people in her District, convincing them by personal discussion and influence, and enrolling them in the District organization. . . . The Party should furnish her with the "Rainbow Literature" to distribute freely. These may be secured from the National Woman Suffrage Co., Inc.

2. The Election District Captains and Party workers should hold parlor and shop neighborhood meetings; they should appear before locals of the unions, men's clubs, political and social groups; they should penetrate into slot machine and moving picture places. They should wear the suffrage button always, that the whole neighborhood will know what they stand for.

3. The Leader should work up a large body of Captains and call Captains' meetings as often as once a month to get their reports and in every way to stimulate the district work.

4. Two or three times during the year there should be a great District mass meeting.

5. Street meetings should be held frequently at the various corners and squares of the District.

6. The politicians, leaders and Legislators of Assembly Districts should be notified of and invited to District activities. While the propaganda work goes on not one motion the suffragists make should be lost politically. . . .

7. It is well to have a leaflet on District activities to give to new recruits who want to do home work in their Districts. . . .

8. Suffrage plays written and acted by members of the District Suffrage Club have been a source of revenue and of propaganda.

9. Assembly District headquarters as a center for the District Suffrage Club are a wonderful help in strengthening the work and in gathering in recruits. The working up of the Assembly District Club with a dues-paying basis from the Captains and active workers and

the non-dues-paying enrollments, is a department of Party activity that requires a pamphlet by itself.

10. Different Districts lend themselves to various forms of propaganda. A sewing circle where women come with sewing and mending while a suffrage book is read and District plans discussed, has been utilized in home Districts.

11. District fairs, District dances, District classes of different kinds have been used for converting and strengthening the District organization.

12. The social settlement for suffrage centers, the suffrage lunch and tea room, the suffrage gift shop, sales of "votes for women" candy and other articles, "votes for women" flower shows, "votes for women" dog shows and cat shows, and District sleigh-rides, are all methods which an alert District worker has used to raise money, increase members, and carry on propaganda.

13. The political reception is a valuable feature of District life. A Leader with her district officers and her Captains has given with great success a reception afternoon or evening and invited all the Legislators of her District.

14. The Flying Squadron of automobiles, or workers on foot with flags and regalia, is a method of stimulating weak districts. The free lances or minute women of the Party, who are not over-burdened with official work, should be organized to go into different districts to do intensive work for a day or a week, covering the district with canvassing, parades, street meetings, etc.

15. Besides all the splendid effective localized activity of the Party which is its basic power, the Central Committee should conceive and carry out plans of an aggressive and dignified character on a larger scale. The great annual city convention of the Party is not only for the adoption of a Party platform and declaring the election of officers, but for presenting to the public a brilliant programme calculated to win converts. . . .

16. On all special occasions, as in time of rejoicing over a suffrage victory, at a legislative crisis, for protest or for jubilation, the Party as a whole should hold great mass meetings.

17. Theatrical benefits are a source of propaganda and revenue. However, for the latter it must be said that not much time and strength should have to go into entertainments for revenue. The Party must always be supported mainly by general contributions and pledges, obtained at big mass meetings.

18. The Party should make the most of all opportunities for unusual demonstrations. In a broad spirit of service for the cause, suffragists should remember that no time or place can detract from the dignity of the cause as long as the suffragist who represents it is dignified, gracious, tactful and earnest. A wonderful way to reach people is by maintaining a tent during the summer months at some popular resort near a city, a different Assembly District taking charge each week. A lunch wagon can be hired and run by suffragists with great effect. Special holiday celebrations can be utilized, such as the decorating of the patriotic statues of a city. A picturesque parade and speeches on the Fourth of July are effective. Places on programmes of other entertainments; booths at pure food, domestic science, governmental and industrial exhibitions; admission for propaganda work at fairs and benefits; an opportunity to take a place on the programme in a vaudeville house or run in lantern slides of suffrage cartoons or sentiments—all these opportunities should be used by the Party.

19. The Party demonstrations should as far as possible emphasize the Party organizations; banners and badges of the Assembly Districts should show in living terms something of the scope and character of the Party.

20. Any unusual occasion, a public celebration or event, a tragedy or a crisis, should be seized upon by suffragists, to drive home the suffrage lesson.

21. The procedure for press work requires a pamphlet by itself. There should be a press chairman and an active co-operating member in each assembly district. The full measure of publicity and propaganda accorded by the press

depends much upon the resourcefulness, adroitness and general efficiency of the suffragists in "getting things over."

EDUCATION FOR CIVIC LIFE

The whole of the Party activity is a wonderful civic education. By making a Precinct Captain and her workers responsible for the few hundred people in an Election District or Precinct and then connecting her activity up to the great systematic organization of the Woman Suffrage Party, not only is the suffrage cause furthered but the workers are wonderfully trained. This sort of organization for team work and united effort is the genius of modern life. Until women, who from lack of training or experience are impatient of or awed by big combinations, are trained up to such standards of work, they cannot be vital factors in the world life of to-day. The patient, careful work which the organization requires is the best training in the world.

1. The Party worker must have some parliamentary knowledge. A class in parliamentary law has been run in some party organizations.

2. The Woman Suffrage Party woman learns to be faithful to political meetings and to be conscientious about coming out to vote. Beginning with her own Assembly District conventions up to the city conventions she learns by practical experience the routine of electing officers and delegates.

3. On its political committees and its legislative committees woman Suffrage Party workers learn the whole technique of government and of political methods.

4. This great volume of volunteer work develops a spirit of social service that is the basis of good citizenship.

5. Perhaps nothing in the Party movement is more remarkable than the education which the Party woman gets in real, not theoretical, democracy. Working side by side with Leaders and Captains from every section, color, race, creed and condition in a big city, she forgets the existence of class distinctions.

6. The speakers' classes, and still better, the experience in drawing room, hall, theatre and street corner, develops a large body of woman speakers.

7. Aside from the development of ability, the general ethical development of women who do this well-built, orderly, persistent, often inglorious work, is very remarkable.

8. A flaming demand for reform and readjustment is aroused in the women of the Party as they are called into close touch with every portion of our great cities, into intimate knowledge of police and political conditions and as they see the degradation and oppression of humanity, especially of childhood and womanhood.

REFORM

It will always be a great question for organized suffragists to decide how far suffrage organizations shall take action upon reform matters. We are more or less solid on the subject of political partisanship. We know that the Woman Suffrage Party must keep free of all political alliances, as we must, as a non-partisan body, take our suffrage demand before committees, legislatures, and bodies of voters of all parties.

But, when it comes to burning social questions, the very form of a Woman Suffrage Party platform . . . shows that we cannot be oblivious of these vital things. It will take tact, courage, judgment, to decide how far to become allied with or to divert our activity toward other great movements. One thing must be remembered—pounds of alleviation will not equal one ounce of the cure which comes with woman's enfranchisement. We are organized for the enfranchisement of women, and we find, because all these other things are of such burning moment to us, because we realize that mistakes are being made which carry tragedy in their train, that we must all the more insist that we be armed with the one weapon known to modern governments, the ballot. However, certain recognition the Party must pay to existing struggles:

1. With social and reform bodies, affiliation is possible.

2. Resolutions and endorsements relative to many social matters are often imperative on the city committee of the Woman Suffrage Party.

3. The primary point at which we must vitally come in contact with reform conditions is in our relation to the labor world. The party will naturally be in close sympathy with the Woman's Trade Union movement.

4. An important part of Party activity is a Wage-Earners' Suffrage League.... A labor chairman should be one of the many chairmen of standing committees on the city committee. She may, or may not, be president of the Wage-Earners' League. Besides their central activities, labor meetings, etc., the Wage-Earners' League members should be distributed and in touch with the District organization.

5. At least once during the year the Party should hold a great labor mass meeting, previous to which the Locals of all the Unions should have been visited with requests to send delegations.

6. The Party should participate in the Labor Day Parade, and other labor demonstrations. Fraternal greetings and fraternal delegates should be sent to great Women's Trade Union and Labor congresses and conventions. Resolutions of sympathy and endorsement are in order in connection with many events in the course of the struggle in the labor world.

7. Adoption of resolutions on various subjects of a social nature are in order to be sent to President, Governor, Mayor, Police Commissioner and other officials.

8. A Leader and her Captains have been known to wait upon the proper city authorities to demand better street conditions, the suppression of factory or smoke nuisances, police protection, etc.

9. Prison reform, abolition not regulation of the White Slave traffic, the struggle against child-labor, reform of criminal court procedure—concerning these the party will protest, pass resolutions, speak on the street corners, endorse organizations specially formed to cope with these matters; but no single-minded suffragist will be diverted by the individual instance, by even the most crying social defect, but will ever remember that causes and conditions are the foes that must be routed and that the one effective weapon is the ballot, and that the most effective way to gain the ballot is through Woman Suffrage Party organization.

39
LUCY BURNS, ALICE PAUL, MRS. JOHN ROGERS, HARRIOT STANTON BLATCH, FLORENCE KELLEY, AND MRS. BAYARD HILLES

Proposed Plan of the Congressional Union (1914)

The second day's business session of the conference was devoted primarily to the consideration of the election policy to be pursued by the Union in the coming congressional campaign. After a persuasive talk by Mrs. Crystal Eastman Benedict on the help which each member of the Union can render in the Federal Amendment work, the discussion of election plans was entered upon. As a preliminary to this discussion, Miss Lucy Burns, vice-chairman of the Union, outlined the record of the National Democratic Party on the suffrage question. Miss Burns showed that the National Suffrage amendment had been persistently blocked by the Democratic Party, which was, as she pointed out, in complete possession of the National Government, controlling the presidential chair and the Senate, and having an overwhelming majority in the House. She analyzed the working of Congress, showing that our Government is a government by party, that no measure of importance had been passed during the present Congress without the backing of the party in

From *The Suffragist*, September 12, 1914.

power, and that no measure could go through the present Congress if opposed by that party. She called attention to the answer given to the seven suffrage deputations to the President and then showed that in addition to the refusal on the part of the President to extend any help, the measure had encountered the opposition of the Democratic leaders in Congress. It was pointed out that the Democratic members of the Rules Committee of the House, who form a majority on the committee, had met and decided by a vote of four to three to oppose the creation of a suffrage committee in the House and then in a full meeting of the Rules Committee had stood together and, by their votes and absences, prevented the creation of the Suffrage Committee, although a majority of the members, as individuals, were for that measure. Reference was also made to the fact that after the suffrage amendment had been reported out of the Judiciary Committee and taken its place on the calendar of the House, it had been impossible to secure time for a vote to be taken owing to the continued refusal of the Rules Committee to allot time for the consideration of the measure. Attention was also called to the fact that the suffrage resolution was lost in the Senate through the failure of the Democratic party to take up the measure and put the party machinery back of it.

The Democratic record during the present Congress was shown to be one continuous course of opposition to the suffrage amendment.

THE ELECTION PROGRAM

Miss Alice Paul then outlined the proposed election program, after having asked the press to withdraw and requested the members of the conference not to reveal the proposed plan until the middle of September, when the Union would be ready to put it into practical operation.

"From the very beginning of our work in Washington," she said, "we have followed one consistent policy from which we have not departed a single moment. We began our work with the coming in of the present Congress and immediately went to the Party which was in control of the situation and asked it to act. We determined to get the amendment through the 63d Congress or to make it very clear who had kept it from going through. Now, as has been shown, the Democrats have been in control of all branches of the Government and they are therefore responsible for the non-passage of our measure.

"The point is, first, who is our enemy and then how shall that enemy be attacked.

"We are all, I think, agreed that it is the Democratic Party which is responsible for the blocking of the suffrage amendment. Again and again, that Party has gone on record through the action of its leaders, its caucus, and its committee so that an impregnable case has been built up against it. We now lay before you a plan to meet the present situation.

"We propose going into the nine suffrage states and appealing to the women to use their votes to secure the franchise for the women of the rest of the country. All of these years we have worked primarily in the states. Now the time has come, we believe, when we can really go into national politics and use the nearly four million votes that we have to win the vote for the rest of us. Now that we have four million women voters, we need no longer continue to make our appeal simply to men. The struggle in England has gotten down to a physical fight. Here our fight is simply a political one. The question is whether we are good enough politicians to take four million votes and organize them and use them so as to win the vote for the women who are still disfranchised.

"We want to attempt to organize the women's vote. Our plan is to go out to these nine states and there appeal to all the women voters to withdraw their support from the Democrats nationally until the Democratic Party nationally ceases to block suffrage. We would issue an appeal signed by influential women of the east addressed to the women voters as a whole asking them to use their vote this one time in the national election against the Democratic Party throughout the whole nine states. Every one of those states with one exception is a doubtful state. Going back over a period of fourteen years each state, except Utah, has supported first one party and then another. Here are nine states which politicians are thinking about and in these nine states we have this great power. If we ask those women in the nine suffrage states as a group to withhold their support from this party as a group which is opposing us, it will mean that votes will be turned. Suppose the Party saw votes falling away all over the country because of their action on the Trust question—they would change their attitude on trust legislation. If they see them falling away because of their attitude on suffrage they will change their attitude on suffrage. When we have once affected the result in a national election, no party will trifle with suffrage any longer.

"We, of course, are a little body to undertake this—but we have to begin. We have not very much money; there are not many of us to go out against the great Democratic Party. Perhaps this time we won't be able to do so very much, though I know we can do a great deal, but if the Party leaders see that some votes have been turned they will know that we have at last realized this power that we possess and they will know that by 1916 we will have it organized. The mere announcement of the fact that the suffragists of the east have gone out to the west with this appeal will be enough to make every man in Congress sit up and take notice.

"This last week one Congressman from a suffrage state came to us and asked us if we would write just one letter to say what he had done in Congress to help us. He said that one letter might determine the election in his district. This week the man who is running for the Senatorial election in another suffrage state came to us and asked us to go out and help him in his state—asked us simply to announce that he had been our friend. Now if our help is valued to this extent, our opposition will be feared in like degree.

"Our plan is this: To send at least two women to each of those nine sates. We would put one woman at the center who would attend to the organizing, the publicity, and the distribution of literature. We would have literature printed showing what the Democratic Party has done with regard to suffrage in the 63d Congress. We would have leaflets printed from the eastern women appealing to the western women for help, and we would have leaflets issued showing how much the enfranchised woman herself needs the federal suffrage amendment because most important matters are becoming national in their organization and can only be dealt with by national legislation. We could reach every home in every one of those nine states with our literature, without very great expense. One good woman at the center could make this message, this appeal, from eastern women, known to the whole state. The other worker would attend to the speaking and in six weeks could easily cover all the large towns of the state.

"This is the plan that we are considering, and that we are hoping to put through. We would be very much interested to hear what you think about it and want of course to have your cooperation in carrying it through."

THE DISCUSSION

Mrs. John Rogers, a member of the Advisory Council of the Congressional Union, and a member of the Executive Board of the Woman's Political Union of New York, then spoke. "This seems to me," said Mrs. Rogers, "a very straight, clear, strong policy by which we have everything to gain and nothing to lose. To those women who say, 'suppose we do not make the Western women rise up and use their power the way we want them to,' I have only to say that many of them will. They are beginning to feel that it is not enough for them alone to be enfranchised; for their own sake they need the co-operation of enfranchised women all over the country. If we are not successful in some states, still it is our plain duty to convince these women that nothing that they could possibly do for their country's welfare could count as much as helping to enfranchise the rest of the women of the United States. In other words, we must appeal to them on the basis of the relative importance of things, and I believe that they will answer to that call. We in New York are facing a referendum in 1915. We do not feel for a moment that the Congressional Union's fight against the Democratic Party will harm us there. We will gain by it. It seems to me a plain and strong policy which I hope very much will be put right through."

Miss Paul then introduced Mrs. Harriot Stanton Blatch, president of the Women's Political Union of New York. She announced that Mrs. Blatch had that morning joined the Advisory Council of the Union, an honor which the members of the Union doubly appreciated because of the fact that a month ago Mrs. Blatch had declined to join the Council.

"The reason I have so recently joined the Advisory Council," Mrs. Blatch began, "is because of something I read in the newspapers this morning. I am one of those who is very fearful of every man or woman suddenly saying, 'Let us be political,' because nine-tenths of the people of the world, men as well as women, have not a political hair in their heads. Now, since I am a person who has a few political hairs in my head, mingled with the gray, and since I profoundly recognize, and with gratitude, that some of the young women have political hairs in their heads, I have today joined the Council. I am thrown into the position where I must take sides, unfortunately. The reason I would not join the Advisory Council was because, as I was centered upon the work in New York State, I saw no reason for taking this side or that side in national affairs, but, alas, now I must; because two policies are presented to me and as an intelligent human being I have to decide on which side I am. And in this position I find myself absolutely standing with the national policy as stated by Miss Paul.

"Yesterday those of you who were at the luncheon may perhaps remember that I referred to one fact in political history—that different classes of men in seeking enfranchisement had always had classes of enfranchised men helping them, but that we women had been singularly lonely in having marched on ever since 1848 without the slightest help from the inside. But at last, as I said yesterday, there is a great band of women voters in the West who can extend their hand to us and help us. My heart as well as my head responds to this suggestion of Miss Paul to go out to those women of the West, reminding them in those nine suffrage states where they can help us, that now at last the opportunity has come and that they can be like the enfranchised men who reached out their hand to men who were struggling for their political freedom—that they can reach out their hand to disfranchised women.

"This proposed election plan means that we ask the Western women to stand against any party or administration that is against us. It simply happens today that the party that has the power in the center of things is Democratic and so we ask them to discipline those men now in power and if tomorrow there comes in another party, then that party shall be disciplined if it does not fall gracefully under the yoke, which I think it will, because, as Miss Paul stated, to nothing are politicians, and statesmen even, more sensitive than to just how a voter is going to vote. So I believe thoroughly in this campaign that the Congressional Union has laid down. I regret that I personally have been forced right into the position of taking part in national affairs, but there seems to have come a parting of the ways, and I feel it my duty not only privately to make up my mind but publicly to state it."

MRS. KELLEY SPEAKS

Mrs. Blatch was followed by Mrs. Florence Kelley, also a member of the Advisory Council of the Union and known the country over as the General Secretary of the National Consumers' League.

"I am quite sure," said Mrs. Kelley, "that what Mrs. Blatch and Mrs. Rogers have said expresses the feeling that will animate the members of the Women's Political Union, but I have to confess that up to noon yesterday I did not understand the proposal. I think there has been a great deal of intentional misunderstanding abroad throughout the country, because garbled statements of the Union's policy have been given out. I do not know by whom. But I had certainly derived the opinion that there was to be a campaign indiscriminately, state, local, and national, against the Democratic Party and I had some fear that there might be a good many cases in which the Democrats may really be the friends of suffrage locally and such a campaign seemed ill judged and disproportionate. I cut off a week from my vacation to come down from Maine for the express purpose of having the Conference make some statement that we are not going to make such a campaign, but after the statement of the policy which has been made this afternoon and which I have been hearing in detail, yesterday and today, I see that the apprehensions which I had been cherishing were unfounded. I do not see how there could possibly be a more statesmanlike proposal than this which has been made this afternoon."

POINT OF VIEW OF A DEMOCRAT

Mrs. Bayard Hilles of Delaware, another member of the Advisory Council of the Union, was then introduced. Mrs. Hilles' remarks were listened to with great interest, as she is a member of an old Democratic family and the daughter of a member of President Cleveland's Cabinet. She said:

"Miss Burns has shown you who are the responsible ones for the failure of suffrage in this country, and Miss Paul has given a program of action. She has told us that we must go to the Western states and we must go to attack the Democratic Party. This question is more important than party—it is a national question—it is a suffrage question first. And until we get suffrage as a national matter, we had better leave off being Republicans or Democrats either. We must have the weapon of politics in our hands before we can choose what kind it must be. It is no easy matter for me as a Democrat to want to defeat Democrats, but I say to you that, though traditionally a Democrat with a long line of male relatives who have served their country in the Democratic Party, I would willingly go out to those states and devote my time to defeating every Democrat if it were going to bring women the right to vote. I hope very much that those of you who had any doubt in your minds when you came here this afternoon about the Congressional Union's policy will now see that it is a very plain, straightforward matter. There is no underhand dealing—we are telling what we mean to do to those men with their own weapon. That is the way that politics goes. Without political action we will gain nothing at all and therefore I beg you, as a Democrat, if there are other Democrats here, to put party behind the great national matter of suffrage and to stand for that until we have it an accomplished fact before us." . . .

40

Lucy Burns

The Susan B. Anthony Amendment (1916)

There are now in the United States over four million women who can vote in national elections.

Women are enfranchised in twelve states, controlling ninety-one electoral votes—more than one-third of the number necessary to elect a President of the United States.

All the states in which women vote are "doubtful" states. Not one of them has gone steadily for any one party in the last five presidential elections. In all of the equal suffrage states during the past five presidential elections,

From *The Suffragist,* June 3, 1916.

a turn-over of nine per cent of the total vote cast would have altered the result of the election and thrown the victory to the other party.

What does this prove? It proves that a comparatively small number of women who will put the issue of political freedom for women above loyalty to party and will chose between parties on the suffrage issue next November can, if necessary, hold the balance of power in the next presidential election and determine who shall be President of the United States for the next four years.

The federal suffrage amendment reads:
"The right of citizens of the United States to vote shall not be denied or abridged by the United States or by any State on account of sex."

This amendment was drafted by Susan B. Anthony in 1875. It was introduced in the Senate in 1878. It has been introduced in every Congress since that time and has received the unwavering support of every suffrage association in America.

There are two ways of winning suffrage for American women: one by amending the Constitution of every state in the Union, and one by amending the Constitution of the United States. Either way is equally proper and constitutional under the laws of our state and national governments.

The Congressional Union for Woman Suffrage prefers to work by the method of amending the United States Constitution, because this method is easier and quicker.

It is clearly easier to amend one national Constitution than to amend all the constitutions of the thirty-seven "unfree states."

An amendment to the Constitution of the United States must first be passed through Congress by a two-thirds' majority of the Senate and House of Representatives.

An amendment to the state constitutions must be passed, usually, by a two-thirds' majority in two successive legislatures; that would have to be done in thirty-seven states.

A national amendment must be ratified by three-fourths of the state legislatures; a simply majority vote suffices to ratify.

A state amendment must be ratified in each state by vote of the male electorate. This would require, before suffrage could be gained nationally, the submission of the question of woman suffrage to the entire voting population of the United States.

It is next to impossible for women to carry on a campaign of education covering all the men of the United States, and to get the vote in their favor registered and counted. The entire machinery of government is in the hands of political parties, almost always strongly opposed to the principle of woman suffrage. It is easy for a party to roll up an "organization vote" against woman suffrage and still entirely escape responsibility for doing so.

In some states it is almost impossible to amend the constitution. New Mexico has recently adopted a constitution in which the provision exists that it cannot be amended for twenty-five years. In Vermont an amendment, if defeated, cannot be reintroduced for ten years. In New Jersey a defeated amendment cannot be reintroduced for five years. In Illinois only one constitutional amendment can be submitted to the people at a given election; and in this state it is said to be the custom of politicians to submit a stock amendment to the people, so as to forestall the consideration of any other amendment. In Kentucky and Indiana only two amendments, and in Arkansas only three, can be submitted to the people at a given election. The suffrage amendment was recently passed by a two-thirds' vote of the Senate and House of Arkansas, but three other amendments were passed before the final vote on the suffrage measure was taken, so that the entire legislative work of getting the amendment submitted will have to be repeated by Arkansas women. In Minnesota a suffrage amendment must secure a majority of the votes cast at the election. This means that if one hundred thousand votes were cast for President of the United States and fifty thousand votes were cast on the suffrage amendment, forty-nine thousand for it and one thousand against it, the suffrage amendment would lose, the votes not cast on the suffrage amendment being counted as against it. This makes it almost impossible to amend the constitution of Minnesota at all. The same provision exists in the constitution of the state of North Dakota.

Under these conditions it would be unwise for women to embark upon the program of amending the constitution of all the states one after another.

The issue of national woman suffrage, always just, has now become politically expedient.

Four million women participating in national elections can demand and secure from national political leaders favorable action on the federal suffrage amendment in the present session.

The women of the entire nation are turning to the women of the west asking for their powerful aid in establishing freedom for women throughout the United States. It is a magnificent opportunity for western women to liberate at a stroke the women of the United States and to establish political freedom throughout America. The coming out of the United States for equal suffrage will be a signal for the nations of the world to adopt it. No moment could be more fitting for such an act than the present, when a great war has shown the close connection of the happiness of women with national destiny and the necessity of women's cooperation in the work of the nation for the nation's success in peace or war. The European war has been the final argument for the principle of equal suffrage in national affairs. Before the war closes, the United States, which advocates as a nation the right of the people to say whether or not they shall embark in war, should give its own people, women as well as men, the right of decision in such grave crises.

41
National Suffrage and the Race Problem (1914)

Among the objections that have been raised in an attempt to defeat the Federal Amendment enfranchising women is the one that it will complicate the race problem.

Without passing on the merits of the methods of preventing the Negroes from exercising the right of the franchise, we will take up the consideration of the situation as it would be today if the women of the South became enfranchised. If the subject is given careful consideration it will become evident that the enfranchising of all women will increase the relative power of the white race in a most remarkable way.

Quoting the United States Census of 1914, we find the proportion of white women to negro women and of white women to the whole negro population as follows:

State	Total Negro Population	White Women	Negro Women	Negro Men	Preponderance of White over Negro Women
Del.	31,181	83,715	15,170	16,011	68,545
Md.	232,250	533,567	117,501	114,749	416,066
D.C.	94,446	121,127	51,831	42,615	69,396
Va.	671,096	685,446	340,554	330,542	344,892
N.C.	697,843	745,659	358,262	339,581	387,397
S.C.	835,847	335,617	427,769	408,078	-92,152
Ga.	1,176,987	707,314	596,724	580,263	110,590
Fla.	308,669	211,089	147,307	161,362	63,782
Miss.	1,009,487	384,055	506,691	502,796	-122,636
Ala.	908,282	602,941	460,488	447,794	142,453
Tenn.	473,088	841,810	239,378	233,710	602,432
Ky.	261,656	997,918	130,164	131,492	867,754
Ark.	452,891	544,606	219,568	233,323	325,038
La.	713,874	460,626	360,050	353,824	100,576
Tex.	691,049	1,533,411	345,108	345,941	1,188,303

To sum up, in the fifteen states below the Mason and Dixon line there are 8,788,901 white women, while there are only 4,316,565 negro women, or 4,472,336 more white

From *The Suffragist*, November 14, 1914.

women than negro women in "Dixie." Not only that, but the total negro population of these fifteen states is only 8,294,274, so that the white women alone outnumber the entire negro population by 494,627.

In only two of these states, South Carolina and Mississippi, are there more negro women than white women, but the same condition exists for the men, and white supremacy could continue to be maintained by the same means as now prevails in these states. The race question would be in no way altered by equal suffrage.

In South Carolina the voter must be able to read and must own and pay taxes on three hundred dollars worth of property. In Mississippi the elector must be able to read the Constitution. The illiteracy of the Southern negro, and especially of those living in the most densely populated sections, is so well-known that it must become evident at once that any educational requirement will prevent a large section of that race from voting.

In four other of the states of the so-called "Black Belt," Georgia, Florida, Alabama, and Louisiana, there are more white women than negro women in each of the states, and there is also a very high requirement for the voting qualification. In Georgia a voter must fill out a registration blank, unaided. He must be able to read and write, or he must own property to the amount of forty acres, or have five hundred dollars in personal property. In Louisiana, he must be able to read and write, or if he cannot, he must then have had ancestors who voted before January first, 1867, and he must, himself, have registered before 1898. In Florida the literacy test is required. In Alabama, there is a rather unusual requirement. A man may vote if he can read and write, and if he owns forty acres or has three hundred dollars *or if his wife does.* If the fact that his wife owns property entitles him to vote, why should it not also qualify her? These tests are such that of necessity many cannot meet them today, neither negro men nor negro women.

In all the other nine Southern States, Delaware, Maryland, Virginia, District of Columbia, North Carolina, Kentucky, Tennessee, Arkansas, and Texas, there are more white women than there are negroes, both men and women, in the state.

An honest study of the race problem, and a comparative study of statistics will convince the student that equal suffrage would go far towards solving this vexed problem, for enfranchising women would not only increase the white vote, but would vastly raise the educational and moral standard of the voters, for, eliminating those negroes born and raised in slave days, the number of illiterate men, both black and white, in the southern states, far exceeds the number of illiterate women. The statistics for crime and immorality are the same in the south as elsewhere, male criminals greatly outnumbering the female. Therefore, it must be at once evident from these facts that the negro question would not be complicated but greatly simplified by the enfranchisement of the Southern woman.

42

ALICE STONE BLACKWELL

The Threefold Menace (1913)

Opponents of equal rights claim to see in the suffrage movement three great menaces to American institutions—militancy, "feminism" and Socialism.

The woman's movement in the main has been distinguished by its mild and peaceable character. From the French Revolution down the struggles of men to gain the right of self-government have usually been accompanied with violence and bloodshed. The women have worked for the same right by gentler methods. At the International Suffrage Congress in Bu-

From Alice Stone Blackwell, *The Threefold Menace* (Boston: Massachusetts Woman Suffrage Association, 1913). Originally published in *Woman's Journal.*

dapest last summer twenty-seven countries were represented. In twenty-six of them the movement is peaceful. In only one do we find a section of the suffragists resorting to violence. It is rational to infer that the violence in England is due to special circumstances peculiar to that country. Clearly it is not an inherent characteristic of the suffrage movement in general—quite the contrary.

NO SUFFRAGE MILITANCY HERE

In America the suffrage movement has always been peaceful, while the anti-suffrage movement has often been marked by violence. Yet so eager are the opponents of equal rights to fasten a charge of militancy upon the suffragists that they cry "Wolf!" upon all occasions, when there is no wolf within a thousand miles. The president of the National Anti-Suffrage Association even stigmatizes as militancy the announced intention of the suffragists to work for the defeat of candidates who are opposed to their measure—a perfectly peaceful and legitimate proceeding, and one that is used by all reformers who mean business.

While peering after an imaginary mote of militancy in their neighbor's eye, the antis quite overlook the big beam in their own—the attack upon the peaceful suffrage parade in Washington last March by hundreds of anti-suffrage hooligans; the pelting of Margaret Foley with breadcrusts and other fragments of a banquet in Ohio; the assailing of suffrage speakers in New York with snuff, pepper, pieces of broken glass, lemons, rolls of ticker tape and paper bags of water; the knocking down and kicking of a woman in Harlem by militant anti-suffragists; the attack upon the annual meeting of the Tennessee Equal Suffrage Association a few weeks ago by ruffians who broke the windows of the hall and hurled a can of explosive and vile-smelling chemicals in among the ladies. No anti-suffrage club has ever passed a resolution condemning any of these acts. If there is any danger of militancy in connection with the suffrage movement in America it is on the part of the opponents, not of the suffragists.

Since Nov. 1, 1912, by purely peaceful methods, woman suffrage has been gained in four States of the Union and in one Territory. It would be inexcusable foolishness for American suffragists to resort to militancy when they are succeeding so well without it.

AS TO "FEMINISM"

Feminism is a word of vague and various meanings. It is often used to cover the general movement in behalf of equal rights for women, which is in different stages in different countries. In some, women have won almost everything but a vote; in others they are still struggling for equal opportunities in education, or for admission to the professions, or, in China, for the use of their own feet. Anything and everything in the line of larger liberty for women is commonly lumped together under the term "Feminism."

By the anti-suffragists the word is always used in a sinister sense, as meaning the abolition of marriage, the destruction of the home and a general reign of immorality. These are about the last things for which women would vote if they had the ballot. Both in their opinions and in their practice, women are stricter than men in the matter of domestic morality. Nothing could well be more fantastic than the notion that, if direct weight were allowed to women's wishes, those wishes would generally be found to favor excessive license. All the vicious interests oppose woman suffrage, from a conviction that women would be severe upon them.

Some persons believe that, in the future evolution of men, women and society, all or most of the principles of old-fashioned morality will go by the board; but these persons are a comparatively small group, and it is made up of anti-suffragists as well as suffragists. For example, some decidedly startling literature of that kind by Emma Goldman was lately sold in the street outside a suffrage meeting in New York—it was not allowed to be sold in the hall—and opponents of equal suffrage have been twitting the suffragists about that literature ever since with vindictive glee. They forget that Emma Goldman goes about lecturing on "The Folly of Woman Suffrage." She belongs to their camp, not to ours.

This was an extreme case. A large number of persons believe that the institutions of marriage and the home, which have already undergone many changes for the better since the days when every man had an unquestioned right to beat his wife, are destined to undergo still further change and improvement. Sentences to this effect, by well-known suffragists, are taken out of their context by unscrupulous opponents and wrested to bear an objectionable sense utterly at variance with their true meaning; or passages really objectionable are quoted from writers whom the great majority of American suffragists never heard of, and these are presented as the true pith and marrow of suffrage doctrine. In this way a grossly misleading argument against so-called "feminism" is built up, and is used as an argument against votes for women.

The results of equal suffrage are no longer a purely academic question. Women are already voting in ten States of the Union, as well as in a number of foreign countries. In some they have had the ballot for many years. As a matter of fact and experience, we do not find that equal suffrage has anywhere led to the overthrow of the home or brought in a reign of immorality. Opponents used to prophesy that it would subvert all the foundations. Now they complain, on the ground that it has made so little difference! Such differences as it has made have been distinctly in the direction of raising moral standards and throwing added safeguards about the home.

Mrs. Julia Ward Howe in 1910 took a census of all the ministers of four leading denominations in the four oldest suffrage States—Wyoming, Colorado, Utah and Idaho—and also of all the editors. She asked them whether the results of woman suffrage were good or bad. She received 624 answers of which 62 were unfavorable, 46 on the fence and 516 in favor. The answers from the editors were favorable, more than 8 to 1; those from the Episcopal clergymen more than 2 to 1; from the Baptist ministers, 7 to 1; from the Congregationalists, about 8 to 1; from the Methodists, more than 10 to 1, and from the Presbyterians, more than 11 to 1. If equal suffrage had promoted those demoralizing results which the term "feminism" is said to imply, their pastors could hardly have failed to find it out.

Instead of equal suffrage having a bad effect upon marriage, every State that has given the ballot to women has declined in its ratio of divorce as compared with the rest of the country. Thus Colorado granted 935 divorces the year before women were enfranchised, and only 597 the year after; and during the twenty years since that happy event, the proportion of divorces to the population has never been anything like so large as it had been before. This is a fact; and "an ounce of fact is worth a ton of theory."

SUFFRAGE AND SOCIALISM

In these days the opponents of equal rights for women are continually harping upon Socialism. "Suffrage means Socialism," is their constant war-cry, both in their public addresses and in their official publications.

There are as many different kinds of Socialism as there are of Heinze's pickles, and the antis always pick out the most extreme variety, and usually caricature even that. "All Socialists are suffragists," they are constantly telling us; and they predict that granting votes to women will mean the speedy bringing in of the Socialist State.

Now, the Socialists themselves do not think so. All Socialists have woman suffrage as a plank in their theoretical platform, but many of them confess that they do not want it to come until Socialism comes, just because they believe that it would delay the coming of Socialism.

The Socialist Party admits women to membership on the same terms as men, but not nearly as many women as men have joined it.

The proportion is said to be about one to ten. In every State in the Union the Socialist vote cast at the presidential election of 1912 showed an increase over that cast at the the presidential election of 1908. Its average increase in the country at large was 112 per cent. But in every State where women have had the ballot long enough to compare presidential election with presidential election, the growth of the Socialist vote was below the average. The general public does not know these things, but the Socialists know them. They are aware that in the United States not nearly as many women as men believe in Socialism. Hence there is a sharp division in opinion among the Socialists, the more consistent members of the party standing up for woman suffrage, while the opportunist Socialists want to keep it from coming until after they have won a nation-wide Socialist victory.

They recall that at the first election in Los Angeles at which women voted, the Socialist ticket was snowed under, and that all the non-Socialists' papers attributed it to the women. In short, while the anti-suffragists are declaring suffrage to be a menace because it would bring in Socialism, a large part of the Socialists look upon it as a serious menace to their success, because of women's conservatism. . . .

When the antis say that "all Socialists are suffragists," it may be true in so far as they are all in favor of it in some ideal future; but many are practical anti-suffragists so far as the actual present is concerned. Some suffragists who had become Socialists are so indignant about it that they have left the party. The Socialists, however, are no worse in this respect than members of other parties. In States where every party has endorsed woman suffrage, we always find some Democrats, some Republicans and some Progressives who do not live up to that plank in their party's platform. But the anti-suffrage plea that suffrage means Socialism is absurd when we observe how many Socialists are afraid of it—and doubly absurd in view of the actual record of the elections in the enfranchised States.

43
Mrs. Paul Laurence Dunbar, Mary B. Talbert, Coralie Franklin Cook, Carrie W. Clifford, Mary Fitzbutler Waring, Nannie H. Burroughs, M. E. Jackson, Josephine St. Pierre Ruffin, Mrs. A. W. Hunton, Maria L. Baldwin, Anna H. Jones, Mrs. B. K. Bruce, Elizabeth Lindsay Davis, Mary Church Terrell, and Lillian A. Turner

Votes for Women (1915)

VOTES AND LITERATURE

By Mrs. Paul Laurence Dunbar

Matthew Arnold defined literature as a "criticism of life." By that he meant life in its entirety, not a part of it. Therefore, if a woman is to produce real literature, not pretty phrasing, she needs to have a firm grasp on all that makes life complete. The completion and perfection of life is love—love of home and family, love of humanity, love of country. No person living a mentally starved existence can do enduring work in any field, and woman without all the possibilities of life is starved, pinched, poverty-stricken. It is difficult to love your home and family if you be outcast and despised by them; perplexing to love humanity, if it gives you nothing but blows; impracticable to love your country, if it denies you all the rights and privileges which as citizens you should enjoy.

George Eliot, George Sand, Harriet Beecher Stowe wrote great novels because they looked at life from the point of view of the masculine mind, with a background of centuries of suffrage. Yet each was peculiarly feminine. It is a significant fact that the American and English women who are now doing the real

From *The Crisis*, August 1915.

work in literature—not necessarily fiction—are the women who are most vitally interested in universal suffrage.

WOMEN AND COLORED WOMEN

By Mrs. Mary B. Talbert

*Vice President-at-Large,
National Association of Colored Women*

It should not be necessary to struggle forever against popular prejudice, and with us as colored women, this struggle becomes twofold, first, because we are women, and second, because we are colored women. Although some resistance is experienced in portions of our country against the ballot for women, because colored women will be included, I firmly believe that enlightened men, are now numerous enough everywhere to encourage this just privilege of the ballot for women, ignoring prejudice of all kinds. . . .

By her peculiar position the colored woman has gained clear powers of observation and judgment—exactly the sort of powers which are today peculiarly necessary to the building of an ideal country.

"VOTES FOR MOTHERS"

By Mrs. Coralie Franklin Cook

*Member of the Board of Education,
District of Columbia*

I wonder if anybody in all this great world ever thought to consider *man's* rights as an individual, by his status as a father? yet you ask me to say something about "Votes for Mothers," as if mothers were a separate and peculiar people. After all, I think you are not so far wrong. Mothers *are* different, or ought to be different, from other folk. The woman who smilingly goes out, willing to meet the Death Angel, that a child may be born, comes back from that journey, not only the mother of her own adored babe, but a near-mother to all other children. As she serves that little one, there grows within her a passion to serve humanity; not race, not class, not sex, but God's creatures as he has sent them to earth.

It is not strange that enlightened womanhood has so far broken its chains as to be able to know that to perform such service, woman should help both to make and to administer the laws under which she lives, should feel responsible for the conduct of educational systems, charitable and correctional institutions, public sanitation and municipal ordinances in general. Who should be more competent to control the presence of bar rooms and "red-light districts" than mothers whose sons they are meant to lure to degradation and death? Who knows better than the girl's mother at what age the girl may legally barter her own body? Surely not the men who have put upon our statute books, 16, 14, 12, aye, be it to their eternal shame, even 10 and 8 years, as "the age of consent!"

If men could choose their own mothers, would they choose free women or bond-women? Disfranchisement because of sex is curiously like disfranchisement because of color. It cripples the individual, it handicaps progress, it sets a limitation upon mental and spiritual development. I grow in breadth, in vision, in the power to do, just in proportion as I use the capacities with which Nature, the All-Mother, has endowed me. I transmit to the child who is bone of my bone, flesh of my flesh and *thought of my thought; somewhat* of my own power or weakness. Is not the voice which is crying out for "Votes for Mothers" the Spirit of the Age crying out for the Rights of Children?

"VOTES FOR CHILDREN"

By Mrs. Carrie W. Clifford

*Honorary President of the Federation
of Colored Women's Clubs of Ohio*

It is the ballot that opens the schoolhouse and closes the saloon; that keeps the food pure and the cost of living low; that causes a park to grow where a dump-pile grew before. It is the ballot that regulates capital and protects labor; that up-roots disease and plants health. In short, it is by the ballot we hope to develop the wonderful ideal state for which we are all so zealously working.

When the fact is considered that woman is the chosen channel through which the race is to be perpetuated; that she sustains the most sacred and intimate communion with the unborn babe; that later, she understands in a manner truly marvelous (and explains only by that vague term "instinct") its wants and its needs, the wonder grows that her voice is not the *first* heard in planning for the ideal State in which her child, as future citizen, is to play his part.

The family is the miniature State and here the influence of the mother is felt in teaching, directing and executing, to a degree far greater than that of the father. At his mother's knee the child gets his first impressions of love, justice and mercy; and by obedience to the laws of the home he gets his earliest training in civics.

More and more is it beginning to be understood that the mother's zeal for the ballot is prompted by her solicitude for her family-circle.

That the child's food may be pure, that his environments all be wholesome and his surrounding sanitary—these are the things which engage her thought. That his mind shall be properly developed and his education wisely directed; that his occupation shall be clean and his ideals high—all these are things of supreme importance to her, who began to plan for the little life before it was even dreamed of by the father.

Kindergartens, vacation-schools, playgrounds; the movement for the City Beautiful; societies for temperance and for the prevention of cruelty to children and animals—these and many other practical reforms she has brought to pass, *in spite of not having the ballot.* But as she wisely argues, why should she be forced to use indirect methods to accomplish a thing that could be done so much more quickly and satisfactorily by the direct method—by casting her own ballot?

The ballot! the sign of power, the means by which things are brought to pass, the talisman that makes our dreams come true! Her dream is of a State where war shall cease, where peace and unity be established and where love shall reign.

Yes, it is the great mother-heart reaching out to save her children from war, famine and pestilence; from death, degradation and destruction, that induces her to demand "Votes for Women," knowing well that fundamentally it is really a campaign for "Votes for Children."

TRAINING AND THE BALLOT

By Mary Fitzbutler Waring, M.D.

Chairman of the Department of Health and Hygiene, N. A. C. W.

In the earlier ages, the thought was common among the nations of the world, that woman was not the equal of man. Socially, religiously and politically she was compelled to take an inferior position and to submit to the will and wiles of man. In some countries she was not even considered as the legal parent of her own child.

The ability to weigh the merits of the persons to fill office and the value of ordinances which govern the people, requires a knowledge of men and affairs. A trained mind, no matter in what profession, is more capable of making logical deductions; therefore the people naturally turn for information to the enlightened. The question of sex is of no importance.

The work of the professional woman just as that of the professional man places her in a position to help the many with whom she necessarily comes in contact, and therefore her influence is a power to be reckoned with. The ethical relations of the professional woman makes her, ofttimes, the confidant and advisor of others and for that reason she should be well informed on political issues and aspirants for public office.

Trained judgment is needed everywhere and it should always be armed with the ballot. . . .

BLACK WOMEN AND REFORM

By Miss N. H. Burroughs

Secretary of the Woman's Auxiliary to the National Baptist Convention

The Negro Church means the Negro woman. Without her, the race could not properly support five hundred churches in the whole world. Today they have 40,000 churches in the United States. She is not only a great moral and spiritual asset, but she is a great economic asset. I was asked by a southern white woman who is an enthusiastic worker for "votes for (white) women," "What can the Negro woman do with the ballot?" I asked her, "What can she do without it?" When the ballot is put into the hands of the American woman the world is going to get a correct estimate of the Negro woman. It will find her a tower of strength of which poets have never sung, orators have never spoken, and scholars have never written.

Because the black man does not know the value of the ballot, and has bartered and sold his most valuable possession, it is no evidence that the Negro woman will do the same. The Negro woman, therefore, needs the ballot to get back, by the wise *use* of it, what the Negro man has lost by the *misuse* of it. She needs it to ransom her race. A fact worthy of note is that in every reform in which the Negro woman has taken part, during the past fifty years, she has been as aggressive, progressive and dependable as those who inspired the reform or led it. The world has yet to learn that the Negro woman is quite superior in bearing moral responsibility. A comparison with the men of her race, in moral issues, is odious. She carries the burdens of the Church, and of the school and bears a great deal more than her economic share in the home.

Another striking fact is that the Negro woman carries the moral destiny of two races in her hand. Had she not been the woman of unusual moral stamina that she is, the black race would have been made a great deal whiter, and the white race a great deal blacker during the past fifty years. She has been left a prey for the men of every race, but in spite of this, she has held the enemies of Negro female chastity at bay. The Negro woman is the white woman's as well as the white race's most needed ally in preserving an unmixed race.

The ballot, wisely used, will bring to her the respect and protection that she needs. It is her weapon of moral defense. Under present conditions, when she appears in court in defence of her virtue, she is looked upon with amused contempt. She needs the ballot to reckon with men who place no value upon her virtue, and to mould healthy public sentiment in favor of her own protection.

THE SELF-SUPPORTING WOMAN AND THE BALLOT

By Miss M. E. Jackson

Of the Civil Service of the State of Rhode Island, President of the R. I. Association of Colored Women's Clubs

Looked at from a sane point of view, all objections to the ballot for women are but protests against progress, civilization and good sense.

"Woman's place is in the home." Would that the poorly paid toilers in field, work-shop, mill and kitchen, might enjoy the blessed refreshment of their own homes with accompanying assurance that those dependent upon them might be fed, clothed, properly reared and educated.

Each morning's sun beholds a mighty army of 8,000,000 souls marching forth to do battle for daily bread. You inquire who they are? Why, the mothers, wives, sisters and daughters of the men of America. "The weaker vessels," the majority of whom are constrained from necessity.

There is no field of activity in the country where women are not successfully competing with men. In the agricultural pursuits alone, there are over 900,000. In the ministry 7,000 dare preach the gospel with "Heads uncovered." And 1,010 possess the courage to invade the field of the Solons, bravely interpreting the laws, although their brothers in all but twelve of the forty-five States (so far as the ballot is concerned), class them with criminals, insane and feeble-minded.

The self-supporting woman out of her earnings, pays taxes, into the public treasury and through church, club and civic organization gives her moral backing unstintingly to her Country.

Imagine if you can the withdrawal of this marvelous economic force,—the working women of America! It is a fundamental necessity of modern civilization.

The laboring man has discovered beyond peradventure that his most effective weapon of defence is the *ballot in his own hand*. The self-supporting woman asks for and will accept nothing less.

"TRUST THE WOMEN!"

BY MRS. JOSEPHINE ST. PIERRE RUFFIN

Pioneer in the Club Movement among Colored Women of the United States

Many colored men doubt the wisdom of women suffrage because they fear that it will increase the number of our political enemies. I have been in suffrage work in Massachusetts for forty years and more. I have voted 41 times under the school suffrage laws. I was welcomed into the Massachusetts Woman's Suffrage Association by Lucy Stone, Julia Ward Howe, Ednah Cheney, Abby Morton Diaz and those other pioneer workers who were broad enough to include "no distinction because of race" with "no distinctions because of sex." I feel that a movement inaugurated by men and women of such wisdom and vision as that of the early workers, cannot dwindle or be side-tracked, and that today, as in those early days, the big women, the far seeing women, are in the ranks of the suffragists. We can afford to follow those women. We are justified in believing that the success of this movement for equality of the sexes means more progress toward equality of the races. I have worked, along with other colored women with those pioneers in the Abolition movement, in the various movements to open educational opportunities for women, business opportunities for women and to equalize the laws; the longer I have been associated with them, the more deeply I have been impressed by this farsightedness and broadmindedness of the leaders, both early and late, in the Woman Suffrage Movement.

Y.W.C.A.

BY MRS. A. W. HUNTON

Formerly Adviser to the National Board of Directors, Y.W.C.A.

A membership of more than a half million, representing some seventeen nationalities, makes the Young Women's Christian Association a world movement.

In the United States three hundred thousand members, distributed in 979 college, city and country associations have as their objective the advancement of the "physical, social, intellectual, moral and spiritual interests of young women."

One of the most unique and wonderful characteristics of the association is the adaptability to meet the needs of all types of women, so that its membership is as diversified as women's lives and interests. This diversified membership, constituting at once the governing and sustaining force of the association, is its strongest barrier to any creed save that upon which the movement is founded.

However, difficult as it is to express any relation between the association and the suffrage movement, it is not difficult to understand that the association spirit dominating womanhood would count for righteousness in the solution of this important question.

Acutely suffering from the wrongs and humiliations of an unjustly restricted suffrage, it is but natural that the colored woman should feel deeply and keenly wherever the question of suffrage arises. But the colored woman within the association, in common with thousands of her sisters who have been touched by other spiritual forces, is animated by a fine spirit of idealism—an idealism not too far removed from everyday existence to find expression in service. Hence she is giving her energy largely to the development of the highest qualities of mind and soul—for these alone can give to the nation the best there is in citizenship.

VOTES FOR TEACHERS

By Miss Maria L. Baldwin

Principal of the Agassiz Public School, Cambridge, Mass.

Woman teachers in those states where school suffrage has already been granted them have found out that even so meagre a share of voting power has given them a definite influence, and has brought about a few notable results. In several cases local schools have been kept, by the women's vote, from the control of persons who threatened all that was best in them. Candidates for election to school boards reckon early with the "teacher vote" and hasten to announce their "rightness" on this or that issue supposedly dear to teachers. It is wholly reasonable to infer that the extension of the suffrage will enable teachers to secure more consideration for themselves, and to have an important influence on the quality of the persons chosen to direct the schools.

At the outset teachers will be confronted by the temptation of power—the temptation to use it for personal or selfish ends. What, as a class, will they do with this temptation! What motives will lie behind their advocacy of men and measures? What tests of fitness will they apply to the candidate for their votes? Will they decline to recognize fine qualities for school service in one who may hold heretical views about increase of salaries, or length of vacations? These questions, which would test any group of workers, I cannot answer. I can only submit what seems an earnest that this group may stand the test.

The profession of teaching has a rich inheritance. These convictions were bequeathed to it, to have and to hold: that the dearest interests of life are in its keeping; that its peculiar service to society is to nourish and perpetuate those noblest aspirations called its ideals; that to do such work one must be devoted and unselfish.

This tradition still inspires the teacher. Some of the unrest, the dissatisfaction with conditions that are everywhere has penetrated her world, but probably no other work is done less in the commercial spirit nor any service more expanded beyond what "is nominated in the bond." Many school rooms are moving pictures of this spirit at work.

One is warranted in thinking that teachers will transfer to their use of the ballot this habit of fidelity to ideals.

WOMAN SUFFRAGE AND SOCIAL REFORM

By Miss Anna H. Jones

Chairman of the Department of Education, National Association of Colored Women

Of the four great institutions of human uplift—the home, the school, the church, and the State, woman has direct controlling force in the first three institutions. In the State her influence at present is indirect. Since her control in the three is unquestioned, should she not have the legal means—the ballot—to widen and deepen her work?

In terms of today, her work is the conservation and improvement of the child; child labor laws, inspection of the health of school children, safeguarding the youth in the home, in the school, in the court, in the street, in the place of amusement. Her work is the prevention of vice with its train of physical and moral evils; the enactment of laws to secure and regulate sanitation, pure food, prohibition, divorce; the care of the aged, the unfortunate, the orphan. All the questions touch in a very direct way the home—woman's kingdom.

When an experiment has been tried for a certain purpose it seems logical to refer to its success or failure. A review of the States in which women have had the ballot will show that their exercise of the franchise has been along the lines of reform mentioned above. Her ballot has not been cast against the forces of right. Is it probable that in the other, the more conservative States, her course will be less judicial?

It may take a little time for woman to learn to make the ballot count for righteousness, but her closer view, and sympathetic touch will be of material assistance in the solution of the social problems that confront her as the homemaker.

The century awaits the "finer issues" of woman's "finely touched spirit."

COLORED WOMEN'S CLUBS

By Mrs. B. K. Bruce
Editor of the Official Organ of the National Association of Colored Women

The national club movement among colored women began definitely in 1895, when a call was sent out from Boston by Mrs. Josephine St. P. Ruffin to a number of prominent colored women to meet in conference.

The special object of that conference was to repel and refute a vicious statement by an evil minded individual who had given currency to his false and misleading statements in book form. A national association called The National Federation of Colored Women, was formed at this conference.

The first convention of the new organization was called to meet a year later in July 1896, in Washington, D. C. In August of 1896 the first convention of the National League of Colored Women was held. The two organizations united under the name, National Association of Colored Women. In 1916 this organization will hold its tenth biennial session in Baltimore, Maryland. One year ago in Wilberforce, Ohio, the largest and most successful convention in its history was held. Over four hundred delegates, representing 50,000 women organized in clubs throughout the country, were present. The delegates came from the East, the West, the North, the South. The burden of the song of the numberless reports and addresses was social service not alone for colored people but for humanity. Miss Zona Gale said of the meeting that she had never attended a convention which so confirmed her belief in the possibilities of the common human race.

One thousand clubs are numbered with The National Association of Colored Women. In 1912–1913 these clubs raised $82,424. Over $60,000 was spent in purchasing property for Orphans' Homes, Working Girls' Homes, Christian Association Homes, Social Settlements and so on. In 1914 the valuation of the various properties exceeded $100,000.

VOTES FOR PHILANTHROPY

By Mrs. Elizabeth Lindsay Davis
National Organizer, National Association of Colored Women

The New citizen is no longer a novelty nor an experiment. She is demonstrating at all times her fitness for her duties and responsibilities by study; by insistent investigation of all candidates for public office regardless of party lines; by an intelligent use of the ballot in correcting the evils arising from graft, dishonesty and misappropriation of public funds; by persistent agitation to arouse civic consciousness, until now she is a potent factor in the body politic.

Men recognize her intuitive ability to think and decide for herself, respect her opinions and bid for her vote.

The keynote in the music of the Twentieth Century is Social Service, and in no better way can systematic philanthropy be done than by using the power of the ballot upon the heads of the great corporations and private individuals to direct their attention to the serious consequences of present day industrial and social unrest, the crime, disease, and poverty emanating from bad housing and unwholesome environment, to train their hands to give systematically to the cause of human betterment.

Woman is a pioneer in the forward movement for Social uplift, racial and community development, whether for the abandoned wife, the wage earning girl, the dependent and delinquent child or the countless hordes of the unemployed.

The highest and most successfully developed philanthropical work depends absolutely upon the control of political influence by the best American citizenship, men and women working in unity and cooperation at the polls.

WOMAN SUFFRAGE AND THE 15TH AMENDMENT

By Mrs. Mary Church Terrell

Honorary President of the National Association of Colored Women

Even if I believed that women should be denied the right of suffrage, wild horses could not drag such an admission from my pen or my lips, for this reason: precisely the same arguments used to prove that the ballot be withheld from women are advanced to prove that colored men should not be allowed to vote. The reasons for repealing the Fifteenth Amendment differ but little from the arguments advanced by those who oppose the enfranchisement of women. Consequently, nothing could be more inconsistent than that colored people should use their influence against granting the ballot to women, if they believe that colored men should enjoy this right which citizenship confers.

What could be more absurd and ridiculous than that one group of individuals who are trying to throw off the yoke of oppression themselves, so as to get relief from conditions which handicap and injure them, should favor laws and customs which impede the progress of another unfortunate group and hinder them in every conceivable way. For the sake of consistency, therefore, if my sense of justice were not developed at all, and I could not reason intelligently, as a colored woman I should not tell my dearest friend that I opposed woman suffrage.

But how can any one who is able to use reason, and who believes in dealing out justice to all God's creatures, think it is right to withhold from one-half the human race rights and privileges freely accorded to the other half, which is neither more deserving nor more capable of exercising them?

For two thousand years mankind has been breaking down the various barriers which interposed themselves between human beings and their perfect freedom to exercise all the faculties with which they were divinely endowed. Even in monarchies old fetters which formerly restricted freedom, dwarfed the intellect and doomed certain individuals to narrow circumscribed spheres, because of the mere accident of birth, are being loosed and broken one by one. In view of such wisdom and experience the political subjection of women in the United States can be likened only to a relic of barbarism, or to a spot upon the sun, or to an octopus holding this republic in its hideous grasp, so that further progress to the best form of government is impossible and that precious ideal its founders promised it would be seems nothing more tangible than a mirage.

VOTES FOR HOUSEWIVES

By Mrs. Lillian A. Turner

Honorary President of the Minnesota Association of Colored Women's Clubs

That the housewife, that great reasoner, will vote intelligently, is my happy conclusion, after reading the ponderous decision of a wise man, who protests that voters should be "only those who are able to substitute reason for sentiment." It is such a relief to have an impartial definition even though its close analysis might exclude a large portion of present voters. But my concern is with the housewife, the future voter, as tested by the wise man's definition.

Now, Sentiment is the housewife's most cherished possession; to this assertion all agree—the man, the anti-suffragist and the rest of us. Furthermore, lack of excessive use will keep it so, for the housewife early learns to substitute Reason for Sentiment. When Sentiment wails because husband walks two steps ahead instead of beside her; weeps because Boy's curls are shorn; foolishly resents the absence of the old attentions, and more foolishly dwells on an infinite variety of things, Reason comes nobly to the rescue and teaches her that none of these things are necessary to life. Reason is the constant substitute for her cherished Sentiment. But Reason's assertion that protection from vice for Son of the Shorn Curls, is impracticable for business reasons, is too difficult for mental gymnastics. Sentiment conquers, and the housewife unreasonably demands the ballot to protect Son! However, Reason being already so well developed through "discipline by substitution" (still quoting the wise man) I have ceased to tremble when I hear dire predictions of the ruin that is expected to follow the rapid approach of woman's franchise.

44
Carrie Chapman Catt
The Crisis (1916)

I have taken for my subject, "The Crisis," because I believe that a crisis has come in our movement which, if recognized and the opportunity seized with vigor, enthusiasm and will, means the final victory of our great cause in the very near future. I am aware that some suffragists do not share this belief; they see no signs nor symptoms today which were not present yesterday; no manifestations in the year 1916 which differ significantly from those in the year 1910. To them, the movement has been a steady, normal growth from the beginning and must so continue until the end. I can only defend my claim with the plea that it is better to imagine a crisis where none exists than to fail to recognize one when it comes; for a crisis is a culmination of events which calls for new considerations and new decisions. A failure to answer the call may mean an opportunity lost, a possible victory postponed.

The object of the life of an organized movement is to secure its aim. Necessarily, it must obey the law of evolution and pass through the stages of agitation and education and finally through the stage of realization. As one has put it: "A new idea floats in the air over the heads of the people and for a long, indefinite period evades their understanding but, by and by, when through familiarity human vision grows clearer, it is caught out of the clouds and crystallized into law." Such a period comes to every movement and is its crisis. In my judgment, that crucial moment, bidding us to renewed consecration and redoubled activity, has come to our cause. I believe our victory hangs within our grasp, inviting us to pluck it out of the clouds and establish it among the good things of the world. . . .

Therefore, fellow suffragists, I invite your attention to the signs which point to a crisis and your consideration of plans for turning the crisis into victory. . . .

MOVEMENT LACKS ORGANIZATION

Shall we play the coward, then, and leave the hard knocks for our daughters or shall we throw ourselves into the fray, bare our own shoulders to the blows and thus bequeath to them a politically liberated womanhood? We have taken note of our gains and of our resources and they are all we could wish. Before the final struggle, we must take cognizance of our weakness. Are we prepared to grasp the victory? Alas, no! Our movement is like a great Niagara with a vast volume of water tumbling over its ledge but turning no wheel. Our organized machinery is set for the propagandistic stage and not for the seizure of victory. Our

From *Woman's Journal,* September 16, 1916.

supporters are spreading the argument for our cause; they feel no sense of responsibility for the realization of our hopes. Our movement lacks cohesion, organization, unity and consequent momentum.

Behind us, in front of us, everywhere about us are suffragists,—millions of them, but inactive and silent. They have been "agitated and educated" and are with us in belief. There are thousands of women who have at one time or another been members of our organization but they have dropped out because to them, the movement seemed negative and pointless. Many have taken up other work whose results were more immediate. Philanthropy, charity, work for corrective laws of various kinds, temperance, relief for working women and numberless similar public services have called them. Others have turned to the pleasanter avenues of clubwork, art or literature.

There are thousands of other women who have never learned of the earlier struggles of our movement. They found doors of opportunity open to them on every side. They found well-paid posts awaiting the qualified woman and they have availed themselves of all these blessings; almost without exception they believe in the vote but they feel neither gratitude to those who opened the doors through which they have entered to economic liberty nor any sense of obligation to open political doors for those who come after.

There are still others who, timorously looking over their shoulders to see if any listeners be near, will tell us they hope we will win and win soon but they are too frightened of Mother Grundy to help. There are others too occupied with the small things of life to help. They say they could find time to vote but not to work for the vote. There are men, too, millions of them, waiting to be called. These men and women are our reserves. They are largely unorganized and untrained soldiers with little responsibility toward our movement. Yet these reserves must be mobilized. The final struggle needs their numbers and the momentum those numbers will bring. Were never another convert made, there are suffragists enough in this country, if combined, to make so irresistible a driving force that victory might be seized at once.

"THE WOMAN'S HOUR HAS STRUCK"

How can it be done? By a simple change of mental attitude. If you are to seize the victory, that change must take place in this hall, here and now!

The old belief, which has sustained suffragists in many an hour of discouragement, "woman suffrage is bound to come," must give way to the new, "The Woman's Hour Has Struck." The long drawn out struggle, the cruel hostility which, for years, was arrayed against our cause, have accustomed suffragists to the idea of indefinite postponement but eventual victory. The slogan of a movement sets its pace. The old one counseled patience; it said, there is plenty of time; it pardoned sloth and half-hearted effort. It set the pace of an educational campaign. The "Woman's Hour Has Struck" sets the pace of a crusade which will have its way. It says: "Awake, arise, my sisters, let your hearts be filled with joy,—the time of victory is here. Onward march."

If you believe with me that a crisis has come to our movement, if you believe that the time for final action is now, if you catch the rosy tints of the coming day, what does it mean to you? Does it not give you a thrill of exaltation; does the blood not course more quickly through your veins; does it not bring a new sense of freedom, of joy and of determination? Is it not true that you, who wanted, a little time ago, to lay down the work because you were weary with long service, now, under the compelling influence of a changed mental attitude, are ready to go on until the vote is won. The change is one of spirit! Aye, and the spiritual effect upon you will come to others. Let me borrow an expression from Hon. John Finlay: what our great movement needs now is a "mobilization of spirit,"—the jubilant, glad spirit of victory. Then let us sound a bugle call here and now to the women of the nation: "The Woman's Hour Has Struck." Let the bugle sound from the suffrage headquarters of every State at the inauguration of a State campaign. Let the call go forth again and again and yet again. Let it be repeated in every article written, in every speech made, in every conversation held. Let the bugle blow again and yet again: The political emancipation of our sex calls you women of America, arise! Are you content that others shall pay the price of your liberty? . . .

Give heed at once to the organization of the reserves; and then to the work that they shall do. Organize in every Assembly District and every voting precinct. It is the only way to make our appeal invincible. Swell the army, then set it upon the trail of every legislator and congressman, for they alone hold the key to our political emancipation. Compel this army of lawmakers to see woman suffrage, to think woman suffrage, to talk woman suffrage every minute of every day until they heed our plea.

All this is mere preparedness to the final drive to victory. The next question is: what shall be our aim?

AIM AT FEDERAL AMENDMENT

We have listened to an exhaustive discussion upon the three-cornered questions: shall we concentrate on the Federal Amendment; shall we concentrate on State Referenda; or shall we proceed as before, supporting both methods. The Convention has voted to continue both forms of activity but there is one further point which should be made clear before we adjourn and that is the exact program to be followed in the support of the two methods. This should be so precisely defined by this convention that every member, every friend and even every foe, may understand it.

We have long known the many obstacles imposed by most State Constitutions and that there are States in which women must wait a probable half century for their enfranchisement if no other avenue of escape is offered than amendment of their State constitutions. But there are other and even graver considerations which, in my judgment, should compel us to make the Federal Amendment our ultimate aim and work in the States a program of preparedness to win nation-wide suffrage by amendment of the National Constitution. I must say, in passing, that this is no new opinion. I have held it for a quarter of a century and the varying suffrage events of the passing years have only served to strengthen and emphasize my conviction. To my mind, the insistence of the enfranchisement of the women of our land by Federal Amendment, is the only self-respecting course to pursue. My reasons, I beg the privilege of presenting. . . .

Rich women, protected and serene, or women well paid by rich women, have grown bolder and more skilful in their unspeakable treachery to their sex. There have been those willing to vilify their sister women from ocean to ocean and to declare them too incompetent mentally and too unclean morally to be trusted with the privilege of self-government. Their motives suffragists will never understand.

The liquor forces have developed an organized opposition, apparently supported by large funds, which has been an active factor in every campaign except two since 1890, and in those two we won. The Secretary of one of the State Liquor Associations recently said to a man of honor, that they would not allow another State to be carried for suffrage within the next ten years. Still another representative of the same force said to another man that they could gather 10 millions of dollars if necessary to throw into any State which gave indications of a suffrage victory. These are doubtless wild threats, but the fact remains that a powerful force is arrayed against our cause, and it scruples at nothing.

In every precinct, there seem to be a few men willing to sell their citizen's right and these may be numerous enough to become a balance of power which added to the normal conservative vote may defeat our amendments. This "triple alliance," the women who work in the open, appealing to the respectable conservative element and the liquor forces secretly conniving with the purchasable vote, forms a combined foe very difficult to combat since its attack is subterranean.

Opposition in the open which meets our arguments with arguments, our claims with defense, must always be welcome. Truth has ever followed in the wake of free and honest discussion. But an opposition which conspires behind closed doors to buy its victory with money or spoils is a criminal so black, so indescribably hideous that it fills the soul, not with discouragement for our cause but with shame for our Republic. We shall never know how many campaigns have been lost by such conspiracies, but it is my own sincere conviction that there have been several. . . .

The liquor interests have been driven to the aggressive defensive by the inroads of the prohibition movement. They are obsessed by the idea that woman suffrage is only a flank prohibition movement. They have the American's right to fight for their own. We cannot relieve them of their notion that woman suffrage will promote prohibition and hence must accept their opposition as normal. But when that opposition ceases to be honest and resorts to conspiracy and bribery to gain its ends, it becomes criminal. . . .

With a vague, uncertain law to define their punishment in most States and no law at all in 25 states, as a preliminary security, corrupt opponents of a woman suffrage amendment find many additional aids to their nefarious acts. A briber must make sure that the bribed carries out his part of the contract. Whenever it is easy to check up the results of the bribe, corruption may reign supreme with little risk of being found out. A study of some of the recent suffrage votes results in significant food for reflection. In Wisconsin, the suffrage ballot was separate and pink. It was easy to teach the most illiterate how to vote "No" and to check up returns with considerable accuracy. In New York, there were three ballots. The official ballot had emblems which easily distinguished it. The other two were exactly alike in shape, size and color and each contained three propositions, those which came from the constitutional convention and the other those which came from the Legislature. The orders went forth to vote down the Constitutional provisions and it was done by a majority of 482,000, or nearly 300,000 more than the majority against woman suffrage. On the ballot containing the suffrage amendment which was No. 1, there was proposition No. 3, which all the political parties wanted carried. It could easily be found by all illiterate as it contained more lines of printing, yet so difficult was it to teach ignorant men to vote "no" on suffrage and "yes" on No. 3 that, despite the fact that orders had gone forth to all the State that No. 3 was to be carried, it barely squeezed through.

In Pennsylvania there are no emblems to distinguish the tickets and, on the large ballot, the suffrage amendment would have been difficult to find by an untutored voter. In consequence, as I believe, Pennsylvania polled the largest proportional vote for the amendment of any Eastern State. . . .

. . . It was easy to teach the dullest illiterate how to vote "No." It might be said that it would be equally easy to teach him to vote "Yes." True, but suffragists never bribe. Both the briber and the illiterate are allies of the Antis.

PARTY MACHINE A SAFEGUARD

The election boards are bi-partisan and each party has its own machinery, not only of election officials but watchers and challengers, to see that the opposing party commits no fraud. The watchfulness of this party machinery, plus an increasingly vigilant public opinion, has corrected many of the election frauds which were once common, and many elections are probably free from all the baser forms of corruption.

When a question on referendum is sincerely espoused by both the dominant parties, it has the advantage of the watchfulness of both party machines and is doubly safeguarded from fraud. But when such a question has been espoused by no dominant party, it is utterly at the mercy of the worst forms of corruption. The election officers may even agree to wink at fraud even when plainly committed, since it is no affair of theirs. Or, they may even go further and join in the pleasing game of running in as many votes against such an amendment as possible. This has not infrequently been the unhappy experience of suffrage amendments in corrupt quarters. With no one on the election board whose especial business it is to see that honesty is upheld, a suffrage amendment suffers further disaster through the fact that most States do not permit women watchers to stand guard over their own question.

When it is remembered that immigrants may be naturalized after a residence of five years; that, when naturalized they automatically become voters by all our State constitutions; that in nine States, immigrant voters are not even required to be citizens; that the right to vote is limited by an educational qualification in only 17 States and that nine of these are Southern with special intent of disfranchising the negro; that there is an unscrupulous body ready to engage the lowest element of our population by fraudulent processes to oppose our amendment; that there is no authority on the election board whose business it is to see that we get a square deal; that the method of preparing the ballot is often an advantage to the enemy; that after the fraud is committed there is practically no redress provided by election laws, it ought to be clear to all that State constitutional amendments when unsponsored by the dominant political parties which control the election machinery, must run the gauntlet of exceedingly unfair conditions. . . .

VOTE

Bear these items in mind and remember that three-fourths of the men of our nation have received the vote as the direct or indirect gift of the Naturalization laws; that the federal government enfranchised the Indians, assuming its authority upon the ground that they are wards of the nation; that the negroes were enfranchised by federal amendment; that the Constitutions of all States not in the list of the original thirteen, automatically extended the vote to men; that in the original colonial territory, the chief struggle occurred over the elimination of the land owning qualification and that a total vote necessary to give the franchise to non-landowners, did not exceed 50 or 75 thousand in any State.

Let us not forget that the vote is the freewill offering of our 48 States to any man who chooses to make this land his home. Let us not overlook the fact every five years of late an average of one million immigrant voters are added to our electors lists,—a million men mainly uneducated and all moulded by European traditions. To these men, women of American birth, education and ideals must appeal for their enfranchisement. No humiliation could be more complete; unless we add the sorrowful fact that leaders of Americanism in Congress and Legislatures are willing to drive their wives and daughters to beg the consent of these men to their political liberty. . . .

To my mind, the considerations aroused by such facts entirely outweigh any philosophy which supports the theory of suffrage by "State rights."

Again, let us not forget that while our struggle continues in this supposedly democratic land, women have been enfranchised within a year in three provinces of Canada nearly equal in extent to all our territory east of the Mississippi; in Denmark and Iceland by majority vote of their respective Parliaments. All signs indicate the early enfranchisement of the women of Great Britain by the same process.

AMERICAN WOMEN HUMILIATED

Why, then, should American women be content to beg the vote on bended knee from man to man, when no American male voter has been compelled to pay this price for his vote and no woman of other countries is subjected to this humiliation? Shall a Republic be less generous with its womanhood than an Empire? Shall the government be less liberal with its daughters than with its sons?

The makers of the constitution foresaw the necessity of referring important questions of State to a more intelligent body than the masses of the people and so provided for the amendment of the Constitution by referendum to the Legislatures of the various States. Why should we hesitate to avail ourselves of the privileges thus created. We represent one land and one people. We have the same institutions, customs and ideals. It is the advocates of the State rights who are championing national prohibition and child labor. It will be a curious kind of logic that can uphold these measures as national and, at the same time relegate woman suffrage to the States. Our cause has been caught in a snarl of constitutional obstructions and inadequate election laws. We have a right to appeal to our Congress to extricate our cause from this tangle. If there is any chivalry left, this is the time for it to come forward and do an act of simple justice.

In my judgment, the women of this land not only have the right to sit on the steps of Congress until it acts but it is their self-respecting duty to insist upon their enfranchisement by that route.

FEDERAL ACTION NOT A SHORT CUT

But, let me implore you, sister women, not to imagine a Federal Amendment an easy process of enfranchisement. There is no quick, short cut to our liberty. The Federal Amendment means a simultaneous campaign in 48 States. It demands organization in every precinct; activity, agitation, education in every corner. It means an appeal to the voters only little less general than is required in a referendum. Nothing less than this nation-wide, vigilant, unceasing campaigning will win the ratification.

Do not allow my comments to discourage you who represent the States where campaigns are pending. Your campaign may win the promise to safeguard your election from the dominant parties. It may so arouse public sentiment that any fraud may be outvoted. You are doing the best work possible. If you win, you have made Federal action and ratification more certain. If you lose, you have organized an army ready for your ratification campaign and have added testimony to the need of Federal action. What you have done in your State must be done in every State. A few women here and there have dropped out from State work in the fond delusion that there is no need of work if the Federal Amendment is to be the aim. I hold such women to be more dangerous enemies of our cause than the known opponent. State work alone can carry the amendment through Congress and through the ratifications. There must be no shirkers, no cowards, no backsliders these coming months. The army in every State must grow larger and larger. The activity must grow livelier and even more lively. The reserves must be aroused and set to work. Let no one labor under the delusion that suffrage can be won in any other way than by the education and organization of the constituencies. Let no woman think the vote will be handed her some bright summer morning "on a golden platter at the foot of a rainbow."

"The Woman's Hour Has Struck." Yet, if the call goes unheeded, if our women think it means the vote without a struggle, if they think other women can and will pay the price of their emancipation, the hour may pass and our political liberty may not be won.

WOMEN ARISE: DEMAND THE VOTE! The character of a man is measured, it is said, by his will. The same is true of a movement. Then, WILL to be free. Demand the vote. Women, ARISE!

45

ANNA HOWARD SHAW

My Position on the Different Policies of the National Association and the Congressional Union (1916)

First, I oppose partisan methods because I want suffrage before I want anything else and while I may be indignant at the attitude of a political party, my indignation should not blind me to the fact that you can't make an enemy of a person who has the power to control the situation in his hands and then expect him to comply with any request you may make in regard to it, that in our country the political situation is such that if the Suffrage Association should line up against any political party, that party would be able not only to block our federal amendment in Congress which requires a two-third vote to pass it, a number greater than any political party has had in Congress since the days of reconstruction but even if this were not so, if by the aid of the members of the other party from the enfranchised states, we were able to pass the measure through Congress, it would be possible to find enough legislatures in the different states controlled by the political party antagonized to defeat us in getting the three-fourth ratification of the amendment after it had passed Congress.

By working for federal suffrage alone we might possibly so block our movement as to make it impossible to get it ratified for the next twenty-five or fifty years under a political policy, while by a non-partisan policy we antagonize no one party politically and are able to win as many friends as possible from every party which sends its representatives to Congress.

Partisan action in favor of a federal amendment is most disastrous when campaigns are pending for the amendment of state constitutions, for it is impossible to carry our movement at the polls in any state without cooperation of suffragists from all parties and I firmly believe that the partisan policy of two years ago lost us Nebraska and South Dakota. If it is attempted this year it will lose us the last chance of winning Democratic West Virginia.

I also try to show that anything bordering on militancy, so called, is disastrous, that women never show up their real weakness so much as when they attempt force, and that it is perfect folly for us to threaten Congress with disaster if they do not grant our request when Congress knows as well as we do and a great deal better than most of us, that we have not the power to carry out our threat.

The boasted four million voters of the women of the West are practically equally divided between the two great political parties and we cannot hope to win many women over from the support of the Democratic Party. Those who are not in either the Republican or Democratic Parties are in some reform party such as the Prohibitionists and Labor and Socialist, and no hope in the world can be held out to win them to the Republican; and we can only defeat the Democrats by increasing the number of Republican votes and therein lies the folly of Miss Martin's last statement to the President, that if neither the Republicans nor the Democrats came out in favor of a federal movement during the campaign, the Woman's Party would "swing the strength of the four million women voters to the Progressive or the Prohibition Party." If anything could show the lack of political acumen, it would be a threat like that to a Democratic President since there is nothing the Democrats would like better than to have the Woman's Party throw its strength, whatever strength it may have, to the Progressives or the Prohibitionists since in that case it would be helping the Republicans to defeat them.

I have also argued that it is unthinkable to expect a man elected on a party platform

From NAWSA Papers, Library of Congress, Box 50. Typescript, dated July 27, 1916.

which is silent upon any subject, who yet when that subject is brought before Congress conscientiously espouses it, works for it and votes it, to be held responsible for the fact that his whole party does not espouse the measure and it is unethical to try to defeat his reelection to the position in which personal loyalty has put him in jeopardy for the sake of our cause. I also urged, in the case which was brought up of the Democratic caucus holding all of its members to vote against bringing the measure before Congress, that they can do so perfectly legitimately. So long as a man accepted election from the Democratic Party and agreed to abide by the decision of that Party, he ethically was bound to do so. The only way he could escape would be to resign his position in Congress and permit the Party to elect in his place a man who would stand by the pledges of his election, in which case I ask to which party would he give his allegiance if he were pledged to help us in Congress and we were defeating known friends to elect a possibly unknown enemy.

The reply has usually been that if we can prove that we are able to defeat the Democrats, it will so frighten the Republicans that they will in the next Congress grant our demand, to which I generally reply that the thing they will do will be that in the next Congress controlled by Republicans they will say that they are in power and they won't put the ballot in the hands of those women who threaten to defeat us whenever we do anything or do not do anything they demand. It is quite as apt to work that way as the other.

The illustration which I use to prove the fallacy of assuming that a political party to which we throw our allegiance will be sure to carry our measure through, if elected, is the case of Sweden.

When the International Alliance was held in Sweden we discussed whether or not the International would favor a partisan or non-partisan action. It was overwhelmingly voted that the International should remain non-partisan although Swedish women attempted to push the partisan policy.

The day following the close of the International meeting the National Alliance of Sweden held its annual meeting and the important question for discussion was the question of partisanship. It seems that in the previous Parliament the Conservatives had voted against the suffrage measure, while the Liberals had voted for it, but the Liberals were in the majority. The question now before the Swedish Alliance was whether or not to turn their influence to the Liberal Party and so put a favorable party in power in the government. After one of the most bitter discussions I suppose that was ever held in that body, it was decided to take a partisan stand and went so far as to demand the Conservative members of the Swedish Suffrage Association should not be permitted to speak during the campaign in favor of the Conservative members of Parliament nor in any way take part in the campaign; otherwise they must withdraw from the Swedish Suffrage Association, and that only work in behalf of the Liberals should be carried on. This, of course, split the Swedish Suffrage Association.

The result of this campaign was that the Liberals were elected and placed in power in the government and now the suffragists were sure that parliamentary suffrage must be granted by Sweden, but the Conservatives, immediately on the assembling of Parliament, introduced a very popular military defense bill. They went out and aroused the patriotism of their country just as it is being aroused in this country to-day, and so the suffrage measure was thrown into the background with every other measure and militarism became the one great issue of Parliament. Suffrage with every other reform measure was forgotten and although the Liberals were a very large majority in Parliament that year they were never able to get the bill moved and we have never heard of Parliamentary suffrage for Swedish women since. It did more to injure the suffrage movement in Sweden than anything which has ever been done. This is my recollection of the case.

The illustration which I gave of the folly of militancy or aggressive nagging military methods was the fact that during the time of the International Alliance in London, Mrs. Pankhurst put a meeting of her society in Albert Hall in the middle of our International meeting, but in order not to let the public know there was anything like dissention in the suffrage ranks, Mrs. Catt and the members of the Official Board of the International decided that it would be wise for us to close our meeting that evening and attend Albert Hall. Mrs. Pankhurst had not the courtesy to invite Mrs. Catt to the meeting although general invitations were issued to all the nations which were gathered at the Council, but Mrs. Catt with myself and some others were invited to occupy Mrs. Belmont's box, which we did. They had boxes decorated for Australia, New Zealand, Finland and the other countries where women already had suffrage and those women were invited to occupy these boxes, but not a single visiting woman, not even the president of the International Association, was invited to occupy a seat on the platform. The speeches of every one who spoke, and they were Mrs. Pankhurst, Chrystobelle, Mrs. Lawrence and Miss Goldthwaite, declared that the only possible way to secure suffrage was by following the methods adopted by Mrs. Pankhurst and her society. They had all the women who had been imprisoned on the platform and gave them their badges, which they all wore with pride to show us what martyrs they had been for the cause and what a lot they were doing for it. It greatly interested and amused some of us to look on the platform at that row of martyrs and then to look around at the various boxes where the enfranchised women sat and to hear Mrs. Pankhurst say that the only possible way by which we could get suffrage was through militancy when, as a matter of fact, not a single nation nor a single state in the United States nor a single province in Canada, has ever secured suffrage through militant methods. In England where the meeting was held, every bit of suffrage that it has was secured before militant methods were attempted and not one bit has been secured since.

When I quote the Swedish position, the answer was made to me that there was this difference between the Swedish position and ours: In Sweden the women had no vote in electing this Parliament but in our country we have that vast number of women voters in the West who can be counted to vote and therefore be a mighty power, and my reply was that while they did not have women voters, they did have influence enough with the men voters to elect their party and if the women voters vote they will vote for men and if men elected by men are not able to, or will not, stand by their pledges to women, what difference does it make whether these men are elected by men's votes or women's votes?

Until we have enough women voters, who can only be secured by states, to hold a sufficient balance of power to practically elect our supporters to Congress on that issue, in which case there could be no greater unwisdom than to organize a woman's political party, men will not stand by their pledges to women. The only political party that would ever have any power to carry out our measure would be a political party composed of men and women pledged to that one thing above all others and strong enough to elect its candidates.

46
The NAWSA Faces World War I (1917)

... Since last we met the all-engulfing World War has drawn our own country into its maelstrom and ominous clouds rest over the earth, obscuring the vision and oppressing the souls of mankind, yet out of the confusion and chaos of strife there has developed a stronger promise of the triumph of democracy than the world has ever known. Every allied nation has announced

From Ida Husted Harper, ed., *History of Woman Suffrage*, vol. 5 (New York: J. J. Little and Ives, 1922), 513–14, 438–40.

that it is fighting for this and our own President has declared that "we are fighting for democracy, for the right of those who submit to authority to have a voice in their own government." New Russia has answered the call; Great Britain has pledged full suffrage for women and the measure has already passed the House of Commons by the enormous majority of seven to one. Canada, too, has responded with five newly enfranchised provinces; France is waiting only to drive the foe from her soil to give her women political liberty.

Such an array of victories gives us faith to believe that our own Government will soon follow the example of other allied nations and will also pledge votes to its women citizens as an earnest of its sincerity that in truth we do fight for democracy. This is our first national convention since our country entered the war. We are faced with new problems and new issues and the nation is realizing its dependence upon women as never before. It must be made to realize also that, willingly as women are now serving, they can serve still more efficiently when they shall have received the full measure of citizenship. These facts must be urged upon Congress and our Government must be convinced that the time has come for the enfranchisement of women by means of an amendment to the Federal Constitution.

Men and women who believe that the great question of world democracy includes government of the people, by the people and for the people in our country, are invited to attend our convention and counsel with us on ways and means to attain this object at the earliest possible moment...."

In a stirring address Dr. Shaw showed what the country expected of women at this critical time, saying:

"We talk of the army in the field as one and the army at home as another. We are not two armies; we are one—absolutely one army—and we must work together. Unless the army at home does its duty faithfully, the army in the field will be unable to carry to a victorious end this war which you and I believe is the great war that shall bring to the world the thing that is nearest our hearts—democracy, that 'those who submit to authority shall have a voice in the government' and that when they have that voice peace shall reign among the nations of men.

"The United States Government, learning from the weaknesses and the mistakes of the governments across the sea, immediately after declaring war on Germany knew that it was wise to mobilize not only the man power of the nation but the woman power. It took Great Britain a long time to learn that—more than a year—and it was not until 50,000 women paraded the streets of London with banners saying, 'Put us to work,' that it dawned upon the British government that women could be mobilized and made serviceable in the war. And what is the result? It has been discovered that men and women alike have within them great reserve power, great forces which are called out by emergencies and the demands of a time like this."

Dr. Shaw described the forming of the Woman's Committee of the Council of National Defense by the Government and her selection as its chairman. She said she had no idea what the committee was expected to do, so she went to the Secretary of the Navy to find out, and continued: "I learned that the Woman's Committee was to be the channel through which the orders of the various departments of the Government concerning women's war work were to reach the womanhood of the country; that it was to conserve and coordinate all the women's societies in the United States which were doing war work in order to prevent duplication and useless effort. This was very necessary, not because our women are not patriotic but because they are so patriotic that every blessed woman in the country was writing Washington, or her organization was writing for her, asking the Government what she could do for the war and of course the Government did not know; it has not yet the least idea of what women can do."

An amusing picture was given of men supervising a department of the Red Cross where women were knitting, making comfort bags, etc. She showed how for the past forty years women in their clubs and societies had been going through the necessary evolution, "until today," she said, "they are a mobilized army ready to serve the country in whatever capacity they are needed. So when the Council of National Defense laid upon the Woman's Committee the responsibility of calling them together to mobilize women's war work, we knew exactly how to do it.... It is not a question of whether we will act or not, the Government has said we *must* act; it is an order as much as it is an order that men shall go and fight in the trenches. It is an order of the Government that the women's war work of the country shall be coordinated, that women shall keep their organizations intact, that they shall get together under directed heads. I said to the gentlemen here in Washington, when at first they feared our women might not be willing to cooperate: 'If you put before them an incentive big enough, if you appeal to them as a part of the Government's life, not as a by-product of creation or a kindergarten but as a great human, living energy, ready to serve the country, they will respond as readily as the men.'

"We must remember that more and more sacrifices are going to be demanded but I want to say to you women, do not meekly sit down and make all the sacrifices and demand nothing in return. It is not that you want pay but we all want an equally balanced sacrifice. The Government is asking us to conserve food while it is allowing carload after carload to rot on the side tracks of railroad stations and great elevators of grain to be consumed by fire for lack of proper protection. If we must eat Indian meal in order to save wheat, then the men must protect the grain elevators and see that the wheat is saved. We must demand that there shall be conservation all along the line. I had a letter the other day giving me a fearful scorching because of a speech I made in which I said that we women have Mr. Hoover looking into our refrigerators, examining our bread to see what kind of materials we are using, telling us what extravagant creatures we are, that we waste millions of money every year, waste food and all that sort of thing, and yet while we are asked to have meatless days and wheatless days, I have never yet seen a demand for a smokeless day! They are asking through the newspapers that we women shall dance, play bridge, have charades, sing and do everything under the sun to raise money to buy tobacco for the men in the trenches, while the men who want us to do this have a cigar in their mouth at the time they are asking it! I said that if men want the soldiers to have tobacco, let them have smokeless days and furnish it! If they would conserve one single cigar a day and send it to the men in the trenches the soldiers would have all they would need and the men at home would be a great deal better off. If we have to eat rye flour to send wheat across the sea they must stop smoking to send smokes across the sea.

"There is no end to the things that women are asked to do. I know this is true because I have read the newspapers for the last six months to get my duty before me. The first thing we are asked to do is to provide the enthusiasm, inspiration and patriotism to make men want to fight, and we are to send them away with a smile! That is not much to ask of a mother! We are to maintain a perfect calm after we have furnished all this inspiration and enthusiasm, "keep the home fires burning," keep the home sweet and peaceful and happy, keep society on a level, look after business, buy enough but not too much and wear some of our old clothes but not all of them or what would happen to the merchants?... We are going to rise as women always have risen to the supreme height of patriotic service....

"The Woman's Committee of the Council of National Defense now asks for your cooperation, that we may be what the Government would have us be, soldiers at home, defending the interests of the home, while the men are fighting with the gallant Allies who are laying down their lives that this world may be a safe place and that men and women may know the meaning of democracy, which is that we are one great family of God. That, and that only, is the ideal of democracy for which our flag stands."

47
Alva Belmont (Mrs. Oliver H. P.)
Excuses for White House Picketing (1917)

To the Editor of the New York Times:

So many letters from eager and intelligent men and women have come to me inquiring as to the purpose of suffrage picketing that I feel it is due these seeking information to be told of the great motive animating the suffrage sentinels to their duty. I hope, therefore, that you will make public this letter which will perhaps in part answer the questions asked.

Few people realize, perhaps, that picketing is just an advance form of demonstration which the women are forced to make in order to call to the attention of a resisting Government and an indifferent mass of people the claim of women, now of all times, to participation in the Government on equal terms with men. Every new form of appeal which women have with great resourcefulness been forced to use has been condemned by the unthinking and the conservative. It was so with processions, beautiful as they were. It was so with street meetings, necessary as they were. It has been so with deputations, conventions, lobbying, automobile and steam car tours of suffragists, and now and we hope lastly, the necessary picketing and unjust imprisonment of the silent sentinels who so courageously plead for the enfranchisement of women.

American women have been imprisoned for holding at the gates of the White House banners demanding democracy at the hands of a Democratic Administration. They have committed no violence, but have stood there quietly, peacefully, lawfully, and gloriously. In return they have been attacked by the metropolitan police and their property destroyed. One of the banners they were arrested for holding bore a quotation from President Wilson's book, "The New Freedom," which read: "We are interested in the United States, politically speaking, in nothing but human liberty."

Another banner bore this legend, "How long must women wait for liberty?"

And still another one carried the noble words of Susan B. Anthony, written at a time when our nation was also at war, which read:

"We press our demand for the ballot at this time in no narrow and captious or selfish spirit, but from purest patriotism for the highest good of every citizen, for the safety of the Republic, and as a glorious example to the nations of the earth."

The other three women who were arrested and sentenced to prison carried the tricolored flags of purple, white and gold, the emblem of the National Woman's Party.

Defenders of democracy abroad become outraged that American women should continue to demand democracy at home. In Italy and France, and even in Germany, the demand by women for participation in the Government is growing more powerful. In new free Russia women have already voted; in England the bill is assured of passage, and yet America, which has laid claim to leadership in world democracy, allows women to be unlawfully arrested through its Government at Washington for merely doing their patriotic duty urging the wisdom and justice of the great ideal of democracy. Women cannot be so unpatriotic as not to complain of a grievous injustice which denies them freedom at home while they are asked to send their sons abroad to fight for world democracy. If democracy is noble, if it is a principle, an ideal worth dying for, then is it not an extraordinary attitude on the part of the President and Congress which allows women no right even to appeal for justice, let alone receive it?

If we were now sitting in the halls of Congress or were represented nationwide in that body, we would not have to take the humiliat-

From *The New York Times,* July 9, 1917.

ing method of printing our appeals on innocent banners. We should then be able to speak authoritatively through legislative channels. As it is we are forced to call to the attention of the world the resistance of our Government by the only method left to us. And shall we not protest when men not only continue to refuse to give us our liberty but decide the manner in which we shall demand our liberty?

Foreign Governments are allowed to present their claims to allegiance in the world war for democracy through representative commissions. These demands are officially recognized by our Government. Since the demands of women are not, we must take the only means left to us. "Militant?" Why all this tenderness and delicacy about "militancy" in the form of banner-bearing when the Governments of all nations are conscripting their men, including our own nation, to be militant? They leave them no choice. Why this horror of mild "militancy" on the part of subject citizens?

We insist that we women would be ashamed to stop trying to win democracy at home—now of all times—when the whole world is dying to possess this precious political freedom. We believe with Garibaldi that "only free men can fight for freedom." All we ask is simple justice. And we ask it now, because we know that the enfranchisement of women as well as men will make the world permanently safe for democracy.

The sentimental ladies and gentlemen who are so afraid lest we fatigue the President are urged to remember that we ourselves are very, very tired, and perhaps the sentimentalists will confer some pity on the faithful women who have struggled for three-quarters of a century for democracy in their own nation.

The Government itself and not the women is responsible for the situation which it has created. It can overcome the embarrassment of having increasing numbers of women expose its shortcomings to the world in one hour's time. Women patriots on behalf of democracy will never rest their labors until the Government has yielded its stupid resistance.

I ask you, Mr. President and gentlemen of the congress, in the words of our valiant and beloved leader, Inez Milholland Boissevain, "How long must women wait for liberty?"

48

Doris Stevens

The Militant Campaign (1919)

A successful young Harvard engineer said to me the other day, "I don't believe you realize how much men objected to your picketing the White House. Now I know what I'm talking about. I've talked with men in all walks of life, and I tell you they didn't approve of what you women did."

This last with warmer emphasis and a scowl of the brow. "I don't suppose you were in a position to know how violently men felt about it."

I listened patiently and courteously. Should I disillusion him? I thought it was the honest thing to do. "Why, of course men didn't like it. Do you think we imagined they would? We knew they would disapprove. When DID MEN EVER applaud women fighting for their own liberty? We are approved only when we fight for yours." "You don't mean to say you planned to do something, knowing men would not approve?" I simply had to tell him. "Why, certainly! We're just beginning to get confidence in ourselves. At last, we've learned to make and stand by our own judgments." "But going to jail. That was pretty shocking." "Yes, indeed it was. It not only shocked us that a government would be alarmed enough to do such a thing, but what was more to the point, it shocked the entire country into doing something quickly about woman suffrage."

People are already beginning to put the proper judgment upon the latest phase of woman's militant fight for political liberty in

From *The Suffragist*, July 19, 1919. Reprinted from *Omaha Daily News*, June 29, 1919.

America. I refer to the last six years of the intensive and courageous agitation conducted by the leaders of the National Woman's Party, which organization centered much of its attack on the government at Washington.

To understand the purpose and effect of this centralization of attack one must remember the long, forty-year fight during which woman's suffrage by national action made scant progress.

Suffragists have exhausted every form of approach known to human imaginations, such as processions, deputations, resolutions, interviews, mass meetings, open air meetings, drawing room meetings, pamphlets, legislative hearings before congressional committees, bazaars, and the thousand usual forms of campaign.

Smiles, sweet words, promises, weak planks in party platforms, empty eloquence at banquets by the slightly more astute politicians had been their main reward.

"What of immediate action?" said the suffragists.

"This is not the time," was the complacent answer from men who were in power, with nothing to win or gain by really standing up and fighting on this issue as they did on issues which affected their political interests and which commanded their fervent support.

"We must make woman suffrage an immediate issue; we must create a political situation so acute that politicians will have to settle it. National legislators must face suffrage as a question on which they will rise or fall, just the same as they rise or fall before an electorate on peace, war, currency, prohibition, tariff and the multitude of other campaign issues."

This was the problem which the younger suffrage leaders faced. This was the task undertaken by that unparalled organizing genius and political strategist, Miss Alice Paul, the frail little Quaker scholar who has inspired the profoundest respect in the breasts of the enemies of suffrage and the warmest devotion and admiration among friends.

The message sent to Miss Paul by Chief Justice Walter Clark of the supreme court of North Carolina typifies this faith and judgment:

"Will you permit me to congratulate you upon the great triumph in which you have been so important a factor? Your place in history is assured. Some years ago when I first met you I predicted that your name would be written 'on the dusty roll the ages keep.' There were politicians, and a large degree of public sentiment, which could only be won by the methods which you adopted. It is certain that but for you success would have been delayed for many years to come."

This was the comment, not of a fiery radical, but of a southern judge. Those of us who have been fortunate enough to have been associated with Miss Paul in the last few years know how true these words are.

A superficial observer might fancy the plan of campaign ill advised, sporadic and fanatical. It must be understood that every step was taken only after the most mature consideration. It was deliberate. It was based on well established political and military strategy, and upon a deep knowledge of the history of all reform movements.

Who were the members of the executive committee who considered, and planned, and executed the program?

Mrs. Oliver H. P. Belmont, always in the first rank of the fight, she who had begun her suffrage work with the more conservative wing and in spite of her years had deserted to the young rebel camp; Mrs. Florence Bayard Hilles, daughter of Thomas Bayard, our first ambassador to Great Britain and secretary of state under President Cleveland (she made a wonderful jail mate); Mrs. John Rogers, Jr., direct descendant of Roger Sherman, one of the signers of the Declaration of Independence; Mrs. John Winters Brannan, daughter of Charles A. Dana, founder of the *New York Sun,* and an intimate friend of Lincoln; Miss Anne Martin, first woman to stand as a candidate for the United States Senate from Nevada, herself state president of the suffrage association in Nevada, which won state suffrage for Nevada women; Mrs. Donald Hooker, wife of Dr. Hooker, of Johns Hopkins University; Mrs. Lawrence

Lewis, sister of Dr. Kelley, famous radium expert, herself a member of Philadelphia's most exclusive clubs, founder of the Lighthouse Settlement and many other charities; Miss Lucy Burns, Vassar graduate and student abroad, formerly a teacher in the New York public schools, and so on. All women of education, scholarly attainments and gentle culture.

The military strategy of the campaign was based upon the military doctrine of concentrating all one's forces on the enemy's weakest point. The weakest point in our country's political lines, especially during the war, was our boasted crusade for world democracy, with the glaring inconsistency of the denial of democracy at home. That was the untenable position of President Wilson and the Democratic Administration.

Our political strategy consisted of opposing the party in power at elections, which had failed to use its power to free women. This not only harassed the offending party, but by example forced down the opposition of the minority party.

The most primer knowledge of history had taught us that no great reform could hope to succeed without a downright fight. Not necessarily a fight with arms; perhaps merely with brains, wits, and devoted sacrifice, but a real fight. That, we decided, was the self-respecting thing to do. We could not knowingly submit to injustice.

To return for a moment to the weakness in the President's armor. Here was a world leader with the almost pathetic trust of the peoples of the world, riding like a knight of old, championing the ideals of liberty, fraternity, democracy, equality and what not; also the self-determination of the Serbs, Poles, Czecho-Slovakians, Armenians, Rumanians—in fact, all the struggling nations of Europe.

Against this beautiful ephemeral hope and promise the women were demanding long delayed action. Action. That was the "acid test" of words, we said.

And so we started out to force action.

We merely sought to so dramatize this weakness with the only weapons at hand to which a powerless class which does not take up arms can resort. Did you ever stop to compare the methods which women adopted in their fight for liberty to those men use in the same struggle?

Bayonets, machine guns, poison gas, deadly grenades, liquid fire, bombs, armored tanks, pistols, barbed wire entanglements, submarines, mines—every known scientific device with which to annihilate the enemy.

What did we do? We could not and would not fight with such weapons.

How were we to make our fight seem more heroic and important by the side of men's world conflagration?

How could we, with reasonable speed, rout the enemy without weapons, and we a class without power and recognition?

Our simple, peaceful, almost quaint device was a BANNER! A banner on which were inscribed pertinent truths and burning questions, fiery challenges and sedate quotations from no less respectable sources than the Declaration of Independence, the Bible, President Wilson's learned volumes on "Liberty and the New Freedom," Abraham Lincoln, the great emancipator, and so on.

How could we possibly know a banner would create such a panic among presidents and cabinet ministers, congressmen and the populace? We must confess we thought this strange and gentle kind of warfare would disturb their afternoon naps and drives, their theater parties and golf games.

That it would alarm the high and mighty to such an astounding course of action our fondest hopes could not have guaranteed.

But the panic was on.

Hurried cabinet meetings, unprecedented meetings of the President himself with the District of Columbia commissioners! The summoning of the military to discuss declaring a military zone around the White House.

Rain and snow storms and freezing temperature did not deter these "unreasonable women." The sentinels, later known as White House pickets, kept up the vigil at the gates of the leader of the nation—the one powerful leader who could compel an unwilling Congress to act.

What would YOU do if you owed a just bill and every day someone stood outside your gates as a quiet reminder to the whole world that you had not paid it?

You would object. Yes.

You would get terribly irritated. Yes.

You would call the insistent one all kinds of harsh names. You might even arrest him. But the scandal would be out.

Rightly or wrongly, your sincerity would be touched; faith in you would be shaken a bit. Perhaps even against your will you would yield.

But you WOULD yield. And that was the one important fact to the women.

RIDICULED? of course. But we had nothing to lose by being ridiculed. Woman is more or less used to that weapon of men anyway. But a president and a cabinet simply cannot stand being made ridiculous, especially by women. That is what hurts.

There must be some way out of this difficulty, the government argued. And so they turned to jail.

Jail is always a convenient institution used by the oppressor when he miscalculates the strength of the oppressed. It would have been easy to jail two women. But what of 200?

When the two hundred mark had been reached the government collapsed. The stream of women willing to submit to the indignities of prison was endless. Obviously, the government must change its tactics.

More cabinet meetings. More hurried consultations. A government agent is sent to visit our leaders in prison to ask if we will abandon "picketing" if Congress passes the measure through one house and not the other.

A firm "No!" from the women.

Finally, unconditional release of all prisoners then serving, and no more arrests on the false charge of "blocking the traffic."

The women had won.

No matter that the higher courts subsequently declared all picket arrests, convictions and imprisonments illegal and unwarranted. The women were not bitter.

They could afford to forgive stupidity which had worked as a boomerang upon the government.

And so I repeat what has never been a secret. We set out to embarrass an administration unwilling to enfranchise women. We succeeded so well that we began to get results. The minute the government began to move we changed our strategy.

Finally, both majority parties were maneuvered into the long-sought position where neither could afford to dally longer. And to good Republicans I would say, "Do not be so sure your own party would have shown such eagerness to pass the amendment this session if it had not had before its political eyes for the last six years the very convincing argument of witnessing the political chastisement of the Democrats by the 'unreasonable women.'" That had a most salutary effect on the most conservative Republican.

The amendment has been passed in Congress, and now comes the last stage of our fight, ratification of the amendment by thirty-six states. Already eleven states have ratified. This stage is less spectacular, less heroic, but very necessary. At the rate we are now going we shall have completed the task by autumn.

49
INEZ HAYNES IRWIN
AND AVA DAVENPORT KENDALL
The Strange Ladies (1921)

... The preceding two chapters have been concerned mainly with the treatment of the pickets at the hands of the law. We now approach a much graver matter—their treatment at the hands of the prison authorities. This chapter describes what is one of the most disgraceful

From Inez Haynes Irwin, *The Story of the Woman's Party* (New York: Harcourt, Brace and Co., 1921; Kraus Reprint Co., 1971), 262, 287–91.

episodes in the history of the United States. It is futile to argue that what happened in the District Jail and at Occoquan Workhouse, and later at the abandoned Workhouse, was unknown to the Administration. The Suffragists, indeed, published it to the entire country. That the treatment to which the pickets were subjected was the result of orders from above is almost demonstrable. It must be remembered that the officials who are responsible for what happened to the pickets—the three Commissioners who govern the District of Columbia, the police court judges, the Chief of Police, the warden of the jail, the superintendent of Occoquan Workhouse, are directly or indirectly answerable to the President. . . .

In the files at Headquarters, there are dozens of affidavits made by the women who went to jail of picketing. It is a great pity that they cannot all be brought to the attention of a newly enfranchised sex. More burningly than anything else, these affidavits would show that sex what work lies before them, as far as penal institutions are concerned. I quote but one of them—that of Ada Davenport Kendall—because it sums up so succinctly and specifically the things that the prison pickets saw.

"I went into Occoquan Prison as a prisoner on September 13, 1917.

"I went in with the idea of obeying the regulations and of being a reasonable prisoner.

"While there I saw such injustice, neglect, and cruelty on the part of the officials that I was forced into rebellion.

"During my thirty days' imprisonment I saw that commissioners and other officials made occasional visits but that the people in charge were usually warned and used much deception on the occasion of these visits. Specially prepared food replaced the wormy, fermenting, and meager fare of ordinary days. Girls too frail to work were hurried off the scrubbing and laundry gangs, and were found apparently resting. Sick women were hidden. Girls were hurried out of punishment cells as the visitors proceeded through the buildings, and were hidden in linen rooms or rooms of matrons already inspected.

"While there I was treated with indignities. I was insulted by loud-mouthed officials at every turn, was stripped before other women, stripped of all toilet necessities, warm underwear, and ordinary decencies, was deprived of soap, tooth-brush, writing materials, and sufficient clothing and bed coverings. I was dressed first in clean garments, but the officials later punished me by putting me in unclean clothing and into a filthy bed in which a diseased negress had slept. In the hospital I was obliged to use the toilet which diseased negro women used, although there was a clean unused toilet in the building.

"With the four other women who were sentenced with me I was fed food filled with worms and vile with saltpeter; food consisting of cast-off and rotting tomatoes, rotten horse meat and insect-ridden starches. There were no fats: no milk, butter, nor decent food of any kind. Upon this fare I was put at hard labor from seven A.M. until five P.M., with a short luncheon out. We were not allowed to use the paper cups we had brought, but were forced to drink from an open pail, from common cups.

"After several days of driven labor this group was ordered to wash the floors and clean the toilets in the dormitory for the colored inmates. I protested for the whole group: said we would not do this dangerous work. For this I was put in solitary confinement which lasted for nearly seven days. Water was brought three times in the twenty-four hours, in a small paper cup. Three thin slices of bread were brought in twenty-four hours. Several times matrons with attendants came in and threatened me and threw me about. They searched me for notes or any writing, and threw me about and tore my clothes. I was allowed no water for toilet, and the only toilet convenience was an open bucket. No reading nor writing materials were allowed. Mail was cut off, as it was nearly all of the time while I was in prison. I was not allowed to see an attorney during this period. The bed had been slept in and was filthy, and there was no other furniture. After six days, influential friends were able to reach my case from outside the prison, and I was taken out of solitary confinement.

"While in prison I heard men and women crying for help, and heard the sound of brutal lashes for long periods,—usually in the evening, after visitors were not expected.

"I saw a woman have a hemorrhage from the lungs at nine in the morning—saw her lie neglected, heard the matrons refuse to call a doctor; and at eleven saw the woman carry a tobacco pail filled with water to scrub a floor; saw her bleeding while she was scrubbing, and when she cried a matron scolded her.

"Saw a young dope fiend who was insane run out of a door, and heard a matron at the telephone order men to loose the bloodhounds upon this girl in the dark. Soon heard the dogs howling and running about.

"Saw men with fetters on legs being driven to and from work.

"Saw matrons choke and shake girls.

"Was continually disgusted with lack of fair play in the institution.

"Inmates were set to spy upon the others, and were rewarded or punished, as they played the game of the matrons.

"Saw sick girls working in laundry. Saw diseased women sleeping, bathing, and eating with other inmates.

"Saw armed men driving prisoners to work.

"Saw milk and vegetables shipped to Washington, and rotting vegetables brought up from city market.

"Saw unconscious women being brought from punishment cells.

"Saw sick women refused medical help, and locked in the hospital without attendance to suffer. Saw them refused milk or proper food. Saw them refused rest, and once I saw the only medical attendant kick at a complaining inmate and slam the office door in her face.

"Found that while the institution was supposed to build and improve inmates, they were ordinarily not allowed any recreation nor proper cleanliness. No classes were held, and no teaching of any sort was attempted. They were deprived of all parcels, and mail was usually withheld both coming and going. Visitors and attorneys were held up, and the prisoners usually absolutely shut away from help.

"Found that no rules governing the rights of the prisoners had been codified by the Congressional Committee responsible for the institution, and was told by the superintendent that the prisoners had no rights and that the superintendent could treat the inmates as he liked.

"Under that management, the matrons, while apparently ordinarily decent and often making a good first impression, were found to be brutal and unreasonable in their care of inmates.

"The inmates were driven, abused, insulted. They were not allowed to speak in the dining-room or workrooms or dormitories. It was a place of chicanery, sinister horror, brutality, and dread.

"No one could go there for a stay who would not be permanently injured. No one could come out without just resentment against any government which could maintain such an institution."

As has been told before Judge Waddill decided that the pickets had been illegally transferred from the Jail to Occoquan and they were sent back to the Jail. But between Occoquan and Jail occurred one night, in which the pickets were released in the custody of Dudley Field Malone, their counsel. They went immediately to Cameron House and broke their hunger-strike—spent the evening before the fire, talking and sipping hot milk. The next day they were committed to jail again and immediately started a new hunger-strike.

The government, however, undoubtedly appalled by the protests that came from all over the country, and perhaps, in addition, staggered at the prospect of forcibly feeding so many women, released them all three days later.

A mass-meeting was held at the Belasco Theatre early in December to welcome them. The auditorium was crowded and there was an overflow meeting of four thousand outside on the sidewalk. The police reserves, who had so often, in previous months, come out to arrest pickets, now came out to protect them from the thousands of people who gathered in their honor. Elsie Hill addressed this overflow meeting, which shivered in the bitter cold for over an hour, yet stayed to hear her story.

Inside, eighty-one women in white, all of whom had served in the Jail or the Workhouse, carrying lettered banners and purple, white, and gold banners, marched down the two center aisles of the theatre and onto the stage. There were speeches by Mrs. Thomas Hepburn, Dudley Field Malone, Mrs. William Kent, Mrs. O. H. P. Belmont, and Maud Younger. Then came an interval in which money was raised. Two touching details were sums of fifty cents and thirty cents pledged from Occoquan "because the Suffragettes helped us so much down there." And Mrs. John Rogers, Jr., on behalf of the pickets gave "tenderest thanks for this help from our comrades in the Workhouse."

Eighty-six thousand, three hundred and eighty-six dollars were raised in honor of the pickets.

On that occasion, prison pins which were tiny replicas in silver of the cell doors, were presented to each "prisoner of freedom."

As Alice Paul appeared to receive her pin, Dudley Field Malone called, "Alice Paul," and the audience leaped to its feet; the cheers and applause lasted until she disappeared at the back of the platform.

It is a poignant regret to the present author that she cannot go further into conditions at the District Jail and at Occoquan in regard to the other prisoners there. But that is another story and must be told by those whose work is penal investigation. The Suffragists uncovered conditions destructive to body and soul; incredibly inhumane! One of the heart-breaking handicaps of the swift, intensive warfare of the pickets was that, although they did much to ameliorate conditions for their fellow prisoners, they could not make them ideal. Piteous appeal after piteous appeal came to them from their "comrades in the Workhouse."

"If we go on a hunger-strike, will they make things better for us?" the other prisoners asked again and again.

"No," the Suffragists answered sadly. "You have no organization back of you."

However, in whatever ways were open to them the Suffragists offered counsel and assistance of all kinds.

I asked one of the pickets once how the other prisoners regarded them. She answered: "They called us 'the strange ladies.'"

50
CHARLOTTE PERKINS GILMAN
Women Are Free at Last in All the Land (1920)

Chant Royal

WAKEN, O Woman, to the trumpet sound
    Greeting our day of long sought liberty;
Gone are the ages that have held us bound
    Beneath a master, now we stand as he,
Free for world-service unto all mankind,
Free of the dragging chains that used to bind,
    The sordid labor, the unnoticed woe,
    The helpless shame, the unresisted blow,
Submission to our owner's least command—
    No longer pets or slaves are we, for lo!
Women are free at last in all the land.

Long was the stony road our feet have found
    From that dark past to the new world we see,
Each step with heavy hindrance hemmed around,
Each door to freedom closed with bolt and key;
Our feet with old tradition all entwined,

From *The Suffragist*, September 1920.

Untrained, uneducated, uncombined,
> We had to fight old faiths of long ago,
>> And in our households find our dearest foe,
Against the world's whole weight we had to
> stand
>> Till came the day it could no more say
>>> no—
Women are free at last in all the land.

Around us prejudice, emotion-drowned,
> Rose like a flood and would not let us free;
Women themselves, soft-bred and silken
> gowned,
>> Historic shame have won by their mad plea
To keep their own subjection; with them lined
All evil forces of the world we find,
> No crime so brazen and no vice so low
> But fought us, with inertia blind and slow,
And ignorance beneath its darkling brand,
>> With these we strove and still must strive,
>>> although
Women are free at last in all the land.

The serving squaw, the peasant,
> toil-embrowned,
>> The household drudge, no honor and no
>>> fee—
For these we now see women world-renowned,
> In art and science, work of all degree.
She whom world progress had left far behind
Now has the secret of full life divined,—
> Her largest service gladly to bestow;
> Great is the gain since ages far below,
In honored labor, both of head and hand
>> Now may her power and genius clearly
>>> show
Women are free at last in all the land.

Long years of effort to her praise redound,
> To such high courage all may bend the
>> knee.
Beside her brother, with full freedom crowned,
> Mother and wife and citizen is she,
Queen of her soul and body, heart and mind,
Strong for the noble service God designed;
>> See now the marching millions, row on row,
>>> With steady eyes and faces all aglow,

They come! they come! a glad triumphant
> band,—
>> Roses and laurels in their pathway strow—
Women are free at last in all the land!

ENVOI

Sisters! we now must change the world we know
To one great garden where the child may grow.
> New freedom means new duty, broad and
>> grand.
To make a better world and hold it so
> Women are free at last in all the land.

51

ALVA BELMONT (MRS. OLIVER H. P.), HARRIOT STANTON BLATCH, FLORENCE KELLEY, MARY AUSTIN, CRYSTAL EASTMAN, AND MARY WHITE OVINGTON

What Next? (1920)

MRS. O. H. P. BELMONT

Women have fought for what they have won in politics as well as in every other field. The vote came to them after a century-long struggle against the greatest odds. We owe nothing—not the least part of our new political freedom—to the old political parties. Our victory has come, not because of them, but in spite of them. We can face the future with a clean political slate.

Women are too prone to give without asking for return and politicians are apt to take advantage of this trait. The widespread tendency among a certain group of women to scramble into the ranks of the old party machines, lending to them the priceless value of their enthusiasm, energy and political gifts, accepting in return miserable doles of political patronage, is to me a very sad spectacle. I want women to have more self-respect, both for their own good and that of the nation.

From *The Suffragist*, October and November 1920.

For I believe that women have a distinct contribution to make to the national good, and that they should be permitted to make it in their own way.

As a means toward securing the fullest contribution from women in our national life, I favor the continuation of the National Woman's Party as a separate political entity, affiliated with no other party, but forming a strategic balance of power group. This organization, united upon a program of equality for women in all spheres, political, industrial and social, could fight for its objects with the weapons of politics—votes. Candidates and parties opposing its measures would be opposed by it. Women candidates for office would be encouraged. Where candidates satisfactory to us were advanced by other parties they would be supported. Otherwise we would nominate candidates of our own.

Obvious planks for the platform of a woman's party occur at once. It should no longer be possible to disfranchise women because of their marriage with aliens. Equal guardianship laws, the removal of any restrictions against office holding by women, are other reforms which should be immediately fought for.

Through a woman's party the ballot may be made the symbol of a new era in which the voice of women shall be heard in the councils of the nation, from the lowest to the highest.

HARRIOT STANTON BLATCH

In winning the vote all was not won. Indeed the ballot is but a tool in the hands of women for the winning of the realities. The politically enfranchised woman is still in need of social and economic enfranchisement. And never was the hour more pressing for her emancipation.

How shall she accomplish her object? Shall she go into one of the existing parties and achieve her freedom through the instrument of party politics? Shall she build a party of her own, or shall she build rather a program and force it through by acting as a nonpartisan force outside party lines?

As many of the things which women want and need form no part of party platforms, it would seem as if feminist propaganda would make small headway under party standards. By all means let women who find in this or that party, principles dealing with several political and economic questions with which they are in agreement, adopt party affiliation, and let them insist upon full recognition of their sex in party management, but when these steps have been taken, each thoughtful woman will find, that though she is expressing quite legitimately her differences of opinion with other women who have aligned themselves with opposite parties, there remain deep and vital questions upon which women of all shades of opinion can and should unite.

It does not seem to me the best way to meet this situation is to create a separate political party, for the reason that on many questions there is no distinctive sex view. There is a Socialist view as to how subways should be financed and managed in contrast to the view of the old parties, but there is in no sense a feminist point of view. In the same way there is a Democratic and Republican manner of regarding the tariff, while there is no distinctively feminine opinion on the question. It seems to me our main object is to forward a program. And no energy should be wasted in building an elaborate machine to accomplish our end.

In order to push the fundamental agreements of women the need is for a nonpartisan, strongly knit group. It is for this reason that I favor the Woman's Party continuing as it is today—namely outside political affiliations, but very much in politics.

The long heartbreaking march towards political freedom for women is ended. The reason it is so difficult to realize that the goal has been reached, is, perhaps, because there seems no chance to pause and take breath as other needs stand facing us impellingly.

I. The most immediate call to action is the need to influence without delay final decisions in international agreements. There should be no League of Nations built up without an effort on the part of enfranchised women to write into such an instrument as a qualification for membership a nation's recognition of women as part of its body politic. Or, if admitted to the League, a nation disfranchising its women should enjoy only curtailed powers. Strangely enough, there is no democratic standard for admission as the covenant now stands. In any just League the test of a nation's power should be its democracy at home. If a country's voting strength is based on aristocracy, on property, on sex distinctions, by just so much restriction should its power suffer as the international centre. When countries begin to feel the unwisdom of degrading women politically, they will mend their ways. The enfranchised women of America, through pressure brought by a Woman's Party, broadening perhaps to an International Woman's Party, could be instrumental in bringing political freedom to the women of the world.

II. A second piece of work close at hand ready for a Woman's Party to undertake is amendment of the 1907 law dealing with the citizenship of married women. And here a world-embracing Woman's Party could function with advantage. Woman's love of country has long enough been a football for her sons to kick about the globe. In regard to these two issues, there could not arise partisan differences between women. They could be of any party and yet unite in furthering a sane foundation for the citizenship of women, and in advocating a democratic basis for qualification for membership in a League of Nations.

III. Nor would divergence arise among women within national boundaries in demands for equality between the sexes in the civil service, of a square deal in politics, in professions, in business, in industry, for the righting of inequalities in divorce laws, in rights of parents, in educational opportunities.

IV. And behind all such social and economic demands lies the most important item in the Woman's program—namely, the endowment of motherhood. Every woman, whether the wife of a millionaire or a day laborer, will in the world built by women, be made to feel that society honors motherhood sufficiently to raise it above all sordid dependence.

It seems clear that to achieve these and other planks of a purely feminist character a union of women is needed armed with the shield of nonpartisanship, and the rapier of political technique such as suffrage groups have developed.

The vote was won by disfranchised women acting as a well-knit, nonpartisan group; surely enfranchised women can win complete freedom for their sex as a trained, nonpartisan Woman's Party.

FLORENCE KELLEY

As one half the constituency our power is immeasurably great. The year 1920–1921 can be made the fit sequel to the year 1848, when, at Seneca Falls, our foremothers made their beginning of that peaceful political revolution now so nearly achieved throughout the western world.

It would be a disaster for the whole planet if we now failed to act in accordance with the greatness of our opportunity.

Each of the following suggestions relates to one or two central aims, *i.e.,* completing the voters' power as citizens or enabling woman to perform more perfectly their especial share in the experience of the race, giving, saving and cherishing life. How far they have been frustrated in this is glaringly shown by existing bad laws, and by good bills lagging on the calendar or in the committee in both houses of Congress.

Our first use of our national political power should aim at immediate improvement of the personnel and activities of Congress. Women should be elected wherever suitable candidates willing to serve can be found. Where it is too late for the primaries but nomination by petition is still available, no effort should be spared to obtain at once for women the balance of power in both Houses.

Anti-suffragists should be retired from elective office. Though still perniciously active, they belong, like cannibals and slaveholders, to a past era.

However incompletely Congress may be modernized in the brief interval allowed us this year, this policy should be inaugurated now and maintained in the face of all future discouragements. . . .

MARY AUSTIN

It is too early to say what women should do with their newly acquired political power. A period of experimentation must necessarily ensue during which they may do anything which will give them the requisite political experience. There are a few precautionary measures which they might take to ensure them against unnecessary handicap when they do make up their minds, as I am afraid must happen before real political effectiveness is secured, to move concertedly as women.

They ought to avoid making any political affiliations which it will embarrass them to dissolve.

They ought not to "play politics" for the sake of any future political plums. Plums don't grow on thistles today any more than figs did when that proverb was a piece of the day's news.

They should never forget that the people who ultimately decide our national policies are the people who are most interested in deciding them. This is just as true when the interests are altruistic as when they are selfish. Women are not going to make any political gains that they do not care as much about as they have cared about winning the political privilege.

Women should never make the mistake of taking men's political promises too seriously. Politics today is not organized around political situations, but around men's reactions to situations. Party line-ups are much more likely to represent temperamental bias than political principles. This is the source of most of our political inefficiency; but only a good-humored, philosophical recognition of the fact will make any headway against it.

Above everything women should avoid any immediate alignment of political interest which will perpetuate or foresee sex antagonism. If it ever becomes necessary for women to pull out on their own initiative it must be because they have seen so clear a light on the political horizon that the difference between men's and women's view of it can be stated in terms not of sex distinctions, but in the length of spiritual vision. . . .

WHAT NEXT?

Women face the future with immense power in their hands. How will they use it? The *Suffragist* has asked women in various fields of activity to answer the question, What shall women do next? What is your answer?

From Crystal Eastman
Why Change Our Tactics?

Marie Tudor Garland, in describing the recent Woman Suffrage Congress at Geneva, says:

"Although attempts were made to break away into a separate feminist movement, dealing with women's rights as apart from men's, Mrs. Catt was able, through her personality, to hold the group to its course—the full democratization of the women of the world, not primarily as women but as joint members of the human family."

In this comment and in the program of the Congress there is revealed a sort of high-minded, altruistic confusion more inimical to the progress of feminism than the edicts of the Catholic Church. The hard practical truth is that there must be a "separate feminist movement dealing with women's rights as apart from men's" because women's rights are at an altogether different stage of development from men's. Women must catch up and they must do it through their own efforts. Few men will even understand the feminist movement, let alone work for it. But women from all classes will understand it, women of opposite economic interests, women with widely divergent views of human progress will understand it and work together for it. Men will help in the need of course. Here and there a man with a taste for adventure and change will applaud us even in the early stages. But the organization of the campaign for woman's freedom, the drudgery of preparation, the burden and heat of the battle, must be borne by the women who want to be free. That is the law of progress. Indeed, a rebel spirit must be born in women, a passionate interest in themselves, which would be utterly dissipated in any attempt to enlist men in the active service of their cause. "But," Mrs. Garland and these eminent suffrage leaders will reply, "we are not proposing to open our membership to men. What we do insist upon is the enlarging of the woman's program so as to include child welfare, educational and moral reforms, international peace, etc., etc."

Here is the very center of the confusion. If the program is to be drawn on large humanitarian lines, including all the more popular human betterment proposals, why is it a woman's program? Have women a corner on progress? Must they jealously guard their right to improve the world? Surely this is man's work as well as woman's. The object of feminism is not to separate the activities of men and women but to unite them. If we cling to these women's reform organizations we but perpetuate the old separation, "charity and church work for women, politics for men." If feminism means opening the doors of the whole wide world for women, it means no less enlisting the efforts of men in our struggle to clean up the world and make it a decent place to live in. Certainly a Woman's International which includes peace, education and child welfare among its objects cannot be said to be consciously feminist in its outlook. And that is not saying that feminists are without human instincts,—women are incurably humanitarian as every unregenerate male can testify. It simply means that a genuine feminist has thought the problem through; she knows that woman's battle for her own freedom must be kept clear of entangling alliances.

There is another very practical reason why the feminist program must not become part of or in any way tied up with a general reform program. A vast number of women have no faith in "reform," no confidence in the vote as a means of abolishing poverty, establishing industrial justice, getting rid of war, or accomplishing any fundamental economic change. It will be the tendency of these women, even though they may be good feminists, to look scornfully upon any effort to win freedom for women by political action. If the feminist program is confused by including in it all sorts of reforms which the direct-actionist knows cannot be brought about by voting, we shall surely lose her support, she will become negligible as a force for feminism. But if the feminist objective is kept clear and definite and single in the framing of our program, even the most convinced industrial communist like myself can honestly support political action to achieve it.

All sorts of changes can be accomplished by voting which are not destructive of the private profit system, which are not inherently inimical to capitalism. Prohibition, daylight saving, woman suffrage itself, are excellent examples. I believe the feminist program belongs in this group. For when we speak of "freedom for women" we do not mean that ultimate freedom for the human race which cannot be dreamed of until the capitalist system is destroyed. We mean such freedom of choice in occupation and such individual economic independence as it is possible for a human being to achieve in the present order. The winning of this measure of freedom for women will not destroy privilege, it will not undermine profits. Vital as this struggle is to the status of women it will not even shake the foundations of this monstrous structure which we call modern capitalism. Therefore feminism will to a large extent cut across class lines, women of all classes who are concerned for their freedom will hang together to achieve it and the vote will be one of their chief weapons.

To break down barriers and discrimination against women in all grades of government service, to repeal the foolish laws which prevent a mother from limiting the size of her family, to establish the principle of motherhood endowment without which economic independence is impossible—for this part of our program we must conduct a political campaign. But this is by no means the whole program. The discrimination against women in trade union rules, in business customs, in professional schools, is after all much deeper rooted than in government service. Women workers by hand and brain must organize and break down these barriers by some form of direct action. There is no other way.

And finally feminism calls for nothing less than a revolution in education. Girls as well as boys must be trained for self-support, not as a matter of bitter and regrettable necessity, but a natural fulfillment of their powers. On the other hand, boys as well as girls must be trained for home-making. Even at the risk of temporarily acting out the old comic cartoon of the man with an apron round his waist about to "wash up," while his wife in hat and coat goes off to business,—we must somehow even up this business of home-making. I wish that for one generation the girls could help father on the farm and the boys help mother in the kitchen. But perhaps that is going a bit too far. The point I wish to make here is that we cannot go very far toward woman's freedom without establishing the feminist ideal in education. And here again the vote will be of little value.

Clearly, then, the vote is not our only weapon, or even our chief weapon. Industrial organization and education can accomplish as much, probably more than political action. This, it seems to me, is the final answer to the question, Shall we have a Woman's Party? A woman's political party, running women candidates for office on purely feminist issues, is unthinkable. But even if it were possible, what a mistake in tactics it would be for a movement which is at most but one-third political!

In so far as the feminist movement is a political movement, what better tactics could possibly be devised than the unique and supremely successful tactics of our present organization? The Woman's Party has demonstrated that the way to make the clumsy, old, outworn machinery of political democracy work for you is to stay outside of it; to be a sort of outlaw political group, strongly organized and very much "on to the game"; wasting no time or emphasis on electing candidates to office, but bringing pressure to bear when and where it will count most.

If women without the vote could get a constitutional amendment in seven years by these tactics, surely with the added power of the vote, *if they do not change their tactics,* they can write a few feminist laws on the statute books....

From Mary White Ovington
Free Black as Well as White Women

During the many years that the women of the United States have struggled for the ballot I have often appealed to suffrage workers and their leaders for help in battling against the disfranchisement of the negro. The answer I have received has been invariably the same, "We must have a single issue; we cannot intrude the negro question until the battle is over. When the fight is won, then will be the time to ask us to take up the cause of the negro women."

Well, the battle is over. The women of the country have received the vote. They will be able in November to go to the polls—that is, the white women will. They have won democracy for themselves. Now is the time to ask them if they have sympathy for other Americans who are disfranchised and whether they are willing to aid the colored women of this country living in the Southern States to exercise the right of franchise. That the colored people alone cannot win this right is illustrated by a story appearing in the *New York Times* of October 6 which runs as follows:

"B. J. Jones, the Negro Chairman of the Columbia County Republican Club of Lake City, Fla., who has been active in urging Negro women to vote, was taken out of his bed on Tuesday night by unknown parties and with a noose about his neck was bundled into an automobile in his night clothes.

"He was carried several miles and after being allowed to think he would be lynched, was allowed to escape. After wandering about, he found a telephone and called up the Sheriff of Columbia County, to obtain an escort so that he might return home in safety.

"Besides urging Negro women to vote, Jones was reported to have been organizing churches, lodges and night schools and carrying on a propaganda to have negro women expelled if they failed to exercise the franchise. He also organized meetings to instruct Negro women how to vote.

"The situation caused by the incident is thought to be serious. The feeling created by the extension of the franchise to Negro women is tense in other parts of the state, and state troops will probably be called to Baker County to guard the election there in November."

What is the attitude of the women of the suffrage movement toward this near-lynching of a man who was endeavoring to instruct the colored woman voter? Are there not many who, having won the ballot, wish to see it used not by the white women of the state only but by all? Surely, as women we cannot remain indifferent to the enforcement of the amendment that we have at length succeeded in incorporating into the Constitution. We must not rest until we have freed black as well as white of our sex. Will not those who wish to see this come to pass write me to that effect?

There are only a few of us in this Negro cause and we need the knowledge that you have gained in your long campaigns. We need your enthusiasm for the cause of woman. We need your splendid ability that at length has won this victory against the great odds of antagonism and, still worse, of indifference.

Will you not show us how to make the Nineteenth Amendment the Democratic reality that it purports to be?

Suggestions for Further Reading

Baker, Paula. "The Domestication of Politics: Women and American Political Society, 1780–1920." In *Unequal Sisters: A Multicultural Reader in U. S. Women's History*, ed. Ellen Carol DuBois and Vicki L. Ruiz. New York: Routledge, 1990, 66–91.

Buhle, Mari Jo. *Women and American Socialism, 1870–1920*. Urbana: Univ. of Illinois Press, 1981.

Cott, Nancy F. *The Grounding of Modern Feminism*. New Haven: Yale Univ. Press, 1987.

Davis, Allen F. *Spearheads for Reform: The Social Settlements and the Progressive Movement, 1890–1914*. New York: Oxford Univ. Press, 1967.

DuBois, Ellen Carol. *Harriot Stanton Blatch and the Winning of Woman Suffrage*. New Haven: Yale Univ. Press, 1997.

———. "Working Women, Class Relations, and Suffrage Militance: Harriot Stanton Blatch and the New York Woman Suffrage Movement, 1894–1909." *Journal of American History* 74 (1987): 34–58.

DuBois, Ellen Carol, ed. *The Elizabeth Cady Stanton-Susan B. Anthony Reader*. Boston: Northeastern Univ. Press, 1981.

DuBois, Ellen Carol, and Vicki L. Ruiz, eds. *Unequal Sisters: A Multicultural Reader in U. S. Women's History*. New York: Routledge, 1990.

Evans, Sara. *Born for Liberty: A History of Women in America*. New York: Free Press, 1989.

Flexnor, Eleanor, and Ellen Fitzpatrick. *Century of Struggle: The Woman's Rights Movement in the United States*. Cambridge, Mass.: Harvard Univ. Press, Belknap Press, 1996.

Giddings, Paula. *When and Where I Enter: The Impact of Black Women on Race and Sex in America*. New York: William Morrow, 1984.

Gordon, Linda. *Pitied But Not Entitled: Single Mothers and the History of Welfare*. New York: Free Press, 1994.

Graham, Sara Hunter. *Woman Suffrage and the New Democracy*. New Haven: Yale Univ. Press, 1996.

Hine, Darlene Clark, and Kathleen Thompson. *A Shining Thread of Hope: The History of Black Women in America*. New York: Broadway Books, 1998.

Kraditor, Aileen S. *The Ideas of the Woman Suffrage Movement, 1890–1920*. New York: Columbia Univ. Press, 1965.

Lane, Ann J. *To Herland and Beyond: The Life and Work of Charlotte Perkins Gilman*. New York: Meridian, 1991.

Marilley, Suzanne M. *Woman Suffrage and the Origins of Liberal Feminism in the United States, 1820–1920*. Cambridge, Mass.: Harvard Univ. Press, 1996.

Matthews, Glenna. *The Rise of Public Woman: Woman's Power and Woman's Place in the United States, 1630–1970*. New York: Oxford Univ. Press, 1992.

Muncy, Robyn. *Creating a Female Dominion in American Reform, 1890–1935*. New York: Oxford Univ. Press, 1991.

O'Neill, William L. *Everyone Was Brave: A History of Feminism in America*. Chicago: Quadrangle Books, 1969.

Rosenberg, Rosalind. *Beyond Separate Spheres: Intellectual Roots of Modern Feminism*. New Haven: Yale Univ. Press, 1992.

Russett, Cynthia Eagle. *Sexual Science: The Victorian Construction of Womanhood*. Cambridge, Mass.: Harvard Univ. Press, 1989.

Scott, Anne Firor. *Natural Allies: Women's Associations in American History*. Urbana: Univ. of Illinois Press, 1993.

Seigfried, Charlene Haddock. *Pragmatism and Feminism: Reweaving the Social Fabric*. Chicago: Univ. of Chicago Press, 1996.

Schwarz, Judith. *Radical Feminists of Heterodoxy: Greenwich Village, 1912–1940*. Norwich, Vt.: New Victoria Publishers, 1986.

Sklar, Kathryn Kish. "Hull House in the 1890s: A Community of Women Reformers." In *Unequal Sisters: A Multicultural Reader in U. S. Women's History*, ed. Ellen Carol DuBois and Vicki L. Ruiz. New York: Routledge, 1990, 109–22.

Wheeler, Marjorie Spruill. *New Women of the New South: The Leaders of the Woman Suffrage Movement in the Southern States*. New York: Oxford Univ. Press, 1993.

PART II

Feminist Politics Beyond Suffrage

I. Political Mobilization

THE TRADITIONAL VIEW OF THE WOMEN'S MOVEMENT is that it died after women won suffrage and was resurrected only in the 1960s when a "second wave" of feminism picked up where the "first wave" (1848–1920) left off. Most women's rights activists, however, felt no sense of an ending on August 23, 1920, when the Nineteenth Amendment finally enfranchised all American women. Instead, leaders of the various suffrage organizations asked themselves and their supporters: What next? As the celebrations quieted, a consensus developed that the fight for women's political equality was by no means won with the attainment of the vote. Socialist-feminist Crystal Eastman eloquently writes in "Now We Can Begin," (1920) "Most women will agree that August 23 . . . is a day to begin with, not a day to end with." Each woman, though, had a different conception of what, exactly, was beginning.

The largest suffrage organization, the National American Woman Suffrage Association, officially dissolved itself at its victory convention in 1920, where its leaders—notably Carrie Chapman Catt—founded the National League of Women Voters (NLWV) as its successor. At least at first, the NLWV conceived of its mission broadly, and at the victory convention six simultaneous conferences covered a broad spectrum of women's issues: women in industry, child welfare, the education of effective citizens, social hygiene, food supply and demand, and the legal status of women. The NLWV continued for a while to support a variety of causes. Its efforts, for instance, were instrumental in passing the first piece of welfare legislation, the Sheppard-Towner Act of 1921, which provided for federal aid to the states to improve prenatal care and child care. However, the NLWV consistently held (some would say, narrowed its focus) to a single political ideal and practice: nonpartisan education. The NLWV self-consciously defined itself as a politically neutral organization that strove simply to send an "enlightened electorate in petticoats" to the polls, as Margery Currey puts it in "The Victory Convention" (1920). Carrie Chapman Catt, the last president of the NAWSA, did more than any single woman to define the purpose of the NLWV. Her speech, reproduced in Currey's article, highlights Catt's belief in a nonpartisan approach to politics, as she urges the new league down the same strategic path on which she had led the NAWSA during the fight for suffrage. She argues that women should work with whichever political party—Democratic or Republican—best represents their own values at a given time and that they should not retain a blind allegiance to any one party.

Catt's speech articulates a persistent dilemma for feminists who want to engage in and affect American politics: Should feminists choose to be insiders or outsiders? Should they join existing political parties and attempt to shape those parties to their own interests? Or should they work in separate women's parties from beyond the machinery of conventional party politics? Catt insists that women can only achieve change by entering the Democratic and Republican political parties, using women's influence within them to "convert" (male) politicians to the NLWV's platform and voting for the parties' (male) candidates. Catt's speech expresses a continuation of conservative NAWSA tactics for achieving suffrage: lobbying state and federal legislators and politicians of either party who seem amenable to the NLWV's cause, and stressing influence on powerful males rather than direct female political action. There is little sense in this document that women will be or should strive to become politicians themselves. Catt shows a realistic understanding of the difficulties women will face in gaining any access to the centers of political power—the "real thing in the center," as she puts it—in order to exert influence there, let alone in getting themselves elected. Throughout the 1920s and 1930s, the broad program of legislative goals that the NLWV presented at the victory convention—goals representing women's distinct interests—slowly diminished as the organization moved away from its feminist roots. Instead, it began to concentrate exclusively on educating voters of both sexes, formerly only one of its aims. By the 1940s there would even be talk of changing the organization's name to the League of Voters, epitomizing its abandonment of specifically women's political issues.

The second major suffrage organization, the National Woman's Party (NWP), also used its victory convention, held in February 1921, as the forum for defining its political future. In contradistinction to NAWSA's official disbanding and reforming of itself as the National League of Women Voters and its slow movement away from feminism, the NWP insisted on its own continuing legitimacy and increasingly came to define what feminism meant in the post-suffrage decades. As usual with the militant NWP, its convention was more contentious than that of the NLWV and its future agenda more vehemently debated. The primary areas of controversy were birth control, black women's voting rights, pacifism, and—above all—the formidable power of NWP leader Alice Paul to define the group's agenda and brush aside what she saw as irrelevant diversions on women's path to formal equality with men. Three articles published in response to the victory convention of the NWP all criticize, to varying degrees, the stranglehold in which they claim Alice Paul grips the organization. Crystal Eastman's "Alice Paul's Convention" (1921), Freda Kirchwey's "Alice Paul Pulls the Strings" (1921), and Belle Case La Follette's "National Convention of the National Woman's Party" (1921) variously construe Paul's ruthless determination to assign the future goal of the party as "a very efficient steam roller" (Eastman); a "tank" and a "machine" (Kirchwey); and utterly single-minded (La Follette). The convention was ostensibly held to discuss the future of the NWP: delegations from women's organizations met with Paul prior to the conference to persuade her of the value of their programs, and they also vied to have their proposals heard by the resolutions committee at the convention itself and to win a chance to address the delegates. What Paul wanted all along, though, finally won the day—a simple and (what she believed to be) "purely feminist" program that calls for the end of all legal discrimination against women. As La Follette articulates the goal of the new organization, it is to end the political and legal disabilities of women, to ensure that political freedom not be lost in any association of nations, and to work for the absolute equality of men and women. Paul believed that a simple statement of the NWP's mission to assert the legal, political, and economic equality of men and women would serve as a unifying rallying point—much as suffrage had been. Paul's critics thought otherwise. Crystal Eastman, for instance, argues that the stated goal of the NWP is tantamount to saying "women are still in subjection and we are going to free them"— which is much too pessimistic and, more important, too vague a declaration (a point with which Kirchwey is in complete agreement). Eastman claims to be speaking for many dissatisfied delegates as she writes that women came to outline "a bill of particulars." Indeed, it seems that the disparagers captured the mood of activist women in 1921, since two months after the convention NWP membership was down to 151 paid members compared to around 50,000 at its height in 1919.

Crystal Eastman, an original founder of the Congressional Union/National Woman's Party, *did* advocate a variegated and specific feminist program aimed at women's emotional, economic, and legal liberation. In "Now We Can Begin" (1920), published in *The Liberator*—a radical journal she edited with her brother Max—Crystal Eastman claims that an organized feminist movement must work for birth control, motherhood endowment, economic independence, freedom of choice in occupation, and a revolution in education. In "Alice Paul's Convention," Eastman enumerates in a six-point plan the broader agenda theorized in "Now We Can Begin." She presented her plan at the NWP convention, but it was summarily dismissed because all of her goals, which included the controversial issue of birth control, were considered divisive by Paul and the party leadership. The plan was incapable, they said, of coalescing all the diverse women who had previously come together to fight for suffrage.

In "Alice Paul Pulls the Strings," Freda Kirchwey highlights the three glaring acts of suppression in Paul's scripting of "her" convention: disarmament, birth control, and the violation of the Nineteenth Amendment by southern states trying to prevent African Americans from voting. All three issues received a tremendous amount of support from members of the NWP, and yet all were rejected by Paul as irrelevant to a "feminist program."

The argument that pacifism should be central to the NWP's agenda, the call that received the most widespread support at the convention, is forcefully presented in Belle Case La Follette's article, "National Convention of the National Woman's Party," published in the journal she and her husband (Senator Robert La Follette) founded and ran in Wisconsin, *La Follette's Magazine*. A proposal that the NWP dedicate itself to world disarmament was, in the end, the only alternative program endorsed by the resolutions committee, seven of whose members signed a minority report that was presented to the delegates for debate. The debate was vigorous, and La Follette voices the arguments of its supporters—primarily that women now have the unprecedented power of their vote and could, together, end war as a "barbarous means of settling differences." Paul, however, ensured that this proposal was defeated. Although there were some "militarist" voices who claimed the United States needed to be able to defend itself, it was ultimately the lack of support of some pacifist women (including Eastman) who swung things Paul's way by agreeing that the fight for disarmament should take place in other, less explicitly feminist, organizations.

The second major point of controversy that surrounded the NWP convention was birth control. Birth control was a central part of Eastman's program, and she argues that any feminist organization must ensure women's ability to limit the size of their families. Initially barred from the program, Margaret Sanger for the American Birth Control League and Mary Ware Dennett for the Voluntary Parenthood League insistently negotiated with NWP headquarters and were finally allowed to address the resolutions committee briefly, winning five minutes in which to speak before the convention itself. Birth control in many states in 1920 was not only controversial but as good as illegal; in New York, for instance, obscenity law banned the distribution of birth control material except for the prevention of disease. Margaret Sanger, who essentially organized the birth control movement of the twentieth century, was herself jailed for thirty days in 1917 for violating this law: she had established a clinic in New York where she distributed diaphragms to poor women.

Margaret Sanger's book *Woman and the New Race* (1920) powerfully articulates her vision of the absolute centrality of birth control to women's freedom, indeed, to the future of the race. It certainly explains why she felt Alice Paul and the NWP should make this issue a keystone of their feminist program. Sanger claims that both the vote and equality before the law are "mere surface"—"weak and superficial"—beside what she considers to be the most vital factor of a woman's existence: voluntary motherhood. The excerpt presented here is notable not only for showing the supreme importance Sanger places on birth control to women's freedom, but also for the way she refuses to shrink from holding women responsible for complicity in their own entrapment. Women, she argues, have allowed themselves to become broodmares, and they have thus not only degraded themselves but all of humanity. If it were not for women's perpetual reproduction, Sanger contends, there would not be the kind of overpopulation and cheapness of human life that have led to the waste and misery of war, that have made political tyranny possible, and that have filled slums, asylums, and jails. Women, according to Sanger's inflammatory rhetoric, have "unconsciously and ignorantly" brought about much of the evil and social disease of the twentieth century.

The third divisive issue at the NWP convention (and the one that dramatizes the most enduring exclusion of the mainstream women's movement) was the voting rights of African American women. Despite passage of the Nineteenth Amendment, black women in the South were being subjected to the same unconstitutional attempts to keep them from voting as black men had undergone for decades. Alice Paul had reconciled southern state legislators to female suffrage by insisting that it would not disrupt states' regulation of voting procedures, sanctioning their imposition of the same discriminatory conditions on women's franchise as on men's. "The White Woman's Burden" (1921) reports the results of a questionnaire that *The Nation* sent to top members of the NWP asking their opinion about the South's systematic attempt to nullify the Nineteenth Amendment and whether that attempt should concern feminist leaders. While the responses were mixed, and some women were certainly very vehement in their disapproval of disenfranchisement, it is disturbing that only one-third of the women written to replied—suggesting NWP officials' overall indifference to the rights of African American women.

That indifference was played out both before and at the NWP victory convention of 1921 (in fact, one wonders where the women were who expressed their displeasure at disenfranchisement to *The Nation*). During preparations for the convention Addie Hunton, a black field secretary of the National Association of Colored Women, led a delegation of sixty African American women from fourteen states to urge Alice Paul to include the enfranchisement of black women as one of the stated goals of the NWP. (Their memorial is included in Freda Kirchwey's "Alice Paul Pulls the Strings.") Paul refused, saying it was a diversionary and divisive issue; all she allowed the delegation was the chance to raise the issue from the floor. Ella Rush Murray, a white delegate from New York, did manage to present the black women's resolution—but it was voted down as an inappropriate goal of the new NWP. In her ambivalent article, "The Woman's Party and the Violation of the 19th Amendment" (1921), Murray both reveals her concern for the rights of African American woman and at the same time claims that it is a fight best fought by black women rather than white. In her suggestion that black women should not wait for white women to win equality for them, Murray separates them from the women's movement and feminism as much as others at the NWP convention had done. The debacle over the NWP's unwillingness to act on the circumvention of the Nineteenth Amendment in the South highlights two major, racially biased attitudes that have consistently surfaced in what many African American critics throughout the twentieth century have called the *white* women's movement. First of all, until recently, discrimination against women of color has almost always been deemed a racial issue, *not* a gender issue, and thus not within the purview of the women's movement. In a letter defending the NWP, which its research chairman, Sue White, wrote to *The Nation* in response to Kirchwey's scathing article, White says "the Woman's Party, as an organization, is concerned only with discrimination on account of sex, and they [the African American delegates] were understood as asking us to protect them against discrimination on account of race."[1] It was only the minority of voices in the NWP who recognized that discrimination against African American women was discrimination against *women*. The second attitude illustrated in Murray's article is that African American women should fight their own battles. Increasingly in the twentieth century, due to the indifference of white women, that is exactly what African American women have done.

Since African Americans had not organized for women's voting rights to the degree that white women had, and since they had largely been kept out of white women's parties because of racism and

---

1. "The Future of the Woman's Party," *The Nation*, March 23, 1921, p. 434.

southern appeasement, no explicitly political organization existed to support the efforts of African American women to enter political life. The National Association of Colored Women, which was an integral part of the club movement, was more interested in social reform than in politics. Some lone black women did begin to engage in political life, however, mostly within the Republican Party—the party of Lincoln, of emancipation, and of attempts to give former slaves some redress in the Reconstruction South. For instance in 1927 in West Virginia, Mrs. E. Howard Harper became the first black woman to hold office in a state legislature (after being chosen to take the place of her deceased husband). "The Negro Woman in Politics" (1922) was written before Harper's success by another such pioneering woman, Mrs. Robert M. Patterson, who ran as a Socialist candidate from Philadelphia for Pennsylvania's General Assembly. Patterson offers a critique of the political activity of black men and urges women to create a new system—one in which votes are not sold or given away and in which the Republican Party is not blindly embraced. In the same way that Alice Paul convinced the NWP just a few years earlier that, despite long-standing allegiances the Democratic Party was not good for women's interests, so Patterson points out the ways in which the Republicans have betrayed African Americans, including failing to pass an antilynching bill. In an incisive remark about the problems of partisanship, Patterson writes that it does no good to put good men and women into offices in corrupt parties, since the party—not a person's own inherent "goodness"—determines the scope of policy making. As a Socialist, Patterson also criticizes the economic exploitation of both blacks and whites; as individual thinkers and strong characters, African American women are the group most likely, Patterson insists, to end such exploitation.

Another group besides the Socialists that explicitly politicized the black working class in the early twentieth century was Marcus Garvey's United Negro Improvement Association (UNIA), which at its height in 1923 had two million members and was the first mass movement among working-class Blacks. Garvey was a black nationalist and encouraged people of color throughout the world to organize to improve the lot of the entire race. Garvey's wife, Amy Jacques Garvey, led the women's division of UNIA and edited in the women's department for the official newsletter, *Negro World*. Her essay, "Women as Leaders Nationally and Racially" (1925) expresses her sense of connection with other Third World women, her impatience with the strategies of mostly middle-class black women's reform organizations, and her critique of the bulk of "vacillating Negro men." Articulating an almost militarist spirit, Garvey promises that her organization will "brush aside the halting, cowardly Negro leaders" and move forward with "arms prepared for any fray." Her document is also interesting for the lack of even a token interest in an allegiance with white women; in fact, Garvey sees the success of white women, and the looming power of "yellow" women, as a direct threat to the empowerment of her race. With Patterson and Garvey, as different as their affiliations and ideologies were, we see the incipience of a black national pride and an impatience with the white tools of power—both of which harbinger the civil rights movement of the 1960s.

The ends to which women would use their newly won political power (as represented by the vote) was not only debated by women's organizations and parties, both black and white, but by many independent feminists in the decades after 1920. One pressing controversy, articulated by Carrie Chapman Catt in her speech defining the strategy of the NLWV and echoed in Patterson's article, was whether women should support Democratic or Republican candidates—or whether they should organize their own party. Anne Martin had been a militant suffragist and an integral part of the NWP: when the Congressional Union became the NWP in 1916, Martin, a Nevada historian, was its chair. After Alice Paul controversially (and narrowly) defined the NWP's goals in 1921, Martin left the party to work for peace. She had also run twice as an independent candidate in Nevada for the U.S. Senate (in 1918 and 1920). In "Woman's Vote and Woman's Chains" (1922), Martin insists that women should form a separate political party to support all women candidates for office, provided those candidates place women's interests above all else—including party affiliation. Martin's "woman's party" is distinct from what she calls "the 'man's party,' whether it be Republican or Democratic." Martin also opposes the NLWV strategy of lobbying for reform and spreading propaganda; in fact, she explicitly condemns the league's presumption that women need to be "trained" as citizens before they can enter political life. Martin insists that women will not have equality until they occupy at least half the seats in legislative halls—until they are making laws rather than trying to influence men who make laws: "Nothing less than woman's actual and equal participation in government, and in all the business of life," she writes, "will establish her equality." Martin's views were controversial (most public women stressed women's right to vote as individuals, like men, and resisted pressure to vote as a bloc), and several women's magazines refused to publish the article that finally appeared in the California regional journal *Sunset*. The editors of *Sunset* clearly anticipated objections, and they encouraged the voicing of opinion, "especially of women and mothers, concerning the views expressed by Miss Martin."

As rare as Martin's opinions were, she was not alone in deprecating women's reluctance to engage political life directly. Rose Schneiderman, president of the New York Women's Trade Union League, criticized women's lack of initiative in failing to run for political office and called for a "woman's bloc" to take the lead in promoting issues of concern to women. Schneiderman expressed her opinion in a symposium entitled "Is Woman Suffrage Failing?" (1924), published in *The Woman Citizen,* the organ of the NLWV. The editors of *The Woman Citizen* wanted to find out what women "in every walk of life and in every branch of industry, every profession" thought about women's three and a half years in public affairs. The media had reported a general lethargy on the part of women in terms of voting, claiming that turnout was low and most women apparently uninterested in the world of politics. In the symposium, women from Molly Lifshitz—a Russian-born former factory worker—to the actress Gloria Swanson insist that woman suffrage has already borne fruit in improving women's social position and will increasingly influence national politics more directly as women became better informed, more involved, and more organized. With varying degrees of impatience, all who answered the symposium's question thought it was far too soon to make judgments about women's interest or ability in political affairs.

The optimism of the 1920s, however, slowly gave way to a widespread pessimism about the efficacy of women's political power. As the women's movement struggled through the 1930s and 1940s—through a depression and another devastating world war—commentators, both feminist and otherwise, proclaimed the movement's demise and insisted that women were losing ground in their fight for equality. In "A Test for the Modern Woman" (1932), historian Mary Ritter Beard sums up the successes of women through the 1920s and describes the changes ushered in by the Great Depression, which lasted from 1929 until the United States prepared to enter World War II. An avid suffragist, trade union supporter, and municipal reformer, as well as a deliberately nonacademic historian of women, Beard was one of the original members of the NWP and in later decades came to believe strongly in the idea of women's separate institutions, both political and civic. In one of the many influential essays she wrote in the 1930s, for instance, she argues that woman's higher education on the male model and in male-dominated institutions has led to "intellectual cowardice" in woman as she becomes merely a mouthpiece for ideologies defined by men. Beard is perhaps best known for her *Woman as Force in History* (1946), which won praise for its elaboration of women's achievements but also drew criticism for Beard's attack on what she saw as the early women's rights activists' emphasis on the victimization of women.

Beard's captious views of the U.S. culture and economy across gender lines as well as of the feminist movement itself are apparent in "A Test for the Modern Woman." Beard uses the waning of "rugged feminism" in a time of economic crisis to point out the shallow foundation of that feminism. She argues against the historical commonplace that the Depression caused feminism to falter and asserts that feminism stalled itself; the Depression was merely a catalyst for what was inevitably to come. Beard has two major concerns in this essay. The first is the intellectual impoverishment of women's organizations. She lambasts, for instance, the mere counting of heads, rejecting the notion that achieving numerical equality in an arena could translate into real equality or real social change. Second, she condemns those organizations' unthinking acceptance of laissez-faire capitalist principles, which are intrinsically exploitative whether practiced by men or women.

The reproof of feminism continues in Genevieve Parkhurst's "Is Feminism Dead?" (1935), which was published in *Harper's*. Parkhurst, a writer and former editor of the *Pictorial Review,* surveys the fifteen years of the women's movement since suffrage and laments that, although the feminist movement is not dead, "We *have* been asleep. We *have* lost a good deal of what we had gained." While Parkhurst recognizes the large role political forces inimical to women's equality have played in this backsliding (notably the rise of Fascism in Germany and Italy—along with entrenched conservatism in U.S. government and business), she also indicts women's organizations themselves. She argues that they have not been able to put aside their differences, working at "often destructive cross-purposes." Citing particularly the schism between those feminists striving for absolute legal equality with men and those interested in piecemeal and pragmatic reform, Parkhurst urges women to unite against the common enemy: the legislative and social drive to coerce women into the "underprivileged class." Parkhurst focuses on women's worsening economic condition, which she recognizes (along with Beard) is in part a product of the Depression. However, while Beard indicts women's too-easy reliance on capitalism, Parkhurst insists that it is not the inevitable fluctuations and injustices of the market *alone* that are hurting women. In a more conventional turn than Beard, she points out evidence of sexism built into the capitalist system—sexism that ensures women will be hired last and fired first. She also discusses a notorious piece of New Deal legislation, designed to help workers hit by the Depression, that seemed flatly discriminatory to most activist women: Article 213 in the Economy Act of 1932 provided that when the government was "reducing personnel" in any of its branches, married persons living with a wife or husband also employed by the government must be the first dismissed. This was, of course, a green light for government officers to start firing married women—on the assumption that they had no one but themselves (if that) to support. Businesses soon followed the example of the government, and married women lost their jobs all over the nation.

The backlash against women's rights in the mid-1930s consisted of more than political movements such as Fascism and pieces of legislation such as Article 213. In "That Much-Maligned Feminism" (1935), Alma Lutz describes the virulent reemergence of many constraining ideologies about womanhood, which worked in tandem with the effort—born of purported economic necessity—to halt women's advances in the workplace. Lutz, born in North Dakota but a transplant to Boston, was a lifelong feminist, a member of the NWP, the American Association of University Women, and later of the National Organization for Women (until her death in 1973). The ideologies that Lutz identifies are certainly familiar, both to the historian and to women who lived through the last two decades of the twentieth century. They foreshadowed, in fact, the pernicious claims the media would bandy about in the 1980s, for instance, and which Susan Faludi identified in her book *Backlash: The Undeclared War against American Women* (1991). They included the myths that single women who have careers are unhappy; women have made no "outstanding contributions to the arts, the professions, to science, business, or government," thus proving themselves inferior to men; women are not only unfit for careers and economic independence, they don't really want them and would prefer a husband who would support them; and women have a certain "spiritual" contribution to make to civilization, associated with maternity and "overlooked in their mad rush to compete" with (in fact, in their attempt to become) men. These beliefs about women purportedly originate with individuals, but their historical persistence signals an alliance with a gender ideology that has supported the interests of American capitalism and patriarchy, bolstering a gendered system of production/reproduction—in which men work and women (re)produce workers—and male supremacy—in which men get much of their sense of identity from women's dependence on them. The cultural beliefs about women that Lutz identifies would reach their height in the 1950s and become the subject of the groundbreaking text of 1960s "second-wave" feminism: Betty Friedan's *The Feminine Mystique* (1963).

During World War II the United States pulled itself out of the decade-long Great Depression, and women's economic situation improved dramatically as women went to work in war industries. Women even maintained some of their economic power after the close of the war. The belief that the women's movement was languishing persisted through the 1940s, however, as commentators continued to insist that women had failed to become a force in politics and to achieve widespread legal equality with men. In *The Saturday Evening Post* article "We Women Throw Our Votes Away" (1948), the grandniece of Susan B. Anthony, Susan B. Anthony II, argues that women still face overwhelming discrimination in the workplace. Women may have more jobs than they had in the 1930s, Anthony points out, but they get paid *half* of what men receive for those jobs. Just as Parkhurst and Lutz did, Anthony locates part of the problem within the women's movement itself. She says there was an "unnoticed crack-up of the American woman movement" in 1920. Agreeing with Parkhurst that women's organizations have been divided by party differences and lack of leadership, and that they have been distracted by concerns irrelevant to women, Anthony further argues that women have failed to gain what they want because they have not been organized as voters and as potential political candidates. In a depressingly familiar refrain, Anthony calls yet again for institutional support for women's work in the home—nursery schools, cooperative housecleaning services, prepared-meal services, and maternity benefits. From Charlotte Perkins Gilman at the turn of the century and the Hull House reformers and activists for maternity benefits, through repeated demands today for better, less expensive, and more available child care, women have consistently recognized that as long as society is indifferent to the work that mothers do and to the efforts of women both to work and raise children, just so long will women be less than free and less than equal citizens.

52
MARGERY CURREY AND
CARRIE CHAPMAN CATT
The Victory Convention (1920)

Women of the United States have attended their last national suffrage convention. They are about to take their first breath of air in a country where, politically speaking, they have what one might have assumed that of course they naturally would have—an equal share with the rest of their nation in the management of things. Suffrage conventions have been held up to the present time for the purpose of planning new means of securing to women that important indication of political equality—the vote; of reviewing forces for the sake of encouragement in the struggle; and of comparing with one another those methods which have been successful in various districts where progress has been made.

With full national suffrage almost gained (perhaps fully so by the time this magazine is printed) what further need for national suffrage conventions!

The Victory Convention, as it was called, held in Chicago, February 12 to 18, was an experience to those who attended it that makes it a fitting session to mark the ending of one epoch and the beginning of another. To one looking back upon it there are two outstanding memories; one is that of the personality and leadership of Mrs. Carrie Chapman Catt, who presided over the sessions with majesty and with justice, even with simplicity and with constantly recurring moments of fun and wit. The other memory is that of the nobility of the task set themselves by the women who represent the millions who are about to receive the privileges of enfranchisement. The program of the League of Women Voters, which was interspersed through the sessions of the convention, indicates that women will use their new privilege to become a factor (not to be adequately described by the term "political" in its old sense) in making a finer democracy, a better world for children and young people to live in, a less harassed life for the aged and incapacitated, and a state in which justice and reason will take the place of much that has been cruelty and stupidity in government. . . .

At each of the conferences held on that first day of the convention speakers from all over the country, noted in their own line of thinking as advocating most advanced measures, were on the program. A resume of the conference proceedings and recommendations was made to the general convention by the leader of each conference, so that all those attending could enjoy the benefit of each of the six important sessions. With guiding policies thus suggested to the women who are about to become full citizens of the United States, and who will report back to their local groups the material obtained at the convention, it ought to be an enlightened electorate in petticoats that will proceed to the polls in every state of the Union when full suffrage is proclaimed!

The League of Women Voters, the logical present-day outcome of the dissolution of an organization formed years ago to secure women suffrage, was explained in a speech made by Mrs. Catt in the course of the convention which proved one of the high spots of the entire seven days' meeting. After pointing out the necessity of women's working through political parties to secure the ends for which they are to use their votes, and the folly of remaining outside of such parties with the present power which political parties have, the great suffrage leader showed how hitherto the women in the various parties have been little more than a sort of "ladies' auxiliary." Said Mrs. Catt:

"As I read the signs of the present political progress of women within the parties, you are going to have within those parties a continuation of the old familiar strife, and it is just this: We have been engaging for sixty odd years in the effort to try to persuade men to believe and have confidence in the capacities of women.

From *Life and Labor*, March 1920.

Now, because you get the vote, it does not mean that every man who is a ward or a county chairman has suddenly become convinced that women can do things as well as men. You have now to begin and convert those men to the new ideas. They may even say it is all right for women to vote, but when it comes to administrative work within the party, that is the man's business. We will hear the old claim again, and you must prove your capacity to those men within the party where you go.

"On the other hand, you are going to find the mass of women as they always have been, hesitant and timid and doubting themselves, and content to stand back and not to use the power and the brains and the conscience that they have. They are going to be inclined to think that everything that they find to their hands that the men have planned for them is all right, and so again you have the same old fight. You must stimulate those women to self-respect. You have got to urge them on, to show them that they are not emancipated until they're as independent within the party as the men are, which is saying, altogether, much.

"You cannot carry on that struggle on the outside. You can only do it on the inside. For thirty years and a little more, I have worked in the first lap of this struggle for women's emancipation. I do not wish to advise where I cannot follow, and I cannot follow in this new struggle that you are going to make; younger and fresher women must do that work. And because I cannot follow, I only wish to tell you that the battle is there, and that we are not going to be such quitters as to stay on the outside and let all the reactionaries have it their way on the inside.

"Within every party, and probably in every state, there is an inner struggle between the progressive elements and the reactionary elements within that party; and there is the platform and the conduct of the party; the candidates, very likely, are a sort of a compromise between these two extremes. Sometimes the progressives get the best of it; sometimes the reactionaries do. When you get into those parties, you will find progressive elements there. And you should make your connections, provided you are a progressive, with that element within your party, and you will not find it all easy sailing. You will be disillusioned; you will discover that having the vote is not bringing the millennium in one election. Perhaps when you enter the party, you will find yourself in a sort of political penumbra, where most of the men are, and they will be glad to see you, and you will be flattered, and you will think how nice it is. And perhaps if you stay there long enough, going to the big political meetings, and whooping it up for your candidate and platform, you will think how charming it is to be thus placed. But perhaps if you stay long enough and move around enough, and keep your eyes wide enough open, you will discover there is a little denser thing there, or the numbra of the political party—and you will not be so welcome there. Those are the people who are planning the platforms and working out the candidates and doing the real work that you and the men, the masses of them, sanction at the polls. You will not be so welcome there, but there is just the place to go. If you stay there long enough and are active enough, you will see the real thing in the center, with the door locked tight, and you will have a long hard fight before you get inside of the real thing that moves the wheels of your party.

"Nevertheless, it is an interesting struggle, and there is one thing about it that I want to warn you about. It is the only thing that I fear about the League of Women Voters. You must go into those parties. They are going to carry your legislation into laws, and you must be in those parties; you must be right up to the center of things and get your influence there; but there is one terrible, terrible evil that lies right across your pathway, and that is the thing we ordinarily call 'partisanship.'

"Now, there are two kinds of partisanship. One is the kind that reasons out that this platform has more things in it that you believe in than any other, and that this party has more capability of putting those things into practice than any other, therefore you say: I line myself up with this party. That is one kind. That is the kind of partisanship that has led the world onward ever since there were political parties. But there is another kind, and that is the kind to be afraid of; a kind of partisanship which makes you a Republican or a Democrat because you were brought up in those parties and your grandfather and your father belonged. You do not know the antecedents of your party, but you know they are all right. You don't know what is in the platform, and nobody does, because we have a turn in the world's road, and it is a new world and a new time, and we do not know what is in those platforms until they are made; but it does not make any difference to you whatever is in them or whatever is left out, you will vote for it. That is the kind of partisanship which leads you to know, if you are a Republican, that all virtue and all wisdom is with the Republicans; and if you are a Democrat, that all virtue and all wisdom is with the Democrats. But it is the kind of thing that blinds the sight and paralyzes the judgment of anybody who has that kind of politics.

"Partisanship is a brand new emotion to some of our people, and they are working it right here. And I find within our body that women who have worked side by side, never knowing what the political affiliations or sympathies of each other were, now are beginning to look a little askance at each other, as if the other one had some kind of epidemic that they never dreamed they had before.

"In the League of Women Voters we have this anomaly: We are going to be a semi-political organization, because we want political things. We want legislation; we are going to educate for citizenship, and in that body we must be non-partisan, all-partisan; the Democrat from Alabama and the Republican from New Hampshire must be friends, and work together for the same thing. And yet those Republicans of New Hampshire have to go inside of the Republican party in New Hampshire; and the Democrats of Alabama, in spite of some recent events, must go inside of the Democratic party in Alabama. But you must convert your parties, your respective parties, to having confidence in you, confidence in your platform, and confidence in the League of Women Voters.

"Now I want to warn you that there is only about one man in twenty-five that will be big enough to understand that you, a Republican, can work with you, a Democrat in a non-partisan body, and be loyal to your respective parties. That is where the danger comes. They are going to criticise you; they are going to discredit you, and if you are timid you may give way and begin to be suspicious yourself. I want to tell you that the suffragists of this country in the last half century, more than any other group of people in this land, have kept flying the flag of the principles of the Declaration of Independence, the principles of the constitution, and have held them before the people of this country. We have educated the public in these principles.

"More, there is another danger. And this danger is that the League of Women Voters is going to be too timid and too conservative. If you are going to trail along behind the Republican and the Democratic party about five years, and your program is going to be that much behind that of the political parties, you might as well quit before you begin. If the league of Women Voters hasn't the power and hasn't the vision to see what is coming, and what ought to come, and to be five years ahead of the political parties, then our work is of no value. Now, to sail between the Scylla of partisanship, which will tear from us some of our principles, and which is sure to bring criticism upon us from the outside, not know [sic] what really is the motive; and the Charybdis of the temptation to be too conservative on the other side—the League of Women Voters may sail through to glorious success, or wreck upon the rocks. I have confidence in the conscientious purpose and the high moral outlook of this body. And I believe that it is coming to a glorious success.

53
CRYSTAL EASTMAN
Now We Can Begin (1920)

Most women will agree that August 23, the day when the Tennessee legislature finally enacted the Federal suffrage amendment, is a day to begin with, not a day to end with. Men are saying perhaps "Thank God, this everlasting woman's fight is over!" But women, if I know them, are saying, "Now at last we can begin." In fighting for the right to vote most women have tried to be either non-committal or thoroughly respectable on every other subject. Now they can say what they are really after; and what they are after, in common with all the rest of the struggling world, is *freedom*.

Freedom is a large word.

Many feminists are socialists, many are communists, not a few are active leaders in these movements. But the true feminist, no matter how far to the left she may be in the revolutionary movement, sees the woman's battle as distinct in its objects and different in its methods from the workers' battle for industrial freedom. She knows, of course, that the vast majority of women as well as men are without property, and are of necessity bread and butter slaves under a system of society which allows the very sources of life to be privately owned by a few, and she counts herself a loyal soldier in the working-class army that is marching to overthrow that system. But as a feminist she also knows that the whole of woman's slavery is not summed up in the profit system, nor her complete emancipation assured by the downfall of capitalism.

Woman's freedom, in the feminist sense, can be fought for and conceivably won before the gates open into industrial democracy. On the other hand, woman's freedom, in the feminist sense, is not inherent in the communist ideal. All feminists are familiar with the revolutionary leader who "can't see" the woman's movement. "What's the matter with the women? My wife's all right," he says. And his wife, one usually finds, is raising his children in a Bronx flat or a dreary suburb, to which he returns occasionally for food and sleep when all possible excitement and stimulus have been wrung from the fight. If we should graduate into communism to-morrow this man's attitude to his wife would not be changed. The proletarian dictatorship may or may not free women. We must begin now to enlighten the future dictators.

What, then, is "the matter with women"? What is the problem of women's freedom? It seems to me to be this: how to arrange the world so that women can be human beings, with a chance to exercise their infinitely varied gifts in infinitely varied ways, instead of being destined by the accident of their sex to one field of activity—housework and child-raising. And second, if and when they choose housework and child-raising, to have that occupation recognized by the world as work, requiring a definite economic reward and not merely entitling the performer to be dependent on some man.

This is not the whole of feminism, of course, but it is enough to begin with. "Oh, don't begin with economic," my friends often protest, "Woman does not live by bread alone. What she needs first of all is a free soul." And I can agree that women will never be great until they achieve a certain emotional freedom, a strong healthy egotism, and some un-personal sources of joy—that in this inner sense we cannot make woman free by changing her economic status. What we can do, however, is to create conditions of outward freedom in which a free woman's soul can be born and grow. It is these outward conditions with which an organized feminist movement must concern itself.

Freedom of choice in occupation and individual economic independence for women: How shall we approach this next feminist objective? First, by breaking down all remaining barriers, actual as well as legal, which make it

From *The Liberator,* December 1920.

difficult for women to enter or succeed in the various professions, to go into and get on in business, to learn trades and practice them, to join trades unions. Chief among these remaining barriers is inequality in pay. Here the ground is already broken. This is the easiest part of our program.

Second, we must institute a revolution in the early training and education of both boys and girls. It must be womanly as well as manly to earn your own living, to stand on your own feet. And it must be manly as well as womanly to know how to cook and sew and clean and take care of yourself in the ordinary exigencies of life. I need not add that the second part of this revolution will be more passionately resisted than the first. Men will not give up their privilege of helplessness without a struggle. The average man has a carefully cultivated ignorance about household matters—from what to do with the crumbs to the grocer's telephone number—a sort of cheerful inefficiency which protects him better than the reputation for having a violent temper. It was his mother's fault in the beginning, but even as a boy he was quick to see how a general reputation for being "no good around the house" would serve him throughout life, and half-consciously he began to cultivate that helplessness until to-day it is the despair of feminist wives.

A growing number of men admire the woman who has a job, and especially since the cost of living doubled, rather like the idea of their own wives contributing to the family income by outside work. And of course for generations there have been whole towns full of wives who are forced by the bitterest necessity to spend the same hours at the factory that their husbands spend. But these bread-winning wives have not yet developed home-making husbands. When the two come home from the factory the man sits down while his wife gets supper, and he does so with exactly the same sense of fore-ordained right as if he were "supporting her." Higher up in the economic scale the same thing is true. The business or professional woman who is married, perhaps engages a cook, but the responsibility is not shifted, it is still hers. She "hires and fires," she orders meals, she does the buying, she meets and resolves all domestic crises, she takes charge of moving, furnishing, settling. She may be, like her husband, a busy executive at her office all day, but unlike him, she is also an executive in a small way every night and morning at home. Her noon hour is spent in planning, and too often her Sundays and holidays are spent in "catching up."

Two business women can "make a home" together without either one being overburdened or over-bored. It is because they both know how and both feel responsible. But it is a rare man who can marry one of them and continue the homemaking partnership. Yet if there are no children, there is nothing essentially different in the combination. Two self-supporting adults decide to make a home together: if both are women it is a pleasant partnership, more fun than work; if one is a man, it is almost never a partnership—the woman simply adds running the home to her regular outside job. Unless she is very strong, it is too much for her, she gets tired and bitter over it, and finally perhaps gives up her outside work and condemns herself to the tiresome half-job of housekeeping for two.

Cooperative schemes and electrical devices will simplify the business of homemaking, but they will not get rid of it entirely. As far as we can see ahead people will always want homes, and a happy home cannot be had without a certain amount of rather monotonous work and responsibility. How can we change the nature of man so that he will honorably share that work and responsibility and thus make the home-making enterprise a song instead of a burden? Most assuredly not by laws or revolutionary decrees. Perhaps we must cultivate or simulate a little of that highly prized helplessness ourselves. But fundamentally it is a problem of education, of early training—we must bring up feminist sons.

Sons? Daughters? They are born of women—how can women be free to choose their occupation, at all times cherishing their economic independence, unless they stop having children? This is a further question for feminism. If the feminist program goes to pieces on the arrival of the first baby, it is false and useless. For ninety-nine out of every hundred women want children, and seventy-five out of every hundred want to take care of their own children, or at any rate so closely superintend their care as to make any other full-time occupation impossible for at least ten or fifteen years. Is there any such thing then as freedom of choice in occupation for women? And is not the family the inevitable economic unit and woman's individual economic independence, at least during that period, out of the question?

The feminist must have an answer to these questions, and she has. The immediate feminist program must include voluntary motherhood. Freedom of any kind for women is hardly worth considering unless it is assumed that they will know how to control the size of their families. "Birth control" is just as elementary and essential in our propaganda as "equal pay." Women are to have children when they want them, that's the first thing. That ensures some freedom of occupational choice; those who do not wish to be mothers will not have an undesired occupation thrust upon them by accident, and those who do wish to be mothers may choose in a general way how many years of their lives they will devote to the occupation of child raising.

But is there any way of insuring a woman's economic independence while child-raising is her chosen occupation? Or must she sink into that dependent state from which, as we all know, it is so hard to rise again? That brings us to the fourth feature of our program—motherhood endowment. It seems that the only way we can keep mothers free, at least in a capitalist society, is by the establishment of a principle that the occupation of raising children is peculiarly and directly a service to society, and that the mother upon whom the necessity and privilege of performing this service naturally falls is entitled to an adequate economic reward from the political government. It is ideal to talk of real economic independence of women unless this principle is accepted. But with a generous endowment of motherhood provided by legislation, with all laws against voluntary motherhood and education in its methods repealed, with the feminist ideal of education accepted in home and school, and with all special barriers removed in every field of human activity, there is no reason why woman should not become almost a human thing.

It will be time enough then to consider whether she has a soul.

54

CRYSTAL EASTMAN

Alice Paul's Convention (1921)

. . . The only thing that makes a convention exciting or worth while is the debate over resolutions and program. But in Alice Paul's convention there were no resolutions and hardly any program! No resolution on disarmament was passed to give expression to the overwhelming pacifist sentiment of the Convention. No resolution of protest against the disfranchisement of Negro women was passed, although the Convention was almost unanimous in its indignation on that subject. Even "simon-pure" feminist resolutions were discouraged.

To all such complaints graduates of the Alice Paul school had one dogmatic reply: "Never endorse anything that your organization isn't ready to fight for. Never protest about anything unless your organization is ready to make that protest good." The more sacred a dogma is the more dangerous it is, and this one has the sacredness of the torn battle flag and the battered sword; it is the legacy of a victorious movement. Vital as this doctrine of extreme consistency was in the heat of the militant campaign—and no one can question that—what bearing had it on the delibera-

From *The Liberator,* April 1921.

tions of this body of women met to consider for the first time the actual status of women and lay the foundations of the movement which is to liberate them?

Last summer I went to Alice Paul with a roughly sketched but fairly complete feminist program. After a little discussion, she said, "Yes, I believe in all those things, but I am not interested in writing a fine program, I am interested in getting something done." This is the way she takes the wind out of your sails. But is she always right? . . .

Alice Paul is a leader of action, not of thought. She is a general, a supreme tactician, not an abstract thinker. Her joy is in the fight itself, in each specific drawn battle, not in debating with five hundred delegates the fundamental nature of the fight. "The Executive Committee have provided a good enough phrase— 'To remove all the remaining forms of the subjection of women.' Let the delegates with the least possible debate adopt this phrase to serve for purpose, program and constitution." Of course she said nothing, but that, I believe, was Alice Paul's notion of what the Conventions' action should be. "I will let you know what the first step is to be, how to act and when. Go home now and don't worry." These words were not printed in the program, but they seemed to be written between the lines.

Perhaps there are times in all movements that call for a leader just like that and for followers just like the majority in that convention who did what they were told. But this was not one of those times, and the proof of it is that the five hundred delegates, whether they voted with or against the leader, went home disappointed, without a quickened understanding, without a new vision. If their discontent could have been articulate it would have expressed itself in some such words as these: "We didn't come here just to state that women are still in subjection and that we are going to free them. We came to discuss and define the nature of our subjection and to outline the terms of our freedom. We came not merely to throw down a challenge, but to bring in a bill of particulars. For we are starting a new movement. We need a program in order to understand each other, we need a program in order to hold our mind and purpose steady and sure in this new field, we need a program as a first step in the process of education with which all new movements must begin."

A minority resolution looking toward such a program was actually introduced as a substitute for the Executive Committee's proposal, but the time limit and a very efficient steam roller disposed of it before the discussion had fairly started. The resolution was as follows:

"Having achieved political liberty for women this organization pledges itself to make an end to the subjection of women in all its remaining forms. Among our tasks we emphasize these:

"1. To remove all barriers of law or custom or regulation which prevent women from holding public office—the highest as well as the lowest—from entering into and succeeding in any profession, from going into or getting on in any business, from practicing any trade or joining the union of her trade.

"2. So to remake the marriage laws and so to modify public opinion that the status of the woman whose chosen work is home-making shall no longer be that of the dependent entitled to her board and keep in return for her services, but that of a full partner.

"3. To rid the country of all laws which deny women access to scientific information concerning the limitation of families.

"4. To re-write the laws of divorce, of inheritance, of the guardianship of children, and the laws for the regulation of sexual morality and disease, on a basis of equality,—equal rights, equal responsibilities, equal standards.

"5. To legitimatize all children.

"6. To establish a liberal endowment of motherhood."

If some such program could have been exhaustively discussed at that convention we might be congratulating ourselves that the feminist movement had begun in America. As it is all we can say is that the suffrage movement is ended.

Is Alice Paul a radical? Is she even a liberal? Is she really a reactionary? These vague reformist terms are inappropriate in describing Alice Paul. Let us use the definite terms of the revolution. She is not a communist, she is not a socialist; if she is class-conscious at all her instincts are probably with the class into which she was born. But I do not think she is class-conscious. I think she is sex-conscious; she has given herself, body and mind and soul, to the woman's movement. The world war meant no moment's wavering in her purpose, in fact she *used* the war with serene audacity to further her purpose. I imagine she could even go through a proletarian revolution without taking sides and be found waiting on the doorstep of the Extraordinary Commission the next morning to see that the revolution's promises to women were not forgotten!

Alice Paul does not belong to the revolution, but her leadership has had a quality that only the revolution can understand.

55

Freda Kirchwey

Alice Paul Pulls the Strings (1921)

The spirit of the National Woman's Party convention at Washington last week was summed up in two striking sentences. Said a disheartened delegate after the last day's session: "This is the machine age." Said one of the leaders of the Party to another delegate who tried to plead for a free consideration of a real program: "At a convention human intelligence reaches its lowest ebb." That was what it amounted to: the leaders acted on the theory of an amiable contempt for their followers; the rank and file, either cynically or enthusiastically, watched the wishes of the leaders become the law of the convention. With quiet precision the Woman's Party machine—a veritable tank—rolled over the assembly, crushing protestants of all sorts, leaving the way clear—for what? If anyone left the convention with a distinct idea of what the Party will do now that it has solemnly disbanded and solemnly reorganized, it is, perhaps, Alice Paul and the Executive Committee and some members of the Advisory Council and a few State chairmen. The rank and file, not realizing that their intelligence was at a low ebb, are vaguely disappointed. They do not know what their party will do; they only know that no action was taken in behalf of the Negro women, who have not yet got the vote in spite of the Nineteenth Amendment; that birth control and maternity endowment and most of the questions that stir the minds of modern women were ignored; that disarmament was ruled out; and that the program finally adopted—the majority report of the resolutions committee—declared vaguely against "legal disabilities" and for "equality" leaving the future definition of those terms and their translation into action to the executive board. The only specific application of the word equality appeared in the demand that it be "won and maintained in any association of nations that may be established"!

It may, of course, be asserted that since this mild and hypothetical program was adopted by a vote of the convention it was therefore the will of the convention, but one is forced to wonder whether the result would have been the same if a dissenting delegate or a minority committeeman had presented the winning report, and if Alice Paul's program had included disarmament or birth control or the enfranchisement of Negro women. I, for one, would back Miss Paul's chances on either side she chose to support. When the minority report recommending disarmament was before the house it was opposed vehemently by several ardent militarists of the order who declare: "I am as much against war as anybody in this room, but when the world is on fire. . . ." From the point of view of the leaders this opposition was undesirable; the majority report would only be weakened by militarist adherents. Presently the floor was taken by a well-known pacifist who

From *The Nation*, March 2, 1921.

set herself squarely on the side of immediate, complete disarmament and then proceeded on other grounds to an effective attack on the disarmament program. Later in the day this same pacifist—who is also a radical and a feminist—had a program of her own in the field in opposition to the majority report. This new dissenting program was specific. It demanded, in addition to the removal of the legal disabilities of women, the rewriting of the existing laws of marriage, divorce, guardianship, and sexual morality on a basis of equality; the abolition of illegitimacy; the establishment of motherhood endowment and of the legal right of a woman who chooses homemaking as her profession to an equal share in the family income; the repeal of all laws against the dissemination of information regarding birth control.

These proposals were sternly opposed by the machine. The leaders declared that such a program was too vague; they declared that it was too definite; they declared that it was too comprehensive; they claimed that the majority program could be interpreted to include all those demands and more besides. But in expounding the majority program they were cautious; not one of the leaders specifically stated, for example, that it should be interpreted to cover the question of birth control. "After all, that's the acid test," said one of the younger delegates. The new program received the support of a few of the less orthodox members of the Advisory Council, but its most persuasive advocates were among the young Party workers who charged that the majority report offered no more inspiration than the programs of other women's organizations which they had long been trained to look down upon as cautious, respectable, dull. Again the leaders were worried; they couldn't let the idea get about that only middle-aged respectability stood for the majority report. And presently a couple of the younger workers rose from their seats and opposed the radical program and swore by all the suffrage prophets that the majority report offered inspiration enough for any feminist. And it was well known to those who hung about in the lobby or watched the play from the wings, that Alice Paul had spoken the word necessary to make the pacifist oppose disarmament and the young radicals oppose the radical program.

Some day the story of the working of the National Women's Party machine will be told. It will be an interesting story, full of strange contradictions. It will tell of valiant self-sacrifice and magnificent defiance coupled with an incongruous willingness to appeal to the tradition of feminine weakness. It will be full of idealism and steadfast purpose and yet of a readiness to use any trick or pretense that might bring that purpose nearer to fulfillment. It will tell of independence and individual heroism existing side by side with obedience bordering on subservience. It will show sympathy and ruthlessness walking together. But that story cannot be written until the people who know it get out from under the spell of the Alice Paul legend. Today any attempt would be futile.

The efforts—finally successful—of the birth control advocates to secure a chance to speak at the convention would form an amusing chapter of that story. At the second day's session representatives of women's organizations with legislative programs made brief addresses stating their aims. Even old-time enemies of the Woman's Party were given a place. For weeks before the convention the head of the Voluntary Parenthood League had been in correspondence with the Party leaders demanding her chance to be heard. First the leaders refused, then they demurred, finally they surrendered; but their written objections to the presence of this organization on the platform of the convention were redolent with the faint fragrance of Victorian delicacy and reserve.

The efforts—wholly unsuccessful—of the representative of the colored women would form a tragic chapter of the same story. A delegation of sixty women sent by colored women's organizations in fourteen States arrived in Washington several days before the convention. They requested an interview with Alice Paul so that they might take up with her the question of the disfranchisement of the women of their race.

They were told Miss Paul was too busy to see them. They said they would wait till she had time. Finally, grudgingly, she yielded. The colored women presented their case in the form of a dignified memorial—which read as follows:

"We have come here as members of various organizations and from different sections representing the five million colored women of this country. We are deeply appreciative of the heroic devotion of the National Woman's Party to the women's suffrage movement and of the tremendous sacrifices made under your leadership in securing the passage of the Nineteenth Amendment.

"We revere the names of the pioneers to whom you will do honor while here, not only because they believed in the inherent rights of women, but of humanity at large, and gave themselves to the fight against slavery in the United States.

"The world has moved forward in these seventy years and the colored women of this country have been moving with it. They know the value of the ballot, if honestly used, to right the wrongs of any class. Knowing this, they have also come today to call your attention to the flagrant violations of the intent and purposes of the Susan B. Anthony Amendment in the elections of 1920. These violations occurred in the Southern States, where is to be found the great mass of colored women, and it has not been made secret that wherever white women did not use the ballot, it was counted worth while to relinquish it in order that it might be denied colored women.

"Complete evidence of violations of the Nineteenth Amendment could be obtained only by Federal investigation. There is, however, sufficient evidence available to justify a demand for such an inquiry. We are handing you herewith a pamphlet with verified cases of the disfranchisement of our women.

"The National Woman's Party stands in the forefront of the organizations that have undergone all the pains of travail to bring into existence the Nineteenth Amendment. We can not then believe that you will permit this amendment to be so distorted in its interpretation that it shall lose its power and effectiveness. Five million women in the United States can not be denied their rights without all women of the United States feeling the effect of that denial. No women are free until all are free.

"Therefore, we are assembled to ask that you will use your influence to have the convention of the National Woman's Party appoint a special committee to ask Congress for an investigation of the violations of the Susan B. Anthony Amendment in the elections of 1920."

Miss Paul was indifferent to this appeal and resented the presence of the delegation. Their chance of being heard at the convention was gone. A Southern organizer told the one active supporter of the colored women—a white woman and a delegate from New York—that the Woman's Party was pledged not to raise the race issue in the South; that this was the price it paid for ratification. But no such sinister motive is necessary to explain the treatment of the colored delegation; they were simply an interruption, an obstacle to the smooth working of the machine. Their leading members were not allowed to ride in the elevators of the Hotel Washington where the convention was held, until finally they made a stand for their rights. And only by the use of tactics bordering on Alice Paul's own for vigor and persistence, did their spokesman—the delegate from New York—get a moment to present a resolution in their behalf—a resolution which was promptly defeated and which left the question precisely where it stood.

The attitude of Alice Paul and her supporters toward these disturbers of the peace—Negro women and birth control advocates alike—was the attitude of all established authorities. "Why do these people harass us?" asked Miss Paul. "Why do they want to spoil our convention?" The answer, that never occurred to her, was this: "For the very same reason that made you disturb the peace and harass the authorities in your peculiarly effective and irritating way: because they want to further the cause they believe in."

In the lobby, among the futile opponents of the machine there was much discussion of the cause of their leaders' hostility to all that was new and clear-cut. The great fighting issue was gone; if the organization was to continue it must turn its attention to other issues and work for them one at a time or several together, not only in Congress but in the States. Would the leaders evolve out of their vague program an issue which they could again attack with military precision and on which they could hope again to raise their disciplined volunteer army? Would they justify their tactics, as they had so often done before by the brilliant success of their results? Or were they only greedy of power, eager to hold the final decision close in their own hands, unwilling to trust to the desires of their followers? Or were they, perhaps, only half awake to the fullness of life? Absorbed in a task of immense proportions, for years they had forfeited, as soldiers must, the common enterprises of life—love, marriage, children, the economic struggle. Had they thereby lost touch with the plain demands of modern women who are more interested in their opportunities for personal expansion and economic freedom and the right to bear children when they choose than they are in the presence of women in the councils of an unborn or dying league of nations? The opponents of the machine never decided those questions; the Alice Paul legend hung too closely over them and its phrases sounded in their ears through the closed doors of the convention hall.

56
Belle Case La Follette
National Convention of the National Woman's Party (1921)

. . . The morning of the third day was devoted to reports of the several national committees. To those accustomed to read the signs and forecast the outcome of conventions, it had early been plain that the future policy of the National

From *La Follette's Magazine,* March 1921.

Woman's Party would be very much in accord with Alice Paul's wishes. It was no great surprise, therefore, when it developed that the rational committees agreed in recommending an exclusively feminist program. This course was upheld in notable speeches by Mrs. Donald Hooker, Mary Winsor, and others.

The afternoon program of this day had been planned to clinch this recommendation. Its manifest purpose was to demonstrate that every field of women's interest other than feminism was well covered by other women's organizations. These short intensive talks were highly interesting and instructive. Taken together they constitute a most valuable survey of women's activities.

Margaret Woodrow Wilson spoke for Community Centre Organization; Julia Lathrop for the Children's Bureau; Florence Kelley for the Consumers' League; Mary Ware Dennett for the Voluntary Parenthood League; Lida Hafford for the General Federation of Women's Clubs; Mary Anderson for the Woman's Bureau, Department of Labor; Ethel Smith for the Women's Trade Union League; Mrs. Ellis Yost for the National W. C. T. U.; Maude Wood Park for the National League of Women Voters; Mabel Kittredge for the Women's International League for Peace and Freedom; Mrs. Henry Villard for the Woman's Peace Society.

If you followed these addresses closely you might have observed there was some overlapping even of the feminist program. One speaker stated that the work of remedying inequality of laws affecting women was already well organized in many of the States.

The fourth day had been assigned to "Discussion of Future of the Woman's Party." Throughout the convention the resolutions committee had been graciously listening to the many different groups appearing before them, it must have been very flattering to the National Woman's Party to have so many advocates of different causes appeal to them for support.

Only three issues reached the floor of the convention, however, and only one of these was supported by a minority report. Seven members of the resolutions committee signed a minority report which differed from that of the majority in proposing that the National Woman's Party take up the fight for world disarmament as an immediate object. This was defeated after a sharp debate under the five minute rule.

Please do not think for one moment, however, that the rejection of the minority report signified that the majority of the delegates to the Woman's Party Convention were not in favor of disarmament. On the contrary, the debate brought out conspicuously that the delegates individually were overwhelmingly for disarmament. As I remember it, only one person opposing the adoption of the minority report, did so from the militarist standpoint—for the reason that we must be prepared. Otherwise the speakers generally announced that they favored disarmament and agreed that it was up to the United States to initiate the movement for world disarmament. The convention divided on the question of whether the National Woman's Party should make the issue of disarmament a part of its immediate program or not, and the majority of the convention voted against making the issue a plank in the platform.

I may be mistaken, but I think this action was a concession to Alice Paul's leadership rather than an expression of the actual wishes of the majority of the delegates. Certainly, there was great disappointment on the part of some of the most enthusiastic supporters of the Party. One delegate, "a farmer," said she had come all the way from Oklahoma, at heavy expense, in the belief that her party was going to help women use their ballots to end war, and she dreaded to go home and report that the convention had refused to support disarmament.

The conduct of the debate on the floor of the convention was fair to both sides. Miss Paul personally spoke to some who were supporting the disarmament resolution and expressed the objection that they were new to the Party and had not earned by long service and sacrifice, the right to shape its future policy. Her point of view seemed to me unwarranted. The invitation to join the Party and to send delegates to the convention had been general and urgent; there was no suggestion of length of service being a qualification; the announcements gave reason to believe that the future policy of the Party was to be determined by the convention and that delegates would be free to express their convictions, and speak for their constituency.

To me, the stake in the adoption or rejection of the disarmament resolution by the convention was this: Now is a crucial hour in history; it will be decided SOON whether mankind shall choose some less barbarous means of settling differences, or whether the world shall continue to waste its substance in preparation of more and more terrible instruments of war; women hold the balance of power; the great masses of women are eager to use their newly acquired vote to end war; never in history could there be greater need or greater opportunity for organization and leadership; the National Woman's Party is ready, it has the experience, the zeal, the power to organize the mass sentiment and bring it to bear on Congress; shall this splendidly equipped organization seize the opportunity to help save civilization and the human race—women's elemental work—or shall it turn a deaf ear to the call of the millions of women it has helped enfranchise, and be content to limit its usefulness to a self-defined field of feminism?

For, it should be noted, the convention under the spell of its desire to follow its leader, refused to specify what feminism might include.

A resolution proposed from the floor for the enforcement of the nineteenth amendment in order to ensure the vote of the colored women of the South was defeated.

Resolutions to rewrite marriage and divorce laws, inheritance laws, guardianship laws, sex laws, on the basis of equal rights, standards, and responsibilities; to repeal laws denying scientific information concerning parenthood; to establish motherhood endowment; to make home-making women partners in the family income; were voted down.

The convention was satisfied to coldly set forth the immediate work of the new organization to be: Removing political and legal disabilities of women; seeing that political freedom shall not be lost in any association of nations that may be established; and working for the absolute equality of men and women.

Alice Paul's genius is her power to concentrate on one issue and to overcome all obstacles in the way of its achievement. She made tremendous sacrifices and suffered real martyrdom for the cause of suffrage. But she fought for it as a right, rather than as an instrument of service. So now apparently she has one goal in view—the ultimate legal, political, and economic equality of men and women.

Miss Paul was chosen chairman of the newly organized party with the understanding she was to have several months' rest before assuming the responsibilities of her position. A board was selected to direct the affairs of the party during the interregnum.

57

Margaret Sanger

Woman and the New Race (1920)

The most far-reaching social development of modern times is the revolt of woman against sex servitude. The most important force in the remaking of the world is a free motherhood. Beside this force, the elaborate international programmes of modern statesmen are weak and superficial. Diplomats may formulate leagues of nations and nations may pledge their utmost strength to maintain them, statesmen may dream of reconstructing the world out of alliances, hegemonies, and spheres of influence, but woman, continuing to produce explosive populations, will convert these pledges into the proverbial scraps of paper; or she may,

From Margaret Sanger, *Woman and the New Race* (New York: Truth Publishing Co., 1920), 1–11, 93–95.

by controlling birth, lift motherhood to the plane of a voluntary, intelligent function, and remake the world. When the world is thus remade, it will exceed the dream of statesman, reformer and revolutionist.

Only in recent years has woman's position as the gentler and weaker half of the human family been emphatically and generally questioned. Men assumed that this was woman's place; woman herself accepted it. It seldom occurred to anyone to ask whether she would go on occupying it forever.

Upon the mere surface of woman's organized protests there were not indications that she was desirous of achieving a fundamental change in her position. She claimed the right of suffrage and legislative regulation of her working hours, and asked that her property rights be equal to those of the man. None of these demands, however, affected directly the most vital factors of her existence. Whether she won her point or failed to win it, she remained a dominated weakling in a society controlled by men.

Woman's acceptance of her inferior status was the more real because it was unconscious. She had chained herself to her place in society and the family through the maternal functions of her nature, and only chains thus strong could have bound her to her lot as a brood animal for the masculine civilizations of the world. In accepting her rôle as the "weaker and gentler half," she accepted that function. In turn, the acceptance of that function fixed the more firmly her rank as an inferior.

Caught in this "vicious circle," woman has, through her reproductive ability, founded and perpetuated the tyrannies of the Earth. Whether it was the tyranny of a monarchy, an oligarchy or a republic, the one indispensable factor of its existence was, as it is now, hordes of human beings—human beings so plentiful as to be cheap, and so cheap that ignorance was their natural lot. Upon the rock of an unenlightened, submissive maternity have these been founded; upon the product of such a maternity have they flourished.

No despot ever flung forth his legions to die in foreign conquest, no privilege-ruled nation ever erupted across its borders, to lock in death embrace with another, but behind them loomed the driving power of a population too large for its boundaries and its natural resources.

No period of low wages or of idleness with their want among the workers, no peonage or sweatshop, no child-labor factory, ever came into being, save from the same source. Nor have famine and plague been as much "acts of God" as acts of too prolific mothers. They, also, as all students know, have their basic causes in over-population.

The creators of over-population are the women, who, while wringing their hands over each fresh horror, submit anew to their task of producing the multitudes who will bring about the *next* tragedy of civilization.

While unknowingly laying the foundations of tyrannies and providing the human tinder for racial conflagrations, woman was also unknowingly creating slums, filling asylums with insane, and institutions with other defectives. She was replenishing the ranks of the prostitutes, furnishing grist for the criminal courts and inmates for prisons. Had she planned deliberately to achieve this tragic total of human waste and misery, she could hardly have done it more effectively.

Woman's passivity under the burden of her disastrous task was almost altogether that of ignorant resignation. She knew virtually nothing about her reproductive nature and less about the consequences of her excessive child-bearing. It is true that, obeying the inner urge of their natures, *some* women revolted. They went even to the extreme of infanticide and abortion. Usually their revolts were not general enough. They fought as individuals, not as a mass. In the mass they sank back into blind and hopeless subjection. They went on breeding with staggering rapidity those numberless, undesired children who become the clogs and the destroyers of civilizations.

To-day, however, woman is rising in fundamental revolt. Even her efforts at mere reform are, as we shall see later, steps in that direction. Underneath each of them is the feminine urge to complete freedom. Millions of women are asserting their right to voluntary motherhood. They are determined to decide for themselves whether they shall become mothers, under what conditions and when. This is the fundamental revolt referred to. It is for woman the key to the temple of liberty.

Even as birth control is the means by which woman attains basic freedom, so it is the means by which she must and will uproot the evil she has wrought through her submission. As she has unconsciously and ignorantly brought about social disaster, so must and will she consciously and intelligently *undo* that disaster and create a new and a better order.

The task is hers. It cannot be avoided by excuses, nor can it be delegated. It is not enough for woman to point to the self-evident domination of man. Nor does it avail to plead the guilt of rulers and the exploiters of labor. It makes no difference that she does not formulate industrial systems nor that she is an instinctive believer in social justice. In her submission lies her error and her guilt. By her failure to withhold the multitudes of children who have made inevitable the most flagrant of our social evils, she incurred a debt to society. Regardless of her own wrongs, regardless of her lack of opportunity and regardless of all other considerations, *she* must pay that debt.

She must not think to pay this debt in any superficial way. She cannot pay it with palliatives—with child-labor laws, prohibition, regulation of prostitution and agitation against war. Political nostrums and social panaceas are but incidentally and superficially useful. They do not touch the source of the social disease.

War, famine, poverty and oppression of the workers will continue while woman makes life cheap. They will cease only when she limits her reproductivity and human life is no longer a thing to be wasted.

Two chief obstacles hinder the discharge of this tremendous obligation. The first and the lesser is the legal barrier. Dark-Age laws would still deny to her the knowledge of her reproductive nature. Such knowledge is indispensable to intelligent motherhood and she must achieve it, despite absurd statutes and equally absurd moral canons.

The second and more serious barrier is her own ignorance of the extent and effect of her submission. Until she knows the evil her subjection has wrought to herself, to her progeny and to the world at large, she cannot wipe out that evil.

To get rid of these obstacles is to invite attack from the forces of reaction which are so strongly entrenched in our present-day society. It means warfare in every phase of her life. Nevertheless, at whatever cost, she must emerge from her ignorance and assume her responsibility.

She can do this only when she has awakened to a knowledge of herself and of the consequences of her ignorance. The first step is birth control. Through birth control she will attain to voluntary motherhood. Having attained this, the basic freedom of the sex, she will cease to enslave herself and the mass of humanity. Then, through the understanding of the intuitive forward urge within her, she will not stop at patching up the world; she will remake it.

Behind all customs of whatever nature; behind all social unrest, behind all movements, behind all revolutions, are great driving forces, which in their action and reaction upon conditions, give character to civilization. If, in seeking to discover the source of a custom, of a movement or of a revolution, we stop at surface conditions, we shall never discern more than a superficial aspect of the underlying truth.

This is the error into which the historian has almost universally fallen. It is also a common error among sociologists. It is the fashion nowadays, for instance, to explain all social unrest in terms of economic conditions. This is a valuable working theory and has done much to awaken men to their injustice toward one another, but it ignores the forces *within* humanity which drive it to revolt. It is these forces, rather than the conditions upon which they react, that are the important factor. Conditions change, but the animating force goes on forever.

So, too, with woman's struggle for emancipation. Women in all lands and all ages have instinctively desired family limitation. Usually this desire has been laid to economic pressure. Frequently the pressure has existed, but the driving force behind woman's aspiration *toward freedom* has lain deeper. It has asserted itself among the rich and among the poor, among the intelligent and the unintelligent. It has been manifested in such horrors as infanticide, child abandonment and abortion.

The only term sufficiently comprehensive to define this motive power of woman's nature is the *feminine spirit*. That spirit manifests itself most frequently in motherhood, but it is greater than maternity. Woman herself, all that she is, all that she has ever been, all that she may be, is but the outworking of this inner spiritual urge. Given free play, this supreme law of her nature asserts itself in beneficent ways; interfered with, it becomes destructive. Only when we understand this can we comprehend the efforts of the feminine spirit to liberate itself.

When the outworking of their force within her is hampered by the bearing and the care of too many children, woman rebels. Hence it is that, from time immemorial, she has sought some form of family limitation. When she has not employed such measures consciously, she has done so instinctively. Where laws, customs and religious restrictions do not prevent, she has recourse to contraceptives. Otherwise, she resorts to child abandonment, abortion and infanticide, or resigns herself hopelessly to enforced maternity....

The problem of birth control has arisen directly from the effort of the feminine spirit to free itself from bondage. Woman herself has wrought that bondage through her reproductive power and while enslaving herself has enslaved the world. The physical suffering to be relieved is chiefly woman's. Hers, too, is the love life that dies first under the blight of too prolific breeding. Within her is wrapped up the future of the race—it is hers to make or mar. All of these considerations point unmistakably to one fact—it is woman's duty as well as her privilege to lay hold of the means of freedom. Whatever men may do, she cannot escape the responsibility. For ages she has been deprived of the opportunity to meet this obligation. She is now emerging from her helplessness. Even as no one can share the suffering of the overburdened mother, so no one can do this work for her. Others may help, but she and she alone can free herself.

The basic freedom of the world is woman's freedom. A free race cannot be born of slave mothers. A woman enchained cannot choose but give a measure of that bondage to her sons and daughters. No woman can call herself free who does not own and control her body. No woman can call herself free until she can choose consciously whether she will or will not be a mother.

It does not greatly alter the case that some women call themselves free because they earn their own livings, while others profess freedom because they defy the conventions of sex relationship. She who earns her own living gains a sort of freedom that is not to be undervalued, but in quality and in quantity it is of little account beside the untrammeled choice of mating or not mating, of being a mother or not being a mother. She gains food and clothing and shelter, at least, without submitting to the charity of her companion, but the earning of her own living does not give her the development of her inner sex urge, far deeper and more powerful in its outworkings than any of these externals. In order to have that development, she must still meet and solve the problem of motherhood.

With the so-called "free" woman, who chooses a mate in defiance of convention, freedom is largely a question of character and audacity. If she does attain to an unrestricted choice of a mate, she is still in a position to be enslaved through her reproductive powers. Indeed, the pressure of law and custom upon the woman not legally married is likely to make her more of a slave than the woman fortunate enough to marry the man of her choice.

Look at it from any standpoint you will, suggest any solution you will, conventional or unconventional, sanctioned by law or in defiance of law, woman is in the same position, fundamentally, until she is able to determine for herself whether she will be a mother and to fix the number of her offspring. This unavoidable situation is alone enough to make birth control, first of all, a woman's problem. . . .

58

THE NATION

The White Woman's Burden (1921)

"In February there will be held in Washington a meeting of women which will be comparable only to their first great gathering in Seneca Falls in 1848." This, though from the Press Chairman of the National Woman's Party, is no overstatement. The three-day convention of the National Woman's Party on the 101st anniversary of Susan B. Anthony's birth will be notable, not merely because of the character of the women who attend, nor because they justly celebrate their important part in winning for this country political sex equality, but also because of the opportunity that this great yet incomplete victory affords.

For incomplete it is. The Nineteenth Amendment has been ratified. The world has been told that America which first lit the beacon of political democracy on earth has at last joined the nations which make no political distinction among their citizens because of sex. Yet some three million women—the women of color—in the States south of the Mason and Dixon line are still disfranchised. In *The Nation* of October 6, William Pickens describes the unconstitutional and illegal devices by which the American woman citizen of African, or of mixed European and African, descent is robbed

From *The Nation*, February 16, 1921.

of her vote. This article was sent to each one of the 160 members of the National Advisory Committee of the National Woman's Party. With it went four questions:

1. Do you approve of the attempt to nullify the Nineteenth Amendment in regard to colored women?

2. What steps, if any, do you purpose to take to help remedy this situation?

3. Do you consider this a matter for official action and effort by the National Woman's Party?

4. What suggestions have you for a course of procedure?

In sending these letters, *The Nation* felt confident that no body of women would be more alive to the issue involved, to its identity with the bitter fight which they had just waged and apparently brought to a triumphant conclusion, indeed, to its inseparability from the whole fabric of our democracy. Would not these "suffrage radicals," fresh from the hardships of disfranchisement and discrimination, see clearly the far graver and greater injustice now being treacherously and dishonestly worked on an integral part of their electorate?

About one-third of those written to replied. The tenor of these responses was most gratifying. The majority declared themselves outraged at the disfranchisement of American colored women and resolved to fight it through. A few were evasive and non-comittal, one or two opposed. Yet if any considerable pattern of the hundred or more who did not reply is even indifferent, the outlook is none too encouraging.

The Nation feels that this issue is fundamental and that whatever the arguments for or against the continuation of the National Woman's Party, as an organization, its members should realize that their goal has not been achieved and the Nineteenth Amendment not won until it means the enfranchisement of every woman regardless of color or race. Will the women of America accept this honor, responsibility, and duty?

Among those replies which appeared to be unfavorable is that of Mrs. Oliver H. P. Belmont [a native of Alabama], from whom was received the following:

Mrs. Oliver H. P. Belmont wishes me to acknowledge receipt of your letter of September 24 asking her to answer four questions. Mrs. Belmont says she finds it needless to give her answers to these questions. She regrets, however, not being able to oblige you.

LOUISE GALVIN, Secretary,

as well as the following from Charleston, S. C.:

I have yours of 24th inst. asking if I approve the disfranchising of the newly enfranchised Negro women. I say emphatically *no*. At the same time I say *most emphatically,* let the South handle its own problems, just as I say let the Californians solve their own problems; one in the North or West, where the proportion of Negro population is about one to every thousand white, cannot possibly undertake to give advice or to help us in the South, where we have communities where the Negro either predominates numerically, or is at rate of half and half. We in the South would not presume to go to the Western coast and undertake to settle the trials and problems caused in California by the yellow race problem, and no more can the North come into the South and undertake to solve our problems. If you were living in a community, like this city, where we have half and half, or in Beaufort, S. C., where the Negroes outnumber the whites and where they are constantly incited by the white race coming from a distance to meddle into affairs of which they know nothing because they have no experience, you would then perhaps get something of the point of view of the South. . . . SUSAN P. FROST.

Somewhat more non-committal is the brief reply:

I'm very sorry to have nothing to say on this important question. Frankly I don't see any clear solution. I shall read with the greatest interest what others have to say about it.

MARTHA B. BRUERE.

Entirely non-committal is that of Mrs. Charlotte Perkins Gilman who writes:

Your second letter about the colored woman voter received. I do not give views or interviews save as I am moved to on my own initiative. In that case I seek to publish them professionally.　　　　　　　　C. P. GILMAN.

A teacher of Latin in a Georgia college, after admitting some haziness on the whole question says:

As you know we white women were prevented from voting in November by the registration clause. The more I think on the race problem the more insoluble it seems.

Becoming slightly more positive is the reply of the National Chairman, who writes:

We have just received your letter of September 24 attached to the October 6 issue of *The Nation*. In reply I am writing to inform you that a bill for the enforcement of the Nineteenth Amendment was introduced last spring in Congress, but was not acted upon owing to the fact that Congress adjourned before ratification of the suffrage amendment was completed. This enforcement resolution will be brought up at the coming session of Congress and we will endeavor to have it passed.　　　ALICE PAUL.

Of the stirring letters, those which breathe the true spirit of militant American democracy, the following are but a few specimens:

1. I disapprove wholly of every attempt to nullify the Nineteenth Amendment, or to infringe in any way upon the right to vote of any colored women or colored men, or any other citizens of the United States who are not actively insane or undergoing punishment for non-political crimes.

2. I propose to work with other voters for the passage of the anti-lynching law and for reduction in the representation of any State which may not obey the Fourteenth and Fifteenth Amendments and uphold, in letter and in spirit, the Nineteenth Amendment.

3. Yes.

4. It is my intention to bring up this subject at the approaching meeting of the National Woman's Party, hoping for official action at that meeting, followed by effective insistence upon equality before the law for all women.

　　　　　　　　　　FLORENCE KELLEY.

And a letter from Mrs. Harriet Stanton Blatch, somewhat too long for reprinting, which includes "an old yellow pencil note of my mother's which shows how she felt in regard to our treatment of the colored race. I feel exactly the same."

From distant California came this letter:

1. Decidedly not. The National Woman's Party, of which I have been a member since its foundation, has fought for sex equality at the polls, subject only to the same limitations as apply to men. Any attempt to disfranchise women on the ground of *color* deals as mortal a blow to the ideal of democracy in general and the purpose of the Nineteenth Amendment in particular as to disfranchise laboring women on the ground of *class*. The Nineteenth Amendment, in other words, is more than skin deep and is color blind. White women who cannot consider this question apart from race prejudice and who are willing that the spirit and purpose of the Nineteenth Amendment be nullified where black women are concerned, should keep in mind the selfish consideration that once the Nineteenth Amendment is tampered with where colored women are concerned it can be tampered with where white women are concerned. It is not that equality which is *justice*. We aimed at *justice*.

2. I shall call attention to this matter in the San Francisco Civic Center, also in any other organizations where public action on their part would prove influential. My association with the National Woman's Party, however, has converted me wholly to the idea of political action on these political questions. Concerted public opinion has to work through those political channels by which alone a movement becomes practically effective. I consider that there has been sufficient education in this country on the subject of political equality and I would therefore recommend that the National Woman's Party with its equipped and well-organized body, its unparalleled leadership and sophistication in politics undertake such action as is necessary to protect the Nineteenth Amendment. *The Nation* probably knows that in the middle of February there is to be a national convention of the National Woman's Party at which time the

matter of dissolution or further continuation of the party is to be voted upon. My personal desire is for its continuation in order that it may carry on its fight for equality in the fullest sense, and I shall recommend to the convention, if it votes to continue, that this matter under present consideration be the first one for which a fight be made by the organization. Sporadic, individual action here and there is of little avail. Even letters to congressmen and senators, unless they are let loose upon them in terrifying numbers, are of little avail. There must be a responsible body, efficient and tireless such as the N. W. P. has proved to be, undertaking the work.

3. My reply to question 2 covers affirmatively this question. . . .

4. I feel this question is one for consideration by people more skilled in political strategy than I am, but in general I would suggest that "the appropriate legislation" called for in the second paragraph of the Nineteenth Amendment, to be passed by Congress for the unqualified enforcement of the amendment, be made as strong as that legislation by which the Prohibition Amendment is protected and that, if necessary, the N. W. P. if it remains an active organization insist on the appointment of Federal officers to protect the rights of citizens to their vote. . . .   SARA BARD FIELD.

And the following from the Atlantic Coast:

On February 15 next there will be held a national convention by the National Woman's Party in Washington, D. C. The paramount issue before that convention will be the question of the future existence of the Woman's Party which at present has attained the only object of its organization, namely, the passage of the Susan B. Anthony Suffrage Amendment. If it is decided at the convention that we continue to exist as a new organization one matter will be paramount, whether our future existence be for political or benevolent purposes. This matter will go with us, whether we indorse it or not, that of the immediate action taken by a large portion of the Southern States after the recent ratification of the Nineteenth Amendment, by which all women, white or colored, have been disenfranchised. In other words, that portion of our country which has so persistently opposed the object of the Woman's Party, has turned its defeat into a practical victory for itself, by callously defying the Nineteenth Federal Amendment, as was the case regarding the Thirteenth and Fourteenth Amendments. Moreover, the situation is much more vital in regard to the Nineteenth Amendment, for never before has there been a trained organization of the leading women of the nation associated together for seven years for the sole purpose of carrying through a Federal amendment. The Woman's Party, if it is to have a future existence, will stand or fall in accordance with the path it chooses in this matter. . . .

    ELLA RUSH MURRAY.

And this from the chairman of the Information Committee of the Woman's Republican Club:

Your courteous inquiry of the 19th inst. in relation to suffrage was delayed in Washington. It is here at last and I hasten to say in answer to your four questions:

1. I do not.

2. Agitation: appeals to Congress, the courts, and above all to the press and the public. Aggressive action all along the line. A man or woman who attempts to deprive a citizen of his or her right to vote should be disfranchised.

3. I do most assuredly.

4. I prefer to submit this in a later communication. It is a proposition involving serious thought. I stand with the women of America, white or colored, in the battle for every right to which they are entitled under the Constitution.   JEAN L. MILHOLLAND.

Finally, a vigorous letter which the writer subsequently forbade the use of "either in the compiling of statistics or otherwise unless you use them in full, including number 5":

1. No—neither in regard to colored men or colored women.

2. I shall join the N. A. A. C. P. if they will send me their membership blanks. I shall urge colored people to join the Socialist Party which

will give them membership in the party on equal terms with the whites and with the triumph of socialism will give them political and industrial justice.

3. Certainly not. The National Woman's Party was formed for the purpose of abolishing discrimination against women—specifically suffrage discriminations. In the task of freeing *all* women—colored as well as white—suffragists were not helped much by colored men voters. On the contrary, the suffrage referendum of 1915 (Penna.) was beaten chiefly by votes in wards (Phila.) where the Republican machine is strongest.

4. The colored voters should demand that this present Republican congress should cut down the representation from the Southern States where the colored voters are disfranchised and should threaten to bolt the party if this is not done. As long as the colored voters continue to bend before the Republican Party, so long will they be enslaved.

5. I don't know why *The Nation* has arrogated to itself the right to catechize the National Woman's Party. *The Nation* was *utterly indifferent* when the members of the N.W.P. were illegally thrown into jail for asking for the vote.

MARY WINSOR.

59
ELLA RUSH MURRAY
The Woman's Party and the Violation of the 19th Amendment (1921)

The National Woman's Party held its final convention in the city of Washington, D. C., from February 15 to 18, with delegates, many hundreds in number, from all over the country. . . .

On February 16, as a member of the National Advisory Council, I presented a Minority Report of the meeting of the council held on

From *The Crisis*, April 1921.

January last. The report covered a motion made by me at that meeting, duly seconded, and defeated, to the effect that the Advisory Council recommend to the National Woman's Party, in event of its reorganization, that a special committee of the Woman's Party be appointed to bring pressure to bear on Congress for a special Congressional Committee to investigate the violation of the intent and purposes of the 19th Amendment.

In explanation of my motion I said to the convention that I was bringing the matter to their consideration on account of the disfranchisement of women of both races in the Southern States at the recent elections, by evasion and perversions of the State Election Laws. That the Enforcement Act enforcing the 19th Amendment cannot meet the situation since it has to be worded like the Amendment which it enforces and thereby can only state that there shall be no disqualification on account of sex. That there never has been and presumably never will be discrimination on account of sex even in the most bigoted sections and that, therefore, it was futile for anyone to argue that the women of the South would be protected by either the 19th Amendment or the subsequent Act enforcing it. That, moreover, the objection that the colored men of the South had found no protection under the 14th and 15th Amendments was equally of no weight since, in the first place, they alone had been disfranchised without similar injustice being done to white men, and that, in the second place, there had been no powerful organization of white men capable of protecting them as the Woman's Party was able, through its national prestige and political experience, to protect women. That the recent disfranchisement of southern women of both races was not only a direct defiance of the very essence of the Susan B. Anthony Amendment but that it was an opening wedge for similar action wherever vested interests of any kind prevail, and upon any subject.

That an unchallenged act of an illegal nature could become, through national disregard of law, an established situation, with the battle to be fought all over again. That the Anti-Suffragist neither slumbers nor sleeps. That there is even now a concerted attempt to prevent women from serving on juries in the State of Pennsylvania. That the Anti-Suffrage League of Women Voters, with headquarters in New York, is not organized purely for the sake of being listed in the New York City Telephone Directory. That in Maryland, the Anti-Suffragist is "walking up and down in the land, and going to and fro in it." That the past history of the Woman's Party will show that the portion of the country which most bitterly opposed Woman Suffrage—the Southern States—was now openly deriding the object for which we had worked so valiantly, viz., the 19th Amendment, and by shameless perversions and evasions of State Election laws, effectually frustrating our efforts.

That aside from the fact that we ought, in the name of all truth and justice, to help our disfranchised sisters of any race, we certainly could not afford, with any degree of dignity, to reorganize along the same general lines without taking official cognizance of the fact that we had not attained our end as long as what we had striven for remained a dead letter in one form or another. That unless we of the Woman's Party went on record with a protest against disfranchisement, we could never consider that our work for the 19th Amendment had been finally achieved.

On Friday morning, February 18, I spoke from the floor of the convention in the form of an objection to the Minority Report of the Resolutions Committee, upon the ground that it did not contain any allusion to the matter in question. On Friday afternoon, just before the convention closed, I succeeded in getting a motion before the convention, to the effect that the Majority Report of the Resolutions Committee should be amended to read as follows:

"That the Resolutions Committee recommends that the reorganized National Woman's Party appoint a special committee to urge Congress to appoint a special committee to investigate the violation of the intent and purposes of the 19th Amendment by evasion and perversions of State Election Laws." The motion was seconded by several delegates, and was defeated by a light majority.

Thus the object for which I had prayed and hoped and worked was attained. The Woman's Party has gone on record, and while it has done so in opposition to any notice of the fact that it has not succeeded in fully enfranchising the women of the country as far as actual voting is concerned, nevertheless an opening has been made, and the opposing vote was not a heavy one. It has been brought up to me that the Woman's Party has provided all women in the United States with the weapon of the ballot, and my reply has been, "If I wish to arm a woman whose hands are tied, which must I do first,—untie her hands, or just leave the gun around somewhere?"

What was most needed at the convention was an emphatic, persistent number of colored women delegates with their own leaders. This is vitally important. Leading colored women should join the State Branches of the Woman's Party and they should be present at the meetings as interested working members, and they should insist that the State Chairman appoint a fair share of colored delegates to the National Annual Conventions, in accord numerically with the total number of delegates allotted to each State Branch. The proof of the value of colored women appearing in a concerted demand for their rights was conclusively shown by the tremendous moral effect produced upon those members of the convention who were present at our National Headquarters when the Deputation of Sixty, representative colored club women, called upon Miss Alice Paul three days before the convention to ask her to state her position regarding disfranchised women. I stood on the stairs as the deputation came up, and listened to the women of my own race as they made such comments as: "What splendid-looking women!" "What a lot of women!" "Where on earth did they all come from?" "Do you mean to say they have come from all over the country just to see Miss Paul?" "Are they all college women?" "Have they got a lot of organized clubs?" etc., etc.

Now the idea of deputations originated in the earliest gloom of time, and its advantage as regards advertising are obvious. What the colored women need now, in the opinion of the writer of this article, is to follow approved political methods. We of the Woman's Party have never broken a law, but we forced the United States Government to do so when it illegally arrested, convicted and imprisoned us for picketing, an act made legal under the Clayton Federal Act. Our Government thereby became "militant," and not the Woman's Party.

It can be clearly seen that the fundamental idea of the Woman's Party, from picketing to deputizing, was to make your opponent put himself in the wrong and incidentally to drag him into as much uncomfortable publicity as possible. Any other organization is at perfect liberty to study our methods, from the early days when we were still working for State Suffrage down to the last hours of political pressure in the two great national conventions of the Republican and Democratic Parties.

The National Federal of Colored Women's Clubs, or the women of the N. A. A. C. P., or any other powerful association can persistently and unremittingly appeal for permission to send speakers to every meeting in the country, down to the smallest Ladies' Auxiliary of the smallest country church. They can work energetically for space in the press to report their speeches wherever made. They can send deputations to every leading woman, calling on her to use her influence to help her disfranchised sisters. Above all, they can picket early and late, all large conventions, the Woman's Party, the League of Women Voters, the Daughters of the Revolution (especially to the point!).

No one except a Woman's Party woman can foresee the train of thought evoked by the sight of fine-faced colored women standing silently at the doors of the conventions of their careless white sisters, with banners inscribed perhaps with some such thought as: "Do you know that (so many) million women are denied the vote?" Or "What are you going to do about the disfranchised women of the Southern States?" Or "Help us to fight for the thing that is nearest our hearts—Democracy,—by enforcing the 19th Amendment in spirit as well as in letter." Liberty is not deserved unless fought for wholeheartedly and with single purpose. We of the Woman's Party can say to you that we placed one object above all others while we fought, and we allowed no other matter to divert us from our goal.

60
Mrs. Robert M. Patterson
The Negro Woman in Politics (1922)

Never was there a time in which there was greater need for sane and sober thought on the part of Negro Women....

A new system must be installed. If we study the history of the Negro men in politics, we will learn some valuable lessons. We will learn, first, that, so far as the Negro is concerned, the Republican Party is the same as the Democratic Party; we will learn that the primary step in the systematic disfranchisement of the Negro in the South was taken when the Republicans betrayed and handed them over to the "White League" of the south in lieu of the acquiescence on the part of the Southern Democrats, in the fraudulent seating of President Hayes. They will learn that lynchings, burning at the stake goes on apace with a Republican President, Congress and Supreme Court. They will learn that the good old Republican Congress cannot or will not pass an anti-lynching bill. They will learn that it was Taft who started kicking them out of appointive positions at Washington. They will note that the Republican Party of Pennsylvania refused to pass a "Civil

From *Women's Voice*, September 1922, as reprinted in Gerda Lerner, ed., *Black Women in White America: A Documentary History* (New York: Vintage Books, 1972), 339–42.

Rights Bill." They will learn that your husbands, fathers, brothers and sweethearts have consistently supported by their votes this abominable condition for a half a hundred years.

All of the phenomena above mentioned have a well-defined and fundamental cause. The Republican Party has not, cannot and will not remedy them because they are not interested in "humanity," they are interested in "property." . . . They represent the owning class in society. The owning class must divide and sub-divide the non-owning class. The poor white and blacks are the non-owning class in America; this non-owning class has been divided on racial lines and sub-divided along economic, industrial, social and political lines. In doing this, capitalistic society is performing its historic mission. The average Negro's lot in life is one long dreary night of the hardest and dirtiest work with the smallest amount of pay; there is not a faint star of glimmering hope in our present social firmament to relieve the monotony of his cheerless watches. He is doubly cursed by a capitalist system which is a savage jungle—a system which forces millions of human beings, black and white, to dwell in poverty—millions of unfortunate women, black and white, to be driven to the bitter bargain of their bodies. A system where few hold sway over body and soul of the many. . . .

The Socialist Party is organizing workers, black and white, on the political field with the aim of putting an end to exploitation. . . . One of the most encouraging signs of the time, to my mind, has been the open-mindedness exhibited by quite a few young women on this momentous question. I have in mind that part of the platform endorsed by the Colored Women Political League, sponsored by Mrs. Somerville Fauntleroy, inviting all parties to present their platforms to the League. . . .

Now the time is ripe for the women to step in and take hold of conditions. . . . The women should form clubs, explain the correct use of the ballot, consult among ourselves the best way this particular principle or policy will benefit society, then make a demand and see to it that it is carried out by those whom you have elected into office. Let us not waste any time talking about voting "good men and women" into office into the various parties when our object is rather to put "good policies" into action. The best man or woman in the world could not possibly do the Negro any good if his or her party's policies and principles were at variance with the Negroes' best interest. . . .

In these times of unrest we need women of the type of Harriet Tubman and Sojourner Truth. Women of mental ripeness, courage and clearness of purpose and a burning spirit to dare and to do. We need women who are not content to trail along in foolish political paths of the Negro men. We need women who will not sell their rights for a mess of pottage. We need women who will not follow kindly a party because of its name, women who will break away from any party that does not stand for absolute equality of opportunity for each and every human being. We should insist that the Negro women get their rightful share of all public offices, and that a common test should be applied to all aspirants.

We should agitate and insist that a larger number of our young women be allowed to qualify as social workers, inspectors and investigators in welfare work, etc.; we should set our faces against the vile and insidious propaganda of separate schools. We must not permit the fight for equal civil rights to cease until it will be possible for every citizen, without regard to race, to have complete civil rights guaranteed to him or her. We should insist that there should be an extended education for all, compulsory education for youth. We should insist upon a system of education where our youths will have every advantage and opportunity to bring out the finer qualities in them. Oh! where are you women of courage? Step out into the battle. Those of you who want the best things in life for all human-kind—you who yearn for that social justice without which the advent of the brotherhood of man is a myth—step out! . . . Vote for Socialism!

61
AMY JACQUES GARVEY
Women as Leaders Nationally and Racially (1925)

The exigencies of this present age require that women take their places beside their men. White women are rallying all their forces and uniting regardless of national boundaries to save their race from destruction and preserve its ideals for posterity. We see them in the law courts pleading as advocates; they preside as judges and administer laws; while in less numbers, yet they are to be seen in parliaments, congresses and council chambers legislating for their people. White men have begun to realize that as women are the backbone of the home, so can they, by their economic experience and their aptitude for details, participate effectively in guiding the destiny of nation and race.

No line of endeavor remains closed for long to the modern woman. She agitates for equal opportunities and gets them; she makes good on the job and gains the respect of men who heretofore opposed her. She prefers to be a bread-winner than a half-starved wife. She is not afraid of hard work, and by being independent she gets more out of the present day husband than her grandmother did in the good old days.

The women of the East, both yellow and black, are slowly but surely imitating the women of the Western world, and as the white women are bolstering up decaying white civilization, even so women of the darker races are sallying forth to help their men establish a civilization according to their own standards, and to strive for world leadership.

Women of all climes and races have as great a part to play in the development of their particular group as the men. Some readers may not agree with us on this issue, but do they not mould the minds of their children—the future men and women? Even before birth a mother can so direct her thoughts and conduct as to bring into the world either a genius or an idiot. Imagine the early years of contact between mother and child, when she directs his form of speech, and is responsible for his conduct and deportment. Many a man has risen from the depths of poverty and obscurity and made his mark in life because of the advices and councils of a good mother whose influence guided his footsteps throughout his life.

Women therefore are extending this holy influence outside the realms of the home, softening the ills of the world by their gracious and kindly contact.

Some men may argue that the home will be broken up and women will become coarse and lose their gentle appeal. We do not think so because everything can be done with moderation. Some women are good cooks, yet because of the call to the other duties they rarely ever cook a meal; but when the necessity presents itself they know how. Others are good business women, yet they would not neglect their children and homes to attend business with their husbands, but if hubby dies or becomes incapacitated, they can fit in his place and save a situation. The doll-baby type of women is a thing of the past and the wide-awake woman is forging ahead, prepared for all emergencies, and ready to answer any call, even if it be to face the cannons on the battlefields.

New York has a woman as secretary of state. Two States have women governors, and we would not be surprised if within the next ten years a woman graces the White House in Washington, D.C. Women are also filling diplomatic positions, and from time immemorial women have been used as spies to get information for their country.

White women have greater opportunities to display their ability because of the standing of both races, and due to the fact that black men are less appreciative of their women than white men. The former will more readily sing the praises of white women than their own, and who is more deserving of admiration than the black woman, she who has borne the rigors of slavery, the deprivations consequent on a pau-

From *Negro World*, October 24, 1925.

perized race and the indignities heaped upon a weak and defenseless people? Yet she has suffered all with fortitude, and stands ever ready to help in the onward march to freedom and power.

Be not discouraged black women of the world, but push forward, regardless of the lack of appreciation shown you. A race must be saved, a country must be redeemed, and unless you strengthen the leadership of vacillating Negro men, we will remain marking time until the yellow race gains the leadership of the world, and we be forced to subserviency under them, or extermination.

We are tired of hearing Negro men say, "There is a better day coming," while they do nothing to usher in the day. We are becoming so impatient that we are getting in the front ranks and serve notice to the world that we will brush aside the halting, cowardly Negro leaders, and with prayer on our lips and arms prepared for any fray, we will press on and on until victory is ours.

Africa must be for Africans, and Negroes every where must be independent, God being our helper and guide. Mr. Black Man, watch your step! Ethiopia's queens will reign again, and her Amazons protect her shores and people. Strengthen your shaking knees and move forward, or we will displace you and lead on to victory and to glory.

62
ANNE MARTIN
Woman's Vote and Woman's Chains (1922)

Woman's equality was not won with the vote last year. Only one barrier fell then. The inadequacy of the national woman suffrage amendment as a step to real equality is shown in striking manner by the economic and political

From April 1922 issue of *Sunset*. Reproduced with permission.

position of American women today. In spite of frequent declarations by President Harding, politicians campaigning up and down the country, Fourth of July orations, and speeches by leaders of women's clubs and civic organizations, this country is not yet a "democracy." Women are not "free" and the equals of men, even with the vote in their hands. The United States today is a sex aristocracy. Professor Einstein to the contrary, American women as a class are ruled by men.

First and foremost, their economic position is abject. Wives are in theory and practise "dependents," although their unpaid labor in their homes earns their own and at least half their families' support. More than ninety per cent of American families do not employ a servant. But the legal view and the theory most wives continue to live and work under is that they are "supported" by their husbands.

In addition to these unpaid home workers, there are upwards of 12,000,000 women wage-earners outside the home, but property laws are still unfair and help maintain woman's inferior status. For example, under Nevada law a lazy husband may collect his wife's salary as a teacher, or her earnings as a washer-woman, and has been known to do it. To retain possession of her separate property the wife must make and file a yearly inventory of it at the court house, otherwise it becomes her husband's. As to community property, I remember watching a very few years ago a "fight" in the Nevada legislature to give the wife some control over this form of property accumulated by her joint efforts. A bill was introduced requiring the wife's signature to legalize its sale. One eloquent legislator rose and said: "Nevada's a suffrage state now, and I'm all for the women (laughter), but this bill would work hardship. I might be in New York City, for instance, selling mining shares, and it might cost me my profits in a fluctuating market or even kill the sale if I had to wait ten days for my wife's signature from 'way out in Nevada." This was a death blow, as there was no woman legislator to point out that such technicalities are arranged beforehand by men partners, and could be arranged by husband and wife as partners. Although the outward rigors of the law have been softened in many states by married women's property acts, in practically every state discriminations continue in one form or another against the wife. The fundamental injustice is that our legal system is a masculine institution. It will be humanized when women as legislators re-make laws, as lawyers interpret them, as judges apply them, as jurors render verdicts. . . .

In defiance of the national suffrage amendment, women were deprived of the right to vote in Georgia and Mississippi last November on technical grounds, which the authorities refused to remove. Women are ineligible to most public offices under a Georgia statute, and special legislation is necessary for them to hold state offices in Massachusetts. A woman candidate in Arkansas at the last election had to withdraw under a decision that she was disqualified on the ground of sex. Women are not permitted to serve on juries in Colorado, Delaware, Florida, Maryland, Massachusetts, Minnesota, New York, Texas, and other states. In Pennsylvania, where the Attorney-General has rendered an opinion that no special legislation is necessary to permit them to serve, judges in Erie and Schuylkill counties have ruled that they can not sit in certain cases, and they do not.

Political parties, national, state, and county, are exclusively controlled by men. It is only through the party organization, of course, that women can be nominated to office, unless they run as independents. The determination of men to keep control in spite of the enfranchisement of women, is seen in the action of the Republican State Committee of Pennsylvania. It met recently and appointed a woman vice-chairman and another woman assistant secretary. At the same time the committee adopted a rule that no woman would be eligible for the offices of chairman, secretary, or treasurer of the committee.

The political appointments by President Harding went exclusively to men. With rare exceptions women hold no high (or low) executive, administrative, or judicial offices, national or state. There are no women ambassadors or consuls. Since the founding of the government more than 25,000 men have been elected to Congress and only two women. Hundreds of thousands of men have been elected to state legislatures, and probably less than one hundred women, although equal suffrage prevailed in our Western states many years before the ratification of the national amendment last year.

The government of the United States is, then, a sex aristocracy. Women are ruled by men. What are they doing to raise their inferior status? Not much. Their passive acceptance of it is the greatest obstacle. They are still satisfied, most of them, with the vote in their hands, to act as ladies' aid societies to men's political parties, doing much of the drudgery of campaigns under the orders of the men in control. They do not see that when swallowed up within the parties they are powerless. They still stand patiently outside convention halls, state legislatures, and the doors of Congress as lobbyists, waiting for their men representatives to appear for a hurried moment to cock an impatient ear toward their pleas for women's measures.

Very, very few women see that the next step toward equality must be winning woman's share, woman's *half* in man-controlled government. They can then remove by direct action as legislators and administrators, no longer by "indirect influence," all discriminations against half the race. But most of them can not shake off the conviction planted in their minds by centuries of teaching, that women as a sex are inferior to men.

Another obstacle is the newspapers, whose news and articles are most naturally accented by the male psychology which controls them, and help to keep women where they are. So do some of the large women's magazines, edited by men with a few exceptions. Just as certain of these magazines were against suffrage until it became popular and inevitable, today they fail to urge women to take the next step. On the contrary, one of the largest ridicules editorially the demand that all jobs be open to women as well as men and that the pay scale be the same, and comfortably concludes: "Where there is the greatest freedom in the world for womankind, she (the feminist) finds slavery and degradation. Where there is new freedom on an ever expanding scale, she strains a morbid fancy to raise bogies and banshees of man tyranny that have been buried since the dawn of the nineteenth century." No wonder millions of women, administered narcotics like this every month in the pages of their favorite journal, are soothed into forgetfulness of their contemptible economic status, and into complacency and gratitude for their "new freedom."

Another woman's publication has taken the cue given by the head of a large woman's organization. She is humbly preaching that women must train for years before holding public office. This magazine has adopted her slogan, "trained citizens versus women politicians." The old double standard "women should not vote because their place is the home" has been succeeded by "women are not ready for office and must be educated first!"

The editorial position of these "women's" publications supports that of the politicians, who are quicker than most women to see that the straight road to equality is not lobbying on the doorstep of legislative halls, but *occupying at least half the seats within those halls*. In their maneuvers to keep women powerless they have attacked even their harmless organizations working outside the Republican and Democratic parties for their modest program of welfare and equality legislation. For example, Governor Nathan L. Miller of New York recently had the New York State League of Women Voters on the carpet, and declared there was no justification for women's political organizations, unless they are formed *within* the "party of your choice;" that any group which seeks to exert political power outside the parties is "a menace to our institutions," which he said can be maintained only by the two-party system of government. He denounced the League for its effort to defeat Senator Wadsworth of New York for reëlection. This senator, it should be recalled, in spite of repeated "mandates" of his party and the protesting gestures of Republican party leaders, prevented for more than a year the passage of the national suffrage amendment. Was the senator punished by his party for insubordination? Not at all; it moved heaven and earth to reëlect him. Yet, ladies, if you do not wish to be considered a "menace," give up your organizations and work *inside* the parties!

Woman's course is clear. One lesson indelibly written in the hearts of some suffragists by the seventy years' struggle for the vote, is that women must work as a separate political force to win equality. A striking example of the effectiveness of this principle is found in the National Woman's Party campaign for the suffrage amendment in 1916. In this vigorous campaign the Woman's Party appealed to enfranchised women throughout the West not to vote for President Wilson because "he had kept us out of war," but to vote against him and the Democratic candidates for Congress, because their party had "kept us out of suffrage." President Wilson's reëlection hung in doubt for days because of his small majority in the deciding suffrage state of California. The woman's campaign raised the Susan B. Anthony amendment from the position of an academic question to that of a national political issue which the President dared no longer ignore. This first important step was taken and the final victory won, not by the political parties but by political pressure exerted upon them from a woman's "balance of power" group outside the parties.

In this way, undoubtedly, women must continue to work to win the next step, the establishment of political equality. Propaganda and appeal to men will not do it, as shown by the suffrage struggle through three generations, and by the failure of groups of women voters, backed by mere pleas of their millions of members, to win their legislative program from the last Congress. The present Woman's Party bill removing all discriminations in every state and abrogating "the common law disabilities of women and the special immunities of men" will not do it, even when passed by the forty-eight legislatures. Nothing less than woman's actual and equal participation in government, and in all the business of life, will establish her equality. To accomplish it a "woman's party" using political pressure is strategically necessary against the "man's party," whether it be Republican or Democratic, which controls our government.

This woman's party need not nominate its own candidates, but should encourage and support qualified women candidates, whatever their political affiliations, if they pledge themselves to place the interests of women above the interests of any political party. Many can thus be elected, and a half share in government secured. Such strategy is necessary only until women have "caught up" with men, and won both political and economic equality. Then sex, both male and female, will be out of politics. As human beings women can freely give their best. The standard of ability, not sex, will be established in the affairs of life, and men and women will move together with increased power toward a more human world.

63
Corinne (Roosevelt) Robinson, Molly Lifshitz, Gloria Swanson, Rose Schneiderman, Mrs. R. F. DeCallies, Rose Pastor Stokes, Mary P. Scully, and Florence E. Allen

Is Woman Suffrage Failing? (1924)

Is woman suffrage a failure?

There are men who say so.

Has the success of the movement, the outcome of nearly three-quarters of a century of tireless, self-sacrificing work of a multitude of women, resulted in nothing but apathy?

There are women who fear so.

From *The Woman Citizen,* March 22, April 5, and April 19, 1924.

Have voting women done nothing but double the votes of men?

Many politicians claim it.

Have women added nothing to the intelligent conduct of public affairs? Have they forgotten the reforms for the sake of which they so earnestly sought the vote?

This charge is made repeatedly.

Are the great organizations of women weak and cowardly in their attitude toward controversial questions?

They have been attacked in print on this ground.

Are women a negligible quantity in local affairs? Is it true that "not a boss has been unseated"? Or a "reactionary committee wrested from the old-time control" through the work of women? Is it true that women have been tried in public office with the result that they are "likely hereafter to be fewer"? That "women will not vote for a woman"? Are women "timid and over-awed in political conventions"? Are "politicians contemptuous of them"?

Is it true that the American woman is not interested in public affairs and cares less to inform herself about them than about anything else under the shining sun? Is it a fact to be faced that American women as a whole "do not care for the vote, that they are not interested in using it and will not accept its responsibilities"?

Are "twenty million women fiddling feeble tunes while the flames of greed, hatred and war creep upon civilization"?

All these charges are being hurled at women, and they come from many sources. Some of the accusations answer themselves. Some find obvious answers in back numbers of the *Citizen,* in story after story of women's political achievements and interest. But we are not answering here, we are asking. For short though the time has been for women's political work, it is not too short to show tendencies. So we are throwing the question wide open.

With a view to discovering how women themselves feel about it, not only the thinking woman, but women in general, we are interviewing women in every walk of life and in every branch of industry, every profession. What does the vote mean to them? Do they use it? Has it made any change that they can see? Would they be wiling to give it up? We are asking the same questions of representative men who are willing to speak frankly and whose opinions count. We are asking some of the women who were well-known leaders in the final years of the suffrage fight whether they are disappointed in the results. We are questioning social leaders, working girls, movie stars, miners' wives, famous singers, business women, authors—in every part of the country.

The series is not intended as a defense for what women have done or an excuse for what they have not accomplished in the three and one-half years since they have had the vote, but it is an effort to get at the facts.

MRS. DOUGLAS ROBINSON

Mrs. Douglas Robinson, born Corinne Roosevelt, sister of the late President Roosevelt, is a member of the New York State Republican Executive Committee, an ardent worker for her party, and a speaker who has much of T. R.'s directness and force.

. . . I have been astounded at opinions advanced in some of our periodicals, implying woman's waning interest in the ballot, and darkly hinting at our failure as voters. I don't know whom the writers can have interviewed to arrive at such conclusions. A wide study of the question, in the interests of my party and in the interests of the women themselves, convinces me of the opposite. There is no failure of woman suffrage. It is true that there are not many women in office as yet, because we want to show ourselves more competent in office first. It is likewise true that the politicians are apparently still somewhat in doubt of women's influence in the parties; they do not take women yet wholly into their councils, which looks as if they were a little suspicious. But I am not a believer in things that come over night. The leaven has already begun to work. It may not make a great showing in this coming election, but in a few years, possibly at the next Presidential election, the women's standard of citizenship will make a great change in this country.

The immediate effect of the vote is not far to seek. My vote means to me the power to make my influence practical. If it were for that alone nothing could make me give it up. It has made a distinct difference in the attitude of men toward me in public life. And while we hear criticisms that all the women eligible for the ballot do not go to the polls on election day, to me one of the great accomplishments in that direction, going on right in New York City, is the remarkable work of the Republican Neighborhood Association, under the leadership of Mrs. James Russell Parsons, in getting out the women's vote in the Fifteenth Assembly District—my own. They have evolved a method which carries education for citizenship right along with it, and is not fugitive but permanent.

MOLLY LIFSHITZ

If you want my opinion, I think it is an insult to women to go around asking what the vote means to them or what they have done with it," Miss Molly Lifshitz, secretary of the White Goods Workers Union, summed up her attitude. (Miss Lifshitz, Russian born, used to be a factory worker, at unskilled labor; by studying in night school she got business training and rose to her present post.)

What have the men done with theirs? They have had it much longer than we have; and no one goes around trying to find out how they have used it.

Of course, it makes a difference to women to have the vote. It is a mark of recognition. But it is only right and fair that they should have it. I don't think they should be expected to accomplish any particular thing with it. After all, they are just a part of the great voting public. They may need education; but so do the men. I don't see that there is any difference.

It is true. I can't see any changes that have been brought through the woman's vote, except that possibly politicians do stand somewhat in awe of the women; and business men may pay more attention to them when organized into groups. Toward individuals their attitude remains unchanged. In the political parties their presence seems to me to find things much the same. I go to the Socialist meetings and can speak only for them. There I think women will find no corruption to uproot. If the party had ever been in power it might be otherwise. Socialists have always paid more attention to women and admitted them on a more equal footing. The fact that they have a vote now has not made any noticeable difference.

GLORIA SWANSON

It would be much more surprising if women's interest in the vote didn't wane," declared Gloria Swanson, an absorbed light in those grey eyes which millions of moving-picture fans adore.

They all concentrated for so many years, worked themselves up to such a pitch of enthusiastic excitement, that when they won the prize a reaction had to come. If they had tried to stay at the top of the peak they'd have fallen over the edge.

It's a lot like the moving-picture business, which leaped ahead with enormous speed. Everyone was interested, everyone was working tremendously hard. Then they achieved the biggest thing they could think of at the moment, and there was a slump. Now it's building up again slowly, and much more surely, on a firm foundation. Women's interest in politics will build again in the same way.

To me, the entire suffrage campaign was a secret and unacknowledged drive or self-expression on the part of women. They had been repressed for so long, being good silent partners of men, never doing the thing they wanted to, nor saying the thing they thought. And one after another they got fed up on it. They were bursting with the desire to express themselves, and because they had been unselfish for centuries, that desire took the form of unselfish service for their fellow women. But it also gave them an outlet for all the things society hadn't allowed them to do or say. Also other women felt that—and I think it was a matter of feeling, for I'm sure no one admitted it even to herself—they joined the campaign. Gradually it became the fashion, but behind it all was the vast, restless urge. It was irresistible, and it burst the dam of custom and won the vote.

And then that desire for self-expression flew into a thousand pieces, channels, avenues, whatever you want to call them.

Women felt a freedom they'd never known, and they set about following their own inborn desires. Some of them went off into business, into various arts, into professions, and some of them stayed concentrated on political affairs.

I don't know whether increasing numbers will find their happiest expression in politics or not. I think the urge is born in a person, is a product of hundreds of generations, and we've been political animals such a short time.

Suffrage hasn't touched me in any tangible way, and yet I think it's the most wonderful thing that ever happened to women. I left Illinois before any intense campaign was under way there, and went to California, where suffrage was a fact and they had stopped talking about it. I was entirely absorbed in making a career for myself, and my twenty-first birthday was like any other. I never thought of voting.

In the movies the only time we talk much about national affairs is when our income taxes are due. Then we growl a lot, but we don't do anything. We haven't time to find out what ought to be done and, anyhow, we get overwhelmed with the powerlessness of a single individual in an enormous population.

But in spite of all that, in spite of the fact that I don't use it, suffrage means more to me than I can possibly put into words. It is a symbol of the freedom of women to do the thing that they have the inborn ability to do, instead of being forced to follow outside orders. I wouldn't give it up for anything. And if they tried to take it away from me, I'd fight!

ROSE SCHNEIDERMAN

I am just as disappointed in women's suffrage as I am in men's suffrage," declared Rose Schneiderman with an upward tilt of that fighting red head which has guided the New York Women's Trade Union League, whose president she is, through so many battles. "Women have done very little in four years of voting, but men have done tragically little in a hundred and fifty years. Why suddenly demand that women do the outstanding thing which we've given up expecting from men?

The women's vote hasn't been of any visible value in the measures which the Women's Trade Union League want. We started twelve years ago to fight for a forty-eight-hour week. We are still fighting for it, and I can't see that it is a bit easier now, that we make any more impression on the Legislature than we did before we could vote.

Women shirk the responsibility for decisive action on public questions. And it's not surprising. For so many hundreds of years they haven't been held responsible for anything outside their own households. Naturally, it is hard to get them to accept responsibility for something which will affect a state, or the entire nation.

And that is true right straight through the whole social organization. Women prominent in public affairs, holding party positions, accepted as leaders, will say, "Oh, yes; I believe in this measure of yours. I think it's fine in principle, and that it will be practical in application. But my party doesn't agree with me. And I can't do anything about it for you. I must abide by the rulings of my party."

We need rebels within the parties, women who won't "follow the leader," who are independent thinkers, and are not afraid to follow up their thoughts with their actions. And the parties need those rebels within their ranks if they are going to save their own flickering lives.

At the other end from the leaders are the masses of working women, and the wives of working men, who stand, not by their party, but by their customs. They don't vote, they don't know anything about political affairs, and no one has shown them any reason why they should learn.

The only thing that can touch the huge, unleavened mass of tenement women is some system of block education, such as was carried on in the suffrage fight. Then we went from house to house, we climbed those long flights of stairs, and brought the women into temporary contact with the campaign. But suffrage was won, and the tenement women dropped back into their own neighborhood life. Their feeling in regard to politics is always typified for me by the answer of a woman who had stood in Union Square watching a suffrage parade. Stooped with work and weariness, she leaned on the handle of the baby carriage while two children scarcely old enough to be out of it clung to her skirts. I asked her if she was interested in suffrage. She shook her head. "No. I haven't any time to go into society."

There's one very important thing that should be done immediately. We ought to send the right kind of women to the Legislature. I wish a non-partisan committee could be formed to name six women to be elected next year. They should be capable, independent, of known ability, able to form a woman's bloc, or to lead action on individual measures. And I would have all the organizations concentrate on the election of these women, and keep close in touch with them during their terms. It would be valuable to see what they could do, and perhaps more interesting to see what they wouldn't do, and why. They would get enough publicity to reach a lot of apathetic women voters, and they would have a salutary effect on the legislators. They would be trail blazers for the right kind of women in political life.

Would I give up the vote? Never. Absolutely not. No matter how poorly the mass of women use it, we are all better off with it than we were without it, and if what I suggest were done, untold benefits would come to all through woman's vote.

MRS. R. F. DECALLIES

Housekeeper and caretaker of a city apartment house gives us an answer of valiant simplicity and directness.

I have never voted and probably never will, but that is because I have not studied public questions. A woman who does not study should not vote, nor should a man who does not study. But the vote has been a wonderful thing for women in general, and it has made some women think. And it has given every woman a better frontage. I mean she turns a better front to the world, and she is more on her own feet.

ROSE PASTOR STOKES

"*The real issues are class, not sex, issues.*"

A prominent Socialist, Mrs. Stokes presents a Socialist point of view in answering the same questions as Dr. Eliot.

I can only think of the value of the vote in its relation to the women of the farms and of the working class. Though its value in arousing consciousness is undoubted, I have no illusions as to its ultimate value at the ballot-box. I am convinced that when the masses demand fundamental change under the increasing pressure of unbearable living conditions, the propertied interests, through their fascist organizations, will meet that demand with violence. The ballot, in other words, will be knocked from their hands by the club or the butt of a gun.

Conditions among the farmers are worse than they've been in decades. The working masses in the cities are exploited more bitterly than before the war. The ballot can help them today only if they are powerfully organized and demand through their organizations a workers' and farmers' government.

Political parties are expressions of class interests, not of struggle between sexes. The old parties, which are the parties of property, may incline men to use more polite language at party meetings, now that women have entered them, but this does not alter the class character of their programs.

In public discussion more women today participate, but I find they line up according to class interest exactly as men do.

Where it is a question of the two old parties, such differences as exist between husband and wife cannot be serious. Usually the two have a common class outlook. It is only in those extremely rare cases where the two are divided in class outlook and class interest that truly independent voting can be said to take place.

Men politicians are not afraid of women's influence because they happen to be women. Where women are radical, politicians are worried. But they equally fear radicalism in men. In other words, the real issues are class, not sex, issues.

MRS. MARY P. SCULLY

"*If women who think would go into politics . . .*"

Mrs. Scully worked in a needle factory, became forewoman in a shirtwaist and dress factory, and because of her success in the famous "shirtwaist strike" became the first woman organizer for the American Federation of Labor.

"Of course the women haven't done anything as voters," Mrs. Mary Scully stated emphatically. "Why should they?—all the leaders have quit, and the women who are now trying to be politicians came away from the fireside when suffrage was accomplished and they don't know anything about politics. The politicians go to the women and hand them a lot of directions, and the women accept whatever they give them. They do not even ask why they were not consulted or why they were not included in the caucus. Women never use their initiative in politics. If you ask them anything, they say, 'Well, I'll ask the men.' The women are simply pawns.

"If you want to teach politics to women, don't hold your meetings in the great hotels. The commoner will not find her way there, and it is the commoner that you want to reach—it is the Italian and Polish families with fourteen and fifteen voters in almost every family that ought to be reached, and they should be taught by people they can understand. I don't mean language, because the second generation can speak English, but people who have worked at machines and in factories and know what their problems are.

"The politicians all gather around those married women who never have been very far away from the kitchen stove and have taken the word of their husbands as law and gospel. I would hate to give up my vote because I worked so hard to get it—not that I think it's of much use to me or anybody else. If women who think would go into politics, they might do something, but they're not there now."

FLORENCE E. ALLEN

Judge of the Supreme Court of Ohio, and the only woman on a state Supreme Court bench.

I believe that women are discussing political and governmental matters much more than formerly, but not nearly so much as they should, of course. I do see, however, a very great gain in that direction. In the state of Ohio I think our interest in governmental matters is greatly stimulated by the jury service, to which the women now are eligible and which they have undertaken for the most part in fine spirit.

For my own part, I believe that the participation of women in the courts alone, not only as attorneys, prosecutors and judges, but as jurymen, has immeasurably raised the tone of the administration of justice. This is particularly marked in the criminal courts, and in my opinion, if no other result had come out of the enfranchisement of women but that of their participating in the work of the courts, the extending of the vote to us would have been amply justified.

64
MARY R. BEARD
A Test for the Modern Woman (1932)

One of the serious consequences of the depression is the disaster which has overtaken rugged American feminism. Just at the hour when it seemed that the women's program of equal rights was to be fully realized after a struggle of eighty years, the crisis came to leave the movement stranded.

American women have been accustomed to a high degree of personal privilege and they are unprepared both physically and mentally to cope with financial calamity. Indeed, they appear to be more stunned than men, judging from the silence among them as to the means of recovery. Women had turned so far from the broad study of life in their effort to emulate the men in the immediate landscape that they failed to foresee that the equality which they coveted might eventually prove to be equality in disaster.

The very transfer in the ownership of wealth to women in recent years in America is in part their misfortune, because property rights are now a heavy burden on their hands. Equal pay for equal work, especially in the teaching field, grows meaningless when an entire staff of instructors has to serve without remuneration; an over-supply of teachers in every city raises apparently insoluble problems for the most ardent egalitarian. An ideal of factory labor on the same terms as men enjoy signifies nothing when neither men nor women can get employment of any sort. Even the battle for the remaining posts loses its heroic qualities to some extent and resembles an atavistic tooth-and-claw struggle in a narrowed and cramped arena. Instead of the benefits which they had confidently anticipated from economic equality, the feminists are unexpectedly confronted with defaults on dividends, a rapidly contracting labor market, a new dependence that the older family system of economy never knew, and the possibility that the capitalist system of production and distribution in which they have been participating so blithely is overworked and doomed.

Everything looked so promising to feminists until the 1930s. Their forward march toward equality was marked by the attainment of important political offices, novel business positions, unexampled wages and salaries,

Reprinted with permission from *Current History* (November 1932). © 1932, Current History, Inc.

educational influence, laboratory advantages, scientific training, honorary degrees, prizes of many sorts, rare chances to explore the earth by land, sea or air, and international recognition. Every few years the press took stock of woman's prowess along man's lines and recorded her gains and liberties. Such inventories led to bolder efforts at acquisition and enjoyment, and thus the general feminist movement was kept alive, encouraged and rendered confident.

For almost a century feminism had been stamping itself on American culture with ever-deepening hues. The Civil War and the World War contributed abundantly to its progress: the domestic struggle by turning half a continent over to free economic exploitation by the two sexes, and the foreign struggle by opening the avenue to full government manipulation to both on equal terms. Indeed, the movement which began with a demand for the prerogatives of men—property rights, cash remuneration for labor, formal education in all its branches, business and professional opportunities and enfranchisement—actually brought such power to women that within a few decades they gained a status amounting almost to dictatorship in the nation's industrial and social order.

At the height of post-war prosperity it was discovered that women were paying billions of dollars annually in taxes and that they were inheriting 70 per cent of the estates left by men and 64 per cent of the estates left by women. Efforts on the part of male relatives to evade taxes and sieges for alimony on the part of wives helped to divert vast sums to this centre of vested rights. Woman's greater longevity was also an asset, and one of the most striking phenomena in this country up to the depression was the horde of aged ladies residing in expensive hostelries and resorts, awaiting the messenger of death as luxuriously as possible.

Personal holdings as a source of privilege and influence were supplemented by the widespread practice which housewives enjoyed of spending their husband's wages and salaries. Although the census shows nearly 1,500,000 more men than women in the population the custom of arming the women with this enormous control over expenditure made them, as the main purchasing agent, the director of industry. As Eunice Barnard phrased it, the "Stop and Go signals for business enterprise" were in women's keeping. Production was largely determined by the feminine choice of commodities, while the profits were flowing in women's direction in a steady stream.

Aware of this control over the economic nerves of the nation, in the heyday of the surplus when the wheels of industry were revolving merrily and women were spending freely, the cry went up from Washington for them to store less food and clothing in their houses and put their money instead into Liberty and Victory bonds, where it could be utilized to finance the war. The slogan then emanating from the White House was "Save!" and women patriotically lent their savings to the government, organized thrift instruction in the schools and made thrift appeals on the streets. Then, in the days of want, when the wheels had ceased to turn and plants stood idle, while the banks were congested with gold, manufacturers and merchants joined politicians and financiers in urging the women to "Share!" and to "Spend!" In other words, women were told to remember that they managed the economic signals and were urged to place them at "Go!"

If feminist operation became highly determinative in the realm of business and finance, it finally assumed a decisive importance in the political theatre as well. A glittering golden age of privilege carried women to the point where they shared in selecting the President of the nation, though none of their sex has yet had a nominating speech for that office made in her behalf at a major party convention. It is true that "Oh, You Beautiful Doll!" resounded through the auditorium when a female delegate eventually nominated a male for the Presidency or seconded the motion, but women were then swept into the common stream of political action with the fanfare and "Hail! Hail! the Gang's

All Here!" Their cheers, their local and national campaigning talents, their financial aid and their emotional novelties were all found stimulating to a full-blown democracy in political assemblage.

The "gang," which included increasing numbers of women delegates after 1918, also comprised party auxiliaries of the same persuasion. These were active in the corridors of the convention buildings and came equipped with platform and radio rights and the funds for travel up and down the land, so necessary for success at the polls. Besides the party delegates and the extra allies, women styling themselves non-partisan achieved a certain influence with the politicians by their united stand for general welfare planks and bills, usually designed with women and children mainly in mind.

In the sweep of feminism the United States became habituated to women Mayors, legislators, national political committee executives, Governors, judges and international commissioners. A European has facetiously remarked that it takes more than a spinster to disarm a male, but at all events, in deference to the insistence of numerous women's organizations, a woman was given a place on the American delegation to the Geneva conference on arms reduction. Thus the circles of feminist politics spread to the periphery of domestic concerns, creating a stronger agitation for the surcease of war.

Rugged feminism in America was refined in some respects and gross in others. It was born of the necessity to recover from the blows administered to the family system of production by machine enterprise. There was vigorous feminine leadership in the old tribal system, and the first group master was no doubt the mother, the logical family maker. About the productive home in the seventeenth century centered economic, political, intellectual and social life, and any one who doubts the forceful rôle of woman in that society should read Alice Clark's volume on domestic industry in England, an economy which migrated with the colonists to the New World. But that system lost its hold over the earth, and nowhere so completely as in the New World. Had women then allowed themselves to be brushed aside forever by the masculine assumption of economic dominance they would have displayed an inertia, a lack of social understanding, a personal sacrifice and a dearth of genius which were not characteristic of the sex. . . .

As a spur to initiative and career-making, the doctrine of equality was useful. Bourgeois men had found it to be such a stimulus when they announced that all persons of their own sex were created equal. And if the doctrine of equality was the best that women could devise in the 1840s, knowing almost nothing of the long past, it served at least to energize their wills and to give direction to their thinking. With the growth of a New World bourgeoisie new values were established in personal ethics for men and women alike, such as the desire to "get on" competitively and the thirst for offices and rewards which are available only in an elastic society. Americans of both sexes could enjoy the rare delights of acquisitive liberties, political privilege and costly diversions with the least check and balance of any people. Their land was long the richest in undeveloped tracts and natural resources. It was the freest from traditional inhibitions. Pioneers in a brief century or two had given it all its recognized history. Its women could profit in a peculiar way through the infinite subdivision of technological processes which marked the course of industry; these specializations made room for women's skill in managing machines and accessories, provided incomparable wages for the working class and unexampled wealth for the owning class. Individualism mounted to favor as the perfect good. So the bourgeois democracy of America reveled in its widely distributed liberties. Its restless feminine contingent found additional exercise for its released energies by inciting women in other lands to organize, to agitate and to acquire.

The social bearings of this economic and political power are still evident. Women own mines and mills in the United States employing child and adult labor. They have stocks and bonds in their deposit boxes representing every kind of investment from a low-rate government security to the most unstable foreign loan. Women are heads of colleges, where at least their own sex foregathers. As doctors and lawyers women contribute to medical and legal opinion. They are ministers preaching the old gospel, and they are founders of new sects. They testify before the Senate committee investigating heavy financial transactions in which they are involved as willful actors. They preside over crime prevention bureaus and over courts. They conduct campaigns for and against a free liquor traffic. The National Woman's Party seeks to abolish by legal means the remaining discriminations against their sex, such as the loss of citizenship by a woman married to an alien. The League of Business and Professional Women sets as its goal "A High School Education for Every Girl"—something no man's organization has yet sought for every boy. The American Alliance for Civil Service Women is working to defeat the "practice of certifying lists by sex at the mere whim or prejudice of the appointing officer." The greatest parliament of women ever assembled is being planned for next Summer at Chicago.

Thus the current of rugged feminism bore women along an exciting course of equality and freedom to the attainment of extraordinary experiences, a broader administrative outlook, unusual racial and political contacts, a personality which felt the wide earth to be its home, and a new consciousness of kind. But there were cross-currents. Because of strict fidelity to the dogma of equality, feminism as it flowered became weakened in its critical faculties. What women members might take to the House of Representatives or the Senate, to caucus or convention, in the way of intellectual or political equipment, seemed to matter little; the point was the counting of women's and men's heads. Every feminist victory at the polls was accorded a paean. Sufficient to all occasions was the idea of an equal participation as between the sexes. To receive army ranking for nursing and other services in time of war was one of the prominent objectives, notwithstanding the movement for peace. To be a butcher, a baker, a candlestick-maker was regarded as excellent in itself if men were butchers, bakers and candlestick-makers. Naturally, it was better to be a speaker, a preacher, a captain of industry, an artist, an efficiency engineer, or a financier, if men believed it so.

Emancipated women settled back to enjoy their new liberties with scant thought of the future. Ceasing to be familial on the former scale, association developed into a herding of adults with individualized interests. In the beginning there were some troubled consciences among the clubwomen, and self-improvement programs demanding intellectual effort on their own part marked the path of club activity, much as Roman women in the early era of a leisure class drew together for the study of arts and letters, music and philosophy. Political discussions and programs were gradually added to the club activities. But soon the clubs adopted as their main attraction the easiest form of entertainment, namely, lectures by native and foreign savants, without the necessity on the part of the members themselves to study the subjects which they heard discussed. Clubhouses were essential for these activities, and of course they had to be financed. Little by little the erection, the maintenance, the tendency toward continuous use, the struggle for a large membership in order that the bills might be paid, induced an intense preoccupation with vested interests until the club building grew so important that even the speakers were viewed as gate receipts. An aggressive, independent, articulate conviction on current events or impending economic and political happenings, such as had provoked the original feminine association, gradually deteriorated into a timid, inarticulate reliance on the opinions of others. The clubhouse had conquered the mind. Other types of leisured association among women developed a similar mental inertia. One leading national organization, not devoted to the clubhouse but bewildered by its very size, its meager aims and its expense, actually called in two men to appraise its objectives and suggest what must be done to save the group.

As long as the *laissez faire* philosophy to which the creed of equality was attached could maintain its economic basis, women did good tail-flying. But the man's kite was always in danger of falling; it was always dipping and diving, and women, racing in the rear, were lamentably blind to the perils ahead. They rejoiced to receive institutional education—just at the time when it had lost its momentum and become hopelessly formalized; they got the vote when it had become least effective, owing to the power of the so-called invisible government; they entered remunerative positions at the period when big business was dropping into a deep air-pocket; they made their main intellectual drive on masculine knowledge at the very stage of man's intellectual collapse.

Perhaps the greatest challenge of history now confronts the women who, led on by the desire for equality, have tasted the sweets of unparalleled liberty. They surely comprehend at last that nine-tenths of the national wealth cannot be diverted to the coffers of the rich, however many women may be included in that category, with any assurance of economic stability for themselves or for other "independent" women. With history as well as recent events to warn them, they must prepare to meet the challenge to bring new ideas to bear on American life and on their own destiny within it.

65

GENEVIEVE PARKHURST

Is Feminism Dead? (1935)

Not long ago I attended a convention of several thousand women who had gathered together to hear from the lips of those who spoke with authority about the change which has taken place the world over in the status of women during the last precarious years. The challenge of the day was issued by two Americans. One, a successful lawyer and a figure in feminist activities, told of the plight of our wage-earning women. She predicted that if heed were not taken, by some compulsion or another, they would be faced with the tepid alternatives of eking out a dwindling existence or of having to return to the home, notwithstanding that the only homes they might have were those they were able to earn for themselves. The other, a journalist or international distinction, used as her premise the statement that during the past fifteen years the women in our western world had lost more than they had gained; that indeed, instead of having progressed, they had retrogressed legally, politically, and economically. She pointed up her declaration with a compact sketch of what had happened abroad, placing a special emphasis on conditions in Germany, and concluded with "to-day the feminist movement is as dead as last week's newspaper."

Not infrequently of late I have heard similar statements among those who are aware of what is going on in the world. In this convention they bore a deeper significance as they were made to so large an audience, most of the members of which are active in one or more of those national and international organizations composed of millions of women in whom is vested the bulk of power in the feminist movement. It was a message they needed to hear, since it looks very much as if they had fallen down on their job of being their sisters' keepers.

This is not to say that they have been wholly without zeal, or that they have not made valuable contributions to the cause. Nor does it imply that they are responsible for all of the ills which have overtaken women during the depression. In any such widespread economic collapse it is inevitable that only the few can escape. But it need not follow, as it has, that they should be made to suffer in undue proportion by being deprived of their hard-won rights as

Copyright © 1935 by *Harper's Magazine*. All rights reserved. Reproduced from the May issue by special permission.

human beings, discriminated against in matters of work and pay, and denied access to the same avenues of recovery as men. And herein lies the culpability of the women's organizations. Had they been awake to the real issues at stake in the woman movement or, being awake, if they could have come to some agreement on principles and procedure; had their leadership been such as to inspire their followers to concerted action, they could have built a stronghold so impregnable that the prevailing injustices of to-day would have been as spray dashing against a rock. Instead of this, with slight exception, they lost sight of their basic need and, unable to agree on processes, they worked at fruitless and often destructive crosspurposes. Their leaders, for the most part, have been uninspiring and lacking in vision. The women whose guardian angels they should have been, have remained indifferent and inert.

In order to arrive at a valid estimate of the present and to predict what the future of women may be it is necessary to go back fifteen years and retrace their line of march, checking up on their gains, marking their losses, and noting the reasons for them. In doing this I shall chiefly concern myself with the American scene, mentioning only those situations abroad which give accent to conditions at home and serve as an example or a warning.

In 1920 it looked as if the first paragraph of a happy ending to the century-long struggle for equal suffrage had been written. In all of the English-speaking countries, and in all of Western Europe except France, Italy, and Spain, woman has been granted the franchise. This did not signify that they had gained absolute equality with men. In several countries, including the United States, there were still in effect numerous laws discriminating against them in relation to property and inheritance rights, to the guardianship of children, to compensation insurance and the collection of accident indemnity, and to choice of occupation. It was believed, however, that through the persuasion of their concentrated vote they could prevail upon their legislators to remove these discriminations from the statutes, thereby establishing equality with men within the law.

But as we look at the feminist map to-day we find that of all the countries in which women have been given the vote the only ones where they enjoy the same civil, legal, and economic rights as men are Norway, Sweden, Denmark, the Netherlands, and Czechoslovakia. . . .

At an international conference of women a year or so ago I met the Scandinavian delegates. From them I learned of a concept of feminism that had not developed on the lines of a sex-war, but on the idea of mutual cooperation between men and women. The delegate from Norway, replying to my questions, said, "We wanted the vote, of course—but only as a step to something much bigger. We wanted security for the entire population. In order to secure this there was need for much legislation. Because of the reactionaries the forward-looking men had to have our help. Before we could help them we had to be established on a solid basis ourselves. We knew that if we were to be constantly occupied with trying to remove a discrepancy in the law here and another there we should have no time for other things. So we educated our women and we stood together in a concentrated voting mass and asked for a complete sex-disqualification removal act. And we got it. So now we work not as women but as citizens. Our people are generally progressive, and we are not indifferent to the problems of the various groups, for we realize that a nation is no stronger than its weakest spot." . . .

III

Here in the United States the drive to defeat women is no longer a menace; it is a condition in fact.

To those who have had occasion, as I have had, to observe maneuvers at close range over a period of years, there is little of the unexpected in the present situation. It has been brought about by the same errors which precipitated the defeat of the German women and are now threatening those of England—errors which have been only slightly mitigated by the virtues which have rendered the Scandinavian women triumphant.

These flaws have been the cleavage in the women's organizations, their acute inaction as a whole, their indifference to the needs of the great body of wage-earning women, a dearth of inspiring and inspired leaders, too great a variety of self-interests, and the inability to stand together on matters of vital importance.

The conflict dates back to pre-suffrage days. On the one side was the conservative element which felt that the franchise could better be obtained through State action. On the other were the militants who favored enfranchisement by constitutional amendment. They reasoned that because of the reactionary attitude toward women in those States where they most needed emancipation, it would take generations of waiting for dead men's shoes to attain their purpose. After years of disheartening effort in legislatures only four Western States had admitted women to citizenship. Then under the able and animating leadership of such women as Anna Howard Shaw, Alice Stone Blackwell, Carrie Chapman Catt, and Alice Paul they came to agreement on the nineteenth amendment which was passed and ratified in 1920.

No sooner was it written into the Constitution than a deeper and wider rift occurred. In every State there were laws which worked great injustice to women. These were hand-me-downs from the old English Common Law, the Napoleonic Code, or the medieval Spanish mores. While both sides were agreed that these disqualifications should be removed, they split on principles and procedure. On the one hand, we had the equalitarians who stood for absolute equality untouched by what they termed advantages in the way of protective laws for women. And to remove all disqualifications from the State laws they advocated a "Blanket Amendment" which would with one stroke of the pen write their definition of equality into the Constitution. Opposing them were the "equalitarians in principle." They maintained that women were at a natural disadvantage because of their biological function and that, this being so, their interests, for the sake of the race, must be safeguarded by protective laws. They reasoned further that if such an amendment were to be passed it would deny the right of the States, and Congress as well, to make laws or appropriations to enforce them which would regulate the condition of women in industry or provide for the care of mother and child.

The equalitarians played a lone hand. Supporting their opponents was an alliance of women's organizations, with a combined membership of ten million and over, which maintained a Congressional Lobby in Washington and in the State capitals. In spite of their interests in common, they, too, were often a house divided. The welfare groups were interested only in welfare. The reformers were not at all concerned with the progress of women but entirely with the promotion of sumptuary legislation. The housewives were largely occupied with questions affecting their own prerogatives such as community property rights, maternity and infant measures. As a considerable group within all of the groups—and I should say they preponderated—were the "Joiners" who had a facility for getting their names on as many lists as possible and then sitting back and doing nothing whatsoever.

Entirely outside of the alliance were the unorganized factions. They included the women of wealth and leisure, the comfortably placed middle class who had never taken part in the suffrage campaign, were indifferent or opposed to the progress of women, and those outside the home who had reached the higher brackets of business and the professions. Safely entrenched in their positions, they were concerned only with their own affairs, or they were complacent and inert. Many of those included in this paragraph would not even take the trouble to go to the polls. Many joined the regular political parties, voting as their men directed. A few, proving amenable, were elected or appointed to subordinate office, as a sop to the woman vote, where they obeyed the mandates of the bosses whether for better or for worse.

Ground between these forces were the eleven million and more women in the middle and lower brackets who must work in order to survive. Inarticulate, or too preoccupied to look after their own well-being, they relied upon the organizations to do this for them.

Out of this mêlée of maladjustment much good might have accrued if we had had enough compelling leaders to effect a compromise—leaders like those doughty old generals of the suffrage campaign—who could have come to an agreement on an amendment which, while removing all legal and economic discriminations from the statutes, would have included clause enabling Congress and the States to enact such necessary measures as mothers' and widows' pensions, an eight-hour day and minimum wage for women in industries. But most of the old leaders were gone. Those who remained were tired or disappointed and had turned their attention to other things. A few of those who have taken their places are able and inspiring, especially those with labor affiliations. They are drawn largely from the leisured who have no conception of what it means for women to compete with men in a man's world.

As a consequence, after fifteen years' growth the family tree is far from robust—a meager efflorescence at the top, roots too feeble to draw sustenance from the soil, and a trunk suffering from malnutrition. . . .

IV

Ever since 1929 it has become an increasing practice with employers when economizing on labor to begin with the women workers, retaining only those whose places cannot be taken by men. Throughout the country, in State after State, married women, without regard to their responsibilities, have been discharged from their jobs in State and municipal institutions and office. They have been stricken from the rolls of teachers in schools and colleges. They have been removed from the staffs in hospitals. And their cue for this came from the government service in Washington where the "marital status clause," known as Article 213 in the Economy Act of 1932, has been taken advantage of by officials who interpreted it according to their own prejudices. This article provides that when reducing personnel in any branch of the service, married persons, living with husband or wife also employed by the government, must be the first to be dismissed. When the Economy Act was submitted to Congress it was seen that the clause could easily be made subversive to women's interests. A number of fair-minded senators rallied to the support of the married couples who would be affected by it. The House, which was already New Deal, passed it. To save the Act in its entirety, the Senate, after a valiant fight to eliminate 213, finally voted the whole bill. When signing it President Hoover protested against the clause and recommended that it should be repealed. The Civil Service Commission did likewise, declaring that it was an attack on the merit system and suggesting that the same amount of money could be saved by granting payless furloughs of a month to all employees. It was hoped that President Roosevelt on creating the Economy Act of March 1933 would delete Article 213. The Act, as submitted, bore no mention of it, and as many of the specific provisions of the former enactment were specifically retained, the question arose as to whether or not it would die a natural death at the end of the fiscal year. A group of women who would suffer if it remained a law called upon Mrs. Roosevelt, who referred them to the Secretary of Labor. She, in turn, sent them to the Budget Director, who said the decision was up to the President. The President said the decision was up to the Attorney General who ruled that the "marital status clause" was permanent legislation.

The first to put it into action was the Adjutant General who immediately let out forty-five women, all of whom had high efficiency records over an average of fifteen years and all of whom had dependents. In addition to their jobs they lost the right to reappointment and to the pension toward which they had been contributing.

During the past two years the Civil and other Federal Services have discharged thousands of married women. On the surface there might be some reason in this if those discharged were in the higher brackets or if the reason were purely economic. But it did not apply to executives nor, curiously enough, to the wives of congressmen who are acting as their husbands' secretaries on a government wage of $5000 a year. According to a recent survey made by the Women's Bureau of the Department of Labor, nine out of ten of those discharged were in real need of their jobs. . . .

V

Bleak as the picture may appear, there is yet light on the horizon. And it is I think, going too far to declare that the feminist movement is dead or that to-day the condition of women in the whole Western world is no better than it was fifteen years ago. We *have* been asleep. We *have* lost a good deal of what we had gained. And the wage-earning woman has come to a point where she *is* eking out a dwindling existence. But in some directions new strides have been taken and they have held some ground. Where we have done this it was because the women in power were aroused to concerted and effective protest. This leads one to believe that if, as a whole, women will face reality they may yet achieve their ideal of emancipation and progress. . . .

Here at home the cleavage is still extant. But within the opposing organizations some of the women have awakened to the need of the hour and are co-operating with the labor groups to bring about the nullification of Article 213 by a Civil Service bill which reads, "And no person shall be discriminated against in any case because of his or her marital status in examination, appointment, reappointment, reinstatement, reemployment, promotion, transfer, retransfer, demotion, removal, or retirement. All Acts or parts of Acts inconsistent herewith are hereby repealed."

In a number of cities and States new organizations are being formed to take care of group interests and they have recorded some victories. An instance of what may be done when women stand together under the leadership occurred in a recent election in Los Angeles. An official in high office up for reelection had proposed that all married women teachers should be dropped from the schools. An unmarried teacher, taking the lead, mobilized ten thousand teachers in a fighting unit against him. Dividing their number into districts, they went from house to house, stating their case, and recording the number of those who promised to vote for the other candidate. The official whom they were opposing had heretofore polled a large majority. Now he was defeated for the first time in his political career, the margin against him corresponding, district by district, to the aggregate votes of the teachers and their converts.

What one can do so may another. Considering the trend of events, it is time for the women everywhere to get together within their organizations and come to some agreement on a federal act which will render unconstitutional any attempt to place them in the underprivileged class. Had we possessed any such guaranty of security as the Sex Disqualification Removal Acts in effect in the Scandinavian countries, our women wage-earners could not have been so ruthlessly discriminated against as they have been in the present emergency. They could not have been penalized because of marriage. They would have had in all forms of government service the same pay as men. All relief measures would have had to apply to them in the same proportion as to men. And it would have removed from the sphere of their activities the necessity for constant nagging bits of legislation which now deter them from directing their energies toward the many problems to be solved if to-day's confusion is not to resolve into utter darkness.

66
Alma Lutz
That Much-Maligned Feminism (1935)

We often hear it said that there is no longer any need for a Feminist movement, that Feminism as a cause and issue is over and done with.

And yet, looking about us, what do we see?

We see Hitler and Mussolini limiting women's sphere by governmental action, taking away women's opportunity of earning a living, spreading the vicious propaganda that woman's one duty and reason for existence is bearing children for the State.

In England and the Scandinavian countries, we find progressive women alarmed at the reactionary attitude toward women workers, at the discharge of married women and the all-too-prevalent belief that only men have dependents to support.

In our own country these same ideas have taken root. Married women have been discharged. Women were not given equal pay for equal work under NRA codes. Men and boys have taken the place of women workers because it has been falsely assumed that men need jobs more than women. Practically all public relief projects have given work to unemployed men. Very little attention has been paid to the thousands of unemployed women who are in desperate need of earning.

From *Equal Rights Independent Feminist Weekly,* August 3, 1935.

The field for to-morrow is rich and inexhaustible. It can be tapped only by the co-operation of men and women with vision and stamina. Are the women of America going to realize the destiny marked out for them when they began their long march of emancipation? Or are they, like the women of Germany, to stand accused of having betrayed themselves?

Then, perhaps more important than all is the fact that the Constitution of the United States does not guarantee to its women citizens full citizenship rights. Conceived in the spirit of English Common Law which respected and protected the rights of men but regarded a woman as a *femme covert,* under her lord or husband, the Constitution is still interpreted in that light. Because of this, when women have claimed the rights of citizens under the Constitution, they have almost without exception been denied them. Many relics of Common Law which rate women as inferiors still remain on the statutes of our various States.

In the face of all this, it is strange to find many women asserting that Feminism is a cause of yesterday and out of tune with today, not realizing that such an attitude is fertile soil for the reactionary propaganda which is sweeping through the world.

The antagonism to Feminism is a strange phenomenon. Ever since women first began to ask for property rights, education, suffrage, equal status under the law, and the ordinary rights of a human being, people in general have looked askance at Feminism. It has aroused in them an unexplainable prejudice and they have regarded it as a pernicious influence destructive to all that they held dear. The first Feminists were dubbed "hyenas in petticoats," sexless creatures aping men. They were accused of wanting to put men in the kitchen and to set them at rocking cradles while they invaded men's domain of business and government.

All this is past and gone, and is worth recalling only to illustrate a certain type of thought which the progress of women has not been able to obliterate and which is again becoming articulate but in changed forms. Feminism still excites in some men a fighting spirit which might be called the last stand of the dominant sex. It reveals in some women a slave complex for which they contend with almost fanatical zeal.

After all, what is this much-maligned Feminism, but asking for a place in the sun? It is not a desire for a matriarchy or feminine dominance, but a chance to work with men on equal terms. It is not a desire merely to follow in men's footsteps, to take over their ideals and their work, but a demand for the opportunity to act and develop as freely as men. It is, as Webster defines it, "the theory, cult, and practice of those who hold that present laws, conventions, and conditions of society prevent the free and full development of women and who advocate such changes as will do away with undue restrictions upon her political, social, and economic conduct and relations."

Men have always stubbornly resisted considering women human beings like themselves and have clung tenaciously to the idea of man's divine right of dominance. Their best weapon in this contest of the sexes has been to make women believe that they were men's spiritual superiors and their inspiration, that because they were on such a high plane they needed protection from the grossness of a man's world.

It would be interesting to know who first started this convenient theory—a shrewd, designing male looking ahead to years of dominance by his sex, or a woman with a sense of inferiority so devastating that she must build for herself a dream world where she could reign supreme.

At any rate the theory has been highly successful. It has given men the dominance they wanted. It has given them that highly satisfactory feeling of protecting the weak and worshipping at a shrine. It has given them the excuse of shying away from idealistic and humanitarian development and sinking themselves in materialism.

Women on the other hand have loved this setting of themselves on a pedestal. It has been gratifying to be told that their special role in life is to point the way to higher, nobler living; that their chastity, their unselfishness, and their goodness is all that stands between men and degradation and damnation. The "better than thou" feeling blinded them to actualities, and like ostriches with their heads in the sand, they declared they had all the rights they needed or wanted. Orthodox religion furthered this myth, binding women to it with fear.

Bitter experience taught some women the folly of believing in such a fairy tale. If men thought (and of course they did not really think it at all) that their salvation depended on woman's goodness, it was time that they learned differently and started to work out their own salvation. These women who had seen through the myth now realized how important it was for all women to face facts and regard themselves not as saints but as ordinary human beings. They were the first Feminists, and their daughters and granddaughters have had the same battle to wage through the years, for women have clung to the myth with the tenacity with which people cling to outworn religious beliefs. It has been the big stumbling block to woman's progress, to her political, civil, and mental freedom. It delayed woman suffrage many years. Men were not eager to give too much power to the noble influence which they lauded in speeches and to which they paid homage in drawing rooms.

The myth has kept women from making the most of their opportunities. Few women have been able to undertake any club work, support any movements, or attempt a political career without feeling that they must reform the world. It is making women apathetic at this crucial point in their history and is clouding the vision of women who in the past have been champions of their sex.

Among certain prominent women it has become the fashion to deride Feminism. Some of them say that women are chasing moths in their new freedom; that their grandmothers without this freedom were much happier; that women were created to be devoted wives and mothers and that nothing else will satisfy them. They point to single women with careers and say that they have missed the greatest thing in life and are unhappy in spite of their worldly success.

They fail to point out the disillusioned wives and the disappointed mothers who too have failed to find happiness. Satisfaction in life and happiness are not the result of circumstances or of any role one may play but are found rather through mental adjustments. Women can be devoted wives and mothers and still be independent human beings. They can be successful lawyers, journalists, and artists, and yet have a full and satisfying life. This rapidly changing world requires many mental adjustments for both men and women.

Others declare that women have not made outstanding contributions to the arts, the professions, to science, business, or government, and have therefore proved themselves mentally inferior to men. They do not take into consideration the short time that women have been free to develop their talents, but assume that women have always been free to do anything they really wanted to do. They point to the few lone women in various generations who overstepped the bounds of their sex and were successful in some line of endeavor. They do not mention that these few women were economically independent, or had unusually sympathetic fathers or husbands; that in spite of a certain inferior fame which they enjoyed, they continually faced, because of their so-called unwomanly actions, the scorn of their contemporaries.

Some maintain that the twilight of women in business has come, that women have not only shown their unfitness for business careers, but have discovered that they are not worth the candle and are glad to find themselves husbands instead. They point out as examples of feminine incompetence those superficial women who now dabble in business as they used to dabble in music and art, and they ignore the large army of efficient women who are making a real contribution to business and the professions and are supporting not only themselves but parents and children as well.

They claim that women prefer being supported to being economically independent and add that after all the idea of economic independence for women is a farce because the depression has proved that there is no economic independence for anyone. The fact that our economic system has glaring faults is no reason for speaking disparagingly of the economic independence of women. It is only because women have earned money of their own that they have gained the freedom they have today. There need be no choice between economic independence and babies. Both are possible and desirable.

Most of the critics of Feminism say that women have a certain spiritual contribution to make to civilization which they have overlooked in their mad rush to compete with men, that while they are failures when in competition with men, they have the ability to exert a spiritual influence which will remake the world. This sounds surprisingly like public opinion of the eighteenth century and shows definitely that the psychological development of some of our brilliant women has not kept pace with the times.

Men of course have joined in gladly with the women critics of Feminism, experiencing with pleasure a revival of that old feeling of superiority and dominance which had begun to crumble. One can forgive the men, ready to grab at a straw to retrieve past glories, but the mental attitude of the women critics is more difficult to understand. Thomas Wentworth Higginson, who was a staunch friend of the early Feminists, told Elizabeth Cady Stanton that he was utterly discouraged by the apathy of women, although his convictions as to their political rights were unchanged.

"I had always taken the ground," he said, "that the acquiescence of the vast majority of women was like that of slaves, but observation has taught me that no such phenomenon is to be found among slaves. The acquiescence of women—for it is not an unwilling, coerced, dogged submission—is an argument hard to answer *for a man*."

Elizabeth Cady Stanton with her characteristically keen judgment held woman's false religious training responsible for this peculiar mental quirk. Although religious dogma does not have the hold that it did even a generation ago, some mentalities are slow to discard the superstitions and chains that bind them.

Feminism has a great work to do to clean house in women's minds, to sweep out the remnants of the myth. The real Feminist will see that the hope of a truly emancipated womanhood lies in future generations and she will make sure that her sons and daughters grow up without those psychological handicaps.

In the meantime it is of utmost importance that women attain equality with men under the law and an equal freedom to choose their work. Given this, they will help men chart a way out of these troubled times. If they are denied this, and the philosophy prevails that one of the main causes of our economic tangle is the fact that women have strayed out of their sphere, progress will be delayed many generations. Therefore women of vision have not found it wise to climb down from the watch towers of Feminism. In fact they are urging a world-wide militant Feminist movement which will do its best to see that women are free to contribute their full share to the solution of world problems.

67
Susan B. Anthony II
We Women Throw Our Votes Away (1948)

My Great-aunt Susan was a stormy, deep-breasted woman who took particular care of her looks. Not that she was vain or wanted suitors. She had many proposals of marriage from ardent gentlemen in tail coats, and she rejected them all. Aunt Susan simply wished to be neat and attractive on lecture platforms, where she exerted a talent for forceful oratory.

I often think she was born before her time. If my Great-aunt Susan were alive and rampaging today—Susan B. Anthony, the nineteenth century's champion of women's rights—political bosses at national conventions would air out the smoke-filled room and usher her to a seat. They would ask her opinion of upstart candidates for the presidential nomination and invite her approval of the party platform. All very respectful, too, because Aunt Susan would be poised to smite them with a crushing bloc of women's votes.

No such bloc exists today. Women have a vote, thanks to Susan B. Anthony and her loyal co-workers, but they don't use it to benefit themselves. The crusade for women's rights, launched with a shout a century ago, has subsided to clubroom murmurings and a few pieces of commemorative statuary. The truth is that the American woman movement has collapsed.

I had occasion to lay a wreath on a stone grouping which depicts Aunt Susan with Lucretia Mott and Elizabeth Cady Stanton, these three being the pioneer fighters for women suffrage. The statue was intended to stand with other sculptured notables on the main floor of the Capitol Building in Washington. I found it in a basement crypt. It has a distressing resemblance to three ladies in a bathtub, due to its expanse of white marble ending in a blank slab. This blank space is reserved, I am told, for a bust of the Woman of the Twentieth Century.

In my view, twentieth-century woman hasn't earned a place of honor alongside the vigorous women leaders of the nineteenth century. Modern women are so poorly led that they skirmish among themselves instead of uniting politically to battle for women's rights. We got the ballot in 1920 under the Susan B. Anthony amendment to the Constitution. We should have promptly voted ourselves equality with men—equality before the law, political, economic and social. Great-aunt Susan planned it that way. But we women have frittered away our massive power at the polls. If we voted together on any issue, 48,000,000 of us, we would make the much-feared "veterans' vote" look like political popcorn. We probably could name the next President of the United States.

From *The Saturday Evening Post,* July 17, 1948.

But we won't. Women had trifling influence, if any, on decisions made this summer at the Republican and Democratic conventions. True, women starred as speakers in 1944. But it was merely Republican glamour—Rep. Clare Boothe Luce—pitted against Democratic glamour, Rep. Helen Gahagan Douglas. It was not a contest between powerful party leaders.

I think it's time for women to take stock, especially since 1948 is the centennial year of the so-called American woman movement, which once packed political dynamite. . . .

. . . But now I wonder: what has happened in the years since women won the vote? Have they used it, as my great-aunt hoped they would, to win a better life for themselves?

Let's look at the right to work. One of Aunt Susan's most famous speeches was entitled: Woman Wants Bread, Not the Ballot. She meant that women should use the vote to win economic independence. In her day, the only paying jobs that women could get were teaching, sewing, domestic service, low-paid factory work and bookbinding. Women surrendered their savings and their earnings to their husbands when they married. We're a little better off in 1948, but not much.

There are more than 16,000,000 women working today, but they form only one fourth of all American workers. Only a third of all women over fourteen years of age have jobs. More important, women are the last to be hired and the first to be fired, just as they were in Aunt Susan's lifetime. Their wages are still low too. Women work at half the pay men get, according to the United States Department of Labor. Even in 1945, when war wages were swollen with overtime, the average annual earnings of women workers were only $1,240. Men averaged $2,570 during this period.

Women have done little with the ballot to write "equal pay for equal work" into law. So far, only nine states have adopted such legislation. A Federal equal-pay bill awaits action; it was introduced twenty-five long years after suffrage. The major women's organizations have not seriously pushed these measures, nor have they united to smash discrimination in hiring by getting a Fair Employment Practices Act for women.

Even if women workers got the same pay as men and an equal chance at jobs, 30,000,000 housewives would still be groping in an economic blind alley. Housewives have no more economic independence now than they did 100 years ago. They clean, cook, shop, sew and care for their families fifty to eighty hours a week—perhaps the longest work week in the land. For all this they receive room and board; no wages. . . .

Have women used suffrage to upset old laws against their property and civil rights? They could have done so. But according to the Women's Bureau of the United States Department of Labor they have not. There remain in the forty-eight states and United States territories some 1,000 discriminations against women handed down from ancient common law. Some state laws on the books in 1948 treat women exactly as they were treated in 1848.

In fifteen states a mother can become the natural guardian of her child only if it is born out of wedlock.

In sixteen states a married woman can't sign a legal document unless her husband consents. When "Ma" Ferguson was elected governor of Texas some years ago, she couldn't take office until "Pa" Ferguson had given his formal approval.

Thirteen states still bar women from jury service. Nineteen states permit women to serve, but allow them to excuse themselves from the jury box on the sole ground of sex.

Four states limit a married woman's right to make contracts. Five states require a married woman to get a court authorization to conduct a business on her own account. If a woman is single, she is presumably smart enough to run a hat shop, but when she marries, these states assume, her good judgment has been sadly impaired.

Six states include the personal earnings of the wife in the common family estate, which is completely under the husband's control by law.

A wife's services belong to her husband, more or less, in forty states. An extreme example was a case decided in Montana in 1924. Mr. and Mrs. Bischoff had run a bakery for years. He did the baking, she did the selling. The business grew until they were able to buy a new bakery for $18,000. Later both sought a divorce, and Mrs. Bischoff asked for an accounting of funds. She felt that she had been her husband's "business partner," entitled to a half interest in the assets they had accumulated. The court ruled that she had not been a business partner, and she got nothing.

The effort to abolish these old discriminations has been led for years by the National Woman's Party, founded in 1916 by Alice Paul, militant suffragist. Since winning the vote in 1920 the party has concentrated solely on an Equal Rights Amendment to the Constitution, introduced at every session of Congress since 1923. The amendment would read: "Equality of rights under the law shall not be denied or abridged by the United States or by any state on account of sex."

The National Woman's Party is controlled by upper-class women, and has hardly increased the 50,000 membership it had twenty-eight years ago. However, the party is supported by thirty-one women's organizations, including the conservative General Federation of Women's Clubs, with 3,000,000 members, and the white-collar National Federation of Business and Professional Women's Clubs, which has stiffened its self-improvement aims in recent years with political action.

Organized women are not unanimous on this issue, however. The suggested amendment to the Constitution is strongly opposed by many women's clubs—thirty-eight altogether, at the last count. Foremost in opposition are the National Women's Trade Union League and the National League of Women Voters, which has less interest in down-to-earth women's problems than in such weighty matters as control of atomic energy and support of the United Nations. These outfits fear that the Equal Rights Amendment would violate state rights and ensnarl state laws which differentiate between the sexes. Under the amendment, for example, state legislation affecting women's wages and hours of labor might be wiped out. There are minimum-wage laws for women in twenty-six states, and maximum-hour laws in forty-three states. The amendment also might erase laws forbidding employment of women in hazardous occupations like mining.

The groups opposing the Equal Rights Amendment form a National Committee on the Status of Women. This committee is lined up for battle against the National Woman's Party, and has introduced its own Woman's Status Bill which they hope will spike the Equal Rights Amendment. The gist of the bill is: "That it is the declared policy of the United States that in law and its administration no distinctions on the basis of sex shall be made except such as are reasonably justified by differences in physical structure, or biological or social function."

I won't take sides here on the comparative merits of the rival legislative proposals. It is enough to point out that women have failed to unite on a specific issue concerning their civil and legal equality with men.

The most incredible blunder of organized women to my mind, is their failure to use the vote to get ahead in politics. Only seven women sit in Congress today; men hold the 524 other sets. There are 7500 state legislators in the Untied States, but fewer than 200 of them are women. A handful of women sit as municipal judges, domestic-relations and juvenile-court judges. One hardy woman, Florence Allen, holds the post of a judge on the United States Circuit Court of Appeals. In election years the Republican and Democratic parties call up the women to ring doorbells and get out the vote. Between elections, when party policy and legislative issues are being decided, the women aren't wanted. The number of women delegates to Democratic national conventions has actually declined.

Eight years of research on women's status have convinced me that our economic, political and social position is only slightly better now than it was in 1920, when we got the all-powerful vote. The right to vote, in fact, is the only unqualified victory we have gained in a century.

Why haven't women won what they wanted? Are we too frivolous, too spoiled? Or is it, as some back-to-the-kitchen propagandists imply, because women are biologically unfit for anything except bearing children and caring for them? I don't think so. I believe that the chief reason for the failure of women to push on to equality with men was the unnoticed crack-up of the American woman movement after the vote was won in 1920.

The end of World War I brought a slogan, "Back to Normalcy," and a general slacking off of progressive movements. The excitement of the fight was over. Great masses of women who had united to struggle for the vote split into weak factions. They could co-operate for a hot political campaign, but they were unready to join hands in a full-fledged woman movement.

Another cause of defeat was the old antagonism to women's efforts to free themselves, which assumed new disguises after women suffrage. The objections to child-care centers, which would let working women support themselves and their children, can only be viewed as a form of opposition to women. Self-styled experts popped up during the depression to say that women should stop competing with men for jobs. Hard times evoked a Federal law that barred married women from Government jobs if their husbands were also employed. And many local boards of education dismissed married women teachers, relenting only during the manpower shortage of wartime.

Another thing: the stupid tradition that political-party action is unwomanly has been kept alive by the inept tactics of major women's organizations. There are exceptions, but most clubs shrink from practical politics, and urge women to study, study, study, and vote by candidate, not by party. They should be advising their members, "Get into political parties with the men and work there; that's where issues are decided, candidates selected and your education and welfare determined."

Housekeeping as usual, fifty or more hours a week, keeps women locked in the home and relatively ineffective as politicians. Until women are freed from endless home chores, it is folly to blather about their "duties as citizens," or their "duties as workers." The phrases sound well in club speeches, but women's organizations would do better to attack the archaic system of household work which handcuffs 30,000,000 housewives.

A new woman movement should campaign for adequate and universal nursery schools for preschool children and co-operative housecleaning services, and prepared-meal services that would deliver hot cooked dinners to homes of double-earner families. Another reform should be professional shopping services; the average woman is just as unskilled in buying as the average man, and the work wastes her time.

These are basic steps to be taken if women are to be free for development as politically potent citizens and intelligent wives and mothers. A new woman movement would not ask identical rights with men. It would ask for rights predicated on the fact that most women are mothers, or expect to be. This means that the Government must insure women's right to have children, through maternity benefits. Families shouldn't have to go broke when a working wife takes time off for childbearing. Nor should women have to worry about job security while they are nursing infants.

American men must share the responsibility for the death of the woman movement. Male political leaders discouraged new voters from getting too near to the levers of party machinery. They feared the formation of an independent bloc of women and diverted the newly enfranchised women to nonpolitical organizations. American women, after grasping the weapon of political action, the ballot, let it rust in their hands. They haven't formed a voting bloc, nor have they joined political parties in enough strength to play the men's game. Consequently they haven't won their economic and legal rights.

More than half of the potential voters in the United States are women. A few—say 6,000,000—are organized in clubs and federations. What if these 6,000,000 women threatened to vote *en masse* only for the party, let's say, that would guarantee maternity benefits to every mother? Would party bosses dare ignore 6,000,000 votes? Not likely; elections have been decided by slimmer margins. The major parties have never faced a united woman electorate. They don't want to, because—I quote a man friend—"It would be like turning the country over to the women."

That's the fear of the politicos of America. So for twenty-eight years since woman suffrage they have been thwarting women voters. And the women voters have hastened to defeat themselves. They take pride in voting just as their menfolk do and staying out of politics. A nasty game, they call it. Oh, my Great-aunt Susan! We need somebody like you now.

II. Equality versus Difference

THE INTELLECTUAL HISTORY OF AMERICAN FEMINISM INCLUDES a multiplicity of goals and ideals that have not always been compatible with each other, a long line of schisms and factions both theoretical and tactical—sometimes offset by farsighted acts, women reaching out to find common cause against masculine power. A great deal of feminist discord has revolved around the issue of exactly who is included in the group of women that defines and drives the "women's movement," or who, in fact, speaks for "women." The same divisions of race, class, and sexuality found in U.S. history at large have unfortunately been incorporated in the social history of feminism. A related source of separation and disagreement has been whether women should strive for full equality (sameness) with men or emphasize women's distinct attributes and perspectives (empower themselves through their difference from men).

This equality-difference split is a basic one, and we find it fully articulated even within the first few years after the word *feminism* joins the American lexicon. In the summary article "The Conflict between 'Human' and 'Female' Feminism" (1914) the equality side of the split is represented by Charlotte Perkins Gilman, who believed that the next stages of human evolution should be guided toward minimizing the biosocial variations between women and men. Gilman implored women to "shake ourselves free" from delimited feminine identities by pursuing (in one of her favorite words) the quality of "humanness." In contrast is the "female feminism," or difference feminism, of the Swedish writer Ellen Key. A pioneer in the study of human sexuality, Key spoke unabashedly of female sensuality, eroticism, and the importance of women's sexual fulfillment. While arguing against patriarchy and economic inequality in marriage, Key also urged women to embrace the natural and penultimate role of motherhood—one of the greatest sources of female strength and distinction. Key was a prolific author, whose books—including *Century of the Child* (1910), *Love and Marriage* (1911), *The Woman Movement* (1912), and *Renaissance of Motherhood* (1914)—were widely read in the United States.

The history of American feminism includes efforts to overcome the equality-difference split, refusals to place women's rights to equality in opposition to women's distinct needs. Such pragmatic rejections of either-or thinking make up a critical vein in feminism, and there is no clearer example of it than the Wisconsin Equal Rights Law of 1921, discussed by the novelist and playwright Zona Gale in "What Women Won in Wisconsin" (1922). With the ratification of the Nineteenth Amendment in 1920, the National Woman's Party (NWP) shifted its focus to abolishing the mass of laws that enforced sexual discrimination. The leaders of the NWP envisioned a strong overarching guarantee of rights, one that could be used in the courts to strike down the many specific instances of women's unequal treatment under the law. In 1923 Alice Paul and the NWP would introduce the Equal Rights Amendment (ERA) to the U.S. Constitution. But before that, in 1921, Mabel Raef Putnam, chair of the Wisconsin branch of the NWP, fought successfully for the passage of the state Equal Rights Law, which declared in its first sentence that "women shall have the same rights and privileges and immunities under law as men in the exercise of suffrage, freedom of contract, choice of residence for voting purposes, jury service, holding office, holding and conveying property, care and custody of children, and in all other respects."

The problem with this broad demand for legal-sexual equality—and this was *the* problem that hounded the pro-ERA feminists at the national level—is that it would in effect erase years of legislative effort intended to protect women. Laws setting the maximum hours of women's work and minimum wages for that work, along with other protective labor legislation, would be in immediate legal jeopardy. So, because of this concern, the second sentence of the Wisconsin Equal Rights Law added that nothing in the law would deny women "the special protection and privileges which they now enjoy for the general welfare." The statute tenuously found a way to avoid the conflict by trying to both meet the demands of equality and recognize women's difference. Alice Paul sent a telegram celebrating the law that made "Wisconsin the only spot in the United States where women have, or ever had since the beginning of our country, full equality with men." But the early legal history of interpretation of the act demonstrates its limitations. Courts narrowed the scope of the law, basically ignoring its broad grant of "equality in all other respects," and primarily recognizing greater rights for married women in Wisconsin. In 1923 the Wisconsin Attorney General refused, despite the Equal Rights Act, to strike down a 1905 law that kept women from being employed in the state legislature. He saw the prohibition as an hours limitation law, because legislative service required "very long and often unreasonable hours." Alice Paul read his decision as a very strong argument against drafting the national ERA with an exemption for protective legislation for women.

Thus, the Wisconsin effort to resolve the dual interests of equality and difference never took hold at the national level in the 1920s and 1930s, for those pushing for an Equal Rights Amendment to the U.S. Constitution refused to include an exemption clause, in part because of the Wisconsin Attorney General's ruling, but also because of the general belief that special treatment of women in the workplace and elsewhere relegated them to a second-class status. Proposed in 1923 by the NWP, the ERA read: "Men and women shall have equal rights throughout the United States and every place subject to its jurisdiction." This simple declaration created decades of controversy and debate. While conservative antifeminists were predictably quick to oppose the amendment, many fully committed but more moderate feminists also fought against it, as seen in Florence Kelley's essay "The Equal Rights Amendment: Why Other Women's Groups Oppose It" (1924). As chief factory inspector for Illinois and then head of the National Consumers' League, Kelley championed shorter hours and better working conditions for women. Therefore, she argued against the obliteration of sex as a classification within the law. The way to proceed, for Kelley, was gradual piecemeal elimination of the most harmful discriminatory laws on the books. "The Equal Rights Amendment: Why the Woman's Party Is for It" (1924), by the journalist Inez Haynes Irwin, represents the other side of the feminist debate: the conviction that women will not be liberated until law and public policy recognize and enforce complete equality between the sexes. A member of the Heterodoxy Club and active in radical-socialist-feminist circles in New York City, Irwin wrote and edited for Max Eastman's journal *The Masses;* among the books she wrote is *The Story of the Woman's Party* (1921).

Ethel M. Smith's article "Working Women's Case against Equal Rights" (1924) points out that the feminist debate over the ERA often followed economic lines of class consciousness: the NWP's desire to clear the way for personal freedom and accomplishment represented the interests of elite business and professional women and tended to overlook the needs of industrial workers who discounted individualism for the sake of power through numbers and the promise of gaining leverage over management through group solidarity. The career woman's aspirations for equal access to the boardroom meant very little to, say, the textile worker who needed time to raise her children while holding down a factory job. Its inability to embrace a broad spectrum of women's perspectives was endemic to the NWP and its losing battle to ratify the ERA. Well-funded and enjoying contacts in government and other positions of power, the NWP remained insular, failing to broaden its base by appealing to younger working-class women. But while inattentive to the ways in which protective labor laws helped a large number of working women at a historical moment when working conditions and wages were often deplorable and only newly and often sporadically regulated, pro-ERA feminists, as William H. Chafe has written, may have been more visionary in arguing that such legislation hindered women's long-term interests in the labor market. The special provisions marked women as inferior, in effect underwriting male priority and privilege in industrial America.[1]

---

1. See William H. Chafe, *The American Woman: Her Changing Social, Economic, and Political Roles, 1920–1970* (New York: Oxford Univ. Press, 1972), 112–32.

A monumental victory in the quest for legal protection of women in the workplace came in *Muller v. Oregon* (1908), the Supreme Court decision that upheld a state maximum-hours law for women. The case was won through Louis Brandeis's renowned legal brief, which amassed sociological, medical, and other scientific data to argue, in his words, that the "two sexes differ in structure of body, in the function to be performed by each, in the amount of physical strength [and] in the capacity for long continued labor." Of course it was precisely this type of public policy that pro-ERA feminists wanted to overcome. Journalist Rheta Childe Dorr, in "Should There Be Labor Laws for Women? *No*" (1925), questions the notion that women need special consideration and criticizes the Brandeis brief for perpetuating the notion of frail womanhood. On the other side of this exchange in *Good Housekeeping,* Mary Anderson, in "Should There Be Labor Laws for Women? *Yes*" (1925), takes a pragmatic approach: protective labor legislation remedies a serious problem for thousands of women. Working women are at a practical disadvantage to men, she says, since many (approximately two million at the time) are expected to handle the added shift of motherhood. Anderson uses her extensive background as a factory worker to lend credibility to the pro-protection proposition. From 1920 to 1944 she served as head of the federal Women's Bureau, part of the U.S. Department of Labor established to investigate and improve female working conditions.

In "Sex and Achievement" (1935), Margaret Mead casts her anthropological eye on the contemporary dilemma of why men excel professionally even in areas thought to be in women's domain, namely cooking and dressmaking. Are there inherent differences between the sexes? Or is male achievement a matter of social expectation? Mead notes that male superiority is true only for public accomplishment, reflecting women's culturally created predilection against competition. She stresses that for men sex membership is based on "positive achievement" in a myriad of prescribed pursuits while women live under a distinct disincentive toward accomplishment. Women cannot strive for professional success without risking the loss of their identity as a woman and consequently their "human heritage"—love, marriage, and children. She concludes: "The remarkable matter is not that there have been so few successful women in masculine fields but that there have been as many as there have been, that so many women have been gifted enough to carry this double load." Mead speaks at least in part from personal experience for she attained a public and professional stature held by no one else in American anthropology. After studying with Franz Boas at Columbia University and earning a Ph.D. in 1929, Mead extended her teacher's work by examining the cultural construction of gender and human sexual relations, proving herself tremendously adept at relating her fieldwork findings to the lives of people in the United States. Mead wrote prolifically: *Coming of Age in Samoa* (1928), *Sex and Temperament in Three Primitive Societies* (1935), and *Male and Female: A Study of the Sexes in a Changing World* (1949) are among her best-known works.

While debated fervently in the nation's magazines and journals during the 1920s and early 1930s, the Equal Rights Amendment didn't get far in Congress until 1972. In 1935 the Equal Rights Treaty—an international version of the ERA designed in part to meet the challenges of worldwide depression and European Fascism—was put before the League of Nations. In response, Mary Anderson, Mary Van Kleeck, and other staunch supporters of protective labor legislation formed a committee and drafted the Women's Charter in 1936. As seen in "The Women's Charter" (1937), it enjoyed support from the American Home Economics Association and other women's groups, asking for full rights and opportunities for women of the world, but also requesting special female privileges and safeguards in the workplace and elsewhere, emphasizing the physical differences between women and men. In her autobiography, Anderson described the Women's Charter as a document that all women could endorse, adding that "perhaps we could, with this charter, bridge the gap between ourselves and the NWP." This statement seems disingenuous, since the type of provision for protective legislation found in the charter had been roundly criticized by the NWP and other pro-ERA feminists. Edith Houghton Hooker enunciates these objections in "Beware of 'Women's Charter'" (1937). In the end, the Women's Charter went nowhere. As Anderson concluded in her autobiography: "The movement was a complete flop."[2]

"How Can We Raise Women's Status? A Symposium" (1938) gives voice not only to familiar arguments about the ERA and protective legislation (Alma Lutz and Frieda S. Miller, respectively), but also to more individualistic "solutions" to raising women's status. Ollie A. Randall urges women to pursue work-related training, and writer Margaret Culkin Banning suggests women use "individual initiative" to run their own businesses. However, as the Great Depression continued through the 1930s, the ERA became a more compelling remedy to the increasing economic burden of U.S. women. Alma Lutz stresses the absolute need for a constitutional guarantee of female autonomy, criticizing the fact that state legislatures and courts still follow the English common law doctrine of *femme covert,* which basically erases the legal identity of a woman once she marries. In 1938 eleven states prevented a wife from holding her own earnings without her husband's permission; married women in sixteen states could not make contracts; and at least twenty states kept women from serving on juries. Individual states enforced laws disempowering women: Maryland, for instance, allowed a husband to divorce his wife if she had had sexual relations before marriage; in Virginia a father did not have to help support an illegitimate child. As part of the New Deal legislation of 1938, the Fair Labor Standards Act set maximum-hour and minimum-wage standards for women and men in all industries involved in interstate commerce. The statute bolstered hopes for the ERA, since it eliminated the need for most state-level protective labor legislation.

As demonstrated by the myriad prominent voices on both the pro and con sides of the forum "Should Congress Approve the Proposed Equal Rights Amendment to the Constitution?" (1943), debate over the ERA heated up again during World War II. Pro-ERA feminists, already emboldened by the Fair Labor Standards Act of 1938, found new support for their position in women's expanded public roles during wartime and in the argument—effectively used in the suffrage campaign during World War I—that since the United States is fighting to establish freedom and equality for the whole world, those values are more than ever needed and deserved at home. During the war, the ERA gained support from such groups as the American Alliance of Civil Service Women, the National Association of Women Lawyers, the American Medical Women's Association, Business and Professional Women, and the National Federation of Women's Clubs. The Republican Party supported the measure in its 1940 platform, followed by the Democrats in 1944. Both the House and Senate Judiciary Committees voted favorably on the amendment in 1942, although it would not be until after the war that the Senate formally debated the issue for the first time. In 1946 it voted in favor of the ERA, thirty-eight to thirty-five, which did not meet the two-thirds majority necessary to submit the constitutional amendment to the state legislatures.

The ERA debate during the 1940s ended in a stalemate. In response to the amendment's momentum, several labor and women's organizations met with the secretary of labor and the director of the Women's Bureau to create a new anti-ERA coalition, the National Committee on the Status of Women. By the beginning of the 1950s the Women's Bureau of the Department of Labor, the National Consumers' League, the League of Women Voters, the YWCA, the American Association of University Women, and the women's representatives of the AFL and CIO were all actively working against the amendment. In 1950 the Senate actually passed a version of the ERA by a two-thirds majority, but it included a rider introduced by Senator Carl Hayden of Arizona safeguarding "all the rights, benefits, or exemptions now or hereafter conferred by law upon persons of the opposite sex."

---

2. Mary Anderson, *Woman at Work; the Autobiography of Mary Anderson as Told to Mary N. Winslow* (Minneapolis: Univ. of Minnesota Press, 1951).

This provision, in effect, killed the amendment for the NWP and other staunch supporters. While some continued to push for the original ERA—as seen in attorney Ethel Ernest Murrell's article "An Equal Rights Amendment" (1952)—the Hayden rider ended, until the late 1960s, realistic hopes for adoption. Meanwhile, as the quest for a constitutional guarantee of female equality died down and the ideal of feminine difference took on new life in the burgeoning suburbs of post-war America, many middle-class women embraced the seeming security of marriage, family, and domesticity with a vengeance—although not without a cost. Sociologist Mirra Komarovsky analyzed this cost, examining gender roles and proposing changes that foreshadow later feminist ideas on balancing work and family, among other things. In "Women in the Modern World" (1953), an excerpt from her book by the same title, Komarovsky criticizes antifeminists for shaming women into "renouncing achievement goals" and at the same time asserts that children-rearing should be granted as much prestige as accomplishments in the boardroom or the courthouse. She also suggests that flexible work schedules, retraining, and "changed attitudes to older students and older workers" are required in society to help women reenter the workforce as their children get older.

68
CHARLOTTE PERKINS GILMAN
AND ELLEN KEY

The Conflict between "Human" and "Female" Feminism (1914)

Hitherto we have had only the antagonism of feminists and anti-feminists with which to puzzle our brains. Now it appears that there are two emergent forces in the feminist movement itself, not only distinct but opposed,—"Human Feminists" and "Female Feminists," thus producing a kind of three-sided warfare. Charlotte Perkins Gilman, in the magazine, *The Forerunner,* calls attention to this division, and she writes: "The one holds that sex is a minor department of life; that the mainlines of human development have nothing to do with sex, and that what women need most is the development of human characteristics. The other considers sex as paramount, as underlying or covering all phases of life, and that what woman needs is an even fuller exercise, development and recognition of her sex." Between the two extremes, of course, there are many shades and degrees of opinion; nevertheless the real struggle lies between these sharply defined forces. Mrs. Gilman continues: "The Human Feminist holds that woman's grave injury is that she has been debarred from this human development; that she has been so preoccupied with being a woman, so happy or so miserable in the range of her feminine relationships, that she has failed to notice her painful deficiencies as a human being. The Female Feminist, on the other hand, holds that woman is preeminently and most valuably a female, and as such she should be indulged, honored, paid, and allowed full and free activity."

Mrs. Gilman herself, according to a writer in the *Nineteenth Century,* is the present "inspiration and authority" of Human Feminism. "Our Humanness" is the keynote of her entire philosophy. Ellen Key is the high priestess of Female Feminism the world over. In a series of articles appearing recently in *Harper's Weekly,* and entitled "Woman in a New World," Madame Key reaffirms her belief in this doctrine. She presents a great paradox. Radical and extremely dangerous to present-day morality in all that concerns marriage and the sex relations, she is yet profoundly conservative, even reactionary, in all that pertains to motherhood. Her ideal of womanly self-sacrifice is very like the antifeminist's; only it contains more. To the duty of self-sacrifice she would add the power of maternal self-assertion. She believes in a consecration and an exaltation of motherhood which amounts to the predominance of the woman over the man, a maternalization of life. "The greatest danger to feminism and to humanity," Ellen Key now writes, "is that so many of the best women do not realize that the duty of motherhood is the most valuable to the nation, the race, and humanity, and that it is all important to reach again on a higher plane the union of self-assertion and self-sacrifice which only motherhood can bring. It is woman's wisdom which the ancients worshiped. It is this wisdom which must be again respected and followed, in order that humanity may rise to the moral and spiritual height to which it has already risen materially, intellectually and scientifically. She concludes her argument with one of her glowing paragraphs:

"Motherhood, which is the fountain head of unselfish ethics and which is woman's special field of action, must become her highest responsibility in thinking, feeling and acting. This is meant not only in a direct sense. When women in youth and early middle age have fulfilled their highest moral duty, to bear and rear the new race, and when in this work they have used all the culture which their new freedom has given them, then the time for spiritual motherhood arrives and occupies their later years. All we dream of for the future may yet be realized, and realized through the women, if the mothers of the next thousand years will consider it their highest happiness to promote through their children the evolution of the race toward a higher humanity."

From *Current Opinion* 56 (1914).

69
Zona Gale
What Women Won in Wisconsin (1922)

TEXT OF
WISCONSIN EQUAL RIGHTS LAW

SECTION 1. Women shall have the same rights and privileges under the law as men in the exercise of suffrage, freedom of contract, choice of residence for voting purposes, jury service, holding office, holding and conveying property, care and custody of children, and in all other respects. The various courts, executive and administrative officers shall construe the statutes where the masculine gender is used to include the feminine gender unless such construction will deny to females the special protection and privileges which they now enjoy for the general welfare. The courts, executive and administrative officers shall make all necessary rules and provisions to carry out the intent and purposes of this statute.

SECTION 2. Any women drawn to serve as a juror, upon her request to the presiding judge or magistrate, before the commencement of the trial or hearing, shall be excused from the panel or venire.

The extension of suffrage to include women left women with legal discriminations against them incompatible with citizenship. By what means would women best call the attention of lawmakers to these disabilities?

By amendment of individual statutes, one would say. But there had been introduced in the 1921 session of our Wisconsin Legislature a bill removing the most obvious discrimination—that of the right to jury duty. This bill, which was only an optional jury-service bill, passed the Senate but was defeated in the Assembly. Wisconsin women admitted to the State bar, admitted to the law school of the State University, and of course sharing in the franchise, still merely because they were women might not sit on a jury as the peers of an accused citizen. And, following the defeat of this jury bill, the judiciary committee of the Assembly introduced a bill expressly barring women from jury service.

This experience led in Wisconsin to the vision of the necessity for a proclamation of a general Bill of Rights for women, to build on. There is the point—to build on. This general grant of power lays down principles similar to the principles laid down in the constitutional Bill of Rights. We know that it must be followed by specific legislation in those instances—and many may arise—in which the issues are not clear. But we hold that a foundation is necessary on which to build, for the guidance of future legislators; and that this foundation is the proclamation of rights embodied in the Wisconsin Equal Rights Law.

Women are going to be vigilant to work for the amendment of individual statutes as these issues arise; and in approaching the legislature Wisconsin women will now have the moral backing of their Bill of Rights. Freudians tell us that an inferiority complex endangers any undertaking, and perhaps this law will operate to sweep away the inferiority complex—not in the minds of women, who have been getting rid of it for some time, but in the opinions which legislators sometimes hold in regard to the rights of women.

The following instances of the actual working of the law in the twelve months since its passage may be cited: The Civil Service Commission of Milwaukee ruled that married women were not eligible to take civil-service examinations. Various women protested, and with the backing of Mayor Hoan and Assistant City Attorney Babcock, both of whom said that this ruling was in direct violation of the Equal Rights Law, after several meetings and much argument gained their point.

Another instance was in regard to two new policewomen. Women had worked hard for the establishment of these posts. Imagine their dis-

From *The Nation*, August 23, 1922.

may when it was announced in the newspapers that married women would be barred. The women again protested. The city officials replied that the newspapers had misstated the case, and that the Equal Rights Law would not permit them to discriminate against married women.

A Wisconsin woman moved with her husband to Montana where he was engaged in the mining business. When their son was of college age this woman returned to Wisconsin to live so that he could enter the State University. The husband remained with his business in Montana. The university ruled that since the husband's home was in Montana the wife also lived in Montana, that the boy was therefore non-resident and must pay tuition. It was not until after our Wisconsin Equal Rights Law was brought forward that the University ruled that the wife lived where she lived.

A Richland Center woman had been deprived of her vote because, although she and her husband live in town with their children, the husband keeps his voting residence in the country district where their farm lies. She could not leave her young children to go to the country to vote and had not voted since the passage of the national suffrage amendment. Under the Equal Rights Law she can now vote in the town where she lives.

The Supreme Court of Wisconsin rendered a decision on last July 7 ordering a Milwaukee teacher reinstated and awarding her back pay for the time she had been deprived of her position. The court held that her dismissal violated the Equal Rights Law. The teacher had been dismissed under a ruling made by the Milwaukee board that a married woman cannot "be transferred, promoted, or permanently appointed to regular teaching positions." The teacher who was dismissed was married March 5, 1921, but continued to use her maiden name and did not inform the school board of her marriage until the following August 30. On September 15, 1921, she was discharged by the school board under the ruling quoted above. Among other specific charges brought against her and on which she was discharged was the failure to report her name promptly and the fact that after her marriage she had signed her maiden name to the school records.

These cases are good examples of the superior merit of a general bill. If we had passed a specific bill in Wisconsin instead of one establishing the general Equal Rights principle it would not have touched points such as these.

Harry Slattery of the District of Columbia Bar makes the following statement on the Equal Rights campaign:

"The adoption of the Nineteenth Amendment . . . enfranchised the women of the United States . . . but it did not provide as thousands of good folk think it did that women should have the same rights and privileges under the Constitution and laws of the United States as men. It did not remove civil or legal disabilities, inequalities, or other discriminations of law against women by reason of sex or marriage. . . . In fact the suffrage amendment is in a sense a half-way house on the road to equal civil, legal, and political rights for women which will place them on an equality with men. . . . In many States today the common-law disabilities of women are comparable to the barbaric laws of the chattel-slavery days. In our Federal laws there are many inequalities that should be removed. Common justice to the women of America requires that both in the nation and in the States these obstacles and injustices be removed. The Wisconsin law recently enacted is a model for State action. But in the last analysis, as in suffrage, a constitutional amendment will best meet the complex situation."

"Barbaric laws of chattel-slavery days" sounds a bit strong. At the other pole from a relationship involving remnants of such days stands the potential relationship, for the future, between men and women. I have tried in this outline to keep to the concrete—will you bear with me for a moment to note this abstract truth: That every man knows what a woman's point of view, when it is wise and sane and kindly, can contribute to life. Of his understanding of this we catch glimpses in his book dedications and in all his moments of greatest articulateness. The difficulty is to generalize, to realize that more women have that wisdom and that sanity or, when they haven't, that we must help them to develop these broadly social qualities. The opportunities of men to express a social spirit in their living are still double and triple those of women. Yet women have a spiritual genius which has never been given social expression. It is precisely this which they could liberate into the world, for the general welfare, if all these meshes of little circumstances hampering them could be swept away and they could be given the moral backing of a general consciousness of equality of opportunity. That is all that any equality can mean in the new status of women—equality of opportunity to express themselves politically and legally, without discriminations against them.

Lady Astor spoke a profound truth when she said at Baltimore recently that women trust to the spiritual and that they can bring the spiritual through to the material world—in time. . . . I am not saying that the Wisconsin Equal Rights Law or any other equal rights law is going to do all that. But I am saying that the Wisconsin Equal Rights Law or any other equal rights law equally well drawn is to be taken as one step in that long progress which women are making—through the doors of education, of the professions, of business, of the franchise, and on to full equality with men; the doors not of their own advancement alone but of that of a race struggling toward the conditions of a just freedom. The status of women in Wisconsin even under our Equal Rights Law is but a stage in that long march.

Meanwhile—"some remnants of the barbaric laws of chattel-slavery days." To emphasize the great work which Wisconsin did in initiating this legislation let me quote from a few of those laws as they exist in some of the other States today. These laws are familiar to you but I beg to recall them. They are collected in a series of booklets issued by the National Woman's Party, a series which is to include every State—save Wisconsin alone.

In Alabama: Mothers are not equal guardians of their children.

In Arkansas: Inheritance laws discriminate against women.

In Delaware: Fathers can will away children from mothers.

In Florida: The father controls the services and earnings of children.

In Louisiana: Married women are classed with children and the insane as unable to contract on their own responsibility.

In Maryland: Divorce laws discriminate against women.

In Massachusetts: Women are ineligible for jury service.

In Mississippi: The husband owns his wife's services in the home and in his business.

In Vermont: Earnings of a married woman belong to her husband.

In Virginia: The property of married women is presumed to belong to their husbands unless proof to the contrary is shown.

"Barbaric laws of chattel-slavery days" certainly and there are many others not listed above. Most of these laws have never existed in Wisconsin. But some of them did exist up to the time of the passage of the Equal Rights Law. And all discriminations against women must be removed. All discriminative laws against women are remnants of chattel-slavery days and all these remnants must disappear.

I see no conspicuous holy of holies in these discriminative laws. And in some States the pedestal does not seem to be high enough to prevent a husband from scaling it to collect his wife's earnings. Whether the discriminations are great, as they are in the Southern States, or less as they are in Wisconsin, the principle involved is the same—all discriminations against all women must be removed.

In this matter there is no woman's standpoint and no man's standpoint. There is only the need of our common citizenship to rid our statute books of these vestiges of the old English common law and to bring our law down to date. To do this for women—yes; and for men;

and for the general welfare; and for the children and the children's children.

70
INEZ HAYNES IRWIN

The Equal Rights Amendment: Why the Woman's Party Is for It (1924)

Before this article sees the light of print, Senator Curtis of Kansas will have introduced into the Senate, and Representative Anthony, also of Kansas, into the House, an amendment to the Constitution of the United States, called the Lucretia Mott amendment. That amendment is the present platform of the Woman's Party. It reads, "Men and women shall have equal rights throughout the United States and every place subject to its jurisdiction."

Now, what does the Woman's Party mean by equal rights?

To answer this question, it is necessary to go back a little distance into history. In 1848 there was held at Seneca Falls, New York, the first woman's rights convention in the world. That convention drew up a declaration of statements and a series of resolutions which we have begun to refer to as the woman's Bill of Rights. Although that convention seemed unimportant in the seething decades which preceded the Civil War, it has grown steadily in significance ever since. It is indeed beginning to loom out of the past like a vast monument marking the forward march of an entire sex. And that Bill of Rights has become as important to the woman's movement as Magna Charta to Great Britain or the Declaration of Independence to the United States. It demanded for women—that extraordinary document—a perfect equality with men before the law and in all other relations to human society. It demanded also an equal moral standard for men and women. And of course it demanded the ballot for women.

Seventy-five years have passed since 1848. Of the whole splendid program outlined by the convention at Seneca Falls, the only right we have gained for *all* the women of the United States is the right to vote. Of course, there are many women who innocently believe that, having become enfranchised, woman has taken the last trench in her struggle for freedom. And it is true that for women to enter the economic conflict without the vote is a little like going into battle without a gun. The present writer has no intention to depreciate the value of the ballot—only that tendency to believe that enfranchisement completed woman's freedom. The majority of women who were interested to see women obtain the franchise pictured her, I think, engaging at once, equally with men, in movements for national and international betterment. But will the mass of women be interested to enter the struggle for—let us say—international peace, or can they effectively engage in such a struggle if they still do not possess such simple fundamental liberties as the right after marriage to their own earnings; to inherit property equally with their husband; the joint ownership with him of their children?

After the United States enfranchised its women, the Woman's Party called a convention of its members to decide whether there was any need for it to continue. It invited every reform organization of women in the United States to send a speaker to present its program to that convention. After listening to these various programs, the Woman's Party realized that not one of them purposed to establish complete equality between men and women. Therefore the party decided to continue its existence and to remove all the remaining forms of subjection of women, beginning with the legal disabilities.

The Woman's Party has always had but one plank at a time in its platform—but back of that plank it has massed the entire Party. In its brief history of a dozen years it has had but two platforms. The first demanded votes for women; the second, equal rights. And just as in

From the March 1924 issue of *Good Housekeeping*. Reprinted with permission.

its work for the suffrage it went straight on, without deviation toward any other cause, until the women of the United States were enfranchised, so in the fight for its present platform, it will go straight on until women stand equal with men before the law in the United States. Until this complete national freedom is won, it is unlikely that the women of the United States can make a big, concerted sex movement toward any great international reform.

In the last two years the Woman's Party has been engaged in an exhaustive research of both the federal and state laws as they discriminate against women. The work is being done in the Law Library of the Supreme Court of the United States by a corps of women trained in the law. From these digests the summaries of twelve states have already been put in pamphlet form. I cite the laws as typical of four states—a southern, an eastern, a middle-western and a far-western state.

In Florida, one discovers that women can not serve on juries and are not admitted to the State University, except the Normal Department, on equal terms with men. A married woman's services belong to her husband. She can not choose her legal residence; does not control her own property; has practically no right to contract or do business on her own responsibility. The father controls the services and earnings of children. The inheritance laws discriminate against women. In Massachusetts, women are disqualified for jury service. The right of married women to carry on business is restricted and mothers have not equal rights with fathers to the services and the earnings of their children. In Michigan, married women have no general capacity to contract; they have not equal rights with husbands over joint property. The husband owns his wife's services in the home and controls her right to work outside the home. Mothers have not equal rights with fathers over their children. In Nevada, marriage revokes a woman's will. Married women have no general capacity to contract or to sue, and are restricted in the right to carry on a business. The husband has the exclusive control of community property, and a widow's share in community property is less than a widower's share. Laws concerning the administration of estates discriminate against women. The apprentice law discriminates against girls. The legal age is less for girls than boys. Prostitution is a matter of commerce. . . .

THE WOMAN'S PARTY TAKES A STAND

The Woman's Party finally decided that just as in their fight for Votes for Women they had demanded an amendment to the Constitution, they would in their fight for Equal Rights also demand an amendment to the Constitution. They adopted this method for several reasons, one being that a federal amendment is permanent and that it prevents the thing which has twice happened in the case of state laws, that a right has been given and then taken away. Again, a federal amendment means the saving of time, money, and strength of women which forty-eight separate campaigns would enormously dissipate. Then, too, the work in the states—where the fight centers around each point of inequality with its personal angle instead of around a fundamental principle—is very difficult. Finally, the Constitution is the supreme law of the land. At one stroke it wipes out past discriminations and prevents new ones. However, the Woman's Party has already been working, though with great difficulty, with state legislatures. It will take every method to get Equal Rights incorporated into the law of the land.

The Woman's Party calls the attention of American women to the fact that all interpretations of the law involving women in our country today are based upon the subject position of women under the English common law instead of on the equal position of women with men. New situations and conditions are always arising which demand a legal interpretation based on equality between men and women rather than on that subject position.

There are few women, I take it, in the United States today—and certainly few women of intelligence—who will deny to women the equal right with their husbands to the guardianship of their children. There are few who will deny women the right to their own earnings; the right to make contracts, to inherit property, to control their own property; the right to equal opportunities in schools, universities, government service, the industries, the professions, the arts; the right to their own identity after marriage. We do not anticipate from so clear-thinking, forward-gazing—so emancipate a group—as the women of America, much argument on any one of these scores. If there is a fight—and our great hope, of course, is that there will be no fight—it may come on the subject of welfare legislation.

The Woman's Party is not a labor organization and does not pretend to say whether benefit should be obtained by legislation or organization, but it contends that if those benefits be obtained by legislation, such legislation should apply equally to men and women.

The Lucretia Mott amendment will make impossible any legislation with a sex basis; so that the law demanding an eight-hour day for women only, and the law prohibiting night work for women only, will apply to women and men equally. A great change has come into the thinking of the world in regard to these matters. The Woman's Party believes that there is a fallacy in special sex legislation, by which it may not work definitely for the betterment of women. In brief, it may result in preventing them from engaging in certain gainful occupations. For instance, where women are enjoined from night work, they may be forced to give up superior night jobs—which are of course eagerly snapped up by men—to take inferior day jobs.

If you have considered this question, I am sure, reader, that you are going to pause at this paragraph—appalled. You are going to say to yourself that the Woman's Party is trying to tear down the fair structure of protective legislation which a band of noble-hearted, self-sacrificing men and women have been, for a quarter of a century, building up. But the Woman's Party designs no such sinister work of destruction. It does not ask the repeal of these laws. It only asks that they apply equally to both sexes.

THE AMENDMENT DOES NOT AFFECT MATERNITY LEGISLATION

The Lucretia Mott amendment will not affect maternity legislation, as it is designed to remove inequalities based on sex, not those based on motherhood. It will not interfere with so-called motherhood pensions, because these pensions are not given to mothers alone. There is an increasing modern tendency toward granting this aid to whichever parent is legally responsible for the child.

The trend of our modern world—and by our modern world, I mean our *after-the-war* world—is toward this complete equality. Seven different European Constitutions, new since the war, have embodied this equal rights idea; those of Germany, Austria, Prussia, Czecho-Slovakia, Lithuania, Danzig, and Esthonia. The United States lagged behind other countries of the world in the enfranchisement of its women citizens, and it can not, alas, now lead in this matter of making them equal with men. But it can be among the first ten to do so. It is the hope of the Woman's Party that it will be number eight.

71

FLORENCE KELLEY

The Equal Rights Amendment: Why Other Women's Groups Oppose It (1924)

As a fortunate and aspiring grandmother, I am hopeful that the doors of the law schools of Harvard and Columbia may be open to all grandchildren, girls and boys alike, when

From the March 1924 issue of *Good Housekeeping*. Reprinted with permission.

mine are ready to enter, and later on perhaps even the portals of the Supreme Court of the United States. Meanwhile, I write as a lawyer admitted in 1894 from Northwestern University to practise before the Supreme Court of Illinois. My bachelor's thesis, a dozen years earlier at Cornell University, had dealt with "The Law and the Child." After that there had followed two winters under the Faculty of Law at Zurich, in Switzerland. But a degree had never seemed important. Suddenly, however, admission to active practise became an urgent necessity, for in 1893, as Chief Factory Inspector of the State of Illinois, I was faced by the baffling fact that prosecutions, started as a part of the official routine for enforcing obedience to the Illinois eight-hour law, applying to women and girls, did not come to trial. That statute was no more self-enforcing than a federal amendment.

These personal items are mentioned because, being related to the legal profession through my father (who was in Congress nearly thirty years continuously, beginning when I was not yet two years old) and by an uncle and a son; and having tried child labor cases in the old-time Chicago "justice shops," I have acquired an attitude of sustained inquiry about methods of improving the law.

This experience may, perhaps, be taken as symbolic also of the organizations which have, since its earliest draft was made public, steadily opposed a proposed blanket equality amendment to the Constitution. They are not newcomers in the field of activity in behalf of women. Many aspects of equality they desire, and have long been, and are now working for. But wisdom born of experience teaches all alike the lesson of caution. Slow and wearisome though the process may be, it is better to keep what has been won, and go steadily on getting good laws by votes backed by organization, than to gamble upon the chance of hoped-for quick winnings, and then lose. In this case the losses might be grievous indeed.

Let us consider some gains which are too precious to be hazarded—among them, equal guardianship, widows' pensions, and the maternity and infancy law. . . .

THE SHEPPARD-TOWNER LAW

Until Jeannette Rankin, in August, 1918, introduced in Congress her bill for the Hygiene and Welfare of Maternity and Infancy, the great mass of grieving mothers accepted with what resignation they could command the deaths of their little ones, which they commonly attributed to the will of God. So widespread, intensive, and enlightening was the campaign for this bill that, in the brief space of five years since Miss Rankin forced the subject upon a most reluctant War Congress, her measure has, under the above title, been accepted by forty states, and death-rates of infants have fallen beyond the hopes of her followers and of the Children's Bureau, which has been administering the law since it took effect in March, 1922.

The Sheppard-Towner law applies explicitly to mothers and babies. In some places the maternal death-rate, which had been slowly rising throughout several years, is stationary. In others it has begun to fall slightly.

There is, however, no possible assurance that this beneficent measure could survive the passage of the proposed equal rights amendment. Talk of its being safe from annulment because it applies solely to children is folly while mothers are expressly included in it. Moreover, the two federal child labor laws have found no charmed life by reason of applying to children! Let us expose this safeguard of the home to no risks. It discriminates indisputably in favor of women. . . .

. . . The speediest method possible is resource to the legislatures. To await a federal amendment would be cruel folly.

A good illustration of this cheerful fact is Virginia, whose legislature passed, in 1922, seventeen of twenty-eight bills introduced chiefly for improving the lot of children. It is confidently expected by the cooperating organizations of men and women who achieved this beneficent success, that the remaining eleven measures will be adopted during the present year.

This procedure commends itself to men and women of experience in the field of legislation for several reasons, of which two are especially obvious. The first is that modifications in state laws can be made with relative ease when needed as social conditions change. But an amendment can hardly be repealed. It can be changed only by the long, slow process of judicial interpretation. The other is that statutes can be obtained without the delays which attend every federal amendment, even one on a subject so popular, for instance, as child labor. It is nearly two years since the second adverse decision of the United States Supreme Court in the child labor cases, and no joint resolution of a federal amendment has yet been referred to the states for ratification. . . .

HARD WORK AND DELAYED RESULTS

The struggle for every gain in statutes and judicial decisions for women and girls in industry has been hard fought and costly in money, time, and effort. It was in the light of twentieth-century decisions of the United States Supreme Court that New York's court of last resort reversed in 1914, its own adverse decision of 1907, thus permanently establishing a night-work law for women in the greatest of all the industrial states. In New Jersey, after many years of persistent effort, women obtained, in 1923, a night-work law so amended at the last moment as to take effect at New Year's, 1925. The delay was explained by legislators as intended to enable mill owners to expand their plants to accommodate the women who would be transferred to enlarged day shifts. Rhode Island is due for successful action in 1924.

In New York, organized working men help pass whatever bills women in industry endorse. There, since 1886, men and women wage-earners have pursued increasingly the policy of cooperation in promoting labor laws. They have, for instance, procured statutes concerning fire, cleanliness, lighting, ventilation, and one day's rest in seven, which apply alike to men, women, and children. They have obtained measures exclusively for men, safeguarding those (commonly known as sand-hogs) who work in tunnels under rivers and harbors, and bills applying to men in the train service of railroads, and on scaffolds in the building trades.

Florida last year prohibited the leasing of men prisoners to labor in lumber camps. Miners in many states have the statutory eight-hour day, having changed their state constitutions to get it. Women obviously do not work in mines and tunnels or on scaffolds. They form no part of train crews under the full-crew laws. Their oldest, most wide-spread, and most insistent demands have been for seats, for more adequate wages, and short, firmly-regulated working hours. This co-operative effort to meet the essential needs of the different groups in industry we consider admirable statesmanship. Whenever union men feel no need of laws, well and good. No one wishes to interfere with them any more than professional women are interfered with today by labor legislation.

On this subject we are immovable. If there were no other reason for opposing the proposed amendment, we should concentrate all our efforts upon this. Even before we had votes, women in general chose to get their shorter day by law, and men by negotiation backed, when necessary, by strikes. Both are legal.

Under the proposed amendment, women could change their hours and other working conditions by law only when men were ready and willing to make the same changes for themselves. This would be a new subjection of wage-earning women to wage-earning men, and to that subjection we are opposed on principle and in practise.

NEGLECTED ROOTS OF TROUBLE

In the long history of human experience there is no record of a quick, sure remedy for an injustice involving fundamental social relations. It becomes daily clearer that much injustice to women is attributable to the general absence from the courts of competent, thoroughly-trained women judges. This situation is obviously not remediable by amending the federal constitution. It requires systematic effort in a different field of activity. The trouble lies oftener in judicial misinterpretation of laws, federal and state, than in the measures themselves. And this is curable by the voters wherever the judiciary is elective.

We can not eat our cake and have it, too. We can not subject ourselves, by a constitutional amendment, to compulsory equality with men forevermore, yet keep our most needed special laws, for lack of which, throughout the long terrible past, women and children have suffered and died.

In this kaleidoscopic world, we are confronted by the perpetual necessity of making choices. The ballot is our most recently acquired instrument of choice and change. With it statutes can be fitted precisely, skillfully, to the needs of every group in the community, as each need is clearly recognized.

LET US MAKE HASTE SLOWLY

If, moreover, the proposed amendment were desirable, its enactment in the near future would be premature. The Eighteenth Amendment is not yet four years old. The uses of the ballot, which it conferred upon women, have not begun to be tested. The first President is yet to be elected, in choosing whom women will vote in all the states.

In many states the election laws were not harmonized with the Suffrage Amendment quickly enough for women to vote in the state elections of 1920. The legislature of Alabama is quadrennial. The new voters have had but one opportunity to share in electing it. Women voters in Alabama State affairs are new voters indeed.

We demand ample opportunity for trying out the possibilities of the ballot in the hands of all the citizens of the whole voting constituency of men and women, before limits are placed upon the freest conceivable use of it. We stand firmly upon the inalienable right of men and women to differ. . . .

72

Ethel M. Smith

Working Women's Case against Equal Rights (1924)

Do you believe in justice? Of course, you do. Do you believe in equal rights for men and women? In this day and age, of course you do—because you believe in justice.

But—do you believe that you can establish justice by decreeing that all people shall deal justly with each other? Probably not, because you know that justice, the abstract principle must needs, for this work-a-day world, be translated into actualities and defined in terms of law. And after that there must be courts to decide the meaning and application of the law in concrete cases. You and I, both believing in justice for all people, may hold exactly opposite beliefs as to what constitutes justice in a given instance. The law, as interpreted by the courts, will uphold one of us and refute the other.

Then consider—do you believe that equal rights for men and women can be secured by decreeing that "men and women shall have equal rights"? If our reasoning is correct, you would not expect that decree to be any more effective than the other. What are "rights" in terms of law? What are "equal rights"? In fact, in view of some court decisions, what are "men and women"; or rather, when?

Our first question above is hypothetical. The second is before us, in fact to be dealt with in the present Congress as a resolution for an amendment to the Federal constitution. As proposals for legislation, either mandate might

From the *New York Times,* January 20, 1924.

mean anything—or nothing. Which might seem to be the end of the matter, were the logic of it all.

But logic is to all, nor are we at the end of the matter. We are at the beginning of a sharp and lasting conflict between an extremist group of feminists on the one hand, and the great mass of the woman movement, together with the entire labor movement, on the other.

The constitutional amendment which is in controversy would provide that "Men and women shall have equal rights throughout the United States and every place subject to its jurisdiction." It has been proposed by the National Woman's Party, which was the extreme left of the woman suffrage movement, and, then, as now, a minority in the whole woman movement. The new proposal, being a minority agitation, might be readily overcome by the women's forces against it but for two facts. The minority has millionaire backing for its undertaking. And, wittingly or unwittingly on the part of the proponents, its program plays conveniently into the hands of a large and well-financed group of men whose commercial self-interest it serves.

OPPOSED BY WOMEN WORKERS

We witness, then, in Congress, the active lobby of well-to-do women of the National Woman's Party demanding the adoption of their "equal rights" amendment; and an equally active, but by no means well-to-do group, protesting against a measure which they consider to be a menace to their actual livelihood and that of their wage-earning sisters.

These latter, the opposing forces of women, are wage-earners belonging to the National Women's Trade Union League and the American Federation of Labor, together with women belonging to such widely representative organizations as the National League of Women Voters, the Young Women's Christian Association, the National Consumers League, the General Federation of Women's Clubs, the National Council of Catholic Women, the Council of Jewish Women, the American Association of University Women, the American Home Economics Association, the National Council of Women, the Girls' Friendly Society, and the American Federation of Teachers.

The opposition to the proposed amendment is based upon legal opinions to the effect that the terms of the measure, undefined as they are and must be in a constitutional provision, would throw into the courts and probably invalidate laws giving rights to women which women need, irrespective of whether those same rights obtain for men or not. The amendment would destroy, without replacing. And in so far as it did not destroy, it would be unnecessary, because everything it demands must now, and would likewise under the amendment, be a matter of separate, specific legislation, by State legislatures or Congress.

Why then, take the risk of destroying, for example, the laws limiting the hours of labor for women factory workers? Or the laws establishing commissions to fix the minimum living wage for women? Or, for that matter, why destroy (until you have a better substitute ready), the laws requiring husbands to support their wives and families? Or laws providing mothers' or widows' pensions? Or laws protecting maternity? Or laws fixing an age of consent for girls?

Grant that any, or all, those laws need amending. Is it constructive, or is it even sensible, to attain equality by the negative process of taking away what one sex has gained, merely because the other sex has it not? Would it have been sensible to achieve equal suffrage by taking the vote away from men?

That is not a far-fetched analogy. The question turns upon the definition of the terms "rights" and "equal rights." The immediate effect of a constitutional amendment is to make unenforceable all State laws that conflict with it. This was a clear-cut result in the case of the Fifteenth Amendment, extending the right to vote regardless of race, color or previous conditions of servitude. It was a clear-cut issue in the case of the woman suffrage amendment, and again in the prohibition amendment. One question only was involved in each of those amendments. The effect was understood in advance.

The proposed "equal rights" amendment is quite a different matter. It assumes that other kinds of rights—social and economic rights especially—are the same as legal rights, or can be secured by legislative enactment. As a matter of fact, legal rights may actually defeat economic or social rights. This has been labor's most bitter experience. It might easily be the experience of women as wives and mothers under the proposed amendment. The injustice might reach to girls of 12 or 14, for courts have called them "women" under some circumstances.

The laws affecting women factory workers are perhaps the clearest case in point, and they are probably the most important, inasmuch as they affect, directly or indirectly, nearly 9,000,000 women wage earners.

Such laws exist in almost every State of the United States. They exist because, however high the ideals and efforts of the best establishments in any industry, there are always some employers who will undercut and drag down the standards of the whole group—unless the law prevents. This undercutter is the very type of employer who makes a point of hiring women, because women workers, as a class, are younger, less experienced in bargaining for their services, and therefore more exploitable then men.

States that have 10-hour laws for women in industry have enacted such laws because without them women had to work 11 and 12 hours a day. The 9-hour States, by their laws, prevent the employment of women for 10 hours a day. And the 8-hour States conform to the still higher standard.

Now these laws, like most labor laws, limit the right of contract, both for the employer and the employed. On the other hand, they confer upon the worker the right to a shorter work day. One right is lost by the worker to gain the other. The right to more leisure, hence better opportunity for health, education, recreation and good citizenship, means more to the worker than the right to work 12 hours a day; or the right to starve on $6 a week.

SAYS PROTECTION ALSO BENEFITS MEN

For the most part, the laws limiting hours of labor apply to women but not to men. A few of them apply to men and women both, or perhaps only to men, as in the case of miners and railroad men, because there are no women in those occupations. They were made to apply to women because women needed them most, the great women-employing industries (textile factories, canning factories, candy factories, sweat-shops for garment making, &c.) having longer hours and lower wages than the great men-employing industries (like the printing trades, metal trades, building trades, &c.).

But what happens is that the laws for women bring up the standards for men in the same industries, because the men's and women's work is interdependent, and when the women stop work at the end of the day the men have to stop also. . . .

They confer, these minimum wage laws do, the right to a living wage, and thereby bring women workers nearer to receiving equal pay with men for equal work. But this economic right, this economic equality, would be destroyed by the enforcement of legal equality.

Consider also some other kinds of rights; say the wife's "right" to her husband's "support." It is fairly obvious to everybody that in the typical family the wife does her share toward the family "support." But the law measures "support" in terms of money, and under non-support laws the wife has a right to sue her husband if he does not provide the money needed for the family.

Legal authorities say these laws would be thrown into the courts by the National Woman's Party amendment on the ground that the rights of husband and wife are not equal. Something must, therefore, be done about it, and it is unquestionably important to know what that something is. Shall we be content merely to take away the wife's right to sue? Or shall we give the husband the same right?

If the mother of six children has no redress against a husband who chooses to evade his responsibility, can she be said to have in fact equal rights with the husband, in spite of their equal legal footing in their like inability to sue each other?

On the other hand, giving both husband and wife the right to sue, what shall the husband recover? Assuming that the average wife is not a wage-earner, and has no independent income of her own, her responsibilities must be measured in other terms than money, presumably in terms of service. But if the services of a wife who has three children to look after be equal to the services of a husband, who contributes $200 a month to the family support—what shall be done to equalize the requirements where the husband earns only $100 a month and the wife has six children to look after?

Or suppose we are concerned with equalizing the responsibility of the father and the mother of an illegitimate child. Generally, the laws discriminate against the mother. They hold her responsible and do not hold the father. The father should, of course, be made equally responsible. But would the National Woman's Party amendment do that? Only in the sense of making neither parent responsible. The mother could claim exemption because the father was not held. And it would take much more than a mere mandate of equality to hold the illegitimate father. The first thing is to find him, to prove his paternity.

Meantime, what of the child? To frame and pass a workable, enforceable law to find and to hold responsible the father of the illegitimate child has baffled many earnest people for many laborious years.

And so with the age-of-consent laws. Nearly everywhere they apply only to girls. The Woman's Party amendment would not automatically extend them to boys. It would throw them into the courts or nullify them for girls until some new law was worked out.

In other words, were the proposed amendment passed, the States and Congress would be confronted with alternatives such as these:

Do without laws making husbands liable to suit for non-support of their families; or make wives equally liable.

Do without mothers' and widows' pensions; or provide pensions for fathers and widowers.

Do without maternity protective laws; or provide corresponding protection for fathers.

Disregard all physical differences between men and women; or make laws applying to both sexes irrespective of those differences.

Disregard the special needs of women; or make the same laws apply to men, whether needed or desired by men or actually undesirable for them.

FIGHTING LEGAL DISCRIMINATIONS

It is a most unreasonable proposal; especially in view of the fact that there is a perfectly feasible, constructive way to remove the legal discriminations against women without courting the inequalities and injustices involved in the "equal rights" amendment of the National Woman's Party.

Everybody knows that there are scores of sex-discriminatory laws on the statute books; various kinds of laws, varying in different States, specific, obvious injustices, apparent to the naked eye. Some of these are hangovers from the old common law or the Code Napoleon. Others are deliberate discriminations of more modern date. Nobody defends such laws today, and practically all thinking women, with the vote now in their hands, are agreed that they should be revised or repealed.

Women's organizations, indeed, are so well agreed upon this that ever since they got the vote they have been diligently working to remove the discriminations. They did not and do not think—excepting, of course, the

Woman's Party—that in order to give the wife in Texas control over her own earnings they should seek a constitutional amendment that would nullify the 48-hour week for women wage-earners of Massachusetts.

What they sought, and what they got, in 68 instances in 28 States within three years' time, was specific legislation removing discriminations or giving women new rights. They are continuing that process, which they believe and have demonstrated is feasible, constructive and quite as rapid as a constitutional amendment would be which merely required the States to do what they are already doing and created chaos meantime.

Women's opposition to the National Woman's Party amendment, therefore, is due to the indiscriminate and reckless destructiveness of that amendment. The language has a plausible, alluring sound, and women do want equal rights with men. But the women of the National League of Women Voters, the National Women's Trade Union League, the National Consumers' League, and all the twelve associated organizations opposing this amendment, are the very women who, in every State, have done most of the hard work to remove the old common law disabilities and other discriminations against women. They know something of the trickery of words. Equal rights may be anything, to suit and purpose, unless the right is defined.

These women, therefore, will buy no pig in a poke. There is a right way, a safe way, to secure equal rights, without imperiling our social standards, without destroying women's labor laws, without sacrificing one group of women to the purpose of another. Legal rights, social rights, economic rights, each need careful, specific consideration and well-drawn statutes to protect or guarantee them. The need is for specific action where laws are discriminatory by the States, or by Congress, as the need may be. That is the program of the women's organizations who are opposing the National Woman's Party amendment.

73
RHETA CHILDE DORR
Should There Be Labor Laws for Women? *No* (1925)

About the time this article is published, women's clubs all over the country will be reassembling, and before long their committee chairmen will be reporting on legislative measures purporting to protect women wage-earners by limiting and restricting their hours of work. I have sat in so many women's meetings and have listened to so many such reports that I know what will happen in most clubs. Without much debate the women will heartily endorse the "protective" measures and go home happy in the belief that they have struck one more blow in defence of mothers, babies, and the home.

All they will have done is to gratify that deep, protective instinct which is so good in women, but alas! sometimes so tyrannical too. Often I wish it could be bottled like a beneficent but pernicious drug, labeled with skull and cross-bones, and inscribed, "To be well mixed with intelligence before taking."

The whole question of restrictive legislation applied to adult women workers is obscured by a fogginess of thought, a confusion of ideas and arguments, based on propaganda rather than on facts. Back of the whole question lie ages of prejudice against any freedom for women, any acknowledgement of their right to function as independent, self-determining citizens. To deal with it properly requires cool thinking, clear intelligence. But if I did not believe that the readers of *Good Housekeeping* were willing to bring intelligence to bear on the subject, I should not be writing this protest against the whole body of laws, those in force and those projected, which on a sex basis alone limit the right of grown women to compete in the industrial world on equal terms with men.

From the September 1925 issue of *Good Housekeeping*. Reprinted with permission.

My first protest is against classing grown women with children under the law. Practically all laws limiting hours of work, prohibiting night work, and providing for a minimum wage are enacted for women and minors. I say "practically" just to be on the safe side. As a matter of fact, it is the routine thing to class woman labor with child labor or with adolescent boy and girl labor.

The reason given is that the vast majority of "females in gainful occupations" are girls of tender years, temporary invaders of industry, pathetic flitters between the schoolroom and the matrimonial altar. I could, if I had space, quote statistical tables to prove the untruth of these generalizations. Few would read the statistics, and besides I would rather have *Good Housekeeping* readers think of working women as human beings rather than rows of figures. However, I will state that the last census gave the number of women, eighteen and over, in industry as 7,593,709. Nearly two million of these adult women workers were married. These wage-earners are not children. Why interfere with their right to earn the highest possible wage by putting them under the police power of the State? All the arguments in favor of such a policy boil down to one sentimental aphorism, "Women are women." Different from men. Weaker. More susceptible to accidents and to industrial diseases. Helpless under exploiting employers, defenceless after dark. Above all, they are mothers or potential mothers. Everybody, especially the women themselves, ought to be thinking about that all the time instead of such material advantages as richer lives, promotion into skilled trades, increased incomes, savings against old age. All so-called protective legislation is based on this "women are women" argument. It was the basis and foundation of the celebrated Brandeis brief supplied by the Consumers' League in defence of the Nine Hour Law in Oregon. On that brief Justice Brewer of the United States Supreme Court wrote his decision (1908) which took away from American working women rights guaranteed all other citizens under the Fourteenth Amendment to the Constitution, the right to "Life, liberty and property," of which the right "freely to contract" is an essential part.

In this Brandeis brief a mass of evidence was offered to show that women, however mature, were by nature unfitted freely to contract. If no police club stood between them and their job, the most horrible consequences might ensue. Among them, ruined health of the women themselves, increased abortions, increased infant mortality, and general social calamity. Every evil enumerated was laid on the single fact that women were working outside the home for wages. Other conditions—poverty, bad housing, poor food, ignorance of hygienic living, diseases of crowding, such as tuberculosis, etc., lack of decent conditions in factories—were minimized or ignored. If you read the brief without knowing any more about the women than Justice Brewer did, or Mr. Louis Brandeis did, you had a picture of an army of happy, rosy-cheeked girls trooping into one door of the factory and a long line of haggard wrecks of femininity staggering out of another. As a piece of special pleading the Brandeis brief was a masterpiece. As a basis for present-day legislation it leaves a great deal to be desired, especially in view of knowledge gained in the World War regarding the relative strength of men and women.

Everybody knows what the women of all the warring countries did during the great conflict. In Great Britain and France especially, and to a lesser extent in the United States, they took over almost every trade formerly sacred to men. For four years more than a million women in Great Britain and France, working in machine trades, produced as good, if not better, results than the trained men they displaced in factories, mills, workshops, laboratories, ship-yards, docks, brick and stone yards, and all other war industries.

Many ancient theories about the feebleness of women were decidedly shaken by that war record, in spite of the fact that as soon as the war ended these splendid workers had to listen to the old argument, "women are women."

Economic experts began to examine industry itself, instead of women workers, for causes of physical breakdown. Even the medical faculty, traditionally reactionary, somewhat modified its previous conclusions. I recommend to all club women who desire to be fair in this matter of restrictive legislation to read a new book, "Protective Legislation," by Elizabeth Faulkner Baker, Ph. D., instructor in economics, Barnard College, Columbia. It is one of the most valuable of the Studies in History, Economics and Public Law, edited by the Faculty of Political Science of Columbia University, and it may be obtained from Columbia, or from the distributing agents, Longmans, Green and Co., New York. Dr. Baker, in this exhaustive study, holds no brief either for or against protective legislation. She simply assembles all available facts. I have space here only to touch on a few of her most important conclusions.

In cautious and scientific fashion Dr. Baker puts her finger on the real disability under which most wage-earning women, at a disadvantage with wage-earning men, labor. The women do a thing which would speedily break down the health and strength of the average man. They carry on two jobs, wage-earning and housework. Young women living at home are expected to do their share of housework after hours, and they not infrequently sew, mend, and wash and iron their own clothes. Everybody expects this of women. Even in the best homes for working girls provision is made as a matter of course for laundry work and sewing. Imagine a Y.M.C.A. hotel for men with a laundry and a sewing room for tired workers! As for married women in industry, they usually do a full days' work after going home from toil. In Fall River, Mass., when I myself was working there as a ring spinner, the conventional hour for hanging out the week's wash was eleven o'-clock at night. The more intelligent women, especially those who are "unprotected" and can therefore earn high wages in superior jobs, never dream of carrying this double burden. They either hire their heavy work done, or they invest in labor-saving devices—vacuum cleaners, electric washing machines, and the like. But great numbers of poorly paid women, kept down to the lower ranks in most trades, still work long hours at home because of poverty, seasonal trades, legal prohibition against working overtime in seasonal trades, and always the fear of unemployment. . . .

What I am trying to urge, in this short article, is that unequal wages and bad factory conditions, and not special laws for adult women workers, are the things in which we all should interest ourselves. Sex has nothing to do with the case. Julia Lathrop and Grace Abbott, in the Children's Bureau reports, have demonstrated that poverty of fathers, rather than wage-earning activities of mothers, are responsible for the ghastly toll of infant life in industrial communities. Of course, the ideal thing would be for all fathers to be drawing such good wages in healthful employment that mothers of children would not have to work at all. But such ideal conditions do not exist. Fathers die, they fall ill, sometimes they desert. For many reasons women, even mothers, have to work, and if they didn't the children would have to. When we limit women's opportunities to work, we simply create more poverty, and we postpone the day when equal pay for equal work will be universal. Without equal work there can be no equal pay, nor anything like a fair field for men and women alike.

Instead of dry statistics I want to give *Good Housekeeping* readers just a few instances of the cruelty wrought by classing women with children and adolescents, and preventing grown women from exercising their Constitutional right freely to contract. If my stories are all of New York women, it is because I live in New York City and know working conditions there.

Mrs. A. is a printer, an expert in every branch of the trade. By the time she was old enough to marry another printer, she was a skilled linotype operator and a member of the union. Her husband died, leaving her with two children to support. In 1913 she was earning, in the composing room of the *New York Times,* about $60 a week, enough to pay for a comfortable little apartment and a capable maid. Mrs. A. worked at night, because the *Times* is a morning paper. But she had had her eight hours' sleep by the time the children got home from school, and she did not leave the house until long after they were in bed. One night, when she reported for work, she was astonished to find a young man at her machine.

"New night law for women's just gone into effect," explained the foreman. "Mean to say you didn't know the uplifters were pushing it through the Legislature? Darned shame. Nothing you can do but look for a job on the day side somewhere."

Early next morning Mrs. A. was looking for a day job on an evening paper. There was no job, but the foreman said she might wait around on the chance some regular man failed to turn up. After two hours of waiting Mrs. A. applied at another evening paper. Every morning she went the rounds, sometimes getting a chance to "sub" for a few hours, once in a great while for an entire day. She soon gave up her apartment and the maid and moved into a few tenement rooms. In order to support even this poor home she was eventually driven into factory work at about a third of her former income. At night she scrubbed, cooked, washed and ironed. Worse than the murderous overwork, worse than her resentment against the law which took her skilled trade away from her, was the agony of seeing her children, especially the boy, running wild in the streets. Organizing other dispossessed women, she managed after two years, and the expenditure of $10,000, much of it contributed by men printers, and women in other trades, to gain an exemption from the night law for women in her trade.

This New York law prohibiting women from working at night originally affected practically all women except those in the learned professions, actresses, office charwomen, and domestic servants. Even women reporters and editors on morning papers were ordered away from their desks. Gradually a few groups were exempted, against protests from the welfare workers, who urged that the favored wage-earners ought to be willing to sacrifice their jobs for the sake of the weakest workers. In other words, to sacrifice all the victories women have won in their long industrial struggle from menial work to independent positions. . . .

. . . I am glad I am in no way responsible for approximately 150,000 women who were thrown out of work by the "protective" laws New York has enacted during the past few years. The women are putting up a splendid fight, especially against the night law. From my twenty years' experience in newspaper work I can testify that there is nothing horrible in night work. One sleeps as well by day as by night, once the habit is formed. Night work is cool in summer, and it is always quiet. Above all, when the night worker goes home there are always seats in the subway and surface cars, instead of the strap-hanging and indecent crowding of the day hours.

I don't want a single woman to relax her war against the crime of child labor, or against the exploitation of adolescent boys and girls. I want them only to turn their intelligence and their great influence in favor of better working conditions and safeguarding of hazardous trades for both men and women. For it takes healthy men as well as healthy women to rear a healthy race. I want them to give up the outworn idea that they can prevent bad conditions by doing women workers out of their jobs. If club women want to work for a shorter work day for all toilers, I suggest that they adopt a plan for which a most intelligent group of women wage-earners are striving in New York. Having killed a forty-eight-hour bill in the last session of the Legislature, they are now sponsoring a bill for a basic forty-eight-hour law for all workers. This law will permit several hours' overtime in busy seasons, with extra pay for each hour. This is a different thing from the usual mandatory legislation, and it puts it up to the individual worker whether or not he or she will work over forty-eight hours in any week. The probabilities are that all who have to endure half-time during part of the year will work as long as they can in order to make up the lost income.

The labor unions are mostly opposed to this law, for few unions want women to advance in skilled trades. The Women's Trade Union League, controlled and to a large extent supported by the men's unions, opposes it. Of course, the welfare organizations oppose it, for it frees women wage-earners from the police power of the old laws. But I pray that public opinion, especially that of the club women, will support it. It's the first law yet proposed that gives working women a man's chance industrially.

"No men's labor unions, no leisure class women, no uniformed legislators have a right to govern our lives without our consent," the women declare, and I think they are dead right about it.

74

MARY ANDERSON

Should There Be Labor Laws for Women? *Yes* (1925)

Probably it is not safe to try to say what a feminist is, but I am convinced that there are at least two types. Both of them feel keenly the discriminations society has imposed upon women through ages past and present, but as a result a difference comes in their attitude toward society—in their sense of proportion. Most women who care greatly about the wrongs and handicaps under which women suffer are willing to admit the importance—the equal importance—of some other social injustices. They recognize, indeed, the interrelationship of the woman question with other great questions. I consider this a perfectly good kind of feminism. There are other women, however, who put the woman question first and above all other issues, and who seem to think that the solution of all others should be determined solely by what is done with women's problems. This type of feminist insists upon woman's rights no matter what happens to other rights.

It is natural, then, that the differences between these two types of feminists should appear in certain other ways. The more moderate type will be the more practical woman, who sees and works with facts. The other type is the theorist, who with a single abstract principle in mind persistently ignores facts, clinging devotedly to abstractions.

This difference between the practical and the theoretical woman is coming to be a serious matter in its effects upon the interests of the great mass of women wage-earners. It is doubly serious because the woman at work for a livelihood is prevented, by the very confinement to her job, from being as articulate about herself and her problems as she might otherwise be, and as her non-wage-earning sisters, or any women more fortunately situated, not only can be but are. So we have over-articulate theorists attempting to solve the working women's problems on a purely feminist basis, with the working woman's own voice far less adequately heard. And these over-articulate, highly theoretical feminists are talking about things and conditions entirely outside their own experience or knowledge. More facts about industry and women in industry are what we need, and less abstract feminist theorizing.

Now I hope I have raised no doubts as to my own feminism. I consider myself a good feminist, but I believe I am a practical one. And I claim a right to discuss the problems of women in industry because I am myself one of those women, and it has been my job in life to understand my fellow workers, their conditions and their problems, group by group, trade by trade, state by state, and in this country as a whole. Eighteen years in a shoe factory are a practical experience which teaches one what the woman worker is up against. Seven years as an organizer of working women add a great deal to one's understanding, and several more years of responsibility for investigating and depicting the conditions of the woman in

From the September 1925 issue of Good Housekeeping. *Reprinted with permission.*

industry to the public through a government bureau give one a keen appreciation of the interrelation of women's problems with other problems. I am convinced that we can not, and we should not, attempt a ruthless application of abstract principle to women's industrial problems. The woman problem in industry is equally a labor problem. Equal rights and equal opportunities for women workers can not be separated from the question of industrial justice for all workers. Above all things, "rights" must be interpreted for women workers as something concrete, and we must start with the world where it is today—not where it might have been had present industrial conditions existed from the beginning.

And now to a specific situation that confronts us:

In two of our great industrial states, New York and Illinois, women are working hard to secure laws which will reduce the present 9-hour and 10-hour working days of women in factories and workshops to 8 per day or 48 per week. Working women are leaders in the movement in both states, so this is not a reform instigated by "outsiders."

The question is a vital one because the shorter working day is the most essential thing in the lives of industrial workers. It means opportunities for life and self-development which are shut out by the whir of the machinery and the routine of the factory job at which the day is spent. It remains also more efficiency on the job and better service to the employer.

So it seems like a cause upon which women would be united, and it has, in fact, the support of nearly all organized women. There are, however, some women in the opposition; and because industrial questions are so widely misunderstood—because, furthermore, a difference of opinion among women always draws a disproportionate amount of attention—the opposition of this minority of women to the laws limiting hours of women workers has seriously confused some sections of the public and some legislators as to the actual issue involved.

The campaign for these 8-hour laws for women in New York and Illinois is the present stage of the movement for labor laws for women which received its great impetus some forty years ago when factory inspection first forcibly drew public attention to the widespread industrial evils which bore with peculiar severity upon women. Today all the states but one have some kind of labor law for women, and about four million women are directly affected by such laws. Indirectly, the better standards of employment thus secured influence the hours of work and the wages or salary of practically all the nearly nine million gainfully occupied women in the United States. Some of the laws are weak—permitting an 11-hour day in North Carolina, for example, and a 10-hour day in 16 states. But other states have gone far above this standard, and 9 of them have an 8-hour day or 48-hour week, while three more with a 9-hour day have a 48-hour week. Thirteen states have minimum wage laws for women, 16 have night work laws, others have laws requiring seats in stores, or otherwise lightening the conditions of employment for women. All such laws penalize employers, not the employees, for failure to conform to the standards. They are based upon the well understood fact that however fair and just the average employer, there exist always, in the absence of compulsory regulation, a laggard few who will not conform to standard and who therefore must be policed, to prevent unfair competition, with all its destructive effects. Such labor laws are to employers a code for fair play in industry. For the workers and the community as a whole, they are primarily public health provisions.

This entire body of law, however, is now under attack by certain ultra-feminists who argue that because the laws do not apply to men as well as women, they constitute a discrimination against women and a handicap to women's economic advance. It is not the provisions of the laws they are opposed to, they say, but merely the limitation to women, and to demonstrate this they propose to amend pending 8-hour bills to make them apply to "all persons." So the issue is reduced, as far as this group of opponents is concerned, to the question of what constitutes discrimination, and the further question of whether women shall have or not have something, merely because men have, or do not have it.

Advocates of the laws believe that those laws are for the most part accomplishing a very necessary purpose which is worth attaining for one group of industrial workers, even if not obtainable for the rest. Therefore, if there is discrimination, it is not women who are discriminated against *by the laws*. It is in industry itself that the discriminations occur, and the laws are equalizing in their effect, for the reason that they obtain for women certain economic rights and benefits which men already have in large measure attained. In other words, the laws for women remove a handicap; and so far as progress is concerned, it is in the states that have good laws for women workers that there exist not only the best conditions for women in industry, but the most important examples of women's advance into new fields of employment.

For my own part, I believe in the laws because, for one thing, I know the meaning *and the feeling* of industrial fatigue. I know because throughout those years of my life in the factory I worked 10 hours a day, six days a week, stitching shoes; drawing $12 in my pay envelope after that amount of toil. I know how we rejoiced in our factory when the state legislature passed an 8-hour law for women factory workers in our state. This meant that the whole working force, men as well as women, went on an 8-hour schedule, because the women did. And I remember well our disappointment when the law was taken away after being in effect just *one* day—taken away because the Supreme Court of the State declared it unconstitutional. Reasonable hours for the industrial worker mean all the difference between health, vigor, the capacity for enjoyment on the one hand, and on the other the horrors of exhaustion, physical ruin, and fear of the human scrap-heap.

I have been speaking especially of 8-hour laws because they are the most necessary kind of labor laws for women, the most important kind of regulation to have for any worker. There are other hour regulations, however, of which night work laws are a more controversial example. They prohibit the employment of women on night shifts. It may be admitted, I think—I for one will admit—that the night work laws are easily capable of misapplication, and the most judicious care should be taken in the drafting of them. Since they have in view fundamentally the health and efficiency of the worker, and night work is usually a hardship there is no question but that means of avoiding it are desirable for men and women *both*. Not equally *necessary* for men and women, however, because men and women do not occupy the same positions in the other half of their lives—their domestic relations. Hence neither the individual nor social cost of night work for men is so high as for women.

A woman at work in a factory, or anywhere outside her home, does not give up her household tasks. If she is married she has literally two full-time jobs when she works in the factory, for she does not earn enough to permit her to employ a servant or a housekeeper. A man does his day's work in the factory, and his job is over for the day. His wife or his sister comes home from the factory and gets his dinner and looks after the children, gets up in the morning, gets breakfast, does the housework, and goes out for another day at the factory. She does this unless she works *at night* in the factory. Then she does her housework during the day—and gets her sleep when she can.

There are, according to the Census, 2,000,000 married women in the United States gainfully occupied. Great numbers of them, mothers of little children, lead some such abnormal life as described above. The night-work laws do not solve their problem, we know. But they do lead to adjustments in industry whereby women get the day shifts, and they do serve, we believe, the greatest good for the greatest number. They can, in all cases, undoubtedly be drawn with exemptions to obviate especial hardships.

Such is the teaching of experience as I see it with reference to night work laws. They should not be abolished, but further studied and perfected. The Women's Bureau is engaged in such studies now.

Then there are that other important group of laws—minimum wage laws. These are based upon the principle that an industry should pay its own way, without subsidy from the workers in the form of unpaid-for service. A wage less than enough to support the individual requires a contribution from some source to make up the cost of living, and if the employer does not pay a living wage the worker's family or the community pays the deficit—unless the worker goes under-nourished and under-cared-for. So the minimum wage law provides that employers in designated industries shall pay *at least* a living wage to any woman they employ, and usually a commission is created to determine, upon the basis of ascertained facts, what is the minimum necessary to keep the worker in health and reasonable comfort. These commissions consist of representatives of employers, employees, and the public, and they base their findings on the cost of living.

All these kinds of regulatory laws have been obtainable for women because women's special needs were more evident to the public than were the needs of other workers, and there was a widespread appreciation of the importance of conserving the health of the actual and potential mothers of future generations. A similar demand for laws for men did not exist for several reasons. Chief of these was and is the fact that men in general work under much better conditions than women; where they work at night they can sleep in the day, and there are in any event no such double demands upon their energies as upon the wage-earning wife and mother; and, though men's wages are too often very low, they are never, I think we can safely say, as low as women's. The ditch-digger, the coal-heaver—any of the very least skilled of men—draw a better wage than do thousands of skilled and semi-skilled women. Porters and messengers in factories I know of are paid more than women who manufacture the products the men cart around on trucks.

It is facts like these that make foolish the feminist claim that minimum wage laws, for instance, work discrimination by causing women to lose their jobs to men. Women's jobs in general are poorer jobs than any man could be induced to take. Men, by the self-action of tradition if for no other reason, can always command more pay and usually better hours than women. Why feminists ignore this fact I never could understand.

Let me say at this point, however, that there is one type of law affecting women which I do not at all defend. That is the prohibitory law which says that women shall not be employed in specified occupations. Such laws are in fact discriminatory, I agree, and should be repealed. Most of them are not of serious practical importance, however, for not many women's ambitions or progress are inhibited by forbidding them to climb telegraph poles, shine shoes, read gas meters, or work in mines—which are the chief kinds of prohibitions, and which, except mining, occur in only a state or two. These laws seem to be a relic of by-gone prudery rather than anything else. The prohibition against taxi-drivers, which exists in Ohio, is probably the most important in its effect, for women chauffeurs in Colorado, for example, have established businesses which illustrate the opportunity Ohio women might very well want to utilize.

The hour laws and minimum wage laws are regulatory laws, fixing standards of employment. That is quite a different matter from prohibiting employment itself.

But, our theoretical feminists say, "we stand on the *principle* that there should be no laws whatever that do not apply to men as well as to women." That theory is good as a theory. If we could make a fresh start with the universe, laying out the whole program from the viewpoint of today, we might agree to have a rigid application of that abstract principle. But certain things have been going on in the world for a considerable time, and industry, as well as human minds, has got "set" in certain ways. Facing facts as we find them, a practical difficulty confronts us which is this:

Conditions of life and of industry are such that while women today are working 9 hours or 10 hours or 11 hours a day in the absence of the 8-hour law, men are at this same moment, in many industries, enjoying their 8-hour day. In other words it is not the 8-hour law, but the *absence* of the 8-hour law for women, that constitutes a discrimination against them as we see it.

Similarly, women's wages are very much lower than men's—will probably average little more than half as much. Minimum wage laws bring up the lowest wages at least within striking distance of an equality with men. Instead of being discriminatory against women, the minimum wage laws lessen the discrimination that already exists.

What the feminist objection to the labor laws for women is really based on is this: The labor laws for women put women on a different *legal* basis from men so far as their jobs are concerned, and to the ultra-feminist *legal* equality means almost everything. The worker prefers *industrial* equality, which is in this case actually *defeated* by *legal* equality. Labor laws limit the worker's technical freedom of contract, yes—and the employer's as well. A labor law limiting the woman worker's technical freedom of contract seems to the feminist discriminatory because she does not know or does not realize how meaningless to the wage worker is the thing called "freedom of contract." A man or woman dependent upon earnings has no real freedom of contract beyond the purchasing power of those earnings. Wage workers must have jobs in order to live, and their freedom to choose a job is determined by the amount of money they possess to buy their meals and pay their rent while they are looking for the better chance. Men think so little of their *legal* freedom of contract in its technical sense that they voluntarily surrender it by joining trade unions. That is the essential principle of a trade union—the collective bargain as a substitute for individual freedom of contract. An 8-hour law, though it takes away the worker's freedom to contract for more than 8 hours of work per day, gives in exchange the economic freedom that the additional leisure brings, with its additional possibilities of health and recreation and self development. It is a substitute for the voluntary limitation through the trade union, thus a sort of collective bargain made through the machinery of the state.

It is a historical fact, however, that working men have always preferred to get their 8-hour day by making their own agreements with their employers through their trade unions and thereby avoiding the machinery of the state. Generally speaking, the organized labor movement is so opposed to having men's wages and hours fixed by law, that any attempt to write the word "persons" into labor laws proposed for women would align the trade union men against that law, insuring its defeat. So there is one fact to face.

Working women, however, are most inadequately organized in all of the great women-employing industries but one. That is another fact to face. These women, then, whose problems are acute and vital, can either use their new tool, the ballot, and with the cooperation of other voters, women and men, seek laws to insure proper working conditions, or they can wait for their 8-hour day until they are themselves sufficiently organized to bargain for it with their employers. Or they can go on working 9 or 10 or 11 hours a day. An 8-hour law, or any other law, comes in recognition of a public demand. All women, and all men, by their votes may help to secure legislation. But if the working woman is to depend upon collective bargaining alone, she must go upon her own and do without help from other women or other men except her fellow-workers. The collective bargain is made between employer and employees.

Now our theoretical feminists are very strong, theoretically, for organization of women workers into trade unions. They are equally inexperienced in organization problems. "Let women do what men have done," they say, adding in effect, with delightful inconsistency: "We who are not ourselves industrial workers, demand in the name of equality that you women who work in factories and shops shall use men's methods of solving your problems. You must get your 8-hour day by the same method men prefer, whether you find that method best or most suitable for you or not. Otherwise we will prevent your getting it at all. Although the laws you want do not apply to us, it is against our *principles* to let you have them unless you conform to men's ways or else convert the entire labor movement to the support of the same kinds of laws for all sections of labor." With which dictum they proceed to the legislature and declare it to be against women's interest to have any law applying to women that does not also apply to men.

I agree that it is above all things desirable for working women to organize, and I have testified to my belief in trade unionism by working for years as an organizer for the National Women's Trade Union League and the American Federation of Labor. Slowly the working women are realizing the importance of collective action for themselves, and there has been a 20 percent increase of women in trade unions in the past ten years, according to some estimates. But there are still millions of women outside the trade unions, and those millions whose hours are disastrously long and whose wages are less than enough to live on are dragging constantly at the standards of the women better situated, and actually impeding organization as well as better standards. It is not always recognized that the farther down the worker is in the economic scale, the harder it is to organize—yet this is proved by the lack of organization among the lowest paid *men* workers all over the world. It is the dreadful vicious circle—the groups at the bottom can not improve their conditions because they are not organized, and they can not organize because their poverty is so great they dare not risk the loss of the miserable jobs they have. For be it remembered that the right to organize is not conceded by employers of the kind who are willing to exploit working people—on the contrary, it is too often bitterly fought....

Meantime, our feminist opponents do not fail, of course, to offer testimony which they claim proves the discriminatory effect of the labor laws for women. They say, for one thing, that businesses and professions do not observe the 8-hour day, and if there is an 8-hour law for women, men will get the salaried positions that would otherwise be open to women. It is impossible for this to be true, for the reason that 8-hour laws for women almost never have applied, and they never need be made to apply, to businesses and professions, or to executive positions.

Some of the strongest advocates of labor laws for women are business and professional women. But of those who oppose, it seems both reasonable and fair to ask that they leave it to the industrial worker to say what she needs for herself. Surely there is ample room for each group to work out its own standards and methods, and to cooperate to their respective ends and purposes, without conflict.

The industrial workers' problems are the collective problems of a great mass of women doing similar or identical work, largely routine. There is not room for more than a few of these women to become forewomen or managers, and the rest of them must remain in the ranks all their working days. Their jobs are usually dull, monotonous toil, not stimulating to mind or body, and lacking almost entirely the creative interest that goes with the job of the business or professional woman. The only compensation for a life of this kind is a work-day sufficiently short to permit relaxation and self-development.

The business or professional woman has an individualized job, which naturally develops in her an individualistic viewpoint. Neither the collective bargain nor the collective principle represented in the labor laws so readily occurs to her for the solution of her own problems. The consequence is that she sometimes attempts to impose her own individualism upon the women in industry, upon whom it inflicts a serious hardship. . . .

Another striking piece of evidence showing that the claims of opponents are not borne out upon investigation is furnished by comparison of numbers of women employed in states which have and states which have not legal regulations for the employment of women. California and Indiana were selected for this survey, which was made by the Women's Bureau, because they have approximately equal population and a similar number and kind of industries employing women. California has an 8-hour law for women and also a minimum wage law which has fixed the highest minimum wages now in effect in the United States; which is to say, has from the legal standpoint imposed the greatest restrictions upon the "freedom of contract" of women workers and their employers. Indiana has no law of either kind.

The survey showed that more women are employed in California with its regulatory laws, than in Indiana with no regulations at all, and that the numbers in California have increased since the laws were enacted.

The Women's Bureau made a study also of the claims that street railway companies could not continue to employ women if women's hours were limited by law and men's hours were not, or if women were prohibited from working at night. In the city of Chicago it was found that the street railway companies had entered into a voluntary agreement with the trade unions not to employ women at night, and to establish an 8-hour day. This agreement was forced by the women ticket sellers—who stipulated in addition that men be barred from selling tickets on the Chicago elevated lines between the hours of 7 A.M. and 3 P.M. and in allotted stations only between 3 PM. and 11 P.M. No women were dismissed as a result of this arrangement. They kept their jobs and the hour schedules for all employees were adjusted, women working only the day shifts. . . .

What usually happens when laws restricting hours of employment are passed, and what almost always can happen, is the adjustment of industry to meet the law. This is what intelligent and fair-minded employers are glad to do, and a law which brings their competitors in line makes it feasible for them to do it. Women have proved their value to industry, and there is not the remotest probability of their being ejected from it. On the contrary, their numbers are increasing constantly, and when a law is made regulating their employment, it serves to bring the whole industry up to the standard required for the women working in it.

The whole question, it seems to me, comes down to this: Shall we let women continue working longer hours than men, for less pay than men, and continue doing two jobs to their husbands' one? And is that sort of thing to continue in the name of some principle of equality? Or shall we agree that the reality of better conditions of employment is more important, both to health and to industrial equality, than is a cherished theory?

Women who are wage-earners with one job in the factory and another in the home have little time and energy left to carry on the fight to better their economic status. They need the help of other women, and they need labor laws. Such laws are a safeguard not only to women but also to the children. They give protection to the family and maintain more satisfactory standards of living. In short, they help to make the country a better place for its citizens.

75
Margaret Mead
Sex and Achievement (1935)

In the long contentions which have waged for the last three generations over the breakfast tables of two continents, as to the relative innate capacity of the two sexes to achieve, the final brick which permitted the man to retire victo-

From *The Forum,* November 1935.

rious behind the one newspaper and left the woman drumming her fingers disconcertedly was his scornful "Even the best *cooks* are men!"—sometimes varied to "Even the best *dressmakers* are men!"

As long as the argument had ranged through the arts and sciences, the advocate of feminine abilities had had an easier task. "Women haven't been in the arts long enough," she would answer, hoping that he would refrain from bringing up that point about how excellent women were in the *interpretative* arts, although they had been allowed to practice them little longer. But when it came to cooking and dressmaking, those activities which she and her critical husband felt to be exclusively feminine (not realizing that there are peoples among whom the husband proudly weaves his wife's wedding clothes and people by whom women are regarded as too profane to approach the important mysteries of cooking), here was a dilemma. Her sulkiness, her scattered, unorganized denials, her scurrying hither and thither for cover proclaimed that, in her mind as well as in his, her battle was lost. Gifted women there might be, but, as long as men could better women in women's own fields, there must be something in the argument that men are superior to women, not only in strength, in endurance, in freedom from the periodic and time-consuming onus of their reproductivity but in innate capacity to achieve.

And then one day, disconsolately murmuring over the old indictment, she unconsciously paraphrased it, "Even the best *chefs* are men," and sat bolt upright in excitement. There was the answer! It was not as cooks but as *public* cooks, professional cooks, cooks in charge of large kitchens with armies of assistants, cooks who worked in great public houses, that men excelled. This was true also of the dressmakers and milliners. It was as heads of the great establishments on the Rue de la Paix that the men excelled the women. The best chefs, the best *couturiers!* All this meant was that women had failed, here as elsewhere, in invading man's field, not that men had outdistanced women

even in their own field of private life, private cooking and private dressmaking. Women simply had not done better than men in the great hotel kitchen and the great competitive dressmaking field.

Her mind paused over the word "compete." Was this another clue? Why must women not compete with men, and what was the penalty for doing so?

The answer was simple. To compete with men in their own field was unwomanly, just as, (come to think of it) to abstain from competing with men in their own field of public and money-making achievement was, for a man, unmanly. The competitive fields, in which one individual was pitted against another in terms of public success—these belonged to men.

This was so—although she did not know it—among all the peoples of the world. One could find peoples among whom men wove or made bark cloth or cooked or played with babies; among whom women built the houses or climbed the tallest coconut palms or did all the fishing. One could find peoples of whom an outsider would say that the work of the women, in basketry or pottery or textiles, was the only enduring and beautiful thing, peoples among whom an outside would pass over as negligible the exclusively male activities, of rabbit hunting or crocheting tiny costumes for doll-like idols. It did not matter; within that society it was the men's occupations which were regarded, by both men and women, as dignified and important, as achievement. To succeed in those fields, defined as masculine, whether it were bear hunting or painting with colors, made a male a man and a female less of a woman.

SEX MEMBERSHIP

The human child, born into a world which regards sex as the most important difference between human beings, wants very much to belong to its own sex, for only so can he or she attain full membership in the human race. A person without full sex membership is worse off than a man without a country.

Nor do human societies believe that mere possession of the appropriate anatomy is enough to ensure membership in the right sex. If this were so, we would not find so much anxiety, so many rituals—cutting the girl's umbilical cord on her yam masher, cutting the boy's on a war club, or sealing the boy's cord up in a pot to ensure him a harsh, deep voice. There is always the chance that the girl may not take to her feminine role, that the boy may not show the hardy, virile character which will proclaim him a man. And the fear of each generation of parents, expressed in ritual, in costume, in admonitions, infects the child with fear: "If I play with dolls, I won't be a man." "If I want to shoot with a gun, I won't be a woman." Fear of being disenfranchised stands at the elbow of every growing boy and girl.

As the boy grows older, he learns that it is not so much playing with dolls which he must avoid as playing baseball and football which he must cultivate. No one will commend him and pronounce him a *real boy* for the things which he abstains from doing. They watch anxiously for signs of positive achievement in the fields of decreed masculine activity. He can neglect the avoidances which were necessary when he was smaller and still longed to play with dolls and hide behind his mother's skirts just in proportion to the skill and enthusiasm with which he wields a baseball bat.

In most historical discussions of sex differences it has been assumed that the little girl learned the same kind of lesson, that she learned that, if she directed enough attention toward dolls, toward daintiness, toward feminine shrinking and fluttering, she too would be safe.

But this is only half the story, and it is the other half which is the more significant. For the boy, as he grows older, the emphasis upon avoiding feminine occupations grows less, until, as the proud captain of the winning eleven he can even hold a baby in his arms and so proclaim his masculinity. For the girl the exact opposite occurs. Her main task is not to achieve in the feminine field but to *avoid achieving* in the masculine. While the boy is merely required to document his masculinity, the girl is required to prove both that she *is* feminine, and that she is *not* masculine, that she will not try to achieve success in any masculine field.

A typical example is the Eskimo woman, forced in her husband's absence to build a snowhouse to shelter her family from a sudden storm. She can build a snowhouse, but it is unwomanly to do so. Afraid that her skill will be held against her, she chatters disarmingly as she works and, when her husband returns and asks who has built the house, she answers: "Just an attempt of a simple woman to put a few blocks together." With such cautious phrases has her formal, many-thousand-years' old culture equipped her to protect her femininity in the moment of achievement.

So the boy is taught to achieve, the girl to prove that she doesn't achieve, will never achieve. The same threat hangs over the unachieving boy and the achieving girl, the threat that he or she will never be chosen by a member of the opposite sex.

But for the small boy the opprobrium of being called a sissy comes early and is usually over; for the girl, the kindness with which the little tomboy is received by boys who have not yet learned to distrust achievement in a girl is a poor preparation for what will come later. For, if she is to be a loved object, the kind of girl whom men will woo and boast of, toast and marry, she must learn to prove that she is a nonachieving human being.

THE DANGER OF SUCCESS

This need to document a lack of achievement is increasing as the special economic role of women within the home decreases with the progress of invention. In the past, while she flutteringly denied any desire to enter a man's field, she could occupy her energies in the domestic field, where she was still permitted positive, solid achievement. But today a man no longer asks that his wife bake bread or hem his shirts; he does ask that she be feminine, which means that, if she does work, out in the world, it must be work which is of a subordinate, routine, badly paid, "feminine" type. The majority of men do not wish to boast that their girls carry motorcycle nuts in their pockets or have ten men under them in the office.

The exceptions, the husbands of successful female innkeepers or female camp directors, serve only to point the moral harder. For who, asks the growing girl, searching anxiously for clues to success in love, wants to be loved by men who have taken their own role so faintheartedly that they are glad to have their wives better them in their own fields?

We may now look again at the field of the interpretative arts, of dancing, acting, singing, in which women have achieved such notable success, fully on a par with men, that their achievement in these fields has even been used to redocument their peculiar feminine incapacities. And we find that here is a field in which the gifted girl can achieve, can attain an outstanding success, and remain an object of love.

Is it not then self-evident? In those fields in which women have succeeded equally with men, it is because they have been able to attain success without denying their human heritage, their right to the love of a member of the opposite sex, to marriage and to children. Every woman who enters a field where this is not so, where in proportion as she is successful she will be voted unwomanly and so remain unwooed, works under a handicap, a handicap of paralyzing fear.

The remarkable matter is not that there have been so few successful women in masculine fields but that there have been as many as there have been, that so many women have been gifted enough to carry this double load. For a woman to succeed in a field defined as male, she must not only compete with men in a difficult and exacting occupation but work under the knowledge that with every success she gains, as a lawyer or a businesswoman, she loses, as a woman, her chance for the kind of love she wants. With every step which a man takes towards success, he also takes a step towards personal happiness: he proclaims himself the more a man, the more desirable as a lover and husband. He steps forward as an achieving individual and forward as a human being. But, for each step which the woman takes in one capacity, she must take a step back in the other. Either she proclaims herself a woman and therefore less an achieving individual or an achieving individual and therefore less a woman.

"My husband is a famous chef. He works at the Ritz." Many a woman would be delighted to make this boast, but who among her brothers would answer with equal pride, "My wife is the chef at the Waldorf"?

Until this dilemma, this identification of achievement and masculinity, is resolved, the world will be able to use only half of its gifted, and always the best chefs will be men.

76
The Women's Charter (1937)

Late in December, the newspapers carried stories about the Women's Charter, and since representatives of the American Home Economics Association were listed among the members of the committee that had drawn it up, the JOURNAL here takes its first opportunity to print the text of the charter and its preamble and to indicate briefly its significance to home economics. The text as sent on December 21 to interested organizations for preliminary study was entitled: "Proposal for a Women's Charter, embodying objectives for legislation in all countries (Proposal drafted by a temporary Joint Conference Group of Women in the United States)." It reads:

PREAMBLE

This Charter is a general statement of the social and economic objectives of women, for women and for society as a whole, insofar as

From *Journal of Home Economics,* March 1937. Reprinted with permission of the American Association of Family and Consumer Sciences.

these can be embodied in legislation and governmental administration. It is put forward in order that there may be an agreed formulation of the purposes to which a large number of women's organizations throughout the world already are committed. It is recognized that some of the present specific needs which it seeks to remedy should disappear as society develops the assurance of a more complete life for every person and some of its objectives would establish conditions which should be attainable for all persons, so that in promoting them for women it is hoped thereby to bring nearer the time of their establishment for all.

WOMEN'S CHARTER

Women shall have full political and civil rights; full opportunity for education; full opportunity for employment according to their individual abilities, with safeguards against physically harmful conditions of employment and economic exploitation; they shall receive compensation, without discrimination because of sex. They shall be assured security of livelihood, including the safeguarding of motherhood. The provisions necessary for the establishment of these standards shall be guaranteed by government, which shall insure also the rights of united action toward the attainment of these aims.

Where special exploitation of women workers exists, such as low wages which provide less than the living standards attainable, unhealthful working conditions, or long hours of work which result in physical exhaustion and denial of the right to leisure, such condition shall be corrected through social and labor legislation, which the world's experience shows to be necessary.

The day after it had appeared in certain papers, the secretary of the Joint Conference Group issued a statement which included these paragraphs:

"The charter has been drawn by a group of 24 women active in various organizations of a civic and educational type. It is now being submitted to these organizations and to others, for study and eventual action in a national delegates' conference to be called in the late spring. This will be preparatory to a similar international delegates' conference, expected to be called in Europe in the summer, to formulate a report and recommendations to the League of Nations and the International Labor Organization. The reason for this action, as explained in the letter of transmittal to the organizations involved, is that a proposed resolution for a treaty ensuring equal rights for women was on the agenda of the Assembly of the League of Nations in 1935, and those aspects related to the sphere of the International Labor Organization were referred to that body for study and report." . . .

Since that statement was issued, the national and international conferences have been postponed, but a resolution is being drafted for submission to the International Labour Organization in June. Also, the Women's Charter Group has formulated a provisional organization with an executive committee representative of various vocational groups as follows: women in industry; agriculture; domestic and personal service; professions, business, and other occupations; household management, including the economic status of housewives and general consumer interests; and social and civic organizations. In addition to representation of occupational interests, advisory committees will be appointed as members of the executive committee including legislation, research, publicity and education, and international cooperation.

The American Home Economics Association accepted the invitation to send representatives to the Joint Conference Group because it has for years been interested in legislation to prevent the exploitation of women in industry. As most JOURNAL readers probably realize, there are two schools of thought on this subject. According to the more aggressively feministic, any legislation which sets up special conditions of employment for women places them at a disadvantage in competition with men, and this disadvantage is considered far more serious than any special dangers to women that arise from the conditions of labor and employment that apply to men. The other side holds that the biological nature and functions of women place them at a disadvantage in industry, with serious dangers not only to themselves but also to their children, and that both for their sake and its own sake society must prevent obviously dangerous and unjust exploitation. Of course, these two sentences indicate only the most essential points in the two theories, but they are perhaps enough to recall why most home economists, with their concern for the welfare of children and families, are in favor of protective legislation under our present social and industrial conditions. They are confirmed in this stand by the fact that it is the one taken by organizations of wage-earning women in this country—the women most closely concerned. It is, therefore, natural that for many years the legislative program of the American Home Economics Association should have included opposition to the so-called Equal Rights Amendment.

The executive committee of the American Home Economics Association has approved of the charter in principle, and copies have been sent to affiliated associations for study and possible action.

77
Edith Houghton Hooker
Beware of "Women's Charter" (1937)

Decisive action should be taken at once by national and international Feminist organizations to expose the disingenuous nature of the so-called "Woman's Charter." This document purports to be a sort of Magna Charta for women, but in reality is precisely the opposite.

The "Charter" is obviously designed, first, to pave the way, in the United States, for "protective" labor legislation for women only; and,

From *Equal Rights,* January 15, 1937.

second, to serve as an instrument to defeat the Equal Rights Treaty in both hemispheres. While the good intentions of the framers of the "Women's Charter" may not be questioned, their mode of procedure is, to say the least, dubious. Not one word appears in the entire document specifically indicating that the purpose of the "Charter" is to shackle women permanently with special sex-linked labor laws; yet any informed and discriminating person must realize that such is its objective. Because of this devious approach Feminists should immediately inform all organizations of women that they can reach, of the true object of the "Charter." It would be nothing short of a calamity to have organizations that oppose "protective" legislation for women only, endorse the Charter simply because they did not understand its significance. Experienced Feminists will, of course, immediately recognize the hooks beneath the bait, but inexperienced Feminists may easily be taken in by the Charter's tempting and ambiguous phraseology. "Full political and civil rights," "full opportunity for education," "full opportunity for employment" and "compensation without discrimination because of sex," sounds like the millennium, but then comes the joker: "Where special exploitation of *women* exists * * * conditions shall be corrected through labor legislation, *which the world's experience shows to be necessary!*"

It would, perhaps, not be polite to laugh, so we cough, discreetly, behind our hand. In the opinion of the framers of the "Charter" the "world's experience" shows "protective" labor legislation for women only, to be necessary. They do not exactly wish to say so, in plain words, for they fear that large numbers of working women are so deluded as to prefer Equal Rights to "protection," and they do not wish to arouse opposition to the "Charter."

The "primer" prepared by a sub-committee of the Joint Conference Group in the United States for the Women's Charter, says: "Women recognize, however, that *equality is not enough,* and that higher standards of living and greater security are attainable for all. The

Women's Charter, therefore, is intended to formulate in this inclusive sense 'the social and economic objectives of women, *for women and for society* as a whole,' as the preamble to the Charter states, adding that 'in promoting them for women it is hoped hereby to bring nearer the time of their establishment for all.'"

Equality is not enough, forsooth! Even when a "woman's wage" is only half that of a man's for the same work. The "world's experience" has never included Equal Rights so how can the framers of the Charter know that "equality is not enough"? In any event it is all that Feminists ask and, according to informed labor women, is precisely what is needed to insure "full opportunity for employment" and equal pay for equal work.

The difficulty is that the framers of the "Charter" are still imbued with the idea that women must be stepping stones for men and that the sob attached to motherhood is the only means available to circumvent the Constitution.

All practical working women, both in the professions and in industry, know that their most serious handicap in earning a decent living, and getting on up in the world, is their sex. Sex is the root of all evil, so far as opportunities and pay for women are concerned. If women could once get their employers and competitors to forget their sex, they might, on a basis of ability, win equal rewards with men. But this the "protectionists" will not permit. Sex, like a sore thumb, protrudes from all their plans. It protrudes from the "Charter" and makes the demand for "compensation without discrimination because of sex," an anomaly. Who will pay a semi-invalid the wages of an able-bodied person? No one, who can stay in business. Who will give wards of the State full political and civil rights, and all the rest of it? No one, in his senses. The question, is Are women the biological equals of men? The "Charter" indicates the negative, on a basis of the "world's experience." Having already successfully challenged the same experience in connection with the "female mind," we accept the challenge anent the female body. Womanhood is not tantamount to a disease; a woman can work as well as a man and equally assiduously. All that a woman needs in order to compete successfully with men for distinctions and compensation is Equal Rights. More than that no self-respecting woman, or man, would accept, and if either one reached for it she or he would be quickly disillusioned.

The "Charter" is false for it pretends to espouse equality and then denies it. The many organizations that oppose "protective" legislation for woman only should speedily join hands to oppose the "Woman's Charter," and should be prepared to defeat the well-meant but archaic designs of its framers. Those who dare to state that "equality is not enough" either disbelieve in the Constitution or disbelieve in women. In either case they are dangerous. Those who have framed the "Women's Charter," unwittingly, we trust, are "framing" women.

78
Alma Lutz, Frieda S. Miller, Ollie A. Randall, and Margaret Culkin Banning

How Can We Raise Women's Status? A Symposium (1938)

EQUAL RIGHTS WILL DO IT

Women's status can best be raised in the United States by giving women the same rights as men under the Constitution. The Constitution was written in the spirit of and under the influence of English Common Law, which regarded women as *femme covert,* or under the control and protection of her lord and master, and it is still interpreted in that light. The rights of a "person" guaranteed under the Constitution are the rights of men—not of men and women. The Supreme Court has repeatedly re-

From *Independent Woman,* September 1938.

fused to apply to women the guarantees of liberty which protect men. In fact, the right to vote, conferred upon women by the Nineteenth Amendment, is the one fundamental right under the Constitution which women now have in common with men.

Through the action of State Legislatures, women have gained rights which raise them legally in many instances above the status defined for them by English Common Law. But they are at the mercy of changing State Legislatures and must continually watch that their hard-won rights are not taken away from them. There is no safeguard for them in the Federal Constitution.

The remedy for this medieval state of affairs is an Amendment to the Constitution which would make applicable to women all the guarantees of liberty which were conferred upon men as a matter of course. Such a measure, the Equal Rights Amendment, is now before Congress and should have the support of every thinking woman. It reads, "Men and women shall have equal rights throughout the United States and every place subject to its jurisdiction."

Some women oppose the Amendment method of raising women's status on the grounds that it will deprive them of privileges which they now enjoy and of the alleged benefits of special labor legislation, which they believe raises women's status to that of men in the labor market. Privileges assigned to women by law and otherwise are questionable things. Only those who wish to be duped or whose judgment is poor would willingly substitute a privilege for a right. Labor legislation for women only is an artificial method of dealing with labor evils which affect women. Never a remedy and at best merely a palliative, it has the most damaging influence on the status of women. Not only does it lower their status in the eyes of employers, who under this system can never be expected to give them equal pay for equal work, but it lowers their status in the opinion of male competitors, and fastens deeper and deeper in their own minds a feeling of inferiority and inadequacy.

You will all agree that in spite of the education and enlightenment of the past century, tradition still keeps women down. Some of you will say, "Change tradition and then such measures as the Equal Rights Amendment will come as a matter of course." I say that the recognition of women's legal rights as full-fledged human beings will do more to change tradition and raise their status than any other one thing.

I am not at all troubled about tradition as it affects men's attitude toward women because this can be changed when women are ready to change it. But I am concerned about tradition as it affects women's minds and muddles their thinking. A great deal of educational work must be done among women to clear out of their minds the shadows of the past. Work for the Equal Rights Amendment is a practical means of arousing them out of their apathy. It will make them think through for themselves the question of their status. It will make them weigh so-called privileges with rights. It will teach them not to be afraid of the word equality, that equality does not mean identity but equal opportunity.

When our forefathers drew up those inalienable rights which we refer to with pride in the Declaration of Independence, they declared that all men were created free and equal. We do not quibble over this, saying that Mr. Jones cannot possibly be equal to Mr. Brown. We accept that statement as a principle and our Constitution expresses that principle as regards men. Let us now put that principle into action as regards women. We can do this with the Equal Rights Amendment.

The Equal Rights Amendment and an improved mental attitude on the part of women, which go hand in hand, are the best and only means of effectively and permanently raising women's status.

ALMA LUTZ

COOPERATION MEANS POWER

Improvement in the economic status of working women has gone hand in hand with the organized efforts of women themselves to better their conditions of work, to gain higher wages, and to achieve greater equality of economic opportunity.

Women entered the industrial world under a great handicap. They came as "cheap and docile labor," seeking employment in factories, stores and offices in increasing numbers as the doors of industry were opened to them, and the old system of family production and home economy gave way to the mass production of goods in factories. As a group, their work remained what it always had been, to assist in the production of food, clothing, and other necessary goods and services. As an individual, however, the industrial woman found a greatly changed mode of work awaiting her in factories. Instead of the variety of tasks which characterized household production, she found she was to spend her day at one small process—seaming up shirts, stapling the corners of paper boxes, packing crackers, shaking out sheets in a laundry, pressing the lever of a punching machine. Instead of determining to a large extent the order of her tasks and the conditions of her work, she found herself an insignificant part of a system controlled by others. If her hours were excessive, her work exhausting, her pay unreasonable, her working conditions all but unbearable, she was helpless as an individual to change them. Not only was she competing for the job against thousands of other women working under the same conditions, but as she was so often reminded, there were countless other women ready and eager to take her job if she was not "satisfied." As an individual she was, and is today, industrially helpless.

It was not until industrial women began to realize the futility of individual action and to group themselves together for "collective bargaining" that they were able to exercise some control over their conditions of work and to improve their economic status. The achievements of the trade unions in the clothing industries afford a striking example of what group action has done to transform an industry once notorious for its sweat shops and exploitation to one in which thousands of workers are today protected by union agreements, and have gained for themselves equal pay for equal work, standardization of hours, unemployment insurance systems, cooperative housing, health services, and educational activities.

There are, of course, other forms of group action besides trade union activity to which industrial women have turned. Their pioneers in trade union organizations of women soon discovered that women were more difficult to organize than men, and even today, only a small proportion of working women are members of unions. Many large women-employing industries are almost wholly unorganized. Even where strong unions exist their members have found that low labor standards for unorganized workers in the industry are a drag on the standards the unions are trying to achieve for their members. There has been good reason, then, not wholly altruistic, for the support which women trade unionists have given to labor legislation providing minimum standards for all women workers.

The increasing number of appeals which have come to the Department of Labor from working women in recent years indicates the extent to which individual workers recognize the need for legal standards and turn to the government for aid. "It's no use for us to complain to the boss—isn't there a law to help us?" In many cases there is, and that body of labor laws in New York State, and in other progressive industrial states, represents the results of years of effort on the part of industrial women and other interested groups to improve the status of working women and hence to bring them a little nearer to economic equality with men.

FRIEDA S. MILLER

BETTER YOUR PERFORMANCE

In the solemn biblical phrase about being "judged every man according to his works" is implicit the most important facet of this perplexing problem, how shall we improve the status of women in what is admittedly still man's domain—the business and professional world. In that world, woman now has a status of sorts, although for two reasons it has not yet been validated as has her legal status as a person and her status as a citizen. First, all women *as women* have never been thoroughly convinced of the serious necessity for their genuinely loyal support, not only of those women who enter the business world, but of the idea that they belong there. Secondly, the so-called "gainfully employed women" have themselves been slow to recognize that their status will be definitely validated only when they have demonstrated their right to that status, because each has prepared herself to be judged according to her "works."

There remains even today an element of opportunism in the way in which many women find their place in business, and by just so much as opportunism is reduced, by just so much will that place be more firmly established as their own. With the increasing complexity and competition for all working persons, actual performance becomes the criterion by which the worker is finally judged, rather than by that of sex or marital status. Excellence of performance is predicated on fitness for the work and ability, combined with the best training possible.

Selection of work for which one is best suited is still difficult, but great strides have been made in developing the vocational knowledge and facilities essential to improved performance. Vocational work for adults is, however, in its infancy, and the need for it is a crying one. Nevertheless it can only become a real force as women accept fully the fact that they cannot justify their place in the business world merely by reason of sentiment or of their need of it. They must be convinced that qualifications including fitness for the work they are planning to do *must be met*.

As for training, the best is never too good. As yet many of the best training resources for work which women are attempting have not been made available to them. And women must realize that until this situation is changed, they are struggling in many fields under a handicap greater than sex discrimination alone can possibly constitute. Even though the preliminary training be sound, women in all kinds of work may well take a leaf from the book of teachers and nurses, who all along the road are constantly taking additional training which keeps them *au courant* with what is latest and best in their professions. Thousands of employment records studied during the years 1930–34 in New York City bore out overwhelmingly the desirability of "training on the job" as a factor contributing to continued employability. If all employed women were sufficiently aware that employability is something which can and should be constantly vitalized, the level or performance would inevitably be raised and women would find themselves firmly entrenched by the soundest method possible.

An individual woman can often improve her own particular status by her own initiative; there is literally nothing women as a group cannot accomplish if they will really work together for it. And legislative action will tend to stabilize much that otherwise might be lost to them. But how futile all these individual and group efforts, and how impermanent the achievements, unless women, once their status is established by any method, prove themselves capable of maintaining that status because they are fitted for it and because they can always be "judged," in the last analysis, "according to their works."

OLLIE A. RANDALL

INDIVIDUAL INITIATIVE HELPS

There are many women in business, industry and the professions who need to be told what to do. Others prefer to work under direction. There are some—not nearly enough of these—who tell themselves what to do and when to do it, who head up their own jobs.

One of the big problems before women today is to increase the number in this last group. This is not for the sake of numbers nor even of balance, but because, if it can be done, the effectiveness of the working world will be increased and new capabilities will be released and proven in many women.

Individual initiative may result in running a candy kitchen or a stenographic bureau or writing the great American novel or in practicing law. It means, very alluringly, all the things that women have not yet tried to do. It means finding out the one thing which you can do better than most other people and in some way putting that ability on the market. It is not a vanity to be your own master. But it does take a certain kind of temperament. No one should try it who can not face strain and worry and responsibility.

Successful private enterprise, whether it is writing or anything else, can not be built up by occasional or sporadic work, or by depending on mood, on inspiration or on luck. If any kind of work demands plan and discipline, and then more plan and discipline, it is work which one carries on without outside direction.

In my opinion there is nothing harder than being your own master. I always feel that the worst traits of the employer come out in you when you run your own job, particularly if you are your own employee. You are a slave driver toward yourself. You feel that you should work harder than is reasonable. You do.

A writer like myself is continually meeting people who believe that because my work has very little overhead and because I can choose my own working hours and place of work that it is an idyllic employment. Furthermore, people say enviously, you can choose your subjects, determine your own product.

None of that is true. The writer who does not set himself sterner hours than any labor organization would tolerate is not likely to succeed. Furthermore, a writer does piece work, on which industry quite properly frowns. Finally, no author is free to write what and how he pleases if he expects a market. I do not mean that a good writer seeks slavishly to please his public and is always apple polishing. But a writer must be able to divine, sometimes against all precedent, what the public will be interested in. He must awake new interest. His work is nearly always produced on a gamble; the risks are great and the competition terrific.

That holds for all occupations which are carried on by individual initiative. A woman may employ others. She may have a big overhead. Each kind of individual job makes its own pattern. That's part of the fun. But two things are true of all of us who run our own jobs, and they are these: we must work harder than do most other people and we must have something to offer the public which is useful or desirable, or, if we are lucky, both.

If wishes are not horses they are still less careers. No one should engage in the risks of private enterprise without a close examination of her talents, her energies, her capacity for punishment, her needs, and her responsibilities.

But if the choice is made for a job which depends on individual initiative, it is the best job in the world even if it is the hardest. The necessary thing to do is to love your work. You should, because it usually has no one but you and its development depends on your loyalty and imagination and devotion to it.

One more thing must be said. If you are your own master and run your own job, it is a struggle not to become self-centered. Your work may be an only child but if you want it to develop normally you must give it companions. The woman who runs a beauty shop all day is better off for an interest in politics. The one who writes in an upper room is wise if she learns about gardening. Put your work first, but don't close it off from the world. That is bad for you and bad for the job.

MARGARET CULKIN BANNING

79

ALICE PAUL, HATTIE W. CARAWAY, MARY T. NORTON, MARGARET C. SMITH, LENA MADESIN PHILLIPS, BURNITA SHELTON MATTHEWS, PEARL BUCK, KATHARINE HEPBURN, GLADYS SWARTHOUT, MOLLIE MALONEY, AND MIRIAM E. OATMAN

Pro: Should Congress Approve the Proposed Equal Rights Amendment to the Constitution? (1943)

ALICE PAUL

In the following statement prepared for this number of the DIGEST, *Miss Paul, Chairman of the National Woman's Party, outlines the party's objective:*

The National Woman's Party is striving to remove every handicap placed upon women by law and by custom. In order to remove those handicaps which the law can touch, it is endeavoring to secure the adoption of an Equal Rights Amendment to the United States Constitution.

The Woman's Party advocates such an Amendment for the following reasons:

1. *A national amendment is the most effective way to establish equality of rights for men and women throughout the country.*

The amendment would, at one stroke, compel both Federal and State governments to observe the principle of Equal Rights since the Federal Constitution is the supreme law of the land. The amendment would override all existing legislation which denies women Equal Rights with men and it would prevent any such legislation in the future.

2. *A national amendment is the most permanent way to establish equality of rights for men and women throughout the country.*

From *Congressional Digest*, April 1943. Reprinted with permission from the Congressional Digest Corporation.

An amendment to the National Constitution would establish the principle of Equal Rights permanently in our country insofar as anything can be established permanently by law. Equal Rights laws passed by legislative bodies, on the other hand, are subject to reversal by later legislative bodies.

3. *A national amendment is the most dignified way to establish equality of rights for men and women throughout the country.*

The principle of Equal Rights for men and women is so important that it should be written into the National Constitution as one of the basic principles upon which our government is founded. The matter is too important to our Nation's welfare and honor to leave it to the States for favorable or unfavorable action, or for complete neglect, as they may see fit.

At this moment when the United States is engaged in a war with the avowed purpose of establishing freedom and equality for the whole world, the United States should hasten to set its house in order by granting freedom and equality to its own women. For the sake of a new and better world, as well as in justice to women themselves, we ask the immediate adoption of the Equal Rights Amendment.

U.S. SENATOR HATTIE W. CARAWAY

The only woman Member of the United States Senate, Mrs. Caraway of Arkansas, Democrat, gave the following reasons for her co-sponsorship of the Equal Rights Amendment:

I want women free to take a larger part in industry, in the professions, and in government. I want them free to assume greater responsibilities as our Nation works its way out of this crisis and plans how to prevent new ones. I want them free to work equally with men to build a better world.

U.S. REPRESENTATIVE MARY T. NORTON

On January 16, 1940, Representative Mary T. Norton of New Jersey, Democrat, Chairman of the

House Committee on Labor, made the following statement in support of the proposed Equal Rights Amendment:

I feel that the time has come when the proposed amendment to the Constitution of the United States, granting men and women equal legal rights, should be submitted to the States for adoption. This seems to me an entirely fair procedure in view of the great difference of opinion regarding the amendment. The wishes of the majority should prevail.

Women throughout the Nation are demanding that restrictions and discriminations against them be removed and that they be safeguarded against further invasion of their rights. A "respect to the opinions" of such a large proportion of our people is in accordance with the democratic principles on which this Government is founded.

Therefore, as a Member of Congress, I shall vote to submit the Equal Rights Amendment to the States, if and when the measure comes before the House of Representatives.

U.S. REPRESENTATIVE MARGARET C. SMITH

The following statement was released by Representative Smith, Maine, Republican, at Washington, D. C., on February 18, 1943:

Many letters have come to me asking my attitude on the Equal Rights Amendment which has been introduced again in both House and Senate. This proposes an amendment to the Constitution saying that men and women shall have equal rights in the United States and all places subject to its jurisdiction. I believe this to be a principle which should be placed in the Constitution.

The amendment has been introduced jointly by many Senators and Representatives. It is supported, among other organizations, by the Business and Professional Women's Clubs, of which I was State President some years ago.

Some of my correspondents ask if the adoption of the amendment would change Maine laws. The Constitution is the supreme law and any State law which violates the principles of the Constitution must yield to the Constitution. There are many laws which are antiquated and unjust. These would be repealed by the equal rights principle. I would not expect any great upheaval from the adoption of the amendment any more than followed the Suffrage Amendment. Many dire predictions were made that giving the vote to women would upset everything, but it has not.

Women gained the vote as free citizens of the United States in the last war period. It is fitting that the principle of equal rights should be recognized in this war period.

DR. LENA MADESIN PHILLIPS

On March 7, 1943, Dr. Phillips, International President of the Professional and Business Women's Clubs, made the following address on the American Forum of the Air. It is supplemented by several paragraphs from her address on January 2, 1943, at the Capitol, Washington, D. C.:

Our Constitution will never protect women as it protects men until an Equal Rights Amendment is passed. When women obtained the vote, their national organizations united in an effort to wipe out discriminations through State legislation. Yet in 20 years less than 150 of them were changed. There are today in the law of the land more than a thousand common law discriminations against women. It would take 150 years to remove them all at that rate.

In addition, State laws do not give the security of a constitutional amendment. What one State legislature does, the next can undo, and often does. Our founding fathers foresaw this and accepted nothing less than a constitutional guarantee of their liberties.

This country is today shedding its best blood and destroying its substance, as it should, for freedom, justice, equality of opportunity. Women are bearing their full share in this. Yet the American woman, the very woman who gladly gives her son, her property or herself, has not equal pay for equal work, equal control of her property, her inheritance, her earnings, her children.

The need of protective legislation for women has been the chief argument against this amendment. Women used the argument out of fear. Men used it also out of fear—that women would obtain jobs desired by men. Experience has proven that "whenever you force one of two competing groups to work for more money or less time, you force that one out of the job."

Whatever the situation may have been in the past, the Fair Labor Standards Act has now set the standard by fixing the same hours and wages for men and women in interstate commerce and the Social Security Act has rightly provided for the children.

America does not want its women penalized because of laws based upon a feudal tradition. America cannot afford to deny to its own women the very things for which we tell the world we fight. The Equal Rights Amendment will pass. It has been favorably reported by the Sub-Judiciary Committee of both the House and the Senate, is sponsored by 23 Senators and by 42 Members of the House. The other day, America's distinguished visitor, Madame Chiang Kai-shek, in endorsing equality of status for women said, "I have never known brains to have sex." Not until we have passed this amendment, as we shall, may we claim to be the equal of this Oriental woman in our understanding and appreciation of true democracy.

Some say women need the so-called "protective legislation," against long hours, night work, occupational hazards. What women? Does it protect housewives and house workers against long hours? Or nurses, war workers and office cleaners against night work? Or one whose hand is deft and whose life expectancy exceeds her brother's against the average strain of the machine? Or is it not rather that woman is thus 'protected' against the better job and in times of unemployment, any job?

Some will say that this is no time to press such matters since the country is at war. At war for what? For freedom and justice, for democracy. Surely we will not refuse to our own that which we purchase for strangers with the blood of our sons.

We who can say with Lucretia Mott, "I am not free to tolerate injustice," do well to seek courage and strength in memories of her life. For the way was not easy then as it will not be easy now. Those who a century ago sought equal status for women faced and bore all indignities from jail to bad eggs, from vilifications to ostracism. They endured courageously because they believed and cared. We should be proud to bear our later share of criticism and misunderstanding.

For we work and endure not alone for the women of our own nation. As President of the International Federation of Business and Professional Women, I know how eagerly in happier days the women of Europe and throughout the world have desired and followed the leadership of American women. "Show us the way and give us the inspiration of example," they said. Now in the darkness and despair which is the lot of so many of them, it is necessary as never before that the women of America be strong and wise—and free. . . .

BURNITA SHELTON MATTHEWS

Mrs. Matthews, attorney at law and counsel for the National Women's Party, issued the following statement on February 23, 1943:

The United States is the center of democracy's fight for the Four Freedoms: freedom from want, freedom from fear, freedom of speech, and freedom of religion. The hour has struck for the women of the United States to unite in a supreme and final effort in behalf of total democracy by adding a Fifth Freedom—the freedom of women from an inferior status under the law.

The English common law which our forefathers brought here from the mother country gave women few rights which men were bound to respect. The Constitution is always considered in the light of the common law. When women have claimed rights under the Constitution they have almost invariably been denied, as the common law gave women few rights, but many duties. Forever behind a man, in every State of the United States, are the rights of a man as a man, while forever behind a woman is the medieval English common law which places upon her the stigma of inferiority.

There are many laws discriminating against women in the various States of the Union. These laws cover numerous points of inequality, some of which are to be found on the statute books of every State. Here are a few discriminations:

In twenty-two States women are considered incompetent to mete out justice—that is, they are barred from jury service.

The "disabilities of married women" relegate women in many States to the realm of children, the insane, and criminals. This classification renders them incapable of conducting many transactions in business and property rights. In Florida the moment a woman marries she is in a class with minors. Her promissory note was described in one case as equivalent to a blank piece of paper. Property owned by a wife before marriage and property acquired after marriage is her separate estate, but her husband has the control and management. Usually she cannot sue without the joinder of her husband. As a rule she is incompetent to make a legal contract.

When Mrs. Ferguson was elected the first woman Governor of Texas she had to petition the court to set aside her legal "disabilities as a married woman" in order that her acts for the State of Texas might be legal. The court solemnly entered a decree reciting that, her husband's consent having been obtained, her disabilities were removed. In the State of Washington a married woman cannot sue for damages for injuries unless her husband joins her in the suit, or has abandoned her.

Nevada is also among the States in which a wife may not engage in a separate business unless the court establishes her capacity to do so. In other words, before a woman marries she is, in the eyes of the law, able to look out for herself. If she wants to operate a beauty shop or a real estate office no one will hold an inquiry as to her capacity to run it. But the moment she marries she must go through a complicated court procedure to satisfy the judge as to her capacity and competency to engage in business. The most ignorant man, married or single, may carry on a business and no inquiry is conducted as to his qualifications.

The wife's rights to make contracts are hampered in some States, as in Michigan and Nebraska.

In forty States property acquired after the marriage by joint effort of husband and wife belongs to the husband and is subject to his control. In South Carolina, believe it or not, a woman's clothes have been held to be the property of the husband.

Massachusetts, Michigan, and New York are among the States where the services and earnings of a minor child belong to the father. In Alabama and Georgia the father is preferred as a guardian of a minor child's property and person. The burden of support of an illegitimate child rests with the mother, and in Idaho and Texas the unmarried mother cannot get assistance from the father for such a child.

In several States, a wife's earnings may be the husband's property. In the Empire State of New York the wife is entitled to pay for employment outside the home, but her earnings from sewing, boarders, and other projects in the home belong to her husband. In Georgia the husband collects his wife's wages whether earned outside or inside the home. In California, unless there is an agreement to the contrary, the wife's earnings become common property and as such are subject to the control of the husband.

In Kentucky a wife may not divorce her husband for drunkenness unless it is accompanied by non-support and property waste, but drunkenness on the part of the wife (though not accompanied by additional faults) entitles a husband to divorce her unless it is shown that he is equally at fault.

Every day in every State, as women heed the call to join the fight to keep democracy alive, they come up against one or more of these discriminations, which cause many of them to wonder how they can fight to retain something they have never had.

The National Woman's Party and other national, State and local organizations are giving support to the Lucretia Mott Equal Rights Amendment. These groups insist that the democracy which the United States has pledged all its resources to guard shall become a true one. The battle cry of these women is "Pass the Equal Rights Amendment—Now!" . . .

PEARL BUCK

The Author

I've been thinking a good deal about the Lucretia Mott Amendment and the more I think about it the more confirmed I am in my conviction that it is only when a nation's people are governed by laws made for its citizens and not for male and female that men and women can live in mutual happiness with each other and with justice toward each other. When one sex is given discrimination, either favorable or unfavorable, the effect works ill for everyone. If women do not have as a matter of course an unequivocally equal place with men before the law, men suffer with them. A mother cannot train her son in the vigor of free thought and action when she herself does not share completely in that freedom. Something of her sense of inferiority shadows him to weaken him in his own moral fibre or to make him feel falsely superior on that utterly untenable ground for superiority, mere sex. When woman does not share in the life of the nation equally with man, with a mental atmosphere as clear as his, and the right to action no more hampered than man's by discriminatory laws and social attitudes, it means that half the nation and the half which has as its peculiarly important work the bearing of children and their early education, is a depressed group and as such affects the whole.

It is as a mother even more than as a professional worker that I say that I believe the Lucretia Mott Amendment is the only self-respecting basis for citizenship in a true democracy.

KATHARINE HEPBURN

The Actress

In the theatre there is complete equality between men and women. We have men and women playwrights, actors, scenic artists, press agents, and stage managers.

If that has worked well for the theatre, why not for all other walks of life? I have just heard that hospitals where internes have gone to war hesitate to take women doctors, although they are available, and industrial concerns that need doctors still discriminate against women doctors. This attitude towards women goes back to the fundamental law of our country. That is why I support the Equal Rights Amendment to the Constitution.

GLADYS SWARTHOUT

In a letter to the National Woman's Party Miss Swarthout, the Metropolitan Opera star, made the following comment on the proposed Equal Rights Amendment:

Thank you so much for giving me an opportunity to tell you how strongly I feel about the necessity of the passage of the Equal Rights Amendment.

The iniquities which are possible in the present dual status are increasingly deplorable as women are coming to be more and more important in every phase of our national life.

You have my heartiest support for any steps which may be taken to secure the inclusion of this amendment in our Constitution.

MOLLIE MALONEY

On the American Forum of the Air program, Mutual Broadcasting Co., of March 7, 1943, Miss Maloney, member of Local 4366, International Brotherhood of Bookbinders, affiliate of the A.F.L., spoke as follows:

I am an industrial worker. I have worked at my trade of bookbinding since I was 11 years old. So I think I know why working women need the Equal Rights Amendment.

I want to tell you what so-called protective laws do to women like me. I mean the night-work laws for women, the laws limiting the hours of work for women, etc. These laws are said to protect women. I want to say to you—they don't PROTECT women. They hurt women. These laws make women lose their jobs. They take away from women all chance to make good and get to the top of their trade.

By the time I was 15 I was an operator of a falling machine and my wages went up until after the war I got $46.50 a week. I liked the night shift better because the hours were shorter and the pay better. And it gave me time to be out in the sunshine, for I got home about midnight and slept until 9 o'clock. I had time to see my friends and get a little enjoyment out of life.

Then they began to enforce the no-night-work-for-women law in the binderies. I was thrown out of my high-paid job and had to go to the day shift.

Then the "protectors" of women got another law passed in New York which kept women from working a single hour overtime. Hurry-up jobs would come from the printers in the afternoon and the binders would have to stay overtime to get them out. But we women could not work overtime, so we lost our jobs to men.

I had to take up table work at about half of what I was getting. My income was cut down so that I could no longer help my family. That is what the no-night-work law for women and the law against overtime for women did to me and to hundreds of other women in my trade. And it worked the same injury to women in other trades.

All my years of training and experience, which made it possible for me to earn a good living and help my family, were junked by those laws that applied to women but not to men.

Now I am growing old. If it were not for the laws I've been talking about I could be laying aside money for my old age, but as long as these unfair laws against women are in force I know I'll never be able to earn more than a bare living at the only trade I know.

These wicked laws have been made largely through the influence of women who were not earning their living but thought they knew how working women should live. These women did not mean to hurt us but they haven't been up against the things we have to face and they ought to let us decide how to run our own lives.

It is all right for the legislatures to decide the conditions of work for children because they are not old enough to look out for themselves. But adult women who have sense enough to learn a skilled trade have sense enough to take care of themselves.

We have our unions. Questions of wages and hours can be settled by them. We working women can protect ourselves if we have equality of opportunity under the law. We do not need the uplifters to take care of us. The laws for the protection of workers should be based on the conditions of the industry and should be applied to all workers, men and women alike. Then we working women will have a fair chance. This is what the Equal Rights Amendment will give us.

MIRIAM E. OATMAN

In a recent article written for Equal Rights, *official organ of the National Woman's Party, Dr. Miriam E. Oatman, political scientist who has been connected with the Brookings Institution, the American University Graduate School, and now with the State Law Index, speaks of women in the war industries.*

Newspapers and magazines are filled with stories of the influx of women into industry. The Office of War Information, in its official weekly bulletin, *Victory,* of January 13, 1943, devotes an article to this subject.

Among the kinds of work being done by women according to this article, are the following: Testing all types of war material, such as tanks, machine guns, trucks and aircraft carriers; sorting ore; cleaning and greasing machinery; railway work, where women serve as engine oilers and wipers, turn table operators and the like; saw-mill operation; precision work on delicate instruments; and ship-building.

The following statements are made as to the percentage of women workers in various war industries: Electrical machinery, 36 per cent.; electrical equipment, 27 per cent.; scientific and technical instruments, 34 per cent.; communications equipment, 48 per cent.; small-arms ammunition, 35 per cent.; other ammunition, 28 per cent.; chemicals and allied industries, 23 per cent.; rubber products, 33 per cent.; firearms, 22 per cent.; aircraft, 17 per cent.

There is a strong demand in the press generally, in official circles and from many private organizations, for having women paid an equal wage with men for doing the same work. There is also a very general agreement that women fill industrial positions acceptably.

This is all very encouraging.

But let us not suppose that the battle for equal economic opportunity between men and women has been won. Industrial work by women is seldom regarded by those who write the publicity stories—or, alas, by some of their readers—as a normal and permanent development. Most of the articles state or imply that when the emergency is past, women will leave industry. Despite the fact that women can do industrial work well, and that all the nonsense formerly talked about their inability to perform the operations and the risks to their health if they should try to do so, is exploded by the facts, there is still a widespread feeling that only an emergency justifies women in doing work of this kind.

To those persons who believe, with the National Woman's Party, that every human being should do useful work, and that the choice of such work should be as free as possible the idea that women should be driven out of any field of labor is monstrous. Not everyone wishes to do industrial work; but if any woman enjoys oiling machinery, for example, more than she enjoys selling goods behind a counter, why should anyone try to prevent her from doing the work that she prefers? Society as well as the individual woman will be the gainer if her choice is free since everyone works best when the work is congenial.

But when the war is over and the soldiers return, should not women stop working and let the men take over the jobs? The foregoing question is asked over and over by persons who do not understand the elementary principles of economics. Such persons suppose that industry can offer a very limited number of jobs, which ought normally to be filled by fathers of families. This economic idea is no longer tenable, nor would anyone hold it who realized that new factories are built and new fields of enterprise are opened every day. Now it is understood that if everyone does useful work, there will be plenty of goods to exchange; and that the surest way to have plenty for everyone is to set everyone to work. Instead of a vicious circle, this is a beneficent one. It means that all human beings can be happy in doing useful work—one of the most certain sources of happiness—and comfortable in the enjoyment of the goods and services produced by such work. From this point of view, to exclude women from any field of labor is to injure them and injure society. It is our task to see to it that this backward step is never taken.

It is sound economy to encourage women to work. Let every woman and every man with faith in democracy resolve that the door of economic opportunity, now open fairly wide, shall never again be locked against women.

80

CARRIE CHAPMAN CATT; MARGUERITE M. WELLS; NATIONAL COUNCIL OF CATHOLIC WOMEN; MRS. J. AUSTIN STONE; AMERICAN ASSOCIATION OF UNIVERSITY WOMEN; THE WOMEN'S TRADE UNION LEAGUE; AND CONGRESS OF WOMEN'S AUXILIARIES, C.I.O.

Con: Should Congress Approve the Proposed Equal Rights Amendment to the Constitution? (1943)

CARRIE CHAPMAN CATT

Through the offices of the Westchester County branch of the National League of Women Voters, Mrs. Catt, Honorary President of the N. L. W. V., issued the following statement on February 28, 1943:

The proposed "Equal Rights" Amendment is a snare and a delusion. All fundamental human rights are bestowed equally on men and women in this country. All these rights are denied to men and women in some countries, but here they have been won.

The women of the trade union occupations enjoy protective legislation and generations of hard work in which women organizations joined brought about this protective legislation.

The workers themselves agree that they have received benefits from this protective legislation, and they are almost unanimously opposed to its repeal through the "Equal Rights" Amendment. The support of the amendment comes chiefly from the white-collar workers and the professional classes. They should remember that if there is any resistance to the enforcement of equal rights their only satisfaction is through the courts.

Prejudices will not melt away because the Constitution decrees equal rights. So many and such varied problems are involved that the "Equal Rights" Amendment would let loose upon the Nation a continuous procession of test cases in the courts.

"Equal rights" will not prevent inequalities in positions held. Proof of ability meriting promotion is the key which will finally open the door of opportunity. Evolution may seem to move slowly, but never forget that it does move, and always onward. Let us not be led astray.

MARGUERITE M. WELLS

Miss Wells, President of the National League of Women Voters, in March, 1943, released the following statement from the League headquarters in Washington, D. C.:

Everyone wants "equal rights" for women—especially now when the work of women is essential to winning the war. But, the proposed so-called "Equal Rights" Amendment to the Federal Constitution raises a lot of questions:

In some States the legal age for marriage is lower for girls than for boys. Is this "equal rights," or would the age have to be raised for girls or lowered for boys? Who knows? Nobody! Who must decide? The courts.

In some States the husband's failure to support his wife is cause for divorce. Under "equal right" may her husband divorce her if she does not support him? Who knows? Nobody! Who must decide? The courts.

In some States a woman reaches the age of majority at 18 years, a man at 21. Does the age for a man become 18 or that of a woman, 21, under "equal rights"? Who knows? Nobody! Who must decide? The courts.

The property rights of married men and women are different in all the States. Would these rights be affected? Who knows? Nobody! Who must decide? The courts.

In California and other States husband and wife own together property acquired during marriage. Would this be true in every State? Who knows? Nobody! Who must decide? The courts.

From *Congressional Digest*, April 1943. Reprinted with permission from the Congressional Digest Corporation.

In some States jury service for women is compulsory, in some optional, in some prohibited; some require women to serve but excuse those who have the care of young children. Which laws would be valid under "equal rights"? Who knows? Nobody! Who must decide? The courts.

Do we want the courts, State and Federal, burdened with litigations to the validity of existing State legislation pertaining to girls and women?

Do we want the Congress to take on the task of legislating in fields now reserved to the States?

The proposed Equal Rights Amendment reads:

"Sec. 1. Men and women shall have equal rights throughout the United States and every place subject to its jurisdiction.

"Sec. 2. Congress shall have power to enforce this article by appropriate legislation."

The amendment would cause great confusion and further burden already over-burdened courts. The mischievous vagueness of the amendment means that every law treating men and women differently would be subject to challenge in the courts.

What does "equal" mean? Identical? That would be the simplest answer. Any law treating men and women differently would certainly be open to challenge in the courts if this amendment were adopted. If "equal" means "identical" the amendment fails to consider the differences between men and women.

What does equal rights "throughout the United States" mean? Does it mean uniform treatment of men and women throughout the United States? Would it mean only equal treatment of men and women within each State?

The amendment is not needed. Legal discrimination against women in State laws or State constitutions will be changed as fast as enough women in those States want them changed. The vote gives them that power.

The amendment would be the greatest single step toward centralization of government control ever taken. It authorizes the Congress to pass legislation in the whole field of social and property legislation—property rights, marriage and divorce—dependency—legitimacy—age of consent—inheritance, etc.

The real discriminations against women result from custom and prejudice—not from laws. A constitutional amendment will not change these attitudes. It could aggravate them.

NATIONAL COUNCIL OF CATHOLIC WOMEN

In a statement of March 4, 1943, the N.C.C.W. summarized its reasons for opposition to the Equal Rights Amendment as follows:

The sponsors of the amendment ask that men and women be treated equally, or identically, in the eyes of the law; but men and women were not created identical.

The amendment is but one phase of a whole movement tending toward the breakdown of the family. Theoretically, the amendment would establish equality in family headship, a condition which would tend to disintegrate the family.

The amendment itself is confusing in its application. Section 1 of the amendment could mean the repeal of all state legislation relating to men or women. Must the standards of California apply in Florida, or vice versa? Which standards shall be accepted—those that are high or those that are low? Certainly the legislation of all States would be thrown into confusion, because no State would know whether its laws or those of another State would be the accepted ones, depending upon test cases in the Federal courts.

The amendment would invade State's rights. Ordinarily, laws governing marriage, family, education, etc., are left to the individual States. These laws, as well as all laws affecting men and women, would then become the concern of the Federal Government, thus increasing an ever growing federalization.

The amendment is unnecessary. Even the National Woman's Party, sponsors of the measure, have admitted in their study of discriminatory legislation, that women now are not debarred from entering any profession. Then, too, the Women's Bureau of the U.S. Department of Labor reports an ever-increasing number of women going into industry. Within the past months, of the number of new people entering industry, 80 per cent. were women. As to wages, the Fair Labor Standards Act, which governs interstate commerce—the bulk of commerce today, guarantees to women equal pay with men for equal jobs.

Where there are inequalities within a State, these may and should be remedied through State legislation, not through an unnecessary change in the Constitution.

MRS. J. AUSTIN STONE

In a letter to the U. S. Senate of May 25, 1942, Mrs. Stone, President of the National Women's Trade Union League of America, presented the views of the following member organizations of the Women's Joint Congressional Committee who oppose the Equal Rights Amendment: National Consumers' League, National League of Women Voters, Girls' Friendly Society of the U.S.A., American Association of University Women, National Council of Jewish Women, National Council of Catholic Women, National Service Star Legion, Nat'l Board of Y. W. C. A.

Representatives of the organizations listed above have asked me to express their opposition to the so-called Equal Rights Amendment. The amendment is opposed by many responsible organizations of women.

Members of these organizations favor equality of opportunity for women; have been instrumental in having State laws discriminating against women changed; oppose the so-called Equal Rights Amendment as being illusory and actually inimical to the goal of equal opportunity for women.

A study of this proposal shows its inappropriateness as a part of the Constitution. It would throw into question State laws treating men and women differently. The courts would be jammed with litigation for an indefinite period. No standard of "equality" is stated in the amendment. Does it mean that a single nation-wide standard shall be established or does it mean that each State could determine "equality" within its own boundaries? The amendment authorizes the Congress to enforce "equality" "by appropriate legislation." Does this mean that the Congress shall act in fields now reserved to the States— marriage and divorce laws, support laws, property laws, etc.? If so, the amendment would constitute one of the most extensive changes in the relation of States to the Federal Government in the history of the country.

The proposed amendment would invalidate State legislation regulating hours of work and setting minimum wages for women workers. Adjustments are being made in the administration of these laws so that they do not interfere with the employment of women in war industries. The protection they afford will be needed in the post-war reconstruction period. Organized women workers consider such protection necessary. Proponents of the amendment, not representative of industrial workers, frankly admit that repeal of this type of legislation is one of their goals in supporting the amendment.

A few serious discriminations against women still exist in the laws of some States. These can be eliminated by action of the State legislatures. Experience has shown that legislatures act when enough women within the State want the laws changed. Most discriminations against women are matters of administration, prejudice and custom rather than law.

In conclusion, we urge you to remember that this amendment is not sought by any considerable number of women; that it will lead to great confusion; will not of itself correct discriminations against women that now exist; and that everything hoped to be accomplished by the amendment can be accomplished without it.

AMERICAN ASSOCIATION OF UNIVERSITY WOMEN

In its summary of reasons for opposing the Equal Rights Amendment the A. A. U. W. makes the following points:

Those who favor this amendment do so because they believe that the writing of a broad affirmation of the principle of sex equality into our Constitution would hasten the day of its acceptance in practice. Those who oppose it on the other hand do so because they see not clarification but added confusion and uncertainty as to its meaning and application, not greater speed in accomplishing the desired end but greater confusion and delay. They see in it a kind of shadow-boxing which, while evidencing a naive confidence in the power of legalisms, cannot possibly have any important effect upon human conduct or upon the psychological barriers to equality which are the really important barriers that remain.

In addition to confusion, delay, and unreality, those who oppose the amendment also see in it an abdication of the responsibility of women for thinking through their own specific problems and a dumping of this responsibility in wholesale fashion upon the judiciary. They see further in the amendment the wiping out of all standards and the destruction of important existing rights, not least among them the right to legislative protection for women in the labor field.

At worst the amendment would be highly destructive. At best it would be wholly ineffective, leaving the job of piece-meal removal of remaining discriminations still to be done. It is because these later arguments seem to the A. A. U. W. far more cogent than those of the proponents of the measure that the A. A. U. W. has taken its stand in opposition to the amendment.

The quarrel is based on method, not on ultimate objectives. Workers all for the emancipation of women, those who oppose the amendment do so because they believe that it is a specious and positively dangerous proposal which, in the field of labor at least, may easily lend itself to reactionary uses, that it is undemocratic in that it takes away from the legislatures and gives to the courts the power to decide difficult and delicate questions of social policy, that it is a device for shirking responsibility in a field that should be the peculiar responsibility of women, that it is an easy but dangerous device to save us from thinking, and that the only sound method for removing discriminations is the method of removing them one by one, by laws specifically adapted to accomplish each particular purpose.

THE WOMEN'S TRADE UNION LEAGUE

The following recent statement of the Women's Trade Union League in opposition to the proposed Equal Rights Amendment was prepared by Blanch Freedman, Executive Secretary, New York Women's Trade Union League:

We oppose the so-called "Equal Rights" Amendment which is dangerous and vicious because:

I. It deprives the State of its inherent right to protect itself

    A. By taking cognizance of the special social role of women as mothers or potential mothers.

    B. By taking cognizance of the physical requirements of women as one of the many categories in its citizenry.

II. By requiring that rights be equal throughout the United States it might involve a complete breakdown of existing concepts of States' rights.

III. The effect of such an amendment would create utmost confusion in interpretation and application.

IV. It asserts as basic public policy a rigid rule of equality of sexes—a fact which is not true in nature or society and would therefore result in grievous contradictions between life and law.

The proposed amendment which is now before the Congress of the United States in essence would do two things:

1. It lays down a rule of public policy that everywhere in the United States men and women shall have equal rights unreservedly, immutably, regardless of time, place or circumstances, and for all purposes.

2. By such declaration of policy it prohibits both State and Federal governments from exercising their inherent police power to safeguard the welfare of the State should such welfare at any point come into conflict with this declared principle.

All progressive people undoubtedly support and advocate the abolition of political and civil discriminations against women that still exist. The proposed amendment is a demagogic attempt to capitalize on that sentiment. Framed to emphasize "equality" its proponents hope that people will believe that this amendment is intended to and will accomplish that purpose. What they do not disclose is that such an amendment would strike from the statute books every law that has been passed to ameliorate the working conditions of women. For in fact and truth that is what they really seek to accomplish through it!

Let it be said at the outset, that we who oppose the adoption of the proposed amendment support wholeheartedly every sincere endeavor to eradicate any disability of women which may still exist; that we have been in the forefront in the efforts which have resulted in resolving many such abuses. It is primarily because of our devotion to that cause that we oppose this amendment whose proclaimed purpose cannot be achieved by it. In addition, the attention and energies of those interested in securing the real emancipation of women are diverted through this misleading and dangerous subterfuge.

Many arguments can be and have been advanced against it during the twenty years that the proposed amendment has been repeatedly introduced into Congress. These arguments cover a wide range, for the proposal is vulnerable in so many respects.

There would be less serious objection to the amendment—however impractical it would be—if it were not for the fact that its adoption threatens all social labor legislation affecting women. In justification of this threatened assault, the defenders of the proposed amendment insist that some of these laws are detrimental and not beneficial to the women involved. Their argument that the adoption of the amendment is a panacea for all such "ills" at one fell swoop is utterly specious. The fact is that 36 legislatures must be convinced to adopt this amendment. Needless to say, if legislation in a State is undesirable, its legislators can be persuaded more easily to remedy it specifically by amendment or repeal rather than by adopting the blanket provisions of this amendment.

As pointed out above, legislation is the method by which the State enacts into law its experience. Since circumstances change and the fund of experience grows, laws necessarily are changed or repealed. In studying the effect of working conditions on women, legislatures have enacted laws which experience deems imperative. Necessarily, time has required and will continue to require modification of such laws as new experiences and changing conditions demand. If it develops that a law enacted to safeguard women in any given occupation is in fact a detriment to them, today the situation is easily remediable. The law can be changed or repealed; in brief, legislation is a flexible and elastic method of dealing with new experiences and changed conditions. But the proposed amendment would prohibit the enactment of *any* legislation for the safeguarding of women alone. An amendment to the U. S. Constitution, such as the proposed "Equal Rights" Amendment, would be a stone wall against which the waves of experience would pound in futility.

CONGRESS OF WOMEN'S AUXILIARIES, C.I.O.

In a press release of March 2, 1943, the Congress of Women's Auxiliaries of the Congress of Industrial Organizations, summarized its opposition to the Equal Rights Amendment as follows:

1. *The simple and fair wording of the amendment is deceptive.* Its two brief sections read as follows: Sec. 1. "Men and women shall have equal rights throughout the United States and every place subject to its jurisdiction." Sec. 2.

"Congress shall have power to enforce this article by appropriate legislation."

2. *The amendment is not needed to provide a general statement of constitutional equality.* It would add practically nothing to the equal rights clause of the Fourteenth Amendment which forbids States to discriminate between persons within their jurisdictions.

3. *The amendment would serve as a dangerous instrument to destroy many hard won rights of women.* It is generally agreed that the effect of the "equal rights" provision would be to abolish those laws which protect the economic, physical and social conditions of women, but do not apply equally to men. It would make unconstitutional hundreds of State, local and Federal laws which represent years of hard won progress, and which have enabled millions of women to achieve a considerable degree of REAL, not legalistic, equality with men.

4. *The amendment would destroy protective industrial legislation and would impose extreme hardships on working women.* It would destroy State wage and hour laws for women, and bring back sweatshop employment standards for thousands of unorganized women who cannot secure better standards without the protection of these laws. It would destroy essential health legislation which safeguards the health of women, and prevents strains and injuries harmful to mothers and pregnant women.

5. *The amendment would create similar hardships for women in other walks of life.* It would deprive wives, widows, mothers, children, of many legal protections they now have and need. It would undermine laws which relate to widows' pensions, the right of dependent wives and children to support of the husband and father, guardianship and many other rights affecting family relationships.

6. *Supporters of the amendment misrepresent its real effects.* They try to leave the impression that its immediate result would simply be to apply all laws equally to men and women. Actually the amendment would do no such thing. It would make unconstitutional every law that does not apply equally to men and women but would leave nothing in its place. New legislative action would have to be taken on every law to determine whether it should be modified, changed or abolished. This would take years of legislative battles and court fights. It would give reactionary groups new opportunities to destroy every progressive measure they dislike.

7. *The amendment would create complete chaos for years in regard to the legal rights and status of women.* No woman would know exactly what her rights are until each law is specifically changed through legislative action. In addition it is expected that the States, the Federal Government and courts would place varying interpretations upon the amendment, and complete confusion would result until each issue is finally settled by the U. S. Supreme Court.

8. *Sponsors of the amendment have shown no concern for the millions of women who would be gravely injured by this amendment.* Some have joined backward employers in opposing State minimum wage and hour laws, although they know that without such legislation, many women cannot get a living wage or decent working conditions.

9. *Legal inequalities which still exist in some State laws can be most effectively eliminated not through the amendment, but through specific legislation in each State.* Some States still have laws which forbid women to serve on juries, to hold certain office, to handle their property without the consent of their husbands, etc. All labor and women's organizations will continue to cooperate in eliminating these discriminations, through specific legislation which will not endanger other gains made by women.

The amendment is not a short-cut to equality, but the road back to economic chaos for women.

Most important national women's organizations are opposed to the amendment. They include: National Council of Catholic Women, Y.W.C.A., Consumers' League, American Association of University Women, League of Women Voters, National Council of Jewish Women, National Women's Trade Union League, and the Women's Bureau of the U. S. Department of Labor.

81
ETHEL ERNEST MURRELL
An Equal Rights Amendment (1952)

The Equal Rights Amendment reads: "Equality of rights under the law shall not be denied or abridged by the United States or by any State on account of sex." It will grant American women full citizenship. "But why," the question is often asked, "why, in order to attain full citizenship, do American women want an amendment to the Constitution?" Is it not enough that state legislation is rapidly giving them as many, if not more rights, than women have possessed since matriarchal Egypt, at least during the period of written history? After all, why quibble about constitutional protection? Cannot women be content to accept their status as limited citizens, provided the states grant them privileges and actual rights?

If there were any stability in state law, this might indeed suffice. Unfortunately, state rights are subject to continual and constant change. There is no safety for women in any legislation that is unbacked by constitutional guarantees.

The American male is a citizen by virtue of rights guaranteed him in the Constitution. None of these guarantees attach to women. Only the right to vote, placed in the Constitution by amendment, includes females in that document. All other rights such as the right to ownership of property, to work, and to choose unrestrictedly the hours for such work, to control earnings and income, to custody of children, to divorce or to freedom of speech, are state rights, subject to change every time state legislatures meet.

The fault lies not in the Constitution, but in the interpretation given the Constitution by the courts. Take, for instance, the Fourteenth Amendment. Ever since its passage women have been trying to come under the liberating and protective clauses. The Supreme Court held that the state cannot bar Negro men from jury duty because to do so would brand them as inferior citizens and deprive them of the equal protection of the laws guaranteed by the Fourteenth Amendment. But, in the same decision, the Court held that jury service may be limited to males.

WOMEN ARE DISQUALIFIED FOR JURY SERVICE

Women are still disqualified for jury service in many states. Other states differentiate between male and female jurors by making service mandatory for one group; voluntary for the other. Since the right to trial by a jury of one's peers is guaranteed all United States citizens by the Constitution and is a right that has been jealously guarded by English-speaking men since 1215, these exclusions are clearly discriminatory; exclusion from jury service is only one instance wherein the limited citizenship of women is apparent.

The International Labor Organization has recently produced a treaty limiting night-work for women. It was transmitted by President Truman to Congress in August, 1950, and recently Secretary of Labor Tobin transmitted it to the forty eight states. If this treaty becomes law, the hours women can work will be limited, thus setting them aside again as a specialized labor group. This is no new thing.

In the twenties New York State passed a law forbidding women to work after midnight. Telephone operators, printers, proof-readers, secretaries and waitresses were among those affected. When it was suggested that such laws were oppressive and that they had been passed for the purpose of removing the competition of women, denials were forthcoming; yet a former New York labor law which prohibited the employment of women printers at night made no mention of women who cleaned printing offices at night. Presumably no male coveted a

From *Equal Rights,* March–April and July–August 1952.

scrubbing job. In 1936 the New England Association of Farmers, Mechanics and other workingmen, expressed the point neatly in a resolution which read:

Whereas, Labor is a physical and moral injury to women and a COMPETITIVE menace to men, we recommend legislation to restrict women in Industry.

Subsequent state legislatures substituted the word "protection" for "restrictive" and produced the same results. Ohio passed a general minimum wage law for women only in 1933. In the dry cleaning industry wages for women were set as much as one-third higher than men were getting under NRA. Within three years one-fifth of all women employed in the dry cleaning industry had been dismissed. Obviously, a republic which purports to extend equal justice under law should not set women apart as workers. Legislation raising the standards of all workers, such as the Federal Wage and Hour Law, should be the criterion and aim of everyone interested in better civic conditions; since the Equal Rights Amendment prohibits laws that restrict on grounds of sex alone, it is the first step to the ideal of higher standards for all workers.

PROTECTIVE LAWS NEED NOT BE AFFECTED

Maternity laws, pension grants and health laws need not be affected. Experience with like measures in New Zealand, the Netherlands and Scandinavia has shown that equality before the law does not affect progressive health regulations. In fact, once we have cleared the books of medieval restrictions we can then concentrate on true protective laws—maternity laws, for instance. The United States, for all its chatter about protecting women, rarely grants leaves with pay to working expectant mothers or periods of rest after birth. In other countries, where equality exists, such laws obtain, shielding mother and future citizen alike. Maternity legislation is comparable with equality for it is similar to legislation for veteran soldiers' benefits. It is granted for a special service rendered to society. It is not sex legislation, as it does not apply to all women any more than veteran soldier legislation applies to all men. Both types of legislation are legitimate forms of "classification" and neither violates the principle of "the equal protection of the law." . . .

Planks supporting the Equal Rights Amendment were written in the national platforms of the two major political parties in 1944 and 1948.

The amendment was reported favorably by the Judiciary Committee of the Senate and of the House of Representatives in the 79th and 80th Congresses, and by the Judiciary Committee of the Senate in the 81st Congress. It received a majority vote in the United States Senate on July 19, 1946, and more than a two-thirds vote of the Senate on January 25, 1950. It was favorably reported out by the Senate Judiciary Committee in the 82d Congress, May, 1951. In 1951 it is considered fashionable on Capitol Hill to be for the amendment. Over 30 million women have declared themselves through their organizations as supporting it—and half as many men's groups have indorsed it.

Yet, logic to the contrary, even in spite of public sentiment, arguments continue for state action. To quote the late Dr. M. Carey Thomas, president of Bryn Mawr College:

"It is strangely unsympathetic for opponents of an equal rights amendment to suggest removing the thousands of inequalities and injustices by slow and piece-meal work in the 48 State legislatures while women are born, living their lives, and dying without the justice for which they have been waiting since the time of the cave man."

The argument that such an amendment would interfere with states' rights is specious. In its favorable report to the Senate, May 28, 1943, the Senate Judiciary Committee said:

"The amendment does not deprive any State of its exclusive dominion over local public policy. Nor does it require uniformity among the several states." [For a full discussion of the subject see *Missouri* v. *Lewis,* 101 U.S. 22.]

To the question: "Would the Amendment cause litigation?"—Charles G. Morris, an outstanding lawyer from Connecticut, stated:

"You tell me that an objection which has been raised to the proposed equal-rights amendment to the Constitution is that it will clutter the courts with cases. All that I can say is that, if that is a valid argument, no legislation should ever be proposed, since any legislation, either in the form of a constitutional amendment or an amendment by the legislature, is necessarily subject to review by the courts to ascertain whether or not it conforms to the constitutional requirements."

Space does not permit the recounting of all the reasons for such legislation, but these alone should answer for thinking people the question asked at the beginning of this article—"Why do women demand an amendment to the Constitution which will guarantee them full citizenship?"—Obviously they demand it because they want to take their places as full-time human beings and to have removed from themselves and their daughters the impediment of dwelling forever at the mercy of whimsical state legislators—an impediment that will hang over them until they shall enjoy full constitutional protection.

Another answer is to employ the Socratic rudeness of replying with a question. "What, gentlemen, would you trade for your constitutional rights?" An earnest thoughtful answer to the second question is the answer to the first.

82

Mirra Komarovsky

Women in the Modern World (1953)

"How should we educate our daughters?" is a question which has bristled with controversy throughout our history. In recent years this controversy has flared up with renewed vigor.

Reprinted with permission of the author.

The whole field of education is in a state of ferment. But if we are uncertain about how to educate men, our confusion with regard to women is doubly great.

What are we educating women for? To raise this question is to face the whole problem of woman's role in society. We are uncertain about the ends of women's education precisely because the status of women in our society is fraught with contradictions and confusion.

Our deep concern with this problem is apparent from the avalanche of books and articles and the continuous flow of words over the radio and in lecture halls on the subject of woman's role. A certain persistent theme is emerging out of this din of voices. We have been repeatedly told in recent years that our predicament is due to the feminist movement for sex equality. Instead of making women proud to be women, the feminists glorified masculine aptitudes and masculine goals. Women were urged to imitate men when they should have striven to develop their own unique talents. Women's education allegedly suffers from the same subservience to masculine values. Feminist educators, disregarding women's special functions in society, educated women "as if they were men in disguise." Our current disappointments and frustrations are the bitter fruit of feminist victories.

We shall examine these antifeminist charges, especially as they apply to the college education of women. While finding a few of these charges valid, this book presents a quite different interpretation of our current difficulties. Correspondingly, the recommendations for educational and social policy also differ from those advocated by the modern antifeminists.

To disagree with an antifeminist does not necessarily make one a feminist. We have suffered from a tendency to debate this issue in terms of extreme alternatives. But we can reject the antifeminist program without having to embrace the old-fashioned feminism with its militant hostility towards men and its disparagement of the home-maker. It is my purpose to explore a course for women's education and for women's lives which avoids both extremes.

The interpretation of women's problems developed in this book is sociological. It is not intended primarily to explain why Mrs. Smith leads a contented and a useful life while Mrs. Jones is a problem-ridden homemaker. Our patient is not the individual but society as a whole. Our problem is to discover what in contemporary society causes such widespread uneasiness in women and tensions in the relations between the sexes. We shall trace the life cycle of the middle-class, and especially the college-trained, woman from adolescence to middle age in order to lay bare the inconsistent social expectations and other social forces which cause conflict at every stage of her life.

Any such attempt to identify the *social* roots of widespread personal maladjustments may create an unintended impression. It may appear that the individual is absolved of any responsibility for her own life. Blaming society for their plight, a few may see in this interpretation a warrant for self-pity. But it is hoped that others will make a better use of this book. Men and women are all too often bewildered by their problems. They attribute them to the perversity of their associates or to personal failure. Blind resentment and humiliation do not make for creative solutions. When, on the other hand, an individual understands how his difficulties came about, his helpless and resentful bewilderment gives way to a degree of detachment and of poise. He is now in a better position to define his dilemmas and to search for constructive remedies. Recognizing the social odds against the good life in his own generation, he may even be inspired to make society better for his offspring.

The title of this book may suggest that it is addressed to women. While it deals primarily with women's problems, as long as men are friends, fathers, brothers, sons and husbands of women, there is no women's problem which is not also a problem for men. It is hoped that men may derive from the pages of this book a clearer understanding of women and also of themselves in relation to women.

Without further study we cannot know the extent to which the problems of the middle class, and mostly college-trained, women analyzed in the following chapters are shared by other classes of women. But, in any event, the experiences of this minority exercise an influence out of proportion to its size. College-trained men and women occupy positions of leadership and have an impact upon the public opinion of the whole community. Similarly, the significance of higher education is not to be measured by the numbers attending colleges and universities. Changing emphases at the top are likely to affect the whole educational system. In other ways, too, the institutions of higher learning set the intellectual and cultural level of the whole society. . . .

Public opinion today tends to hold education responsible for all the ills of our society. We observe the restlessness of educated women and in our chagrin point the accusing finger at the colleges: "Why haven't you made women content with their lives?" But if the analysis of women's problems presented in this book is sound, education alone cannot solve them. Education should help women make the best possible adjustment to current contradictions, but wider reforms will be required to eliminate these dilemmas for the daughters and granddaughters of the present graduates.

Consider for example the valid charge that, in glorifying careers, we have robbed some women of self-respect who would, otherwise, have led contented and useful lives as homemakers. Mrs. Peterson, the ex-career women who winced at having to admit that she became "just a housewife," may be an exception. And yet, as Margaret Mead pointed out, unless the most gifted college housewife can take the same pride in her status as professional women take in theirs, we face the risk that her discontent will permeate wider strata of women.

But what ailed the career-minded housewives was, after all, their wholehearted assimilation of the dominant values of our society. They believed that it is good for an adult to earn his own living and not continue being an economic burden upon his family. They held it to be a duty of the individual to strive to make the best of his endowments and opportunities, and that such a goal is to be pursued mainly through one's occupation; that the kind of work one does is pretty much the measure of the person; that everyone should have the right to whatever occupational level he can attain through merit and ambition; that highly specialized occupations are superior to the unskilled ones and intellectual activities to manual labor, and so on. Possessing what it takes to meet the challenge of such values, they organized their lives and, what is more, they fashioned their self-image accordingly. Marriage suddenly called for a major reorganization of their mode of life and its supporting values.

In the face of these beliefs, what must we do to raise the prestige of domesticity among educated women? As we explore this problem, it becomes clear that colleges could not effect any significant changes in our values unaided by society as a whole.

If the prestige of domesticity can be raised among educated women, it will probably not be through the emphasis on housekeeping. In our era of specialization, a specialist will inevitably outrank a jack-of-all trades. Excellent as the housekeeper may be, she will not equal the specialist chef, the interior decorator, or the dietitian. That her function is socially important is not enough to earn her high prestige. The farmer is indispensable to our very existence, but a cross-section of the American public ranked some thirty-eight other occupations higher than farming. The ex-professional woman may be relieved to escape the strain of her career and may find deep happiness in housekeeping, but, being a child of our society, she will experience the change as a demotion in the occupational hierarchy.

What can give the necessary prestige to domesticity is the spotlight on family relationships and, particularly, on child rearing. Indeed, it has been said that if we could only make women understand that no job in the world can equal in importance or challenge the job of rearing children to be fine human beings, no one would need to worry about the self-respect of the housewife-mother. But what stands in the way of such understanding? If educated women do not accept the obvious fact, it is certainly not from want of repetition. Torrents of words are continually directed towards them from the pulpits, from the loud-speakers, from the press concerning the importance of motherhood.

It is quite true that building bridges, writing books, and splitting the atom are no more essential to society or more difficult than child rearing. But, in our opinion, women cannot be made to believe it unless men believe it too; unless, that is, the whole of our society becomes oriented towards values quite different from those which dominate it today.

Otherwise, a dozen times a day events would belie, even as they do now, the sermons directed to women alone. If our whole society endorsed these values, a nursery school teacher would rate a salary at least equal to the beginning salary of a street cleaner, and the curtailment of social services to children would not be the first economies that politicians feel safe to propose in a period of retrenchment. The young settlement worker who was the first to succeed in pacifying neighborhood gang warfare would have as good a chance of draft deferment as a brilliant engineering student.

If men believed for a moment that the rearing of children is as difficult and important as building bridges, they would demand more of a hand in it too. It would become unnecessary for child psychologists to campaign for more active fatherhood. A man could derive prestige and self-esteem from spending weekends with his children even if this called for a less single-minded dedication to occupational success. The conflict between occupational and family interests would then become a problem also for men, and each would have to strike his own balance between the conflicting interests. One can imagine a male sociologist writing a book to show that, though women are the child bearers, nature did not intend to bar men from the honorable task of educating the young. He would seek to demonstrate that, whenever their environment demands it, men too exhibit psychological insight, and that a good salesman, politician, or psychoanalyst can match any woman in intuition.

To sum up, what defeats our appeal to women to find dignity in domesticity is the fact that our society is saturated with other values and that the experience of the educated and the gifted housewife flies in the face of the unconvincing assurance that she is doing the most important job in the world. She knows that when her husband says: "But in rearing our children you are doing something more creative and difficult than anything I can do in a lifetime," he does not quite believe it himself.

It used to be possible to maintain a system of values for women only and to insulate them against the dominant masculine goals of society. But the conditions of life and the ideologies which supported the sharp demarcation between the feminine and the masculine goals have greatly changed. Having to earn a living, women are exposed to the incentives of the economic world. Urged to participate in cultural and political activities, women are bound to absorb values pervading those sectors of life. If not the majority of women, at least those gifted and able to attain our highly prized goals of economic, intellectual, or artistic attainment will continue to feel that in becoming "just housewives" they are losing status—unless, that is, our whole society begins to regard the "nurturing" activities more highly. There is another alternative. The modern antifeminists attempt to shame women into renouncing achievement goals by claiming that such goals lure only the neurotic women, and that the male emphasis on achievement is but a compensation for his inability to bear children. Such an ideology can succeed only by elevating into dogma many unproved theories about feminine personality, and by suppressing what we have learned about the overlapping of mental traits of men and women.

Apart from the low rating of nurturing activities, another factor lowers the status of the housewife: the term "housewife" is applied to the effective and to the incompetent alike, to the woman at the peak of her contribution and to others, still in their prime, who no longer render any useful service. "If everyone who could change a fuse were bracketed with the designers of power plants under the designation of 'electrical engineering,' we should have an analogy to the present status of homemaking."

Conversely, what would add to the prestige of the housewife would be the social expectation that as children get older and demand less of her, the mother will turn to some other worth-while pursuit, volunteer or paid. It is right that some social honor should go to any mother for having borne and reared children. But rearing two or three children should hardly exempt the woman for life from any other responsibility, especially when her children have left the parental home.

But, here again, urging the "retired mother" to find some constructive pursuit is not enough. She will require the assistance of some social measures, such as more part-time jobs, better vocational guidance, retraining courses, changed attitudes to older students and older workers, and so on.

Raising the prestige of domesticity, desirable as it is, will not solve the problems brought to light in the chapter on the homemakers. Those mothers had some legitimate grievances. Mrs. Sanders, the overworked mother of young children, would have been a better mother if she had had some leisure to pursue individual interests apart from her family. We have shown that the sense of intellectual deprivation expressed by the homemakers cannot be dismissed lightly, nor can their need to feel themselves occasionally persons and not merely mothers.

The solutions to these problems are far from simple. But it is better to see the situation in all its complexity than to delude ourselves with pseudo remedies. A proper diagnosis is bound to release creative thinking and give an impetus to social reconstruction. As long as the conscientious housewife was led to believe that all dissatisfactions with housewifery were due to a neurosis, she was much more concerned with personal salvation than with any co-operative search for remedies. On the other hand, given social endorsement, all kinds of social inventions are bound to emerge. A number of them, such as "sitting" pools, co-operative play groups and nurseries, are already in existence in various localities. Co-operation of neighbors has in many places broken down the isolation of the individual family and has extended to wider circles some of the benefits which a well-to-do family derives from servants, children's camps, or a country club.

Co-operative effort of neighbors is not the only means of social adjustment. Public action must be taken, for example, to make good nursery schools available to all children who could profit by them, and it is a rare child who could not. That some well-to-do mothers have seized upon the nursery school, the afternoon play group, and the summer camps to escape responsibilities of motherhood is no argument against these agencies. Irresponsible parenthood must be attacked directly, through better parent education, better mental health, closer co-operation between parents and teachers. It would be foolish to ignore the pressing needs of the multitude and be paralyzed into inaction because some have misused a constructive service. Public in addition to private action must protect the children of working mothers, through pensions where such are indicated and also by extension of child care centers, recreational facilities, school lunches, family and child counseling services, and other social services.

One of the most constructive measures of all would be an increase in part-time jobs for married women. Part-time jobs may not be feasible in every occupation, but we have not scratched the surface of possibilities for economically sound and socially advantageous utilization of part-time workers.

Some more radical innovations have been recommended to give a homemaker more leisure and a chance to pursue individual interests. Many writers have observed that the urban household is too small and inefficient and that economies could be effected with greater division of labor among a group of housewives in an apartment house or in a housing project. One such plan envisioned a series of neighborhood businesses, each specializing in some housekeeping function. A woman interested in cooking, for example, might run a neighborhood restaurant. Another might take care of young children for a few days at a time, while their mothers were away. If such novel arrangements could be worked out, they would permit women to specialize in those housekeeping functions in which they have a special talent and would tend to shorten the working day for all.

There is no contradiction between such proposals and the plea that we increase the pride of the individual homemaker in housekeeping arts. All housewives must strive to provide nourishing meals and a comfortable home for their families. Some women will choose to develop housekeeping arts to a high level and they should be given encouragement and acclaim. But if other women and their families agree to simplify standards of housekeeping (or to purchase such a service as was just described) in order to be able to do more of something else (a part-time job, a volunteer activity, a cultural hobby)—that, too, should be an acceptable choice. Far from lowering the quality of food, families might enjoy better meals if women who really liked cooking supervised meal preparation for several families. To widen the range of acceptable choices need not, of course, mean to endorse anything and everything. The irresponsible housewife whose housekeeping is neglected to allow time for gossip or window shopping need receive no encouragement.

Is social approval to extend also to careers for mothers? The full-time and demanding careers will continue to be difficult for all but the exceptional mothers. On the other hand, women who are willing and able to restrict their occupational goals may succeed in striking a good balance between economic and child-rearing functions. Everything we know and believe today about the development of the child points to the importance of mother-child relations. The child, and specially the young child, needs *enough* consistent care, *enough* loving, *enough* contact with the mother to insure the proper depth and range of this relationship. But whether this can be accomplished in four or fourteen hours a day with the mother depends on many factors, of which the quality of the mother's attitude during the time spent together is the most important. But other factors matter too: the personality of the child, the duration and quality of the father's contacts with him and the quality of the person who assists the mother.

We do not want a mother to yearn for a job merely because her social group deprecates housewifery. But neither do we want a woman like Mrs. Merrill, who could have combined teaching with motherhood, to refrain from doing so because of the attitude of *her* group and her husband. Public opinion should recognize the legitimacy of her interests, even if that would call for a considerable adjustment on the part of her husband. Public opinion should also accept marriages in which both husband and wife choose to share more symmetrically the economic and domestic functions.

A society must take a stand on certain essentials. We must aim to rear women so that they will be capable of mate love and of mother love. Women must be prepared to follow a pattern of economic and domestic activities which will, in general, differ from the masculine pattern. But within such limits the great need today is to widen the range of sanctioned patterns to suit the great variety of personalities and circumstances. Too many divergent influences impinge upon women to contain them all in a rigidly defined role. There is no need to place the homemaker and the professional woman on a seesaw and to link the elevation of one with the degradation of the other. We endorsed the antifeminist plea to raise the prestige of the homemaker. But we outlined ways of accomplishing this without, at the same time, debasing the intellectual and the professional woman.

These shifts in social attitudes are advocated out of concern for men, as much as for women. We place an intolerable burden upon men by re-emphasizing a model of "masculinity" which is increasingly difficult to attain in modern society. Young men frequently need the temporary financial assistance of their wives, if marriage is not to be delayed. In order to protect their self-esteem, instead of proclaiming that man is the natural provider, we might remind the young husband that wives have always made an economic contribution to the home. It is not the fault of the husband that this contribution must now take the form of earning money outside the home, rather than weaving cloth within it. But this change requires in all fairness a corresponding shift in men's duties within the home and they must be prepared to accept it. Defense needs may again make us appeal to women to take up everything from accounting to welding. Multitudes will develop a proficiency in hitherto "masculine" fields. Is it timely, then, to revive the stereotypes of "masculine" and "feminine" aptitudes? What anxieties will be stirred up in men unless we weaken (rather than strengthen) the expectations of male superiority which experience is bound to belie with increasing frequency.

It was one thing to rear men and women in the expectation of male superiority at an earlier era. When men received superior schooling, enjoyed legal advantages and wider economic opportunities, had the exclusive right of political participation and the like, they could *in fact* excel in the "masculine sphere." Today, under the influence of old attitudes, men continue to expect too much of themselves in a world which no longer gives them the former advantages. Only mischief can come from such a discrepancy.

It seems unlikely that we could bring back, even if we desired it, the economic and the social conditions which in the past caused the sharp demarcation between the masculine and the feminine spheres. And if we cannot give men their former advantages, the best chance of adjustment would come through less rigid definition of masculine and feminine roles and a wider range of accepted patterns of life. The early feminists who led the crusade for sex equality often revealed a hostility towards men. Today the antifeminists, who clamor for the dominant male, may paradoxically have less basic good will towards men than the advocates of a more equalitarian companionship between the sexes.

An appeal is currently directed to women to redeem our overcompetitive and conflict-ridden world through the exercise of the distinctively feminine virtues. It is uncertain whether nature and motherhood have really made the feminine sex, in general, more kindly, humane, understanding, sympathetic, and co-operative. Be that as it may that appeal will begin to bear fruit only when men, too, accept that challenge and, together with women, carry on the task of making a better world.

III. Work, Labor, and Socialism

CERTAINLY A BASIC COMPONENT OF TWENTIETH-CENTURY U.S. feminism has been contestation over work, both in the home and out of it. How can women be relieved of sole responsibility for housework? Who cares for the children and under what conditions? What barriers to working outside the home do women face? How can women gain economic independence? What does "worker solidarity" mean in a union if it does not accept and help women? How do racial and ethnic factors combine with sex discrimination to create even greater economic inequality for working women of color than for their white counterparts? Such questions have permeated modern American feminism, especially since passage of the Nineteenth Amendment.

Women have always worked, but as the engines of industrial capitalism demanded more and more cheap labor, early-twentieth-century American women (composing almost 24 percent of the workforce by 1920) found themselves drawn into different kinds of work—namely manufacturing and clerical positions—even while assumptions regarding their domestic duties remained intact.

The early-twentieth-century feminist effort to improve working women's lives included initiatives at various institutional levels. Unionization would become integral to improving wage and working conditions, but the American Federation of Labor (AFL), the leading national association of trade unions, refused to represent women's interests; therefore, at the 1903 AFL convention, settlement house workers and labor officials founded the Women's Trade Union League (WTUL). Originally designed to direct union organization, the WTUL quickly turned to education and legislative goals, serving as a type of clearinghouse for working-class and middle-class industrial-reform lobbying. Progress in the workplace was slow. (Indeed, like coeducation, equal opportunity and treatment for the female workforce are still in contention at the turn of the twenty-first century.) Public policy and social attitudes have long regarded the millions of gainfully employed women as secondary to working men and judged their lives as fundamentally—even morally—different. A long tradition of writing by working-class women, which began with the Lowell mill girls in the 1830s, has served to debunk resultant myths about their lives of purported promiscuity and ease. In "The New York Shop Girl" (1908), socialist-activist and intellectual Anna Maley responds sarcastically to patronizing middle-class male assumptions regarding the woman worker. She paints a harsh portrait of the desolate life of a shop worker trying to get by in New York City on six dollars per week. Maley's realism includes the hunt for a husband with the promise he brings of a "steady meal ticket" and, as an alternative, the lure of relative material comfort through prostitution.

Maley's essay exhibits empathy toward women workers—their welfare is very much her concern—and this quality of class-conscious sisterhood is also displayed in "The Diary of a Shirtwaist Striker" (1910), Theresa Serber Malkiel's testament to the solidarity of her fellow strikers in the New York City garment industry walkouts of 1909–1910. For Malkiel, a high point of the strike came during the Hippodrome meeting sponsored by WTUL millionaire Alva Belmont: "There, more than anywhere else, I felt the kinship between all the girls and myself. It seemed to me that their joy was my joy, their sorrow my own." She transcended herself. "It seemed as if I had grown a pair of wings that lifted me nearer to heaven." The New York shirtwaist makers' strike, or the "Uprising of the Twenty Thousand" as it came to be called, was overseen by the radical International Ladies' Garment Workers' Union (ILGWU) as well as the WTUL. Eventually it affected more than five hundred shops, bringing production in the city's garment industry to a virtual halt. Most of the strikers were young women—the majority of them recent Jewish immigrants, like Malkiel herself, with a propensity toward risking their jobs for the sake of long-term improvement. Born in Russia in 1874, Malkiel immigrated to the United States in 1891, found a job in the garment industry, and quickly proceeded to join seventy women in forming the Infant Cloak Makers Union of New York in 1894. This avowedly radical union eventually made connections with the Socialist Trade and Labor Alliance, with Malkiel's genius for labor agitation leading her to high positions in the Socialist Labor Party and the Socialist Party of America. Malkiel's biography, as Mari Jo Buhle puts it, "helped create the legend of the Jewish woman *qua* militant unionist."[1]

The push for strong unions in the garment industry only increased after the Triangle factory fire of 1911, in which 147 (mostly women) workers were trampled, burned to death, or killed jumping from the eighth-floor shop windows. The business's owners had rejected demands for fire escapes. They had also chained the factory's doors to keep out would-be union organizers. A few days after the fire, some eighty thousand people joined an ILGWU-organized funeral procession up Fifth Avenue. Later, upper-class civic leaders as well as immigrant workers attended a mass meeting at New York's Metropolitan Opera House. There, a twenty-nine-year-old Russian emigre, WTUL organizer Rose Schneiderman, told those in attendance that they had not done enough to prevent the tragedy. The story is recounted in "The Triangle Fire" (1911), an except from Schneiderman's 1967 autobiography, written with Lucy Goldthwaite. This event helped push New York's governor to appoint a state factory investigating commission that drafted laws to shorten the work week and improve safety in business and industry. Schneiderman would go on to enjoy a long career as a labor activist and to serve as a WTUL president.

There is great overlap between the history and rhetoric of socialism, modern American feminism in general, and labor activism among women in particular. Many feminists throughout the twentieth century believed that socialism—defined generally as a postcapitalist political system that includes both public control of the means of production and broad-based economic leveling—is a precondition for full sexual equality. In the U.S. labor movement before World War I, women workers and unionists benefited from the organizational mélange of local and national socialist groups and parties, including the Socialist Labor Party (founded in 1877), the Socialist Party (founded in 1900), and the Industrial Workers of the World (founded in 1905). And yet, as Mary White Ovington writes in "Socialism and the Feminist Movement" (1914), socialism and feminism have had an uneasy and unequal relationship, with "pure" socialist theory subsuming the interests of women by insisting that economic relations between male industrial workers and the bourgeoisie and consequent class consciousness is *the* factor in determining social structure and human history. By the early twentieth century, male socialist leaders begrudgingly acknowledged women's place in wage labor and their role in the class struggle while at the same time refusing to consider women's domestic work a part of real production. Within the dominant socialist framework, such work was part of the *re*production of the worker, not production itself.

The publication date of both Ovington's article and "Low Wages and White Slavery" (1912) by Pauline M. Newman marks a high point for U.S. socialism: Eugene V. Debs of the Socialist Party received approximately 900,000 votes in the 1912 presidential election (6 percent of the total); in that same year more than two thousand socialists served in public offices; and by then women had created their own organizations and agendas within the socialist parties' frameworks. Newman, a former worker at the Triangle Shirtwaist Company and a member of the New York Socialist Party's women's committee, published her article in *The Progressive Woman*—a leading socialist women's magazine founded in 1909 and edited by Josephine Conger-Kaneko. The article demonstrates the invaluable critical perspective that arises from socialist feminism: working from the Marxist tenet of the alienation of one's labor under capitalism, Newman explains the lure of prostitution by minimizing the moral and physical difference between receiving a wage for the bodily work in a shop or factory

---

1. Mari Jo Buhle, *Women and American Socialism, 1870–1920* (Urbana: Univ. of Illinois Press, 1981), 176.

and being paid for sex work. In fact, Newman warns, when adopting the point of view of young destitute women most concerned with food and shelter, the higher pay of prostitution is most attractive.

Early-twentieth-century African American women held the most precarious place in both the industrial and nonindustrial U.S. workforce. Not only having to fight systemic biases against women's work and women workers, African American women contended also with the legacy of slavery and the economic degradation and political powerlessness that long outlasted Lincoln's Emancipation Proclamation. The fact that their grandparents if not their parents or themselves had been born into involuntary servitude and its elaborate centuries-old system of forced unrecompensed labor suggests the difficulty African American women had in breaking through the collective barriers to gainful employment in modern America. Along with effectively disfranchising African American men and women (the latter after the 1920 ratification of the Nineteenth Amendment) the post-Reconstruction South placed African Americans in the economic hole of sharecropping, tenant farming, and other extremely low-paying agricultural work. Thus, beginning in the late nineteenth century and peaking during World War I, the push of the Jim Crow South and the pull of potential jobs and a new beginning created a steady stream of migration to the urban industrial North. Once there, however, African Americans continued to find racial discrimination—although in different, more subtle forms (perhaps even more difficult to resist). African Americans were the last to be hired for and the first to be fired from factory jobs. And, with few exceptions, the nation's labor unions shut out African American membership and equal representation until well into the mid- to late twentieth century.

The deep structure of racial discrimination in early-twentieth-century employment is described personally in "My Experience as a Clerk in a Government Department" (1917–1918/1940), an excerpt from Mary Church Terrell's autobiography. The daughter of the South's first African American millionaire, Terrel received an excellent education, graduating from Oberlin College near the top of her class, and took several tours through Europe, where she perfected her knowledge of French, German, and Italian. Despite the very high demand for people speaking those languages during World War I, the federal government denied her a position in intelligence because of her skin color. Eventually, she was placed in an office comprised solely of "colored clerks." Terrell's partially ironic account points out the element of absurdity that she found in Washington, D.C.'s segregated federal wartime offices. She describes the humiliating experience of light-skinned African American women who could "pass" being pulled from designated white positions after office managers deliberated over the truth of their race regardless of their job performance. Terrell eventually gained prominence as a professional speaker in the United States and abroad, addressing on several occasions the International Council of Women, held in Europe.

As Mary E. Jackson writes in "The Colored Woman in Industry" (1918), published in *The Crisis* (the journal of the National Association for the Advancement of Colored People), American entrance into World War I opened up jobs in railroad yards, wire works, lumber yards, glass works, tile roofing plants, clay yards, and countless other areas previously closed to black women in particular and in some cases women in general. African American women are proving themselves in filling these positions successfully, writes Jackson. In turn, they finally have an opportunity to push for improvements in working conditions, integration of black and white women workers, and the acceptance of African American women into unions. This strategy of using the end of the war and women's hard work on the home front as a historical pivot for female labor can be seen in the National Women's Trade Union League's "Post-War Program Proposal" (1919); no mention of African American workers can be found in this document, although in other ways it is quite ambitious in scope, calling for nothing less than a new progressive era of domestic reform. The continuing subordinate status of African American workers is charted in "Two Million Negro Women at Work" (1922) by Elizabeth Ross Haynes, an examiner for the Employment Service of the U.S. Department of Labor. Haynes points out that the vast majority of African American women workers in the early 1920s still hold nonstandardized jobs in agriculture and domestic service, even while nonblack women have started to achieve a more secure place in modern industry. Both Haynes and Jackson mention the importance of education for African Americans' long-term success in the national workforce: employers have to learn of African Americans' abilities, and the girls and women need better education to prepare themselves for employment. Such was the impetus behind the heroic founding and development of Bethune-Cookman College, which Mary McLeod Bethune describes in "Faith That Moved a Dump Heap" (1941). Bethune's faith in both African American solidarity and interracial cooperation led to her extraordinary success as an educator. Bethune's school opened in 1904 in a one-room shanty with five girls enrolled; by 1941 Bethune-Cookman College had expanded into fourteen modern buildings on a thirty-two-acre campus, with a student body of over six hundred. Bethune's life itself serves as an inspiration to achievement. Born to former slaves, Bethune served in Franklin Roosevelt's administration, was a friend and teacher to Eleanor Roosevelt, and used her White House connections to push for equal treatment of African Americans in New Deal agencies. Her career is often likened to the turn-of-the-century African American leader Booker T. Washington.

Despite the quality of women's work during World War I and the fact that it dispelled many myths of inherent female inferiority, women in the 1920s still faced numerous barriers to equality in labor, not the least of which was continuing discrimination within unions. In "Women Workers and the A. F. of L." (1921), Katharine Fisher criticizes the insidious ways the American Federation of Labor leadership avoids engaging "the woman question" and thereby maintains what she calls its belief in "men's right of dictatorship over women." By claiming that it could not create policy for individual unions like the barbers' and carpenters' brotherhoods, the AFL implicitly supported the exclusion of women from these craft unions while avoiding openly discriminatory language itself. In addition to holding on to notions of inherent male prerogative, the AFL approach to this issue betrays the widespread fear that, because of the lower female pay scale, women could displace men. The 1930 census suggests the results of antiwoman union policy: of the nearly eleven million gainfully employed women, only two hundred fifty thousand were organized in trade unions, and half of them were in the garment industry; nationwide, one in nine male workers belonged to a union, and only one in thirty women workers.

Women workers' efforts to join trade unions were helped little by the Women's Bureau, even though it was headed by trade union veteran Mary Anderson. Established under pressure from the WTUL and the National Consumers' League, the Women's Bureau was founded in the U.S. Department of Labor in 1919 as a permanent successor to the Women in Industry Service set up during World War I. "What the Women's Bureau Has Accomplished" (1930) reports that in its first decade the office was long on studying the problems of female labor—publishing more than eighty pamphlets by 1930—but short on achieving actual solutions. In alliance with those women and organizations favoring protective labor legislation, the Women's Bureau generally did not envision complete sexual equality in the workplace and thereby tacitly supported union bias toward men. In "Women and Machines" (1921), Mary Van Kleeck, cofounder of the Women's Bureau, reflects the office's antagonism toward the Equal Rights Amendment and the National Woman's Party, using the word *feminism* to categorize pejoratively those opposed to sex-based labor legislation.

Within the history of early-twentieth-century labor activism, an American original was Mary Mother Jones, author of "You Don't Need a Vote to Raise Hell" (1925). Beginning her career as a labor organizer of Pennsylvania and Illinois coal miners in the 1880s and 1890s, often working for the United Mine Workers, Mother Jones gained public notoriety for her sharp wit, militant speeches, and overall dramatic flair. These qualities are well demonstrated in her leading of miners' wives in a moonlight march over mountains and then banging on tin pans to block strikebreakers trying to start the morning shift. Despite the daring of Mother Jones in labor struggles, her views on women's issues were traditional. As loudly suggested by the title "You Don't Need a Vote to Raise Hell" (1925), she opposed women's suffrage, and she understood her own activism as driven by the moral authority of the mother within a family.

With the stock market crash and the beginning of the Great Depression in 1929, female labor became at once less valuable and more common. Women workers (generally faring better than men) increased in number throughout the 1930s: women's paid wage labor outside the home grew from nearly eleven million women in 1930 (24 percent of women in the United States) to fourteen million by 1940 (27 percent). Besides the increase in wage labor, the economic hardship and social dislocation of the Depression made work within the home more demanding—with the drastic decrease in male earning power women had to find new ways to get by with far less. Meridel Le Sueur's grim account of "Women on the Breadlines" (1932) depicts the particular suffering of jobless women often without home or family. By 1935 there were seventy-five thousand homeless women in New York City alone; and, as Le Sueur points out, compared to men, unemployed vagrant women had fewer charitable institutions like flophouses and soup kitchens to depend on. Gnawing hunger, "like the beak of a terrible bird at the vitals," was the predominant concern for destitute women. Even prostitution offered less of a way out, since like other work it paid far less during the Depression.

The Depression brought an unprecedented effort by the federal government to regulate the economy and provide relief for its citizens. Innovative New Deal legislation like the Fair Labor Standards Act of 1938 helped working women by setting hour and wage standards for those employed in businesses and industries engaged in interstate commerce. Greatly strengthening the labor movement was the National Labor Relations Act of 1935—or the Wagner Act, named after its sponsor Senator Robert Wagner of New York—which guaranteed workers' collective bargaining rights by outlawing company unions and creating the National Labor Relations Board to oversee management's response to the new law. Union organization thrived during the Depression, with the most dramatic successes coming through the efforts of John L. Lewis's Committee on Industrial Organizations, founded in 1935 and renamed in 1938 the Congress of Industrial Organizations (CIO). Unlike the AFL, which still ignored unskilled industrial workers, the CIO helped organize the millions of men *and* women employees in the steel, automobile, rubber, and electrical industries. This rather rapid development in the late 1930s and early 1940s marked the most important advance for women in trade unionism. And, as Sabina Martinez explains in "Negro Women in Organization—Labor" (1941), the nondiscriminatory CIO improved African American women's subordinate position in basic industry. As an example, Martinez draws from her own role in the CIO's organization of New York City's twenty-seven thousand (predominantly African American women) laundry workers into a union affiliated with Amalgamated Clothing Workers of America.

Intersecting with the success of the labor movement during the 1930s, socialist and even communist thought flourished. The human suffering of the Great Depression seemed to call for radical change. While relatively few Americans actually joined the Socialist Party or the Community Party (founded in 1919 after splitting from the Socialist Party), many union organizers, industrial workers, and young intellectuals embraced Marx's vision of moving past the cutthroat economic competition and gross inequities of industrial capitalism. Beginning in 1935, under direction of the Soviet Union, American communists supported the New Deal and U.S. liberalism overall in an effort to form a broad coalition or Popular Front against the rise of European Fascism. Adding to this radical-liberal synergy was the further development of socialist feminism. As Grace Hutchins writes in "Women under Capitalism" (1934), an excerpt from her influential book *Women Who Work,* middle- and upper-class women enjoy comfortable and autonomous lives while working-class women along with African Americans bear the brunt of industrial capitalism with their undervalued labor. In addition to her sharp class consciousness, Hutchins looks to the Soviet Union as a model for feminist progress: communism, she believes, accepts responsibility for women workers; differences between the sexes dissolved with the end of capitalism. Similar socialist-feminist optimism can be found in Rebecca Pitts's essay "Women and Communism" (1935), which is particularly valuable for its explanation of how the advent of private property destroyed the equality accorded women in communal prehistoric societies and is, in turn, directly responsible for female subjugation. Pitts also demonstrates acute awareness of the hyperconservative changes to women under Fascism—what she describes as the most complete political manifestation of capitalism.

Conventional U.S. women's history has American women serving valiantly in heavy industries and military women's corps during World War II, then returning quietly to domesticity as the Cold War and the rise of middle-class suburbia usher in a long period of conservatism that lasts until the early 1960s when Betty Friedan's liberal critique of "the feminine mystique" appears, followed by the radical women's liberation movement. Daniel Horowitz and other historians are currently revising this history, finding strands of socialist feminism from the early Cold War era that connect the radicalism of the 1930s and early 1940s to the progressive tumult of the 1960s. A compelling aspect of this new intellectual history is Horowitz's uncovering of an early stage in Friedan's life when she was a strong-minded class- and race-conscious labor journalist, writing pieces for publications like *The UE News*—the newspaper of the United Electrical, Radio, and Machine Workers of America (UE), the most radical union in the postwar United States. Horowitz—author of *Betty Friedan and the Making of* The Feminine Mystique: *The American Left, the Cold War, and Modern Feminism*—believes Friedan to be the author of the pamphlet *UE Fights for Women Workers* (1952), which harshly criticizes the contradictory glorification of women's power as consumers while they are underpaid and virtually ignored as workers. Another connection—one that may have influenced the young Friedan—can be seen in the wide-ranging socialist-feminist essay from the postwar era "Woman against Myth" (1947–1948), by Betty Millard, which was published in *The New Masses* (a radical communist-oriented journal). Writing in the early days of the Cold War, Millard trashes the spurious ideal of genteel femininity and then goes on to praise the Soviet Union for instituting state-run nurseries, paid maternity leave, free health care, and other measures making women workers' lives more manageable. Another communist-influenced response to resurgent domestic ideology was Irene Epstein's article "Woman under the Double Standard" (1950), which seizes on the economic contradiction whereby capitalism, in trying to keep women subjugated in the home, also demands their cheap labor in the industrial workforce. Writing in *Jewish Life,* Epstein also praises the freedom and equality Israeli women enjoy in communitarian kibbutzes.

Socialism played a major role in the evolution of second-wave feminist theory, too, specifically in the transformation of radicalism into a practical program for achieving female power and equality. The goal of directing liberationist energy into "wresting control of the institutions which now oppress us" is stressed in "Socialist Feminism—A Strategy for the Women's Movement" (1972), published by the Hyde Park Chapter of the Chicago Women's Liberation Union. Women's oppression, according to this paper, stems from two intertwined and deeply rooted sources: capitalism and sexism. Rather than targeting one of these over the other, rather than constructing a monolithic theory of feminism, the Chicago Women's Liberation Union formulates a decidedly pragmatic approach to opposing female subordination. Since, as the group explains, "at different periods our oppression may be greater in one area than another," it is crucial to remain adaptable and strategic in the struggle rather than intellectually pure and consistent in doctrine.

83
ANNA A. MALEY
The New York Shop Girl (1908)

In the recent issue of *Van Norden Magazine* there appeared an article by Remsen Crawford, entitled "Her Majesty the Shop Girl," in which the writer contends that the "muck rakers" have created in the minds of the people a condition of discontent for which there is no justification in fact. He instances the much commiserated shop girl of New York City. The daughter of the farm, he states, who wastes her pity on the New York shop girl, might see, could she stand on a down-town corner of Broadway at eight o'clock in the morning, "a smiling throng of dimple cheeked girls neatly attired in pretty shirt waists, jaunty jackets and smart frocks, all marching and counter-marching with elastic, buoyant steps on trimly booted feet, toward factory, warehouse, office and store. There are just 130,691 of these wage earning girls in New York City, and be it said to their credit, they make $41,994,400, or an average of $350 each."

More than a dollar a day, comments the author, when Sundays and holidays are deducted.

Having proved to his own satisfaction that a shop girl can live comfortably in New York on one dollar a day, and having dislodged from our minds the haunting superstition that it costs money to live in this city on Sundays and holidays, Mr. Crawford proceeds to set some posers which are altogether worthy of the discernment displayed up to this point in his discussion. To quote:

"Having thus established by a somewhat tedious process as accurately as it can be established just about what the shop-girls of New York earn in a day, and a week, and a year, the real interesting part of the subject is before us: What does she do with this money? How does she spend it? Why has she toiled to earn it? Is it being used for her moral and mental uplift? Has the privilege of earning this dollar a day so fascinated her with her own independence that she thinks less and less of marriage–of taking her place at the fireside of a growing family? Does the dollar a day go to gratifying the feminine follies, dads and capricious fancies which have held women in their fetters since the gate of Eden closed behind Eve?"

During a residence of two months in the same house with a shop woman employed with the firm of Simpson-Crawford, I gained some intimate knowledge touching the questions raised by Mr. Crawford. She may be taken as representative of the 130,000, and I take pleasure in giving the details: This blithe marcher was a widow who was employed in the toy department at a wage of six dollars a week. She was forty years of age. She lived in an inside room, a room on the air-shaft, altogether cut off from the great outdoors. In it were a narrow bed, a trunk, a small table and one chair. Among this furniture one could wriggle one's way if one were thin—and careful. For this room she paid weekly $1.75.

And she was thin: for she paid fifteen cents for her best meal on weekdays and twenty-five cents for her Sunday dinner, a weekly dinner bill of $1.15. For dinner and supper she ate bread without butter and drank cocoa made from water. These two meals cost her not to exceed ten cents a day or seventy cents a week. She would have drank coffee instead of cocoa but as she surreptitiously used the landlady's gas for cooking she must use odorless foods. Distances are great in New York and there was an inevitable weekly bill for carfare of sixty cents. These items total $4.20. Out of the remaining $1.80, her majesty must pay her laundry bill. She might have washed her own shirt waists, but to dry and iron them would have meant sure detection by her watchful landlady and a calling to account for the gas. During my acquaintance with this woman she paid every week without exception a fine amounting to at least twenty-five cents, most frequently for wrong addresses. Her majesty explained to me

From *The Socialist Woman*, November 1908.

that most of these errors arose from the fact that foreign speaking customers did not give addresses clearly. One week my princess had fines to the amount of seventy-five cents and then she wept. She had been trying for three months to accumulate the price of a pair of shoes. She used a paste-board inside sole to keep her feet from the ground, and her stockings had been darned until none of the original feet was left. She had a fading beauty. In her pretty white teeth the black rocks shone but her ladyship elected to spend her dollar a day in gratifying her feminine follies, fads and capricious fancies and would not give her money to a dentist.

Such is the reward, such is the struggle of the New York shop girl. The value of her services is well expressed in Mr. Crawford's own words:

"Those who have taken so much pains to exploit the shop-girl's wrongs and woes might have been generous enough to exploit also her achievements. When one stops to consider the great part the working girls of New York City alone play in the trade and commerce of this country one sees her as a cogent factor in the national welfare in very truth. She sews on the buttons of a continent. Her handiwork is displayed on the counters of village stores from Mexico to Maine. The dainty bonnets she bedecks with ribbons and flowers make glad the feminine heart at Easter time in every little hamlet and nearly every great city of the northern half of the hemisphere. She stitches together the garments for hundreds of thousands of men, women, boys and girls of Brother Jonathan's country. By the activity of her nimble fingers great dry-goods emporiums thrive, and countless village stores do business. For the dollar which gladdens her heart every day she gives garments fine enough to be playthings of plutocrats, or cheap enough to be bought by the needy in the remotest corner of the land. With a self effacement that is beautiful to contemplate the shop girl goes about this great work seemingly unconscious of her very great importance in the clothing, millinery and dry-goods business of the country. She rarely joins a labor union. There are only 8,000 such working women in all New York out of the 367,000 counted by the last census."

Contented, patient, modest without being meek, unselfish, happy—these are the attributes of "Her Majesty—the Shop Girl."

My sister of the shop, this author tells you that your self-effacement, your blotting out of yourself and your rights is beautiful to contemplate. But we ask you, is it beautiful? What does it mean for you? A weary, neglected body, a stunted mind, a narrow soul, a bitter spirit. Are these things beautiful? Is the husband hunt, the chase for an opportunity to exchange yourself for a steady meal ticket—beautiful? Is the lure toward prostitution created by your poverty—beautiful? In what is your sacrifice beautiful? No child is happier because of your pain. To be sure, the children of your master are pampered and overfed and taught to despise you. Your master's class despises you. They could give no stronger proof of this than that they ask you to live in New York at a dollar a day. The masters and not, we insist upon class divisions and distinctions. Any group from Fifth Avenue may come with their curious vulgarity to inspect the slums. They would not suffer for a moment that the slum dwellers should inspect their drawing rooms.

So we tell you that your self-effacement is not beautiful. It is hideous. Yet all the workers of the world must consent to self-effacement as long as the masters own the land, the mills, the mines and shops where the workers earn their bread. The Socialist party stands for the ownership by the workers of the things with which they must work. We ask you to join our ranks. We call you to a destiny, not of self-effacement but of full and free womanhood and manhood. Rise in holy protest against the betrayal of yourself and your brothers, join the congregation of the fighters for industrial freedom, and forge steadily forward to the day when all the workers of the world may celebrate themselves.

84

THERESA SERBER MALKIEL

The Diary of a Shirtwaist Striker (1910)

DECEMBER 1.—People say that a new month is sure to bring new luck with it, but I fail to see it in our case. The fight is now worse than ever; though many of the bosses have settled there are still so many strikers that one imagines they grow over night.

As the days go by the girls suffer more and more. During the tedious picket duty they get frozen, catch colds, go without food until they're nothing but shadows of their former selves—it's real disheartening.

When I got down to the headquarters this morning I had to go and help out at the information bureau. Lord! complaints were coming in faster than I could put them down.

"A ruffian tore my coat and broke my glasses," cried a girl at the top of her voice. "I haven't another coat and can't make a step without the glasses."

"Be glad it ain't your head," consoled another whose face and eyes were swollen and bruised. She told me later that she was beaten by a thug while out on picket duty.

"I got no more hair," complained a third one. "Tim that works by Cohen, he pulls them all out of me."

"Ach Got, mein Got!" pleaded a stooping man with a long, unkempt beard streaked with gray. "Mine children, they hungry. I want one job."

It almost broke my heart to listen to his plea. I think it's a shame that a man of his age should have to work and go out on strike. But it seemed rather strange—the man knew his children were hungry and that he could get work if he wouldn't be so scrupulous and become a scab. But I really admire him more than blame him.

From Theresa Serber Malkiel, *The Diary of a Shirtwaist Striker: A Story of the Shirtwaist Makers' Strike in New York* (New York: The Co-operative Press, 1910), 17–19, 21–31.

"I'm that mad I can't see straight!" assured me a girl of about sixteen. "I stay out until 4 o'clock this morning in the night court—close to a lot of drunken bums and street women. I know the judge; he do it for spite; he just loves us poor people. And when I got home my ma gave me terrible scolding; she didn't believe I was in court. She thinks I was fooling around somewhere."

I was dreadfully excited by that girl's story. One could scarcely believe that men with families of their own would be so deaf to all sense of justice. Who could blame this young girl if she would go wrong?

"Hey, children, children, I say nothin'," murmured an old, toothless woman, her wrinkled face propped up with both hands. "I make $5 one week to keep myself and my two childs. The girls in my shop they go on strike. I no stay one scab. But it's bad; my children they no eat nothin' today."

Five dollars a week for three people! How is it possible? What sort of a life must they lead? I must admit that I'm beaten. I've always thought that I was bad off—but Lord! we live in perfect bliss in comparison to this woman and many others like her. I'm just beginning to find out what real misery means. It's simply dreadful—dreadful is hardly strong enough a word for it. And people wonder why we are out striking! The only thing that takes me is the bravery of the girls—one would think that this sort of life ought to crush every bit of energy in them, but it doesn't look it. I guess their energy thrives on suffering; it seems to grow with it.

Why! this one day at the information bureau broke me up completely, I could almost write a whole book from the tales I heard and sights I saw there. I felt like dazed on going home and when I got there I found Jim waiting for me. I forgot all about that this was Wednesday night—beau's night. Jim thought it wasn't proper for me to stay down town so late, that the day was long enough for this tomfoolery and that I'm getting to be as lawless as one of them darn anarchists. Just for the fun of it I'd like to meet one of them and see if they're really as black as they're painted. For it seems that Jim can't find anything worse to compare me with. And yet—I doubt if he knows what an anarchist is like—it can't be that he does, or he wouldn't call us girls anarchists. If the people at large weren't worse than us girls it would, perhaps, be easier to live in this cold, merciless world.

And it wasn't all in words, either, my falling out with Jim, for there were others around; it's our looks that told more than the words.

December 2.—I was so tired last night that I left the sitting room before Jim was gone and this morning Ma informed me that they had talked it all over—that is, Jim and Pa, for Ma ain't got much to say when Pa's around.

Funny—they've decided my fate for me. I'm to quit going down town, Jim to try and rush things up for our marriage and Pa'll manage to keep me in clothes for the time being, until Jim'll take me off his hands.

And they are considered sensible men! What did they think? I was their baggage, perhaps. It must be so, or they could never have thought that they had a right to dispose of me at their own sweet will. I wonder if they thought of keeping me under lock and key or permit me at large?

To think of it—just because I happened to be born a woman! Well, what of it? Ain't I of the same flesh and one as a man? I, too, was carried under a mother's heart. And since I was born I've suffered from almost the same diseases and was healed by exactly the same medicines. I walk under the same sky and tread the same earth as men do. I, too, have senses, moods and reasons, am old enough to judge for myself; but they didn't seem to think so. Well, I must say—they've made the mistake of their life if they think that I'll abide by their resolution.

Of course, even while Ma was telling me all about last night's conference I was getting ready to go down town. But I couldn't help thinking of it until I got to the meeting rooms. Here they're talking of my marriage to Jim when I'm just commencing to think that we don't even know each other well enough. That is, I've come to think so of late, for it seems to me that he ain't the Jim I took him for. I disagree more and more with him and am shocked at times at his ignorance of things that concern everyday life. And what is even worse than his ignorance is the fact that he thinks he knows it all and I ought simply listen to what he tells me.

Well, this was certainly the day for feeling blue—it poured cats and dogs, as if nature itself was sympathizing with me. But I forgot myself as soon as I came face to face with the bigger sorrow. And I don't see how anybody can look into the gulf on the brink of which our girls are standing without feeling a pang of keenest grief, without a desire to do something only to make their lot easier.

Poor devils! their worn clothes and torn shoes were just soaked by the peltering rain. To tell the truth, we were all a sorry sight to look at—the dirty water pouring from the hats down upon the face and neck. But even then I couldn't help laughing at Annie's beaver hat; it looked too funny for anything—all shriveled up and out of shape. This lasted only a moment for I bethought myself that it is the only hat she has and may not be able to buy another this winter.

I think that even the cops pitied us this morning, while some old gentleman offered to buy us rubbers. The girls refused his offer, but I've been wondering whether he really meant it out of the goodness of his heart or was it some new scheme to trap us girls.

Everybody tried to make love to the little coal stove when we got back to the meeting rooms. But I wouldn't be a bit surprised if many of the girls will be laid up with sore throats by tomorrow. It is terrible; they go down like flies. There's scarcely a shop but has a number of girls sick in bed. This makes it so much harder for those who are still up. Poor Ray, her teeth were just rattling when she got back this afternoon; even the cup of hot water we gave her didn't help much. She ain't fit to work or strike, either. It's a sanitarium and good care that she needs, but where is she to get it, and what will the others do without her?

How is it that people walk around with their eyes open and yet don't seem to see all these things? . . .

DECEMBER 4.—These are days of excitement—yesterday the parade, tomorrow the Hippodrome meeting. I wonder what next. The girls were just wild about tomorrow's affair; you could hear them talk of nothing else but Mrs. Belmont; they've even forgot their own troubles for a while. It is rather strange, her offering to pay for the big place. I wonder what made her do it? She must surely be better than the rest of her kind if she is willing to spend her money to help us girls rather than give a monkey dinner or buy a couple of new pet dogs.

But then, why shouldn't she? She's got plenty of money. And to think how much the papers make of her. I think that she and the rest of her kind ought to be thankful to us girls for giving them a chance to do a good deed. I know I felt fine when I spent my last quarter for the Bloom kids, and Mrs. Belmont doesn't have to give her last, I am sure.

In a way I think it's really a shame that the very rich get so much free advertising while little Violet and many others like her, who are really sacrificing themselves to help us out, shouldn't be mentioned at all, except when they are arrested and taken to jail.

Stopped on the square this afternoon and listened to them that talks votes for women. It's all very true. I also say that a woman is every bit as good as a man and should have the same rights with him. But us girls have something else to think of just now. We must see to it that we win the strike for bread and then we can start one for the ballot.

As I was leaving the square I met a girl going to the headquarters; her face was all swollen, one of her teeth knocked out, her clothes in tatters and she running around since early this morning unable to find a policeman willing to arrest the brute who beat her so terribly. I wonder if this is what our good Mayor is doing for us?

As I said, we have our hands full just at present—a number of girls went back on us. The fools got scared because Hayman told them that he'd rather go out of business than give in to us girls. I don't believe a word he says—what else would he do if not be in business unless he turned dog catcher? But it wouldn't pay as well as the waist making business does.

The pity of it is that us working people don't really realize what a power we are. I fully agree with that speaker who said that in spite of all their money our bosses couldn't get along without us working people. For if they had even a hundred times as many machines, and the whole world built of factories, they couldn't deliver a single order unless the working people chose to make them up.

But how are the girls to know all these things? I'm sure not by sitting day in and day out at the machine, rushing, pushing and hustling all in order to make another couple of cents. And one can't blame them for doing it; it's precious little they make, even at that.

The Lord knows that they're near enough to starvation. The worst part of it is that very few can realize what it means to lead a life like the most of our girls are leading. For somehow it seems to me that if the people would really know the true state of affairs, if they could be brought to realize that the girls have ventured out on this strike because they can't stand it any longer, they wouldn't remain quietly at their comfortable homes while thousands of girls are being driven to the dogs.

The papers say that Mrs. Belmont is worth millions; that each of her hats and suits is worth hundreds of dollars. If this be true and if she is affected by the girls' sufferings, why doesn't she try to do something more for us. If she really feels about it the way I do why don't she come down among us, feed the hungry and warm the cold? I didn't see her even once and I don't believe any of the girls did. Perhaps she thinks she's too high-toned to come down here. Well, then, she can just stay where she is, and us girls will try to fight our own battles. I'm anxious to have a look at her tomorrow.

DECEMBER 5.—Lord! I never saw anything like it in my life—that Hippodrome meeting.

The place was so crowded that I had trouble in getting in, though I did come rather early. But once I was in it was worth all the trouble of getting there. It did my heart good to see how happy every one of our girls looked. There, more than in any other place, I felt the kinship between all the girls and myself. It seemed to me that their joy was my joy, their sorrow my own. It seemed as if I had grown a pair of wings that lifted me nearer to heaven. I sang and laughed, and was happy like all the rest of them. For I felt as though I had been born anew and became a power. I knew that if I should happen to be hurt or abused all these thousands of men and women would stretch out their hands to lift me out of danger.

It is really a wonderful feeling that comes over one when a body finds itself surrounded by thousands of people all assembled for the same purpose, breathing the same hopes and thinking the same thoughts—it's like an immense giant born for the purpose of doing justice to all.

I think the speaker must have felt the same way when she said that one person in himself is something like a lone tree planted in a desert. It is bound to wither and die under the steady burning of the hot sun and the heavy gales of wind. But all the people united together are like a great shady forest where every tree, small or large, is protected by all the others, so that all have their chance to grow and prosper. Yes, when I come to think of it I realize that one person by himself, no matter how rich or clever he may be, can't exist very long, unless he is helped and protected by everybody else.

It is strange, that I've lived for over twenty years, gone through school and Sunday school and never gave it a thought until to-day. I'm beginning to think that this strike is the best thing that could have happened to me, though it may cost me Jim's love.

He was with me at the meeting and said that I've surely gone crazy, the way I behaved down there. I believe he was touched to the quick by the votes for women speaker—she said that woman, married or unmarried, has as much right to live and enjoy life as any man. That the women are foolish to permit themselves to be ruled and patronized by men.

"I can see my finish," snapped Jim at me when we left the place. "I guess I'll have to quit if you continue to keep company with these loons."

And mighty sane loons they are at that. I wonder if Jim ever heard a talk that had more common sense in it than he did this afternoon at the Hippodrome. But as the saying goes, none are so deaf as those that will not hear. He thought he'll scare me by his warning. A lot I care! What is my little trouble compared with the suffering of the great big forest of people?

I was anxious to see Mrs. Belmont, but the meeting proved so interesting that I forgot all about her. To tell the truth—I ain't got much use for these rich, especially since I've learned how miserable the poor are. Somehow I can't believe they are human—if they were they couldn't stand for all this misery.

The most of our girls had to walk both ways in order to save their car fare. Many came without dinner, but the collection baskets had more pennies than anything else in them—it was our girls themselves who helped to make it up, and yet there were so many rich women present. And I'm sure the speakers made it plain to them how badly the money is needed, then how comes it that out of the $300 collected there should be $70 in pennies?

I'm sorry I couldn't help with the collection. Jim wouldn't let me. I could have found out for myself just who gave the most. Make believe I wasn't furious at Jim, but what could I do? I wouldn't start a quarrel with him right there and then. But I'm afraid it's coming, this real quarrel is. All these little disagreements bode no good to either of us. We seem to be drifting apart daily. I often think it's a good thing that it all happened before we were married, for the Lord knows how it will all end.

December 6.—Lord! my nerves are all on edge, but I'm glad that I read the law to her. The scab on the body, as a rule, comes from hunger and privation but with Mame it is nothing but a case of sheer cussedness. She's just a mean, vile, paltry scab from scabby land!

Talk about the proud, independent American—I must admit I'm ashamed of my country-women; they're the worst scabs living. One can't really do a thing with them but beat it into their heads. Anybody that knows me knows that I ain't the kind to go in for a fist fight; in fact, I don't think I've ever laid my hands on anybody before this, but I'm not a bit sorry for giving her that lesson; she needed it badly.

It seems almost incredible that she was my best friend once upon a time and that I was, in a way, as bad as she is today. And I'm mighty glad of the change; I wouldn't want to get back to her way of thinking for a fortune.

What set my blood a-boiling is the manner in which she commenced to yell as soon as Fanny and I came near her. This was a signal for that ruffian Ben to fall upon poor Fanny and pound her with all his might. And what could I do but lay it in to Mame, even if she had been my friend? In love and in war everything, they say, is fair.

Fanny's face is black and blue, her eyes are all swollen, but she won't hear of complaining against that hoodlum, for fear that they may get after me then. No wonder that Christ had sacrificed himself for all mankind; it seems to run in the Jewish blood, this spirit of self-sacrifice. But somehow I have a premonition that they'll get me just the same. It wouldn't be like Mr. Hayman to let a thing like that slip by.

The way they stick to their union, or make believe they do! I only wish our girls would be as wise as all that, but they ain't; they carry their troubles on their sleeves. When we started to discuss the strike this morning, some of the girls, and even more so the men, were for giving up the fight and going back without the union. I think these men of ours would surely take the first prize in cowardice. To think that they don't lift a finger to help win the strike, but are ready on the job when there's any kicking to be done. I had occasion to know some of the white trash that lives in the South, and, honestly, as I watch these so-called men of ours I can't help calling them—man-trash.

I was proud, though, of some of the girls and the fine arguments they've put up in favor of holding out. "What do we lose?" asked Minnie. "We've gone cold and hungry before this, and a little more or less won't matter. If we can afford to starve on the boss' account we can also afford to do it on our own; perhaps it will help in the long run; perhaps the sun will still shine even for us. I think we're entitled to a bit of it."

"If you had brains in your head instead of corn mush," admonished Ray, "you'd readily understand that if Mr. Hayman objects to having a union you ought to stick up for it. The bosses are smarter than us working people; they know that hundreds and thousands of girls and men bound together for the purpose of helping all are a terrible power, and, therefore, they are fighting this power and nothing else, but you people don't know your own strength; you're ready to cut your own throats. By urging us to give up the strike you're rushing to your doom. And all because you can't see farther than your nose, you're willingly shutting your eyes to the future."

"It's only lobsters that creep backward. People with common sense move on all the time. Lot's wife was changed into a mountain of salt for turning back, and you'll be sure to shed enough tears to make a salt lake," warned them Sarah.

"I ain't going back just the same," assured us Rose. "But Lord help those of you who do—we'll break every bone in your body."

So we argued and threatened and quarreled until we won—we ain't going back until we get a signed agreement. But who can foretell how it will all end? Hunger and want are pressing more and more upon the girls, their strength, too, is giving out, while the bosses are waging a more bitter fight than ever. But what's the use worrying?

DECEMBER 7.—I thought so—Mr. Hayman wasn't the kind to let things slip by—he went after me bright and early, as soon as I got near the shop. And now I'm a real striker—felt the grip of a policeman's hand, had a free ride in a patrol wagon, spent a few hours at the police station and was arraigned in court. One may imagine things, but not until you meet them face to face do you really know what they are like.

Not until I was placed in a real cell and the door shut behind me did I realize what it means to be a prisoner, to be deprived of freedom of action and speech. And yet—ain't we deprived of it every day of our lives, I mean us working girls? We go to the factory bright and early in the morning and after that until we leave we are practically prisoners, except that we don't know it and imagine that we are there of our own free will; but it ain't so, we are there because we must or we would starve.

This is, perhaps, one of the reasons that us girls don't mind the jail as much as other people do, for we're used to the filth and dirt and a good many other things. But what shocked me beyond words was the horrible behavior of the policemen. And they kept to protect us from harm!

"How late were you out last night?" asked one of them.

"Oh, I don't think she has caught him yet," chimed in another; she's looking for a match right now."

"They are silly, these girls are," assured a third. "Where's the sense of their going on strike when a woman can earn plenty of money without working?"

It's sickening to repeat all the things they did say to us girls as we sat in our cells huddled in a corner, afraid to breathe or even look up, for their eyes were full of beastly poison.

I don't know what I looked like, but it was certainly a pity to watch the other girls—they were too scared for anything—on the one end the horrid policemen, on the other four drunken women. Every time the policemen said something nasty the women let out a shriek that could be heard two blocks away. Across the hall from us a man kept walking back and forth like a caged animal. The terrible look in his eyes made me think of the tigers in the park —it was enough to make anybody refrain from approaching him.

A good thing that the captain got word that another batch of strikers were coming and he had to make room for them, so he took our names, asked a whole lot of questions and gave us another free ride to the court house. And I was mighty glad at that—didn't have to go to the night court or tell anything about being a jailbird to the folks at home.

Now I always thought that a court house was a magnificent place where sits a grave dignified judge, many clerks, stenographers and great lawyers. But what a sad disappointment—the place they brought us to wasn't much better than the station house. The judge looked as though he had been out on a spree. The lawyers—a lot of cheap guys that you see hanging around the corner saloons. And the audience—well, they beat it all! One could have made up a funny museum of them. And talk about cases—a husband charged with licking his wife; a German woman accused of pouring out the leavings upon her neighbor; a wife deserter, a pickpocket, a drunken woman, a sneak thief, a dozen or more strikers.

One couldn't really recall them all. What I'm wondering at is how Miss Elizabeth could stand it all—to be there day in and day out and she not striking, either, except against everything that's wrong.

I thought it rather silly when they made me swear that I'll tell the truth—everybody else swore to do it, but as far as I could judge, very few told the honest truth.

"Your honor," says I when my turn came. "I saw them fight with each other and I knew them all, so I stepped in and took them apart. I'm sure you would have done the same if you were there."

And he had to admit that he would, but it seemed so funny to him that he had to laugh right out. "Discharged," said he, "and try to keep out of my way."

DECEMBER 8.—Another wrinkle—a conference of all the arrested girls. I only wonder where they find names to all these different conferences, but, then, what is the difference? You learn something new every time.

But it really amounts to this: The League women saw at last there ain't no use sending committees to the Mayor, or telling our troubles to a policeman, so, to please the girls, they got us to tell our troubles to that good soul—Helen. Of course, we understand that she can't do much for us in that line, but if she'll only give us a few of her kind smiles it will make it easier to bear the burden. And of this we were pretty certain, for Helen has always a smile for us girls, even when her heart breaks from sorrow. It's my belief that the kind soul will go down to her grave with a smile on her lips.

And still and all, I was startled to see the room filled with girls, each eager to tell her tale of woe, but it did my heart good to see their temper of rebellion—every one of them was prepared to face the music to the bitter end. And if those that hound us had only been present they would have understood the folly of their policy of trying to subdue us by such outrageous treatment.

Why, it's hardly believable that all these girls were arrested in a free land, for no bigger crime than the desire to stand up for their rights. Talk about being anarchists—I really wonder if that name doesn't suit the police better than it does us girls? And my pa, a good union man, has the courage to say that it ain't a girl's place to belong to a union!

I just wondered this morning where the protectors of all these girls were hiding. It's on our own responsibility that our parents sent us out to hunt for a job, and get in and out of all sorts of traps—then what sort of a love can they have for us when they deny us the right to band together for mutual protection?

In a way, I think we girls are to blame for being so timid all along and now everybody got so used to it that they take it for granted—it must be so. But, I'm glad to say, we left off creeping, and if we can do this much at the first attempt we're sure to be able to stand on our feet before very long. Once your eyes are opened you can't help seeing and protesting against everything that's wrong. They might as well stop the incoming tide as stop a body from fighting for liberty to lead a decent life.

The judges and police make the mistake of their lives if they hope to stop us by keeping up this jail business—every new arrest makes a firm convert to the cause. The girls' sense of justice becomes sharpened by the fact that they are persecuted for telling the truth. Helen tried to assure us that they'll impeach the judges—I'd like to know who'll be brave enough to do it. But anything is good, so long as it quiets the girls.

Some of the League women rushed off in a hurry, they said, to hold a conference with the bosses. I do hope they'll come to some understanding this time, for this strike is just killing many of the girls. But some of them labor leaders needn't think that they can bunco us into any tom fool settlement, for we won't stand for it. Us girls have come to realize that the welfare of one means the welfare of all, and this is likewise true about the hardships. Annie and Rosie don't amount to anything as long as they remain only hands and stand up each one for herself and let the devil take the hindmost.

But there are a few sleek go-betweens, smooth-tongued spiders I'd call them, and it's them that's trying hard to entangle us girls into a net. One of them mistook me for somebody else this morning and said more than he would have had he known I was a striker. That's how I came to know that they would like the League women to sign an agreement with the bosses and declare the strike off without consulting us girls about it. I listened quietly to all he had to say and never said a word to contradict him—it's good to keep your views to yourself once in a while and somebody else's, too, for future reference.

DECEMBER 9.—I tell you, life seems to be made up of surprises, and I certainly had one this afternoon when I went down to a meeting at the Thalia Theater arranged by those Socialists. I herd of them before this, of course, but only when pa was very much disgruntled with his union, then he would come home and put all the blame for it on the Socialists, which made me think that they were the worst ever.

But it wasn't really the Socialists that attracted me to the meeting—I was curious to see that woman the papers have written so much about, the one everybody calls mother. I couldn't understand how she could be a mother to everybody when it's real hard to mother one's own family.

To be sure, I know better now. One glance into her glittering eyes, a glimpse at the noble face and outstretched arms that are anxious to embrace the whole human race, is enough to make you understand how she does it, not to say anything of the words of wisdom that flow from her lips.

And suppose she gives her whole time to help others—that's what I call worth while living for. She's as happy as she can be, and if I was to compare her with my mother I'd surely take the latter for the martyr. And the reason for it is probably the fact that we're but one great family after all; that is, all the people the world over, no matter what color we are or what religion we believe in, and it's the welfare of that big family that should by rights interest us first, for isn't the whole bigger than the part, and each small family is but a part of the big one.

I must say, what with all the things we see for ourselves, and the different speeches we hear, a body can't help getting new ideas; but I know Jim would be sure to say that I've graduated into an anarchist. Let him. I think our people smell a rat and are bound to let me know it pretty soon.

But coming back to the meeting—I've learned a great deal there. That two armies of fighting soldiers isn't the only war in existence; that there is a terrible war raging just now and I'm a soldier in that war and that is the war for a bit of bread. I suppose I've felt it for some time, only I couldn't reason it out for myself; it took the people's mother to do it.

I could see that we working people were standing by ourselves, while on the other side stood our bosses, also a bunch by themselves, and now the way Mother Jones explained it to us it is clear that our bosses can't have any love for us, for every time we make a cent more they have a cent less left for themselves, and every time they can squeeze an extra cent from us they're that much the gainer. And from what I've seen for the last few weeks with my own eyes I can't help realizing that they've become so hardened in their growing greed that they're just ready to fight us to the end.

The mother said that it didn't have to go on that way, that all of us could have enough to live on if we only managed our own affairs in the right way, and if this is what the Socialists teach I earnestly believe they're talking common sense.

If one has patience to listen to their string of talk it becomes self evident that they've certainly learned what ails the people nowadays, and, I suppose, that by understanding the injustice they were able to find a remedy. To tell the truth, I don't see what we working people have to lose by trying their way of management. We can't be much worse off than we are today, I'm sure.

And I think they've pretty good people among them. They say that the little Jew girl who married one of them millionaires, the lucky dog—well, she's a Socialist, and she's certainly been good to her kind, especially to us girls during the strike. Why, she don't think anything of coming right among us, as if she was still a working girl, and doing all sorts of jobs—nothing is too small or too hard for her. And here's brave Mother Jones and many of the other people who have been our best friends during this trouble, and, as the saying goes, a friend in need is a friend indeed.

As I said once before, if only us girls could bring ourselves to reason out things for ourselves.

DECEMBER 10.—I'm really surprised at myself and all the courage I'm working up. But I've come to think that heroes ain't born, but made by circumstances. When I got near Levinson's factory this morning it just made me wild to see that high iron fence put up in front of the entrance—it came so much nearer being a prison than ever. And all to keep away the union people from taking down the girls. He thought he was smart, but us girls are just as smart, or even smarter, than he is. I made believe I wanted to work for him; told him what a good worker I was, where I was employed and a whole string of fibs why I'm out of a job just now. Mr. Levinson was delighted, took me up to the workroom and promised to employ me steadily. But when the afternoon whistle blew for the girls to get back to their machines the most of them had come down with me, not to return until the union is recognized.

As I expected, the conference proved a failure—we're to strike on. I'm not disappointed, for I felt it all along that the bosses won't give in so easily, and why should they? There's still over two weeks to the real season. They've time to lose then. And, considering the condition the most of our girls are in, I'm not surprised that the bosses hope to starve them into submission. But they forget that it ain't easy to starve these girls; they're pretty trained hands at that job.

I felt happy over this morning's success, but the afternoon put a damper over me. We were holding a joint conference with the Levcovitch people and it goes without saying that Sam, who is such a wonderful exception to the most of our men, was the chairman. Poor devil! when we were in the heat of discussing a new scheme of dealing with the scabs we were all startled by an irritated woman's voice: "For shame on you, Sam; you're chinning here with the girls, while your poor wife is most dyin'."

Terribly frightened, Sam jumped from the chair and ran right out, leaving hat, coat, meeting and all. And no wonder—he's just married one year and didn't have time to tire of his wife. This is the reason he worries so much because he can't support her just at present, when she needs all the care and attention—the woman is to become a mother any minute.

This makes me think of the fuss some people make of their first born and I don't know as they can be blamed for doing it, but here is one coming and not a cent in the house for the most necessary things, not to say of a doctor, medicine, nurse and all such things that follow sickness. People throw up to us that we needn't strike, for we're sure to get married. Here's a girl that had worked for many a year side by side with the man she married, always for a little less than he did, with the result that she didn't help herself, but dragged him down.

Poor fool! she married him and hoped to be happy, but how could she when the shadow of starvation is always hovering over their door.

The baby was born dead; perhaps it's better for it, but the mother is very ill, and in such circumstances! Big, handsome Bill heard of it and gave me $5 for Sam. Bill's all right, he is. I've often watched his actions to his good wife Bertha, and I've come to believe they're more like two good chums than husband and wife. That's what I call worth while being married. They say Bill is a Socialist, and I must add, if all the Socialists treat their wives as good as he does it's worth while marrying a Socialist.

The five-dollar bill will come in very handy for Sam, but how long will it last? So far the young wife clung to every bit they had in the house, for the articles were mostly wedding presents, but now I can see Sam taking them one by one to the uncle who prospers on the people's misfortunes. I know Sam; he's the kind that would rather die than go back on his fellow-workers. He'll just keep on fighting and believing as long as there's life in him. But why should this world be divided up so unevenly—so much misery on the one end and too much happiness on the other? This can't be right. I say the Lord bless the Socialists, if they mean, earnestly, to change things for the better.

85

ROSE SCHNEIDERMAN

The Triangle Fire (1911/1967)

A serious problem was the strike-breakers' inability to understand our message of trade unionism. I mean literally to *understand* because

From *All for One*. Reprinted by permission of P. S. Eriksson.

language was a great problem to organizers during those years. At a mass meeting one had to have at least four interpreters—for Polish, German, Yiddish, and Italian, and sometimes a fifth one for Slovene. On the other hand, the language problem was an asset to employers like the Triangle Waist Company. By hiring newly arrived immigrants from several different countries who not only spoke no English but could not communicate with each other, they protected themselves against the union.

But the union was determined to organize the workers at Triangle and continued to campaign for over a year until March 25, 1911. Then suddenly it was all over. At five o'clock on that Saturday afternoon, when union shops were enjoying their newly won half-holiday, passersby in the neighborhood of Washington Square saw great clouds of black smoke coming from the building at Washington Place East and Greene Street. It was the Triangle factory and before the fire was out, 143 girls and women had perished. Trapped behind locked doors—locked to protect them from the union organizers—many of them died in the flames. Others, in their effort to escape, clawed their way to windows, only to plunge to their death on the pavement eight floors below. But all were victims of wanton and criminal disregard of fire and health hazards.

For a week the city was saddened by the funerals of the victims who could be identified. Then the League and Local 25 of the ILGWU got permission from the city to hold a funeral for those who could not be claimed by anyone. More than 120,000 of us were in the funeral procession that miserable rainy April day. From ten in the morning until four in the afternoon we of the Women's Trade Union League marched in the procession with other trade-union men and women, all of us filled with anguish and regret that we had never been able to organize the Triangle workers. But in our grief and anger we, who were dedicated to the task of awakening the community to the plight of working women, would not remain silent. Already we had taken steps to make sure such a catastrophe would never be repeated.

The day after the fire, while the lifeless bodies of the women were still being gathered from the charred debris, a special joint meeting of the executive boards of the League, the Shirtwaist Makers Union, and the Hebrew Trades was called by the League at its headquarters. A relief committee to cooperate with the Red Cross in its work among the families of the victims was formed, and another committee was appointed to broaden the investigation and research on fire hazards in New York factories which was already being carried on by the League.

The League also established and played a vital part in another committee, the New York City Citizens Committee on Safety. First, it called a mass meeting on May 2 to protest the lack of safety and the inhuman conditions in the factories. Through the generosity of Anne Morgan the meeting was held at the Metropolitan Opera House. There was not an empty seat by the time it began. Jacob Schiff, the well-known financier and philanthropist, was chairman. Among the speakers were eminent civic leaders, churchmen, lawyers, labor-union officials, and representatives of women's organizations. The latter included not so eminent me.

After Monsignor White, Bishop David H. Greer, Rabbi Stephen Wise, and E. R. A. Seligman, the well-known economist from Columbia University, had spoken, the meeting asked for the adoption of a resolution calling for the appointment of a fire-prevention bureau, more factory inspectors, and some sort of compensation for workmen. Many in the audience were tired of resolutions being passed but never acted upon. There were shouts and hisses from the galleries and interruptions from the floor. The meeting seemed doomed to break up in disorder.

Then it was my turn to speak. I was so overcome that I could hardly talk above a whisper, but for some reason in that huge auditorium my voice carried. I think I shall let the *New York Times* tell the rest of the story as it appeared in the paper the next day. I could never write a speech that amounted to anything. But once I got on the stage, the words poured out and I am grateful to the *Times* for preserving my words that night:

". . . There was one moment when feeling grew tense to a snapping point, and the audience was held too closely by the speaker's words to interrupt or applaud as the girl who had been speaking went back up the stage to her seat.

"Rose Schneiderman, who led the workers out of the Triangle factory in their strike two years ago and bailed them out after being arrested, found words difficult when she tried to speak. She stood silently for a moment and then began to speak hardly above a whisper. But the silence was such that everywhere they carried clearly.

'I would be a traitor to these poor burned bodies,' began Miss Schneiderman after she had gained possession of her voice, 'if I came here to talk good fellowship. We have tried you good people of the public and we have found you wanting. The old Inquisition had its rack and its thumbscrews and its instruments of torture with iron teeth. We know what these things are today: the iron teeth are our necessities, the thumbscrews the high-powered and swift machinery close to which we must work, and the rack is here in the fire-proof structures that will destroy us the minute they catch on fire.

'This is not the first time girls have been burned alive in the city. Every week I must learn of the untimely death of one of my sister workers. Every year thousands of us are maimed. The life of men and women is so cheap and property is so sacred. There are so many of us for one job it matters little if 143 of us are burned to death.

'We have tried you, citizens; we are trying you now, and you have a couple of dollars for the sorrowing mothers and daughters and sisters by way of a charity gift. But every time the workers come out in the only way they know to protest against conditions which are unbearable, the strong hand of the law is allowed to press down heavily upon us.

'Public officials have only words of warning to us—warning that we must be intensely orderly and must be intensely peaceable, and they have the workhouse just back of all their warnings. The strong hand of the law beats us back when we rise into the conditions that make life bearable.

'I can't talk fellowship to you who are gathered here. Too much blood has been spilled. I know from my experience it is up to the working people to save themselves. The only way they can save themselves is by a strong working-class movement.'"

86
Mary White Ovington
Socialism and the Feminist Movement (1914)

Socialism and Feminism are the two greatest movements of to-day. The one aims to abolish poverty, the other to destroy servitude among women. Both are world movements. No matter how backward the nation may be that you visit, you will find your revolutionist there preaching that poverty is unnecessary, and that a great organization is working to destroy private capital and to build a co-operative commonwealth. And throughout western civilization, and even in the heart of the Orient, you also find the woman revolutionist telling her enslaved sisters of the effort among women to attain their freedom, to gain the right to live, not according to man's, but according to their own, conception of happiness and right. Ideas fly swiftly about the globe, and we are learning to think on the lines not of family or nation or race but of common interests and common suffering.

But while Socialism and Feminism are world movements they present an immense difference in that Socialism has a well defined

From *The New Review*, 1914.

policy carried out by a marvelously coherent international organization, while Feminism has an indefinite policy and little organization. The feminist who creeps into the harem and whispers into the ear of the Turkish wife that there are women working to lift the veil from her face cannot at the same time invite her to the feminist local in her nearest precinct. Nor has she any world program by which salvation is to be gained. She is only voicing a discontent with woman's subserviency to man.

Now, the relation of Feminism to Socialism is a matter of profound importance to many women Socialists. They read the party platform, demanding that women shall have equal rights with men, they attend the Socialist local and find these rights recognized by their comrades; and this should perhaps assure them that Socialism and Feminism are one. But they are not satisfied. They know that in any big movement certain propaganda is pushed to the foreground, to be striven for without cessation, while certain other is left behind, only to be considered when more important matters are disposed of. Where, they then ask, does Feminism stand with the Socialist party? Is it forward or is it in a dusky background from which it is rarely brought to light?

In putting this question I realize my incapacity adequately to answer it. This would require a knowledge of both Socialism and Feminism far beyond anything I posses. I can only give a few suggestions that may provoke interest among others more competent to discuss the matter than I.

The feminist movement as we have noted, is difficult of description because it deals with women under all stages of masculine rule; but, broadly speaking, it is a revolt. As Mary S. Oppenheimer tersely put it in the NEW REVIEW, it is "a reaction from the long rule of man and the consequent repression of womankind." The Socialist party in America as elsewhere always recognizes its political aspect when in its platform it demands a universal franchise for men and women alike, and when in its party organization it gives women an equal vote with men.

This is a great deal, but the Progressive party has done as much. Is the Socialist party continually carrying on a woman's suffrage propaganda? Is it showing woman's economic condition, the injustices she suffers not only because she is poor but because she is a woman? That is, is it laying emphasis on the aristocracy of sex, on the fact that men to-day are still exercising extraordinary power over one-half the population, and are thus making democracy a farce? Is it doing these things?

Individual Socialists are undoubtedly doing them very often, especially women Socialists. But among many men prominent in America as Socialist writers and party leaders there exists a strange apathy on the woman question. Under Socialism, they assure you, women will have everything, but they are not interested in seeing that she secures her modicum now. They subscribe to the party platform, but they do not think the woman's suffrage plank of vital interest....

Perhaps the whole matter may be explained by saying that the majority of the men in the Socialist party recognize no division but the division of class, and no struggle but the class struggle; while many, but by no means all, women Socialists recognize also a woman's struggle, the struggle of a sex for the full development of its powers and for the right to the full use of those powers. And while the woman undoubtedly sees that such development is sadly incomplete for the majority in a capitalistic society, she knows, as the man does not seem to know, that men have gone a long way toward freedom, else the political party of Socialism would not have been born. And she knows too, that the coming of Socialism is not purely material. It does not mean simply a full stomach—that was often attained under chattel slavery—but a full life; and while she looks forward to the Socialist society she desires all the fullness of life that she can get now.

William Englsh Walling has said that the difference between a conservative and a radical is a difference of time. Both see the wretchedness of conditions and both want a change; but one is willing to wait while the other wants the change *now*. It is this way with woman and Socialism. The Socialist tells her to work for Socialism and she will then receive all she desires; but the woman intends *now* to get legal equality with man, the vote, equal pay for equal work, and all the educational privileges open to men. She has no more idea of waiting for Socialism to give her these things than the man has of waiting for the co-operative commonwealth before he enters upon his trade or casts his vote. This is the meaning of the militant suffrage agitation in England. Undoubtedly suffrage will be given to English women in good time, but the militants want it now, and they do not brook waiting with placidity.

The mass of men Socialists, as I have said, recognize no struggle but the class struggle, and thus logically they have no interest in enfranchising any women but those of the working class. Theodore Rothstein, writing in the NEW REVIEW, assures us that women are adequately represented by their fathers and brothers and husbands because these represent their economic rights, and that the Social-Democrat of England favors universal woman's suffrage, "not on general grounds of so-called citizenship, justice and the rest, but because it will add to the political power of the proletariat."

That women are represented by their fathers, their brothers and their husbands is surely gravely open to question. It is only since women have persistently agitated for their rights that the woman of property has been able to control her fortune or the working woman her wage. This, perhaps Comrade Rothstein would say, does not concern the class struggle—the money, whether husband's or wife's, remains in the same class—but it does concern the individual wife. And it is such masculine talk as his that must convince every thoughtful woman of the need of a movement for her release from masculine domination.

But there is a more serious aspect to Comrade Rothstein's reasoning. If as Socialists we think of democratic movements simply as a means of increasing a *class* vote, are we not in danger of thinking of them as increasing a *party* vote, and of refraining from enfranchising those who will not vote with the Socialist party? This is a real question in America where we have the disfranchised Negro. And while the Socialist party is pledged to woman's suffrage, it is quite conceivable that where it has scored a victory it may be lukewarm, if not indifferent, to giving the vote to women even though by so doing the proletarian vote would be increased. It may inquire regarding the character of the woman proletarian. Is she not more conservative than the man? Is she not likely to be ruled by the priests? Isn't it better, now at least, to postpone universal suffrage until Socialism is more strongly entrenched in the proletarian mind?

Such reasoning as this seems very dangerous to some of us women who believe in democracy. It is a far-away cry, that of the Declaration of Independence, "that governments derive their just powers from the consent of the governed," but it is one that women are obliged to declare daily. And perhaps the reason men take so little interest in the declaration is that they fought this question out a century ago, and are now in "fresh fields and pastures new." The woman who lives in a country where the franchise has not yet become universal may perhaps obtain it with more ease than the one who lives in America where men have forgotten that there was a time when but few males could vote. A belated movement is the most difficult of movements in which to interest mankind.

I find that my feminist argument has centered about the suffrage movement. But I believe that women for a long time to come, whether they have suffrage or not, will need to be banded together against oppression. They have a work to do in backward countries as educators, as physicians, as preachers of the divine right of revolt. Doubtless Socialist women will be in the forefront of the battle, and their Socialism will give them courage for the conflict. But they will also recognize that as women they have their obligation to stand with all other women who are fighting for the destruction of masculine despotism and for the right of womankind.

87
Pauline M. Newman
Low Wages and White Slavery (1912)

Say what you will, low wages are bound to go hand in hand with white slavery. Wages paid to women workers, and especially to girls in department stores, are NOT enough to live on decently.

The average wage paid to a girl in a paper-box factory, sweatshop and department store will range from $4 to $5 a week. In cities like Chicago, New York and Boston these girls must pay $1.50 a week for a room. Out of the remainder they must buy clothes and food, pay their doctors' bills, get their amusements, etc. Clothes are expensive. The cost of living is high. Work is hard and tiresome. The hours are too long. Work is also monotonous because it is so arranged to-day that the worker is nothing more than a part of the machine. The desire for nice clothes is there whether the wage is little or big. The yearning for something more pleasing than making a garment or a paper box or selling over a counter is within a girl regardless of how much she earns. And the everlasting question arises, "What is to be done?"

Many of these girls pick up sufficient courage to tell the foreman or superintendent that they can't possibly get along on the wages they get, and they hope that he will give them a raise. Instead of her hope coming true, he looks at her, sizes her up from head to foot and asks, with a friendly smile, "Why don't you look for a friend on the side?"

If you don't believe this, gentle reader, go and try a job in one of the big department stores and convince yourself of its truth.

From *The Progressive Woman*, February 1912.

Unfortunately for the girl of small intelligence, this suggestion works oftentimes. She doesn't bother the foreman again, but thinks over what he has said to her. In her imagination she sees herself with one who would really be a friend to her. She is tired of cheap moving picture shows and would like to be taken to real theaters, to nice restaurants, and to many attractive places. So she decides to do what other girls have done and look for a "friend." It is easy enough to find one, for there are thousands of "friends" whose chief *business* it is to pick up these tired-out, underpaid wage slaves and get them into a life of hell by giving them a "good time" for a little while.

The little shop girl's "friend" takes good care of her. He takes her to a theater and after the theater to a "swell" place for supper. There she meets many men and women who eat, drink and are merry. Music, dancing and wine are all for her. She is told by her "friend" that he loves her and that he always will. He buys her new and pretty clothes, and, in short, sees that her desires are satisfied. He finally persuades her not to go back to the store and work her life away. And what is the use of going home? Did she not leave enough of the wretchedness, misery, poverty and worry there? And so the girl, intoxicated with the excitement of the new life, quits the store and leaves her home to live with the "friend." Then follows the tragedy.

There are many girls who do not go into this business because of getting nice clothes. They are forced into it because there are families to support and not enough to support them on—that is, not enough to buy the actual necessities of life. Some of us who have worked in factories KNOW THIS TO BE A FACT, for we have seen it with our own eyes.

In the year 1907 the statistics of New York showed that more than 65 per cent of the prostitutes came from the slum districts. What does that mean? WHO LIVES in the slum districts? The working class, of course. Low wages paid to the father, low wages paid to the girl, and THAT IS WHAT FORCES HER INTO THE RANKS OF THE WHITE SLAVE. Don't forget that.

What is to be done, then? GIVE THE GIRL WORKER A CHANCE TO LIVE, A SHORTER WORK DAY, WAGES SUFFICIENT TO COVER PRESENT-DAY NEEDS. Make her working and living conditions human and there will be little or no temptation to go out at night for pleasure or to look for a "friend."

How to do it? Join the union. Organize one if there is not one in your trade. Start today. Don't wait for to-morrow—to-morrow may never come.

Remember that white slavery is an economic problem. Yes, a bread and butter question, and the evil of white slavery, together with all other evils such as child labor, industrial robbery, political corruption, hypocrisy, will exist just as long as a system which produces these things exists.

The problem of white will be solved when all economic problems are solved. And many other problems may be solved when the working-class man and woman learn to use their power on the economic as well as on the political field.

Intelligence and organization are the watch-words!

88

MARY CHURCH TERRELL

My Experience as a Clerk in a Government Department (1917–1918/1940)

This is the story of a colored woman living in a white world. It cannot possibly be like a story written by a white woman. A white woman has only one handicap to overcome—that of sex. I have two—both sex and race. I belong to the only group in this country which has two such huge obstacles to surmount. Colored men have only one—that of race.

From *Colored Women in a White World*, "Introduction to Chapter 25," by Mary Church Terrell. © 1940 The Gale Group. Reprinted with permission of The Gale Group.

White women of Great Britain showed what a serious handicap they considered their sex by the desperate methods they used to obtain the suffrage. The white women of the United States proved they entertained the same view by working continuously and hard for more than seventy years to secure the rights which citizenship usually confers upon men. I wonder what they would have done if they had been obliged to overcome two handicaps instead of one.

In relating the story of my life I shall simply tell the truth and nothing but the truth—but not the whole truth, for that would be impossible. And even if I tried to tell the whole truth few people would believe me. I am well aware that truth will be interpreted by some to mean bitterness. But I am not bitter.

I have been obliged to refer to incidents which have wounded my feelings, crushed my pride and saddened my heart. I have touched upon this phase of my life as lightly as I could without misrepresenting the facts. I do not want to be accused of "whining." I have not tried to arouse the sympathy of my readers by tearing passion to tatters, so as to show how wretched I have been. The many limitations imposed upon me and the humiliations to which I have been subjected speak for themselves.

I have recorded what I have been able to accomplish in spite of the obstacles which I have had to surmount. I have done this, not because I want to tell the world how smart I am, but because both a sense of justice and a regard for truth prompt me to show what a colored woman can achieve in spite of the difficulties by which race prejudice blocks her path if she fits herself to do a certain thing, works with all her might and main to do it and is given a chance.

Some of my white friends tell me that colored people must work out their own salvation. I hope the efforts which I have made will convince them that I have tried not only to work out my own salvation, but to help others in my group to work out theirs.

I do not want to wage a holy war or any other kind of war upon a group which is strong and powerful enough to circumscribe my activities and prevent me from entering fields in which I should like to work. I wish to insist upon this with all the emphasis which I can command. No colored woman clothed in her right mind who has had as many genuine friends in the dominant race as I have had and who has been given by them as many opportunities to render the service which I have tried to give could be bitter toward the whole group. . . .

During the world war almost everybody in Washington who knew how to write and spell was taking an examination of some kind, so as to get a job in one of the Government departments. The officials were calling loudly for assistance, as the volume of business incident to the war continued to increase, and they were urging citizens all over the country to take an examination for the various clerkships, so that they might have the extra help required to do the work. Accordingly, I decided to take an examination as typist and presented myself with my machine at the building designated for that date.

I knew I had passed, but I took it for granted that it would be a long time before I would be called if, indeed, I ever received an appointment. So I thought very little about it. Ten days after I took the examination our doorbell jangled one morning between two and three o'clock and a telegram addressed to me was handed to me. "Come immediately to the Aetna Building, Room 305," it read, and was signed by General Crozier.

At first I was speechless with surprise, for I did not connect the telegram with the examination I had taken. It came at such an unearthly hour in the morning I thought it must be very urgent indeed. I asked my husband whether it was not my duty to answer the summons immediately, as I was requested to do. He laughed heartily at the idea, saying that even if I went to the Aetna Building at three o'clock in the morning, nobody would be there to receive me.

About nine o'clock, therefore, I presented myself at Room 305 and handed the telegram to General Crozier's secretary. The young man soon ushered me into his presence, and I found him reading a paper. It was my questionnaire at which he was looking, for everybody who took an examination for Government service was required to answer certain questions showing what his preparation and record were.

When General Crozier first saw me, he merely glanced at me but greeted me very cordially, nevertheless. His eyes were fastened upon my questionnaire, which showed that I had received the A.B. and A.M. degrees from Oberlin College, that I had traveled abroad, that I could speak, read and write both German and French and that I had once spoken Italian quite well. Perhaps I should state here that, in replying to the question concerning race, I simply wrote "American," without specifying what particular kind of an American I am.

After the General had carefully read my record, he laid it on the table and looked at me squarely for the first time. "You have had very fine training indeed," he said. "We need the services of those who understand German and French." Then he studied me intently for a second and a shadow passed over his countenance. He began to appear puzzled and then displeased, as he looked at me. The longer he looked, the more puzzled and displeased he became. A light of some kind seemed to be dawning upon him. The General picked up my questionnaire and looked at it again. "I see you have taught in a high school here," he said, eyeing me closely. "Which one was it?" he inquired. "I taught in the M Street High School." Instantly an expression of pronounced displeasure swept over the General's face, and I knew my doom was sealed. He tossed the paper aside immediately.

"Mrs. Terrell," he inquired, "have you ever had any office experience?" His tone was that of a man about to offer a criticism of some kind. "I have had none, General," I replied. "I have stated that in my questionnaire." "Well, I'm sorry you haven't had any office experience. I hoped you had." As he said this, he flicked my questionnaire farther away from him. "I do not see how anyone who summoned me here could have hoped I had had any office experience, unless he thought I would tell a falsehood," I ventured, "for in answer to the question 'Have you had any experience in office?' I stated on my questionnaire 'Absolutely none.'" "So you have," agreed the General, picking up my questionnaire again. "Good morning." I knew then that my name would be among the uncalled.

By those in a position to know I have been informed that at that time college graduates were being eagerly sought, especially those who could speak and translate both German and French. Had I been a white woman there is no doubt I would have secured a responsible and lucrative position in the Government service at that time.

Shortly after that I was summoned to the War Risk Insurance Bureau and appointed to a clerkship. The man before whom I then appeared did not consume enough time in giving me the "once over" to note any peculiarity in my complexion which would suggest to him that I was "different from the rest." That little oversight on his part undoubtedly accounts for the fact that I was placed in the room with white women. After I had been appointed and assigned to this room, I learned that the women who were known to be colored had been placed in a section to themselves.

In the division to which I was assigned it was the duty of the clerks to send in the records of the soldiers who were ill or insane. One of the young women in the room was designated to give me the necessary instructions and did so cheerfully. All the clerks in the room were very cordial and pleasant indeed, and I entered upon my duties with enthusiasm and zest.

I had been working about two months in this section when suddenly, I received a letter saying I had been suspended from duty from October 15 up to and including October 20, during which time I was requested to prepare my defense in answer to the following charges preferred against me: "It has been reported that you have taken action on cases contrary to the rules and regulations of the Bureau and contrary to the regulations of the chief medical adviser. It has been found that you have made numerous mistakes, and when these mistakes were called to your attention you cause considerable disturbance and tend to deny responsibility. You do not want to understand or can not understand the requests of your superior in the matter of properly performing duties assigned to you."

There was not a scintilla of truth in any of these charges. It was a case of "framing" a colored woman, so as to remove her from a room in which she had been placed by mistake where they did not want one of her race to work. If I had really "taken action contrary to the rules and regulations of the Bureau and of the chief medical adviser," those responsible for the proper conduct of the office would have called me to account the very first time they learned I was guilty of the infraction of the rules. If they allowed me to persist in such a disobedient, inefficient course, they themselves were derelict in their duty, and deserved to be punished as well as the offending clerk.

But I had never seen any rules and regulations in print, nor had anybody stated any to me which I had violated in any way, shape or form. As careful as any colored woman would be in an office in which she knew her slightest mistake or dereliction of duty would be greatly exaggerated and summarily punished, it is inconceivable that she would fail to obey to the letter every rule or regulation enforced. I realized that I was treading on thin ice all the time, and I was very careful to do the work exactly as I was instructed. Several times I observed (for I kept my eyes and ears open every second to catch anything new floating around in the air) that a change in the manner of making out certain records had been ordered by those higher up without notifying me as they had the other clerks in the room. As soon as I was aware of this, and it was easy for me to discover it by constant vigilance, I would ask a young woman from the far West, who was very cordial, to show me how to do the work, and she always complied with my request cheerfully. On several occasions, without being asked to do so, she slipped me papers showing the new way of filling out certain records, as soon as she herself had been instructed, for she knew that I would not be notified.

Nobody who understands conditions in the National Capital would believe that a colored woman working in one of the Government departments in a room with white women "would cause considerable disturbance" when mistakes were called to her attention if she were sane and wished to retain her job. Colored women know all too well if they make themselves conspicuous or objectionable, either to their fellow clerks or to their superior officers, they are courting disaster and ruin. The few colored women who are assigned to rooms in which white women work are constantly in a state of suspense and apprehension, not knowing the day or the hour when the awful summons of removal or dismissal will come. They know they are there either by mistake or suffrance, and they would as soon think of "creating a disturbance" as they would plot to dynamite the White House. All they ask is to be let alone and be allowed to do their work in peace.

Young women with only a high school education were able to perform the duties in the room to which I was assigned. It could scarcely be possible, therefore, that a woman who had graduated with a good record from a reputable college, who had studied all her life and had taught school, could not surmount the difficulties which these girls could master with ease.

If any woman known to be colored who was working in a Government department during the World War had been "either unable or unwilling to understand requests of her superior officers," she would not have been allowed to retain her job a single week.

A very interesting episode happened once when I was told by a substitute to change the wording of a printed slip during the absence of the woman who had charge of the room. I thanked the substitute for the information she gave me, but I stated at the same time that the director in charge had instructed the clerks to make the slip out as I had done. The clerk who sat next to me overheard the conversation and volunteered to corroborate what I said. Each and every clerk in the room did the same thing. During the conversation between the clerks and the substitute I preserved the silence which is always golden for a colored woman similarly situated.

Very much irritated at the unanimous decision against her, the substitute went to consult the doctor in charge of the section and returned to the room saying she, and not we, was right. When this incident was related to the regular director on her return to the room, she calmly remarked that so many changes were being constantly made in methods of doing the work that nobody could tell one day what would be done the next. I saw to it, therefore, that I kept up with the newest methods of doing the work, for I knew that the slightest error on my part meant embarrassment and loss of my job. There is no doubt that it irritated some of the higher ups, who were hungry for reasons to dismiss me, that I was constantly on the alert and kept abreast of the times.

My relations with both the officer in charge of the room and with the clerks were most cordial. For instance, whenever the clerks brought candy to the room, they always passed me some, and if I refused to take it, they insisted upon giving me a piece anyway. One afternoon, just before I left the building, the director asked me if I would help her inspect some of the files the next day because she had a great deal to do and no one to assist her. I readily consented. But the next morning she requested some one else to help her and ignored me completely. She showed plainly that she was embarrassed. Undoubtedly she had been warned by somebody higher up not to allow me to assist her in inspecting the files. She would never have requested me to help her in the first place if she had not believed I understood the work very well.

The truth of the matter is that when some of the superior officers of the Bureau saw that a colored woman was working in that particular room, they decided to remove her at all hazards.

The easiest way to do this was to prefer charges against the colored woman, and they decided to resort to this method to get rid of me.

I am certain I know by whom the agitation to remove me was started. A doctor, who hailed from the South and who had charge of the section in which I worked, walked into the room one day and saw me at my desk. He stood looking intently at me for several seconds and then left abruptly without transacting the business to which he came presumably to attend. Either he had been informed that a colored woman was working in that room and he entered to see whether it was true, or he came on a tour of inspection and observed for the first time that was the case. It was shortly after this doctor's visit that the notice of charges preferred against me was received.

Colonel Wainer, who wrote the letter containing the charges, was a Jew. When I urged him to give me a square deal, presented facts to show that the charges were trumped up, and requested him to get my record directly from the woman in charge of the room, he turned a deaf ear to my appeal. I did not want to allow myself to be dismissed from that clerkship without waging a hard fight against such cruel injustice. It was one of the most galling experiences of my life. If my husband had not occupied such a prominent position in the city, I should never have submitted to that outrage without waging a righteous war against it. I knew that any contest on my part would embarrass him and might easily hurt his standing as a judge in the Municipal Court. I have always believed that a wife has no right to injure her husband's career by what she says or does.

Shortly after this experience I was appointed by the Census Bureau. Here I was placed in a section, one portion of which was set aside exclusively for colored clerks, although white clerks sat in another part of the same large room. From the building on Pennsylvania Avenue, which was once occupied by the Census Bureau and in which I worked when I was first appointed, all of the colored clerks were transferred to one of the temporary structures erected in another section of the National Capital during the World War. Here they were herded together in a room with a colored man as director who was very efficient and whom it was a pleasure to assist.

One day a clerk sitting near me wrote me a note telling me to stop work a second and look ahead. Then I saw a woman, who I knew had been working in another section of the Bureau, come into our large room carrying her hat, her umbrella and her purse. The white man who accompanied her then left and she was given a seat by the colored director of our division. In a few minutes another woman was ushered into our room and given a seat. And this was repeated half a dozen times. Then it suddenly dawned upon me what the advent of these newcomers signified.

They were colored women so fair that they had been assigned to sections set aside exclusively for white women. By fair means or foul their racial identity had been disclosed to somebody "higher up," who was opposed to allowing the women of two races to work in the same room together. Suddenly on that beautiful spring afternoon somebody pounced upon those fair colored women, snatched them from the places to which both their ability and their personal appearance had caused them to be assigned, and removed them to the room to which "they belonged."

It was doubtless a very depressing and humiliating experience to these victims of race prejudice to be forced publicly to leave their desks at which they had been happily doing their duty and marched like culprits into strange surroundings, the cynosure of all eyes. They themselves had done nothing to justify this humiliation to which they had been subjected. They had not tried to deceive anybody. They had simply neglected to place a placard on their backs notifying the world that they belonged to a socially ostracized race in the United States.

One of these women who had to "walk the plank" came from Florida. She told me she was summoned to the office of the man in charge of her section and subjected to a searching examination about the racial affiliation of her parents. "As a matter of fact," probed this inquisitor, "aren't you a colored woman?" "Yes, I am," she replied. "I have never denied it. It was not my fault that I was placed in a section with white women. I made no request to be assigned there, but I have been very happy attending to my duties where the authorities placed me."

"Didn't you know it was not customary to put white and colored people together here in Washington?" she was asked. "No, I was not aware that was the case," she said. "Before I came here, I heard that in some of the departments the two races sat together, so I did not know that by remaining in the room to which I was assigned I was violating any hard and fast rule. Now that I know there is a new rule in force, I shall be much happier in a room set aside exclusively for colored people than I would be working where they are excluded. But I am sorry I had to be publicly humiliated to learn this fact."

A short while after that drastic separation of the two races occurred, one of the young women came to tell me that an order had been promulgated whereby the colored women clerks in our section would no longer be allowed to enter the lavatory which they had used up to that time because it had just been set aside for the women of the other group. Then and there I made up my mind I would do everything in my power to prevent that order from being executed. I knew it was just another device to humiliate colored women. There was no earthly reason for excluding colored women from a room they had been using ever since they had been working in that building.

After a painstaking investigation I learned that the colored clerks had done nothing to cause them to be embarrassed by being subjected to such treatment. First, I went to the colored supervisor of the section. He stated that the order advising him to notify his women clerks not to use the lavatory to which they had been accustomed to go had been sent to him, but, since it was not signed, he did not intend to pay any attention to it. Soon after that conversation with him, however, he told me that the order had been signed by the proper authorities, and that he intended to talk with them about it before issuing it.

The next day some of the women came to me to ask me if I would not go to see the man who issued the order because our own supervisor had been unsuccessful in persuading him to withdraw it. I complied with their request. Even if it were possible to give a verbatim interview with two of the men I tired to induce to spare the colored women clerks an unnecessary humiliation, I should not do so. Although one of the men was reasonable and courteous, he gave me no assurance that the objectionable order would be withdrawn. Then I decided to resign and sent in my resignation immediately. As my reason, I stated that I was unwilling to remain in a Government department in which colored women were subjected to such an indignity as we had been.

A few minutes after the author of the order had received my resignation he sent for me to come to see him immediately. "Why are you resigning?" he inquired. I told him that the reason assigned in my resignation was the correct one. Under the circumstances, I declared, there was only one thing for me to do to maintain my self-respect. After a long conference with him in which I had a splendid opportunity to reveal to him a colored woman's point of view, I agreed to modify the reason of my resignation if he would rescind the objectionable order which he had issued. This he agreed to do. After weighing the matter as carefully as I could in the short time given for my decision, I felt it would be foolish to stick to the original statement when, by making a slight compromise, I could relieve the women of my group from embarrassment and humiliation without sacrificing my self-respect.

The head of the division in which I worked urged me to remain in the Bureau, but I decided to resign. The work was enjoyable and I needed the money, to be sure. But the idea of remaining in a section over which were placed men who had no regard whatever for the feelings of colored women was abhorrent to me. I simply could not stay even for the sake of the salary which would have filled a long felt want.

During the World War when so many were taking examinations for positions under the Government it was very hard for colored women who showed plainly to what race they belonged to secure the positions to which they were entitled by their records. Some of the teachers in our public schools who made high marks failed to receive an appointment. Several told me they had been marked as high as 95 per cent, but had not been given jobs. On the other hand, young colored women who were fair enough to "pass" secured positions without any difficulty whatever, even though their examination papers were marked comparatively low.

Several of these fair colored women came to ask my advice as to what they should do about accepting positions offered them, knowing as they did they would never have received them, if the appointing power had been aware they were colored. I could see no good reason why these women should refuse to take positions which they had earned and for which they would be paid, because those in authority did not know they had a few drops of African blood coursing through their veins. Some of them who received these good positions under "false pretenses," so to speak, held them for four or five years, and a few have retained them up to the present time.

89
Mary E. Jackson

The Colored Woman in Industry (1918)

Just as colored men are going into the Army, so colored women are being recruited into industry. Thousands and thousands of eager boys

From *The Crisis*, November 1918.

have gone to France; we all know about them. Few of us realize that at the same time an army of women is entering mills, factories and all other branches of industry.

I undertook an industrial survey of these women for the National Board of the Young Women's Christian Association. I investigated the increasing numbers employed, the kinds of work, wages, working conditions, what has been done, and what more can be done to raise the efficiency of the workers. At the same time I began in each city the organization of industrial women into clubs.

A great alteration has come in manufacturing sections like Philadelphia, Baltimore, Cleveland, St. Louis, Louisville, Detroit and Chicago. The shifting of so many thousands of negro laborers and their families from the South during the past two years, has brought a large supply of women's labor into these districts, where it is much needed. The matter is well summed up in a letter from Rachel S. Gallagher, Director of the City Free Labor Exchange, Cleveland, Ohio, written in the spring:

"If you had asked me two years ago about the colored girls as wage earners, in Cleveland, I would have told you that they could be found in housework, as laundresses and cleaning women, as maids, in a few cases in banks and offices, and there were a few employed by a cigar box manufacturing concern.

"Today, however, when I started to list the firms where they were employed, I found that they had entered nearly every field of women's work, and some work where women had not previously been employed. To be sure, at times in small numbers, but they have made an entrance.

"We find them on power sewing machines, making caps, waists, bags and mops; we find them doing pressing and various hand operations in these same shops. They are employed in knitting factories as winders, in a number of laundries on mangles of every type, and in sorting and marking. They are in paper box factories doing both hand and machine work, in button factories on the button machines, in packing houses packing meat, in railroad yards wiping and cleaning engines, and doing sorting in railroad shops. They are found in cigar factories stripping and packing, and in an electrical supply manufacturing plant doing hard work. One of our workers recently found two colored girls on a knotting machine in a bed spring factory, putting the knots in the wire springs." . . .

The Ohio letter mentions only a few of the lines of work in which we find women newly employed. They are in both the skilled and unskilled trades. This comes out clearly in a report from Pittsburgh, where two different factories are especially mentioned. A garment factory making raincoats for the Government has had about twenty girls. They are careful to employ the better educated type of girl, but they work on a separate floor and do not mingle with the white girls who are prejudiced against them. Wages and conditions, however, are exactly the same for both. The work is machine sewing and sticking with glue. The other company, which uses untrained labor, has employed colored girls for three years. About fifty of the seventy-five girls they employ are colored. The other girls are foreign, evidently low grade labor. The work is picking and sorting rags, papers, bottles, etc. Wages and conditions are the same for both races. They work together and apparently there is no antagonism on either side.

The change brought about by war conditions is in many cases spectacular. Women are working in the tobacco fields in Connecticut; Indiana reports them in glass works; in Ohio, they are found on the night shifts of glass works; cotton chopping and harvesting claim them in Texas; they have gone into the pottery works in Virginia; wood-working plants and lumber yards have called for their help in Tennessee, while in St. Louis, where the special investigation has been carried further than in the other places, they dip tile in roofing plants, shovel rock into wagons in clay yards, truck brick and load scrap iron; on railroads they are utilized as section hands and engine wipers. So great a change as this deserves close attention in the matter of wages and of working conditions.

Wages among women are unstandardized. There are several reasons for this: In the first place, the labor of colored women is almost entirely unorganized. The attitude of the unions toward them is evasive. Of the six labor secretaries with whom I talked last December, in New York City, only one set up any objection to colored members. The others agreed that the colored woman was not only welcome to the unions but that she must be made to see the mutual advantage of her joining. But the fact remains that there is practically no colored membership. In the 30,000 members of the Ladies' Waist and Dressmakers, only about one hundred are colored, although the needle trades stand first among those which the colored women are now entering so rapidly.

A significant and encouraging incident, however, was reported from Philadelphia in the early summer. A strike was called by this union in an establishment where colored girls were being paid one cent for which white girls had been paid three cents. The colored girls promptly joined the strike and the union and the pay was raised.

Again, at this period much of the colored labor is unskilled, and unskilled labor is helpless in the matter of wages unless organized. Then, too, in many of the industries the women are beginners and, therefore, unable to deal with the situation intelligently. Added to this is the general assumption that women should be grateful to be paid anything at all and that their wages have no relation to their standard of living. Piled on top of all of these disadvantages is the fact that the women belong to the Negro race. Some people have actually said that the standards of Negro life are so much lower than those of the white that the colored woman does not need as high a rate of wage.

The most encouraging case that I have come across was in a Detroit factory, where we found one colored girl making as much as $4.50 a day working at a punch press. In startling contrast to this is the small amount paid for unskilled work. In nutshelling factories, where the women pick out the meats after the shells have been cracked by machinery, a woman makes from $6.00 to $7.00 a week. She is paid ten cents a pound for whole meats and five cents a pound for broken meats. Although it is possible for a woman to make as much as $12.00 a week, this seldom happens.

In another big factory the women's wage was until recently only $6.00 a week. When I was lecturing to a group of business women of that city, I mentioned the very low pay of this factory. By good fortune the welfare worker, a white woman, who has an equal interest in the welfare of the colored workers, was present. She took the matter up with the manager of the factory and the $1.00 a week raise was announced.

The pay for heavy unskilled work, formerly performed by men, is higher than the rate paid for what has been known as women's work, although unusually lower than the amount which men received for the same work. The following figures illustrate this:

. . . Dipping in glaze and stacking: 9 hr. day at 25c. hr.

Clipping impurities from clay, shoveling and wheeling rock: $2.00 to $2.50. (Men's wage $3.00.)

Shoveling clay, trucking brick, etc.: $2.50 to $2.75.

Feeding brick to furnace, rolling clay balls: 9 hr. day at 30c. hr.

Loading scrap iron: 9 hr. day at 80c. hr. Bonus of 8 per cent a week if not absent.

One must not rely upon the given rate because it is so nibbled away by absences, perhaps because of the unhealthy nature of the work, by fines, and various other methods. In many cases the workers themselves do not realize how much less they received than the regular rate.

The serious part of this matter is that women are undercutting men in wages. This has the effect of lowering wages all over the country. Of course, women have always done this. Every possible precaution must be taken to avoid it. A protest has been sent in one state to the Director-General of Railroads, pointing out that women were being employed in freight yards and round-houses for twenty-two cents an hour, while men were paid thirty cents an hour for the same work.

The working conditions vary as much as the wages. When large numbers of colored girls are employed, they usually work in rooms separate from those of the white girls. When there are any hazards or disadvantages, it is the colored woman who is subjected to them. Conditions depend absolutely upon the attitude of the firm. Some old, well-established companies provide equally well for all women. One firm which I found in the West, under the guidance of an expert welfare worker, has provided for white and colored women alike: lunch rooms, shower baths, a circulating library and dressing rooms with steel lockers.

The tobacco factories all through the South have very bad conditions. I was once shown a coat room as if it were a remarkable concession on the part of the management. As a rule the women sit at their work stripping the tobacco while they eat their luncheon to eke out their meagre pay. The same factory which raised the wages, although it has at present most unhygienic conditions, is about to put up a new building in which the colored women are to have the same good accommodations that are provided for the white workers.

A letter from a small Kansas city presents a situation which must be occurring in many places:

"We have about fifteen colored girls working at our Santa Fé Railroad Round-House wiping engines. The hours are from seven until five and the wages two dollars and forty-seven and a half cents a day. These are the only women working in the shops. They are forced to walk almost two miles in their greasy overalls to their rooming places as a colored person cannot rent a house near the shops. Their own people are too poor to board them so they are forced to prepare their own meal when they get home, wash their clothes and prepare their lunch for the morrow.

"We plan, if possible, to rent a small house in that vicinity where the girls may change their clothes and rest." . . .

The altering of the bad phases of employment depends in the end upon the progress of education. We must educate the public, the employers and the girls themselves. It is especially important that leaders among colored people—like ministers, club leaders, teachers, social workers—thoroughly inform themselves on this matter, which is of more than momentary importance. Last summer the Young Women's Christian Association had this far-reaching vision, realizing that such work was both a war measure and a preparation for after the war. Now is an especially good time to present the matter to the general public in the proper light, because it is now to the national advantage to give the Negro a square deal.

Employers must be won to employ colored girls. Sometimes we are able to obtain from a Chamber of Commerce a list of manufacturers who might be willing to take on colored help. The accomplishment of one worker shows how much can be accomplished by patience, ability, tact and persistence. She opened fifteen factories, including cigar factories, packing and novelty companies, clothing companies, knitting mills, trunk factories, a foundry, a toy factory, an undergarment manufactory and a fur factory; and placed 346 women in them.

Individual girls can accomplish much if they go about it the right way. A girl walked into a wholesale drug company in a southern city and asked for work. She was taken on as an experiment. A few days later she brought six friends with her. They all made good. By the time the Y.W.C.A. investigator got around to that store, twenty were working there and the superintendent promised to take thirty-five more to fill capsules and label bottles. The best of all was that he bore witness to the girls' good work by saying:

"Show the colored girl what you want done, and she does it quicker and better than the white girl."

All this effort, of course, is of no value unless the girls give satisfaction. We must educate them both to individual effort and to group effort. Girls come to me constantly for interviews about their industrial future. It is natural that they should become discouraged. When a girl has been refused positions time and again, she may not have the persistence to apply at the very time that she would be accepted. We found, for instance, a graduate of a normal school mending bags at $6.00 a week. She needed our encouragement and assistance to get into a position in which she could use her ability.

In one city we found in three office buildings twenty-six high school girls who were answering telephones and dusting, at an average wage of $5.00 a week without any hope of further advancement. Girls like these must be encouraged to further effort. The one greatest barrier of all lies in their own minds. Before outside obstacles may be overcome, we must convince the girl of the possibility of success.

The group education is equally important. The colored girl has never before been held responsible to other girls and to the community. She is now in a new relation toward her country. She must come to see that she is no longer "different;" she must learn to look upon herself as a part of a unit. The future of all girls rests partly upon the accomplishment of the individual girl.

The supervision of colored factory girls by colored forewomen is of the utmost importance. The girls are more efficient and have more interest in their work because the forewoman herself is interested in what they accomplish. I found this strikingly illustrated in one factory where one room full of girls was under the charge of a white forewoman while the second was under the charge of a colored woman. In the first room, a happy-go-lucky atmosphere prevailed; in the second room, the girls were quiet and industrious. The forewoman had pride in her room. She set a certain standard for girls to live up to.

The Young Women's Christian Association is organizing clubs among the workers of all factories as rapidly as possible. These clubs offer constructive, continuous recreation which is linked up to the community needs. Organization is, after all, the solution of industrial problems, and every possible method of achieving it must be utilized.

90
Elizabeth Ross Haynes
Two Million Negro Women at Work (1922)

The thought realm in which the two million Negro women in the United States, gainfully employed, live and work, vibrates with pathos and humor, determination and true heroism, belief and expectation that with the coming years, they too, as a group, with training and larger opportunities, will come into their own as real women.

The three types of occupations in which the majority of these women are engaged are (1) domestic and personal service, (2) agriculture, (3) manufacturing and mechanical industries.

To-day they are found in domestic service, nearly a million strong, with all their shortcomings—their lack of training in efficiency, in cleanliness of person, in honesty and truthfulness, and with all of the shortcomings of ordinary domestic service; namely, basement living quarters, poor working conditions, too long hours, no Sundays off, no standards of efficiency, and the servant "brand." In spite of migration during the World War they are found on the farms, with all of the inconveniences and health hazards of Southern plantation life, in larger numbers than in domestic service. Before the World War there were over 67,000 of them in the unskilled processes of the manufacturing and mechanical industries and 3,000 in the semi-skilled processes. These numbers were greatly increased during the war. In 152 plants visited in 1918–1919, by Department of Labor representatives, more than 20,000 were found employed.

DOMESTIC SERVICE

During the past twelve months some decided changes affecting Negro women have taken place in domestic and personal service. For instance, in Detroit, Michigan, to-day, from eighty to ninety per cent of the calls for domestic workers are for white girls. The average wage in that city for general houseworkers is from $8 to $12 a week as against $15 to $20 a year ago. Women working by the day receive from $.40 to $.50 an hour as against $.60 to $.70 one year ago. The calls for office, elevator, and stock girls are no longer for Negro girls.

In Washington, D. C., with the fixing of the minimum wage in the hotels, restaurants, etc., at $16.50 for a forty-eight-hour week, and the increasing number of available white women, Negro women were to a very large extent displaced. Wages for domestic service for the rank and file have fallen in the past twelve months from $10 a week without any laundry work to $7 and $8 with laundry work. In the parlance of the women, "general housework" now means "cook, wash, and ine (iron)." The numbers driven into domestic work are very large. At one employment agency in this city there are often as many as 200 Negro women a day applying for work. A large majority of them are untrained, inefficient, and poorly equipped with the one thing needful—a good reference.

Only two of the Washington laundries are to-day paying the minimum wage. The average wage in the other laundries is $9 per week, and a few workers get as little as $6. Ninety per cent of these laundry workers are Negro women. As soon as some of the laundries began to fear that they would be forced to pay the minimum wage they began to ask the employment bureaus about the possibility of obtaining white girls. Now that they are not paying the

From *The Southern Workman,* February 1922.

minimum wage they are perfectly satisfied with Negro women. A few of these have been in the laundries from fourteen to thirty-eight years, working through from the flat-work department until they are now "finishing" shirt-bosoms—which one who understands must term really artistic work. In Los Angeles, California, Negro women cooks get from $60 to $100 per month, chambermaids from $40 to $75, nurses from $50 to $75, mothers' helpers from $20 to $40. Day workers receive from $.45 to $.50 an hour. These women are, however, through the unions, excluded from even the laundries.

Some very evident changes have come about in personal and domestic service during the past twelve months, and yet there is much the same restlessness and change from one employer to another; much the same wear and tear on households and housewives; many of the same old customs and conventions. The bond between mistress and maid in many cases is not sufficiently strong for the mistress to learn her maid's surname or her address. Neither seems personally interested in the other and often neither knows, even when they separate, just what the other has been thinking. When one deeply interested in the whole problem analyzes the conditions and sympathizes with mistress and maid sufficiently to get the whole truth, she must conclude that in too many cases the feeling of each borders on real dislike for the other. Neither has for the other that priceless possession—confidence.

Recently, a gentleman applied to an employment agency for a maid or, more correctly speaking, a general houseworker. Upon being asked how many there were in his family, he said, in a somewhat hesitating manner, "Just two in the family, except two boys who don't amount to much—one is six years old and the other is eight." No idea of taking advantage of anyone entered his mind, for his were the thoughts of a man! but the women domestics who heard him at once came to the conclusion that he was trying to "slip something over." On the other hand, a lady advertised for a maid and fifteen came at different times during the day to see her. She engaged every one of them to begin work the next morning and not one of them "showed up." When maids wish a holiday or Sunday off, death in their families, falls by which they are seriously injured, automobile accidents, faked special-delivery letters (especially when they live with the employer's family), annual meetings of lodges in distant cities, and all sorts of other make-believe excuses are given. The night they are paid off they often arrange everything for breakfast, saying they will be back in the morning, but they never return. Often, on the other hand, when a maid applies for a place, if she is not suitable she is told by the lady of the house that her former maid has just come back.

Letters, cards, telephone calls, the people themselves, bespeak the pathos, the restlessness, the ignorance, the inefficiency, the absolute need of the standardization of domestic service as an occupation or industry, and also the absolute need of domestic-training schools in connection with public employment agencies.

AGRICULTURE

A woman owning over a thousand acres of land in the Black Belt of Alabama wrote me, saying:

"Farm conditions are as bad as we have ever seen them. The cotton crop is very poor. Women can pick on an average of from 85 to 110 pounds of cotton per day, for which they get 40 cents a hundred. The peanut farms also furnish some work for women at the rate of 50 cents a day. They pull up the peanut bushes and let them dry. The bushes are then taken to a steam peanut picker which picks off the peanuts; these are then sacked and sent to the factory.

"Down here women do almost any kind of work on the farm from handling a two-horse plow, and hoeing and pulling fodder, to cleaning new ground. Women in domestic service here get from $7 to $8 per month."

Allowing much for migration and giving due credit to the General Education Board, the Slater and Rosenwald Funds, the Jeanes supervisors, and the farm-demonstration agents, who are doing a great work in rural districts of the South, there are many thousand Negro women on the farms to-day eking out such a bare existence as is described in the above letter. They are out early in the morning afoot and on horseback going to near-by fields and, in many instances, on wagons going to fields four and five miles distant. If the fields are near by, they hurry home in the heat of the broiling sun to cook their families' dinners, often over a blazing fire on the hearth, and after dinner they return to the fields in what seems to city people sweltering heat. They tarry late in the fields because, as they say, they can work better "in the cool of the evenin'."

In many sections almost the only recreational or social contacts enjoyed by such women come through the monthly church meeting, the occasional burial of a friend, or the annual trip to town at cotton-seed time. Better prepared ministers, more missionary school-teachers and welfare workers, and many district nurses would make the life of the average agricultural woman worker more endurable.

MANUFACTURING AND MECHANICAL PURSUITS

Many well-informed persons are apt to think that there were no Negro women in manufacturing or mechanical industries until the World War. On the contrary there were and are still some thousands of Negro women in the cigar and tobacco factories of the country. They are poorly paid, of course, their wages ranging from $6 to $10 for a sixty-hour week. The work is dirty, and most of the factories are poorly ventilated, being without an air shaft for the expulsion of the dust; the result is that the tobacco fumes and dust almost suffocate new workers. Then, the work being more or less seasonal, women are sometimes out of employment for weeks at a time. In most tobacco factories the only seats for the women are boxes or stools without backs; and in a few factories women stemming tobacco sit flat on the floor humming a tune while they work. Even fairly reputable lunch rooms and decent toilet facilities are lacking.

Before the World War unskilled Negro women workers in small numbers were in the clothing, food, and metal industries. They were to be found especially in slaughtering and meat-packing houses, crab and peanut factories, and in iron, steel and automobile industries. They were also working in furniture and shoe factories, printing and publishing establishments, and in cotton and silk mills. There were semi-skilled workers in electrical-supply, paper-box, and rubber factories, and in the textile industries. Finally there were a few skilled tailoresses, tinsmiths, coppersmiths, and upholsterers. The story of their entrance into industry in large numbers during the World War is too familiar to warrant repetition here. The part they played in winning the war will probably not be told for many years to come.

Just before the beginning of the unemployment crisis the Women's Bureau of the Department of Labor made a survey of Negro women employed in 150 plants in 17 localities of 9 States. In those plants, covering food, furniture, glass, leather, metal, and paper products, tobacco, and textiles, there were 11,812 Negro women employed. Some of these were even making and decorating lamp-shades; some were making cores in foundries; and others were competing successfully (according to their employers) with girls of many years' experience in the textile industries. Still others were serving as stenographers, typists, etc., in two large mail-order houses in the Middle West.

The questions in the minds of us all are these: How many of these industries still employ Negro women in appreciable number in the skilled and unskilled processes? Are there many Negro women in other industries? And how will Negro women bread-winners, unused to domestic service, weather the storm of the unemployment depression? Information to date from industrial plants in the East, West, North, and South indicates that a larger number of Negro women have lost their places within the last twelve months. One large garment factory in the Middle West, one of the first to take on Negro women and one that seemed proud of its experiment, says now, "We have discontinued the use of Negro women." A Southern mill that used some Negro women before the war says, "We use Negro women only occasionally now for odd jobs."

In spite of such reports, at least some Negro women are still employed in factories. For instance, the Virginia and Maryland crab factories employ 5,000 to 8,000 of these women. Some of them, now forty or fifty years of age, have been in the same factory since they were twelve years old. Crabs are brought in barrels placed in large, iron, crate-like kettles, which are set down into steam for the purpose of cooking the crabs. A newer method is to use cars with seven barrels of crabs to a car. The cars are run on tracks into a steam chest which cooks the crabs in a few minutes. When they are cold each woman receives a certain number of shovelfuls at a long wooden table, or, in a more up-to-date factory, at a better arranged table for two workers. The woman sits on a box, or a "backless" stool, strikes a crab one blow with the handle of a small knife with curved blade, taking off a part of the shell, and, often without even looking at the crab, cuts out what is called "the dead man" and then the white meat, which falls into a pan, and the dark meat, which falls into another. The work is done so rapidly that women pick from forty to seventy-five pounds a day, thus earning $3 or more a day. The crab factories are built over the water, many of them having cement floors. A woman who has worked in such a factory for many years, upon being asked about the healthfulness of such an arrangement, said, "Yes, ma'am, the floors gen'ally fills you full o' rheumatism. Some mo'nin's I kin hardly git out o'bed, I'se so stiff and painful." In spite of the lack of any arrangement that might be called sanitary, except in a very few factories, one never saw a happier group of workers anywhere than the Negro women in the crab factories.

Women who have never worked out and whose husbands have lost their jobs after ten or twenty years' service on the railroads or in both places, and others who have worked out but have not been inside of an employment agency for twenty-five or more years, are now trying, through such agencies or through friends, to find a day's work—cleaning or washing or sewing; hair-dressing or manicuring; acting as agents for selling goods; assisting undertakers; or doing anything else whereby they can earn a living. Struggling against lack of training and against inefficiency, restricted in opportunities to get and hold jobs, more than two million Negro women and girls are to-day laboring in domestic service, in agriculture, and in manufacturing pursuits with the hope of an economic independence that will some day enable them to take their places in the ranks with other working women.

91

Mary McLeod Bethune

Faith That Moved a Dump Heap (1941)

I was first stirred to serious thinking as a child by the custom of holding family prayers every morning and evening. In the corner, by our huge clay fireplace, sat my old grandmother, Sophia, a red bandanna around her head, nodding, and smoking a long-stemmed pipe. All day she talked to God as if He were a person actually present: "Dear God, I am so happy to be living in this loving family circle, where I can get hot biscuits and butter, and coffee with cream, sitting at my own fireside." Mother,

From *Who: The Magazine About People* (1941). Reprinted with permission of Bethune-Cookman College.

more restrained, would thank God for giving her freedom, shelter, and the privilege of having her children with her.

On Sundays, Mother always took us to church and Sunday school. The minister used to visit us on occasion, his pockets full of books. He would read and preach to us, and we would all sing hymns and spirituals.

I was born in Maysville, South Carolina, a country town in the midst of rice and cotton fields. My mother, father, and older brothers and sisters had been slaves until the Emancipation Proclamation. My mother, Patsy McIntosh, belonged to the McIntosh family of South Carolina; my father, Samuel McLeod, to the McLeods. Like all the slaves of that period, they took the family names of their masters. After Mother was freed she continued in the McIntosh employ until she had earned enough to buy five acres of her own from her former master. Then my parents built our cabin, cutting and burning the logs with their own hands. I was the last of seventeen children, ten girls and seven boys. When I was born, the first free child in their own home, my mother exulted, "Thank God, Mary came under our own vine and fig tree."

Mother was of royal African blood, of a tribe ruled by matriarchs. She had dark, soft skin, thin lips, a delicately molded nose, and very bright eyes. Throughout all her bitter years of slavery she had managed to preserve a queenlike dignity. She supervised all the business of the family. Over the course of years, by the combined work and thrift of the family, and Mother's foresight, Father was able to enlarge our home site to thirty-five acres.

Most of my brothers and sisters had married and left home when I was growing up—there were only seven or eight children still around. Mother worked in the fields at Father's side, cutting rice and cotton, and chopping fodder. Each of us children had tasks to perform, according to our aptitudes. Some milked the cows, others helped with the washing, ironing, cooking, and housecleaning. I was my father's champion cotton picker. When I was only nine, I could pick 250 pounds of cotton a day.

But my great joy was in those moments of spontaneous prayer and song which relieved our days of ceaseless toil. Young as I was, I would gather a crowd around me, and like a little evangelist, I would preach, teach, or lead the singing.

Both Grandmother and Mother had taught me Bible stories. I would sit at their feet, picturing myself as the hero or the heroine of every tale. Then, as we were sitting around the fireplace one evening, it flashed through my mind with the intensity of flame that if my favorite, Queen Esther, had been willing to risk her life and plead with the king for her people, I could and would risk mine to do the same for my people.

"WHOSOEVER BELIEVETH"

But my mind dwelt on earthly, as well as on heavenly, subjects. On market days, when my father let me walk to town with him, I noticed the contrast between the lives of the masters and their servants. I looked at the white people around me who were living in homes with real glass windows. Their little girls wore white silk dresses and soft shoes, and rode in carriages, with piles of books on the seats beside them. I glanced down at my own brogue shoes, with brass tips, and my neat but tattered clothes. I had no books. I could not even read!

Dimly it began to permeate my mind that these things came with education. I saw my people still in darkness; unable, in spite of their being free, in spite of all their heartbreaking toil, to experience the good things of life.

But how was I to help them? I could not even help myself. For it was almost impossible for a Negro child, especially in the South, to get education. There were hundreds of square miles, sometimes entire states, without a single Negro school, and colored children were not allowed in public schools with white children. Mr. Lincoln has told our race we were free, but mentally we were still enslaved.

A knock on our door changed my life overnight. There stood a young woman, a colored missionary sent by the Northern Presbyterian Church to start a school near by. She asked my parents to send me. Every morning I picked up a little pail of milk and bread, and walked five miles to school; every afternoon, five miles home. But I walked always on winged feet.

The whole world opened to me when I learned to read. As soon as I understood something, I rushed back and taught it to the others at home. My teacher had a box of Bibles and texts, and she gave me one of each for my very own. That same day the teacher opened the Bible to John 3:16, and read: "For God so loved the world, that He gave His only begotten Son, that whosoever believeth in Him should not perish, but have everlasting life."

With these words the scales fell from my eyes and the light came flooding in. My sense of inferiority, my fear of handicaps, dropped away. "Whosoever," it said. No Jew nor Gentile, no Catholic nor Protestant, no black nor white; just "whosoever." It meant that I, a humble Negro girl, had just as much chance as anybody in the sight and love of God. These words stored up a battery of faith and confidence and determination in my heart, which has not failed me to this day.

I could scarcely wait to run home and tell my mother. For the first time, I gathered the family in a circle around me and read aloud to them from the Good Book. "Praise the Lord," cried my mother. "Hallelujah." That night I drove the first nail of my life work.

By the time I was fifteen I had taken every subject taught at our little school and could go no farther. Dissatisfied, because this taste of learning had aroused my appetite, I was forced to stay at home. Father's mule died—a major calamity—and he had to mortgage the farm to buy another. In those days, when a Negro mortgaged his property they never let him get out of debt.

I used to kneel in the cotton fields and pray that the door of opportunity should be opened to me once more, so that I might give to others whatever I might attain.

THE WAY OPENS

My prayers were answered. A white dressmaker, way off in Denver, Colorado, had become interested in the work of our little neighborhood school and had offered to pay for the higher education of some worthy girl. My teacher selected me, and I was sent to Scotia Seminary in Concord, North Carolina. There I studied English, Latin, higher mathematics, and science, and after classes I worked in the Scotia laundry and kitchen to earn as much extra money as I could.

Scotia broadened my horizon and gave me my first intellectual contacts with white people, for the school had a mixed faculty. The white teachers taught that the color of a person's skin has nothing to do with his brains, and that color, caste, or class distinctions are an evil thing.

When I was graduated I offered myself eagerly for missionary service in Africa, but the church authorities felt I was not sufficiently mature. Instead, they gave me another scholarship, and I spent two years at the Moody Bible School, in Chicago. Again I offered myself for missionary service, and again I was refused. Cruelly disappointed, I got a position at Haines Institute, in Augusta, Georgia, presided over by dynamic Lucy C. Laly, a pioneer Negro educator. From her I got a new vision: my life work lay, not in Africa but in my own country. And with the first money I earned I began to save in order to pay off Father's mortgage, which had hung over his head for ten years!

SEVEN YEARS' SERVICE

During my early teaching days I met my future husband. He too was then a teacher, but to him teaching was only a job. Following our marriage, he entered upon a business career. When our baby son was born, I gave up my work temporarily, so that I could be all mother for one precious year. After that I got restless again to be back at my beloved work, for having a child made me more than ever determined to build better lives for my people.

Like Jacob, who served seven years for Rachel, I was to serve seven years, going as an instructor from one small mission school to another, before I could locate a hearthstone to call my own. Whenever I accumulated a bit of money I was off on an exploring trip, seeking a location where a new school would do the greatest good for the greatest number. I would leave my son with relatives or with his father, who was not altogether sympathetic. He would chide me: "You are foolish to make sacrifices and build for another. Why not stop chasing around and stay put in a good job?" Common sense whispered he was right. But I was inspired by the noble life and work of Booker T. Washington, whose writings had become a second bible to me and now urged me on.

In 1904 I heard rumors which sent me off on another of my many pilgrimages. Henry Flagler was building the Florida East Coast Railroad, and hundreds of Negroes had gathered in Florida for construction work. I found there dense ignorance and meager educational facilities, racial prejudice of the most violent type—crime and violence.

CREATING A COLLEGE

Finally I arrived at Daytona Beach, a beautiful little village, shaded by great oaks and giant pines. A wondrous light filled my mind—this seemed the place and time to plant my seed!

Next morning I combed the town, hunting for a location. I found a shabby four-room cottage, for which the owner wanted a rental of eleven dollars a month. My total capital was a dollar and a half, but I talked him into trusting me until the end of the month for the rest. This was in September. A friend let me stay at her home, and I plunged into the job of creating something from nothing.

I spoke at churches, and the ministers let me take up collections. I buttonholed every woman who would listen to me, told people I was going to open a new type of school, to give more than mere reading or book learning. I told them I proposed to teach the essentials of homemaking, the arts, the skilled trades—and good citizenship.

On October 3, 1904, I opened the doors of my school, with an enrollment of five little girls, aged from eight to twelve, whose parents paid me fifty cents' weekly tuition. My own child was the only boy in the school. Though I hadn't a penny left, I considered cash money as the smallest part of my resources. I had faith in a loving God, faith in myself, and a desire to serve. Although I saw my work would have to be done on a day-to-day basis, I built a fence of trust around each day.

We burned logs and used the charred splinters as pencils, and mashed elderberries for ink. I begged strangers for a broom, a lamp, a bit of cretonne to put around the packing case which served as my desk. I haunted the city dump and the trash piles behind hotels, retrieving discarded linen and kitchenware, cracked dishes, broken chairs, pieces of old lumber. Everything was scoured and mended. This was part of the training to salvage, to reconstruct, to make bricks without straw. As parents began gradually to leave their children overnight, I had to provide sleeping accommodations. I took corn sacks for mattresses. Then I picked Spanish moss from trees, dried and cured it, and used it as a substitute for mattress hair.

The school expanded fast. In less than two years I had 250 pupils. In desperation I hired a large hall next to my original little cottage, and used it as a combined dormitory and classroom. I concentrated more and more on girls, as I felt that they especially were hampered by lack of educational opportunities. And besides, they are the mothers of the race, the homemakers and spiritual guides.

I had many volunteer workers and a few regular teachers, who were paid from fifteen to twenty-five dollars a month and board. I was supposed to keep the balance of the funds for my own pocket, but there was never any balance—only a yawning hole. I wore old clothes sent me by mission boards, recut and redesigned for me in our dressmaking classes.

At last I saw that our only solution was to stop renting space, and to buy and build our own college.

FIVE DOLLARS DOWN

Near by was a field, popularly called Hell's Hole, which was used as a dumping ground. I approached the owner, determined to buy it. The price was $250. In a daze, he finally agreed to take five dollars down, and the balance in two years. I promised to be back in a few days with the initial payment. He never knew it, but I didn't have five dollars. I raised this sum selling ice cream and sweet-potato pies to the workmen on construction jobs, and I took the owner his money in small change wrapped in my handkerchief.

That's how the Bethune-Cookman College campus started.

We at once discovered the need of an artesian well. The estimate was two hundred dollars. Here again we started with an insignificant payment, the balance remaining on trust. But what use was a plot without a building? I hung on to contractors' coat-tails, begging for loads of sand and secondhand bricks. I went to all the carpenters, mechanics, and plasterers in town, pleading with them to contribute a few hours' work in the evening in exchange for sandwiches and tuition for their children and themselves.

Slowly the building rose from its foundations. The name over the entrance still reads Faith Hall.

I had learned already that one of my most important jobs was to be a good beggar! I rang doorbells and tackled cold prospects without a lead. I wrote articles for whoever would print them, distributed leaflets, rode interminable miles of dusty roads on my old bicycle; invaded churches, clubs, lodges, chambers of commerce. If a prospect refused to make a contribution I would say, "Thank you for your time." No matter how deep my hurt, I always smiled. I refused to be discouraged, for neither God nor man can use a discouraged person.

Strongly interracial in my ideas, I looked forward to an advisory board of trustees composed of both white and colored people. I did my best missionary work among the prominent winter visitors to Florida. I would pick out names of "newly arrived guests," from the newspapers, and write letters asking whether I could call.

One of these letters went to James N. Gamble, of Procter & Gamble. He invited me to call at noon the next day. I borrowed a watch from a friend, jumped on my trusty old bicycle, and arrived early. I hid behind some bushes until the clock hands pointed to exactly twelve. Then I pressed the bell.

Mr. Gamble himself opened the door, and when I gave my name he looked at me in astonishment. "Are you the woman trying to build a school here? Why, I thought you were a white woman."

I laughed, "Well, you see how white I am." Then I told my story. "I'd like you to visit my school and, if it pleases you, to stand behind what I have in mind," I finished.

He consented. I scurried around town and persuaded the mayor and the leading real-estate dealer to act as a reception committee. When Mr. Gamble arrived the next day, everything had been scrubbed with soap and water until it glistened—including the pupils. He made a careful tour of inspection, agreed to be a trustee, and gave me a check for $150—although I hadn't mentioned money. For many years he was one of our most generous friends.

Another experience with an unexpected ending was my first meeting with J. S. Peabody, of Columbia City, Indiana. After I had made an eloquent appeal for funds he gave me exactly twenty-five cents. I swallowed hard, thanked him smilingly, and later entered the contribution in my account book.

A WHITE LIE

Two years later he reappeared. "Do you remember me?" he asked. "I'm one of your contributors." I greeted him cordially. He went on:

"I wonder if you recall how much I gave you when I was here last?"

Not wishing to embarrass him, I told a white lie: "I'll have to look it up in my account book." Then after finding the entry, I said, "Oh, yes, Mr. Peabody, you gave us twenty-five cents."

Instead of being insulted, he was delighted that we kept account of such minute gifts. He immediately handed me a check for a hundred dollars and made arrangements to furnish the building. When he died, a few years later, he left the school $10,000.

Experiences like these taught me that an apparent disappointment may be the prelude to glorious success. One evening I arranged a meeting at an exclusive hotel, expecting to talk to a large audience of wealthy people. But so many social functions were taking place that same night that I was greeted by an audience of exactly six. I was sick at heart—but I threw all my enthusiasm into my talk. At the end a gentleman dropped a twenty-dollar bill in the hat.

The next day he unexpectedly appeared at the school. He said his name was Thomas H. White, but it meant nothing to me. He looked around, asked where the shabby but immaculate straw matting on the floor came from. I said, "The city dump." He saw a large box of corn meal, and inquired what else there was to eat. I replied, "That's all we have at the moment." Then he walked about the grounds and saw an unfinished building, on which construction work had been temporarily abandoned for lack of funds. That was nothing new—there were always unfinished buildings cluttering up the landscape of our school. But I think the crowning touch was when he saw our dressmaking class working with a broken-down Singer sewing machine.

He turned to me, saying, "I believe you are on the right track. This is the most promising thing I've seen in Florida." He pressed a check in my hand, and left. The check was for $250. The following day he returned again, with a new sewing machine. Only then did I learn that Mr. White was the Singer people's principal competitor.

Mr. White brought plasterers, carpenters, and materials to finish our new building. Week after week he reappeared, with blankets for the children, shoes and a coat for me, everything we had dreamed of getting. When I thanked him, with tears in my eyes, for his generosity, he waved me aside.

"I've never invested a dollar that has brought greater returns than the dollars I have given you," he told me. And when this great soul died, he left a trust of $67,000, the interest to be paid us "as long as there is a school."

Do you wonder I have faith?

I never stop to plan. I take things step by step. For thirty-five years we have never had to close our doors for lack of food or fuel, although often we had to live from day to day. . . .

As the school expanded, whenever I saw a need for some training or service we did not supply, I schemed to add it to our curriculum. Sometimes that took years. When I came to Florida, there were no hospitals where a Negro could go. A student became critically ill with appendicitis, so I went to a local hospital and begged a white physician to take her in and operate. My pleas were so desperate he finally agreed. A few days after the operation, I visited my pupil.

When I appeared at the front door of the hospital, the nurse ordered me around to the back way. I thrust her aside—and found my little girl segregated in a corner of the porch behind the kitchen. Even my toes clenched with rage.

That decided me. I called on three of my faithful friends, asking them to buy a little cottage behind our school as a hospital. They agreed, and we started with two beds.

From this humble start grew a fully equipped twenty-bed hospital—our college infirmary and a refuge for the needy throughout the state. It was staffed by white and black physicians and by our own student nurses. We ran this hospital for twenty years as part of our contribution to community life; but a short time ago, to ease our financial burden, the city took it over.

Gradually, as educational faculties expanded and there were other places where small children could go, we put the emphasis on high-school and junior-college training. In 1922, Cookman College, a men's school, the first in the state for the higher education of Negroes, amalgamated with us. The combined coeducational college, now run under the auspices of the Methodist Episcopal Church, is called Bethune-Cookman College. We have fourteen modern buildings, a beautiful campus of thirty-two acres, an enrollment in regular and summer sessions of 600 students, a faculty and staff of thirty-two, and 1,800 graduates. The college property, now valued at more than $800,000, is entirely unencumbered.

When I walk through the campus, with its stately palms and well-kept lawns, and think back to the dump-heap foundation, I rub my eyes and pinch myself. And I remember my childish visions in the cotton fields.

But values cannot be calculated in ledger figures and property. More than all else the college has fulfilled my ideals of distinctive training and service. Extending far beyond the immediate sphere of its graduates and students, it has already enriched the lives of 100,000 Negroes.

In 1934, President Franklin D. Roosevelt appointed me director of the division of Negro affairs of the National Youth Administration. My main task now is to supervise the training provided for 600,000 Negro children, and I have to run the college by remote control. Every few weeks, however, I snatch a day or so and return to my beloved home.

This is a strenuous program. The doctor shakes his head and says, "Mrs. Bethune, slow down a little. Relax! Take it just a little easier." I promise to reform, but in an hour the promise is forgotten.

For I am my mother's daughter, and the drums of Africa still beat in my heart. They will not let me rest while there is a single Negro boy or girl without a chance to prove his worth.

92

NATIONAL WOMEN'S TRADE UNION LEAGUE

Post-War Program Proposal (1919)

The National Women's Trade Union League Committee on social and industrial reconstruction presents the following program:

The Great War has ended. The peace of the world, to be based on the covenant of free peoples, is to be written into history. Democracy was challenged on the battlefields, and millions of men died that she might be triumphant.

The war of today has ended, but the world-old struggle of freedom and justice has not ended. In a thousand contests, men and women have struggled for more liberty, for greater justice, for a deeper brotherhood. Under a thousand names the battle has been waged. Yesterday the challenge rang on the battlefields of Europe. Today it is heard in the political and social and industrial life of the peoples. Yesterday the nations answered through their soldiers; today they must answer through their citizens. Yesterday Democracy called to the nations to train their men to fight; today Democracy calls to the nations to train their citizens to think. Yesterday millions of men died that the democratic purpose of life might be achieved. Today Democracy must win through living men. Valor and sacrifice were demanded of the soldier in the trenches; valor and sacrifice are demanded of the citizen at home.

The citizens of today are not a group of men and women set apart for a specific service; the citizens of today are the men and women in the factories and workshops and counting houses, in the mills and the mines, in the fields and forests, tillers of the soil, workers of hand and brain, hewers and thinkers.

From *Women's Work and War* (published monthly by The National Women's Trade Union League), January and February 1919.

Yesterday the nations united to train and equip the soldier and all the resources of society were called into service to give him a fighting chance. Today the nations must unite and all the resources of society must be called into service to train and equip the citizen, to set free his powers of mind and spirit, for he is the defender of that democracy for which our brothers died, he is the builder of the new world to be founded in freedom and justice and self-government; to him is entrusted the Covenant of the World. The summons has come to the citizen. The hour calls for consecration of will and purpose to the high resolve that these dead shall not have died in vain and that under God the Nations shall have a new birth of freedom.

The first essential of a democracy is a standard of life for the citizens of the commonwealth. We declare for a standard of life which shall insure to all citizens, both men and women, free opportunity to work with hand and brain, and secure to them a full measure of health, education, recreation and fruitful leisure; such a standard as shall guarantee to every child the certainty of a high school education and the possibility of a university education in preparation for citizenship.

As a step toward this end, we ask that the following Labor Standards be included in the Treaty of Peace, to take effect within a given time:

Compulsory education up to 16 years of age, and part-time education up to 18 years.

Abolition of Child Labor.

An 8-hour day and 44-hour week.

No night work for women.

One day rest in seven.

Equal pay for equal work.

Equal opportunity for men and women in trade and technical training.

Social insurance against sickness, accident, industrial disease, and unemployment.

Provision for Old Age and Invalidity Pensions and Maternity benefits.

We urge a complete restoration at the earliest possible moment, of all fundamental political rights—free speech, free press, and free assemblage, and the removal of all war-time restraints upon the interchange of ideas and the movements of peoples among communities and nations. We ask an immediate amnesty for all political prisoners.

We ask that the principle of self-government in the workshop be established in all industry, both public and private, and that the right of the workers to organize into trade unions be recognized and affirmed.

We urge the full enfranchisement of women, and that they be accorded political, legal and industrial equality; and further, we urge the adoption of the most modern methods of representation for the establishment and maintenance of political democracy.

We ask for the establishment of universal social standards, a single-standard of morality, the protection of motherhood, and the guarantee to every child of the highest possible development, physical, mental and moral.

Believing that a government that demands universal service from its citizens in time of war should provide universal employment at a living wage for its citizens in time of peace, we ask for the establishment in every country of a Commission on Demobilization, on which Labor shall be fully represented by men and women, to formulate plans which shall ensure employment for all workers at standard rates of wages that the Army be not demobilized in greater ratio than industry can absorb; and that munitions workers and other war-contract workers be considered equally with the soldiers and sailors in the plans for demobilization.

We ask, further, that to crippled soldiers and sailors be afforded a just opportunity, through education, allotment of public land (intelligently directed, as under the law of the State of California, or otherwise), and other means, to reestablish their individual lives and homes, and that equivalent provision be made for all men and women incapacitated through service in war industries.

(The above action was unanimously adopted by the National Women's Trade Union League of America at its Biennial Convention,

June, 1917. As no Reconstruction Commission has been appointed as yet by the Government of the United States, we now ask that the Secretaries of War, Navy, Labor, Agriculture, and the Interior, be designated to formulate the proposed plans.)

We re-affirm our stand in favor of the government ownership of public utilities and the nationalization and development of natural resources—water and unused land.

In order that the problems of women wage-earners in the United States may be dealt with as intelligently as possible, we further urge:

That the Women in Industry Service of the United States Department of Labor be placed upon a permanent basis.

That in every State Department of Labor a Woman's Bureau be established, to care for the protection and welfare of women workers.

That provision be made for increased appropriations for State Factory Departments, and for the appointment of women inspectors in the proportion of one for every 15,000 women wage-earners.

That women workers be represented upon all State and Federal administrative boards.

That the Federal and State Employment Agencies be co-ordinated and standardized and all private agencies be abolished.

That the use of the Injunction in labor disputes be abolished by embodying the principles of the federal Clayton Act in state legislation—this we ask for the protection of the organization of the workers.

We, the Committee on Social and Industrial Reconstruction of the National Women's Trade Union League of America, recognizing that the problem here presented concern—in whole or in part—working women the world over, urge again the calling of an International Congress of Working Women for the exchange of thought and the concerted action required by the task before us.

93
Katharine Fisher
Women Workers and the A. F. of L. (1921)

The woman question appeared at the 1921 convention of the American Federation of Labor in a resolution to amend the constitution of the Federation to secure to women opportunity for union membership on the same terms as men. The convention answered the question by a substitute resolution which leaves the women's case where it was before, in the hands of the national and international unions. Last February a conference of representatives of the A. F. of L. and of these unions put at the top of a list of rights which it called on the public to recognize and support, "the right of the working people of the United States to organize into trade unions," and appended their names to it with the statement: "To the above declaration and appeal we pledge ourselves and those whom we represent."

Among those who made this appeal and pledge are the President and another representative of the International Molders' Union, and the President and the Secretary-Treasurer of the Journeymen Barbers' International Union, both of which unions expressly exclude women from membership. The names of Samuel Gompers and all the other members of the Executive Council of the A. F. of L. appear as representing the Federation and pledging it to "the right of the working people of the United States to organize into trade unions." Yet, a few weeks later Secretary Frank Morrison wrote in answer to an inquiry: "The American Federation of Labor would have authority to issue charters to women members of a trade only where such course would be authorized by the international organization having jurisdiction."

An example of how this works is that when the women barbers of Seattle, denied member-

Originally published in *The New Republic,* August 3, 1921. Reprinted with permission.

ship in the Barbers' Union, asked the A. F. of L. for a separate charter, it was refused, because the Barbers' Union objected.

Either the A. F. of L. and its affiliated organizations do not recognize and support the right of the working people of the United States to organize, or they do not recognize women as people. The second assertion contains the most truth. The stock defense of the A. F. of L. for not living up to its "stand," and its "declarations" in favor of "organizing all the workers, regardless of sex," is, "The A. F. of L. cannot dictate to the internationals." In this matter, "the autonomy of the internationals" is stretched into a dictatorship of a single international over the A. F. of L. But the real trouble is that union men, too many of them, believe in men's right of dictatorship over women.

The fact that only five internationals explicitly exclude women, and also the fact that discrimination of various sorts against women occurs in organizations that are most firmly on record as favoring equality for women, have been considered reasons for not demanding action by the A. F. of L. in convention. But women who believed that a step toward industrial equality for women would be taken by forcing the question upon the attention of the Denver Convention, formed the Women's Committee for Industrial Equality and drafted the following amendment, which was introduced in the form of a resolution by Delegate Ethel Hague:

"Nothing in this constitution shall be construed as recognition of any right on the part of the American Federation of Labor, or of any affiliated union, or of any officer or officers of such union, to deny or abridge the right of workers to membership and to all the privileges of membership in the union of their trade or industry on account of sex; and women in a trade under the jurisdiction of a union which does not admit women to membership on the same terms as men shall not be denied a separate and direct charter from the American Federation of Labor for lack of the consent of that union."

This amendment made the principle of industrial equality paramount. It provided that if one door of entrance to the A. F. of L. was closed to a group of women, another should be open. But it avoided direct interference with "autonomy" by not being mandatory on the internationals.

The substitute resolution which was adopted reads: "Resolved, that those international and national organizations that do not admit women workers give early consideration for such admission." This is even more meaningless than it sounds, because two of these organizations, the Barbers' Union and the United Brotherhood of Carpenters and Joiners, will not hold conventions until 1924; another, the Molders' Union, has not yet set the date for its next convention; and each of the three Presidents of these organizations admits that no consideration will be given the subject by his union until its convention is held. As President Hutcheson of the Carpenters was a member of the Committee on Law, which reported the substitute resolution, the committee certainly knew just how "early" the consideration of the women-carpenters' case would be.

In the June number of *Life and Labor,* Mabel W. Taylor, organizer for the Women's Trade Union League, reports from Grand Rapids, Michigan, where many women are employed in furniture making, a branch of carpentry, that efforts to organize women there have failed. In giving reasons for this, she says:

"The men in the shops are to blame for not taking the girls into their organizations when they first entered the shops. In many instances they have antagonized the girls by trying to have them discharged, by belittling the amount and quality of the work they do, and by making the girls feel that they are interlopers. . . . In most of the organizations of men, where women are in competition with them in their various crafts and trades, you will find men who declare that they will never admit women into their union. These men, in my opinion, have the interests neither of the working man nor of the working woman at heart. The employers know only too well that once the men and women unite, by their combined strength they can get anything they wish. If only the men, now that most of them realize their mistake, would put their shoulders to the wheel to rectify that mistake, what a wonderful amount of progress could be made for the good of humanity!"

Things seem from this account, to be reaching a pass at which the A. F. of L., instead of leaving the internationals to their own destruction, will have to take a hand. It will have to teach the short-sightedness of trying to keep women out of a trade by keeping them out of a union, a lesson unions have been learning, one by one, painfully, for sixty years. Women are excluded, ostensibly for their own good. "It isn't a woman's trade." But it is dollars to doughnuts that when a man talks of protecting a woman from an unsuitable job that he is trying to protect *his* job from the woman.

Pages of the Proceedings of the Barbers' Convention in 1919 are filled with speeches to the effect that a woman cannot cut a man's hair and remain respectable. Carpenters hint darkly of untellable things in plants where men and women wood-workers are employed. President Valentine of the Molders' Union, to show the dire effect upon a woman's modesty of working in a foundry, told of seeing a woman (she happened to be the owner of the foundry) tuck her skirt between her knees when she stooped to look into a furnace. But the risks to women involved in turning them clean out of their jobs do not worry him at all. He told members of the Committee for Industrial Equality how he got every woman core-maker in a plant discharged by notifying the employer that union men would not use the cores they made. "Because they were made by non-union workers, or because they were made by women?" Mr. Valentine was asked. He replied. "Because they were made by *women*." Running a wood-working machine in a furniture factory is highly unwomanly, to the mind of President Hutcheson, of the Carpenters' Union; but he was surprised that barbers should object to women in their trade. "Barbering,"—he said, "now, that's a nice, light trade for women. They can do that without losing their *femininity*."

Secretary-Treasurer Fischer of the Barbers' Union was frank enough to say, "Immorality isn't the real reason for excluding women barbers." A molder, not a delegate, declared, "They can't get away with that bunk about work in foundries being too heavy for a woman. It's dirty, but women, like the men, have helpers to do the heavy work, like shoveling sand. Women are better than men at making small cores." This man was strong for the amendment for the reason that women were "running the union molders and core-makers out and breaking up the unions" in foundries in Massachusetts which he named. He said the rank and file wanted the women organized, but the officers were opposed. "These men here," he added, "don't represent the rank and file."

Perhaps it is because they have nothing at stake that when called on to act in accord with A. F. of L. declarations about "organizing all the workers," they are content to make a gesture of impotence. But it is encouraging that the rank and file are, as Miss Taylor says, "finding out their mistake."

The industrial equality amendment proved in a measure a touchstone to test the live elements in the convention. The numbers of delegates and delegations who readily pledged their support to it surprised the Industrial Equality Committee. Although only a small fraction of the delegates were interviewed, over 12,000 votes out of the 38,294 cast by the 523 voting delegates were pledged in favor of it. The women who worked for it hoped for a record vote, but the reporting of a substitute resolution and the impossibility of getting a roll-call at half-past five from a convention facing an evening session, prevented. The amendment made hundreds of men think and talk of women's relation to the labor movement. It brought speakers to its support, and there were more of these ready than time allowed to be heard. After its defeat, the Committee for Industrial Equality continued its propaganda and increased its membership. It has changed its name to the National Woman's Union and plans to secure the adoption of the same or an even stronger resolution at Cincinnati in 1922.

94
THE WOMEN'S BUREAU,
U.S. DEPARTMENT OF LABOR
What the Women's Bureau Has Accomplished (1930)

At the end of its first decade as a permanent agency in the Federal Government the Women's Bureau can boast of a steady development and expansion of activities. Handicapped by a small appropriation and a very limited staff, the bureau nevertheless has made a creditable record in the performance of its task as outlined by Congress "to formulate standards and policies which shall promote the welfare of wage-earning women, improve their working conditions, increase their efficiency, and advance their opportunities for profitable employment.". . .

With over eight-and-a-half million women wage earners in the United States, according to the 1920 census, with one in every five women a wage earner and one in every five wage earners a woman with women engaged in all but 35 of the 572 occupations listed by the Census, the Women's Bureau, charged with the responsibility of studying and safe-guarding the interests of these workers, has indeed had a big job to perform. But at no time has the appropriation granted for the work been commensurate with the task assigned the bureau.

The variety of elements composing this vast army of working women has added greatly to the complexity of the problems confronting the bureau. In the ranks of the wage-earners are found young girls, middle-aged and even elderly women, married, widowed, and divorced women, Negro and foreign-born workers, each type with its own set of problems requiring attention and solution. There are women who support not only themselves but dependents as well, those who must enact the double role of homemaker and wage earner, or even carry a triple burden with the addition of motherhood.

The great variety of jobs in which women are found has complicated the work of the bureau, and has necessitated considerable versatility on the part of the members of its staff, who have had to analyze the individual problems of women in the different occupational groups and their subdivisions. Also in any consideration of the complicating factors connected with the employment of women in the United States and affecting the program of the Women's Bureau, it is necessary to call attention to the many variations of labor legislation for women in the 48 States, probably no two States being identical in this respect.

In general there have been two chief divisions to the activities of the bureau—fact-finding and fact-furnishing. On the one hand, it has collected information, planned scientific studies, and made technical investigations pertaining to wage-earning women; on the other, it has classified, analyzed, published, and disseminated these collected data, for the purpose of informing and interesting the public and stimulating into action, to effect better conditions, those forces directly concerned with the employment of women.

As a Government agency the Women's Bureau has had the weight of authority, even though it is not vested with any powers of law enforcement. As an organization unrelated in any personal sense to the industrial and business world it has had the impartiality of a court of justice. With a number of experts and economic specialists on its staff it has had the solidarity of a scientific foundation.

During its existence the bureau has conducted many and varied investigations, the results of most of them having been published and

From the records of the Women's Bureau, U.S. Department of Labor, [unpublished] report, dated April 30, 1930.

given wide distribution. It has to its credit 80-odd bulletins which have been of real interest and value to many different groups—to industrialists, business men, and employers from the point of view of dollars and cents and efficient production; to sociologists, psychologists, educators, physicians, and scientists concerned with human welfare, conduct, and relations; to forward-looking women interested in the progress of their sex; and to labor groups striving to gain a firmer and higher foothold on the ladder of industrial progress. The bureau's mailing list of those to whom its bulletins have been sent is varied, comprising economists, research foundations, schools, universities, professors, students, libraries, employers, employers' associations, labor organizations, industrial specialists, women's clubs, periodicals, newspapers, free lance writers, State departments, and organizations in foreign countries.

Cooperation with State departments of labor has always constituted an important feature in the bureau program of activities, since the States in so many instances lack the funds, personnel, and equipment essential for conducting investigations of the type possible for the Women's Bureau. Accordingly this Federal agency has made surveys of women in 20 States, in each instance in response to a request from the State—investigating working conditions, hours, and wages of women employed in such establishments as factories, stores, laundries, mills, hotels, restaurants, telephone exchanges, and canneries.

The bureau has conducted also a number of intensive studies of special industries employing large numbers of women, such as candy manufacture, fruit harvesting, canning, textile mills, five-and-ten-cent stores, laundries, meat-packing plants, and cigar factories.

In general these investigations reveal that although many women are employed under satisfactory conditions, the majority still fail to receive an adequate wage for efficient service and thousands continue to operate on a 10-hour schedule and under working conditions detrimental to health and safety.

According to the 1920 Census there were in this country more than a million women in agricultural pursuits and considerably over two million in domestic and personal service. Each of these two big groups is characterized by a number of difficult employment problems. The Women's Bureau has to its credit several investigations of the hardships and handicaps of women in such types of employment and has thus made available data of value and importance, stressing the need for considerable improvement in standards. Much remains to be done, however, in the way of education before such ends are achieved.

Although the lion's share of the bureau's program has been given to women in the producing and distributing trades this is as it should be, since these workers are involved in such a severe struggle to earn a livelihood and to meet the many demands made upon them. Nevertheless, women in business and the professions, whose progress is so often checked by prejudice and other barriers, have not been neglected, their problems forming the subjects of discussion in several of the bureau's reports. Outstanding studies of this nature deal with women's occupational progress, women in the realm of invention, the status of women in Government service, and the employment status and opportunities of women doctors. Similar studies of the difficulties attendant upon women in other fields are urgent.

Matters of health and safety as related to women workers have called for constant attention and investigation on the part of the Bureau. Not only are these problems the raison d'etre for several special bulletins, but such vital questions as these run through practically all of the bureau's publications as the essential framework on which other discussions are hinged. Studies of the physiological basis for the shorter workday for women, industrial poisons, industrial accidents, the employment of women in hazardous industries, the effect on women's health of employment at night are some of the most noteworthy contributions by the bureau along the line of industrial hygiene and safety. With changes in industry and the development of new processes other aspects of the health situation are constantly arising and confronting the bureau with the need for more scientific research and analysis.

Special labor laws for women have called for considerable library research and first-hand investigation by bureau specialists. At least ten of the Women's Bureau publications deal with various phases of this subject. The history of special labor laws, the detailed analyses of the various types, and the effects of such legislation on women constitute the main lines of discussion.

Other problems pertaining especially to wage-earning women which have been the subject of intensive and extensive study by the bureau are occupational progress of women, based largely on detailed analysis of census data, opportunities for employment and for training for special trades, the family responsibilities of single women, the breadwinning activities of married women, the handicaps and hardships of special classes of women such as Negroes and immigrants, industrial home work by women, and lost time and labor turnover of women workers.

The activities of the Women's Bureau in broadcasting its material have not stopped with its published bulletins. Since the material contained therein is largely of a scientific and statistical nature, it has been necessary to translate it into popular form with emphasis placed on the human interest aspects.

News stories and many special articles of both a popular and a technical nature have played a steady and important part in the educational campaign which the Women's Bureau has considered it essential to maintain.

A number of popular exhibits, such as models, motion pictures, maps, charts, posters, folders, have been prepared and have been circulated by the bureau in every State in the United States and also in a number of foreign countries. The bureau participated in the National Sesquicentennial at Philadelphia, and in the Iberian-American Exposition at Seville, special exhibits made for these occasions having attracted considerable attention and won gold medals as awards from the commissions.

Two conferences on women in industry have been called and conducted by the bureau, the first in 1923 and the second in 1926. The object in each instance was to bring together the women in the country concerned with the industrial and economic problems as related to women workers and to give opportunity for the presentation of facts about women in industry by experts and the discussion of such problems by the delegates. These conferences made possible an interchange of experiences and ideas among employers, workers, and the general public for the purpose of developing policies for broader opportunity and more profitable employment of women under modern industrial conditions, and for securing by such means the best results for both industry and society. All national women's organizations and all national organizations having a large proportion of women members were asked to send delegates. Employers, industrial and business organizations, and specialists along many lines also participated in response to invitation from the bureau.

Throughout the past ten years the bureau has made it a policy whenever feasible to comply with requests for its representatives to attend and participate as speakers, advisors, and consultants in important conferences and conventions called by other organizations interested in the problems pertaining to women wage earners.

Each year, as the bureau has become better known, the demands upon it have steadily increased, and the volume and variety of its work have expanded. With the number of women workers steadily growing, with the constant increase in married women wage earners, with the share of women in family support and economic responsibility assuming greater proportions, with acute problems of employment and unemployment piling up as a result of our present machine age, and with the development of new industries and new processes giving rise to new hazards and additional strain for women workers, the task of the Women's Bureau becomes each year more extensive and complicated.

95
MARY VAN KLEECK
Women and Machines (1921)

"As much a woman's job as a man's," said a manufacturer, commenting on the work of women recently initiated into the operation of milling machines. By what mysterious process 'milling' (which has to do with metals, not flour) is accomplished, is unimportant. Its claim to distinction is its power to break through the barriers between women's work and men's work, and to become, as it were, a sexless job. This is but one of several hundred mechanical tasks of industry described as women's new opportunities in a forthcoming report of the Women's Bureau of the United States Department of Labor and the War-Work Council of the Young Women's Christian Association, under the title, *The New Position of Women in American Industry.*

The volume does not indulge in prophecy, but confines itself to the security of comprehensive statistics (from nearly fifteen thousand firms, employing almost two and a half million workers), setting forth for the first time the official record of the occupations of women during the war, and their retention since the Armistice in new tasks. With so definite a foundation on which to stand, it is tempting to analyze the more elusive factors and tendencies in women's present industrial status. For women in industry represent one of many undetermined forces in a generation of uncertainties, and prophecy requires rash courage; but to invite others to observe changes that have already taken place, and to measure the direction of influences now operating, is not too bold an undertaking.

Originally published in *The Atlantic Monthly* (1921). Reprinted with permission.

I

The war record, at least, is clear. Management in industry, and not feminism, opened the way to novel work for women. The usual explanation is that the war did it. Superficially, the war appears to have released the powers of women in industrial processes more effectively than all the preaching of economic independence during the past fifty years. Actually, however, by no known alchemy can war be converted into spiritual kinship with feminism. The war played a part because the strain which it put upon industrial capacity forced industry into the service of the community; and the prejudices against women's employment in the more skilled mechanical processes were relaxed because there was no one else to produce while the men were fighting. Prejudices were laid aside "for the period of the war," but not shaken out of men's minds permanently. Nor has industry, although temporarily controlled for national service, lost its power to exploit women as cheap and docile labor. This, however, anticipates a comment that belongs later.

The gain made in the war was the practical demonstration of women's unsuspected industrial capacity. Their record is an accomplished fact, which may be destined to modify, alike, prejudices and the customs which they influence. But the condition to be modified is made of sterner stuff than men's opinions....

In brief, so extensive were the changes in the claims of industry upon women that five and a half pages of close, small type of a government report are required for a mere listing, in paragraph form, of the processes in which women were actually substituted for men. They ranged in their main divisions from blast-furnaces and steel-works to logging-camps and sawmills. The details included, in multitudinous diversity, the making of chemical analyses of steel, the operating of cranes, core-making, acetylene welding, stamping tin, loading cartridges, caning chairs, operating lathes, and many other tasks with technical names so unfamiliar as to give no picture to the reader except an impression of variety and complexity.

For women, the varied jobs opened to them not only offered a chance to try their hands at unfamiliar occupations: they gave opportunity for release from a restricted group of industries hitherto open to them. Before the war three-fourths of the women employed in manufacturing and mechanical industries were concentrated in shops making textiles, personal apparel, gloves and shoes, food, and tobacco products. The notable fact of the war experience is the drift of women from these traditional pursuits to novel adventures in mechanics.

More important than the industries opened to them was the work they did. That the proportions of women increased so greatly in the iron and steel industries and the metal trades is interesting as part of the history of the war; but more promising for the future is the fact that they learned how to operate the same machines that are used in making scientific instruments, automobiles, optical goods, and motorcycles. In managing these successfully, they were acquiring a skill which could be turned to account in manufacturing many products used in the normal times of peace. The lathe is a good illustration, because practical knowledge of its principles of operation gives the mastery of other cutting machines.

Were these large increases in the proportions of employed women due to the fact that it takes two or more women to do the work of one man? In crane-operating, yes; because women were employed in three eight-hour shifts, where men had worked in two twelve-hour shifts—a practice, by the way, which many managers in industry have now made obsolete; here, then, three were employed in place of two men. But in all the industries considered together, with this kind of exception, ninety-eight to a hundred men were released for every hundred women employed. Hundreds of jobs, like milling, became sexless. The wise and the esteemed employer was not the one who clung to past practice, but the pioneer, who discovered new ways of releasing men for the army by successfully initiating women into their jobs.

Did the women succeed? "No," said one group of employers. "Women are not desirable in our work because of lack of physical endurance and training; nor are they temperamentally capable of attaining the same efficiency in machine work as a man." "Yes," said another group, much larger in numbers. "Women, if properly trained, can do as well as, if not better than, men in any kind of mechanical work."

More important than opinions, however, was the analysis of conditions in the plants where success or failure was reported. Results apparently depended less on the kind of work, or even in the degree of skill required, than on the intelligence with which women were initiated into their new work, the mechanical changes planned where they were necessary (to the advantage of men as well as women), and especially the training given....

When the fighting stopped, industry, of course, faced another revolutionary transition from war-products to the work of peace, and many plants curtailed their force. In some instances, work done by women—making gas-masks, for instance—came to an end. Extra shifts were disbanded in many plants. Indeed, forty out of every hundred were, in the language of industry, "laid off." Of every hundred men in the important war industries, sixty-two were retained; of every hundred women employed in November, 1918, forty-three were at work in August, 1919. The larger proportions of women displaced in the transition from war to peace are accounted for, in part, by some previously wageless women of the "leisure class," by part-time workers, and by some married women who had been lured into industry by the war-emergency, with no intention of continuing. With the importance of the lathe in mind as the key to success in mechanical industries, the fact is impressive that of the firms questioned in 1919 who had recruited women for this job during the war, more than half were retaining them.

II

In accomplishing these changes, ideas and public opinion have lagged behind tangible and practical adjustments in the shops. We are almost prepared to assert that, if women are on the way to enlarged opportunities in industry, business, and not feminism, will open the way. But no one who has had even a glimpse of the new spirit of women can doubt that, if the managers of business undertake to make changes affecting them, they will have to deal with feminism, whether or not they understand that name and its purposes.

Machinery versus feminism—this is the real issue. Machinery—or, to use its more abstract title, business—does not know yet that feminism has any connection with it, or lives in the same town. Feminism is immensely interested in machinery just now, and does not know its dangers. She calls it "equal opportunity," and she thinks that, like a brave David, she needs no more power to conquer than she can carry in her bare hands. She has won the vote. Economic opportunity seems to her no more difficult to attain.

Thus these two forces stand over against each other—industry, never more problematical, transitional, uncertain of the coming phase of control, and women, confident that economic freedom is their next goal after political equality, but not yet cognizant of the burdensome and baffling ways of winning it. They seem to have forgiven industry all its past. Or, perhaps, some of them do not know that it has ever oppressed women more than men.

Some women—feminists also—know it by practical experience. These are the women in industry, who are urging laws to improve the conditions of their employment. Other women, not in industry, but familiar with its problems, stand with them in these efforts. Feminism, therefore, is by no means a unit.

The most audible interest of one group just now seems to be to forego all labor laws which are limited to women, lest they restrict women's "opportunities." Surrender of all special protection for all women is the price they offer to pay for a novel job. And it must be said that it has often been the women in the professions who have been willing thus to offer up the present safeguards affecting their sisters in the factories—without consulting those sisters.

III

A chance to learn to operate a machine is not a woman's most important claim on industry. A distinction must be made between technical skill and the status of an individual or a group in the industry. If technical skill were all, we could predict women's future from the recent past. Careful selection of workers, healthful physical conditions, adequate training, would ensure success. But all the trouble men have had with industry arises out of much more puzzling conditions. If, as some pessimists declare, industrial organization is in danger of collapse, it is not because it is unskillful technically, but because it is blind socially.

Industry has a bad record for the social hopes of men, and its conspicuous victims have been women and children.

'Tis the Brute they chained to labor!
  He has made the bright earth dim.
  Stores of wares and pelf a plenty,
    but they got no good of him.
Quietude and loveliness,
Holy sights that heal and bless,
They are scattered and abolished
    where his iron hoof is set.

This is merely a poet's summary of official reports, Blue Books of Parliament, lawyers' briefs in defense of the constitutionality of labor laws. These have massed the evidence concerning wages too low to support life; hours too long to maintain health or to sleep, without even counting, as normal needs, time for recreation or for the duties of citizenship; too much noise, too rapid a pace, too little air, too much crowding—just being cogs in the wheels, one process hour after hour, uninteresting and uninspiring, and not enough return to buy the goods and service from other people's labor that one has no time or energy left to produce for one's self.

Technical skill?—the individual has about as much as is necessary, or he can acquire it by easily recognized methods. But status—a claim upon industry, a share in society, the opportunity to relate one's self to one's fellow workers and one's fellow citizens in a common enterprise with equal power? This it is that men and women are vaguely challenging the state and employers to give them. This it is that is withheld less by the will or greed of any man than by the intricacy of organization in industry, which gives opportunity for the greed and selfishness of a few to oppress a large number. In surrendering to a process essentially coöperative in a mechanical sense, because of its subdivisions and specializations, men have not yet learned how to establish, also, coöperation in control, which shall force industry to yield diffused happiness and economic security instead of concentrated financial success. The war, with all its record of technical achievements, wrought no change in this fundamental tendency of the industrial organization.

That this tendency, as it affects women in industry, is not universally recognized, especially among professional women, is due probably to the inherent difference in their outlook. Successful professional women are conscious of power in themselves, not inherently dependent upon the strength of their relationships with others. They have known what it means to suffer as pioneers; but they knew that they were pioneering, and success was, in a sense, their personal achievement. Not so in industry. There the enterprise is less thrilling. The nation, or even the city, is not vitally interested in a woman's achievements even in operating the newest machine on the market, except in war-time; and the labelers of cans and packers of hair-nets never dream of exciting anybody's interest in their accomplishments.

Women work in factories, not primarily for the joy of working, but because they must earn a living, for themselves, and often for others. In too many instances they have had neither joy, nor enough earnings for a living. Managers employ them because they need their labor, and, often they want it cheap. Neither the underpaid girl nor her employer is aware of the movements of history which thrill the hopeful prophet of women's economic emancipation.

Both would be astonished if they knew that the feminist is becoming convinced that, in an age founded on iron and steel, it is the success of women in mechanical industry that must be the first step toward her economic freedom. Nor is it a mere whim that is leading so many professional women, and the victorious leaders in the fight for suffrage, to turn their attention to women in their relation to machines.

IV

On the surface, the fundamental incompatibility of feminism with modern industrial organization seems at present to be an insurmountable obstacle for women. Feminism has been concerned with the removal of prejudices and customs that make sex the barrier against woman's freedom in the choice of her activities. Its essence is voluntary choice—in marriage, in motherhood, in politics, and in a career. The freedom of the individual, and the release of powers suppressed by artificially imposed limitations, are its goal.

Industry affords a striking contrast. Merely because of its technical developments, quite apart from the selfish use of power, its method of getting results is to give the individual a place in a complex body of inter-relationships, determined by the mechanical processes of manufacture. Management, at its best, not through lack of humanitarianism, but through technical necessity, knows it to be a virtue to standardize jobs, to discover standard speed, standard belts, standard tools. The standard man is the inevitable result. The environment is made ready and he is put into it. "Man . . . was a machinate mammal." This, elaborated, says Samuel Butler, was the argument of the only man who made serious protest against the complete destruction of machinery throughout Erewhon.

Experience is abundant to show that, whatever may be the scope ultimately for the individual to control conditions, his economic power, like his mechanical accomplishment, cannot be complete unless he acts as one of a group. In brief, it is the method of industry to attach the individual to his limited, specified place in the whole scheme of production; while the aim of feminism is to make the whole recognize a hitherto unrealized obligation to the individual, or, at least, to relax its stranglehold on the freedom of personality.

Feminism is not, and has not, a definite programme. Like democracy, it is a spirit and not an invention—not an institution, but a changing life within the changing forms of institutions. And feminism, like democracy, busies itself with the issues that the times create.

V

The economic issues of the time, as they are reflected in woman's industrial status, were never more baffling. She must win a more secure place in the shop as a skilled worker. She has as yet only a limited and, at times, grudging recognition in the labor movement through which men are seeking to protect their own rights, giving as yet little attention to women's needs. She is accused of aiming to undermine the home, just when she may be working hardest at uncongenial tasks to support it. So discouraging is the outlook in some of its large aspects, that one is almost inclined to agree with certain anti-feminists about the effects of industrialism on all our social institutions, including the family as a whole and women individually. Not feminism, however, but industrial organization, uncontrolled in the common service, has done the damage, and feminism has not yet been able to exert an appreciable influence.

Consider, for example, hours of work. The early tendencies of mechanical industry were all in the direction of the maximum use of machinery without regard to the health of the operator. Machinery had seemed to make production independent of physiological limitations, and women and children were drawn into the general wreckage. The story is too well known to need retelling: how labor laws, first for children, and then for women,—with advantageous results, also, for men,—registered public protest and compelled industry to recognize its obligations by restricting hours of work to limits humanly endurable. As years went by, humanitarianism became firmer in its insistence through laws that industry should achieve socially desirable standards. Much later, the scientific basis in physiology for these humanitarian measures reinforced the whole effort; and gradually management is realizing that it pays to take care of the workers' health.

In some degree these laws have been extended to men, as in the requirement for one day's rest in seven. But, in general, the trade-union movement of the United States has opposed, though by a divided vote, suggestions that they support legislation as a means of shortening hours for men. They have preferred to rely on trade-union efforts to secure the eight-hour day. Thus, in a more or less opportunistic fashion, legislation applying to women exclusively has been sought and continued. . . .

Not only in practice, but in theory also, is the wage of women a debatable issue. "Equal pay for equal work," as a principle, received, to be sure, official sanction from governments during the war, and in the Peace Treaty itself. But this was merely part of the shell of progress. It applied, at best, only to those jobs in which women took the places of men, and then only if no change of any kind was made in the process. In practice, it was often ignored, even when the work was not only equal, but identical. Failure to clarify, however, the fundamental basis of women's wages, either in a man's job or in a woman's job, was its real title to superficiality. On this subject disagreement continues, unaffected by the experience of the war.

The British War Cabinet's Committee on Women in Industry disagreed. The majority declared that no woman should receive less than a "reasonable subsistence-wage," and defined it as "sufficient to provide a single woman over 18 years of age . . . with an adequate dietary; with lodging to include fuel and light in a respectable house not more than half an hour's journey, including tram or train, from the place of work; with clothing sufficient for warmth, cleanliness, and decent appearance; with money for fares, insurance, and trade-union subscriptions; and with a reasonable sum for holidays, amusements, and so forth."

Note that "subsistence" for herself alone is the normal woman's claim on industry. If she has an old father or mother to support, of if she is sharing the life of a family with younger brothers or sisters in school, she is regarded by the British War Cabinet as exceptional, not modifying in any particular industry's social obligation to women. . . .

This conclusion had already been reached in the United States by the Women's Bureau, when, in formulating the standards found desirable during the war, the Bureau advocated a wage based on occupation and not on sex, and including provision for dependents.

At no other point do the present dangers of women's position in industry emerge more conspicuously than in this matter of wages. Even with all the stress of war, women's wages, although they increased with the general rise in wage-levels, never overcame the handicap of long years of lower rates. Nor was universal public support enlisted in favor of overcoming the unfavorable comparisons in the earnings of women and men. Yet in no other aspect of industry are the interests of the family, on the one hand, and men, on the other, so involved with those of women as a group. If experience has demonstrated women's capacity for handling complicated machines, but no controlling influence has modified the tendency to pay a woman lower rates than a man, what power can prevent the lowering of rates for men by the competition of women? . . .

The first ventures of the feminists in the problem of wages seem to be taking the form of protests against minimum-wage laws, as, again, in their view, constituting a restriction on opportunity, and a denial of woman's political equality by classing her with a specially "protected" group. As a matter of fact, minimum-wage legislation does not necessarily perpetuate the old conception of a different basis for women's wages. The law merely gives women a voice in determining what considerations should affect their wages, by providing for a commission to set minimum rates after recommendations have been made by a board in each industry, made up of representatives, in equal numbers, of employers and of women at work. Not the fixing of wages by law, but the setting up of instruments for registering the voice and vote of the women who work and the vital concern of the community in their wage, is the immediate practical purpose of minimum-wage laws. Some day, perhaps, they will apply, also, to men; but no one with any dependable information about present conditions believes that this could now be urged successfully. The choice is between minimum-wage laws for women, with the hope that they offer of immediate relief and practical experiment, and indefinite postponement of any action at all by the community.

No present issue could more effectively illustrate the dire need of cultivating a realistic respect for the slow, intermediate steps necessary for the attainment of distant aims. One group of women seems to be engaged just now in a wasteful conflict, which, if successful, can have no other result than to weaken the too slowly developing power of the community to control the leviathan of industry. . . .

Industry will never yield the spiritual opportunities that women so hopefully desire, unless it changes. That is one reason why economic freedom is so much more difficult to attain than the vote in politics. Men, in the generic sense, must learn how to make the machine their servant. Economic freedom is not a woman's fight alone. It is not anybody's fight alone. All workers must learn to think and act coöperatively, not merely because co-operation is necessarily the best philosophy of life (though it may prove to be so), but because their work is mechanically coöperative.

Even so pessimistic a critic of feminism as Brooks Adams gives boundless hope when he declares, in discussing the "Degradation of the Democratic Dogma," that "the family system is the creation of the woman," Woman "has acted as the social cement, and she has sustained the arch on which the social fabric has rested." If woman has accomplished the creation of the family system, in the midst of all the hazards of primitive existence, which have constantly threatened life itself and tempted man to wander, perhaps so powerful a force, if it is allowed to permeate industrial organization, will help to create relationships designed to conserve, and not to dissipate, spiritual values in our mechanical, economic order.

96

Mother Jones

You Don't Need a Vote to Raise Hell (1925)

. . . In Lonaconia, Maryland, there was a strike. I was there. In Hazelton, Pennsylvania, a convention was called to discuss the anthracite strike. I was there when they issued the strike call. One hundred and fifty thousand men responded. The men of Scranton and Shamokin and Coaldale and Panther Creek and Valley Battle. And I was there.

In Shamokin I met Miles Daugherty, an organizer. When he quit work and drew his pay, he gave one-half of his pay envelope to his wife and the other half he kept to rent halls and pay for lights for the union. Organizers did not draw much salary in those days and they did heroic, unselfish work.

From *Autobiography of Mother Jones* (Chicago: Charles H. Kerr and Co., 1925), 89–93, 200–204, 236–40, 242.

Not far from Shamokin, in a little mountain town, the priest was holding a meeting when I went in. He was speaking in the church. I spoke in an open field. The priest told the men to go back and obey their masters and their reward would be in Heaven. He denounced the strikers as children of darkness. The miners left the church in a body and marched over to my meeting.

"Boys," I said, "this strike is called in order that you and your wives and your little ones may get a bit of Heaven before you die."

We organized the entire camp.

The fight went on. In Coaldale, in the Hazelton district, the miners were not permitted to assemble in any hall. It was necessary to win the strike in that district that the Coaldale miners be organized.

I went to a nearby mining town that was thoroughly organized and asked the women if they would help me get the Coaldale men out. This was in McAdoo. I told them to leave their men at home to take care of the family. I asked them to put on their kitchen clothes and bring mops and brooms with them and a couple of tin pans. We marched over the mountains fifteen miles, beating on the tin pans as if they were cymbals. At three o'clock in the morning we met the Crack Thirteen of the militia, patrolling the roads to Coaldale. The colonel of the regiment said "Halt! Move back!"

I said, "Colonel, the working men of America will not halt nor will they ever go back. The working man is going forward!"

"I'll charge bayonets," said he.

"On whom?"

"On your people."

"We are not enemies," said I. "We are just a band of working women whose brothers and husbands are in a battle for bread. We want our brothers in Coaldale to join us in our fight. We are here on the mountain road for our children's sake, for the nation's sake. We are not going to hurt anyone and surely you would not hurt us."

They kept us there till daybreak and when they saw the army of women in kitchen aprons, with dishpans and mops, they laughed and let us pass. An army of strong mining women makes a wonderfully spectacular picture.

Well, when the miners in the Coaldale camp started to go to work they were met by the McAdoo women who were beating on their pans and shouting, "Join the union! Join the union!"

They joined, every last man of them, and we got so enthusiastic that we organized the street car men who promised to haul no scabs for the coal companies. As there were no other groups to organize we marched over the mountains home, beating on our pans and singing patriotic songs.

Meanwhile President Mitchell and all his organizers were sleeping in the Valley Hotel over in Hazelton. They knew nothing of our march onto Coaldale until the newspaper men telephoned to him that "Mother Jones was raising hell up in the mountains with a bunch of wild women!"

He, of course, got nervous. He might have gotten more nervous if he had known how we made the mine bosses go home and how we told their wives to clean them up and make decent American citizens out of them. How we went around to the kitchen of the hotel where the militia were quartered and ate the breakfast that was on the table for the soldiers.

When I got back to Hazelton, Mitchell looked at me with surprise. I was worn out. Coaldale had been a strenuous night and morning and its thirty mile tramp. I assured Mitchell that no one had been hurt and no property injured. The military had acted like human beings. They took the matter as a joke. They enjoyed the morning's fun. I told him how scared the sheriff had been. He had been talking to me without knowing who I was.

"O Lord," he said, "that Mother Jones is sure a dangerous woman."

"Why don't you arrest her?" I asked him.

"O Lord, I couldn't. I'd have that mob of women with their mops and brooms after me and the jail ain't big enough to hold them all. They'd mop the life out of a fellow!"

Mr. Mitchell said, "My God, Mother, did you get home safe? What did you do?"

"I got five thousand men out and organized them. We had time left over so we organized the street car men and they will not haul any scabs into camp."

"Did you get hurt, Mother?"

"No, we did the hurting."

"Didn't the superintendents' bosses get after you?"

"No, we got after them. Their wives and our women were yelling around like cats. It was a great fight." . . .

In January of 1915, I was invited to John D. Rockefeller Jr.'s office with several other labor officers. I was glad to go for I wanted to tell him what his hirelings were doing in Colorado. The publicity that been given the terrible conditions under which his wealth was made had forced him to take some action. The union he would not recognize—never. That was his religion. But he put forth a plan whereby the worker might elect one representative at each mine to meet with the officials in Denver and present any grievance that might arise.

So with Frank J. Hayes, Vice President of the United Mine Workers, James Lord, and Edward Doyle we went to the Rockefeller offices. He listened to our recital of conditions in Colorado and said nothing.

I told him that his plan for settling industrial disputes would not work. That it was a sham and fraud. That behind the representative of the miner was no organization so that the workers were powerless to enforce any just demand; that their demands were granted and grievances redressed still at the will of the company. That the Rockefeller plan did not give the miners a treasury, so that should they have to strike for justice, they could be starved out in a week. That it gave the workers no voice in the management of the job to which they gave their very life.

John Rockefeller is a nice young man but we went away from the office where resides the silent government of thousands upon thousands of people, we went away feeling that he could not possibly understand the aspirations of the working class. He was as alien as is one species from another; as alien as is stone from wheat.

I came to New York to raise funds for the miners' families. Although they had gone back beaten to work, their condition was pitiful. The women and children were in rags and they were hungry. I spoke to a great mass meeting in Cooper Union. I told the people after they had cheered me for ten minutes, that cheering was easy. That the side lines where it was safe, always cheered.

"The miners lost," I told them, "because they had only the constitution. The other side had bayonets. In the end, bayonets always win."

I told them how Lieutenant Howert of Walsenberg had offered me his arm when he escorted me to jail. "Madam," said he, "will you take my arm?"

"I am not a Madam," said I. "I am Mother Jones. The Government can't take my life and you can't take my arm, but you can take my suitcase."

I told the audience how I had sent a letter to John Rockefeller, Junior, telling him of conditions in the mines. I had heard he was a good young man and read the Bible, and I thought I'd take a chance. The letter came back with "Refused" written across the envelope.

"Well," I said, "how could I expect him to listen to an old woman when he would not listen to the President of the United States through his representative, Senator Foster."

Five hundred women got up a dinner and asked me to speak. Most of the women were crazy about women suffrage. They thought that Kingdom-come would follow the enfranchisement of women.

"You must stand for free speech in the streets," I told them.

"How can we," piped a woman, "when we haven't a vote?"

"I have never had a vote," said I, "and I have raised hell all over this country! You don't need a vote to raise hell! You need convictions and a voice!"

Some one meowed, "You're an anti!"

"I am not an anti to anything which will bring freedom to my class," said I. "But I am going to be honest with you sincere women who are working for votes for women. The women of Colorado have had the vote for two generations and the working men and women are in slavery. The state is in slavery, vassal to the Colorado Iron and Fuel Company and its subsidiary interests. A man who was present at a meeting of mine owners told me that when the trouble started in the mines, one operator proposed that women be disfranchised because here and there some woman had raised her voice in behalf of the miners. Another operator jumped to his feet and shouted, 'For God's sake! What are you talking about! If it had not been for the women's vote the miners would have beaten us long ago!'"

Some of the women gasped with horror. One or two left the room. I told the women I did not believe in women's rights nor in men's rights but in human rights. "No matter what your fight," I said, "don't be ladylike! God Almighty made women and the Rockefeller gang of thieves made the ladies. I have just fought through sixteen months of bitter warfare in Colorado. I have been up against armed mercenaries but this old woman, without a vote, and with nothing but a hatpin has scared them.

"Organized labor should organize its women along industrial lines. Politics is only the servant of industry. The plutocrats have organized their women. They keep them busy with suffrage and prohibition and charity." . . .

Other strikes come to mind, strikes of less fire and flame and hence attracting less national notice. The papers proclaimed to stockholders and investors that there was peace and there was no peace. The garment workers struck and won. In Roosevelt, New Jersey, the workingmen in the fertilizing plant of Williams and Clark struck.

Two strikers were shot dead—shot in the back by the hired gunmen. The guards were arraigned, let out on bail, and reported back on the job. The strikers were assembled in a vacant lot. Guards shot into their midst, firing low and filling the legs of the workers with bullets.

"Mother," the strikers wrote to me, "come help us with our women!"

I went. "Women," said I, "see that your husbands use no fire arms or violence no matter what the provocation. Don't let your husbands scab. Help them stand firm and above all keep them from the saloons. No strike was ever won that did not have the support of the womenfolk."

The street car men struck along in 1916 in New York City.

I spoke to a mass meeting of carmen's wives and we certainly had those women fighting like wildcats. They threatened me with jail and I told the police I could raise as much hell in jail as out. The police said if anyone was killed I should be held responsible and hanged.

"If they want to hang me, let them," I said. "And on the scaffold I will shout 'Freedom for the working class!' And when I meet God Almighty I will tell him to damn my accusers and the accusers of the working class, the people who tend and develop and beautify His world."

The last years of my life have seen fewer and fewer strikes. Both employer and employee have become wiser. Both have learned the value of compromise. Both sides have learned that they gain when they get together and talk things out in reason rather than standing apart, slinging bricks, angry words and bullets. The railway brotherhoods have learned that lesson. Strikes are costly. Fighting them is costly.

All the average human being asks is something he can call home; a family that is fed and warm; and now and then a little happiness; once in a long while an extravagance.

"I am not a suffragist nor do I believe in "careers" for women, especially a "career" in factory and mill where most working women have their "careers." A great responsibility rests upon woman—the training of the children. This is the most beautiful task. If men earned money enough, it would not be necessary for women to neglect their homes and their little ones to add to the family's income. . . .

I had passed my ninety-third milestone when I attended the convention of the Farmer-Labor Party and addressed the assembly. "The producer, not the meek, shall inherit the earth," I told them. "Not today perhaps, nor tomorrow, but over the rim of the years my old eyes can see the coming of another day."

I was ninety-one years old when I attended the Pan-American Federation of labor held in Mexico City in 1921. This convention was called to promote a better understanding between the workers of America, Mexico and Central America. Gompers attended as did a number of American leaders.

I spoke to the convention. I told them that a convention such as this Pan-American Convention of labor was the beginning of a new day, a day when the workers of the world would know no other boundaries other than those between the exploiter and the exploited. Soviet Russia, I said, had dared to challenge the old order, had handed the earth over to those who toiled upon it, and the capitalists of the world were quaking in their scab-made shoes. I told them of the national farce of prohibition in America.

"Prohibition came," said I, "through a combination of business men who wanted to get more out of their workers, together with a lot of preachers and a group of damn cats who threw fits when they saw a workingman buy a bottle of beer but saw no reason to bristle when they and their women and little children suffered under the curse of low wages and crushing hours of toil.

"Prohibition," said I, "has taken away the workingman's beer, has closed the saloon which was his only club. The rich guzzle as they ever did. Prohibition is not for them. They have their clubs which are sacred and immune from interference. The only club the workingman has is the policeman's. He has that when he strikes."

I visited the coal mines of Coalhulia and saw that the life of the miner is the same wherever coal is dug and capital flies its black flag.

As I look back over the long, long years, I see that in all movements for the bettering of men's lives, it is the pioneers who bear most of the suffering. When these movements become established, when they become popular, others reap the benefits. Thus it has been with the labor movement. . . .

In spite of oppressors, in spite of false leaders, in spite of labor's own lack of understanding of its needs, the cause of the worker continues onward. Slowly his hours are shortened, giving him leisure to read and to think. Slowly his standard of living rises to include some of the good and beautiful things of the world. Slowly the cause of his children becomes the cause of all. His boy is taken from the breaker, his girl from the mill. Slowly those who create the wealth of the world are permitted to share it. The future is in labor's strong, rough hands.

97
MERIDEL LE SUEUR
Women on the Breadlines (1932)

I am sitting in the city free employment bureau. It's the woman's section. We have been sitting here now for four hours. We sit here every day, waiting for a job. There are no jobs. Most of us have had no breakfast. Some have had scant rations for over a year. Hunger makes a human being lapse into a state of lethargy, especially city hunger. Is there any place else in the world where a human being is supposed to go hungry amidst plenty without an outcry, without protest, where only the boldest steal or kill for bread, and the timid crawl the streets, hunger like the beak of a terrible bird at the vitals?

We sit looking at the floor. No one dares think of the coming winter. There are only a few more days of summer. Everyone is anxious to get work to lay up something for that long siege of bitter cold. But there is no work. Sitting in the room we all know it. That is why we don't talk much. We look at the floor dreading to see that knowledge in each other's eyes. There is a kind of humiliation in it. We look away from each other. We look at the floor. Its too terrible to see this animal terror in each other's eyes.

So we sit hour after hour, day after day, waiting for a job to come in. There are many women for a single job. A thin sharp woman sits inside the wire cage looking at a book. For four hours we have watched her looking at that book. She has a hard little eye. In the small bare room there are half a dozen women sitting on the benches waiting. Many come and go. Our faces are all familiar to each other, for we wait here everyday.

This is a domestic employment bureau. Most of the women who come here are middle aged, some have families, some have raised their families and are now alone, some have men who are out of work. Hard times and the man leaves to hunt for work. He doesn't find it. He drifts on. The woman probably doesn't hear from him for a long time. She expects it. She isn't surprised. She struggles alone to feed the many mouths. Sometimes she gets help from the charities. If she's clever she can get herself a good living from the charities, if she's naturally a lick spittle, naturally a little docile and cunning. If she's proud then she starves silently, leaving her children to find work, coming home after a day's searching to wrestle with her house, her children.

Some such story is written on the faces of all these women. There are young girls too, fresh from the country. Some are made brazen too soon by the city. There is a great exodus of girls from the farms into the city now. Thousands of farms have been vacated completely in Minnesota. The girls are trying to get work. The prettier ones can get jobs in the stores when there are any, or waiting on table but these jobs are only for the attractive and the adroit, the others, the real peasants, have a more difficult time.

From *The New Masses,* January 1932.

Bernice sits next me. She is a large Polish woman of thirty-five. She has been working in peoples' kitchens for fifteen years or more. She is large, her great body in mounds, her face brightly scrubbed. She has a peasant mind and finds it hard even yet to understand the maze of the city where trickery is worth more than brawn. Her blue eyes are not clever but slow and trusting. She suffers from loneliness and lack of talk. When you speak to her her face lifts and brightens as if you had spoken through a great darkness and she talks magically of little things, as if the weather were magic or tells some crazy tale of her adventures on the city streets, embellishing them in bright colors until they hang heavy and thick like some peasant embroidery. She loves the city anyhow. Its exciting to her, like a bazaar. She loves to go shopping and get a bargain, hunting out the places where stale bread and cakes can be had for a few cents. She likes walking the streets looking for men to take her to a picture show. Sometimes she goes to five picture shows in one day, or she sits through one the entire day until she knows all the dialogue by heart.

She came to the city a young girl from a Wisconsin farm. The first thing that happened to her a charlatan dentist took out all her good shining teeth and the fifty dollars she had saved working in a canning factory. After that she met men in the park who told her how to look out for herself, corrupting her peasant mind, teaching her to mistrust everyone. Sometimes now she forgets to mistrust everyone and gets taken in. They taught her to get what she could for nothing, to count her change, to go back if she found herself cheated, to demand her rights.

She lives alone in little rooms. She bought seven dollars worth of second hand furniture eight years ago. She rents a room for perhaps three dollars a month in an attic, sometimes in a cold house. Once the house where she stayed was condemned and everyone else moved out and she lived there all winter alone on the top floor. She spent only twenty five dollars all winter.

She wants to get married but she sees what happens to her married friends, being left with children to support, worn out before their time. So she stays single. She is virtuous. She is slightly deaf from hanging out clothes in winter. She has done peoples washings and cooking for fifteen years and in that time she saved thirty dollars. Now she hasn't worked steady for a year and she has spent the thirty dollars. She dreamed of having a little house or a house boat perhaps with a spot of ground for a few chickens. This dream she will never realize.

She has lost her furniture now along with the dream. A married friend whose husband is gone gives her a bed for which she pays by doing a great deal of work for the woman. She comes here every day now sitting bewildered, her pudgy hands folded in her lap. She is hungry. Her great flesh has begun to hang in folds. She has been living on crackers. Sometimes a box of crackers lasts a week. She has a friend who's a baker and he sometimes steals the stale loaves and brings them to her.

A girl we have seen every day all summer went crazy yesterday at the Y. W. She went into hysterics, stamping her feet and screaming.

She hadn't worked for eight months. "You've got to give me something," she kept saying. The woman in charge flew into a rage that probably came from days and days of suffering on her part, because she is unable to give jobs, having none. She flew into a rage at the girl and there they were facing each other in a rage both helpless, helpless. This woman told me once that she could hardly bear the suffering she saw, hardly bear it, that she couldn't eat sometimes and had nightmares at night.

So they stood there the two women in a rage, the girl weeping and the woman shouting at her. In the eight months of unemployment she had gotten ragged, and the woman was shouting that she would not send her out like that. "Why don't you shine your shoes," she kept scolding the girl, and the girl kept sobbing and sobbing because she was starving.

"We can't recommend you like that," the harassed Y.W.C.A. woman said, knowing she was starving, unable to do anything. And the girls and the women sat docilely, their eyes on the ground, ashamed to look at each other, ashamed of something.

Sitting here waiting for a job, the women have been talking in low voices about the girl Ellen. They talk in low voices with not too much pity for her, unable to see through the mist of their own torment. "What happened to Ellen?" one of them asks. She knows the answer already. We all know it.

A young girl who went around with Ellen tells about seeing her last evening back of a cafe down town outside the kitchen door, kicking, showing her legs so that the cook came out and gave her some food and some men gathered in the alley and threw small coin on the ground for a look at her legs. And the girl says enviously that Ellen had a swell breakfast and treated her to one too, that cost two dollars. . . .

"I guess she'll go on the street now," a thin woman says faintly and no one takes the trouble to comment further. Like every commodity now the body is difficult to sell and the girls say you're lucky if you get fifty cents.

It's very difficult and humiliating to sell one's body.

Perhaps it would make it clear if one were to imagine having to go out on the street to sell, say, one's overcoat. Suppose you have to sell your coat so you can have breakfast and a place to sleep, say, for fifty cents. You decide to sell your only coat. You take it off and put it on your arm. The street, that has before been just a street, now becomes a mart, something entirely different. You must approach someone now and admit you are destitute and are now selling your clothes, your most intimate possessions. Everyone will watch you talking to the stranger showing him your overcoat, what a good coat it is. People will stop and watch curiously. You will be quite naked on the street. It is even harder to try and sell one's self, more humiliating. It is even humiliating to try and sell one's labour. When there is no buyer.

The thin woman opens the wire cage. There's a job for a nursemaid, she says. The old gnarled women, like old horses, know that no one will have them walk the streets with the young so they don't move. Ellen's friend gets up and goes to the window. She is unbelievably jaunty. I know she hasn't had work since last January. But she has a flare of life in her that glows like a tiny red flame and some tenacious thing, perhaps only youth, keeps it burning bright. Her legs are thin but the runs in her old stockings are neatly mended clear down her flat shank. Two bright spots of rouge conceal her pallor. A narrow belt is drawn tightly around her thin waist, her long shoulders stoop and the blades show. She runs wild as a colt hunting pleasure, hunting sustenance.

It's one of the great mysteries of the city where women go when they are out of work and hungry. There are not many women in the bread line. There are no flop houses for women as there are for men, where a bed can be had for a quarter or less. You don't see women lying on the floor at the mission in the free flops. They obviously don't sleep in the jungle or under newspapers in the park. There is no law I suppose against their being in these places but the fact is they rarely are.

Yet there must be as many women out of jobs in cities and suffering extreme poverty as there are men. What happens to them? Where do they go? Try to get into the Y.W. without any money or looking down at heel. Charities take care of very few and only those that are called "deserving." The lone girl is under suspicion by the virgin women who dispense charity.

I've lived in cities for many months broke, without help, too timid to get in bread lines. I've known many women to live like this until they simply faint on the street from privations, without saying a word to anyone. A woman will shut herself up in a room until it is taken away from her, and eat a cracker a day and be as quiet as a mouse so there are no social statistics concerning her.

I don't know why it is, but a woman will do this unless she has dependents, will go for weeks verging on starvation, crawling in some hole, going through the streets ashamed, sitting in libraries, parks, going for days without speaking to a living soul like some exiled beast, keeping the runs mended in her stockings, shut up in terror in her own misery, until she becomes too super sensitive and timid to even ask for a job.

Bernice says even strange men she has met in the park have sometimes, that is in better days, given her a loan to pay her room rent. She has always paid them back.

In the afternoon the young girls, to forget the hunger and the deathly torture and fear of being jobless, try and pick up a man to take them to a ten cent show. They never go to more expensive ones, but they can always find a man willing to spend a dime to have the company of a girl for the afternoon.

Sometimes a girl facing the night without shelter will approach a man for lodging. A woman always asks a man for help. Rarely another woman. I have known girls to sleep in men's rooms for the night, on a pallet without molestation, and given breakfast in the morning.

It's no wonder these young girls refuse to marry, refuse to rear children. They are like certain savage tribes, who, when they have been conquered refuse to breed.

Not one of them but looks forward to starvation, for the coming winter. We are in a jungle and know it. We are beaten, entrapped. There is no way out. Even if there were a job, even if that thin acrid woman came and gave everyone in the room a job for a few days, a few hours, at thirty cents an hour, this would all be repeated tomorrow, the next day and the next.

Not one of these women but knows, that despite years of labour there is only starvation, humiliation in front of them.

Mrs. Grey, sitting across from me is a living spokesman for the futility of labour. She is a warning. Her hands are scarred with labour. Her body is a great puckered scar. She has given birth to six children, buried three, supported them all alive and dead, bearing them, burying them, feeding them. Bred in hunger they have been spare, susceptible to disease. For seven years she tried to save her boy's arm from amputation, diseased from tuberculosis of the bone. It is almost too suffocating to think of that long close horror of years of child bearing, child feeding, rearing, with the bare suffering of providing a meal and shelter.

Now she is fifty. Her children, economically insecure, are drifters. She never hears of them. She doesn't know if they are alive. She doesn't know if she is alive. Such subtleties of suffering are not for her. For her the brutality of hunger and cold, the bare bone of life. That is enough. These will occupy a life. Not until these are done away with can those subtle feelings that make a human being be indulged.

She is lucky to have five dollars ahead of her. That is her security. She has a tumour that she will die of. She is thin as a worn dime with her tumour sticking out of her side. She is brittle and bitter. Her face is not the face of a human being. She has born more than it is possible for a human being to bear. She is reduced to the least possible denominator of human feelings.

It is terrible to see her little blood shot eyes like a beaten hound's, fearful in terror.

We cannot meet her eyes. When she looks at any of us we look away. She is like a woman drowning and we turn away. We must ignore those eyes that are surely the eyes of a person drowning, doomed. She doesn't cry out. She goes down decently. And we all look away.

The young ones know though. I don't want to marry. I don't want any children. So they all say. No children. No marriage. They arm themselves alone, keep up alone. The man is helpless now. He cannot provide. If he propagates he cannot take care of his young. The means are not in his hands. So they live alone. Get what fun they can. The life risk is too horrible now. Defeat is too clearly written on it.

So we sit in this room like cattle, waiting for a non existent job, willing to work to the farthest atom of energy, unable to work, unable to get food and lodging, unable to bear children; here we must sit in this shame looking at the floor, worse than beasts at a slaughter.

It is appalling to think that these women sitting so listless in the room may work as hard as it is possible for a human being to work, may labour night and day, like Mrs. Gray wash street cars from midnight to dawn and offices in the early evening, scrubbing for fourteen and fifteen hours a day, sleeping only five hours or so, doing this their whole lives, and never earn one day of security, having always before them the pit of the future. The endless labour, the bending back, the water soaked hands, earning never more than a week's wages, never having in their hands more life than that.

It's not the suffering, not birth, death, love that the young reject, but the suffering of endless labour without dream, eating the spare bread in bitterness, a slave without the security of a slave.

Editorial Note: This presentation of the plight of the unemployed woman, able as it is, and informative, is defeatist in attitude, lacking in revolutionary spirit and direction which characterize the usual contribution to *New Masses*. We feel it our duty to add, that there is a place for the unemployed woman, as well as man, in the ranks of the unemployed councils and in all branches of the organized revolutionary movement. Fight for your class, read *The Working Woman,* join the Communist Party.

98
SABINA MARTINEZ
Negro Women in Organization—Labor (1941)

Organized labor has rescued the Negro woman from her obscure position in basic industry, where she once toiled and labored from ten to twelve hours a day under most inhuman conditions and at a starvation wage. Some women have come timidly, others very sure of their convictions, and some with mental reserva-

From *The Aframerican,* Summer and Fall 1941.

tions. But all have secured better wages, in many cases as much as 60 per cent increase. All their hours have been reduced to eight hours a day, and all their positions have been rendered more secure. The bosses, who formerly subjected them to their whims and fancies, through their participation in unions, have learned to respect them.

In bringing this about organized labor found it no easy task; not because women did not appreciate unions, but because of the false anti-union propaganda that had been handed out to our women by the bosses . . . and because of the definitely Jim-Crow policy of the high executives of the A. F. of L., which ignored Negro people. . . . This policy, along with corrupt Negro leadership, has made it difficult for progressive labor . . . to win the confidence of the Negro people, especially that of the Negro women. However, this mass movement seeking to improve social and economic conditions can no longer be ignored. . . .

Negro women workers welcomed the birth of the C.I.O. and the partially open door of the A. F. of L. and are now a part of such unions as: Laundry, Cleaners and Dyers, Textiles, Teachers, Domestic and others. Negro women helped to lay the basis for these unions and in many instances were on the first committees that helped to formulate the policies of these unions. . . .

The Laundry workers were unorganized for thirty years in the city of New York. In six months the C.I.O. has organized this industry into a compact body of some 27,000 Laundry workers, the great majority of whom are Negro women. Negro women helped lay the foundation, formulate the policies and now hold executive offices in this union, which is an affiliate of the Amalgamated Clothing Workers of America. Some of those who serve on the executive staff of this group are Charlotte Almond, Phoebe Symond, Roberta Randolph, and Sabina Martinez.

The Cleaners and Dyers Union which is only four years old was given its first impetus toward C.I.O. by Ida J. Dudley, a negro woman. Seeing the need for organization in this field, she started to round up the clerks, being able to organize a vast number of them. The Textile and Domestic workers, who are only partially organized, have brought into the ranks of organized labor hoards of miserable, exploited workers who are denied protection under Social Security or State Labor laws.

Dora Jones, backed by many progressive labor groups, is preparing an extensive drive for organization of Domestic workers....

In 1930, 3 out of every 5 Negro women employed were in the field of domestic or personal service. Many Negro women have started upon their careers in business as domestic workers, and should be willing to help gain some protection for those who because of circumstances, are forced to remain in this field.

The Sharecroppers Union, the Tenant League, and many of the new organized unions owe their existence to the unselfish contributions of Negro women.... Organized labor owes women as a class more than a union book. It must rid itself of the old idea that women must be subordinate to men, or that women do not provide as good leadership as men. Organized labor must make a sincere effort to increase the women personnel of its membership.... Once a woman has entered her field of industry, she must join that union. She must become a part of the union just as she is a part of her shop. She must attend meetings, participate in discussions and be ever eager to improve the position of herself and her fellow workers. She must consider herself a worker, and be conscious of all political and economic struggles that affect the working group to which she belongs. She must never pass a picket line or buy anything that labor has requested boycotted. She must seriously question herself on the wise use of her vote.... [M]ost of all she [the black woman] must have complete confidence in herself and ... in the principles of organized labor, or she will never be able to convince any fellow workers.... She must continue to contribute to the cause of organized labor as a laborer and as a leader.

99
Grace Hutchins
Women under Capitalism (1934)

Freedom. What do the women of the middle and upper classes mean when they speak of freedom and equal opportunity with men? They mean freedom to enjoy the rights of property and the rights of citizenship on an equality with men. They mean "getting the opportunity to do the interesting and important work at any scale of pay." They mean freedom to pursue a career, to do creative work, to study for any one of the professions they may choose and to practice that profession without being hindered by sex discrimination. Much of this freedom has already been won by women of the privileged class. Legal disabilities and disqualifications have for the most part been removed in the United States. Most of the institutions of higher education are now open to women. The professions have yielded a grudging recognition of women's intelligence and ability and achievements. An Amelia Earhart flies alone across the Atlantic; a Madame Curie discovers radium; and their success is hailed as a remarkable achievement or as an outstanding contribution to the sum of human knowledge.

In the privileged groups mothers have been able to hire some one to help in the house work at home; they have had information on how to space and limit the number of their children; they have parked the smaller children in private nursery schools or employed a mother's helper or a nursery governess, and thus have been almost as free as single women to work outside the home without neglect of the house or children. In this special group of the middle and upper classes, married and single women alike have had the opportunity to do creative and interesting work, to write books and articles on every imaginable subject;

From *Women Who Work* (New York: International Publishers, 1934). Reprinted with permission.

to do original, scientific research; to hold responsible positions in the business and professional worlds.

But for women of the working class in capitalist society, this freedom of women in the comfortable middle classes is a mockery. Working women have no such freedom. While still in their teens, they are forced to work long hours in the mills, in domestic service, or in the fields, in order to add a few dollars to the meager family income. When married, they are bound down by the labor of the house and the kitchen, "that little penitentiary," and then by the care of children. Throughout their lives they are exploited, haunted by the fear of unemployment, of illness, of old age, of destitution. A girl earning $12 a week or less in a mill or shop has about as much "freedom" and "opportunity" as a rose-bush in a desert of sand.

Many a working class woman must do the work of two persons, and more, in an effort to keep the family alive, not only the work at home with all its exacting tasks, but also a full-time job outside. What this means to the worker's family has been ably described by R. Palme Dutt:

"Capitalism extracts from her the labor of two persons; and at the same time the whole family and home life, which the capitalists affect to worship with such holy piety, is broken up and destroyed, the care of children neglected, maternity becomes a disaster for which no adequate time, rest or attention before or after can be given, and the younger generation has to grow up under conditions destructive of health or of the possibility of development."

These women at work in industry outside the home have followed production into the factories. As part of the process of social production they are now making outside the household many of the things that women formerly made inside the individual home. So, for instance, cloth, clothes, shoes, soap, candles, bread, preserves and other articles of food were all made at home not so many years ago, and the women and girls made these necessaries of life. With the introduction of machines and the rise of modern capitalism more and more of these goods were made in factories. First clothing, then household supplies, and then all kinds of foods and other goods were taken over by the capitalists who found they could produce them in quantity and sell them for profit, and thus the old hand-made goods were displaced by modern machine production. The productive labor of women was to a large extent transferred from the home to the factory. . . .

Marx was the first to point out that with all the brutality of modern capitalism in its treatment of women workers—underpaid, exploited, ruined in health and then cast out on the scrap heap of unemployment and old age— yet modern capitalism itself has created the conditions for women's final freedom. By drawing increasing millions of women and girls into social production it has opened the way for a wider and fuller life for women which, however, can never be secured under capitalism. Only a communist society will make social provision for the needs of motherhood and the care of children. Only a communist society will do away with the exploitation of the weakest, and put an end to the private profit now taken by the capitalists out of the wealth created by the workers. But in spite of the immediate, terrible effects of women's being drawn into capitalist industry, the final result, through working class organization, must be the true freedom and equality of women in a communist form of society. Thus Marx wrote:

"However terrible, however repulsive, the break-up of the old family system within the organism of capitalist society may seem, none the less, large-scale industry by assigning to women, and to young persons and children of both sexes, a decisive rôle which has to be fulfilled outside the home, is building the new economic foundation for a higher form of the family and of the relations between the sexes."

Lenin repeatedly called attention to the fact that only as women share in the general process of social production can they be truly free but that only a communist society will so organize production as to provide for the basic needs of women and children. In a speech to a Moscow Conference of Working Women he stated this plainly:

"The full liberation of woman and her real equality with man requires a communist economy, a common social organization of production and consumption and the participation of women in general production. Only through this will women take the same place in society as man."

So, the working class republic, the Soviet Union, is increasing year by year the number of women employed in social production. But one basic difference between capitalist society and the socialist republic is that socialist society accepts full social responsibility for the health and welfare of women and children. The U. S. S. R. has already established not only the most complete system of social insurance in the world, for the protection of all workers, but also coöperative kitchens and dining rooms, coöperative laundries, day nurseries and nursery schools which are freeing the women from the impossible task of caring for home and children while working also outside the home. . . .

Capitalist society, on the other hand, while talking sentimentally about the welfare of children, of mothers, and about the care of the sick and aged, has nevertheless left upon the individual working class family the full burden of insecurity. The wage worker is thus tied down by anxiety for his wife and children; he is terrified of losing his job, of becoming ill and unable to work, of dying and leaving them destitute. He is terrified into submission to the ruling class. And the working class wife, in turn, becomes the slave of a slave, bound down to the narrow interests of her own household, often holding back her husband when his anger rises in revolt against the capitalist class. As Palme Dutt puts it:

"Each wage-slave's household becomes a small exclusive unit fighting for existence with every other; the daily deprivations, cruelties, anxieties and harassment of proletarian conditions of life are magically turned aside from becoming the basis of anger and revolt against the capitalist class, and made instead the basis of family worries or family quarrels. Capitalism does not without reason make the economic institution of the family, or the family household, with its subjection of women, the pivot of its system. . . . The subjection of women is bound up with the conditions of capitalism."

ECONOMIC BASIS OF WOMEN'S SUBJECTION

The working class housewife is supposedly dependent upon her husband's earnings; yet if he has a job at all his wages are totally insufficient to provide for a family's needs. The wife and mother has the daily struggle to make ends meet. Her days are full of a great burden of work; as cook, dishwasher, scrub-woman, laundress, chambermaid, seamstress, errand girl and nurse, to say nothing of the skilled profession of a mother with little children. Almost a dozen trades, skilled, semi-skilled and unskilled, are represented in the housewife's work. She must also be ready to serve her husband whenever he wishes to use her. She is subordinate because she has no money of her own. Of these unpaid housewives there are still 23,000,000 in the United States, according to Wm. M. Steuart, director of the Census Bureau.

Nor does the working woman who goes out to earn her living in capitalist industry find that her earnings bring her freedom and equality with men. The employer can buy a woman's labor power at even less than a man's, and the woman therefore remains subordinate. The capitalist class is of course interested in buying women's labor power at the lowest possible price and therefore wishes to keep the masses of working women in this position of submission.

Propaganda to this effect is seen everywhere in the capitalist world, in advertisements, in the daily press, in the schools and churches, on the radio and in the "talkies." Take, for example, a hundred advertisements in the press or on the billboards and see what a high percentage of such "ads" are addressed to women as subordinate to men, simply as vehicles of sex charm, as if their sole end and aim in life should be to attract and please the man.

Kept on unskilled or semi-skilled jobs, the girl worker still has less chance than the boy to be a machinist, for example, or to learn any one of the more skilled trades. She is expected to stay in the "inferior," less well-paid occupations and every influence is against her earning more. The man who is her fellow-worker has been taught by boss class propaganda since his earliest childhood to regard girls as less important than boys and he does not usually encourage the girl to learn a more skilled job. It is only as he becomes class conscious in the workers' own movement that he recognizes the interests of all workers, men and women, white and Negro, as bound up together.

Petty bosses, superintendents and capitalists insist upon women's subordination in order to forestall the demand for equal pay for equal work. It is a common practice to fire men workers and hire women for the same work at lower pay, and so the myth of women's inferiority is kept alive. Whether the boss is a factory foreman, a restaurant manager, an office executive, or a hospital physician, his girl worker, his waitress, his typist or his trained nurse must be kept subordinate.

American Federation of Labor officials have been as ready as the employers to preach and teach women's subjection. Jealous of women's coming into the more skilled trades to take men's jobs, these officials of the craft unions have steadily opposed equal opportunity for girls and have established restrictions against taking women into the A. F. of L. unions on any equal basis.

Women workers themselves react to this propaganda in different ways. Often it has been effective in creating a submissive attitude on the part of girl workers who have been too docile to revolt against conditions. Taught to expect marriage and motherhood as a sufficient life work in itself, girls have thought of the outside jobs as temporary and have usually been less ready than men workers to organize and demand wage increases. Many girls have what might be called an "inferiority complex" as the result of the capitalists' teaching and it is only as they have been made bold in strikes or in other struggles of the workers' movement that they overcome this sense of inferiority to men and take their place in the ranks of active workers, striving to improve their conditions.

As a result of the ruling class propaganda, among some of the men workers who should know that their strength lies in working class solidarity, there still exists an attitude of superiority toward women workers. And just as white workers may not recognize in themselves the "white chauvinism" toward Negro workers which is felt keenly by Negroes, so also the men workers may not recognize in themselves their attitude toward women. The result is that women have not been encouraged to take positions of leadership and the workers' movement has been weakest on the very front where it might be strongest—among the masses of unskilled and semi-skilled women workers. When once aroused to class consciousness and to the possibilities of organization women have proved themselves among the best and most active fighters in the labor struggle.

Every word that is said about the exploitation of white American-born women workers is doubly true for Negro and foreign-born women of the working class. White women's wages are lower than men's, but Negro women's wages are lowest of all. They are discriminated against in every imaginable way and the discrimination is by no means confined to the southern states. Negroes everywhere have been forced to submit to the white ruling class. Jim-crowism runs through every phase of capitalist society in every part of the United States.

So also with the foreign-born women workers. Their pay is lower than native white women's, as is shown in studies of the U. S. Women's Bureau; their jobs are harder, and they have less chance to get into the better-paid occupations. They are not only discriminated against but terrorized by the American ruling class.

Capitalism depends for its very existence on a large body of surplus labor power ready to be bought at the lowest possible price. It is therefore to the interests of employers to keep these Negro and foreign-born women workers in a condition of "inferiority" ready to underbid white workers, just as it is to the interests of employers to keep women to under bid men in the labor market. One group of workers is played off against another group—foreign-born against American, Negro against white, women against men. So long as the boss can point to a body of workers ready to work for still lower wages, he has the whip-hand over his employees.

"If you don't like it, you can get out; I can get plenty more glad to work at half the pay," is the spoken or unspoken answer of the employer to any protest from the workers who have jobs.

This desperate competition for jobs between different groups in the working class, between men and women, white and Negro, adults and children native-born and foreign-born, is admitted by most economists in the capitalist world....

These years of crisis have merely intensified the suffering of working class women under capitalism. Even in times of so-called "prosperity," the total income of a working class family is barely enough to provide for the most immediate needs of life, and the burden of work, of trying to get food enough for the children, falls with deadly effect on the woman, making her old before she is middle-aged, breaking her health and her spirit. The worker's family cannot save to meet the unemployment, illness and old age that are sure to come. Never under capitalism can a working woman find adequate social provision for her needs, for maternity, for the proper care of the children, or for her own protection and health at home and at work.

Revolt is beginning. Spontaneous strikes of industrial women workers against wage cuts and speed-ups have been followed by rent strikes and bread strikes of working class tenants and housewives. Farm women and agricultural workers have engaged in a series of notable struggles. Negro women have shown what solidarity between Negro and white workers can accomplish....

This story of organization and struggle must be told against a background of concrete conditions as they are in capitalist industry and in the worker's household. Women on the farms and in the fields need to see their problems in relation to those of women in the mills and in the shops. All workers under capitalism, in order to organize intelligently and permanently, need to know what other workers are doing in other industries and other plants....

BOURGEOIS WOMEN'S ORGANIZATIONS OPPOSE CLASS STRUGGLE

It is true that "thousands, even hundreds of thousands, of women" are organized in religious, social, and educational organizations. These religious, feminist, social, patriotic, political and educational organizations are used by the employing class to take the edge off the class struggle. They are made up largely of middle-class women who run true to form as petty capitalists. The great majority of these groups foster in the community around them, among the workers as well as among middle-class associates, the idea that the individual can climb out of the working class, can get on top of other workers and become in turn an exploiter of the workers. They cultivate also notions of individual "culture" as attainable by the woman worker who can raise herself above her fellows and become a "success" in the business or professional world. They hail the stenographer who forgets other office workers in the general scramble for promotion and personal advancement, or they repeat the ancient myth, still the theme of many a moving picture, of the poor working girl who marries the rich man's son!

In all these ideas, so harmful to the interests of the working class as a whole, the middle-class women's organizations reflect and maintain the basic principle of capitalism—that the entire profit system of production is for the benefit of the few on top, who can live without work on the wealth created by the workers. Everything around us, the advertisements, the success stories in *Liberty, The Saturday Evening Post,* the *Ladies' Home Journal,* the tabloids, all the papers that are read by millions in the United States; the daily propaganda that issues from comic strips—note the open anti-strike and other reactionary preaching in "Little Orphan Annie"—radio and the talkies; the teaching in a thousand schools and colleges; the sermons in a thousand churches; all accept the profit system as desirable and final, all urge the individual worker to forget her class and feather her own nest. Rare indeed is the bourgeois woman's club or organization that questions the profit system or the idea of individual advancement. For the most part the members of these organizations uphold the *status quo* and promote it eagerly and gladly even while they may salve their consciences by dabbling in charity, in "relief" for the "worthy" poor, or in reforms that will still leave the profit system intact.

This teaching of *individual* advancement and success as all-important is exactly the opposite of the teaching in the Soviet workers' state where every influence, from infancy up, teaches the child and the grown-up that working *coöperatively* and for the good of society as a whole is the highest good.

While we may lump together most of the bourgeois women's organizations in the United States in describing their subtle influence against the workers, yet each group and each organization has its own special emphasis. Some of them count working girls and women among their members and in these the influence against strikes and against the class struggle in general is more direct and definite. Such groups as the Young Women's Christian Association, the Young Women's Hebrew Association, the young peoples' organizations of the Roman Catholic as well as the Protestant churches are usually engaged in teaching young workers to be submissive to employers, taking the fight out of them, and encouraging them to act against their own class. Many of these societies conduct classes for the "industrial girls" and carry on educational work that encourages individual "culture" but definitely discourages mass action by young women workers, to better their economic conditions. . . .

In political activity these women's organizations almost invariably support the ruling class parties, Republican and Democratic, and expect the working women of their communities to do likewise. Two of these organizations, the National Woman's Party and the League of Women Voters, are a direct outgrowth of the campaign for woman's suffrage and the "Votes for Women" days. Since the suffrage was secured working class women have been used for the most part by the Republican and by the Democratic machines to swell the number of votes for their candidates.

In this policy of asking the votes of working class women for Republicans or Democrats, the League of Women Voters plays a prominent part by presenting certain candidates as if they were "progressive" and likely to promote social legislation of a kind beneficial to the workers. They come into working class neighborhoods to make "good American citizens" and to advise the working women to vote for "good government" and for so-called nonpartisan candidates. These so-called good government candidates, however, are still tied to the old party machines. As soon as elected they conveniently forget their preëlection promises about the "forgotten man" or the "forgotten woman," and do nothing about unemployment insurance or about any other protective legislation that would really improve the workers' conditions.

The National Woman's Party, while sounding progressive in relation to equal rights and equal opportunities for women, is essentially reactionary in upholding the capitalist system and in opposing legislation that would in any way benefit working class women. As has been shown in describing its campaign against special hours legislation the chief interest of its members lies in equal opportunity for professional and business women, as its membership consists mainly of middle and upper class women. Their slogan is "Equal Rights with Men in All Laws and Customs," and their propaganda tends to spread an idea of hostility to men as men, not of hostility to capitalists as opposed to workers.

Politicians of the Republican and Democratic parties make good use of these organizations to catch the women's votes. These political leaders realize the importance of women as nearly one-half of the voting population and they have begun to appoint some women leaders to political office. In a burst of confidence, however, these women political officials admit that the men do not really grant the women complete equality and do not include them in some of the private conferences at which the most important matters of party policy are decided.

The Socialist Party worked for woman suffrage and nominally stands for equality of the sexes, but it has lost its working class perspective. It makes its appeal to the petty bourgeoisie and to middle class reformers. It tends to mislead the workers and turn them away from the path of struggle. The idea that not only the achievement of women's freedom but the solution of other social and economic problems is inseparable from militant working class struggle and working class revolution has faded out from the Socialist Party picture.

It cannot be denied that most of the religious, social and educational organizations among women are acting as a sedative to lull the workers of the community to sleep—misleading them into thinking that the authorities, local, state or national, are really doing something "progressive" to aid the working class. The fact that so many women workers have been thus misled into trusting the ruling class is one reason why comparatively few are now organized in labor unions to demand and secure for themselves the gains that capitalists will never bestow freely. . . .

Battling for immediate demands, for unemployment insurance and for other forms of social insurance, workers find themselves involved in political struggles. Indeed, as Marx and Lenin stated, "Every class struggle is a political struggle." Political action, moreover, is necessary if we are to gain at least some measure of social insurance and other labor legislation such as can be secured even under the capitalist system.

Workers in the United States are gradually awakening to the fact that the ruling, capitalist class, through its older political parties, will always organize, legislate and carry on in its own behalf, never in behalf of the working class. The ruling class acts only to try and protect itself in the making of profits and more profits. None of the much-heralded "progressive" legislation of the present Roosevelt régime, for example, the National Industrial Recovery Act, the farm act, the banking act or any other measure, really increases the workers' buying power, shortens working hours or lessens unemployment. Real wages, representing the buying power of the masses are, as we have seen, less now than before the "New Deal." Workers are now learning, in acid disillusionment, that they cannot expect working class legislation from capitalist political parties. Nor can they expect any effective legislation that will advance the workers' cause from social reformist parties that advocate class collaboration and find their present roots among liberals, intellectuals and petty capitalists, rather than among the workers.

For these reasons, increasing numbers of workers are turning year by year to the Communist Party of the United States as the only party with a revolutionary objective, that enters into the day-to-day struggles of the working class. It is the only political movement that brings together workers as workers and keeps them together in a struggle not only for immediate demands but for the final elimination of the profit system.

In this long, organized struggle, women workers have a most important part to play and they have already achieved some notable successes. . . .

. . . There are ten million women at work. Women workers have proved they are ready for organization. It is of the utmost and immediate importance to the entire working class, for the protection of men workers and their union standards no less than for the women and girls themselves, that working women should be organized in unions that are not afraid to fight. So organizing, the women who work in the United States, Negro and white, find themselves united with millions of other workers, men and women, all over the world, in the common movement to overcome capitalism and build a workers' society. Only so will they carry forward the struggle to the real emancipation and equality of women.

100
REBECCA PITTS
Women and Communism (1935)

"In the case of female education the main stress should be laid on bodily training, and after that on development of character and last of all on intellect. But the one absolute aim of female education must be with a view to the future mother."   HITLER, *Mein Kampf*

"Let German women breed warrior men and take pleasure in breeding them. Woman is to be neither comrade, nor beloved, but only mother."   SPENGLER, *Years of Decision*[1]

"The Soviet Union is the first state in the world in which the government authorities and the whole public are consciously working at the solution of the woman's question."
CLARA ZETKIN[2]

There is a specific dilemma involved in being a woman, and few ever solve it triumphantly. In general it may be stated as a conflict between *sex* (with its biological needs and social demands) and our *humanity*. There are certain powers and possibilities latent, we assume, in every human being; they achieve clear expression, however, only in very highly conscious individuals. Important among these powers is a capacity for impersonal creative living—by which I mean no renunciation of private and personal experience, but a transcending of such experience: a conscious participation that is, in the processes of nature and history. Without doubt this relation to the world is an important condition—a rich soil, so to speak—for the growth of genius. But in women there has existed (ever since the development of *property*) a tragic battle between the demands of personal life and this capacity for impersonal living.

The conflict has been sharpened rather than eradicated by our recent gains in freedom. Formerly only the woman of "genius" was aware of it—trying to reconcile her needs and duties as lover, wife, or mother with some urge toward a more conscious human development. But today the difficulty is wide-spread among cultivated middle-class women, who have a leisure and intellectual awareness not yet reached by working-class women. We have—theoretically—every political and cultural advantage open to our brothers. Nevertheless it is still bitterly hard for us—whether we are geniuses or not—to find a personal, emotional fulfillment and at the same time live a creative social life. The dilemma still exists. As a result we have heard a good deal recently about the "biological tragedy" of being woman. Women—so the theory goes—have at last been granted complete freedom to develop. If

From *New Masses*, February 1935.

1. Quoted by R. P. Dutt, *Fascism and Social Revolution*, p. 220.

2. Quoted by Fannina Halle, *Woman in Soviet Russia*, p. 267.

such a life were really natural, therefore, women would combine some socially creative work "outside the home" with the functions of sex and motherhood. But what has been the case? To begin with, there has been no great flowering of genius in any field, in spite of all hopeful prediction. Individual women may have achieved, perhaps, at no tragic personal cost, a degree of genuine eminence; but such women are exceptions. Ordinarily the division among us is bitterly distinct: on the one hand a growing army of restless, unsatisfied women—sometimes neurotic, often emotionally sterile—who do not, of course, admit that when they chose a "career" they chose ill; on the other hand an even greater army of those whose *real* talents—within the framework of marriage—are never used. So much for the bourgeois woman. For working-class women the problem has a more deadly simplicity. Most of them have no choice; they are forced into productive work "outside the home"—but with heart-breaking results for their own health and the welfare of their children. These facts make an impressive case for the theory that our sex is a disability: that "genius" is rare among us and a personal tragedy when it appears; that for the vast majority fullness of life is to be attained *only* in marriage; and that married women ought never to be obliged to work.

Now if we were content (in spite of our theoretical freedom) to accept the old restrictions, women could be regarded as unfit *by nature* for independent (productive) activity. But we do not accept this doom as inevitable. In spite of a personal cost that is often tragic, thousands of women demonstrate what a vital urge drives them—married or single—into creative effort: in science, the arts, or the professions. On such a large scale the very presence of desire indicates the presence of a capacity crying to be used. Quite as much as men, then, women need (for keen and conscious living) to do some kind of socially productive work.

As a matter of fact, we realize now that the root of our dilemma is *social* rather than biological. This becomes clear as we see women everywhere stirring in discontent. Even the relatively free middle-class woman is coming to suspect that it is her *status in society*—not her sex in itself—that makes it hard to lead a balanced life. But the factor of social tyranny is laid bare, in all its ugliness, only by the plight of women in the working class. These women, who are usually married, have been driven (not by a need for wider arenas but by a simple hunger) into socially productive work in industry. And what is the result? Savage discrimination against their sex, although often they work better than men; and a vast complex of conditions making it impossible for them to do their necessary work without endangering their health and their children's welfare. In their case two brutal facts are clear: that women today are an exploited group in society, and that the competitive wage-system offers them no hope of better things. The suffering of working-class women then, arises from the fact that they are exploited as workers and doubly exploited as *women*. It is also true—and I shall make it clear—that, *for every woman in capitalist society,* the suffering, defeat, and frustration too often involved in womanhood arise wholly out of our enforced status in society.

The question of the status of women, all over the world today, is a bitterly living issue. Obviously this is so in Nazi Germany, where women are denied higher learning and degraded into breeders of cannon-fodder. Not so obviously but just as truly is it an issue for us. For in our so-called "emancipation" (as I shall indicate later) we cherish only the husk, not the reality, of a truly human freedom. But even this husk is not guaranteed forever. *When we drift toward Fascism, we drift inevitably toward a degradation of women.* The reason is clear when we analyze our real status today—historically tied up with property and the psychology of property.

The continued subjection of women was necessary to early capitalism: there was need of the primitive family to bring up children, to support the aged and the unemployed, to consolidate property, and to perform those tasks of "domestic" labor that society could not yet conveniently take over. Hence women were forcibly compelled to marriage as the one honest way to get a living. (In this way society merely italicized the treatment it had accorded women since the age of barbarism.)

At a certain stage in its growth, however, capitalist society had to take a progressive stand with regard to women. In the search for more workers to exploit, industry began to hire female labor. In spite of brutal discrimination against us (on the theory that we have no dependents) women have, nevertheless, gained a foothold in the economic order. Political "rights" and cultural "opportunities" reflect this basic economic fact; they are impressive—although theoretical—concessions. To this extent, then, (and because a thriving capitalism found it profitable) women have been set free.

Now, however, capitalism is falling into decay: it no longer needs a large labor-army; it does, on the other hand, need to spread poverty—so that as many dependents as possible may live on the wretched pay of one worker. The political expression of this decaying economy is, of course, Fascism—a reactionary and brutal dictatorship set up solely to preserve the profit-system. It is quite logical that Fascism (in its effort to enlarge the circle of one worker's dependents) should reverse history with regard to the status of women.[3] Woman as cook, domestic toiler without pay, breeder of Fascist Storm Troopers: that is the new ideal, and signs of its approach are not wanting even in this country. It is no longer profitable for capitalism that women should be free; as the system decays, then, we must lose—like the workers—our hard-won rights.

In the light of these facts, it is now possible to define the real position of women under capitalism. And the definition is not pleasant. In spite of political "rights," cultural "opportunities," and every other pleasant fiction about equality we delude ourselves with, one fact emerges clearly. Capitalist society has granted us a relative liberty for precisely the same reason that it "freed" the Negro slaves. In other words, women *constitute a reserve labor-army maintained in the interests of the employers.* So that all labor may sell itself cheaply in the open market, there must be some who are discriminated against and forced to sell themselves much too cheaply.[4] In industry there are two such groups: Negroes—and women; and this basic discrimination is reflected also in the professions.[5] Capitalist society could free neither women nor Negroes until it became *profitable* to free them. And as soon as a dying profit-system finds it more profitable to degrade us to our former position, (for reasons I suggested in the preceding paragraph) we shall lose, as in Germany, our relative and illusory liberty.

We find ourselves thus bound to an evolving capitalism because of one simple fact: since the beginning of history *women have been degraded and oppressed.* Even folk-lore and fable reflect that in the days of the heroes women were subject to men. It would seem, therefore, that a good reason for discrimination is given by our innate "inferiority." Bourgeois law-givers could enjoy, in fact, a glow of generosity in liberating us, while all the time maintaining the old oppression in all important respects. Of course the process has worked out without reference to the will or desire of individuals; but the interests of capitalism have been well served by our historic status as inferiors.

Women were not always oppressed, however, as the evidence of anthropology reveals. In primitive times, and, indeed, until shortly before the dissolution of tribal communities, women were free, productive members of the group. But during the late Neolithic period (the Middle Status of Barbarism, as Lewis H. Morgan called it) they were enslaved. It is very interesting and important to notice that women lost their liberty precisely when primitive communal life broke down and *private property* developed. Only then was the ancient "mother-right" destroyed.

---

3. R. P. Dutt, *Fascism and Social Revolution*, p. 220 *ff.*

4. Grace Hutchins, *Women Who Work*, p. 76.

5. *Ibid*, p. 132.

This primitive dignity of woman—this mother-right—was rooted in the collective form of barbaric society. The wholly promiscuous herd-family of savagery had evolved into the *tribe* with its minor sub-division, the *clan.* The tribe was a "political" unit; the clan (really an enlarged family) was an economic unit, resting upon an absolute community of property. Within the clan all were considered brothers and sisters: hence, to avoid incest, one had to marry someone from another clan in the tribe; and, by an equally severe rule, no property could be taken out of the clan. Inevitably, according to such rules, there were only two alternatives: to reckon descent through the mothers and expel men from the clan when they married; or to reckon descent from the fathers and expel women upon marriage. Now in this early communal life both men and women were free; they all held their property in common; and they all shared in the labor of the clan. No one, in other words, had any motive for constraining another; neither men nor women had anything to gain or lose. Naturally, therefore, they reckoned descent through the mothers, for the obvious reason that maternity cannot be doubted. (So when a man married, he entered his wife's clan.) A few peoples—for example, the Lycians, whom Herodotus mentions—persisted in this custom after the beginning of history; and to this day there are traces of it in many primitive tribes.

But the development of agriculture put an end to the mother-right nearly everywhere. Increased wealth brought more leisure and a division of labor; and the upshot was that the *men* came into possession of farm-tools and means of production. At the same time the various clansmen (who had formerly hunted, or tended herds, in common) began to acquire their own plots of ground. Thus by slow degrees *private property* arose, and the economic basis for clan-life was undermined. In many parts of the world, however, (for instance, Rome) the clan was retained as a means of reckoning descent, but with one very significant change. Since property now belonged to the man, the *father-right* was set up so that his wealth could be handed down to his own heirs; and—in order that the children be unquestionably his own—he forced upon his wife the command of absolute faithfulness. In this way women were slowly degraded—from a position of freedom and productivity in the community to a completely subject role. Of course they did not suffer this shame without resistance; the legend of the Amazons has a basis in fact.[6] But they were doomed to defeat: the long upward spiral of conscious history had begun; and only by means of property and class-division could a part of human energy be released for progress. Through the evolution of private property, therefore, woman herself became the property of man: from an end in herself she became a sexual commodity and a means to an end.[7]

Today all women under capitalism bear the marks of this servitude in their lives. It is hard for us to be clear about this; the forces that mould us are too subtle and pervasive. It is not merely a matter of economic discrimination, although that alone is bitter. Equally in our so-called "feminine" reactions to the world, in our frustrations and baffled struggle, in our failure to attain genius—we are stifled by the old historic bondage. Not one of us has reached (nor *can,* conditioned as we are) the stature that ought to have been ours. For if a man or woman is to develop his capacities to the full, he must take his part in the two chief functions of mankind: *work* and *sex.* The tragedy of woman, however, is that society has denied her a free creative part in the world's work; and that as a result even sex, about which her life has centered, has been warped for her and unnaturally twisted.

In the communal life of barbarism women shared, as free individuals, the productive work of the clan. There is abundant anthropolitical evidence that the focal values of that time lay in the

---

6. See Emanuel Kanter, *The Amazons.* Chas. H. Kerr, Chicago.
7. The reader is referred to: Bebel, *Women Under Socialism,* Chap. I. Fannina Halle, *Woman in Soviet Russia,* Chap. I. Friedrich Engels, *The Origin of the Family.*

group, not the individual; that all early culture arose out of *group* needs—whether statue of Fertility, spring rite for adolescents, or majestic animal fresco in the caves of Altomira. Un-self-conscious, impersonal as Nature is impersonal, these early people must have felt an organic unity with the world that civilized men have not recaptured. Up to a certain point their growing cultural complexity (their richer productive forces) merely made life more human and more conscious. In these last stages of pre-history, then, *work* must have had a very great dignity and importance for every person in the clan. It was man acting upon his environment—creating, discovering, growing—and not only for himself but for the group. In this creative activity women shared to the full.

With the further development of tools and agriculture, however, and the rise of private property, all this was changed. Women were gradually degraded, imprisoned in the "women's quarters," and denied all participation in community life. And not only *women* were enslaved, of course, but great masses of toilers who had lost out in the scramble for wealth. Work—for the few—became personal, ambitious, acquisitive; for the masses—meaningless drudgery.

Now for happiness in work, people need to feel that what they toil at has some value and meaning behind a mere subsistence. In actual practice only society can confer this value upon anything; that is, we need to feel our work (even if it is revolt) as integral to the social process. No doubt many medieval craftsmen shared this happiness—taking pride in their contribution to the community and in an honest job well done. Genius itself (burning with an intense flame) is only this same double passion: a love of one's craft and an imaginative sense of larger wholes. But since the beginning of history women have been shut off from a vital contact with society. Only with capitalism have we entered a wider arena; and yet, we are not free. Nor do the chaotic, egoistic values of capitalism permit—to most people—any real happiness in work. With the rise of property and class society, then, women were robbed of their dignity as productive workers.

But this was not all. At the same time, and in the same way, women were robbed of their *sexual* dignity. Sex may be a very personal matter, but our reactions are shaped by the social psychology about us; and this psychology, of course, reflects the basic economic structure of the period. Under primitive communism the sexes were equal, all members of the clan were productive workers, and value resided not in the atomic person but in the organic group. In a very real sense the individual found his happiness and liberty in the communal whole. This absence of egocentric aims must have deeply colored their attitude toward sex—rendering it less personal than it is today, and freed of jealous obsessions. With the rise of private property, however, there was a great change. The seizure of economic goods by the individual gave rise inevitably to conflicting aims and a psychology of *power*. In man's fight to amass wealth and give it to his legitimate heirs, he compelled woman to a faithfulness based not on desire but on necessity. No longer was mating a free choice of equals; man had come to regard woman as his own property, made for his personal use and pleasure.

Throughout history, then, women were *owned*—and kept at home—until factories needed their labor. Today, however, the property-theory is absurd among the working classes; too often the woman—not her husband—feeds the family. It is quite true, however, that even among the middle classes a new woman is emerging—and a more comradely ideal of marriage. But we need not delude ourselves. The historic view that women are property still fosters the myth of our "inferiority"—employed so usefully today in unfair discrimination against us. And now with the decline of capitalism, as Fascism invokes again our old servility, we see clearly that we are still used as property.

Upon this view of women, indeed, bourgeois society founds its whole theory of marriage: that in return for the use of her body (to give him pleasure and to breed his children) a man is obliged to support his wife at home. (As I have pointed out, the theory seems not to operate among working-class people. But the bourgeois woman is a sexual commodity; and to be respectable her husband must demonstrate his ability to pay for her.) Hence the opposition even yet between marriage and a "career," which in practice condemns most wives to domestic slavery. And from the same theory of purchase stems the man's right to woo, to select, to impose his own taste upon women who bid for his approval.

This view of marriage is enforced by three factors—deriving from a competitive system. First, for most men an early marriage is impossible. Second, by unfair discrimination society renders productive work unattractive in itself to a majority of women. Third, for economic reasons there are always more women than men who are eligible for marriage. It is impossible to overestimate the pain and injustice inflicted upon women by these circumstances. The economic necessity for late marriage implies (if not prostitution) the brief liaison; and no matter how we glorify or become used to such compromise affairs, they have tragic shortcomings. The fact that women are discouraged by unfair discrimination, moreover, means that most of them look forward to *marriage* rather than *work* as the principal end in life. And the fact that marriageable women greatly outnumber the men who can marry means simply this: that from early youth the competition for male favor is fierce and of primary importance. This implies for every woman an intense preoccupation with sex.

But sex itself—in the civilized world—has been twisted into an ugly mockery of conscious living. Except for a mature minority, human sexual behavior is based largely upon egotism, self-worship, and personal conquest. With the rise of private property, value shifted from the *group* to the *individual*—where it has stayed ever since. Of course barbaric society was crude and simple, and evolution could occur only by means of this development; but at the same time a violent dislocation took place in human personality. The sex-relation was altered; the element of autocratic preference on the man's part, and submission on the woman's had been introduced. Upon a psychology of power and egotism, therefore, civilized man has built his vast complex of attitudes on sex and love. *Sex* has been transformed into *sexuality;* from an impersonal end (participation in life) it has become a personal means. Sometimes, transmuted by an elaborate ritual of romance, this ego-sexuality becomes the "in love" state so characteristic of our culture: naively greedy in popular songs and screen plays; subtly disguised in the lamentations of a Byron or De Musset. Whether "in love" or not, however, each sexual partner desires in the other the mirror and gratifications of his own self-love. So wide-spread is this personalism that we crown it with social approval and call it "normal."

If women are to escape celibacy, therefore, they must play incessantly and with passion at this game of conquest. For a man, sex may be a means to personal pleasure; but by virtue of his power to choose a woman when he will, he can forget this personalism and become absorbed in larger interests. For women, however, there is no such easy solution. At all times—since husbands are won by clever angling—women must be "alluring." Confronted by an imperious sexual need (often complicated by economic need) no wonder the majority find work to be secondary, and ambition hollow.

Woman under capitalism, therefore, finds herself not only oppressed as a worker, but kept (by means of this basic tyranny) in a position of *sexual* servility as well. Daily she is told, of course, that she is the equal of the male; but daily the quiet, inexorable force of social reality shapes her tragic dilemma. If she is to escape celibacy and lead a "normal" life, she is forced, in most cases, into a definite pattern. To get a husband (even lovers, even admirers) she must please the dominant male—"normally" an undeveloped egotist who regards her as a means to his own pleasure. It becomes her business, therefore, to arouse desire; to play by means of sex-allurement, dress, and personal charm upon male ego-sexuality. Instead of being a rounded, creative personality she is warped and twisted (by this overemphasis upon sex) into a creature who really is inferior to man. Vain, spiteful, personal, petty: so often these epithets are well deserved. It is proof of a strong urge in woman that so many really do—in spite of this terrific pressure from bourgeois society—lead creative lives.

From even so brief a scrutiny, we see that the tragedy of womanhood is not biological at all—but *social*. To begin with, we are confronted by a false and warped choice between marriage and work. The mother who leaves six children to work in a factory is no exception. She has been forced by need and exploitation; her work is drudgery and her family life precarious. The young middle-class wife who ekes out her husband's income with her own is likewise no exception. For in her case, too, the work has neither meaning nor independent dignity: it is something to do one season and drop the next. *The fact remains that most women are unable to marry, to have children, and still pursue any absorbing, satisfying work.* This is partly a result of discrimination; more frequently, however, it is the consequence of their early conditioning that women are literally ruined for such work. But the necessity for such a choice is vicious and unnatural—as a growing rebellion among women indicates.

Even more vicious than the fact of choice, however, are the alternatives themselves. If a woman prefers marriage she is driven, in most cases, to be "normal" with a vengeance; to become absorbed, that is, in a highly personal, self-regarding manipulation of sex. But if her urge to work is deep and strong, she is confronted by an even more deadly alternative. Discrimination is very real, for one thing, against married women; and for the right to persistent, sustained effort in science or the professions a woman must almost take a vow of celibacy. As a result of discrimination, therefore, and the difficulties of celibacy, many talented women are denied real satisfaction in their work. Just as the poison of individualism has withered sex into sexuality, so the poisons of unfair competition, anxiety, and denial of natural instinct warp and shrivel the creative urge.

From the beginning of history, then, society has denied to women the reality of life. From the experience of those who have learned to live consciously, we can understand what life *ought to be:* a conscious cooperation with—participation in—the process of universal growth; not any infantile "happiness" or "security," but a great awareness of the world and the will to labor for the unfolding of its possibilities. But to live at such a level the individual must be free. His experience of sex cannot halt at self-adulating romance or sensuality; it must mature into an identification with life. His productive labor cannot remain mere drudgery; it must be integrated in some real way with the labor of society—so that he feels it to have value and dignity. It is unnecessary to point out that although most men have never been able to reach this level, they have had far more chance than women have had to do so.

Denied this reality of conscious living, women have, broadly speaking, adjusted themselves to their dilemma in two ways: by acquiescing in their socially imposed fate they have become "normal" or "feminine"; by rebelling against it they have substituted some kind of more obvious compensation. It is important to realize, however, that the "normal" adjustment is just as false—just as empty a shadow of reality—as any of the varieties of rebellion. The "normal" is approved for purely statistical reasons; but the term carries no implication whatever of the *natural* or organically *right*. It is as much a mockery of life for woman to be vain, petty, and personalistic, as for her to erect any other system of replacement.

A sturdy minority, indeed, *have* rebelled in one way or another—repudiating with pain or violence this servile necessity to "please." Of course we cannot guess how many wives have instinctively desired a richer and more honest relation with their husbands; or how many (failing, perhaps, to hold their men) made motherhood and religion compensate for the loss. And it would be equally hard to estimate how many women—married or single—have dashed themselves into fanatical reform movements because their desire for creative work had been frustrated. Modern psychology, however, is very suggestive on these points.

But a more intense (although unconscious) repudiation of social tyranny takes place in the nightmare pain of the neurotic. In both men and women this conflict arises when a highly sensitive personality fails to become organically adjusted to the world. Only a rare minority, of course, ever do attain any wholeness, any depth, any reality of experience but the "normal" person accepts a set of facile substitutes, a shallow pasteboard imitation of organic life. From this falsity the neurotic recoils with horror—his fear of life arising from a sense of its mocking emptiness, and from his own failure to reach a three-dimensional *participation* therein. Thus painfully aware that life is slipping by, he clutches at shadows and symbols and weird replacements of his own; all the while, of course, cutting himself off the more sharply from reality. Now it is the custom to deal with neurosis and insanity as if they were isolated cases; as if, in short, the disorder arose in the individual and could be healed there. Nothing could be farther from the truth; it is *society* which thrusts mental anguish upon so many. By denying to human beings a valid sense of the dignity and meaning of their toil, society creates in sensitive people a feeling of frustration and strain. And by fostering (on a basis of economic individualism) a collective psychology of shallow cruelty and warped display, society destroys our power to find creative self-realization in sex. And of course economic worry is a source of terrible tension. In the light of these facts, we need not be surprised that a great majority of neurotics are women.

Whether "normal" or neurotic, however, (and in spite of the fact that a few women can transcend these limitations) most of us stagger today under a crushing inner burden imposed not by nature, but by the social order.

By now it should be clear to every woman that *within class society* she has nothing to expect but a return to slavery. Women were enslaved to begin with by the rise of property and class divisions, and they have been regarded ever since as inferiors and sexual commodities. Our "liberty" today is not true freedom: freedom hardly exists, in class society, even for many men; and I have labored to show the added burdens (economic, sexual and psychological) which are thrust upon women. Our emancipation is merely the right to work—if we can—thereby driving down *all* wages for the fat profit of the owners. From this one fact it is plain that while the profit system endures women cannot be free: we are too useful in a servile position. With their usual bluntness the Nazis have made this brutally clear.

Only when exploitation, therefore, is destroyed—and the psychology of power and profit—can women be free. We all need to see this: the oppressed industrial worker, to be sure; but also the professional woman, the ambitious college girl, the wife who has stifled her native talents in domestic slavery. For in a classless society—a democracy of free workers—we shall have for the first time the conditions for a truly human development. Only Communism offers woman the right to be an *independent productive worker:* recognizing that sex and parenthood are important for women and men alike; but that while they *are* important they do not fill every need nor exercise every capacity. Only communism, likewise, offers woman another right (so closely related to that of independent work): the right to a freer, more natural sex happiness.

In the Soviet Union we already find proof that to liberate woman as worker means to liberate her also as *sexual being*. For since women can enter any work they choose (except the heaviest physical labor) and are not discriminated against in any way, no economic need can turn marriage for them into a means instead of an end. And since even very young people can be self-supporting, they do not need to endure the pain and frustration of chastity, or the brief pathos of a clandestine affair. An early marriage may prove unstable, but it can be decently dissolved; meanwhile the very naturalness and ease with which it has been formed are safeguards against unhealthy obsessions. And as for the strictly "biological" problem of womanhood—adequate contraceptive aid, so that when a child comes it is *wanted;* four months' leave from work, with pay for the mother; and nurseries where young children are cared for during working hours: these provisions *by society* are a sane solution. Of course all these factors make for a freedom and honesty in sexual matters (and therefore a new happiness for women) that we merely dream of under capitalism.

We have reason to hope, however, for an even deeper change—under Communism—on our attitude toward sex: a change arising from the basic revolution in property relations. I have already hinted at the unity of the barbaric clan: its simple, organic sense of communal interests that transcend those of the individual. This unity was based on a common ownership of productive goods and was therefore shattered with the rise of private property. Now, after a history of conflict and bloody greed, humanity returns (but on a higher, more conscious level) to *another* communal ownership of wealth. When no individual—no class—can exploit another; when all resources are owned by society, the very idea of private interest will disappear. Rid of this age-old mental burden (like insanity dividing man from man) people can live natural lives again. It will no longer be reserved for saints and sages to experience the unity of life; every member of society will find his own happiness in serving a truly human whole. In such a world sex, too, must inevitably take on new meaning.

In recent years there have been many prophets of a sexual "transvaluation of values." Of these D. H. Lawrence was undoubtedly the greatest—by virtue of the loathing he poured upon a petty generation; and by virtue of his terrible vision of sex itself, as an *impersonal plunging into life,* a rebirth into the natural order. Instinctively he knew that beneath the experience of civilized men lies the great perversion: that in seeking "love" (no less than pleasure) we use life for personalistic ends. But he could not understand the emergence of *mind* as a creative force, so he rejected it; and he failed to see that men are social beings as well as biological. In his effort, therefore, to avoid ego-sexuality he sought identification with "Nature" in a mindless, sensual darkness; but such a quest for reality was only a more strenuous form of the very perversion he wished to escape. This was inevitable, since in rejecting mind and society he came to Nature as a naked atom, looking for his own salvation. Thus his fate is a paradox: he felt the stale horror in the property-perversion of sex; and yet throughout his work we find prophetic hints of the cruelty and lust of Fascism. The men of the future will not follow Lawrence in his rejection of mind and society; they will, on the contrary, see Nature risen to supreme self-consciousness *in the human community.* But will they not find in sex (as he confusedly prefigured) a means of identification with the natural order? Not personal pleasure; certainly nothing mystical; but an experience that is natural and deeply real. This can come, however, only when the economic and psychological foundations have been laid. And any such revolution in sexual attitudes cannot fail to affect women (since they have been slaves, historically, of sex) far more than men.

Today, of course, it is impossible to prophesy in detail—to say that women will be like this or that in a classless society. An attempt at any such forecast would be an attempt to make a blue-print for one phase of the future—a most un-Marxian procedure. It is even impossible to state categorically that women are not inferior to men. From a social point of view, however, these questions are merely speculative: the one essential thing now is to give every human being, regardless of race or sex, the chance to develop freely, to grow, to live to the limit of his capacity. And from the foregoing analysis it is clear that in class society every woman bears a heavy load of disabilities imposed by that society: a burden of economic discrimination, psychological strain and sexual inferiority, all of which are a wholly adequate explanation for our apparent failures in the field of productive work. Only in a classless society, then, only under Communism, we can free ourselves as workers and as women. Meanwhile the Soviet Union gives embryonic hints of the future: hints of rich growth in personality, and socialist virtues—courage, tenacity, self-subordination—which ennoble the new woman as well as the new man.

101
BETTY MILLARD

Woman against Myth (1947–1948)

"How did woman first become subject to man, as she now is all over the world? By her nature, her sex, just as the Negro is and always will be to the end of time, inferior to the white race and, therefore, doomed to subjection; but she is happier than she would be in any other condition, just because it is the law of nature. . . ."

When James Gordon Bennett made these observations in 1852 it was indeed true that woman was subject to man all over the world. In America it had been held to be self-evident that all men were created equal, but only a few female crackpots and a couple of male fellow-travellers made the ridiculous contention that men and women are created equal. It was self-evident to the Philadelphia *Public Ledger and Daily Transcript* in 1848 that "women have enough influence over human affairs without being politicians. . . . A woman is nobody. A wife is everything. A pretty girl is equal to ten thousand men, and a mother is, next to God, all-powerful. The ladies of Philadelphia are resolved to maintain their rights as Wives, Belles, Virgins, and Mothers, and not as Women." To the *Transcript's* women readers it must have come as a surprise that they had rights in their sexual and family relations with men, for they were being offered at the same time advice similar to that still being given to their daughters by the Reverend Knox-Little of Philadelphia in 1880. To her husband a wife "owes the duty of unqualified obedience," he said. "There is no crime which a man can commit which justifies his wife leaving him or applying for that monstrous thing, divorce. It is her duty to subject herself to him always. . . . If he be a bad or wicked man, she may gently remonstrate with him, but refuse him never." (Eugene A. Hecker, *A Short History of Women's Rights*.)

But if the Philadelphia ladies were surprised to learn in this roundabout fashion that they had rights, there were still greater surprises in store for them. For 1848 was the year of the first Woman's Rights Convention in Seneca Falls, N.Y., when a woman got up in public and for the first time openly demanded the vote for women. The events that followed were enlivened by great drama, participated in by towering figures, full of meanings for us today. Yet we have all but forgotten this struggle and the people who led it. Who in 1947 remembers Elizabeth Cady Stanton or Lucretia Mott? How many students of the history of oppressed peoples remember the mountains of abuse heaped on these women for disputing the "law of nature" which declared woman to be man's property? In short, why does the history of woman's battle for equality no longer seem to have meaning for many of us?

The only conclusion one can come to is that most of us feel the fight is more or less won. We do not leave the history of the Negro people to the historians—even the good ones—because we know that all of us who want to achieve equality for the Negro people need this weapon. If we felt the same way about

From *New Masses,* December 30, 1947 and January 6, 1948.

the women's struggle, we would make use not only of the challenging life of Frederick Douglass but of that of Susan B. Anthony as well.

But is it true that the fight is practically won? Should we perhaps turn our attention to other more pressing matters? In general women have the vote: they can hold property, make contracts and run businesses (with exceptions); divorce is no longer a calamity and they can usually get custody of their children. Few of these rights were theirs a hundred years ago. Furthermore, women are not lynched—as women. They have met these violent ends only as Negroes, Jews or anti-fascists.[1]

The old legal rule that permitted a husband to beat his wife "within reason," with a stick no thicker than a man's thumb, has been superseded. In most countries wife-beating is no longer good form.

For women there is generally reserved a quieter, more veiled kind of lynching. Many of the thirty-eight million American housewives are doomed to circumscribed, petty lives, to the stultification of whatever abilities and interests, outside of motherhood, they may have had. The 15,400,000 women wage-earners are discriminated against in almost every field of employment, are notoriously paid less than men for the same work, are the first to be laid off. Yet according to a survey conducted by the Women's Bureau of the Department of Labor, 84 percent of working women work because they have to in order to support themselves and their dependents. The Bureau of Census estimates that there are now from two and a half to three million unemployed; of these, according to the Congress of American Women, over two million are women.

Legally, many of the discriminations of old British common law against women are still on our statute books and enforced by the states. In eight states the husband controls all the property of the marriage without regard for the contributions of the wife. Women are excluded from jury duty in sixteen states; in six states a married woman is no more allowed to keep her week's wages than was the slave Frederick Douglass, who when he worked in a Baltimore shipyard also had to turn his pay over to his master every Saturday night. Politically, twenty-seven years after the nineteenth amendment was ratified there are still only seven women in Congress. The Republicans and Democrats make no serious attempt to nominate women, in accordance with their potentialities, and even in progressive circles there is a tendency to give only lip-service to "the need to bring women forward into full citizenship."

It would require a volume to describe all the economic, legal and political barriers against women. I do not want to multiply examples here because, while this aspect of the woman question is crucial, these articles will deal primarily with some of the less discussed aspects of the question. For instance: how does a woman in such a society feel about herself as a woman? She is a majority of the electorate; does the fact that she hasn't yet achieved equality mean that she doesn't really want it after all? Is it true or is it a myth that "women like to be dominated"?

It is hardly remarkable that the great majority of women are from earliest childhood convinced—if only subconsciously—of their inferiority to men. Woman's inferiority is

---

1. It might be interesting, however, to consider the question of rape as a form of violence practiced against women. Rape can only happen to a woman, just as anti-Negro attacks can only be made on Negroes and anti-Semitic attacks on Jews. It seems to me the first is a reflection in brutal form of the underlying values of our society just as are the other two. True, rape, unlike attacks on Negroes and Jews and other minorities, is not deliberately employed as a means to terrorize and keep in subjection an oppressed group. But it is a criminal act of a special kind—an anti-woman act—just as the other two are crimes of a special kind. The lynching of a Georgia Negro is the violent expression of a pattern of white supremacy; rape is a violent expression of a pattern of male supremacy, an outgrowth of age-old economic, political and cultural exploitation of women by men. When a Negro woman is raped by a white man these two aspects of our society merge. But it's only then that we tend to think of it as a crime against an oppressed group.

embedded in the very language she uses. Take Webster's definition of the word "man" (and the definition occupies twenty lines in the Collegiate Dictionary, third edition, as against five for the word "woman"). Man is: "(1) A human being. (2) The human race; mankind. (3) The male human being." Only in the third is man specifically a male. In the first man is synonymous with "person," in the second with "people." Where does that leave woman? Webster's says woman is: "(1) An adult female person. (2) Womankind." The word is derived from the Anglo-Saxon *Wifmann*, or wife-man. Hence a woman is the wife of a man, a sort of appendage of the human race, or "mankind." In other words, the word "woman" historically occupies the same position in our language as woman has occupied in society.

Further "he" means "one." ("If anyone wants a copy of this pamphlet, will he see me after the meeting?") It's "men and women," not the other way around. All men are created equal, and they hope to establish Liberty, Equality and Brotherhood. "Sisterhood" not only doesn't include men (assuming that the brotherhood men hope to establish does include women), but it's a fairly comic word in itself. As for the language we use when we get emotional, the choicest insults in the English (and probably every other) language reflect either on the animal kingdom or on women, especially the insultee's mother. A whole psychological study could be written on the fact that among men a four letter word relating to sex has become one of the most common expressions of anger and aggression, reflecting as it does a society in which the sexual relationship itself often has exploitive characteristics.

Language changes as society changes—though of course it may lag behind a century or two. What's going to become of the verb "to man," for instance, now that Soviet and Yugoslavian ships are being womanned as well as manned? If the trend continues—and it's sure to—it will pose us a semantic problem.

Philologists of 2147 are going to be interested in how we solve such problems. We can see that in the present state of our society it would be all but impossible to eliminate from our language reflections of woman's inequality: and even if it were possible it would, by itself, be futile, for our job is to attack the inequality and the chauvinistic concepts themselves. Then the language will take care of itself.

So many factors operate to impress upon women a sense of inferiority that it would be impossible to touch upon all of them.

All major religions, for instance, hold woman to be a sort of necessary evil. When God created the world, he made man in his own (male) image, and then created woman as a sort of afterthought from one of man's inconsequential spare parts. Everyone knows that when Eve disobeyed God and bit into the Apple of Knowledge she became responsible for all the ills that have befallen the world, or Man, ever since. (Pandora in opening that box played a similar dirty trick on the ancient Greeks.) The Bible says: "But I suffer not a woman to teach, nor to usurp authority over the man, but to be in silence." (I Tim. 2:12). Confucius says: "It is a law of nature that women should be kept under the control of men and not allowed any will of their own." In the Jewish religion the men pray: "I thank thee Lord that thou hast not created me a woman." The Hindu woman who burnt herself on the funeral pyre of her husband did so because of her religion. A Turkish woman is held in the harem through religion. In the place of worship orthodox Jewish women are fenced off by a grating; Christian women cover their heads—a relic of the Eastern veil, the symbol of subjection. Women cannot become priests or rabbis. As for the Christian marriage ceremony, only recently has the word "obey" been generally omitted; we still follow the custom of "giving the bride away," which originated at a time when a daughter was a form of property to be given away as the father would dispose of any other form of property; and the twelfth-century Church authority Gratian says, "Women are veiled during the marriage ceremony that they may know they are lowly and in subjection to their husbands." (In fact, he adds that woman must never, under pain of excommunication, cut off her hair, because "God has given it to her as a veil and as a sign of her subjection." He offered no explanation of the fact that men can grow long hair not only from the tops of their heads but from the front of their faces as well, thus beating any shroud God ever gave to a woman.)

Laws, customs, language, religion—they all conspire to keep woman in her place. But by themselves they couldn't do the job. Day-to-day attacks in books, films, radio shows and magazine articles are called for, since women are more and more coming awake, discovering that their problems are tied up with the great overall struggle for democracy.

In 1853 the editor of *Harper's New Monthly Magazine* warned of the "intimate connection [of the women's rights movement] with all the radical and infidel movements of the day. A strange affinity seems to bind them all together. . . . This female Socialism presents a peculiar enormity of its own: in some respects more boldly infidel than any kindred measure." . . .

This commentator put his finger on a remarkable heritage of common struggle. A century ago women's fight against oppression was closely linked with that of labor and, especially, the Negro people. The leaders of the women's movement took part in the struggle against Negro slavery; the Abolitionists gave their support to the women. The two movements have been considered dangerous and upsetting to the social structure for much the same reasons.

It boils down to this: Negroes can be paid less; women can be paid less. As long as both are not organized on an equal basis with white men and work under equal conditions, they form the most vulnerable sections of labor; they are labor's Achilles' heel. In a general period of assault on labor they especially must be attacked relentlessly.

So that in this year of Taft and Hartley it is no accident that there is a crescendo of abuse levelled against women. Gone are the wartime editorials saluting women in industry, the magazine articles praising her newfound mechanical abilities. Today we read about the "foolishness" of women, their "immaturity." Above all, we get a barrage of the familiar propaganda that woman's place is in the Kuche with the Kinder. Paradoxical as it may seem, this is essential to a supply of underpaid women for industry: a favorite employer argument is that women leave their jobs when they get married or have children and therefore they are not as valuable as men, and should be paid less. Hence it is necessary to preserve and reinforce the general opinion that a woman's job is transitory and unimportant and that her only real fulfillment comes as a wife and mother. ("A woman is nobody. A wife is everything.")

The difference is that the authority quoted is no longer God but Freud. In 1947 women are attacked by Ferdinand Lundberg and Dr. Marynia Farnham in their best seller, *Modern Woman—The Lost Sex*, not for attempting to subvert God's will but for unconsciously seeking to deprive the male of his power, to castrate him. They reach into history to perform a psychoanalytical autopsy upon that great pioneer Mary Wollstonecraft, whose *Vindication of the Rights of Women* appeared in 1792. "Mary," they say, unconsciously "probably wished to . . . kill her father, but this desire, though powerful, was powerfully deflected as untenable. It came out only in her round scolding of all men. The feminists have ever since symbolically slain their fathers by verbally consigning all men to perdition as monsters." Similarly, Elizabeth Cady Stanton is said to have agitated for votes for women because of her envy of the male sex organ.

This kind of use of Freudian concepts has become a political technique which is increasingly effective among people who are no longer susceptible to religious argument, for it seems to deal "scientifically" with real problems. Women *do* envy men. But they have good cultural reasons for doing so. The majority of women who try to combine running a home and a full-time job find great difficulty in doing either satisfactorily. Economics, religion, customs, taboos impose conflicting roles and wishes on women, who are unable to function fully in society as both mothers and citizens not because of their special biological natures but because every society until the advent of socialism has made it economically and socially impossible for them to do so.

There are few women who do not look forward to marriage and children. And certainly raising a family of happy, useful citizens is an accomplishment of which any woman can be proud. But it is not in any way belittling a mother's hard work and achievement to assert that time may prove that motherhood no more exhausts a woman's potentialities as a human being than fatherhood does a man's. To him fatherhood is part of a normal, happy life: he does not become a "house-husband."

The day will come, I believe, when it will no longer be necessary for any woman to refer to herself as merely a "housewife." And when that day comes there will open out before women such a future of accomplishment and satisfaction as we can only dream of today. . . .

Women's attempt to achieve equality with men involves an especially difficult, concealed and subtle struggle because women are not isolated in ghettos but live in intimate daily relationship with the "superior" sex, a relationship infinitely complex and entangled with biological, economic and social factors.

Even many otherwise progressive men cling to their vested interest in male superiority, and many women are so committed to the seeming security of their inferior yet "protected" position that they echo the voteless, propertyless, completely dependent women of a century ago who declared to Elizabeth Cady Stanton and Susan B. Anthony that they already had "all the rights they wanted." In this sense one might say it is true that "women like to be dominated," that they tend to take on the convictions and standards of fathers and husbands, of any men on whom they become dependent. It is an attitude common among people who have found that their security depends on approval of some powerful individual or group. Some women lose no opportunity to attack members of their sex; the Dr. Marynia Farnham who with Ferdinand Lundberg wrote *Modern Woman—The Lost Sex* (and followed it with "The Tragic Failure of America's Women" in the September *Coronet* magazine) is no less contemptible in her betrayal of her sex, and especially of those great women who fought to achieve for her the advantages she enjoys today—such as a medical career—than is Milton Mayer, who as a Jew attacked the Jewish people in the *Saturday Evening Post,* or Warren Brown, a Negro who insulted his people in the *Reader's Digest*.

The assumption of woman's inferiority has too long been accepted by both sexes as a biological fact. The James Gordon Bennetts of the world say that woman is doomed to subjection "because it is the law of nature." Frederick Engels, however, has a different slant on it. In earliest gens society, according to him, there was no place for domination and subjection, either social or sexual. The division of labor was natural: the man waged war, hunted and fished; the woman looked after the house, prepared food and made clothes. Each was supreme in his own sphere; the man owned his tools—weapons, etc.—and the woman the household equipment. Housekeeping as well as marriage was communal (the group marriage), and whatever was made and used in common was common property of the tribe.

It was the domestication of cattle that led to the undoing of this primitive communism. At first the herds were owned in common, but as they grew and cattle became increasingly an article of exchange, ownership passed from the tribe to the individual heads of families. Prisoners of war were transformed into slaves to provide the labor necessary to this widening field of production, and there arose the first great cleavage of society into two classes: masters and slaves, exploiters and exploited. At the same time a revolution came over the family. It had always been the man's job to procure the means of existence; they therefore belonged to him, along with the commodities and slaves taken in exchange for the cattle. The woman had no share in the ownership of this surplus. As Engels puts it in *The Origin of the Family*, "The woman's household work had now dwindled in comparison with the man's labor in procuring the means of existence; the latter was all-important, the former an insignificant adjunct." At the same time monogamy arose—for the woman—because of the man's desire to bequeath his private riches to his own children and no other; it set the pattern, of course, for those as well who had no wealth to hand on. And with this unilateral monogamy came prostitution.

Hence with the rise of private property and the master and slave society woman herself became an object of exploitation. Her inferior status has persisted in every society based on the exploitation of one class by another, whether the exploited be slave, serf, or wage-earner. The great majority of women became the vassals of vassals. Cut off from the productive process, they were confined to household drudgery, were uneducated and took no part in public life. Then, much as when Negroes are excluded from education they are then accused of being ignorant, women were declared to have no brains worth mentioning. Marriage based on love—on other than property and prestige considerations—was a rarity. It was not until the beginnings of capitalism, undermining the rigid traditions of feudalism and substituting the concept of free contract for that of inherited right, that the revolutionary concept of marriage based on love began to gain ground. Until that time a woman was supposed to remain absolutely under the power of father, husband or guardian, and do nothing without his consent.

The earthquake that cracked the old prison walls around women was the industrial revolution. The introduction of machinery created a demand for cheap labor—and that meant women (and children). Working fourteen hours a day for two or three dollars a week, women found themselves in a new and more brutal kind of slavery; but at the same time, learning painfully the lesson of organization, they laid the groundwork for their freedom. For as Engels says, "*The emancipation of woman first becomes possible when she is able, on an extensive, social scale, to participate in production, and household work claims her attention only to an insignificant extent*. And this for the first time has been made possible by modern large-scale industry, which not only admits woman's labor over a wide range, but absolutely demands it, and also strives to transform private household work more and more into a public industry."

This emancipation by no means took place automatically. Every inch of the gains women have made has had to be fought for. They were fought for on the picketline in 1834 when 2,000 factory girls in Lowell, Mass., struck against a wage-cut, when women umbrella-makers went out in 1863 against seventy cents for an eighteen-hour day—conducting their struggles not only against their employers but against the overwhelming prejudice against "un-feminine" women who asserted their rights in any form. They were fought for in legislatures, on the platforms, in the church, in the home. They were fought for within men's trade unions and within Abolitionist circles, where women had to do battle for their right to help end Negro slavery.

The greatest leaders of this struggle in the nineteenth century were Susan B. Anthony and her life-long collaborator Elizabeth Cady Stanton. Susan Anthony is at least a remembered name today, although there are a few who have any idea of her momentous contributions. But Elizabeth Cady Stanton is truly America's most forgotten woman. Yet when she died in 1902 she was called by some "the greatest woman the world ever produced." It is hard to accuse her admirers of over-enthusiasm, for it is doubtful if any woman had ever done more for the human race than Mrs. Stanton. While Susan Anthony provided the great organizing talent, and the single-minded drive to achieve the vote for women, Mrs. Stanton might be called the theoretician of the movement: she attacked along the political, economic and psychological fronts.

From the day in 1848 when, discouraged in such a revolutionary step by all her friends but Frederick Douglass, she demanded the vote for women at the first Women's Rights Convention, she brought forward one issue after another—divorce, education, sensible clothing, religion—and brilliantly showed their relation to woman's struggle for equality. She was an ardent Abolitionist. The abuse heaped on her by outraged men and women alike merely made her more militant as the years passed. In her old age she became, though of middle-class background, increasingly pro-labor and attracted to socialist thought, alienating the conservative younger women for whom suffrage had become "respectable." In addition to bringing up seven children she wrote and spoke— she agitated—continuously throughout her long life. It is an indication of the shameful neglect of the heritage of the women's rights movement that such a woman can be virtually forgotten today. (Her life is described in an excellent biography by Alma Lutz, *Created Equal*.)

Of course, the roll of honor in the women's struggle is a long one: Mary Wollstonecraft, Lucretia Mott, Wendell Phillips, Frederick Douglass, William H. Sylvis are there, to name only a few. Every woman today who votes, speaks her mind, gains an education or enters a career owes them an immeasurable debt.

Yes, women are in industry and public life to stay. But still after a century a draftsman (f.) will be turned down in nine shops out of ten solely because she belongs to the wrong sex; if she's hired she'll be paid less; and if she should have children she might just as well forget the whole thing. For since capitalism's preferred use of woman is as a source of cheap labor it only reluctantly makes use of her higher talents as she develops them, and makes little provisions for the mother who must (or wants to) work. For a society that eagerly welcomes woman's entrance into new fields and lays the economic and legal foundations for her full participation, we must turn to socialism and the Soviet Union.

It is not a mere matter of expediency that women have been brought into social production in the Soviet Union. True, in a society in which there is no class of profit-makers to stand as a barrier against full production and full employment every mind and pair of hands is welcome; but there are larger issues involved. They can be summed up in Lenin's famous phrase, "Every cook must learn to govern." No Soviet woman is forced to work if she would rather stay home and live on her husband's wages (and many still do); but it is a basic principle of Soviet thought that woman must assume responsibility outside the home if she is to realize all her potentialities as citizen, wife, mother and creative individual.

To this end the Soviet Union has established a network of aid to women, and especially mothers, that is without parallel in other countries. Space forbids extensive description here: most notable are the factory and neighborhood nurseries that, staffed by trained specialists, care for the children while their mothers work; the three months' maternity leave with pay; the free medical care and the monthly grants for each child after the third. No job is barred to a Soviet woman on account of her sex. The only limitations are: (1) her physical ability (and the picture changes as rapidly as mechanization progresses and her muscular inferiority becomes irrelevant); (2) her educational and technical qualifications. Soviet women do not yet hold an equal number of skilled jobs or directorial posts, for they are still paying for centuries of ignorance. But this handicap is fast being overcome. Every factory and farm has become an educational center; women who were eighty percent illiterate in 1917 already by 1939 formed half the student body in higher institutions of learning. By 1946 women constituted twenty-one percent of the deputies in the Supreme Soviet. In other fields they have forged ahead even more rapidly: today, for instance, over half the Soviet Union's doctors are women.

As a consequence a momentous change has taken place in Soviet family life. With women no longer economically dependent on fathers or husbands the groundwork has been laid for completely free marriages based on equality and mutual love. The Soviet family has, after the early upheaval of the civil war period, been constantly strengthened through the years. At the time of the Nazi attack prostitution and venereal diseases had been all but wiped out—a revolutionary achievement in itself, done not through jailing prostitutes but primarily through an attack on the economic causes of prostitution. The divorce rate is steadily declining; even when "postcard divorces" were still obtainable they were used less and less frequently. Women have become more intelligent mothers and more interesting companions as wives. As mothers, they not only have learned improved techniques from their contact with the nurseries but because of their activities outside the home they do not fasten themselves upon their children as their only means of fulfillment—to the detriment of the children as well as themselves—and do not end up "ex-mothers," with no function left to them, once their children have grown—as is often the case in our society. As wives, an indication of the changed attitude was the play *Tanya*, produced in Moscow about ten years ago, in which the heroine gave up her medical studies when she married and stayed home, becoming the "little woman." As a result she had nothing but trivialities to offer her husband in the way of conversation and he became attracted to another woman who had an interesting job. The happy ending came only when the heroine went back to her career—the Hollywood thesis in reverse.

In America today one out of three marriages ends in divorce, a startling fact which has been the subject of innumerable magazine articles and sermons. But no moral preachments can disguise the fact that it is Communist Russia that is establishing new highs in family stability while capitalist America is witnessing an increasing breakdown in family relationships.

The conclusion is unavoidable that the one is a reflection of the cooperative relationships that permeate the whole of socialist society, while the other mirrors the insecurity and corrosive stresses of our competitive system.

Freedom, as Engels noted, is the recognition of necessity. When Frederick Douglass as a slave in Baltimore came to understand the basis and meaning of the slave system he was already in a profound sense freer than the man who "owned" him. As we grow in understanding of the historical impulses involved in man-woman relationships we begin to free ourselves of ancient concepts concerning women and begin to see more clearly the path toward equality.

For instance: we are told that "you can never trust a woman," that women are tricky and devious. What is the reality? The reality is that any oppressed people who cannot meet their oppressors on an equal footing resort to guerrilla tactics—whether they are Greek antifascists, Negroes, Chinese peasants or women. The woman who has to beg, wheedle or nag her husband for a new coat—or maneuver him into thinking that he had the idea in the first place—is talking to a man who holds a position of economic superiority and she cannot discuss the question with him as an equal.

Again, it is a fact that there are fewer good speakers among women than men. It is usually the man who can order his thoughts better, can proceed on a direct course to the logical end of an argument. It is a woman more often than a man who substitutes emotion for reason. If, on the other hand, she thinks logically, then she "thinks like a man."

Of course there are many exceptions to these generalizations, and as women grow in activity and self-confidence the generality in regard to them becomes increasingly less valid. For it is precisely because woman has been excluded from the productive process and hence from the larger activities and problems outside the home that she does find these difficulties in expressing herself as a human, thinking person. In a society in which every young girl learns that the worst thing she can do is appear more intelligent or better informed than the boy who takes her to the movies it is hardly surprising that those same girls later find difficulties in expressing themselves which no man could ever possibly encounter.

Hence when we talk about the need to bring women into leadership in unions and other organizations we face a double problem. For it is true that women are not today as equipped for leadership as men—for reasons which by now should be clear. Even in the Soviet Union women do not as yet occupy the highest political positions: the newsreels show that the May Day observers on Lenin's tomb are still all men. But while the Soviet government has a conscious political philosophy and program designed to bring women into equality, ours does not; and it is here that we reach the other aspect of the problem. For it is up to the progressive movement to supply that conscious leadership. Women must continue to be a major force in their own liberation, but they can move ahead only in common action with the working class. And that means activity based on Marxist understanding: it means the trade-union organization of millions of women as yet unreached; it means a serious attack on male chauvinism, and its reflection among women; it means the conscious effort to find abilities among women where they are not immediately apparent. It means that a man who does half of the household chores after he and his wife have come home from work will not feel that he is doing his wife a favor; for equality cannot be given as a favor but only recognized as a fact.

And it means, finally, struggle together with such organizations as the Congress of American Women for price and rent control, for the rights of the doubly-oppressed Negro women, for nurseries, for protective legislation and equal pay—in short, for a fuller democracy. Without this larger struggle the attempt to throw off woman's historical restrictions cannot be successful.

This new year, as we mark the hundredth anniversary of the publication of the *Communist Manifesto*, we will mark also a hundred years of the organized fight for equality of American women that began with the Seneca Falls convention. Those two events are linked by more than a common date. More and more we come to see that it is only the socialism foreshadowed by Marx and Engels, abolishing as it does all forms of exploitation of one human being by another, that can make it possible for women to achieve real equality. That can give substance to the ringing declaration adopted at that woman's convention holding it to be self-evident "that all men and women are created equal."

102
United Electrical, Radio, and Machine Workers of America
UE Fights for Women Workers (1952)

FOREWORD

Since our Organization in 1936, our Union, the UE, has carried on an unceasing fight against the longstanding discrimination of companies against women's rates of pay, their job security and their right to work at all jobs in the plant. Basic to this fight for the rights of our women members was the understanding that this discrimination against women was a weapon that employers daily used to undermine all rates and to reap billions of dollars of extra profits.

In this struggle to end discrimination, UE has won many victories and has been able to prove before government agencies how companies discriminate and the extent of the discrimination. These victories, precedents and experience can be of invaluable help in overcoming the substantial discrimination still practiced by companies against women workers in the industry.

The purpose of this pamphlet, therefore, is to expose the trickery used by companies to

Reprinted with permission of United Electricians.

conceal and "explain" the double exploitation of women workers, and to set forth how UE locals have been able to win the elimination of rate discrimination against women. Armed with this knowledge, UE locals who put up a determined fight can force the companies in our industry to end discrimination against women.

There are other problems facing women workers—adequate care for their children, the need for a government program of day nurseries, problems of maternity leave, health protection—the need to train women for leadership in the union. UE members must pay increasing attention to these problems. But the key problem for the union at this time is the elimination of the basic economic exploitation of women workers, a problem the entire union can and must attack now in the interests of all our members.   ERNEST THOMPSON, Secretary, National UE Fair Practice Committee

HOW INDUSTRY EXPLOITS WOMEN WORKERS

In advertisements across the land, industry glorifies the American woman—in her gleaming GE kitchen, at her Westinghouse Laundromat, before her Sylvania television set. Nothing is too good for her—unless she works for GE, or Westinghouse, or Sylvania or thousands of other corporations throughout the U.S.A.

As an employee, regardless of her skill she is rated lower common labor (male). She is assigned to jobs which, according to government studies, involve greater physical strain and skill than many jobs done by men—*but she is paid less than the underpaid sweeper, the least skilled men in the plant.* She is speeded up until she may faint at her machine, to barely earn her daily bread.

Wage discrimination against women workers exists in every industry where women are employed. It exists because it pays off in billions of dollars in extra profits for the companies. According to the 1950 census, the average wage of women in factories was $1,285 a year less than men. Multiply this by the 4,171,000 women in factories and you get the staggering total of 5.4 billions dollars. In just one year, U.S. corporations made *five billion four hundred million dollars in extra profits* from their exploitation of women.

Here are just a few examples of the double standard on wages in the electrical manufacturing industry:

"At a large GE plant, women who make up one-fourth of the workers are hired in at $1.22 an hour, while men are hired in at $1.47, except for common labor, which is $1.43. Most of the women work on production jobs whose highest rate is $1.34—nine cents less than the rate of an untrained sweeper. Women doing the same work as men on punch press, motor winding, stator bar insulating, wiring, electronic-tube assembly, are getting from 20 to 30 cents an hour less. GE pockets the difference—a profit on sex.

"At a large Westinghouse plant, the minimum hiring-in rate for women is $1.33. The hiring-in rate for men starts at $1.51. The highest rated job held by a woman pays $1.54½, only 3½ cents more than the male sweeper. Only a few women are in labor grades 5 and 6, equal to or slightly higher than the bottom sweeper's rate on the male key sheet. Most of the women are in grades 1 to 4, below the starting point of the male key sheet.

"At another Westinghouse plant where women do *all* the production work, and men are only used for maintenance, the common labor rate for the men is $1.42—the *highest* rate a woman can get is $1.44. These situations exist throughout GE, Westinghouse and Sylvania chains as well as in the smaller plants of the industry.

"In the lamp industry, all production work is done by women, who make up three-fourths of the total working force. These women production workers are hired in at from five to twenty cents less than men, and the *highest* rate they can make is several cents *less* than the male common labor rate. As a result, the companies make $2,619 per year on every employee in the lamp industry, compared to $1,540 per employee in the motor and generator plants where only one-quarter of the workers are women. An extra profit, on sex!"

GOVERNMENT REPORT PROVES "EXPLOITATION"

Valuable ammunition for this battle is contained in the document issued by the National War Labor Board[1] in 1945 as a result of UE's case exposing discrimination in women's rates in GE and Westinghouse. The document was based on extensive material presented by both UE and the companies at government hearings and on an inspection of plants of both companies by members of the government board.

The "exploitation" of women workers which they found exists in the same way today. The information in this document is extremely important in exposing lies the companies still are using to justify lower pay for women. The majority of women in our industry are still *segregated* by the companies on jobs to which the companies do not assign men at all. They may not actually be labeled "women's jobs." But the companies deliberately maintain an artificial separation of the work done by women from the work done by men in order to prevent comparison on the basis of the actual content of the jobs. This War Labor Board report of the historic UE case shows how to PROVE discrimination against women in the plants, not only in GE and Westinghouse, but in any company.

EVIDENCE FROM WAR LABOR BOARD

In its analysis of the job content of so-called men's and women's jobs, the Board used approaches originated by UE which are extremely useful today in determining whether discrimination exists.

[1]. Do not confuse President Roosevelt's War Labor Board of World War II with the Wage Stabilization Board which was set up under Charles E. Wilson, ex-president of GE, to freeze wages without any freeze on prices, and which cleared all decisions with the big businessmen running the mobilization setup.

They found, first, that discrimination was embodied from the beginning in the job evaluation systems of the companies.

Both GE and Westinghouse determined the content of each job by assigning points based on the skill, effort conditions of work, etc.

In Westinghouse, "the occupations or jobs filled by women are point rated on the same basis of point values for requirements of the job and responsibility, with the same allowances for job conditions as on the jobs commonly filled by men." *But then the company goes ahead and artificially assigns a lower rate to women's jobs.*

The company itself admitted that for women "the rate or range for Labor Grades do not coincide with the values on the men's scale. Basically, then we have another wage curve or key sheet for women below and not parallel with the men's curve. . . ." The company conceded that women are paid less than men for jobs which, by point evaluation, fall within the same labor grades.

In General Electric, a similar system was used assigning points to the job on the basis of the requirements, both for men and women. But after these points are assigned, the GE Job Evaluation manual states the payment for the points is on the following basis: *"for female operators the value shall be two-thirds of the value for adult male workers."*

Both companies have since claimed they do not use this type of job evaluation system anymore. But once jobs held by women have been assigned discriminatory lower rates, all other such jobs which are subsequently set up are rated on the same basis as the original jobs. Therefore, the original pattern of discrimination has continued down to the present, regardless of the kind of rating system the companies claim they are using now.

COMPARISON OF THE LOWER-RATED "WOMEN'S JOBS" AND MALE COMMON LABOR

The companies claimed that the large rate differential between the lower-rated "women's jobs" (janitress, packer, waitress, scrubwoman) and male common labor was due to a difference in physical effort.

The government board cited UE's evidence to prove this was false, by showing that the companies paid very little, if any difference, in rate where a much greater difference in physical effort was involved between two men's jobs, such as male sweeper versus a laborer digging ditches.

They cited a case in GE where the rate differential between the janitor and the scrubwoman was four times the rate differential between the janitor and the male sweeper, for no greater difference in physical effort and job conditions.

The fact that at Schenectady GE "at one time, due to war conditions, over one-quarter of the common labor force consisted of women, would seem to indicate that the element of physical effort attached to the common labor work does not warrant the large differential between that work and the lowest paid women's jobs," the board concluded.

At Westinghouse, the board stated that "the physical effort involved in the work of the male common laborers, whose work was observed, clearly did not justify the substantial difference between their rates and the rates for the least skilled women's jobs." Janitors and janitresses were doing similar work vacuuming rugs, cleaning rugs, cleaning floors, washing, waxing and mopping laboratory floors, yet were being paid substantially different rates.

COMPARISON OF THE MORE SKILLED "WOMEN'S JOBS" AND MALE COMMON LABOR

The government board stated flatly that at General Electric: *"All but a small fraction of the women's jobs are rated substantially below male common labor, despite the fact that many, if not most, of these jobs clearly involve more skill, mental aptitude and responsibility than the male common labor jobs."*

For example, the board found that assembly and insulating jobs held by women required up to twelve months of training and were given up to 120 points for skill, while a sweeper job took no training time and was given zero points for skill. For physical application, the sweeper was given 35 points, the janitor 15 points, and women on assembly jobs were given 25 to 35 points, women on insulating jobs from 30 to 35 points. The sweeper and janitor were given no points for working conditions, while some of the women's assembly jobs and most of the women's insulating jobs were given 5 points for working conditions.

"These jobs (assembly and insulating)— the two largest groups of women's incentive jobs—carried total point values ranging from 475 to 610, as against 440 for sweepers, 475 for male janitors and 480 for male 'inside shop labor,'" the board reported. *"Yet, by virtue of the one-third markdown factor in the translation of these points into rates, all of these women's jobs were rated below the male common labor jobs."*

Thus a comparison of production jobs held by women with male common labor *on the company's own job evaluation scale* shows clearly that the "women's jobs" had higher requirements. Yet the company, using the arbitrary standard that "for female operators the value shall be two-thirds of the value for male operators," put rates on women's production jobs below common labor.

COMPARISON OF THE MORE SKILLED WOMEN'S JOBS AND SIMILAR JOBS PERFORMED BY MEN ON INCENTIVE

Noting that many of the women's jobs were on incentive, and therefore many of the women (by speed-up) earned up to and above common labor day rates, the board found by comparing these jobs with similar men's incentive jobs that the differential in the base rates still could not be justified. *To find out if discrimination exists on women's incentive jobs, it's still true today as the UE showed the War Labor Board in 1945 that you have to disregard incentive earnings and compare base rates.*

Sometimes men, and even women, fall for the company's trick figure if a woman is able to increase her earnings on incentive; there is no discrimination. They fail to see that if the woman's base rate was set in terms of actual job content instead of being based on discrimination, she would not be forced to speed up in order to earn enough to exist on.

For both GE and Westinghouse, the government board found that "in comparing women's jobs with men's jobs which correspond more closely to the operation performed by the women, and which are also on incentive, differences appear which cannot adequately be explained by reference only to differences in job content."

At GE for example, in winding jobs there are differences of 31 cents between men and women on similar jobs, working on the same size of wire, under identical conditions, except that men were working on larger frames. In coil insertions, there was a difference of 40 cents an hour between men and women. While the men's work in coil insertion required double winding instead of single winding and the use of a heavier hammer, the women, in addition to the hammer, had to use a tool similar to a screw driver which called for considerable physical effort involving hands, wrists and forearms. According to the board, *"it seemed particularly strange that jobs of this sort should be rated even below the job of male sweeper."*

Coil winding jobs in GE, where a difference of 50 mills (one-twentieth of an inch) in the size of the wire on the men's and women's jobs was the only basis for a 41-cent wage differential, were cited by the board to *"illustrate rather dramatically a condition running all through the plants involving a differential between men's and women's rates, which in its full extent cannot fairly be explained as attributable solely to differences in job content."*

In Westinghouse also, the differences between men's and women's rates for similar jobs could not be explained on the basis of comparison of the jobs. The 19-cent difference in rates between male and female packers working side by side in Westinghouse and performing identical tasks except that the men pack larger cartons could not be justified "on any usual theory of job evaluation," said the board. Male winders working with wires only slightly heavier than women winders received much higher rates. Enormous differences appeared in the rates for male and female punch press operators, drill press operators and testers of instruments and relays.

BOARD CONCLUSION AS TO EXTENT OF SEX DIFFERENTIALS

The government document stated: *"On the basis of the entire record, we conclude that the union has established the existence in the plants of both companies of substantial differentials between rates for women's jobs and men's jobs which cannot be justified on the basis of comparative job content.... In our final discussions with the parties, the representatives of both companies virtually conceded that the differentials could not be justified on the basis of job content."*

It must be emphasized that although the UE case before the War Labor Board was concerned with GE and Westinghouse, the findings are applicable to every plant in the industry where discrimination exists.

Is There Any Justification?

The companies claimed there were other grounds for paying women lower rates. Their arguments—still being used by industry generally to justify wage discrimination against women—were completely exposed by the UE before the War Labor Board as company propaganda. They can be met with statistics from other government sources that also prove them lies.

The Companies Say:

"Women are young, temporary workers. They quit after a few years to get married." "The greater turnover of women, the special services they require, make it necessary to pay them lower rates."

The Facts Are:

The U.S. Census Bureau reveals that one out of every two women workers in American industry is at least 35 years old, and most of these older workers have held onto their present jobs for at least five years.

The National War Labor Board rejected these company arguments in World War II, laying down the principle that "intangible alleged cost factors incident to the employment of women could not legitimately be used to reduce the rates to which the women would otherwise be entitled on the basis of job content." In the GE and Westinghouse cases, the Board said, "no evidence of such costs was introduced."

The Companies Say:

"Women don't have families to support. They work for pin money." "General sociological factors justify lower pay for women."

The Facts Are:

According to government figures, one out of every four women workers have children under 18 whom they must support. One out of every five is either widowed, divorced or separated from her husband. Many have to work because they are war widows, wives of disabled veterans, or of men now in the army. But most women work because their husband's pay is inadequate to support the family needs. *93% of all women work because they have to support themselves or their families.*

The Companies Say:

"Women are simply worth less for purposes of factory employment than men."

The Facts Are:

The attitude on the part of GE management—that women are somehow inferior workers "worth less" to the company—was revealed by UE's government case to be the greatest hoax of all to justify wage differentials. Stated the National War Labor Board, after its survey of GE and Westinghouse plants:

"If men were to be substituted for women on the so-called women's jobs there would probably be a very real loss in efficiency and productivity, since it is recognized that men are not as well adapted as women for light, repetitive work requiring finger dexterity. The productive worth of women on the jobs to which they are customarily assigned, if fairly weighed, might well offset any added production costs resulting from such factors as absenteeism, transient character of service, etc."

Even the National Association of Manufacturers stated, in May 1942: "There is little difference between men and women as regards their satisfactory performance in industry."

The Companies Say:

"Women aren't as strong as men. They need extra help for heavy lifting etc."

The Facts Are:

The overemphasis on physical effort is a trick often used by companies to justify sex differentials. Actually, physical effort alone has little to do with the value of a job on the company's own scales, which place common labor digging ditches at the lower end and tool and die makers at the top. But, insofar as physical effort is one factor in a job's value, the Women's Bureau of the U.S. Department of Labor, in a survey in 1951 of the electrical industry, pointed out that:

"The constant arm and finger movements involved in many women's jobs were, in the course of a day, probably more wearing in many cases than the occasional lifting of a 30- or 40-pound box." The jobs done by women "often involve close attention to work and concentration that is fatiguing."

It's true that women can't lift as heavy weights as men, even though the companies used to demand it of them before they had the protection of a UE contract.

But the ability to lift heavy weights is actually only a very small part of the valuation placed on a job by the companies themselves. Out of 33 sample jobs rated by the National Electrical Manufacturers Association, only two were given as many as 40 points for "Physical effort" out of a total possible evaluation of 500 points. Physical effort at the most constitutes less than 10% of the evaluation the company places on the job.

On more skilled women's jobs where they may be doing the same work as men except for a difference in the size or weight of the material, the difference in physical effort required is hardly ever sufficient to justify as great a rate differential as the companies claim.

The Companies Say:

"Our rates for women are in line with established community practice. Industry has always paid women less. We're justified because every company does it."

The Facts Are:

This argument was rejected by the government board in the GE and Westinghouse case, as follows:

"If this contention were sound, it would follow that no exploitation of any group could be ended (save by voluntary action) if it constituted the common practice of the employers in the locality. The real question is whether any exploitation exists. If it does exist, as we believe that it does from the evidence in this case, it should be ended, and the fact that others practice it ought not to stand as a bar."

"The claim of community and industry practice cannot be advanced as a sound reason for doing nothing to correct an injustice which patently exists," the board stressed. "Moreover, these companies as the whole or dominant employer in the community in many instances, may have themselves initiated or supported the practice."

The Real Reason for Discrimination

Big business has found it profitable to maintain the old superstition that women are "inferior" to men. Not long ago women were considered men's "chattels," with no rights at all of their own. They had no vote, could hold no property separate from their husbands.

It is no accident that big business all over the world fought the movement for votes and equal rights for women. For in their factories, the public acceptance of women's equality would mean the loss of a huge source of labor they could segregate and exploit for extra profits, and as a means to hold down the wages of all workers.

The following memorandum from the government's Women's Bureau was quoted by the Board as the explanation of why women were originally discriminated against when they came into industry and why they are discriminated against still.

"In any early period when women were first entering industry as a new part of the labor force, carrying over into the factory household skills that were not given a high money value in the public mind, women were paid at lower scales of wages than those usually paid men. In this they suffered from the same type of wage exploitation that ordinarily has occurred with the entrance of any new group to industry, such as migrant workers or those of different nationalities or races. . . .

"From this, two parallel wage structures grew up, one for men and one for women, the latter fixed on a lower scale, frequently without valid reasons that would hold up under objective tests. Frequently, and especially where women are involved, wage rates have been determined by tradition or custom or prejudice wholly unrelated to the requirements of the job or its exactions from the workers. . . .

"These low pay scales for women were continued long after women had demonstrated their efficiency in various skilled occupations, even though industry came to depend on their work to an increasing extent. There were several reasons why this was so, not the least being that there has been little public understanding of the serious effects of this situation on the American economy as a whole."

A GE company representative admitted to the investigator from the Women's Bureau of the Labor Department, in 1951, the real reason for lower rates for women: "because women's job opportunities had been relatively limited in industry in the past, it had been possible to get them to work for less than men, and employers took advantage of this fact to underpay women."

"I'd hate to have to be the one to have to sit across the bargaining table trying to justify differentials," the GE representative said.

Then why do the companies keep on trying to justify lower pay for women?—*because it means extra profits*. That's why they try to convince the men in the plant, and the women themselves, that women shouldn't get as much as men. That's why for fifteen years they have so bitterly opposed the UE's demands to end rate differentials against women.

The Situation Today

After UE exposed the exploitation of women in GE and Westinghouse before the War Labor Board in 1945, GE claimed it threw away the old job evaluation plan under which all women's jobs were automatically paid for at two-thirds of the rate paid to men. It also allegedly discarded its separate key sheet for women. GE merely re-designated the "women's jobs" as "light" or "simple" jobs in each category and the "men's jobs" as "heavy" or "complicated." The rate differential remained unchanged.

Then to further confuse the situation and make it more difficult to detect the discrimination against women, GE discarded even the "light" and "heavy" distinction and set up a single key sheet—in which jobs held by women were simply added to the bottom of the men's scale, below the common labor rate. In many cases the code number of the job remained the same during each change, as did the rate differential. See below how an assembly job held by women at a large GE plant has remained unchanged in its relation to a male sweeper's job even though the company now uses a single key sheet. The special adjustments for women won as a result of UE's fight in 1945 and 1946, and all the other wage increases won by UE for both men and women, still left the women's production job, with requirements well above the sweeper's job, at a rate below sweeper.

Actually, the above woman's assembly job with an AER of $1.34 should not be compared with the sweeper's job but with the lowest man's assembly job with an AER of $1.47. The lowest man's assembly job at this GE plant has a rate of $1.47, and these men's assembly jobs complement and are performed on the same assembly lines with the women's jobs rated at $1.34. Moreover, the discrimination against women is measured not only by the difference in AERs between men and women, but also by the fact that the lower AER means a lower take-out on incentive earnings.

The above job held by women was one of thousands the company upped in 1945 and 1946 as a result of UE pressure. But many other jobs held by women, including jobs at the lowest rates, and the hiring-in rates, did not get special increases to eliminate the discrimination. Consequently, the differential in cents per hour between the hiring-in rates of men and women is the same as it was in 1945 when the War Labor Board ruled that the company take steps to eliminate the differential—that is, about 15 cents per hour. If starting rates of women production jobs at GE are compared with starting rates of men's production jobs, the differential is about 25 cents an hour.

Through UE efforts in GE women's straight time earnings, which were only 70.3 percent of men's in April 1945, were raised to 78 percent of men's earnings in 1952, but the differential is still substantial throughout the chain.

A parallel situation exists in Washington, although UE was able there to raise not only individual women's jobs, but entire women's labor grades. As a result, the differential in hiring-in rates as well as between men's and women's labor grade rates has been narrowed. . . .

At some Westinghouse plants such as Jersey City and S. Philadelphia, the differential between men's and women's rates has been entirely eliminated by UE.

In the Sylvania chain, UE's battle on wage discrimination against women also forced the company to discard its separate women's key sheet. Sylvania, like GE, set up a single key sheet, but simply took all the women's jobs and added them at the bottom of the men's sheet below common labor, as the first six labor grades. Since the new key sheet was supposed to be based on proper job evaluation, they had to create a new basis for rating the women's jobs lower than men's.

So they arbitrarily set up a base factor of 200 points for all jobs done by men, and a base factor of 100 points for all jobs done by women, before adding in the factors for actual job content. If the man's job and the woman's job received an equal valuation on every single factor, this arbitrary base factor would still make the man's job rate 100 points higher.

Now Sylvania has started to put men into those first six labor grades, which were created to maintain lower rates for women. As a result of this rate discrimination against women, Sylvania has been able to put men on production jobs at rates below common labor.

The situation in the electrical machinery industry as a whole reflects the situation in General Electric, Westinghouse and Sylvania. As of July 1948, the latest date for which such information is available, the differential between men's and women's average hourly earnings in electrical manufacturing was 35 cents. Not only were women's average hourly earnings considerably below the average for men, but women's earnings were even 7½ cents an hour below the average for *unskilled* men. In other industries the differential is even greater.

Special Situation of Negro Women

The situation of Negro women workers today is even more shocking.

Even more than white women, Negro women have to work to live. For the discrimination that keeps Negro men at the bottom of the pay scale forces their wives to work to supplement the pitifully inadequate income of the family.

But Negro women are barred from almost all jobs except low-paying domestic service in private homes, or menial outside jobs as janitresses and scrubwomen. In the basic sections of the electrical, radio and machine industry, as in industry generally, Negro women are not employed. In lamp plants and others where Negro women have been hired as a source of cheap labor, they suffer the exploitation of all women working under discriminatory rates of pay because of their sex.

UE's fair practices committees in many local unions have been fighting the discrimination against hiring the Negro women in the electrical and machine industry, and the discriminatory practices that restrict Negro women to the most menial, lowest-paid jobs. But electrical apparatus plants and other basic sections of the industry still discriminate on a large scale against Negro women, and for the most part today Negro women are not employed in the industry. Negro women workers have a real stake in the UE's fight to end rate exploitation of women in industry, but their problems also require a special fight to lift the double bars against hiring of Negro women.

How to Tackle Rate Discrimination

The campaign that UE is waging today to wipe out rate discrimination against women is realistic. It recognizes that legislation has not succeeded in wiping out this discrimination—for in the 11 states which now have laws requiring "equal pay for equal work" most women in industry are still working at lower pay than men.

UE's program demands an investigation of the actual rate structure in every plant and reslotting of all jobs held by women on the basis of the actual job content, starting with common labor as a base as it is for jobs held by men.

The Labor Department's 1951 *"Case Studies in Equal Pay for Women"* revealed that "equal pay" state laws do not keep companies from underpaying women workers unless the union tackles the actual rate structure to wipe out lower rates on jobs done by women. Most of the women in the electrical manufacturing industry are employed on jobs which the companies segregate as exclusively "women's jobs" so that they cannot so easily be compared to jobs done by men. The Labor Department revealed that GE actually set up "women's jobs" where they didn't already exist in order to get around equal pay laws and keep on paying the women lower rates.

Describing a GE plant in New York State, the Labor Department said:

"When the State equal-pay law was adopted in 1944, those women doing the same jobs as men were either raised to the same rate that men were getting, or their jobs were broken down or altered in some way so that they were no longer doing exactly the same work as the men." For instance, GE's regular packing department "was divided into a light packing department staffed and supervised by women and a heavy packing department staffed and supervised by men, and the men were paid a higher rate than the women."

But this same study by the Women's Bureau of the Labor Department was able to cite examples in the electrical industry where specific contract guarantees won by the UE and the union action on the rate structure not only achieved equal pay for men and women on the same job, but prevented the company from paying lower rates on any jobs done by women.

The Labor Department described a radio plant in New York City where UE Local 430 has completely wiped out lower rates for women on an industry-wide basis:

In 1942, in the plant, women were being paid between 42 and 55 cents per hour and men's rates ranged from 52 cents to $1.26 per hour. Women doing the same jobs as men were paid from 5 to 24 cents less. Today women are paid the same as men not only where they are doing the same jobs but in all jobs in the plant. The dual wage structure has been eliminated.

The UE obtained a clause in its contract spelling out: *"There shall be no discrimination against any employee either in hiring, promoting, advancement or assigning of jobs or with respect to any other terms or conditions of employment because of such employees' union membership or activity, sex, race, creed, color or religious affiliation."*

The union also won company agreement for a job evaluation, on which the Labor Department document says: "The company wanted to continue the sex differentials in the rates to be set, on the ground that the women's work was lighter. The union opposed this. The case went to the War Labor Board, which ruled in favor of the single rate scale, and women's rates were adjusted to bring them into line with men's."

There are no lower paid "women's jobs" in this UE plant. States the Labor Department: "There is a job classification plan, with job descriptions and rates for key jobs. . . . Rates are set with reference to these key jobs, and without regard to whether they are performed by men or women."

Here are a few other examples of successful UE battles against rate discrimination:

"At International Harvester, women's rates used to be 20 cents an hour lower than men's. The union fought for and succeeded in establishing a single rate structure, slotting jobs for both men and women upward from the common labor rate. This not only raised rates for Harvester women, but for men too.

"At General Cable, there were two separate rate structures and two separate seniority lists for men and women when UE organized the chain. The UE won a single rate structure and a single seniority list, with no discrimination between men and women. Not only are there no discriminatory lower rates for women, but no separate women's jobs in General Cable. Under the UE contract, women are upgraded up to the highest skilled jobs in the plant, such as precision tool and diamond die-making. The segregation of women on separate jobs at the bottom of the rate scale has been completely eliminated by the UE in this chain."

In summary, wiping out discriminatory lower rates for women requires setting up a single rate structure, from the common labor rate to the highest skilled job, with jobs held by women reclassified according to their actual job requirements to eliminate discrimination as compared to jobs held by men. When this is done, the women's rates that fall below common labor are abolished. For *rated according to the employer's own job evaluation categories*—education, experience, physical effort, responsibility, working conditions, mental and visual effort, hazards, etc.—*the simplest production job held by women falls at least as high as common labor and in most cases higher.*

Note that the simplest women's assembly or production job requires at least three months training. In lamp, electronics, radio tube and television plants, production jobs held by women require the most concentrated use of the eyes up to actual assembly under a microscope, to the extent that eye defects are common among women after several years at this work. The great majority of women workers in these plants work under very disagreeable working conditions of heat and ventilation, in temperatures up to 120 degrees, to the point that fainting on the job is not uncommon. They are liable to danger from flying glass, beryllium poisoning and exposure to other chemicals that cause dermatitis and other skin eruptions.

The employers' most frequent excuse for rating these women's jobs below the male sweeper is "less physical effort." Many women's jobs require a great deal more physical effort than sweeping floors. Since physical effort comprises less than 10% of the total value of the job on the employer's scale and since the difference in physical effort between the sweeper's job and the simplest woman's assembly job is more than outweighed by the greater skill and mental and visual concentration required of the woman assembler, all jobs held by women should be reclassified to bring them at least to the common labor rate. The more skilled women's jobs should be reslotted at the proper point above the common labor rate by comparison with similar production jobs held by men in the plant.

Men's Business Too

Companies make so much extra profit out of their exploitation of women that they bitterly resist attempts to make them stop it. That's why over the years they've filled men workers and even the women workers themselves with propaganda that women aren't worth as much as men in a factory—and that if women got more they'd be taking money or jobs away from the men. The last thing the companies want is for the women and men to get together to fight this profitable double standard on wages, as they are doing today in UE.

That's why the UE can't fight this battle merely over the bargaining table with the company but must conduct an educational campaign in the shop and the community to expose the bosses' propaganda and show how the exploitation of women hurts all the workers in the plant.

It's an actual fact that lower rates for women are being used by the companies today to cut rates for men. In Westinghouse, East Pittsburgh, the company took jobs paying $1.45 to $1.48 an hour when done by men and put women on them for $1.30 to $1.38 an hour. UE Local 601 members fought together with IUE rank and file workers to stop this, but IUE-CIO made a deal with the company which is now introducing the same system throughout the plant. In GE's Locke Insulator plant in Baltimore, UE Local 120 is fighting an attempt by the company to layoff the 13 most senior men in a large department by putting in new machines to be run by women at below the common labor rate.

It's obvious that as long as these discriminatory women's rates below common labor exist, all men's rates are endangered. It's an established principle that the lowest rates in a plant are the basis upon which all other rates are constructed. Thus, low rates for women hold down the entire rate structure.

The Illinois Department of Labor pointed out in its October 1951, bulletin: "Establishment of the principle of equal pay for women is essential to a healthy economy. It protects wage levels, not only of women workers but of all workers and thereby sustains consumer purchasing power.

"It is an axiom that when large numbers of workers can be hired at lower rates of pay than those prevailing at any given time, the competition of such persons for jobs results either in the displacement of the higher paid workers or in the acceptance by them of a lower rate. Over a period of time this tends to depress all wage levels, and unless this tendency can be halted, it results eventually in lower levels of earnings for all, with a resulting reduction in purchasing power, and in standard of living."

It's not higher rates for women that threatens men's earnings, but the present lower rates for women that now exist in some plants. For all companies are introducing these new processes and machines to be run by women at lower rates. The higher-paid men are to be laid off. Eventually the company may put men on the job at the lower rate they established for the women—unless these discriminatory rates are abolished now.

It works the same way with speedup. *Because women's base rates are so low, they are forced to speedup to make a living wage. The company is then able to force the men in the plant to speedup accordingly.*

WOMEN MUST HAVE RIGHT TO ALL JOBS

Along with the battle to end rate discrimination against women, UE is fighting to eliminate double seniority lists wherever they exist and to win for women equal opportunities for upgrading to jobs throughout the plant.

Double seniority lists are a part of the whole pattern of discrimination the companies use to keep women segregated as "inferior" workers and confined to certain under-rated jobs so that their low pay rates can be used to keep all wages down. They are a way of keeping the workers divided and weakening the strength of the union.

The companies don't want to put women on "men's jobs"—not because they don't have the skill, but because the *segregation* of women is the only way they can maintain the discriminatory rates of pay from which they reap those extra profits. They don't want to put men on "women's jobs" in time of layoff because they'd lose the sex excuse for lower rates and they know they'd have to raise the rates for the job.

UE men and women have fought together in a number of plants recently to end these discriminatory practices in seniority and job opportunities. At Westinghouse Airbrake in Pittsburgh, UE Local 610 eliminated the dual seniority list that had existed in the plant and established in their contract that layoffs be conducted strictly in accordance with length of service, guaranteeing to both men and women the right to bump into any job in any department for which they had seniority, regardless of sex.

Recently 1,500 workers were laid off. The company wanted to transfer women only into jobs that they considered "women's jobs"—which would have meant that long-service women would have been laid off. The union told the company that the only principle operating was seniority, not sex—and that women, and men, must be laid off and transferred according to seniority throughout the plant.

As a result, 50 women were transferred into jobs and departments where no women had ever worked before—into the machining department, assembling departments, into turret lathe, milling machine, drill press, and grinding jobs. In one department 29 long-service women went in as grinders where never before had there been women grinders. Women replaced sweepers—and men from the machine shop who might otherwise have been laid off replaced shorter service women in the rubber department on what had formerly been "women's jobs."

The women who transferred into these machine, drill press and grinding jobs, etc. were given a breaking period, just as the men were. The fact that women are working alongside men on these skilled jobs in a heavy industry plant like Westinghouse Airbrake shows that it can be done in any plant in the industry.

In another basic section of the industry, the West Pullman plant of Intl. Harvester in Chicago, UE-FE Local 107 fought successfully to save 160 women from discriminatory layoff, and to give them the right to transfer jobs formerly only held by men. The company had tried to hire men from the street rather than recall these women according to their seniority.

UE'S PROGRAM FOR WOMEN

The UE 17th convention resolved to adopt and give its unqualified support to the following program in the fight for women's rights:

The lowest rate in every plant shall be the common labor rate of men or a sweeper's rate. No women shall be paid any rate lower than the common labor rate.

The rate structure should be re-examined, and all jobs, particularly those performed by women, should be reclassified above the common labor rate according to job content.

Make the company provide adequate health and safety safeguards for all workers.

Eliminate double seniority lists for men and women wherever they exist.

Give special attention to problems of married women growing out of family responsibility, such as shifts and absenteeism.

Eliminate discriminatory hiring practices against married women, Negro women, etc., where they exist.

Campaign for government-financed child care centers for working mothers as were provided in World War II.

Press fight against speedup which is causing accidents and ill health among women workers.

Guarantee the life and militancy of the union by developing, training and electing women to all levels of leadership.

See that Fair Practices Committees are functioning in every shop.

103

HYDE PARK CHAPTER, CHICAGO WOMEN'S LIBERATION UNION

Socialist Feminism: A Strategy for the Women's Movement (1972)

INTRODUCTION

We have written this paper to express and share with other women ideas for a new strategy for the women's movement. Currently there are two ideological poles, representing the prevailing tendencies within the movement. One is the direction toward new lifestyles within a women's culture, emphasizing personal liberation and growth, and the relationship of women to women. Given our real need to break loose from the old patterns—socially, psychologically, and economically—and given the necessity for new patterns in the post-revolutionary society, we understand, support and enjoy this tendency. However, when it is the sole emphasis, we see it leading more toward a kind of formless insolation rather than to a condition in which we can fight for and win power over our own lives.

The other direction is one which emphasizes a structural analysis of our society and its economic base. It focuses on the ways in which productive relations oppress us. This analysis is also correct, but its strategy, taken alone, can easily become, or appear to be, insensitive to the total lives of women.

From Heather Booth, Day Creamer, Susan Davis, Deb Dobbin, Robin Kaufman, and Tobey Klass, Socialist Feminism—A Strategy for the Women's Movement (Chicago: Hyde Park Chapter, Chicago Women's Liberation Union, 1972), 1–8.

As socialist feminists, we share both the personal and the structural analysis. We see a combination of the two as essential if we are to become a lasting mass movement. We think that it is important to define ourselves as socialist feminists, and to start conscious organizing around this strategy. This must be done now because of the current state of our movement. We have reached a crucial point in our history.

On the one hand, the strengths of our movement are obvious: it has become an important force of our time, and it has also succeeded in providing services and support for some women's immediate needs. Thousands of women see themselves as part of the movement; a vaguely defined "women's consciousness" has been widely diffused through rap groups, demonstrations, action projects, counter-institutional activity, and through the mass media. Women in the movement have a growing understanding of common oppression and the imperative of collective solutions. With the realization that what we saw as personal problems were in fact social ones, we have come to understand the solutions must also be social ones. With the realization that all women lack control over their lives, we have come to understand that that control can only be gained if we act together. We have come to understand the specific needs of various groups of women and that different groups of women have different ways in which they will fight for control over their own lives.

On the other hand, the women's movement is currently divided. In most places it is broken into small groups which are hard to find, hard to join, and hard to understand politically. At the same time, conservative but organizationally clever entrepreneurs are attaching themselves to the movement, and are beginning to determine the politics of large numbers of people. If our movement is to survive, let alone flourish, it is time to begin to organize for power. We need to turn consciousness into action, choose priorities for our struggles, and win. To do this we need a strategy.

Our movement's strategy must grow from an understanding of the dynamics of power, with the realization that those who have power have a vested interest in preserving it and the institutional forms which maintain it. Wresting control of the institutions which now oppress us must be our central effort if women's liberation is to achieve its goals. To reach out to most women we must address their real needs and self-interests.

At this moment we think that it is important to argue for a strategy which will achieve the following three things: 1) it must win reforms that will objectively improve women's lives; 2) it must give women a sense of their won power, both potentially and in reality; and 3) it must alter existing relations of power. We argue here for socialist feminist organizations. We are not arguing for any *one* specific organization but for the successful development of organizations so that we may be able to learn from experience and bring our movement to its potential strength.

I. SOCIALIST FEMINISM

We choose to identify ourselves with the heritage and future of feminism and socialism in our struggle for revolution. From feminism we have learned the fullness of our own potential as women, the strength of women. We have seen our common self-interest with other women and our common oppression. Having found these real bonds as women, we realize we can rely on each other as we fight for liberation. Feminism has moved us to see more concretely what becomes of people shaped by social conditions they do not control. We find our love and hate focused through our feminism—love for other women bound by the same conditions, hate for the oppression that binds us. A great strength we find in feminism is the reaffirmation of human values, ideals of sisterhood: taking care of people, being sensitive to people's needs and developing potential.

From feminism we have come to understand an institutionalized system of oppression based on the domination of men over women: sexism. Its contradictions are based on the hostile social relations set into force by this domination. This antagonism can be mediated by the culture and the flexibility of the social institutions so that in certain times and places it seems to be a stable relationship. But the antagonisms cannot be eliminated and will break out to the surface until there is no longer a system of domination.

But we share a particular conception of feminism that is socialist. It is one that focuses on how power has been denied women because of their class position. We see capitalism as an institutionalized form of oppression based on profit for private owners of publicly-worked-for wealth. It sets into motion hostile social relations in classes. Those classes too have their relations mediated through the culture and institutions. Thus alliances and divisions appear within and between classes at times clouding the intensity or clarity of their contradiction. But the basic hostile nature of class relations will be present until there is no longer a minority owning the productive resources and getting wealthy from the paid and unpaid labor of the rest.

We share the socialist vision of a humanist world made possible through a redistribution of wealth and an end to the distinction between the ruling class and those who are ruled.

We have come to understand that only through an organized collective response can we fight such a system. Sisterhood thus also means to us a struggle for real power over our own lives and the lives of our sisters. Our personal relations and our political fight merge together and create our sense of feminism. Through the concept of sisterhood, women have tried to be responsive to the needs of all women rather than a selected few, and to support, criticize and encourage other women rather than competing with them.

OUR VISION—SOCIALIST FEMINISM IS DESIRABLE AND NOT POSSIBLE UNDER THE EXISTING SYSTEM

The following would be *among* the things we envision in the new order, part of everyday life for all people:

- free, humane, competent medical care with an emphasis on preventive medicine, under the service of community organizations
- people's control over their own bodies—i.e., access to safe, free birth control, abortion, sterilization, free from coercion or social stigma
- attractive, comfortable housing designed to allow for private and collective living
- varied nutritious, abundant diet
- social respect for the work people do, understanding that all jobs can be made socially necessary and important
- democratic councils through which all people control the decisions which most directly affect their lives on the job, in the home, and community
- scientific resources geared toward the improvement of life for all, rather than conquest and destruction through military and police aggression
- varied, quality consumer products to meet our needs
- an end of housework as private, unpaid labor
- redefinition of jobs, with adequate training to prepare people for jobs of their choice; rotation of jobs to meet the life cycle needs of those working at them, as well as those receiving the services
- political and civil liberties which would encourage the participation of all people in the political life of the country
- disarming of and community control of the police
- social responsibility for the raising of children and free client-controlled childcare available on a 24-hour basis to accommodate the needs of those who use it and work in it

- free, public quality education integrated with work and community activities for people of all ages
- freedom to define social and sexual relationships
- a popular culture which enhances rather than degrades one's self respect and respect for others
- support for internal development and self-determination for countries around the world

We outline this vision to be more concrete about what a socialist feminist society might mean or try to be. This vision of society is in direct opposition to the present one which is based on the domination of the few over the many through sex, race and class. While there are concessions that it can make, the present form would not or could not adjust to the kind of people-oriented society outlined above.

CONTRADICTIONS— AN ALTERNATIVE IS NECESSARY

Socialist feminism is not only desirable but it is also necessary because the current system of capitalism is not stable and cannot last in its present form. However, this does not mean that the society will inevitably become socialist. A fascist or barbaric form is also an alternative. The system that will replace capitalism will be determined by the orientation and power of groups fighting for alternatives. Hence, we must struggle to bring our vision of socialist feminism to fruition.

Contradictions are phenomena necessary to maintain the system but by their own internal logic produce forces destructive to it. A knowledge of them helps explain the chaos around us, giving a stable context to understand the historically changing process, points for defense and attack. Examples of these contradictions are all around us in varying degrees of severity. Sexism and capitalism reinforce one another, shape each other and have shaped us.

CONTRADICTIONS IN OUR POWER

Any analysis of the distribution of power and its effects on society's institutions must recognize the historical context of our oppression. Our oppression is different from that of our sisters at the turn of the century who had no legal rights, were confined to the home, and bore children from maturity to death. Thus, what is liberating at one time may be a factor of oppression at another. For example, women were denied their own sexuality because of social attitudes, inadequate birth control, the shelter of the family, women's private role in the economy, and the lack of knowledge about their bodies. The development of a more advanced technology (the pill and machines) and education objectively gave more freedom to our sisters. At the same time, these developments also made possible new forms for the oppression of women, increased sexual objectification and abuse.

In the realm of women and work, legislation which protected women was of great benefit in easing their burden. Currently, however, in the name of easing our burden, such legislation is used to deny women equal opportunity. Of course, women and all people have a right to safe and good working conditions; but these need to be fought for all workers.

Understanding our changing history helps us to avoid stereotyping our opposition or our own notions of what liberation means. The development of a strategy makes it clear that technological advances, legislative changes or educational developments are not good or bad in themselves. When we know the *context* in which any specific change occurs, we can judge the value of that change for our goals.

We have learned from history that, in fact, what is progressive for the system as a whole is also the seeds for its destruction. For example, increasing the availability of jobs for women and encouraging talented women to enter the labor force helps employers and strengthens capitalism but at the same time gives women an opportunity to come together physically and unionize as a collective force for change. Other women, seeing this, will raise their expectations and demands on the system for a larger share than it can offer all.

Knowing that these contradictions are the reality in which we live, we can fight that otherwise supposed "monolith" of control at its weak points and gain strength for ourselves. If our analysis is correct, on the basis of those contradictions, women and other powerless people will find concrete bases for unity to struggle in their self-interest. Now we see severe contradictions and possibilities for fights for structural changes on issues of childcare (for adequate care and community control), inclusion in the political system, jobs and working conditions for workers' control, etc.

MULTI-LEVEL CONTRADICTIONS

Many analyses have identified various institutions (e.g., the family or sexual relations) as the crucial contradiction of sexism. However, these contradictions reflect the social relations of a sexist society, or institutions in which sexism occurs. Eliminating these "prime factors" would neither eliminate sexism nor necessarily create supportive alternatives for women. As the factory may be the locus for capitalist exploitation, it is not *the basis* of that exploitation. Private ownership and profit *is* the basis, giving rise to the class relations. Similarly, the family is a crucial locus of sexist oppression but *it is not the basis of that exploitation*. Control by men over women and the relegation of women to secondary roles is the basis of sexism, giving rise to a sexist society.

We do not find helpful the constant cry that before we organize, we need to develop a complete theory of the nature of our oppression or find the *prime* contradiction of our oppression (as if there is just one). Some analyses, in fact, have led us only to further inaction with the rationale of not having the whole picture.

Every institution oppresses women as long as the society is based on the oppression of women. Our struggle against sexism is against those institutions, social relations and ideas which divide women and keep them powerless, and subservient to men. At different periods our oppression may be greater in one area than another, and this should direct our struggle.

The social relations of society—its institutions, culture and ideology—grow out of this system. But these ideas take on a life of their own, no longer dependent on or necessary to the economic base. In fact, they can develop in contradiction to that base. So, for example, racism or sexism serve much more than narrow economic function. Thus, what is important is not just redistribution of goods but a change in authority, control and ideas. Clearly, all elements of a class society are not reflections of the economic relations; however, *in the last instance* (at the point where contradictions become revolutionary in dimension) economic relations are the crucial link.

Contradictions at every level of society influence each other and within each level (economic, social, ideological) they are mirrored and overdetermined. That is, the pace at which contradictions develop is complex, sometimes reinforcing, sometimes cancelling each other. Thus, long range planning and a carefully worked out strategy are needed to continually respond to the complexity of the contradictions in American society. But we reflect in our theory that there are contradictions and that an alternative system is 1) desirable and not possible now, and 2) necessary to provide a true end to hostilities (between classes, sexes, races, nations).

We find it futile to argue which is more primary—capitalism or sexism. We are oppressed by both. As they are systems united against our interests, so our struggle is against both. This understanding implies more than women's caucuses in a "movement" organization. What we as socialist feminists need are organizations which can work for our particular vision, our self-interest in a way that will guarantee the combined fight against sexism and capitalism. At times this will mean independent organizations, at other times joint activity recognizing specific situations and general conditions.

THE AMERICAN CONTEXT OF THE CONTRADICTIONS

The forms of oppression we face are filtered through the unique conditions of the American situation. We have a very heterogeneous working class, more diversified by ethnic background, race and job status than most other countries. This gives us many different strengths but also many internal divisions. Also, we have a heritage of slavery with an oppressed black and minority population. This now is as basic to the society as is sexism and is linked with it.

In addition, the power of the ruling class is widespread and disseminated through every aspect of the society. This makes for a difficult enemy—hard to isolate, focus on at its root, and hold accountable while its ideas filter into our minds. As the leading world imperialist power, our national struggle must consider strategic relationships linking our struggle with those around the world. Also, we live in a society with relative material comfort. This means that what we have to offer must not be just economic solutions. The question of quality of life is not only to be raised but also ideas for a new social order.

We also are cut off from our history of left struggle since the destruction of the left in the fifties. To our great lack this has sometimes denied us a sense of long-term struggle and strategy development. One of our overriding responsibilities at this particular historical period is to develop a strategy which will both call into question the validity of current economic and social relations and at the same time make socialist feminism a meaningful possibility. This will not occur except as more and more people gain the political experience necessary to develop a concrete understanding of the viability of our vision.

ROLE OF IDEOLOGY IN THE DEVELOPMENT OF STRATEGY

The preceding section outlines our ideology—socialist feminism. It is this ideology which guides the development of our strategy and tactics, sets our priorities, and gives us an overall focus for our work. The key ideological understanding is that all issues are political, are based on power, and that our actions have political implications.

We develop this ideology both out of practice and in reading and discussion—matching theory to the real world. To an extent ideology plays the role of consciousness—it is a clear picture of reality which strengthens our ability to communicate and argue for our position. Stated explicitly, ideology helps provide links for women, in seeing how one struggle is related to others. Some individuals, aware of many social contradictions, may make an intellectual leap—understand the parts as a whole through a socialist feminist ideology.

Most people are guided by an ideology. Our own particular relationship to ideology has two special functions. First, it provides ideas which guide us, defining the framework and reason for our actions. Second, it defines our view of the world concretely, thus providing a system of analysis through which women can understand socialist feminism as a world view.

The ideological underpinnings for a socialist feminist strategy are laid out here and should be evident in the paper. But this paper is designed primarily to propose a strategy. It flows from and should help us define our ideology even better in the future; but it is a different undertaking—determining what we should do NOW.

This is one reason we feel confident in describing a strategy when we do not have the full blueprint for how revolution will occur. One is not developed full blown and then the other becomes possible.

Neither is this an attempt at overall strategy. Overall strategy helps us to see the way to seizure of state power and the critical break from the past, developing new institutions and a new social order based on equality of people and redistribution of wealth and resources. We can only develop an understanding of exactly how this will occur as we gain experience in building our movement. Continually moving from political work to further theoretical development and back to political work is a necessity. Revolution has several stages and it is important to have an understanding of the historical period we are in.

Therefore, given the ideology presented here, we have developed the following priorities for this particular point in time:

1) We must reach most women. We must work toward building a majority movement. Our analysis tells us this is possible if we proceed in the right way.

2) We must present intermediate goals that are realizable as well as desirable to show the necessity and possibility of organizing.

3) We must develop collective actions.

Now the crucial need is to weaken the power of the ruling class, give women a sense of their own power, and improve our lives so that we are welded together as a force prepared to struggle together. Concern with these issues is the basis for the socialist feminist strategy we outline in the next sections.

IV. War and Peace

A CENTRAL TENSION IN AMERICAN FEMINISM, THAT between the quest for civic equality and the conceptualization of women as inherently different from men, runs through much of the thought and literature concerning women, war, and peace. On the one hand, feminist peace activists have stressed the creative and nurturing nature of women, the sex's intrinsic ability as mothers to empathize with other women about the death of those they brought into the world. On the other hand—and in sharp contrast to the essentialist notion of the distinct female capacity for creation, compassion, and protection—some American feminists have pushed for the military to open itself up to women who want to serve and realize the prestige and benefits U.S. society has historically bestowed on its citizen soldiers. In coming to terms with the maternalistic dimension of early-twentieth-century feminist pacifism, keep in mind that the nurturing benevolent feminine ideal was one half of a modern gender ideology that viewed men as inherently aggressive, violent, and brutish—traits that could and would be emphasized in motivating American men to kill and risk death in modern warfare. Rooted in Darwinian theories of evolution, this sharp differentiation in predispositions between the sexes grounded maternal feminism in social science and further legitimated it as a source from which to draw in fighting the male impulse of war.

On August 29, 1914, less than a month after the outbreak of World War I, more than fifteen hundred women in mourning dress marched down New York City's Fifth Avenue in silence, led by a large white flag with a dove carrying an olive branch. This protest, as Roland Marchand has said, marked the beginning of a new chapter in the history of the U.S. peace movement, as it led to the founding of the Woman's Peace Party in January 1915. With some of the era's most prominent women in its membership—Emily Balch, Carrie Chapman Catt, Alice Hamilton, and Charlotte Perkins Gilman—and with Jane Addams as its first president, the Woman's Peace Party emanated from a perceived solidarity of all women's inborn opposition to war. Although American women had not yet gained universal suffrage, the organization called itself a "party" to suggest its intentions for political action; in fact, the "Program for Constructive Peace" (1915), the initial declaration of the Woman's Peace Party, includes the demand for women's suffrage, urging the extension of self-government as a remedy to nationalism and international hostility. The primary purposes of the program are to delineate the means by which the war should end; to propose guidelines for a settlement that would prevent future wars; to suggest how an international system of governance could be established that would "place the future of the world upon securer foundations"; and finally, to make a series of recommendations to guide the United States' course of action away from intervention and armament, toward neutrality and the role of international diplomat. Though the party's efforts to maintain American neutrality appeared successful with the 1916 election of Woodrow Wilson (who promised peace and neutrality), the president's decision to enter the war made many of the party's members the targets of intense public ridicule and government prosecution for violation of the Sedition Act of 1918.

In 1915 Aletta Jacobs of Holland, Rosika Schwimmer of Hungary, and other leaders of the International Woman Suffrage Alliance called on women of belligerent and neutral nations alike to take action against the war that was tearing the world apart. The result was the formation of the International Congress of Women at The Hague, Netherlands, in May of 1915. The American Woman's Peace Party responded to the call with a forty-two-woman delegation made up of leading suffragists, social workers, labor activists, prison reformers, and members of the Women's Trade Union League. Jane Addams headed the U.S. delegation and was also named president of the congress, giving its concluding address "Women and War" (1915). Addams begins by praising the "heroism" of those women in attendance from countries at war; their courage in differing from their male compatriots' killing and dying for country bodes well for the cause of peace. She goes on to speak inspirationally of the "spiritual internationalism" that brought this congress together. Women, Addams implores, must tap their exceptional "moral energy"—their instinctive capacity for nurturing—to help end the world war. Addams means this literally: the May 1915 congress served as the staging point from which Addams, as its president, sent out its delegates to visit the heads of state of the key nations and to generally work for peace in both Europe and the United States.

After World War I the United States went into a long period of isolation, with the U.S. Congress rejecting American membership in the League of Nations, passing immigration restriction acts in the early 1920s and the Neutrality Acts in the mid-1930s. This period ended on December 7, 1941, when the Japanese attacked the U.S. naval base at Pearl Harbor, Hawaii. With the United States at war with imperial Japan and Fascist Germany, the nation mobilized like never before. Women were indispensable. Millions took up jobs in ship and airplane building, steel making, and other war industries. And with the establishment of the Women's Auxiliary Army Corps (WAAC), a women's division of the Navy called Women Accepted for Volunteer Emergency Service (WAVES), the Women's Airforce Service Pilots, and the Marine Corps Women's reserve, more than 350,000 American women served in the military itself during World War II. Thousands of other women volunteered in civil defense programs.

Women's unprecedented work and service during World War II prompted writers to take stock of women's roles as U.S. citizens, to examine their heightened duties and responsibilities during world war, and to consider what more could be done to advance women's interests in step with their responsibilities. In "Defense and Girls" (1941), First Lady Eleanor Roosevelt discusses the merits of instituting a year of compulsory service for girls and young women that would parallel the draft of men for military service; women's service, in contrast though, would be in education, home economics, farming, or health care—pursuits that would benefit the nation and also develop skills and build confidence in the participants. Mrs. J. Borden Harriman puts forward a similar idea in "Women Enlist Now!" (1941). She calls for a "volunteer draft army" of women to take charge of such assorted duties as food distribution, community defense, and (in a component somewhat like the New Deal all-male Civilian Conservation Corps) such areas as "slum clearance, housing, [health] clinics, social welfare and the like." In "We Too Must Fight This War" (1942), Minnie L. Maffett, M.D., is unimpressed with government's use of women. Compared to Britain and the Soviet Union, for instance, the United States has been inefficient and shortsighted in tapping its "womanpower." Why are so many qualified women not called upon, Maffett asks, in a time when doctors, engineers, and government administrators are so desperately needed? She also points out the absence of women in positions of power.

Although relatively few Americans opposed U.S. entrance into World War II—it was commonly agreed that Hirohito's Japan and Hitler's Germany had to be stopped—the genocidal scale of human history's most destructive war brought new urgency to the quest for lasting world peace. Consequently, some women writers began to reemphasize the feminine role in opposing and ending war. For instance, Pearl S. Buck in "Women and War" (1941), a chapter of her book *Of Men and Women,* offers a sophisticated heartfelt appeal to peace and, more specifically, to women's responsibility to draw from their deep-seated "trait" of caregiving to counteract the "atavistic" male mind-set that leads to war. In her repeated use of the concept of atavism, the Nobel Prize–winning novelist ventures into a sociobiological explanation of war: not very far removed from its beginnings in the animal world, the human species is "not yet free of the wild; the love of blood and the kill," which still drives "man" toward self-destruction. In a roughly similar analysis, Dorothy Thompson in "A Woman's Manifesto" (1947) uses cultural anthropology to compare masculine aggression to the cross-cultural instinctive nature of women toward cooperation and community. Thompson did not, however, oppose World War II. A prominent columnist and political commentator who traveled the world as a newspaper reporter in the 1930s and 1940s, hers was an early voice against the dangers of Hitler and the need for American intervention.

With the United States' dropping of atomic bombs on Hiroshima and Nagasaki, Japan, bringing World War II to a close, Americans soon found themselves in a different type of war—a Cold War with the Soviet Union and China (after Mao Tse Tung's Communist takeover in 1949). In the summer of 1950 the United States also entered a hot war in Korea, when Communist forces of North Korea invaded American-supported South Korea. With China intervening on the side of North Korea in November, 1950, the United States—as Charlotta A. Bass points out in "You Can Vote for Peace" (1952)—was perilously close to fighting a World War III. Editor for forty years of the West Coast's oldest African American newspaper, *The California Eagle*, Bass worked for black civil rights, fighting the Ku Klux Klan and seeking an end to violence against blacks from at least the 1920s to her death in 1969. In the late 1940s she became a founding member of the Progressive Party and in 1952 became the first African American woman to run for the vice presidency. "You Can Vote for Peace" includes the text of a radio campaign address Bass gave in Texas in which she presents her party as the only one in the race with an actual solution to the Korean War: immediate withdrawal. In the address she makes a deliberate appeal to women as "52 percent of the national vote" to end the "slaughter . . . of our loved ones."

The organization Women Strike for Peace (WSP) was founded by self-defined housewife and mother Dagmar Wilson in the fall of 1961 to protest above-ground nuclear weapons testing and, generally, the nuclear arms race. WSP's first major action was a one-day strike for peace held on November 1, 1961, at city halls and federal buildings in more than sixty U.S. cities. According to Amy Swerdlow, author of *Women Strike for Peace: Traditional Motherhood and Radical Politics in the 1960s*, WSP membership—which included pacifists, Quakers, communists, and socialists—played down its highly politicized background and exploited the age-old ideal of mothers as creators and protectors of life. WSP tried to project an image of middle-class peace ladies in white gloves and flowered hats. In any event, as Sophia Wyatt recounts in "One Day Strike for Peace" (1962), WSP's first strike was effective in gaining national and international attention and also in bringing heretofore disconnected "sisters" together for the common cause of ending the arms race. The organization's lobbying effort paid off in the 1963 Test Ban Treaty between the United States and the Soviet Union. WSP would go on to play a central role in protesting the Vietnam War.

Bound by its Cold War strategy of checking community expansion abroad, the United States drew itself into the Vietnam War. It was the nation's longest war, lasting a decade after the beginning of direct participation in 1964, and one of its costliest—with fifty-eight thousand Americans losing their lives in action and the American people irreparably losing trust in their government. In addition to the geopolitics of the Vietnam War, a critical source of the domestic discord that engulfed the United States in the late 1960s and early 1970s was the military draft. Organized opposition to the draft began in early 1967, as young male student radicals burned their draft cards and, more important, urged all men to refuse to cooperate with conscription. Women of the student movement joined this opposition, with the unanticipated consequence that the antidraft campaign helped expose a growing gendered division within the New Left. As the movement tackles human rights violations in the world at large, it must also come to terms with the second-class citizenship of women in its own ranks, argue the authors of "Anti-Draft and Women's Rights" (1967), by Karen Koonan and Bobbi Cieciorka, and "Women and Draft Resistance: Revolution in the Revolution" (1968), by Jill Severn. This wedge issue led to female student radicals splitting off from the Student Nonviolent Coordinating Committee, Students for a Democratic Society, and other male-dominated radical organizations and sparked the beginning of the women's liberation movement.

By 1968, after the Tet Offensive by the North Vietnamese and the continued massive American bombing of North Vietnam (with seemingly little strategic effect), protests against the war reached a new intensity, and Women Strike for Peace played a key role in that opposition. In "Testimony before the 1968 Platform Committee of the Democratic National Convention on Behalf of Women

Strike for Peace" (1968), Bella Abzug urges the Democratic Party to break with Lyndon Johnson's administration and nominate a presidential candidate committed to full withdrawal from Southeast Asia. At the time, Abzug was a labor lawyer and chairman of WSP's legislative committee. She went on to serve two terms in the U.S. House of Representatives (1971–1974) and became a cofounder of the National Women's Political Caucus in 1971. "A Woman's Declaration of Liberation from Military Domination" (1970) is a short bold statement from WSP's national office decrying, among other things, the billions of dollars being spent on war while American "cities decay and fester." The declaration further demands that Congress stop funding the war, repeal the military draft, and simply end the war. In "The Longest Day of the Longest War!" (1971), the WSP calls for women to refrain from all consumer spending on June 21, 1971, and to devote the day instead to lobbying Congress to cut military appropriations and end the hostilities.

Some hope of peace came after Johnson decided not to run for reelection and Richard Nixon won the presidency, in part on his "secret plan" to end the war (he had none). With little material evidence of change and a growing distrust of Nixon, however, opposition to the Vietnam War escalated, and radical feminists like the author of "Women and War" (1970) continued to examine how women are affected by a dominant political culture devoted to making war. Writing in one of the many underground or alternative newspapers of the time, the author signed her article, simply, as "maude." Among the ways women are hurt by war, maude explains, are by its reducing the standard of living through inflation, cutting social services as the federal budget is devoted to war, and increasing emotional and financial pressure after their men are forced to go to Vietnam. In the spring of 1970 antiwar protests on college campuses reached a fever pitch after Nixon announced, contrary to his explicit campaign promise in the 1968 election, that he ordered the invasion of Cambodia, thereby spreading the war in Southeast Asia. On May 4, 1970, three days before the Bread and Roses "Speech at the Women's Anti-Imperialist Rally" (1970), the Ohio National Guard shot and killed four students at Kent State University; ten days after these murders, Mississippi police opened fire on black students at Jackson State College, killing two and wounding twelve. It had truly become a war at home. In 1973, the United States signed an agreement with North Vietnam, South Vietnam, and the Viet Cong calling for a cease-fire and American withdrawal from Southeast Asia.

The divisiveness of the Vietnam War along with the role the peace movement played in launching the women's movement tended to keep issues related to women within the military toward the back of the feminist burner. After the war, some feminists focused more attention on women's place in the military and on the desire among some women to serve their country in the military—thereby gaining the full social, economic, and political rights of equal citizenship with men. The article "Women and the Volunteer Armed Forces: First Report on a Rocky Romance" (1977), by Linda Alband and Steve Rees, describes the changes in the armed forces that were affecting women and that women were influencing. Its conclusion "presents a brief critique of mainstream feminist and pacifist views about women in the military." The mid-1970s, write Alband and Rees, saw the extremely unusual and "momentary coincidence of interests between the voluntary military's insatiable demand for qualified labor, and the women's movement's demand for equal access to, and equal rights within, public and private institutions." The result was the military's breaking with some of its "anachronistic traditions," although sexual harassment, discrimination against gay and lesbian soldiers, and many more serious problems remained. According to Alband and Rees, along with equal citizenship, what women want most from the military is rather practical in nature—education, travel, training, and a steady paycheck. Writing in the journal *Radical America*, Alband and Rees urged leftists to avoid the standard dismissive attitude toward the armed forces; to change the military, it must be closely studied and understood as a dynamic but permanent institution in American life.

104
WOMAN'S PEACE PARTY
Program for Constructive Peace (1915)

I. TO SECURE THE CESSATION OF HOSTILITIES:

1. We urge our government to call a conference of representative delegates from the neutral nations to discuss possible measures to lessen their own injuries, to hasten the cessation of hostilities, and to prevent warfare in the future.

2. In case an official conference of the kind named above proves impossible or impracticable, we pledge ourselves to work toward the summoning of an unofficial conference of the pacifists of the world to consider points named.

II. TO INSURE SUCH TERMS OF SETTLEMENT AS WILL PREVENT THIS WAR FROM BEING BUT THE PRELUDE TO NEW WARS:

1. No province should be transferred as a result of conquest from one government to another against the will of the people. Whenever possible, the desire of a province for autonomy should be respected.

2. No war indemnities should be assessed save when recognized international law has been violated.

3. No treaty alliance or other international arrangement should be entered upon by any nation unless ratified by the representatives of the people. Adequate measures for assuring democratic control of foreign policy should be adopted by all nations.

III. TO PLACE THE FUTURE PEACE OF THE WORLD UPON SECURER FOUNDATIONS:

1. Foreign policies of nations should not be aimed at creating alliances for the purpose of maintaining the "*balance of power*" but should be directed to the establishment of a "*Concert of Nations,*" with

(a) A *court, or courts,* for the settlement of all disputes between nations;

(b) An *international congress,* with legislative and administrative powers over international affairs, and with permanent committees in place of present secret diplomacy;

(c) An *international police force.*

2. As an immediate step in this direction, a permanent League of Neutral Nations ("League of Peace") should be formed, whose members should bind themselves to settle all difficulties arising between them by arbitration, judicial, or legislative procedure, and who should create an international police force for mutual protection against attack.

3. *National disarmament* should be effected in the following manner: It should be contingent upon the adoption of this peace program by a sufficient number of nations, or by nations of sufficient power to insure protection to those disarmed. It should be graduated in each nation to the degree of disarmament effected in the other nations, and progressively reduced until finally complete.

4. Pending general disarmament, all manufactures of arms, ammunitions and munitions for use in war should hereafter be national property.

5. The *protection of private property at sea,* of neutral commerce and of communications should be secured by the *neutralization of the seas* and of such maritime trade routes as the British Channel, the Dardanelles, Panama, Suez, the Straits of Gibraltar, etc.

6. National and international action should be secured to remove the *economic causes of war.*

7. The democracies of the world should be extended and reinforced by general application of the principle of self-government, including the extension of *suffrage to women.*

IV. IMMEDIATE NATIONAL PROGRAM FOR THE UNITED STATES:

1. We approve the Peace Commission Treaties which our country has negotiated with thirty nations, stipulating delay and investigation for the period of a year before any declaration of war can take place. We express the hope that all other countries will be included.

From Woman's Peace Party, Program for Constructive Peace, January 10, 1915, as reprinted in Marie Louise Degen, *The History of the Woman's Peace Party* (Baltimore: Johns Hopkins Press, 1939), 44–46.

2. We protest against the increase of armaments by the United States. We insist that the increase of the army and navy at this time, so far from being in the interest of peace, is a direct threat to the well-being of other nations with whom we have dealings, an imputation of doubt of their good faith, and calculated to compel them in turn to increase their armies, and in consequence to involve us in an ever-intensifying race for military supremacy.

3. We recommend to the President and Government of the United States that a commission of men and women be created, with an adequate appropriation, whose duty shall be to work for the prevention of war and the formulation of the most compelling and practical methods of world organization.

105
Jane Addams
Women and War (1915)

At this last evening of the International Congress of Women, now drawing to its successful conclusion, its president wishes first to express her sincere admiration for the women who have come here from the belligerent nations. They have come from home at a moment when the national consciousness is so welling up from each heart and overflowing into the consciousness of others that the individual loses, not only all concern for his personal welfare, but for his convictions as well and gladly merges all he has into his country's existence.

It is a high and precious moment in human experiences; war is too great a price to pay for it but it is worth almost anything else. I therefore venture to call the journey of these women, many of them heartsick and sorrowful, to this Congress, little short of an act of heroism. Even to appear to differ from those

From Jane Addams, "Women and War, Address Given at the Hague, May, 1915," as reprinted in Lucia True Mead, ed., *The Overthrow of the War System* (Boston: The Forum Publications, 1915), 1–9.

she loves in the hour of their affliction or exaltation, has ever been the supreme test of woman's conscience.

For the women coming from neutral nations there have also been supreme difficulties. In some of these countries, woman has a large measure of political responsibility and, in all of them, women for long months have been sensitive to the complicated political conditions which may also easily compromise a neutral nation and jeopardize the peace and safety of its people. At a Congress such as this, an exaggerated word may easily be spoken or reported as spoken which would make a difficult situation still more difficult; but these women have bravely taken that risk and made the moral venture. We from the United States, who have made the longest journey and are therefore freest from these entanglements, can speak out our admiration for these fine women from the neutral as well as from the fighting nations.

SPIRITUAL INTERNATIONALISM

Why then were women from both the warring and the neutral nations ready to come to this Congress to the number of 1,500? By what profound and spiritual forces were they impelled, at this moment when the spirit of Internationalism is apparently broken down, to believe that the solidarity of women would hold fast and that through them, as through a precious instrument, they would be able to declare the reality of those basic human experiences ever perpetuating and cherishing the race, and courageously to set them over against the superficial and hot impulses which have too often led to warfare.

Those great underlying forces, in response to which so many women have come here, belong to the human race as a whole and constitute a spiritual internationalism which surrounds and completes our national life, even as our national life itself surrounds and completes our family life; they do not conflict with patriotism on one side any more than family devotion conflicts with it upon the other.

NEW CHANNELS NEEDED

We have come to this International Congress of women not only to protest from our hearts and with the utmost patience we can command, unaffrighted even by the "difficult and technical," to study this complicated modern world of ours now so sadly at war itself; but furthermore we would fain suggest ways by which this large internationalism may find itself and dig new channels through which it may flow.

At moments it appears as if the excessive nationalistic feeling expressing itself during these fateful months through the exaltation of warfare in so many of the great nations, is due to the accumulation within their own borders of those higher human affections which should have had an outlet into the larger life of the world but could not, because no international devices had been provided for such expression. No great central authority could deal with this sum of human will, as a scientist deals with the body of knowledge in his subject irrespective of its national origins, and the nations themselves became congested, as it were, and inevitably grew confused between what was legitimate patriotism and those universal emotions which have nothing to do with national frontiers.

UNNECESSARY MENTAL CONFLICT

We are happy that the Congress has met at The Hague. Thirty years ago I came to this beautiful city, full fifteen years before the plans for international organization had found expression here. If I can look back to such wonderful beginnings in my own lifetime, who shall say that the younger women of this platform may not see the completion of an international organization which shall make war impossible because good will and just dealing between nations shall have found an ordered method of expression?

We have many evidences at the present moment that, inchoate and unorganized as it is, it may be found even in the midst of this war constantly breaking through its national bounds. The very soldiers in the opposing trenches have to be moved about from time to time lest they come to know each other, not as the enemy but as individuals, and a sense of comradeship overwhelm their power to fight.

This totally unnecessary conflict between the great issues of internationalism and of patriotism rages all about us even in our own minds so that we wage a veritable civil war within ourselves. These two great affections should never have been set one against the other; it is too late in the day for war. For decades, the lives of all the peoples of the world have been revealed to us through the products of commerce, news agencies, through popular songs and novels, through photographers and cinematographs, and last of all through the interpretations of the poets and artists.

Suddenly all these wonderful agencies are applied to the hideous business of uncovering the details of warfare.

SOLEMN PROTEST

Never before has the world known so fearfully and so minutely what war means to the soldier himself, to women and children, to that civilization which is the common heritage of all mankind. All this intimate and realistic knowledge of war is recorded upon human hearts more highly sensitized than ever before in the history of man and filled with a new and avid hunger for brotherhood.

In the shadow of this intolerable knowledge, we, the women of this International Congress, have come together to make our solemn protest against that of which we know.

Our protest may be feeble but the world progresses, in the slow and halting manner in which it does progress, only in proportion to the moral energy exerted by the men and women living in it; social advance must be pushed forward by the human will and understanding united for conscious ends. The slow progress towards juster international relations may be traced to the distinguished jurist of the

Netherlands, Grotius, whose honored grave is but a few miles from here; to the great German, Immanuel Kant, who lifted the subject of "Eternal Peace" high above even philosophical controversy; to Count Tolstoy, of Russia, who so trenchantly set forth in our own day, and so on from one country to another.

Each in his own time, because he placed law above force, was called a dreamer and a coward, but each did his utmost to express clearly the truth that was in him and beyond that human effort can not go.

WOMAN'S SYMPATHY

These mighty names are but the outstanding witnesses among the host of men and women who have made their obscure contributions to the same great end.

Conscious of our own shortcomings and not without a sense of complicity in the present war, we women have met in earnestness and in sorrow to add what we may to this swelling tide of purpose.

It is possible that the appeal for the organization of the world upon peaceful lines has been made too exclusively to man's reason and sense of justice, quite as the eighteenth century enthusiasm for humanity was prematurely founded on intellectual sentiment. Reason is only a part of the human endowment; emotion and deep-set racial impulses must be utilized as well—those primitive human urgings to foster life and to protect the hopeless, of which women were the earliest custodians, and even the social and gregarious instincts that we share with the animals themselves. These universal desires must be given opportunities to expand and the most highly trained intellects must serve them rather than the technique of war and diplomacy.

They tell us that wounded lads lying in helpless pain and waiting too long for the field ambulance, call out constantly for their mothers, impotently beseeching them for help; during this Congress we have been told of soldiers who say to their hospital nurses, "We can do nothing for ourselves, but go back to the trenches again and again so long as we are able. Cannot the women do something about this war? Are you kind to us only when we are wounded?"

WOMAN'S RESPONSIBILITY

The time may come when the exhausted survivors of the war may well reproach women for their inaction during this terrible time. It is possible they will then say that when devotion to the ideals of patriotism drove thousands of men into international warfare, the women refused to accept the challenge and in that moment of terror failed to assert clearly and courageously the sanctity of human life, the reality of things of the spirit.

For three days we have met together, so conscious of the bloodshed and desolation surrounding us, that all irrelevant and temporary matters fell away and we spoke solemnly to each other of the great and eternal issues, as do those who meet around the bedside of the dying.

We have formulated our message and given it to the world to heed when it will, confident that at last the great Court of International Opinion will pass righteous judgment upon all human affairs.

106
PEARL S. BUCK
Women and War (1940)

Women have for too long left men to struggle alone with the problem of evil in the world. And what is the problem of evil except the problem of wicked and ruthless individuals, the gangsters in a community, whether that community be a town, a nation, or a world? Protected by the walls of her home, busied in the

From *Of Men and Women* (N.P.: Cornwall Press, 1940).

peaceful pursuits of cooking and caring for children, woman has taken no responsibility for the control of wicked men, with the result that we see in the world today. In her security she has been too sentimental even to her own children. Women's sons stand at this very moment behind the machines of aggressive war and kill millions of innocent people. Women's sons are murdering and looting on a scale never before known in history. Is this not colossal proof of the failure of women to create moral character in her sons while they are in the home? If woman cannot create moral character in her sons while they are in the home, then she must help man to control evil character outside. For clearly it is beyond man alone to cope with evil, now that the will to evil of even a single man can be so magnified by modern weapons of war.

If we are ever to have peace, it will be accomplished not by vaguely organized individuals passing resolutions. It will be accomplished only by bitterly determined men and women who will study and use every means in their power to enforce and indoctrinate the ideas and performance of peace. But the first step toward peace as the foundation of human relations will be a complete knowledge of what war is. We shall all have the knowledge of how war works when it breaks and what its effects are—that will be enforced upon us. But we need to know how it begins and who begins it and where and when.

War is, of course, endemic as yet in human society; and, like all endemic diseases, given certain conditions, it becomes epidemic at regular or perhaps irregular intervals. Those conditions are, if one reads the history of wars, two: first, discontent in a human group, that discontent being in the main economic; and, second the rise to power of a certain type of mind. That type of mind is endemic, too. It is atavistic, cruel, simple, or cunning. But whatever it is, it is basically uncivilized. Thousands of years hence, unless such minds have destroyed us all, the creatures of a wiser age than ours will look back and recognize them for what they are—the persistent traces of our beginnings in the animal world from which we have so newly sprung. We are not free yet of the wild; the love of blood and the kill is still in us. Here is our true enemy, the enemy of us all, whatever our race and nation. These atavistic minds, hostile to kindness, resentful of slights which anyone must accept in life, remembering even the mishaps of childhood, resort to violence inevitably as their means of vengeance. We are too soft toward them. We are too apt to forgive them, saying, "Ah, if their childhoods had been better, they would have been better."

There is no proof of this. On the contrary, many of the best, the kindest, the most civilized and humane of men and women have suffered cruelty in childhood. But they were better for such suffering. They forgot it as they pressed on, or remembered it only to see that others were spared what they had suffered. They did not want to make all the world suffer because they once suffered, or dispel their youthful frustrations by machines of war crushing the bodies of the innocent and unknown. The suspicious jealousies of an ignorant tyrant who kills his intellectual superiors is an evidence not of an unhappy childhood but of an atavistic and undeveloped mind; and, however shrewd and cunning and clever that mind may be, it is undeveloped if it proceeds against human society in tyranny and war. Let us not deceive ourselves. We have rightly discarded the old idea of Original Sin. And yet there is a truth in it. We are sprung from dark and earthy sources, and the mud clings to us yet in these atavistic minds who resort to animal force to gain their ends, an animal force heightened a million times when it extends itself through machines of war and death. These are dangerous minds, both dangerous first through confluences of blood and heredity we do not understand, made more dangerous by certain environmental conditions, and reaching their final climax when they are able, through finding at certain times, as they do, an environment suitable to them and an economic situation which they can exploit. War is the inevitable result of this meeting of the atavistic individual and the environment surrounding discontent.

What are we to do with such minds? Discern them, watch them, and bar at every step their rise to power. Let them function as individuals in a democracy and never as officials or demagogues. How discover them? As children in school, as youths in college, as men in life. There should be psychiatrists' reports on them, and heed should be given the reports. We were all shocked a few years ago by a peculiarly brutal and it seemed aimless murder committed by a young man of some genius. That murder could have been prevented if a psychologist's report made upon him years before had been kept in mind. "This child," the report read, "will one day resort to violence." He did.

The minds which lead us to war are few. It would not be difficult to stop their rise to power. But it takes a method, a watchfulness, an energy for action which only determination for peace can provide.

To discover and to watch and to prevent the rise to power, therefore, of the atavistic individual is the first necessity for peace. Genghis Khan, Napoleon, Hitler—the mind is the same. It is as uniform as the symptoms of a known disease. It can be recognized, it can be prevented, and half of the basic cause for war eliminated.

The other half of the basic cause for war has to do with economic adjustments in a nation and between nations. Population pressures, unequal treaties, unjust tariff, the unfairnesses of trade, deprivation of raw materials, make national and international discontents which provide breeding places for war. There is full information on such places in newspapers, magazines, books. Foundations make constant research into such conditions. But nobody uses the information with the aim of discovering possible sources for war. We need as clear, as cold, as sacrificial a spirit for this as doctors have when they determine to eliminate a source spot of yellow fever or Asiatic cholera which threatens the world. War is the most devastating endemic and epidemic disease the human race has to endure, and yet too little has been done to discover and eliminate its cause by intelligent early control.

There must be a reason for this delay. It is to be found, I believe, in the mistaken estimate which men have made and still make of war when they do not see it as the inescapable result of certain knowable and removable causes. It is not possible to prevent war when all the causes which produce it have been allowed to flourish. But the causes can be prevented. That they are not prevented, that war is still accepted as a possible fate and destiny, even a glorious one, is the false notion which men still hold. The habit of men's minds is toward war. It may be that men alone can never make an end to war.

But women do not share the glories and pleasures of war. They are the ones who are left behind. They do not have the joy of comradeships, the excitement of adventure, the possible glory of victory or death. None of the glamour of war is theirs. They remain at home alone, that for which they lived gone. They take up the drab work in factories and fields which men have left. And when the men do not return, theirs is the burden of the postwar world. If the men do come back, nothing is the same, for no man goes through a war without being deeply wounded in spirit. Women have no illusions, or should have none, about what war is.

I believe that it is women who must end war if it is ever to be ended. It is women who must determine by whatever ways of reason and deep emotion that they can use, that they will not go on having their work of bearing and rearing wasted by war or even the fear of war. Such determination is the first step. With it anything can be accomplished. Without it, we shall go on endlessly, generation after generation, with the sort of thing which faces us today.

To end war by the discovery and elimination of its individual and economic causes— here is a task great enough, human enough, useful enough to invite all women.

Hard? Yes, but not as hard as war!

Difficult to organize women? But not more difficult than to organize for war.

An international task? Yes, but do not imagine women anywhere like war any better than we do.

A complex job? Yes, but not more complex than war.

It would bring women into national and international affairs? Why not? She is able.

A long and slow job? Yes, but how endlessly long and slow war is, when its effects are felt generation after generation!

And what aim more suited to woman's creative nature than the bringing about of peace through the control of the two chief causes of war, the maladjusted individual and the depressed social group? Here is a field in which woman would have no competition with man, through which she could penetrate into thorough understanding of human problems, by means of which she could, if she would, influence government, by active participation or by group pressure. It is said too often that women have made no notable contribution to humanity except to bear children. Yet to continue to bear children only to have them slaughtered is folly. But to take as a solemn task the prevention of war would be an achievement unmatched. In the process women would become inevitably concerned in human welfare, to the betterment of all society as well as of themselves. It is the only hope I see of the end of war.

And it would give woman a job in the world. Actually women are becoming less and less necessary to the running of the world. It takes no great wisdom to see that woman is increasingly on the periphery of management. She was once the center of it. But those were the days when the center of civilization was the home, and she was the center of the home. Those were her days of power. In the whirl of centrifugal motion which is the movement of the human race the center of civilization has changed. Rather, it is changing. Where it will pause none knows yet, but it is now veering in the direction of the state. It will not end there finally, for it is in ceaseless motion. In history that center of civilization has been in many places. For long it was in the church, for long it was in universities. In pioneer countries it was always in the home. In periods of great industrial development it was in industry. In periods of expansion the center of civilization passed even into exploring. This is the political age, and human thought is centered in the ideologies of governments and in the organization for power, and never has woman been so remote from the vital growing centers of life as she is now.

For she is still struggling with the old, old question of whether or not she should stay in the home, without perceiving that the home as the center of life is already gone. Its roof is there and its four walls. Her beloved bric-a-brac is there, and the utensils for eating and sleeping and listening to the radio, which are the few necessities of life today. Yet even the necessities of life do not center in the home any more. Eating can be done anywhere at little cost and no trouble, and hotel beds are clean and comfortable and maybe less expensive than one's own. The truth, dreadful to women, is that the home is more and more of a luxury these days and less and less of a necessity except as a place to put women to keep them out of the way. Unless it can be brought back in some more necessary way, some day men are going to find that it is cheaper just to keep women in cells and cages or barracks or harems whence they can be summoned when service is wanted or the state needs new recruits. Women have always been relegated whenever men have relapsed into thinking that the sole important functions of women are to service men and to breed children. Those are the times when the nonessentialness of women is evident on every hand.

I have had a cold foreboding since the day I heard an important executive in New York fume against the appointment of a woman to a government post in Washington. "But we'll soon change all that," he exclaimed. "We don't want any women cluttering up things in Washington now."

In other words, when action is required women must be got out of the way because they have no part in the vital and actual work of the nation. All that they do can be dispensed with in strenuous times except breeding and possibly caring for the sick and wounded. They enter industry, it is true, in menial ways when men are called out of it for war, but when men return they must again withdraw. In the days of highly mechanized industry which are inevitably ahead of us there will be no use for women at all. More than ever in that future women will have to knit, and not only knit but unravel and knit again, just to have something to do. The managerial age is approaching, and unless woman can somehow educate herself to take her share in the management of the world she will be relegated entirely. She is very nearly relegated now.

I do not feel disposed to blame men for this state of affairs. I should be glad to hate them, for that would be the simplest way of fixing blame. The simplest way of starting a reform for women always is to begin by an attack upon men. Actually, the fault, if there is a fault, lies in women themselves. The fault does not in every country lie with women. Obviously, one cannot expect the Japanese woman, for example, oppressed by centuries of chatteldom, to take her place now by man's side, especially when the last thing a Japanese man wants is a woman at his side instead of under his feet. The recent announcement in Japan that women are to be kept out of all public office since their place is in the home is merely a laughable imitation of Japan's big brother for the hour, Germany. Japanese women never have come out of the home. It is significant, however, that no such announcement has come from China, and certainly in our country woman has had a good chance to take her place by man's side. Many men have waited for her to take it. She has had the liberty to do so.

But hers has been the fatal weakness of hesitation. Hesitating upon the threshold of her home, uncertain whether to stay in or come out, she has tried to make her individual decision, not upon the basis of woman's worth or ability, but upon what man wants or would like. She has doubted the strength of her femaleness. She has been afraid of losing her femininity. And she has feared, if she lost it, that she would have nothing left wherewith to hold man's heart or attention. Instead of going boldly forth to join him, confident of the eternal female strength in her, sure of her own undying power to attract him when she wished to do so, she has settled back into her home and shut the door and waited, how often in vain, for him to come to her. Or she has sallied forth in shamefaced fashion, apologetically, as though she, too, thought she belonged at home, or she has come forth with hostility and hardness, and those are ugly traits.

The truth is that if a woman is a real woman and proud to be one, nothing can quench the essential femininity of her being. She may sit upon a throne and rule a nation, she may sit upon the bench and be a judge, she may be the foreman in a mill, she could if she would be a bridge builder or a machinist or anything else; and if she were proud of herself as a woman her work would be well done and her femininity deepened. It is when women undervalue themselves as women that they ape men and become mannish and arouse dislike in all their fellows, men and women. No kind of work can spoil the quality of a woman unless she has first spoiled it herself by wishing consciously or unconsciously that she were not a woman. This undervaluation of herself has made woman uncertain when she leaves the security of the familiar environment of home, and in her uncertainty she has too often imitated man, whom she fears, and she alternates in her behavior between repulsive mannishness and an apologetic, overexaggerated, false femininity that is equally repulsive.

For the real female quality is something tough and strong and resistant. Women are not weak, except when they are uncertain of themselves. Once they are certain, they are whirlwinds of power and wells of strength. If they could have some sort of certainty that their femaleness was natural and right and ought not to be changed or quenched, they could and would take their places willingly by man's side. But they have for so long heard their qualities derided, they have for so long been called the weaker sex, they have for so many generations been told that they have no head for business and no understanding of government, that it would be more than human to expect them to have resisted the subtle degeneration of self-doubt.

The one good that men have conceded to women is moral superiority. Men have, or have pretended that they have, always expected women to be morally superior to them. So now, when a few independent women have gone out into business and government and have made use of the financial and legal and political tricks which men employ as a matter of course, there has been loud indignation that women are as dirty in business and politics as men are.

"What's the use of having women in politics," these furious males inquire, "if they are as bad as men?"

What use, indeed, are bad women anywhere, or bad men, or liars, male or female, or thieves or robbers or murderers, men or women? And what of the possibilities of good women, if woman were working at man's side, or are good women too troublesome outside the home?

This moral superiority which men have so generously given to women is as a matter of fact a very degenerating influence upon women. For, having no other superiority allowed her by man, she snatches at this poor rag of righteousness which he throws her out of the abundance of his strength and power over her, and she tries to make it cover her nakedness. If man had wanted to keep moral superiority too, of course he would have done so. But he found it inconvenient in everyday life. To be as white as snow is not practical in business. Every little spot shows. It was a man cook I once had in China who conducted an earnest campaign in my house for several years to persuade and finally to force me to yield in the matter of dish towels of black instead of white linen. It would, he said, spare us both—me the trouble of incessant worry over dirty towels, and him the trouble of washing them every day. We parted at last, he male and I female to the end, on this matter of purity even in so utilitarian a matter as dish towels.

So have men always parted from women on practical righteousness. There is much to be said for men. Obviously it was easier for women to be good than men when women were shut up at home away from temptation to any of the major sins. If they developed the minor ones of laziness and pettiness and indifference and small lies and gossip, these became feminine weakness and did not greatly interfere with the bolder outlines of chastity and—I find I cannot think of another virtue for women, so let it go at chastity.

But why should men be astonished when woman coming forth at his side seems to be much the same stuff as he? The wonder is that she is not worse than he, because her righteousness is, after all, a hothouse thing, untried and untempted; and she has no real strength of her own to resist. She has not even his strength of experience to help her. He at least has sinned often enough to know the folly of sinning beyond a certain point. But she has had so little experience of sin that she cannot be blamed for folly or failing.

Besides, her righteousness, so long imposed upon her, has had very little reward. All the real rewards of goodness man has still kept for himself. Thus, though she is the angel, he is the priest, the prince of the church. It is he who addresses God, not she. She, poor thing, though so good that even he says she is better than himself, must sit in the pews and listen while he preaches, and she must bow her head when he prays to God on her behalf, and she must put in her bits of money when he passes the contribution box. I have always thought women got small reward from the church for all this righteousness of theirs. It does seem as though at least in the church, where moral worth is supposed to be required for entrance, woman ought to have some power. But no, man even devised a means of escape there. Though he demanded righteousness of woman he invented a religion which excused him from it. Righteousness was after all but filthy rags if one trusted to the blood of Christ for salvation, he proclaimed. The forgiveness of sins was made the great mercy of God, so that in a sense the greater sinner a man was, the more glory to God for washing him clean and accepting him as spotless. Thus did man make superiority out of his inferiority.

But practically he demanded righteousness of women, because it is inconvenient for a man to have an unrighteous wife. For one thing, if she is unrighteous he cannot be sure that he is the father of his sons, and there is fury and inconvenience in this. An unrighteous wife may bring trouble of all sorts in the home, and man cannot have trouble when he comes home at night. Indeed, women have had so little practical benefit from their superior righteousness that the sensible woman ought to discard righteousness altogether and take man's standards for her own. This would put men and women on an equal basis of moral worth and would do them both good. Men would see women as they are, and women could be rid of the degenerating effect upon them of a false valuation which they have taken far too seriously.

For, incredible as it may seem to the rational mind, many women do really believe that merely because they are women they are more moral than men—"nicer," if you like, more fastidious and purer and more spiritual. I cannot pronounce that word "spiritual" aloud. I have not done so in years. It arouses such feelings of repulsion and ferocity in me that I feel my tranquillity menaced. For, content with their so-called spiritual superiority, women have let their souls rot into pettiness and idleness and vacuity and general indifference in a world crying and dying for want of real superiority of spirit and moral worth, so that the spectacle does not bear contemplation. If women were really superior to me in righteousness or spirituality, could they sit blind and deaf and dumb, knitting their interminable knitting, crocheting and talking and going to teas and bridge parties and knitting again, and filling the theaters day in and day out, and rolling bandages and knitting again, and exchanging recipes and knitting, and re-arranging their furniture and curling their hair and painting their nails and going to style shows and knitting, knitting, knitting, while the world goes down to darkness and dismay through lack of bold goodness and moral integrity and real unselfishness? Where is this moral superiority that will do nothing but knit while heads roll off in revolutions and war crashes upon our great cities so that ruins are all that we shall have left if the world goes on as it now is?

Women have no moral superiority to man so long as she will not come out of her selfish retreat and by man's side work out with him the sort of democratic organization that the world must have if we are to live. We shall have no change for the better until she does. We shall have only increasing chaos and trouble as new wars release new weapons upon us. For man has gone as far as he can without woman. The constant repetition in our life proves it. Man by himself has not been able to make war obsolete, as it should be among civilized people. Habituated to war, conditioned to it as an inevitability, trained to consider it as opportunity for his highest heroism, man can scarcely be expected to look cold-bloodedly at what has for so long been his best chance for excitement, freedom, and glory. The Nazi belief in the catharsis of war for men may be partly true. It is a human necessity to find a certain release of self in sacrifice of self. Anyone is happier who does not live for himself alone.

This loss of self is easier for woman than for man. However, complex and selfish a woman is as an individual, when she has a child she goes down into a simple and elemental experience which drives self away, which divides that self into another and brings all of life into its simplest primeval terms. There never was a woman who was not the better for it, however inadequate she may be afterwards in nurturing and training her child. Women are cleansed in soul by this return to the elements of death and life that make childbirth, and any woman who has not had the experience is and feels incomplete. Sublimation there may be, but she searches for it, aware of her incompleteness.

But in our changed world man has no such opportunity left him any more for return to the elemental. Once he had it, perhaps, in the hunt, the chase, the risk of death. For the loss of self carried with it always the risk of death, and death has a fearful and endless charm for the human creature. It is as though in the dark places of his being there hides always the awareness of his end, and that awareness leads him, as moth to candle, to approach death again and again. The risk of death in childbirth exalts the woman. She goes down to the gates of death and she comes back triumphant over death. But man has no equivalent of this experience, and his being craves it and he devises it out of war. Generation after generation he devises it in one way and another, and as it approaches he dreads and fears it, and when it is come he welcomes it and exalts himself through it.

For war to man, like childbirth to woman, is simplifying in its emotions and activities. All the real problems of life can be put aside while the one thing is done and little thought is needed to do it. He gives himself up to the familiar process. There is for him an actual relief in having an expected war break. His hatreds can be expressed without censure, he can let his emotions run free, he can behave as dramatically, as heroically as he likes, and no one laughs at him. It is almost impossible for a man to behave heroically in the cool and ordinary times of peace. But in war anything is allowed him, he is praised and applauded and made much of, as women are excused and allowed for in pregnancy. It is inevitable then, in a world controlled by men without women, that we shall have wars and disorders recurrent. Only when women take their full share in the directing of history can there be a balance which will then do away with such disturbances.

What can be offered to man as a substitute for the blood bath of war? Where shall he go for glory? That question man must answer for himself. The skies are open to him with all their stars and suns, the earth is beneath him full of materials he does not know. The very air in which he moves is waiting with its secrets for him to plumb. How necessary is the blood bath for men and women? Civilized women by the million these days must do without the elemental experience of childbirth. Only a return to polygamy could give children to all women. It may be not too much to ask that civilized man do without war.

But war, of course, carries to men sweets beyond itself. War automatically puts men in places of power. All men who wish women to retreat, love war, for war helps them. Every war sets women back a generation, and this in spite of industrial gains for them. For those gains are in small places, and women have to give a good share of them up again when the men come home. They would be called ungrateful if they did not; and, besides, they may as well, for laws would be devised to compel them. Psychologically and emotionally, war sets women back both in man's mind and their own. For man comes home from war a spoiled creature, and one too often weakened by self-pity and conceit. He has had to be pampered and praised into considering himself a hero so that he would be a hero, and everyday life is flat after war, and his wife must go on with the pampering and praising or he will feel her unappreciative. It is for him amazingly like childbirth for the woman. She behaves like that after she has successfully had a baby.

Men and women will have to work out some sort of compromise on this matter of having wars and babies. They manage to negate each other as it is. Women fulfill themselves in having the babies, and men fulfill themselves in destroying them. There ought to be some other more profitable form of pleasurable sacrifice for the human race than this sacrifice of the innocents.

107
Eleanor Roosevelt
Defense and Girls (1941)

"Dear Mrs. Roosevelt: What can I do? I feel that the women and girls of this country ought to be doing something just as well as the young men, but I don't know just what to do. I am nineteen and my young man has just gone to camp, and it doesn't seem right for me to sit at home and go around doing the same things I have always done."

Granted that a year of service for boys is finally satisfactorily adjusted, I personally hope that a year of compulsory service will also be considered for girls. I do not, of course, think of girls as taking the same training, or doing the same kind of work that the boys will probably do, nor do I think of them serving in camps. However, just as there are boys whose interests and capacities vary, so have girls varied interests and capacities. I think the opportunity should be offered to girls to work and train themselves along many different lines.

To be specific, I think of girls doing their year of service, in large part, in their own communities. For instance, they could obtain training in a local hospital during part of the year. In this way not one, but two things might be achieved. The girl would be getting something which would be valuable in her own life in the community later on. The hospital would be better able to meet the needs of the community because of the service which she could give. I have seen many a woman facing an illness of a husband or a child with trepidation because she did not even know how to take a temperature or what an ear syringe looked like. A little early training in sanitation, home nursing and diet would make a great difference in the health of the nation as a whole.

I should like to see set up, in the schools, highly efficient courses in home economics.

From *Ladies' Home Journal* © 1941, Meredith Corporation. Reprinted with permission.

The schools could be used as laboratories by providing free hot lunches for every child, or the girls could run school cafeterias by way of practice in properly feeding groups of people. This again would achieve a double end by improving the health of the children of the community, and by giving the girls the knowledge and experience which would help them to raise the standards of their own future homes.

I know of a community in which cooking for the nursery school was the first time that some of the mothers had any intimation that such things as cold coffee and pancakes were not desirable diets for one and two year old children.

This course should teach buying and cooking for large numbers. Such preparation might be valuable in cases of evacuation of people, either because of fire or flood or disaster of any kind, even including war.

In order to vary the training, some girls could work out budgets for different income levels and run an ordinary sized family on such budgets as part of their training. Of course, you may say that for some girls, who are never actually going to cook the meals for their families later on, this kind of training would not be useful. I insist that it is useful training for any girl, even if she never cooks another meal in her whole life. It gives a girl a sense of self confidence. Further, it makes her better able to judge other people's work when and if she is later an employer. If a girl is going into business or one of the professions, it trains her in the planning of her time and in the handling of people. Both these things are important, no matter what she does during the rest of her life.

In rural areas, farm-management courses in schools would be valuable. I believe that a sense of the value of co-operation could be learned through such courses. For example, gardens could be grown co-operatively for the hot school lunches. Every person in the community could feel that she was contributing in this way toward the better health of the children in her community. I have seen projects of this kind used to increase the practical knowledge of the use of co-operatives. I think this would be of value to people in urban as well as rural areas.

I can imagine that some girls might want mechanical training of some kind, which might be better acquired in resident centers such as the National Youth Administration has already set up. That would, of course, be optional; but if a girl wished to go there, she could obtain training for a job, in case of an emergency, ordinarily filled by a man. And there is mechanical work suited to a woman's ability in many peacetime industries.

As a matter of fact, I saw ten girls on an NYA project in Boston, Massachusetts, who were learning to make some parts for trucks for the use of the city government. I was told that a larger project was being set up where girls would be taught how to assemble these machines before they went to work on them. There was certainly nothing beyond the physical ability of any girl in this work; and with the opportunities opening up in the future, an increase in mechanical skill seems to me wise for girls if they are interested in this type of training. Many a housewife would find it extremely valuable and economical if she could make small repairs in her own home. And I have seen women who were handier with tools than some men!

I can hear some of my young friends, particularly those so influenced by certain political beliefs, bringing up the question as to why this year's service should be compulsory. They would claim that this is a Fascist or Nazi scheme leading us straight to the system of German work camps. I feel that these young people, and even some of the other people who think the same way, are ignorant of the principles of democracy.

Thomas Jefferson himself believed in a compulsory school law. We have accepted that compulsion as an ideal ever since the public-school system was originally established. In fact, the idea that education belonged solely to the privileged class is one of the beliefs which democracy has attempted to destroy. If we compel our children, for their own good, to go to school, I see nothing undemocratic in giving the people of the country an opportunity to decide at the polls whether they believe a year's service at a given age for the boys and girls of the nation would be of value to them as individuals and to the nation as a whole.

I believe that girls, if it is decided to require of them a year of service, should be placed on exactly the same footing as men, and they should be given the same subsistence and the same wage.

Of course, if a girl lives at home, what is allowed the boys as subsistence in camps should be allowed to the home for the girl's subsistence and she should receive the same cash remuneration which the boys receive. The difference in the type of service rendered makes no real difference, and they are entitled to remuneration on the same basis as the young men.

This year of service should give us an opportunity to check on the health of our girls also, and we should be able to remedy defects which might have been overlooked in the preceding years.

It should also give girls a good opportunity for understanding what democracy really means. Girls are the potential mothers of the future generation, and with a full realization of what democracy means, what its obligations and responsibilities are, they can teach the children at home to supplement what is taught, or what we hope will be taught, in our schools.

This year of service should give our girls new friends and a wider knowledge of the people who make up this country. They will learn to co-operate in work and in play.

All of this could be accomplished on a voluntary basis, but it would not be. My main reason for believing that it is important to have this year of service compulsory is that I believe so much in the value of knowing many sides of our national life. While I know quite well that there are a good many of our young people who would gladly volunteer for this year of service, I also know that there are a considerable number who would not volunteer. They constitute the very group who force the majority of the nation to make the opportunity for training and education compulsory.

Another important reason why girls should give a year of service to our country is that through so many years we have been constantly increasing our placid acceptance of what the men in our country provided, and that frequently includes their participation in government and their defense of us in wars. Wars today are back where they used to be, and women stand side by side with the men.

Our forefathers fought a daily fight for the preservation of their hard-won liberty. The women of the pioneer days stood side by side with their husbands, shared every hardship, and were often left to fight the battle of life all alone.

We accepted our freedom as a gift from the pioneers and from heaven, and yet it is more than evident today that there are constant assaults on our liberty, perhaps not the least of which is our own apathy. If we wish democracy to survive we must be constantly alive to the many-sided battle we wage.

Take the question of freedom of religion. That was established in our Constitution. It made our country a haven for persecuted people, but feeling runs high today—against Roman Catholics in certain sections, and against Jews in other places. We are a nation of many races and yet there is feeling against the Negroes. I have heard different derogatory names applied to various other racial groups, and this scorn of different races is tied up closely with religious intolerance. All intolerance is based on fear, and fear is usually a lack of understanding. The elimination of these threats to our freedom requires a continuous battle on our part for the principles of democracy.

I feel, therefore, that young people who have worked and played and lived together in groups in communities or in camps for the period of a year will understand one another better throughout their lives.

There would be no strikes, for instance, in which the public would not know on which side it stood, and would not speedily force a conclusion through the weight of public opinion. The fear which now seems part of the psychology of the young people, as well as of the older generation, would speedily depart from their consciousness. They would realize how little real security there is in the world unless we create it, and that that security is bound up with the better cooperation which must exist between all individuals in the community, in the state and in the nation.

In the case of a real emergency such as we are facing at present, of course, older people and even young people below draft age should be willing to render whatever services they are qualified to give, but today I am not discussing what I consider home defense for an emergency period. I am writing of what I consider participation in home defense should be as we look at the future. It should include training for our girls, and a thorough understanding on their part of democracy as a way of life. This will lead to the determination to hand on this democracy to their children, not as a permanent, static thing, but as an ideal to grow as future generations grow, and they will continue to strive for something better for all of us.

108
Mrs. J. Borden Harriman
Women Enlist Now! (1941)

The great thing about democracy is that where it is true to itself it cannot fail. This means it must live as a set of burning ideals put into action. Action without belief has a hollowness which dooms it to failure; and belief without action renders that belief vapid and defenseless. Democracy must embrace both belief and action, or else it cannot be true to itself.

Moral armament of our youth. To build a better democratic future for the world, our youth

From *Independent Woman,* June 1941.

must be taught to understand clearly the full nature of our democratic concepts. American youth is not naturally cynical or frivolous or pessimistic, but they have been brought to such an attitude by a generation marked by disillusionment and inertia. This attitude must be reversed—immediately. The Nazis have their Hitler Youth and Labor Corps with which to indoctrinate young German boys and girls by drilling into them the nihilistic philosophy of fascism. We, in quite a different way, must educate our youth so that they, too, are aware of the beliefs that give our nation its strength.

Reaffirmation of eternal verities. The strength of democracy is built upon the vitality of certain spiritual values, best expressed in the concept of the brotherhood of man. This concept finds manifestation in all our institutions, but chiefly in the home, the bulwark of the whole democratic structure. Reassertion of the ethical values of democracy will strengthen our homes and provide a defense against the propaganda directed at these values—the propaganda which seeks to set man against man, class against class, group against group, and church against church.

Necessity for the bolder life. The gigantic task of defense of America cannot succeed unless we are willing to make definite sacrifices of individual interests for the broader needs of our country. We must learn to accept, willingly and eagerly, such things as smaller profits for the business man, longer hours for the worker, fewer luxuries, less leisure, and higher taxes. We must give something of ourselves, or, in the end, America will have nothing to give to us.

Widening the defense front. It is not enough to *believe* in America; we must *act* for America. And that doesn't mean the government or the military forces alone. It means every one of us. No talent is too slight to be harnessed in the service of democracy. The woman with clear voice and stout lungs can stand on a soapbox or behind a microphone and speak out for democracy. Other women can study local and regional food problems, planning how to budget food supplies if these were to be curtailed or study the defense needs of the community—the adequacy of shelters and hospitals and transportation; or how to cooperate best with the officers of the nearest draft army camp. There is much to be done in long-range planning, too—slum clearance, housing, clinics, social welfare and the like—for the driving power of a democratic people depends upon its hopes for an increasingly brighter future.

Voluntary draft. We women of America should consider ourselves a volunteer draft army, disciplining our bodies and our minds so that we may be ready at any time to do our part for American democracy, in whatever capacity we may be called upon by the government to serve. This business of the defense of America is a job for every person in the land. Your number has been called; the induction center is your own home—enlist now!

109
Minnie L. Maffett, M.D.
We Too Must Fight This War (1942)

For several months now we have been at war with the most treacherous foes to civilized opinions and practices that America has ever faced, or probably will ever be called upon to face again. It is pertinent that we survey calmly but honestly our government's utilization of the total manpower, inclusive of the womanpower of America. Most informed people in this country feel that both will probably be needed before total and decisive victory shall be ours. And this victory you and I both know *must* be ours if it takes the last American dollar, the last drop of American blood, and the remainder of our lives to win it.

The women of our democracy represent one-half its adult population, equal men in education and training and share a reasonable por-

From *Independent Woman,* August 1942.

tion of our war effort. Women probably face greater dangers in case of defeat than do men and are, I well know, anxious to make their contribution to the safety of a country they love before again we must face the tragic verdict, "Too Little and Too Late."

This contribution to the war and to the peace they would like to make as intelligent American citizens and not as classes—privileged or otherwise. They desire only that such service be rendered in high places or low, wherever their greatest contribution can be made. I am open to conviction, with the warning, however, that the argument must be better than any I have heard to date that "low places" are the only ones in which women can serve loyally and well.

In considering the service that we in America can, will, and must render, it is well to remember the trite but true fact that "smart people don't make mistakes that other people have already made." Look at our great ally, England, after more than two years of devastating war. Learn from Margaret Biddle's book, *The Women of England,* and other authentic sources about the great part that more than 7,000,000 women of that country who are now mobilized directly for war are playing. They are doing everything, in fact, other than actually pulling the trigger that fires the gun. (And who knows when anti-aircraft guns may need to be fired by women?) Think of the facts today and remember Mr. Churchill's statement in one of his magnificent broadcasts soon after England's entrance into the war when he declared over a world-wide hook-up that, "not until the last gasp of our national life will we permit women to fight in this war."

What constitutes actual fighting is subject, of course, to individual interpretation, but it is my belief that the girl in the factory who makes the fuse, the worker who assembles the bombs, the pilot who guides the ship and the bombardier who releases the "eggs" on the enemy are equally effective fighters. If this philosophy is true, women today constitute a great potential part of America's effective fighting force.

In one of your Denver papers since my arrival, I noticed that one hundred women—most of whom were army nurses—were left on the rock when Corregidor fell. I leave it to you whether they were an important part of MacArthur's fighting forces!

In another western newspaper, I saw pictured two or three days ago Chinese guerrillas, many of who are women, making life unhappy for the Jap bandits infesting that great country. No one can deny that *they* are actually a part of China's fighting forces.

Looking again and more critically at England, we are convinced that she is at last utilizing her womanpower not only in the field of production but in the planning and direction of the war effort.

When Caroline Haslett, the British engineer, was in America early in the year, she told us that the British government had appointed a womanpower committee, to advise the Minister of Labour on all problems affecting the employment of women. Miss Haslett herself is serving as an adviser to the Ministry of Labour, with the title of Undersecretary of Women in Industry. She is working daily with Mr. Bevin on developing plans for the increasingly effective participation of women in the production area.

And other women have been given responsible posts which call for planning and administration. Florence Horsbrugh is parliamentary secretary to the Ministry of Health. Lady Reading was asked by King George to recruit the Women's Voluntary Services, in which 1,000,000 women are now serving.

The highly trained professional woman—who at the beginning of the war may have taken on a job that any amateur could equally well fill—is being transferred to her proper work. Women scientists are busy in research in the forces, in various government departments, and in industry. The government training scheme, for instance, offers a special six months' course in aircraft inspection to women who hold university degrees in science, and has sponsored training courses for women welfare and personnel managers in factories.

In Russia, womanpower is being used probably as extensively as in any country at war in the planning and direction of war production and in every part of the total war effort, even on the firing line with the men.

An inventory shows that our own American women have done a great deal during these first seven months of war. They are now taking their posts with the armed forces of the United States, through the newly created WAAC. They are taking over lathes and work benches, they are serving as nurses in military hospitals, they have taken courses in engineering and many semi-skilled industrial operations, and they have played vital roles in civilian defense activities.

But there is one glaring weakness. Even today when, as everyone knows, production is the key to victory, opportunities to serve are given to women usually with the greatest reluctance. While our country is now fighting for the right to be free, it is paradoxical that its women citizens must still fight for the right to fight to be free.

As we take an inventory of the place of women seven months after war has been declared, we find them *in* practically everything except the higher policy-making and administrative posts—be these in business, in labor, or in government. The prejudice against women in high positions, of course, has its roots in our tradition and culture.

In the large labor groups in the country, in both the American Federation of Labor and in the C.I.O., there are no women in any of the inner councils. Even the top positions in the Women's Trade Union of Auxiliaries of the A. F. of L. are held by men! The unions predominantly composed of women are governed by the few *men* who are members. Eighty-five per cent of the members of the International Ladies' Garment Workers Union, for example, are women—but the executive board is made up of men and *a* woman!

The non-existence of women in upper executive posts in business and in banking is an old story, though some 400 women have gained executive status in banks in the past two decades—a few as active presidents. War is forcing many firms to take on more women workers—women messengers, women research workers and women bank tellers—but the portals of the council rooms are still closed.

Perhaps most striking of all is the absence of women in high policy posts in our own government. Here is the roster taken from the very latest pamphlet issued by the Office of Emergency Management:

In the War Production Board—among the 146 highest ranking officials listed, there is not one woman.

In the Office of Price Administration—among the 69 officials listed, there is one woman.

In the Office of Facts and Figures—among the 8 top-ranking officials, no women.

In the Office of Civilian Defense—among the 29 top-ranking officials, no women.

Office of Lease-Lend Administration—12 officials, no women.

National War Labor Board—45 members and associate members, no women.

Office of Defense Transportation—16 officials, no women.

Office of Scientific Research and Development—11 officials, no women.

Office of the Coordinator of Inter-American Affairs—23 top-ranking officials, no women.

Office of Defense, Health and Welfare—8 top-ranking officials, no women.

War Manpower Commission—9 top-ranking officials, one of whom is a woman.

Board of Economic Warfare—25 top-ranking officials, no women.

The absence of women in policy-making posts has its humorous side as well as its more serious aspects. I was told that recently the Women's Bureau received an excited call from the Office of Production Management. The deep bass voice at the other end of the telephone was saying, "We are at a meeting and are trying to allocate rubber for women's undergarments. How much rubber must be used in a woman's corset?" I would like to ask, where are the women from the wholesale and retail stores, the factory executives who make them and who know the answer to this question?

Why is it that women are not at the council tables helping make these decisions that affect not only our armies abroad but our wartime living conditions at home? Is it because there are no qualified women? I leave you to answer. We have in this country women trained and experienced in practically every profession and occupation. We have, for example, 131 women engineers; over 10,000 women physicians; 4,000 women lawyers; about 423,000 women managers, owners, and executives—to mention only a few.

These numbers are not as high as they might be because women have been discouraged from going into these highly trained fields. But there are enough.

Let's take the field of psychological warfare. People in the know maintain that the United States is losing the battle of psychological warfare abroad. We have not begun to do a job in this vital area. Why not give some of our superlatively qualified women a chance? I want to ask why such women as Anne O'Hare McCormick, Dorothy Thompson, Clare Boothe Luce, Mrs. Ogden Reid—to name just a few of the many—have not been given the opportunity to help plan and direct our foreign broadcasts?

Our government is engaged in spreading American ideals and democratic principles on the air waves to invaded and enemy countries. There are women in this country with real knowledge of those countries and with real knowledge of the thought processes and the thought patterns of these people. Yet few of them are being heard on government programs. I refer now to such women as Lisa Sergio, Neyan Watts Stevens, and Sigrid Arndt. Failure to use our ablest womanpower in this way is a shortsighted and suicidal policy.

I want to know why some of our able women engineers like Lillian Gilbreth, Edith Clarke, and Mrs. Mabel Rockwell are not in big posts, working side by side with men in directing scientific problems in this war that affects everyone?

I want to know why some of our trained and equipped women surgeons and doctors are not being used in the armed forces? I know something of women in medicine, as well as the civilian and military medical needs at this time, and some estimate of these needs for the future.

The Army and Navy are demanding 6.5 doctors per 1,000 enlisted men. Five thousand are needed in the immediate future and, according to Dr. Leonard Rountree, Medical Director of the Selective Service, 15,000 additional doctors must be secured before the end of 1942. With an Army of five to ten million, you can estimate the medical needs for the future. Twenty-five per cent of the active physicians in my town are already in the service. More than a year ago 3,000 women doctors answered a questionnaire regarding their attitude toward military service. Two thousand expressed a desire for such service—1,300 preferring civilian assignments, and 700 with the armed forces.

These doctors are from the best American medical schools and cover approximately every specialty in medicine.

In response to an opinion expressed by a representative of the Surgeon General's office a year ago, that women doctors "do nothing but diseases of women and children," I made and submitted to that office a survey of the twenty-six women doctors practicing in Dallas and they probably represent a fair cross-section of other medical centers. These twenty-six come from such medical schools as Baylor University, Texas, Cornell, University of Chicago, Woman's Medical University of Pennsylvania, University of Paris, University of Minnesota, Johns Hopkins. Many of them are well trained in endocrinology, pathology, surgery, dermatology, eye, ear, nose and throat, pediatrics, orthopedics, etc. Only two are doing obstetrics!

I had an opportunity to have a personal conference with Colonel Rountree the day the Senate passed the Rogers Bill creating the

WAAC, and offered him the services of these highly trained scientists for such portion of the medical personnel of the WAAC as might be considered equitable and advantageous.

As many of you know, we have been working with the American Medical Women's Association in trying to open the Army and Navy Reserve Corps to women doctors. English women are today serving in this capacity; in fact the British have actually recruited an American woman, Dr. Barbara Stimson, who is now in England working with the British armed forces. Eleven American women doctors were sent to England in response to their call for American doctors a year ago, but none has been used at home so far.

Now, I want to be quite clear, that in making our protests public, I am not attacking the present administration in Washington. We are all for it, we pray for its success, and we are aware that under any other administration and any other political party the situation as regards women would be the same.

Yet I feel that it is my duty, in a democracy, to point these things out, that we may get on with the winning of the war. We have no time to lose.

Some government agencies such as the United States Employment Service, and some private groups, particularly colleges, and organizations like our own, are already trying to supply women with information about training and job openings, so that those who foresee the inevitable future can find their useful place in the war effort. But some war plants still refuse to hire or train women; many labor unions look upon women as unfair competition—and many government agencies apparently never heard of them. Will they see the need for women in time?

Total war means total production. We as a Federation must take on the responsibility of seeing that training is given to women, especially to white collar women. When trained, women along with their brothers in the various fields of production, must be made to appreciate the epitaph that Kipling wrote for a British battalion wiped out when their ammunition was exhausted: "If any mourn us in the shops, say we died because the shift kept holiday." American women at this time will not keep holiday while American boys are fighting and dying on the battlefields of the world.

As a Federation, we shall marshall our strength to see that women are used wherever they can best serve. We are not fighting for women's rights; we are now fighting for human rights and in that fight women have an essential place.

All this year we have taken steps in this direction. We have only recently, for example, urged the creation of a women's advisory committee to the Manpower Board to advise on all plans and policies affecting the mobilization of women. "Because we are so well aware of the many difficult problems that are bound to arise," we wrote Paul V. McNutt, director, "we believe an advisory committee of women should be created composed of women who know and understand these problems. Such an advisory committee of women who are experts in personnel and production problems could help sift and reflect the best thinking of women themselves. Such a committee could be of real assistance to you and to the entire nation."

And so when these just and desirable measures shall have become realities, what will again prevent such a progressive program from retrogression? I feel definitely that the greatest safeguard will be a strong, organized body, such as this, devoted to the democratic philosophy of fair play for every American—man or woman—Jew or Gentile—white, black, red, or brown—whether an American-born or an American-made citizen—and dedicated to this unselfish task of seeing to it that this great democracy, born in blood and tears, shall remain forever the land of freedom and opportunity in fact and not in theory alone.

Women, as well as men, will meet national demands without a murmur, and I can definitely assure our friends and our government that the total resources of this Federation are intensively being used to win this war.

And when this great victory shall be ours and the battle for the peace becomes paramount, we in America will not again have to call for a Pilate's bowl to wash our hands of the responsibility for failure to join the other democracies in establishing and maintaining a just, reasonable, and lasting peace.

110
DOROTHY THOMPSON
A Woman's Manifesto (1947)

The time has come for the women of the world to speak to the leaders of states, who control the destinies of men and nations. For centuries—yes, from the beginning of the history of civilization—we have performed our functions to the family, and through it to human society, for the most part in humility and largely in obscurity.

Despite our historically recent enfranchisement, and despite the opening for us of economic opportunities outside the home, we recognize our primary function, as it is still our primary occupation, to be the reproduction and nurture of children to adulthood and the maintenance of the home, as the basic unit of all civilizations.

We call attention to the fact that woman was the original creator of settled civilization and thus of the state.

In the most ancient times, man, an adventurous nomad, went forth to hunt and to kill for food, taking his woman and offspring with him. In these wanderings, families were separated, and the young and tender members fell by the wayside. Then it was woman, as a mother, mindful of her young ones, who demanded that they be settled in one place, where they could be kept at her side until they were old enough and strong enough to fend for themselves. Thus, out of the deepest and most profound of all instincts and loves—the maternal instinct, and maternal love—the first homes were created, the first estates, and the forerunners of all states.

Woman, as all the myths and sagas of the world describe her, was the founder of agriculture. It was she who turned her mate from huntsman to tiller of the soil. She saw in the earth into which seed was dropped by Nature, to generate new life and come to fruition in regular time, the reproductive process of her own experience, and all nations and all languages recognize the deep symbolic affinity between the mother and the earth.

She, the mother, desired stability and peace. Thus came the first household, the first farm, the first garden, the first industrial arts, and the beginning of the first *community.*

We may take it that in those still savage and nomadic days, new-founded homes and communities had to be protected from still roaming and savage marauders, and the man, being physically the more powerful, assumed the role of fender off of assaults upon his family. For this he armed himself with whatever weapons the status of his civilization made possible. He emerged as the warrior, associating himself in tribes of kindred warriors, and the pre-eminent among these became the chiefs. Thus the warrior became the statesman, and the original creative role of woman was relegated to secondary place.

The mark of that fact is upon the whole of human society, now, as it has been for millennia. Our societies, national and international, are in a perpetual state of naked or veiled war; and force, naked or veiled, is its arbiter.

This condition belies the most profound and anciently rooted experience of women as the nurturers of families. It belies the experience of government in the primary center of government: the home.

The condition of the home is peace. The condition of the home is harmony, between all its members. Though within a single family of children of identical parents there is a wide variety of gifts; though one be stronger than another, one more brilliant, another more industrious, the basis of the home is mutual aid

From *Ladies' Home Journal* (1947).

based on love. Neither the weak are sacrificed to the strong nor the strong to the weak. The strong are turned from predatory to protective inclinations and the weak strengthened by the example of the strong.

The condition of the home is law—of justice tempered with mercy. The rules of the home are established for the welfare of all. They are not established to favor the strong members over the weak, nor to shackle the strong with the disabilities of the weak. Each has the duties and responsibilities suitable to his capacities, and each the reward necessary to his sustenance and development.

The discipline of the home is merciful. When punishments are meted out, it is not to satisfy some vengeful god nor to return evil for evil; nor to establish authority as arbitrary force. No, its purpose is the protection of the family and of the wrongdoer himself, as a member of it; it is to train the young to respect authority which is reasonable and affectionate, to prepare them for self-control, and for eventual law-abiding membership in a larger community than the home.

The home is not an organization. It is an organism, a part of organic life itself. As Nature attracts man and woman to each other that out of their love for and pleasure in each other life should be renewed, so it endows the father with pride to care for and support his offspring and the mother with the instinct to serve and sacrifice for them. Her body is the very earth in which they are bred; her bones unjoint themselves in agony that they be born; her breasts offer them their first nourishment; her hands perform for them their first services. No matter what her personal achievements may be, there is no joy in them comparable to joy in the achievements of her children, and there is no creativeness of her own, as an individual person, to rival the life-giving, life-serving creativeness of her motherhood.

Thus, in nature, she is the nurturing, stabilizing, balancing and conservationist force, bent toward the renewal, protection and perfecting of the race.

Her occupation—the primary occupation of the overwhelming majority of womankind—falls outside the pattern of the rest of economic life.

Men work for gain expressed in money, the convertible value. This gain goes in large part to the support of the family and the home. But the woman's contribution finds no recompense in, nor is it measurable by, such values. Her services are rendered for love, and the conditions of her work set only by capacity and necessity. Performing so wide a variety of tasks that half a dozen persons would be needed for them were she to resign from all; matching the length and intensity of her toil to suit, not her own whims, but the habits and emergencies of the whole family; asking no compensation for herself beyond what is left over from expenditures for the others; she, the homemaking, home-serving woman, belongs in no organized body or category of workers or employers; operates under no recognized economic codes or laws; and falls into no recognizable economic class. For economic classes are in constant struggle with one another, and the dominant motive of all is self-interest. Her dominant motive is love, the service of love and the interest of her loved ones.

Or if it be that the services of men are rendered to the state, whose prime characteristic is that it is an instrument of force, she is still not a servant of the state, unless or until she is divorced from her primary service, to the family.

Thus her experience of life is unique. She is bound less to organized class, and less to the force of the state, than is her mate. She is bound at its prime source to life itself, life which comes before class, or state, or nation. As she first recognized the soil as the source of sustenance, so she is cosmically tied in other ways, her very reproductive system being part of the rhythm of seasons and tides responsive to the laws of Nature.

There is on this earth, and would be wherever in this universe organic life exists, a solidarity which has hitherto been largely silent. It needs no governments, nor unions, nor organized associations to bring it into being. It needs no flag to raise. No boundaries delineate it, whether they be boundaries of nation, or race, or class. It is the solidarity between women as mothers. It is the solidarity of a function and vocation transcending all ephemeral patterns of organized society—the function and vocation of protecting, through nurture, the human race.

Even war does not destroy it, nor the hates of war obliterate it. Battles rage between great nations of men, and all are mobilized, women too, and shouts are raised that this nation or that must be forever rendered impotent, and in the madness of war people become abstractions to be named en masse with the name of a state or of the leader of a state.

But to woman people are not abstractions and not masses. People are living beings, each one of them unique, each born in suffering and each to unavoidable suffering as well as joy before his life is done; each, though, endowed with life, with life due him from his fellows in life, and in the mother there is great compassion for all the children of men.

The boy hurtling to his death from a burning plane may be a classified enemy. But the woman's heart tells her he is a boy, his life perverted to the will of a state, and otherwise the natural companion of her boy. The lad shattered on the battlefield is a lad, on whichever side of the line he may fall. The girl raped in the savagery of war is a girl, some father's love, some mother's care, whatever her language and name.

This is true, and every woman knows it is true, no matter how, under certain conditions, her tongue may hold silence.

The woman knows that war is the cancer of society, the running amuck of its cells, the destroyer of its focusing point, the home, and as such the violator of the purposes of all human activity.

For all states, all organized order and economies are exclusively created to serve the home and the communities of homes. As the home was the beginning of civilized order, so its prosperity and protection are the end purpose of civilized order.

Warring nations and warring classes forget this. The simple, practical and even banal fact that the state exists as an extension of the family, and in service to it, is lost in struggles for power and grandiose dreams of new orders of power.

These struggles deny the moralities of the home, overturn its carefully inculcated inhibitions and values, corrupt its most sacred lessons, deny the natural human solidarity and harmonies which it affirms, and create an absolute breach between its realities and the realities of the organized state.

The great historic and biological function of woman is wrenched from her. She is crippled in her primary vocation and wounded in her deepest social impulses. All she performs and that women before her have performed is brought to naught. The child to whom she has taught love is instructed to hate; the strong boy whom she has taught to protect others is called off to wound or kill, or be wounded or killed by, others.

The gentle and just authority of the father is torn from the family, and the authority of reason and love replaced by the authority of brute force and blind obedience. The weak are called to duties and responsibilities normal to the strong. The son, in whom the mother has invested not only the services of her body, but her own aspirations of achievement, is killed, or maimed, or perverted from the standards the home has bred in him.

Waywardness enters the home, as the reflection of the wild waywardness of war. Sons and daughters mature precociously, the presence of death making them lustful of life, and happiness whose postponement may be forever, marrying in haste and creating foundationless families.

Since lawlessness is the very cause of war, and war itself the violation of the primary law of life, all laws come to be held in contempt, and waves of crime sweep society, sucking into them even the carefully reared.

And all this happens in warring nations even when they never hear at home the sound of battle; even when they are safe from the indiscriminate havoc of bombs.

What, then, of those societies, those communities of homes, where the maelstrom is centered? In them the home itself is destroyed—its physical existence. The mother and children are driven underground into communal shelters where there is neither privacy nor normal decency. The children live in perpetual terror, developing nervous illnesses, reduced by shock to near or actual insanity, and are often crippled or blown to death before the mother's eyes. Or she herself is killed, and with the father dead or far away, the child is orphaned, and in the chaos of destruction left to wander, to fend for itself, to live on society as a wild predatory animal, and become familiar with all forms of delinquency and crime.

The wild dynamism of war knows no checks of inhibitions. To win becomes the sole goal of entire human societies, and to win by any means. All the conventions of war created in the reasonableness of peace lapse one by one. The enemy becomes, not an army, not a state, but an entire people, infant and aged, living and unborn. There is no weapon which is illegitimate, and none which, once discovered, remains unused, if its use can be regarded as decisive.

Her heart paralyzed, her eyes widened to ever-mounting horrors, the woman hears of plottings to destroy the organic life of the earth itself—the earth, to which her finger first pointed as the source of sustenance.

She learns with fascinated, almost hypnotized terror, that the secrets of the cosmos have been penetrated, that cosmos to which she is so intimately attached, and of which she is so perpetually and gratefully aware. That which holds the world together is untied for war; the very neutrons and electrons are unloosed in fury to destroy in a single moment a hundred thousand lives.

The cessation of hostilities does not check the awful dynamism. The woman prays for a just peace, and when it comes it wears the face of war. Now, has thought the woman, comes the rebuilding, but its foundations are corroded by revenge. A new order is proclaimed by this or that one of the victors, and for it new millions of families are uprooted and cast adrift, the barbed-wire cage their habitation and pariahhood the curse upon their children.

With the dissolution of more families, the dissolution of society progresses. For every crime committed, another is compounded, and for every atonement of guilt new scapegoats are found. Each state points the finger of accusation against another, and says, "For this hapless state of affairs, you, or you, or you are to blame," thus selecting the new enemy, against whom a new war must be fought, or from whom the nation must again be defended. Thus each war breeds the next in dreadful succession, each truce being briefer than the last, and each new war more fearful.

This competition between armed, sovereign states has its own awful laws. For each weapon in the hands of one, a worse weapon must be found by the other. For each state subjected as a satellite, a satellite must be attached by the other. For each man conscripted by one, two men must be drafted by the other.

The destruction of society proceeds in preparation for renewed war.

Agents are sent into open states regarded as potential enemies, to set class against class, race against race, and undermine the possible belligerent from within. Even pacifism and the nobler instincts of man are perverted into instruments of war, as those with aggressive intentions use them to weaken the resistance of their victims.

Puppets are set up as despots over doubtful allies, or eased into governments to serve the interests of mighty contenders approaching each other.

The military takes precedence over the civil, the heads and diplomats of states appear as marshals or generals.

The Moloch of war preparation eats up the revenues needed for home building and the erection of plants for production for the people's needs.

Fear again permeates the whole of society. The laws of the free become grudgingly permitted, and laws for informers and spies are enacted.

Privacy of thought and freedom of conscience fall prey to suspicions, and loyalties are impugned.

Honesty and candor are corrupted, lest they aid a possible enemy, or precipitate a crisis too soon.

And all these are committed and justified only as measures of defense in anticipation of probable war.

What condition of affairs is this, asks the woman, that perpetuates as peace the very evils for which she has sacrificed children and home? Did she not endure once again the scourge of war only that those who embodied its spirit and seized its weapons should be repulsed and eternally tamed, and that all, with them, should learn the lesson? What condition of affairs is this, whereby nations and states adopt the spirit and methods of their defeated enemies, commit their very crimes, repeat their very patterns, and all in the name of defense and security?

The mind and the instincts of the mother cry: Halt! They cry warning.

The mother points to the earth, poisoned with human blood, from which even in peace are driven its native husbandmen for fear of another war. The mother warns: Beware! For the earth will take her revenge. She will lie fallow and men will hunger; she will grow sterile and children will weep.

The mother regards the heavens, the sun, the stars, the changing seasons, the rising and waning moon, the grandeur of their rhythms, the beauty of their cosmic harmony, the majesty of their laws, and her heart, full of reverence and wonder, trembles with fearful premonition that this planet, one among them, shall be displaced and hurtled into blackness by violent interference with their integrating forces.

The mother searches the faces of men, and sees in them fear and the angers begotten of fear. She listens to the voices of statesmen, her ears acute to long-yearned-for words. What she hears are harsh cries for Peace and Armed Power, Armed Power and Peace. What she listens for are the words: Peace, Love, and Law.

Again she sees, as her mother and her grandmother before her have seen, the forces dividing and armies forming. Already she sees the minds of the peoples rebent to war. Already she sees the revenues of states expended in prodigious wastage for armies and weapons of war. And already she sees the subtlest scientists of war from among the late enemies welcomed by both sides into the newly forming camps.

Already she sees all institutions, hopes, ideals, promises perverted to war and the propaganda of war. Because they are the social systems of powerful states, the question is asked: Can communism and capitalism exist in the same world? If not, by what means shall one or the other perish?

The woman knows the answer to this question. Life and society are manifold. Life is a growing, a waning, birth, passing and rebirth, and so it is with social orders, as they experiment and change to adapt themselves to the habits and needs of peoples. In all of them are true values, in all of them some evils, and none promises unchanged permanence. For all of them one can have tolerance, if their carriers and promoters are but inhibited from forceful subjection of others.

It is not communism and capitalism which cannot live in the same world. It is *armed* communism, and *armed* capitalism, bending their theories to become instruments of combat, facing each other with mighty armies and frightful weapons, which threaten all order, all social systems, and the very life of the humanity which each of them claims to serve.

The time of decision is here, is due and overdue, the time when the promises perennially made to the mothers of men should be fulfilled.

Let, therefore, the nations and the leaders of nations gather together, and let them make unto themselves a law.

Let them select from among themselves a judge.

Let them create from among themselves a police to enforce the law and the judgments of the law, and let the judge and the police be responsible to no state or nation but to the body of mankind.

Let the law be against the great collective crime of mankind, so long adjudged as such by the conscience of mankind: the crime of war.

Let the law strike from the hands of states the weapons of mass destruction, which are the terror and menace of the world, and strike from the power of states the right to manufacture what will otherwise, in the devil's own time, bring all civilizations and much of organic life to certain end.

Let the law be written into the constitutions of all states and be the definition of "peace-loving."

Let no man and no state infringe the prohibitions of this law to prepare for war with conscript armies and weapons of mass destruction, except with certainty of immediate punishment.

Let all frontiers be open to inspection by the defenders of this law, and let offenders, before their actions become dangerous, be brought before judgment, and if guilty be banished forever from communication with mankind.

Let this law be proclaimed in all languages and on all wave lengths of the world, in repeated remainder that it exists to protect all peoples. And let them know to whom they can report violation, or suspicion of violation, of this law, and let there be agencies for their protection.

And let no state dare veto this law of life, lest it be immediately recognized by its own people and by the people of the whole earth as the enemy of mankind.

Thus shall the home again be secure, the state be an instrument for its protection, its standards and values be rehabilitated in society, and its body and soul have peace.

The brow of the woman has been gentle, her will compliant, her patience enduring.

Now the crisis demands that her brow be stern, her patience be indignation and her compliance be translated into purposeful power. For she must contribute to fulfill on a world scale the beneficent functions of her nature and the purposes of her destiny.

111
Charlotta A. Bass
You Can Vote for Peace (1952)

Except for signs such as "For Whites," "For Colored" in railroad stations, theatres, and most public places and recreational centers, the pattern of discrimination against Negroes in Texas differs but slightly from Washington, D. C., and from Governor Stevenson's home town and state capitol, Springfield, Ill., where I and other Negroes have been refused service in jimcrow restaurants.

At 10:30 A.M. Saturday, Oct. 4, I reached Dallas, Tex. At the station to meet and welcome me were many leading citizens. . . .

After several hours rest, at 6:30 P.M. we went to station WFAA, and I delivered a fifteen-minute speech which was broadcast over the entire state of Texas. When I entered the studio to make the broadcast, the receptionist and some of the other personnel scowled and were obviously unfriendly. But after hearing the speech on ending the Korean war now, and negotiating the lone remaining issue later, they were all smiles and several insisted on shaking hands with me. After the broadcast we were dinner guests of friends, which afforded us the opportunity of meeting many of the leading people of Dallas. . . .

When I talked to the Texas radio audience, I told of some of my observations as our train

From *The Daily Worker,* November 2, 1952.

rolled over the vast plains of the West of Texas. Then I talked about the issues uppermost in the minds of all Negroes today—and of all Americans. This is what I told the radio audience:

"117,000 casualties have been suffered by our forces in the Korean 'police action.' 117,000 families have grieved the loss or injury of sons, husbands, and loved ones. For what purpose is the youth of our country being sacrificed? What do we hope to gain by flirting so very dangerously with all-out World War III by bombings on the Yalu River at the border of China? We, the ordinary everyday Americans trying to raise our children to be good future citizens have everything to lose and absolutely nothing to gain. This is not the case of the war profiteers, the generals, and the politicians for whom 'peace' is the forgotten issue in this campaign.

"Our prisoners of war in prison camps for up to 27 months have everything to lose. Our youth, spending their approach to manhood in being trained to kill, have everything to lose. The small businessman, even here in Texas where war dollars from mining camps may put money in his right-hand pocket, but taxes filch it out of his left-hand pocket to pay for a war economy that costs 85 cents out of every tax dollar. The small businessman, as well as the housewife who can't balance her food budget because of war spending, has everything to lose in a war that even generals, high in command, say can't be won on a military level.

"I am speaking to you tonight as Vice Presidential candidate on the Progressive Party ticket. I feel great pride that the Progressive Party saw fit to name as the first woman in our history, no less the first Negro woman, to be a candidate for high national office.

"The reluctant Democratic candidate, Governor Stevenson, says, and I quote, 'I have no tidy solution for the Korean problem.' His Republican counterpart states—and again I quote—'I have no prescription for bringing the Korean war to a decisive end.' Only the Progressive Party, my party, the People's Party, for which I ask your support, has a simple plan to end the Korean war. We demand—Stop the shooting war NOW—Negotiate the difference later! Whoever heard of a war being fought over the exchange of prisoners? Yet that is exactly what is happening. The stated reason for the beginning of the war no longer exists. We have long since reached the 38th Parallel. The American people yearn for peace. But the war goes on. Every single opinion poll bears out this deep-rooted conviction.

"Especially are we, the American women, comprising 52 percent of the national vote, opposed to the continued slaughtering of our loved ones. As women, we play a creative role. We bear and bring up children. We guide and hold together the home. The destiny of the nation is in our hands. We create, because it is against our very nature to destroy. We will not stand idly by while senseless war destroys what we sought to build.

"I assure each and every one of you in the listening audience that I solemnly pledge to work for peace on your behalf, and I earnestly solicit your vote for the Progressive Party candidates to insure this end.

"As I rode across the vast expanse of Texas I could see from my train window the havoc wrought by the drought, regarded as the worst in 25 years. I could see herds of white-faced cattle searching the sun-baked plains for a blade of grass. Acres and acres of burned-out cotton on which Texas farmers had toiled long and hard, had planted and replanted, and yet had no money crop to show for their efforts.

"Occasionally, I saw some irrigated land where the cotton grew green and healthy. In wide-dry-land farming areas in Texas, wells can be drilled to provide adequate irrigation. The uncertainty of the farmer who has to pray for rain, and for the past three years without much success, can be eliminated by government aid in irrigating these vast areas. Yet how can the government aid the farmer if 85 cents out of every dollar goes to bolster foreign governments rejected by their peoples, in attempting to influence internal policies of European countries by buying their loyalty, and for all-out war. The peace program of the Progressive Party means aid and prosperity to the farmer, while the say-nothing attitude of the two major presidential aspirants portends continued disaster. Both candidates have ignored the facts as reported by the Federal Reserve Board that soaring farm production costs have been 'set in motion or magnified' by war in Korea 'and by the subsequent acceleration of defense activities.' Neither mentioned that 'farm debts have increased about 80 percent since January, 1946.'

"As the farmer continues to get a smaller and smaller share of the national income, the man in the city, both the small businessman and the salaried man, gets caught in the squeeze. Ask any Texas rancher how much he received a head for cattle. He'll probably tell you that he sold for less than he paid, in addition to feed costs. Ask any housewife how much she paid for a pound of beef. The great difference in price goes into increased production costs, as well as profits, caused by the war. The American public has long grown used to the illogical assertions of campaign oratory. Yet a new low, even in political promises, is made by General Eisenhower when he calls for military spending on one hand, and sweeping tax reductions on the other. At least Gov. Stevenson tells you not to look for reduction in taxes; he plans to pour more dollars and men into the war. Is this what you want?

112
Sophia Wyatt
One Day Strike for Peace (1962)

It had apparently all started with a few women in a living-room in Washington discussing in alarm the way world affairs were rocketing out of control. They wondered what they could do about it and somebody had the idea that women ought to stage a one day "Strike for Peace" throughout the nation. I shall never know by what alchemy the word went around, but on November 1 in 20 major cities in the nation, women marched out of their homes to demonstrate for peace.

The word came quietly to me in Los Angeles when an old friend rang me up and said she was sending me some literature which was the most exciting thing she had ever read, and would I pass it on to the neighbours, talk to my friends and be a darling and give her a lift on November 1st. When I started to ask who and what, she cut me short. There were no names; it was no organization; would I just read it and come.

An anonymous pamphlet like an anonymous letter tempts me to reach for the wastepaper basket, and in this mood I began to read the literature. Who would be so stupid as to respond to a call that is not even signed by a Mrs. Smith? My misguided friend must be told that only Communists would distribute literature without name in the name of peace. In America, status is the hidden persuader, and anyone with status would certainly proclaim it. I would not go, but to preserve old friendship I would merely say that since I am a working woman and November 1 was another working day, I could obviously not go.

Yet as I held the pamphlet poised over the wastepaper basket, I was restrained from tearing it up by the same idiocy that mastered reason when as a girl I invariably passed on every chain letter for fear of breaking the charm of luck that it carried. I reread the sentence that held me against my will. "We don't make foreign policy but we know to what end we want it made: the preservation of life on earth."

I made a note of the instructions for the Los Angeles area. We were to meet at 10:30 AM on the steps of the old State Building at First and Spring streets in the heart of Los Angeles and there join the line of march. "Placards will be prepared. Please do not bring your own."

From Women Strike for Peace pamphlet, 1962.

I took the pamphlet to my office and tried a bit of agitation on my fellow workers, but like the salesman who does not believe in the product he is trying to sell, my voice grew weaker and weaker before their argument, which deep in my heart was my own, "What's the use?"

I started to get ready for this foolish trek in an unjust and mounting irritation with my friend who had got me into this. But the pamphlet was exercising its spell. Although Los Angeles is a town where slacks and pincurls are more at home on the street than gloves and hat, I suddenly changed into a respectable dress, hauled my one and only hat out of mothballs and put on gloves. The telephone rang. It was one of my colleagues who had thought it over. Could she come in my car? When we got to my friend's house she too had picked up another passenger, so the Morris Minor was full.

All the way down the Hollywood Freeway, we kept abreast of the wierdest vehicle I had ever seen. It looked like an oversized white gasoline truck, but on its belly in blood red letters we read, "Fallout Shelters, Inc., A Division of Western Swimming Pools, Inc."

We reached the steps of the old State Building half an hour before the scheduled time and my heart started down. A handful of women were fixing up arm bands and placards. A television truck stood by and a few policemen rocked on their heels eyeing the empty steps. My friend the instigator, sorrowfully avoiding my eyes, mumbled, "It doesn't look so hot. Let's go and have some coffee."

We came out of the restaurant 20 minutes later and saw a miracle. The steps had come alive, teeming with women, young, old, white, yellow, black, with babies and buggies, some bearing babies unborn. A long line of chartered buses looking like the return to the depot after a day's run, moved slowly up the street to the crowded steps. They disgorged women, women and more women. Reinforcements of police were called in. Who were these women? Where did they come from? I turned to my neighbor, a bright young woman, and asked, "What organization do you belong to?" She laughed. "I don't belong to any organization. I've got a child of 10."

All stood ready and waiting. In a great arc across the steps like the banners of the Knights of the Garter in St. George's Chapel, the placards were lifted proclaiming the purpose for which they were gathered. "End the arms race, not the human race," "Choose peace while there is a choice," "The Soviet 50-megaton bomb is an outrage against humanity," and quoting Mr. Kennedy, "Mankind must put an end to war or war will put an end to mankind."

Punctually at 10:30 the voice of a woman magnified through the loud speaker rose in the crowd. This frail woman was no professional speaker but in the passion of her sincerity she spoke for us all. The Governor of California, attending state affairs in Sacramento, was represented by the Attorney General of California. Even a politician did not sound like one on this day, as in his response he introduced a literary analogy to this occasion in the gathering called by Lysistrata at the square in Athens. Courteously and with admiration he wished us well and read a telegram from the Governor and one from his wife.

Silently and with banners raised the women lined up and proceeded eight deep and in a line stretching, for blocks and blocks, into thousands, to march to the City Hall and the Federal Building. A blossoming of faces appeared at every window to the uppermost storeys of the surrounding buildings as the police, halting all traffic, shepherded us across the road like kindly fathers. The messages were delivered, and with their mission completed the women disbanded.

That evening the Women's Strike for Peace took precedence over all the news. Commentators even made it the theme of their remarks and to a man said, "Well done," to the women.

As I sat back with my feet propped up watching the other demonstrations on television—the women in Washington leaving a petition at the White House for Mrs. Kennedy and another at the Soviet Embassy for Mrs. Khruschchev; Faye Emerson addressing the crowd and saying, "I felt I *must* do something."—I relived the moment mysteriously beyond all knowledge, when women standing shoulder to shoulder as strangers became sisters.

"Now tell me," said Lysistrata, "if I have discovered a means of ending the war, will you all second me?" As in Athens so in America the cry went up, "Yes, verily."

113
Karen Koonan and Bobbi Cieciorka
Anti-Draft and Women's Rights (1967)

We want to talk about a couple of things: How the draft is an issue which affects women, and why women should fight this thing which both symbolizes and sustains our oppression.

Because women in this country are oppressed—people in this country are oppressed, but women in special ways—and we are oppressed, very directly by the draft.

THE DRAFT

The draft needs to be understood in the full scope of its coercive power. Not only does it gobble up our young men, warp their minds and get a lot of them killed, it also controls how the rest of us will live in order to escape its clutches. An official Selective Service System memo which we read recently points out that procuring manpower for the armed forces is only a small part of the SSS operation. More important is the "channeling manpower through (the) deferments aspects of the Selective Service System." The memo makes it quite clear that this is very conscious manipulation. Time and again it comments on "the ever increasing problem (of) how to control effectively the service of individuals who are not in the armed forces. . . . Many young men would not have pursued a higher education if there had not been a program of student deferment, many young scientists, engineers, tool and die makers and other possessors of scarce skills would not remain in their jobs in the defense effort if it were not for a program of occupational deferment. . . . Selective Service processes do not compel people by edict as in foreign systems to enter pursuits having to do with essentiality and progress. They go because they know that by going they will be deferred. Delivery of manpower for induction . . . is not much of an administrative or financial challenge. It is dealing with the other millions of registrants that the system is heavily occupied." . . .

In other words, that student deferment, that defense industry job which seems like such a clever maneuver, has all been planned ahead. Where you work and what you work at and a whole lot of things about what ought to be your PRIVATE life are shaped by the SSS lurking in the background.

WOMEN

How do women fit in? Well, you notice that the memo doesn't mention them. That's because women aren't really important to the power structure which designed the draft. Those politics and those economics can pretty much get along without women. And that's why women are second class citizens in this country. And that's why our status isn't going to change until the power structure is changed. Until changes are made, women are going to have to put up with second class education, second class jobs and second class wages. And something else: Ain't nobody gonna make those changes FOR us. We have got to do it for ourselves.

WOMEN & THE WEEK

Stop the Draft Week made us think about broad issues. The Week wasn't just another moral protest; it was the beginning of a move

From *The Movement*, November 1967.

toward POWER. We learned that it wasn't just Stop the Draft/Don't Feed the War; it was the really broad issues of power in this country, the need for self-determination, the need for people to control their own lives. In other words, some pretty basic changes in this old country. And we thought about what that means for women, because it's a little different for us than it is for men. Some observations: Women do play secondary roles in this society, roles which are perpetuated by the society. Any serious attempt to liberate the society has to reject secondary roles for women. As a movement, we can't talk about taking power over our lives while within that movement men still dominate women. Men can't talk about self-determination and at the same time refuse self-determination to women. That just ain't freedom, ain't equality and ain't gonna lead to taking power. So, as women, seeing this, we have a duty—which is to emancipate ourselves, NOW, so that we can be fully functioning individuals in the struggle, able to act without relying on men.

MOVEMENT WOMEN

Even in the movement in the past we've usually played secondary roles. We've been the typists and teachers, the office managers and cooks. We have not been projected as leaders or spokesmen: we have rarely BEEN leaders and spokesmen. We existed to BACK UP the men and be around for the social aspects of their political lives. When we have participated equally with men, when we have led demonstrations, been on steering committees, etc., it's been very difficult. We have to work twice as hard as a man to prove ourselves before we are accepted. We have to deal with snickering, being called "unfeminine" and just plain being ignored. Some of us have done these things; a lot of us haven't.

THE WEEK

In the Stop the Draft Week organizing, women faced the usual problems. Somehow there we were doing the office work and the agit-prop theater. But some of us demanded in the planning sessions that we be listened to as political, thinking people. We came to realize that when the guys joked or called us "ball breakers" we could respond with "That's your problem, baby," and it would be true; it wasn't our problem. We knew what we were doing; we knew we weren't "trying to be men." If men were threatened by women acting as independent political people, it said something about their confidence in themselves, not about our femininity.

When the heat was on—in the demonstrations—many of us participated, some as monitor captains. In the face of possible violence by cops there was no need and no time to worry about women acting like men. It has been the same in ALL people's struggles for power—in Cuba, in Spain, in Vietnam—woman have participated as equals with men. Battlefield conditions both allow and require us to become fellow warriors. During the Stop the Draft Week demonstrations we worked along side the men, protecting demonstrators, rescuing people from the cops, building barricades. Now we all know that we can do those things and that's a good feeling.

WHAT NEXT?

What needs to happen next is that we must extend the legitimacy for which we struggle so hard, the legitimacy to which Stop the Draft Week has in some measure added, particularly around the draft issue. Women have to become increasingly militant. We have to learn to assert ourselves, to demand both our rights and our right to equal participation in the struggle. We think the draft is a good issue for women to work around. When the draft is understood as a coercive force which attacks both men and women, and when it is seen in the context of our larger struggle for power to control our lives, it is obvious that women are just as involved as men. We don't pretend to say that this increased militancy will be easy. The system legislates against it. Our own insecurities and the prejudices of our men increase the difficulty. But the stakes are high. That ancient goal, freedom for all people, can only be attained when women as well as men are free.

114
Jill Severn
Women and Draft Resistance: Revolution in the Revolution (1968)

The objective status of women in this country is as much one of second class citizenship now as it was in 1920 when suffrage for women was first won. That was nearly 50 years ago. Today, we are still discriminated against in jobs, housing, legal redress, and in the social freedoms we are allowed in a post-Victorian society. To put it plainly, we are oppressed.

From this oppression there is coming now a growing consciousness among women of all walks of life that something in our lives is being denied, and that we cannot tolerate the roles assigned to us by this system and still be whole people. There is a mounting consciousness among women not only of our own oppression and a determination to fight it, but a consciousness of the inter-relation of our victimization to the rest of the struggle against a system which finds oppression so necessary to its own survival.

Women's groups are springing up all over the country to fight for women's rights, for they feel an identity with all other oppressed sectors of the U.S. and the world and share their militancy. This growing consciousness, and the new organizations which express it, deserve the support of all radicals who aspire to an equalitarian society. If we are to effect the kind of social changes that will produce an equalitarian society, we dare not overlook or ignore the right of women to equality on precisely the same grounds as we demand it for Black people, youth, and every other oppressed minority. Discrimination on account of sex is no less inhuman than discrimination on account of race or age, and should be afforded as little tolerance.

The status of women in the radical movement is little better than a reflection of the norms of second-sexdom of society at large. Women are discriminated against and taken advantage of inside the movement as much as outside it. They are denied leadership and the opportunities to develop as political because, in the case of Black women, it is feared they will "castrate" their male counterparts, and in the white old and new left, they are primarily and expediently exploited for white technical secretarial skills, or they are at best allowed to operate as spokesmen where a vacuum of male leadership exists; they rarely operate in top leadership positions. The absurdity of a movement with our goals perpetuating this kind of degradation and internal hypocrisy is becoming more apparent and more resented by women activists.

There are those both inside and outside the anti-draft movement who would deny women full participation in this movement on the grounds that since we aren't directly confronting "the man," we are not entitled to leadership in the anti-draft movement. But to deny us full and equal participation here is only to add another dimension to our already existing oppression. . . . Refusal of induction is one of the few potent forms of protest and resistance to American imperialism. That is not to say that we will fight to participate in the Vietnamese war, but that draft exemption means a *denial of full participation in the struggle against the military* at a time when that struggle is one of the most important things happening. Exemption for women is not a privilege, but another indication of the inferior status of women in this country.

There was a time when Blacks were excluded from military service too, and it is

From a typescript, drafted by Jill Severn on behalf of Radical Women, April 1968.

doubtful that anyone ever successfully used that discrimination as proof of their "privileged" status. Exemption from the draft is only one more "special consideration" designed to perpetuate the dependency of women, and at this point in the history of American politics and the development of the movement, the denial of this avenue of expression is many times over as crucial as the denial of the vote was to women prior to 1920.

For these reasons, it is incongruous and offensive to us that we should be denied leadership or equality in the movement on the basis of our supposedly priviledged and protected special position. If anyone confronts the oppression of "the man," and confronts him on every social level of life, it is women!

We demand, and deserve, the right to participate in the movement on exactly the same basis as anyone else: on the grounds of our political beliefs and our equal stake in the future. We reject the concept of ladies' auxiliaries, of special political roles based on our "finer nature and gentler instincts," and of the whole gamut of supportive, subordinate, and "inspirational" political functions for women. We can fight at least as long and as hard and as consistently for we are doubly oppressed and doubly angry and accordingly, have a double stake in the movement.

What we demand from Draft Resistance is support of our struggle to achieve equal rights and recognition of the connection of women's equality with every other goal of the movement. To those who say it is irrelevant and devisive to make an issue of this question when there are so many other "more decisive" issues to fight on, we answer that we have been intimidated by this contemptuous approach too long already and that the time for our fight for freedom is now.

Freedom is indivisible, and oppressions cannot be value-judged in an order of priority. Solidarity of *all* the oppressed is the key to freedom for any one of the sectors. Morale and mutual aid is the name of the tactic of liberation. To attempt to "unify" the movement by demanding that it rally around a single issue is to fracture the movement internally by separating, isolating, and demoralizing the various victims of different but inter-related exploitations. To demand that a victim of injustice stifle her cries until "more decisive" victims are rescued is to demoralize a potential vanguard and inject chauvinistic unconcern into a movement that must respect *all the oppressed*. The movement can only grow by recognizing and encouraging its most vital and militant supporters and spokesmen, and is insulting to women as well as sheer folly for the movement, to allow itself to be divided along lines imposed by the masculine mystique of the ruling class.

115

BELLA ABZUG

Testimony before the 1968 Platform Committee of the Democratic National Convention on Behalf of Women Strike for Peace (1968)

I speak today on behalf of Women Strike for Peace, a movement of thousands of American women who found their political voice less than a decade ago when they cried out against the threat to human survival implicit in the deadly nuclear arms race and the testing of atomic weapons that menaced the children of this earth. Five years ago, the forces for peace and sanity won a tiny victory—the limited nuclear test ban, which President John F. Kennedy described as the first step in the thousand-mile journey toward peace. The second step has not come. Instead, we have—

- the horror of Vietnam.
- a monstrous military behemoth that consumes more than half of our national budget.

From Women Strike for Peace (New York), [unpublished] typescript.

- the futile peace talks in Paris in which the Administration refuses to take any of the minimal measures necessary for a political settlement.
- a punitive draft system that confronts our young men with the agonizing choice of participation in an illegal war, jail, or flight.
- the weakening of the United Nations, with the Johnson Administration rejecting every suggestion for peace in Vietnam made by United Nations Secretary General U Thant.

And, a national atmosphere of despair and violence fed by poverty, neglect and frustration at the spectacle of a power structure that is still—despite all the talk, investigations, nation Commissions, promises, etc.—only nibbling away at the massive problems of the cities, where a deepening split between black and white feeds on the continued and systematic denial to the black and the poor of their legitimate share of the resources and opportunities of American life.

As a women's peace group we have participated in the American protest movement and the political campaigns which have laid the groundwork for the present challenges for alternative policies and leadership within the Democratic party. We have sensed a great stirring among the electorate, an overwhelming desire for an end to the war in Vietnam, to racism and poverty at home, and a searching for leaders whom they can respect and trust. As we work among women (and incidentally women constitute more than half of the electorate), especially with women of the ghetto, the poor and the oppressed, we find that they are becoming more political, but also more militant in their demand for change.

This is a trend that goes beyond the traditional confines of the Democratic party, a clear signal that this is no year for politics-as-usual. The support that has been eroded by the Johnson Administration's Vietnam policy can be summoned again—but only by new leadership that is not tainted with participation in the Administration's policy decisions. There are great new resources of strength available to the Democratic party, if only it will place people politics ahead of machine politics.

We state flatly that under no circumstances will we support the nomination or candidacy of Hubert Humphrey or any other political leader identified with President Johnson's disastrous policies. We believe that the survival of the Democratic party as a majority party depends upon its capacity to reject the President's Vietnam record and domestic failure, and to nominate as candidates for President and Vice-President political leaders who are prepared to take the necessary steps to get the United States out of Vietnam and to turn to the monumental task of rebuilding our cities, giving equal rights, dignity and opportunity to all Americans, and improving the quality of our life. We believe that unless the votes of a majority of Democrats in the primaries for new directions and fresh leadership are reflected throughout this convention, the American electorate and particularly American women (whose vote by consensus of all polls is a significant peace vote) will look beyond the Democratic party for political solutions.

We believe the selection of a national ticket genuinely committed to peace and progress must be strengthened by the adoption of a national platform that clearly rejects the incorrect premises of our foreign and domestic policies and blue prints new priorities for our nation, both in its domestic and foreign goals.

We also believe that the Democratic party must restructure itself to restore political power to the people by the guarantee of full franchise and representation for those who thus far have been barred from decision making by reason of race, poverty, class or sex.

We propose specifically that the following points be included in the 1968 platform of the Democratic party:

1. The Democratic Party repudiates the United States intervention in Vietnam and the entire concept of a foreign policy which uses military power to sustain unpopular governments, interfere in the political life of other

countries, and suppress the national aspirations of other peoples.

2. To bring a speedy end to the war in Vietnam, the Democratic Party should call for an immediate and unconditional end to the bombing of North Vietnam, withdrawal of U.S. support from the Saigon government (which sends peace advocates to jail) and prompt recognition that the National Liberation Front, The Alliance of National Democratic and Peace Forces and other anti-Thieu regime movements have a legitimate role in the political life of South Vietnam. The Democratic Platform must commit itself to the prompt withdrawal of all United States military personnel and bases from Vietnam, to allow the South Vietnamese to determine their own future. This to be followed by negotiations for the withdrawal of all American firepower and manpower from the rest of Southeast Asia.

3. The Democratic Party must call for a restatement of the powers of Congress that were intended as a restraint upon the excessive exercise of power by the Executive branch of government, particularly in the area of foreign affairs. It should specifically reaffirm that only Congress has the constitutional right to declare war, so that never again will such a deceitful tactic as the Tonkin Gulf resolution be employed to maneuver our nation into an illegal war. Furthermore, the leaders of the Democratic Party must be prepared to reform the Seniority System in Congress through which a handful of Southern militarists exert inordinate influence by preventing the passage of progressive domestic legislation and by supporting increased military expenditures to satisfy their economic lust for military profit-making installations in their own states.

4. The Democratic Party, having accepted the expenditure of almost one trillion dollars for military purposes since World War II, must call for substantial cutbacks in United States military spending. As a token of faith in its program of new priorities, it should propose that Congress rescind the $5.5 billion appropriation for a futile anti-ballistic missile system which can only touch off an even more futile and costly arms race. A minimum of $30 billion now wasted annually on the Vietnam war must be earmarked specifically in the Democratic Party platform to provide a massive program of jobs, job training, education and housing for all Americans.

5. The Democratic Party must give meaning to the recently signed non-proliferation treaty to halt the spread of nuclear weapons by insisting that the major nuclear powers reduce their existing nuclear arsenals. As a significant step toward the goal of international disarmament—that long awaited second step on the journey to peace—the U.S. should announce that it will hold no more underground nuclear tests and pledge that it will never initiate a nuclear attack. The United States should ban the manufacture and use of chemical and biological weapons, and take steps to initiate international agreements to effectuate same. We believe that such measures can be extremely helpful in creating an atmosphere conducive to achieving further agreements for peace.

6. The Democratic Party platform must pledge that the United States will work for the development of effective United Nations peacekeeping machinery that will be honored by big and small nations alike, in the Middle East as well as the Far East and in Africa where millions starve as conflict rages. The bilateral American military commitments with some forty-two governments around the world must be replaced by international agreements, including provision for effective enforcement that respects the national independence and territorial sovereignty of all states. The Democratic Platform must accept the concept of universal membership in the United Nations, withdraw its opposition to the admission of the People's Republic of China, and take other steps to arrive at a detente with China, including diplomatic and trade relations. The Democratic Party should also call for normalization of trade and diplomatic relations with Cuba.

7. The Democratic Party should call for the elimination of the draft and a general

amnesty for the hundreds of men who have been imprisoned for challenging conscription in an illegal war. The concept of conscientious objection should be enlarged to recognize the right of Americans to assert their dissent from war on the basis of moral, humane and political reasons.

8. Finally, the Democratic Party must recognize that the people are weary of Cold War and racist concepts that have made the United States a symbol of repression in many parts of the world, alienated the black people, the poor and the young. Women Strike for Peace shares with millions of other Americans a desire to see the enormous wealth, genius, and great traditions of our nation dedicated to bringing peace to the world and to making a better life for millions at home.

You, the delegates to the Democratic National Convention, face an awesome responsibility. The viability of our society and civilization itself may well rest on your selection of a standard-bearer. We ask you to face the reality of political life in 1968, and to look not to a discredited Administration for leadership, but to the American people's unbounded desire for peace and a decent America.

116
Women Strike for Peace
A Woman's Declaration of Liberation from Military Domination (1970)

We women will no longer tolerate the domination of our lives and the lives of our families by the war-makers in the Pentagon and their spokesmen in Congress and the White House.

In the past twenty-five years, men who live by and for war have spent one trillion dollars of our tax money on armies and weapons—and they want still more.

The slaughter in Vietnam has killed over 48,000 Americans, wounded 250,000 of our young men, and destroyed the lives and homes of millions of Vietnamese. It is brutalizing our nation and bringing shame to us all.

Despite the protests of millions, the war goes on and now engulfs Laos, Cambodia and Thailand. But the Pentagon demands still more—$73 billion this year for the military establishment, additional billions for the ABM, and more of our sons and brothers to be brought home in coffins.

This unparalleled military plunder of our resources has brought our nation into crisis. Cities decay and fester. People are denied decent homes, jobs, schools, medical care, protection from pollution, and crime. Thousands of young men who refuse to be impressed into an unjust war have been forced into exile or jailed for dissent. Millions of black and minority group Americans live in malignant neglect.

The Nixon Administration spends 70 times more of our tax money for war than for housing, 9 times more for war than for education, 5 times more for war than for health.

A great and terrible wrong is being inflicted upon our country, and we demand redress of our grievances. The continued appropriation of our tax dollars for war without the clear consent of the American people is taxation without representation. This must be stopped.

We demand the birthright that our forefathers pledged to all Americans in 1776. We women declare our liberation from military domination which deprives us and our loved ones of life, liberty and the pursuit of happiness.

We demand that the President and the Congress of the United States live up to their Constitutional obligation to promote the general welfare.

We demand an end to the war in Vietnam and Laos NOW and the withdrawal of ALL troops, supplies and bases from Southeast Asia.

We demand repeal of the Draft.

From Women Strike for Peace (Washington, D.C.), broadside, dated March 18, 1970.

We demand that Congress vote "NO" on appropriations for the Pentagon.

We demand priority for human needs.

WE SAY NO MORE MEN—NO MORE MONEY FOR WAR!

117
SHIRLEY MARGOLIN, AMY SWERDLOW, AND IRMA ZIGAS

The Longest Day of the Longest War! (1971)

Following-up on the initiative of a new group of young women in Ann Arbor, Mich. and our old friends in North Shore Chicago, the National Consultative Committee of WSP has endorsed a June 21st, *DON'T BUY WAR* action.

Ann Arbor women singled out June 21st *THE LONGEST DAY OF THE LONGEST WAR* to call upon their sisters to use their consumer power to say "NO" to the war by spending NO MONEY on that day and using their time instead to pressure Congress to vote "NO" on war appropriations and "YES" on Legislation to end the war in 1971.

So far, the LONGEST DAY Campaign has been endorsed by many prominent women and organizations, including Barbara Avadon of Another Mother For Peace, Jane Hart, Representative Bella Abzug, Jane Fonda, WSP and Women's International League for Peace and Freedom.

Communities such as Santa Barbara, Calif.; Madison, Wisc.; Syracuse, N.Y.; Albany, N.Y.; Tenafly, N.J.; St. Louis, Mo.; Flint, Mich.; Chicago, Ill.; Great Neck, N.Y. have already started organizing, and have reported broad based support.

Ann Arbor has prepared a press release for distribution to Women's Page editors in almost 600 dailies across the country. In addition, local groups are urged to do their own publicity.

GUIDE TO WSP ACTION!

(1) Call a meeting as soon as possible of your WSP group and leaders in your community to organize local actions for the 21st. Enclosed is a flyer and suggestions for local activities. The flyer can be adapted to insert your local action, be it a film showing, a luncheon or a coffee klatch to rap about how women can withdraw their support from the war,—a mother's march through town,—tables at supermarkets for collecting post cards to send to Congress—or a special day of counseling on the draft and tax resistance. Another flyer "War Prices Peace Prices" including the "Pentagon Shopping List" and a post card to be sent to Congress, is in preparation to be used on the 21st. It will be sent out as soon as possible.

As usual—*TIME IS SHORT.* Each WSP Chapter has to move fast and adapt the program to the local situation. Feel free to do your thing. June 21st is the first day in the Summer Offensive. Do your part, and let us know what it is. We need to spread those brilliant ideas around.

118
MAUDE

Women and War (1970)

War has always been a man's game—the cruelest, most oppressive form of politics known to humanity. Using military force as a tool of imperial aggression, the United States and other imperialist powers have taken the lives of hundreds of thousands, both Americans and those called "the enemy"; and have laid waste to land needed by others for survival—all in order to maintain economic toeholds, and extensions of international power.

From Women Strike for Peace (New York), letter, dated May 28, 1971.

From *The Great Speckled Bird,* March 9, 1970.

Women of other nations, fighting for national liberation from great power domination, have taken major roles in the struggles: in Algeria, women fought alongside men against France; in Vietnam, women have picked up the gun to end U.S. aggression and domination.

From its inception, women have provided major support in the movement against the war in Vietnam. We have supported our brothers who have refused military induction and who have organized within the armed services. We have swelled the antiwar marches, and have carried a heavy load of antiwar organizing shitwork. But war does not oppress only men.

Now we raise our voices to the ways that the U.S. imperialist wars directly oppress women "left behind."

While few American women are asked to play the capitalist war games of the United States, all women must pay. Three women of the Student Mobilization Committee, Laura Dertz, Mission High School, San Francisco; Ruth Getts, Northern Illinois University; and Jaquiline Rice, Detroit, issued the following list of ways in which women are directly affected by war:

1) The war is currently creating unemployment. Women and Third World people are its first victims. But when women leave a tight labor market, they are generally forced out of the market entirely, or only allowed back in as domestic or seasonal workers.

2) In racist America, where most women are paid less than men, black, brown, red, and yellow women are paid least of all—they are last hired and first fired—and many must support families. In wartime, these conditions are only made worse.

3) The war erodes the current standard of living by inflationary prices. Fruit and meat become a luxury many cannot afford, and women have to stretch the budget to satisfy their families. Rents increase, forcing us to live in cramped quarters. That is true for all workers, but particularly for women who receive only 30–60 per cent of what men earn. It is a disaster for a family where the women is the breadwinner, as in one of ten U.S. families.

4) As long as the money is spent on war, free 24-hour child care facilities, free and adequate health care, equal access to education, and equal, adequate salaries will not be implemented. Even the ruling elite does not pretend there can be both "guns and butter."

5) The war adds an additional burden on a woman whose husband is forced to go to Vietnam. She must assume total responsibility for the home and children, while living in fear that her husband may never return.

A male dominant society such as ours puts a premium on those human characteristics which lead to war: toughness, competitiveness, material profit over human gain. Sensitivity, gentleness, cooperation—the traits assigned to women are kept neatly in their place.

Women's Liberation has every reason to support both the liberation struggles abroad and the antiwar movement at home: we recognize the right of peoples to control their own lives, because we as women are uniting in struggle against oppression by men, and particularly against being seen as property. We also see that the wars pursued by the United States in Vietnam, in Laos, as well as the threatening military presence in South America and elsewhere, result from our male dominant, competitive, profit-oriented society. We as women will band together to overcome this most vicious game of men.

119

BREAD AND ROSES

Speech at the Women's Anti-Imperialist Rally (1970)

What brought us here today? Was it the events of this week—the invasion of Cambodia, the resumption of bombing of North Vietnam, and the murder of 4 students in Ohio? Or was it be-

From Bread and Roses, [unpublished] typescript, dated May 7, 1970.

cause of other events . . . last December when Fred Hampton and Mark Clark were murdered, because the L.A. Black Panther office was laid under siege or was it when Bobby Seale was chained and gagged in a court room and thrown into jail for four years without trial. Or when the Conspiracy was convicted, or was it because in two separate places 5 of our sisters and brothers were blown up, or is it the massive attempt to destroy the Panthers by so-called legal means as in New Haven where 9 Black Panther women and men are on trial for their lives. Or is it because of all the events the press hardly covers, like 3 people being sentenced to 6 years for operating a GI coffeehouse in Columbia, S.C., or Kevin Moran being killed by the pigs in Santa Barbara, Calif., or Linda Evans indicted on conspiracy charges sitting in jail several months pregnant. Or several women in women's liberation in the Boston area fired from their jobs, others beaten, and most recently four women busted, for spray painting, all fighting for our liberation.

But those events are not the only reason why women have come here together today. We are angry about the invasion of Cambodia and the repression of the Panthers, but we are also enraged about what we have to face everyday in order to survive and stay sane—walking down the street, on our jobs, at home and at school. They make survival sound simple; we are told that whenever anything goes wrong, it is our fault. If we are afraid or unhappy, they make us feel that we are guilt-ridden pieces of shit. It is not paranoid to be afraid of the violence that surrounds us—we are beaten and raped on the streets and in our homes everyday. It is not neurotic to feel like we can't be a good mother to our children when we are taught that we are responsible for the health and welfare of our children yet decent medical care, housing, and education are luxuries reserved for the rich. It is not ungrateful to resent being imprisoned in our home when home is a sink full of dirty dishes, a vacuum cleaner, piles of dirty laundry. It is not petty to be concerned about a 20¢ rise in the price of hamburger meat when we are responsible for making ends meet to insure the survival of our family. We are not being piggy, it is not that we want more but inflation is making it impossible to meet basic needs. It is not frivolous to spend our money and time on clothes and cosmetics when it is necessary to decorate ourselves to sell our bodies in the job market and to get men. It is not castrating for us to demand that we, not husbands, doctors, priests, pimps, or legislators, that *we* control our own lives and bodies. All our lives we have been told that these are our own hangups, our personal problems. But what more and more women—housewives, single women, black, white, middle class, welfare mothers, factory workers, high school students—are rapidly learning is that those men who plotted the invasion of Cambodia, who are systematically ripping off the Black Panthers, who are responsible for the murders of the students at Kent State, are the very same men who have enslaved us—by trying to destroy our minds and control our bodies, by exploiting our labor on the job and in the home. They are the very same men who have enslaved us for the purpose of enslaving people the world over.

That attempted enslavement has become fully exposed to us as white Americans. The horror of the events of this past week have finally forced us to face what Third World people from the colonies of Southeast Asia to Roxbury have been saying to us for years—that the United States ruling class is the world oppressor. While horrified at the brutal act of power that the United States government is willing to commit, we must see that aggression as an act of desperation, in response to the overwhelming growth of movements for liberation from American imperialism.

The war in Vietnam and the invasion of Cambodia have been in response to liberation movements there. Corporate control as well as military dictatorships, CIA infiltration and counter-insurgency programs have been designed to perpetuate U.S. power and suppress struggles for self-determination in countries like Greece, Haiti, Bolivia, and South Africa. The mounting repression against groups like the Black Panther Party and the Young Lords is a direct response by a racist system to the rebellions of black and brown people within this country. The court-martialing and imprisonment of GIs and National Guardsmen are a response to the increasing resistance of young men who are rejecting their assigned pig roles, pig roles essential to repressing liberation movements within and beyond the borders of the United States. Finally, the murders of the Kent State students and the armed presence of troops on campuses across the country is a response to a growing white movement which is wreaking havoc on the stability of this society by closing down universities, by burning down or blowing up ROTC buildings, Banks of America, police stations, Standard Oil offices.

Women have played a crucial part in all these struggles and have not been spared from repression, as dramatized by the imprisonment and brutal conditions experienced by many Black Panther women particularly in New Haven and New York jails; by the deaths of countless, nameless Vietnamese heroines; by the beatings and jailings of welfare women in many cities. Women have always been fighters. Throughout our history women have helped forge struggles for human dignity: in the abolitionist and labor struggles, in the thrust for suffrage. And within our lifetimes, women have been the backbone of the civil rights and antiwar movements. But women have been fighters not only in mass movements—since the beginning of the human race women have had to fight for our own survival and that of our families in a male supremacist world which has relegated us to the position of slaves.

Women are becoming a powerful force in and of ourselves. The women's liberation movement is transforming the strength we have had to have as individuals in other struggles and in our daily lives into a collective strength. We have learned that we cannot postpone the struggle for our own particular needs until after the resolution. It is because of our rage at our own oppression that we are fighting hard. We are fighting not just for ourselves but for all people. It is through our experience of sexism—our oppression *as women*—that we understand in our guts what racism and imperialism mean to other oppressed people.

We are revolutionary feminists. We must build an independent women's movement, to destroy male supremacy. We must fight in solidarity with all other oppressed people because we understand that our liberation depends on the total liberation of all people.

We know that there will only be thousands of millions of women people to discover, touch, and become one with, who will say with a Vietnamese girl, "let us now emulate each other," who will understand you when you say we must make a new world in which we do not meet each other as exploiters and used objects. Where we love one another and into which a new kind of human being can be born.

POWER TO THE SISTERS!
POWER TO THE PEOPLE!

120

Linda Alband and Steve Rees

Women and the Volunteer Armed Forces: First Report on a Rocky Romance (1977)

Former Army Secretary Howard Callaway announced in 1975, with all due authority and a straight lip, the Army's latest scientific discovery: "a woman could do about anything a man could." Young women recruits are now trained in rifle marksmanship and defense combat tactics, and trudge on night marches evading simulated rifle fire and real tear-gas cannisters. WAC First Lieutenant Andrea Kopolka boasts that "The Army's where it's happening for women." Her enthusiasm is shared by her 18-

From *Radical America,* January–February 1977.

year-old trainee Jean Mehorczyk, who testified at her basic-training graduation, "It's the greatest thing that's ever happened to me." Female non-commissioned officers now exercise immediate authority over hundreds of enlisted men. Of the few dissenting female voices within the ranks, most belong to lesbians who are battling, not to leave the institution, but to stay in.

Are these changes to be celebrated as the gains of the women's movement, dreaded as dangerous signs of the military's new-found legitimacy, or dismissed as token concessions but nothing more? Let's not be too hasty in choosing. Our intent here is not to prove once again beyond the shadow of a doubt that despite these reforms the military remains a bastion of anti-feminism. Nor are we intent on proving that these internal reforms, or any other reforms for that matter, do not alter the basic function of the institution. While believing that both assertions are true, we're not interested in reducing these or any other of the left's commonly-held ideas about the military to a catechism. Rather, we intend to test those ideas against the reality of a military which is breaking with many of its anachronistic traditions. If the left refuses to examine these changes, its understanding of the U.S. military, not to mention its attempts to change it, will become equally outmoded.

THE CONTEXT

After being defeated in Indochina and humiliated at home, the military had to either adapt or die. The Nixon doctrine of Vietnamization on a global scale made a change in the military's function possible. The Indochinese Revolution and the antiwar movement made it necessary. The all-volunteer-force concept soon followed. What resulted was an overhaul from top to bottom: an end to the draft, a 40% reduction in force, and hundreds of internal reforms, not the least of which was the attempt to make soldiering a job just like any other. In fact, the relation between GIs and the command soon came to resemble that between labor and management. For motivation, patriotism was replaced by a paycheck. . . .

This trend toward a more modern, streamlined armed forces made it easier for the Department of Defense (DoD) to bring its attitudes and treatment of women more up-to-date. But it was the women's movement that set the standard against which the military's progress would be measured. Not only did the women's movement begin to influence masses of working-class women, but it also spread from one generation to the next. Ten years ago, teenage girls were considered daring if they dreamt of the independent life of an actress or stewardess. Today, many of those teenage girls shudder at the thought of marriage and kids, a dull job, or living with parents, and strike out on their own by turning to soldiering. Ten years ago, women shouting insults at gentlemanly military officers would have been considered unseemly and unfeminine. Today, the women's movement has helped remove these obstacles to action. Enlisted men's wives have, in the last three years, shouted, picketed, petitioned, and press-conferenced their way into many a confrontation with the command. The battered post-war military is in no position to do battle with a trend as compelling as this. Unable to lick 'em, the military has, in a sense, joined 'em. The military has been changed in the process, but not without turning some aspects of the women's movement to its own advantage.

ENLISTED WOMEN

In the midst of this flurry of reform activity characteristic of an enormous bureaucracy scrambling for its survival, one factor more than any other determined the military's new turn toward women: the demand for labor. Stripped in mid-1973 of its power to conscript, the military was forced to compete on the open market for the recruits it needed. In addition, it had to improve the quality of military life to encourage its career soldiers to stay. Even after the unemployment and inflation percentages climbed into double digits, the military still had profound "manpower recruitment" difficulties. It faced the unprecedented task of recruiting one out of every three available and qualified non-college males. And all this even after a 40% reduction in the number of DoD employees in uniform, and the civilianization of many jobs traditionally held by soldiers. As recruiters fell further behind their quotas (even in the first year of the volunteer armed forces), and as the enticing enlistment bonuses and benefits became too expensive to maintain, the DoD began to realize how important women could be in fulfilling its "manpower" requirements. . . .

Even after the economic slump enabled recruiters to meet their quotas, and reenlistment officers to halt the mass exodus of experienced career personnel, several branches still faced personnel shortages. The Army was still short in the combat arms: artillery, infantry, and armor. The Navy lacked boiler techs, machinist mates, and nuclear engineers. If women could be recruited and trained for many of the non-critical slots, more men could be channeled into the critical specialties. Furthermore, the more far-sighted of the military's manpower managers knew that an economic upturn and a decline in the number of available male recruits due to the decline in the birth rate could eventually push the military's recruiting capabilities to their limits. The prestigious Defense Manpower Commission, it its April 1976 report, recommended that the military prepare to tap the pool of available female GIs-in-waiting as one of the least disruptive responses to this dilemma.

The military's need for women recruits is only half the story. Why do these women need the military? Every survey reveals the same collection of motivations: the desire for education, travel, and training, and the lack of other opportunities. Recruiting ads echo these sentiments: "Who says men don't listen when a woman talks?" "A new life and a new world of travel." "Making her own way." "You can find yourself." Women from poor families, from racial and ethnic minorities in the U.S., or from smaller, rural towns have even fewer economic options than do their male peers. Unlike men their age, they are not encouraged to strike out on their own. The military offers a package deal within an authoritarian structure that leaves little risk of having to make choices about one's life. Some of the recruitment propaganda plays up to this family-substitute angle, stressing "something different, but not so really different" and "It's more like what you're used to."

In an article in *Ms.* several years ago, B. J. Phillips assembled a composite of the typical WAC she met during her week at Ft. McClellan. "She had been out of high school for a year, and in a recession economy, found jobs nonexistent or dull and low-paid. Unable, for financial reasons, to go on to college or into some type of vocational training program, she chose the army because it offered her both job training and GI Bill benefits for further education after she leaves." In a word, these young women, like their male counterparts, enlist because they lack options elsewhere.

Ultimately, the desires of these recruits and the requirements of the military in time of war will clash. . . . But so long as the defense of the nation requires no extraordinary sacrifices by those in the ranks, that clash may be postponed.

Although the impact of these women on the military has been significant, this is not mainly because of their numbers. Enlisted women make up only slightly more than 5% of the total DoD active-duty force. But even that modest figure is a threefold increase over its 1971 level. And when measured as a percentage of new recruits, women figure more prominently: 9.2% for the Army, 11.4% for the Air Force, and an average of 7.7% for the entire DoD. By 1978, women are supposed to make up over 6% of the DoD active-duty force.

These enlisted women have insisted that the military no longer restrict them to "women's work." The military's need for women was so critical that it had to accommodate the demands that women were making both inside and outside its ranks. In the last two years, the military has announced new plans to provide women with equal opportunity, and has authorized the following changes:

- Rules banning mothers from military service were lifted. The military had reserved the right to judge whether a woman could adequately perform her duties and cope with motherhood, but this reservation was dropped as of July 1975.
- Women can adopt children.
- Women can get married after enlistment, and still stay in.
- Married women can enlist both in the regular service and in the reserves.
- Women are now eligible for the same family benefits as men.
- Women are now full-fledged members of promotion boards, no longer confined to evaluating women only.
- Pay is the same for men and women of the same pay grade.
- Job restrictions have been lifted. Women were previously restricted to 39% of the Army's job categories, but are now eligible for 94%—all but the combat arms.
- College ROTC programs are open to women. One school commandant remarked, "We are finding that competition between the sexes is a good motivator."
- Military academies, such as West Point with its 173-year all-male tradition, are opening their doors to female cadets.
- Policy has changed to permit women to command men, except in the combat units. Several WAC officers have been selected for colonel-level commands.
- All enlisted women in the Army are now required to take defensive weapons training....
- Separate detachments for women are being gradually eliminated, with the result that women are now assigned to duty wherever job vacancies exist. And, in mid-September of 1976 the WAC (Women's Army Corps) was eliminated—now both women and men enlist in the Army.

Two items from this list of reforms are worth examining in more detail: basic training and the opening of non-traditional jobs to women. These are the two most troublesome changes for the Pentagon, and the most fascinating for the young women who join.

Beginning in basic, the Army vacillates between training its women recruits to be soldiers and training them to be ladies. True, fatigue-clad, booted women recruits march, jump, climb, and hurdle their way through an "unladylike" and rigorous physical-training program—a program not always equal in intensity to that of the men, but demanding nonetheless. They drill in formation, dig foxholes, bivouac, and range-fire the M-16 rifle. The content of the 13-week basic-training program has remained essentially what it was during the Vietnam era; physical-fitness training, marching, warfare-technique classes, and instruction in the use of hand grenades, the M-60 machine gun, and the M-16.

There are, however, two major differences in the training programs for men and for women. One of the two is in the area of tactical-weapons training. Men receive 143 hours of rifle marksmanship and defensive tactics, while women receive 72 hours. The other difference is in the "feminine" arts. Women sit through mandatory classroom instruction in hair care, skin care, weight control, rape prevention, and "family planning" (birth control). The closest equivalent on the male side of the balance sheet is venereal-disease prevention—in itself an interesting comment on the Army's notion of who's responsible for what.

Despite these differences, and despite the Army's admittedly inadequate preparation of these women trainees for combat situations, the camaraderie of a shared ordeal and the pride of discovering previously untapped abilities is the core of basic training for women. They don't leave basic any more patriotic, war-hungry, or infatuated with the military than when they went in. Doctrinal training, or motivational training, is not stressed.

Equal opportunity in the military, as elsewhere, has its limits. Admiral Holloway, Chief of Naval Operations, explained the Navy's limitations in an interview in *U.S. News and World Report:* "ship billets must by law be filled with men, and secondly, we must preserve some billets for those men at sea to rotate to. Otherwise, we would be putting our men on open-ended sea duty." In the Army, women are still unable to join combat-arms specialties. The Air Force prohibits women from flying. And these are only the more visible limits.

More to the point is to ask what happened when the Army suddenly opened up 415 of its 451 occupational fields to women? According to the Defense Manpower Commission, not much. Their report claims, "Women entering the services are opting for the more traditional female jobs. Many have not had the background or exposure to nontraditional areas. Two-thirds of the military women still work in the traditional medical and administrative fields, with no significant concentration in any of the mechanical or electronic career fields."

This picture should come as no surprise. Recruits have to qualify for the job they request by passing a battery of tests. Even if everyone has an equal opportunity to take the same tests, everyone is not equally prepared to take them. Like other equal-opportunity employers, the military can do no more than reproduce the same division of labor which is already present in this society.

Since the institution of the All-Volunteer Military, lesbians have been one of the most coherent forces which have put pressure on the Pentagon to make good its claims of being an equal-opportunity employer. Some of these lesbian enlisted women are the victims of witch-hunt-like sweeps of the women's barracks by military-intelligence officers who grill women on the details of their barracks-mates' private lives. The military conducts these witch hunts to purge itself of its "undesirable elements." They usually begin when the authorities select one woman they suspect—or say they suspect—of being a lesbian. They threaten her with a less-than-honorable discharge. Then they offer to either let her out with a better discharge, or let her stay in if she gives them the names of other lesbians. This tactic is repeated with subsequent victims, so that the investigation might grow to include dozens or even hundreds of women. Interestingly enough, one lesbian ex-WAVE told us that it is more often the case that straight women get busted in these purges. She went on to say that most lesbians knew how to "cover their ass" and were real good at projecting the "proper military image." Another lesbian WAVE who knew that she was going to be called before a Naval Intelligence Service (NIS) investigation board, prepared herself in this way: "I went into the ladies' room, took off my butch watch with the wide strap, put on my lipstick and mascara, and I was ready for 'em."

Still other enlisted women openly defy the military by announcing their lesbian preference. In the past, both men and women have admitted to being homosexual to get out of the military, whether or not they actually were. But today, the armed-forces code is being challenged from within by individuals who have stood up and declared themselves to be gay and have demanded that the military change its treatment of homosexuals.

The military's response in both cases is invariably to initiate discharge proceedings. The soldiers who are targeted for this treatment range from model soldiers-of-the-month to feminists and the disaffected. Of the many who fight to stay in, not all do so out of any love for the military. As Army Reserve Sergeant Miriam Ben Shalom remarked, "I am defending my basic constitutional rights to work, to privacy, and to the freedom of my lifestyle." Whatever their reasons, the consequences of their actions are questioning the line between the citizen and the soldier. They are challenging the military's determination of what they do after work. Having taken to heart the military's own message that it's a job like any other, they are now setting about to make it just that.

It is not as if the handful of lesbians who are now fighting the military for the right to stay in, or even those 2,000 others booted out every year in semi-secret shame, constitute the entire homosexual population in the military. Two Kinsey Institute scholars estimated in 1971 that the percentage of homosexuals in the military hardly differed from their percentage in civilian society—10%. The various defense lawyers and experts in the current cases use this standard estimate of 10%. Others believe this is an extremely conservative estimate, and point to the massive network of bars, clubs, and newspapers which make up the ghettoized gay military.

While the movement of lesbians in uniform has been a reflection of the larger movement for equal rights for homosexuals, it may soon become its test case. The ACLU lawyer who defended two gay WACs at Ft. Devens last year speculated, "Sooner or later, one of these cases will produce a court decision declaring discrimination against homosexuals unconstitutional. The military is the key institution. Just as the racial integration of the military in the late 40's set the stage for a national social policy of integration, the critical sexual battles are going to be fought here."

ENLISTED MEN'S WIVES

The recent leap into the twentieth-century of the military's treatment of enlisted women has only underlined the medieval status of those nearly one million women whose husbands are soldiers. The Army has an orientation pamphlet for the "Army Wife" (Does the woman marry her husband or the Army?) which best articulates the contrast. "Although no serviceman's career was ever made by his wife, many have been hindered or helped by the social skills of their wives, their flexibility, and their loyalty toward the Army and its customs. . . . As an Army wife, never forget that you are the 'silent member' of the team, but a key 'man.' . . . A wife should try to keep her husband from feeling bitter about the system. If she feels the system isn't too bad, he'll probably agree. . . . Your whole scheme of life revolves around your husband, your children, and a happy home." Captured here is the tension between the military's genuine dependence on its "military wives" and its simultaneous denial of the wives' existence independent of their husbands. When, for instance, an enlisted man's wife steps out of line, the woman's husband is reprimanded by his commanding officer. In fact, the wife is formally outside the jurisdiction of military law. Furthermore, the contribution of the "silent member of the team" is rewarded, not in the form of wages to the woman, but as a dependent's allowance attached to the husband's paycheck.

The young working women who settle with their husbands in the trailer parks and stucco apartments of stateside base towns face a tougher ordeal than most non-military wives. These women experience divorce, alcoholism, and stress at rates far above the national average. With most of their husbands working irregular shifts and logging fifty or sixty hours a week, more and more of the work at home falls to them by default. Women whose husbands are ship-stationed have to reckon with six-month cruises when their husbands are on sea duty, and week-long sea trials and irregular, often very long duty shifts even when their husbands' ships are in port. If a woman's husband is assigned to an overseas base, the military will help her move and cover the moving expenses only if her husband's rank is sergeant (E-5) or up. If not, she can come along only if she can afford the move on her own. A skimming of the conservative bi-weekly women's supplement to the *Army Times* reveals more trials and tribulations than we have room to list here: an entire issue on rape—one of the fastest-growing crimes in the military community; boredom and its remedies—service clubs, volunteer work for the Red Cross, and wives' clubs; how to cope with waiting; and base-town crime.

Any institution which, in the 1970's, produces this quality of life and then insists on a woman's total identification with her husband

and his job is asking for trouble. In the last three years, the military's found plenty of it! Not uncommon is the following letter from a Norfolk, Virginia woman whose husband was in the Navy: "A free test of a good marriage is about the only benefit enlisted people are given during their struggle to get by. Up to this point I've tried with difficulty to accept the way things are and the fact that the Navy and the system will always run my life for me. I really don't think it's selfish to say I'd like some control over the situation.". . .

In at least two recent instances, this sentiment has been translated into collective action. In San Diego, enlisted men and their wives organized a group to contest the Navy's illegal nonpayment of reenlistment bonuses. (See the May/June issue of *Radical America*.) For almost two years, the group—VRB/OUT (meaning, give us our variable reenlistment bonuses or let us out)—fought the Navy in the courts and in the papers. The enlisted men in the group, though, were often at sea, leaving the bulk of the responsibility for the organization with their women. The women leafleted the bases, planned legal strategy, and picketed recruiting stations—actions which tarnished the Navy's public image and hurt recruiting. Their public statements were confined to the issue, but off the record the women explained that much more was at stake than the loss of a several-thousand-dollar bonus; forced six-month separations, notoriously inadequate on-base medical care, flimsy finding for family services.

In Alameda, California, women whose husbands were crewmen on the aircraft carrier USS *Coral Sea* publicly charged the ship's captain (at a well-attended press conference) with a long list of health-and-safety-regulation violations. They petitioned Congress requesting that the ship be put in drydock for an overhaul, and not be allowed to sail on a six-month Western Pacific cruise. Working night and day, they circulated their petition. . . . [T]he Navy dodged the women's charges. In a press release, they credited the women with being well intended but slightly misinformed. After a quick cosmetic clean-up, the ship's captain escorted select news crews through the more modern and least critical parts of the ship. And when the women raised hell on the pier the morning of the *Coral Sea*'s departure, they were gently and tactfully escorted off-base. What would the Navy gain, after all, by calling attention to a group of enlisted men's wives who dared to challenge the Navy's judgment of a ship's seaworthiness, and who refused to suffer the anxiety, hard work, and loneliness customarily expected of a dutiful Navy wife?

CONCLUSION

Having described these relatively new trends toward reform, we can venture an interpretation of our own, and a brief critique of mainstream feminist and pacifist views about women in the military. What makes any interpretation difficult, however, is the momentary coincidence of interests between the volunteer military's insatiable demand for qualified labor, and the women's movement's demand for equal access to, and equal rights within, public and private institutions. This convergence has meant that the reforms in the military related to equal rights and access for women were established at the top, without much agitation or direct action by women in the ranks below. The challenges to which the military responded took place, for the most part, outside the military itself. One cannot simply argue, then, that these reforms in the military were merely cooptive measures designed to head off rabble rousing in the ranks, or alternatively that the reforms were concessions squeezed from a weak bureaucracy through the dynamics of class struggle. Like all half-truths, both observations accurately describe two parts of a much more complex totality.

Some radicals, especially within the anti-imperialist and pacifist trends, have decried the recent influx of large numbers of women into the armed forces, and their integration into a more accommodating and up-to-date institution, as signs of the militarization of women. Ultimately, they argue, no one, man or woman, should submit to or volunteer for the profession of soldiering. In the short run, their political activity is geared toward discouraging women from enlisting at all. So reforms which make military life more attractive to potential recruits can only serve to make these radicals' tasks more difficult to realize. In fact, the more just the reform, the more they dread it. These radicals resemble those who believed that the way to abolish capitalism was to dissuade people from working. Those who worked were considered bourgeoisified, and reforms which improved the lot of those who worked were considered sops, crumbs, which could only make the ultimate revolutionary act more remote. During times of revolutionary upsurge, they may have commanded some following. But in times of relative stability, they can do little more than soapbox to uninterested passers-by. Our disagreement with these radical soapboxers today is not that we would encourage young working-class women to join up, but that it is through their joining that the stability of the all-volunteer, peacetime military might be undermined. The pacifist perspective is more suited to wartime anti-military work with soldiers, and does not grapple with the possibilities of the present period. Furthermore, they consider the military's women-related reforms statically, fixed in their present scope and form, and ignore the opportunity to drive these reforms beyond their intended limits.

At another extreme, the National Organization for Women (NOW) pose sexual equality as an absolute principle which determines their relationship to the military. Consider these remarks of Pat Leeper, a lobbyist for NOW and a coordinator of their Committee for Women in the Military, offered to the Department of the Army in the first months of 1976: "Should women go into combat? To us the question is completely irrelevant. We only need to know that there are capable women who want jobs." Her recommendations included accelerated entry programs and assertiveness training for women, lifting quotas which limit the number of women recruits, and the use of physical (not gender) standards for every job. If NOW holds any position critical of the military's mission, it is not apparent from Pat Leeper's policy paper.

NOW and the Pentagon's more radical critics certainly have conflicting concerns. NOW's advocates are cheering on the waves of female recruits who appear to them to be successfully assaulting one of the last great bastions of male power: soldiering. And the radicals who fear the imminent militarization of women do what they can to head it off. But neither group's perspective focuses on women in the ranks. Our balance sheet, drawn up after a three-year accounting of the all-volunteer, peacetime force experiment, finds the new situation something to be welcomed, not dreaded.

1. At least in the area of women's rights and sexual equality, the military has been compelled to get in step with the rest of society. This goes directly against the grain of traditional military thinking which insists upon the institution's separateness from the rest of society. The old-time military moguls argue that separated courts, laws, prisons, hospitals, schools, and codes of conduct are made necessary by the military mission. They justify distinct social relations within the institution on the same grounds: laws against fraternization between enlisted men and women; separate quarters, dining halls, and bathrooms for officers; saluting and "yes, sir"-ing; grooming and appearance regulations; an enlistment agreement between the GI and the government that saddles the soldier with the obligations of an indentured servant and gives him or her none of the protections of a contractual agreement. Even during wartime, these habits, rules, and regulations are questionable. But during peacetime, they seem even less justifiable to the enlisted men and women who are degraded by these customs daily. So when the ways of the civilian world begin to intrude on the military's erstwhile separate society, it is often to the advantage of the soldier in the ranks, and rarely to the advantage of the command. If one

distinction between the civilian and military worlds can be dispensed with, why not the rest? (This is as true in the area of soldier's First Amendment rights as it is in the area of sex discrimination.) The military's recent opposition to formal sex discrimination, however limited, is one step away from an army of professional legionnaires, and one step toward an army of citizen-soldiers. If there are to be any soldiers at all, better that they march in step with the hesitating syncopation of popular music than the goose-stepping four-four time of John Phillip Sousa.

2. These reforms in the military may have a ripple effect, encouraging similar reforms in institutions outside the military. It's still too early to point to any proof, but there is a strong historical precedent. The military's desegregation program after World War II, and its insistence since 1967 on open-occupancy housing agreements from civilian landlords, contributed to the attack on segregation in some of the regions and institutions most resistant to change. The military has at times been not just a reflection of social movements, but also their dynamo.

3. As young women recruits are called upon to do the work of soldiers, their conception of their own capabilities can only expand and improve. And hopefully, after having discovered the social restrictions on the development of their abilities up till then, they will be even quicker to challenge those restrictions next time they encounter them, and not mistake them for natural ones. In addition, the demand for equal rights and access is on the face of it a just demand, although by no means a revolutionary one at this present time and place.

4. As long as these women continue to question the remaining obstacles to equality, the reforms which initially encouraged their questioning can have a destabilizing effect, creating new tensions even while resolving old ones. First, once the catechism of female equality is officially attacked, even ridiculed, then why restrict the percentage of women in the military to 6% or even 10%, as Pentagon planners do? Why shouldn't women have 50% representation? Second, if equal rights implies equal obligations, shouldn't women be assigned to the combat specialties if they meet the physical requirements? Military planners are not opposed to this in principle, but oppose its implementation on the grounds that the country isn't ready for it yet. Third, the institutionalization of all these reforms concerning enlisted women has only made "dependent" status less excusable than before. In fact, a recent article in *Army Times,* headlined "Professor Expects Surge of Feminism by Service Wives," summarized the findings of a Mills College sociologist, Dr. Lynne Dobrofsky, who predicted that military wives will become radicalized as they realize that they have no status or identity other than their husbands'. Enlisted men's wives have already shown signs of independence in two significant campaigns—the movement to stop deployment of the attack carrier USS *Coral Sea* over health and safety hazards in November-December 1974, and the variable-reenlistment-bonus suits—and will probably continue to be a thorn in the Pentagon's side.

Suggestions for Further Reading

Banks, Olive. *Faces of Feminism: A Study of Feminism as a Social Movement.* Oxford, U.K.: Martin Robertson, 1981.

Becker, Susan D. *The Origins of the Equal Rights Amendment: American Feminism between the Wars.* Westport, Conn.: Greenwood, 1981.

Black, Naomi. *Social Feminism.* Ithaca, N.Y.: Cornell Univ. Press, 1983.

Buhle, Mari Jo. *Women and American Socialism, 1870–1920.* Urbana: Univ. of Illinois Press, 1983.

Chafe, William H. *American Woman: Her Changing Social, Economic, and Political Roles, 1920–1970.* New York: Oxford Univ. Press, 1972.

———. *The Paradox of Change: American Women in the 20th Century.* New York: Oxford Univ. Press, 1991.

Chatfield, Charles. *The American Peace Movement: Ideals and Activism.* New York: Twayne Publishers, 1992.

Cott, Nancy F. *The Grounding of American Feminism.* New Haven: Yale Univ. Press, 1987.

Diamond, Irene, ed. *Families, Politics, and Public Policy: A Feminist Dialogue on Women and the State.* New York: Longman Publishing, 1983.

Dye, Nancy Schrom. *As Equal Sisters: Feminism, the Labor Movement, and the Women's Trade Union League of New York.* Columbia: Univ. of Missouri Press, 1980.

Early, Frances H. *A World without War: How U.S. Feminists and Pacifists Resisted World War I.* Syracuse: Syracuse Univ. Press, 1997.

Eisenstein, Zillah R., ed. *Capitalist Patriarchy and the Case for Socialist Feminism.* New York: Monthly Review Press, 1979.

Harley, Sharon, and Rosalyn Terborg-Penn, eds. *The Afro-American Woman: Struggles and Images.* Port Washington, N.Y.: Kennikat Press, 1978.

Hartman-Strong, Sharon. "Challenging 'Woman's Place': Feminism, the Left, and Industrial Unionism in the 1930s." *Feminist Studies* 9 (Summer 1983): 359–86.

Hoff-Wilson, Joan, ed. *Rights of Passage: The Past and the Future of the ERA.* Bloomington: Indiana Univ. Press, 1986.

Horowitz, Daniel. *Betty Friedan and the Making of "The Feminine Mystique": The American Left, the Cold War, and Modern Feminism.* Amherst: The Univ. of Massachusetts Press, 1999.

———. "Rethinking Betty Friedan and *The Feminine Mystique*: Labor Union Radicalism and Feminism in Cold War America." *American Quarterly* 48 (March 1996): 1–42.

Kessler-Harris, Alice. *Out to Work: A History of Wage-Earning Women in the United States.* New York: Oxford Univ. Press, 1982.

Koven, Seth, and Sonya Michel, eds. *Mothers of a New World: Maternalist Politics and the Origins of Welfare States.* New York: Routledge, 1993.

Lemons, J. Stanley. *The Woman Citizen: Social Feminism in the 1920s.* Urbana: Univ. of Illinois Press, 1973.

Marchand, Roland C. *The American Peace Movement and Social Reform, 1898–1918.* Princeton: Princeton Univ. Press, 1972.

Muncy, Robin. *Creating a Female Dominion in American Reform, 1890–1935.* New York: Oxford Univ. Press, 1991.

Rupp, Leila J., and Verta Taylor. *Survival in the Doldrums: The American Women's Rights Movement, 1945 to the 1960s.* New York: Oxford Univ. Press, 1987.

Savarsy, Wendy. "Beyond the Difference versus Equality Policy Debate: Postsuffrage Feminism, Citizenship, and the Quest for a Feminist Welfare State." *Signs* 17 (winter 1992): 329–62.

Scharf, Lois, and Joan M. Jensen, eds. *Decades of Discontent: The Women's Movement, 1920–1940.* Westport, Conn.: Greenwood, 1983.

Schramm, Sarah Slavin. *PloughWomen Rather Than Reapers: An Intellectual History of Feminism in the United States.* Metuchen, N.J.: Scarecrow Press, 1979.

Simon, Rita, and Gloria Danziger. *Women's Movements in America: Their Successes, Disappointments, and Aspirations.* New York: Praeger, 1991.

Sochen, June. *Movers and Shakers: American Women Thinkers and Activists, 1900–1970.* New York: Quadrangle/The New York Times Book Co., 1973.

Storrs, Landon R. Y. "Gender and the Development of the Regulatory State: The Controversy over Restricting Women's Night Work in the Depression-Era New South." *Journal of Policy History* 10 (1998): 179–206.

Ware, Susan. *Beyond Suffrage: Women in the New Deal.* Cambridge: Harvard Univ. Press, 1981.

Swerdlow, Amy. *Women Strike for Peace: Traditional Motherhood and Radical Politics in the 1960s.* Chicago: Univ. of Chicago Press, 1993.

Zahavi, Gerald. "Passionate Commitments: Race, Sex, and Communism at Schenectady General Electric, 1932–1954." *Journal of American History* 83 (September 1996): 514–48.

Index

abortion, women and, 248, 249
Abzug, Bella, 454–55
action: communal v. individual, 98–99; from knowledge, 98
Acts. *See specific acts*
Adams, Brooks, 400
Addams, Jane, 97–99; on widow's pensions, 134; and Women's Peace Party, 452–53
AFL. *See* American Federation of Labor (AFL)
African American(s): after emancipation, 381; as leaders, 259; women's voting rights, 228, 230–31, 246; workers, 347. *See also* men, colored; Negroes; women, colored
African American women: appreciation of, 258–59; deputations and, 255–56; discrimination of, 230, 250–54, 367; disfranchisement in South, 244, 251; equal rights for, 257; in government, 367–72, 373; in industry, 373–77; National Woman's Party (NWP/CU) and, 230, 242, 243–44, 255–56; occupations for, 373, 441; other races and, 231; Republicans and Democrats on, 231, 256–57; segregation of, 373; in state legislature, 231; treatment of fair, 371, 373; Woman's Party and, 230–31. *See also* women, colored
African American women's club, 99–100
agencies, employment, 380
ages, equal rights and, 330
agriculture: colored women in, 378–79, 381; mother-right and, 419; three branches of, 72–73; women as founders of, 475
Airforce Service Pilots, Women's, 453
Alband, Linda, 455
alimony: right to, 26; as unfair, 19
amendment(s): of 1907 law, 218; Blanket, equalitarians and, 273; changes to, 297; democratic blockage of suffrage, 180; Eighteenth, 298; Equal Rights (ERA), 281, 284–87, 299, 302, 330, 332; Fifteenth, 141, 161, 196, 254; Fourteenth, 161, 163, 254; Lucretia Mott, 293–95, 327; National/Federal Suffrage, 179, 184–85, 199–200, 202, 238; Nineteenth, 3, 149, 150, 252; ratification procedure for, 203; state, 201; Susan B. Anthony, 183–85; Thirteenth, 253; U.S. Constitution and passage of, 184–85; Woman Suffrage, 174, 298. *See also specific amendments*
American Alliance for Civil Service Women, 270, 287
American Association of University Women, 287, 299, 332–33
American Birth Control League, 229
American Federation of Labor (AFL), 266, 311, 472; colored women and, 408; and ERA, 287, 299; and Women's Trade Union League, 345; women workers and, 348, 388–91
American Federation of Teachers, 299
American Home Economics Association, 315, 317
American Medical Women's Association, 287
American Suffragette, The, 145
American Woman Suffrage Association (AWSA), 141
amnesty, for draft, 490
anarchists, 354, 359, 360
Anderson, Mary, 286
androcentricism, 48–49
anger, as destructive principle of universe, 111
Anglo-Saxons: South and, 157–58, 162; as standard of ages, 157; supremacy of white, 5
Anthony, Susan B., 141, 147, 149, 164–65, 169, 208; Amendment, 183–85, 244, 254, 279; interview with, 166; as organizer, 430
Anthony, Susan B., II (grandniece), 234; on Susan B. Anthony, 279
antifeminist(s), 341; feminism and, 338; homemaking and, 343

Anti-Suffrage League of Women Voters, 255
anti-suffragist(s), 23, 29; attacks of, 187; feminism and, 187–88; man as, 196–97; retirement of, 219; socialism and, 188–89
Appeal to Reason, 144
armament(s): increase in, 457; moral, 469–70
armed forces, 484; volunteer, 495, 501; women in, 494–502. *See also* military
arms race, 454, 483
Army, 496, 499
art(s): career in, 45–46; Chicago Arts and Crafts Society in, 115; chief characteristic of, 114–15
Assembly District Club, 176
atavism, 61, 453, 460
Atherton, Gertrude, 6
at-home women, support for, 234
atomic bombs, 454

Backlash: The Undeclared War against American Women (Faludi), 233
Baker, Elizabeth Faulkner, 304
balance of power, 456
ballot(s): attainment of aspirations through, 153–54; intelligent, 160; for officers, 155; philanthropy and, 195–96; protective value of, 153–56; self-supporting woman and, 192–93; as sign of power, 191; as stimulus to women's education, 155; training and, 191
banners as weapon, 211
Banning, Margaret Culkin, 287
Bartels, Paul, 92, 94
Bass, Charlotta A., 454
Bax, Belfort, 31–33
Beard, Mary Ritter, 232–33
being, revolt of pretense of, 21
Belasco Theatre, mass-meeting held at, 214–15
Belmont, Alva E. Vanderbilt (Mrs. Oliver H. P.), 149–50, 210, 251; garment industry and, 355, 356
Benedict, Crystal Eastman, 5
Benedict, Ruth, 49
Bethune, Mary McLeod, 348
Bethune-Cookman College, founding of, 383–86
Bible: banner based on, 211; inference to women as inferior, 55
bill(s): Hygiene and Welfare of Maternity and Infancy, 296; introduction of legislative, 174–76. *See also* Sheppard-Towner Act/Law
biology, inferiority of women and, 92–93, 429

birth control: Crystal Eastman on, 229; feminism and, 240, 243, 249; Margaret Sanger on, 229–30, 247; NWP and, 228–29; overpopulation and, 229–30, 240, 248–50; Voluntary Parenthood League and, 229; women's freedom and, 229–30, 240, 248–50, 409
Bjorkman, Edwin, 26–27
Black Panthers, 493
Blackwell, Alice Stone, 141, 148
Blackwell, Henry, 141
black women. *See* African Americans; Negroes; women, colored
Blanket Amendment, 273
Blatch, Harriot Stanton, 144, 147, 150; on joining Advisory Council, 182; on winning of vote, 217–18
bloc, women's, 232, 265, 279, 282–83
block education, 265
Bonaparte, Napoleon, 461
bonds, Liberty and Victory, 268
bourgeois women: communism and, 417; organizations for, 413–15; as sexual commodity, 421
boycott, 409
brain, inferiority of women's, 92–93
Brandeis, Louis, 286, 303
breadlines, women in, 406
British War Cabinet on wages, 399
Bruere, Martha, 251
Bryn Mawr, 48, 337; academic organization of, 56–57; nutrition/sanitary conditions of students at, 58
Buck, Pearl, 327, 453
Burns, Lucy, 146, 211
Business and Professional Women, 287, 324
business(es): and feminism, 396; neighborhood, 342; social separation in, 49–50, 85–86, 88; women in, 239, 258, 278, 287, 311, 321, 392. *See also* industrialism
Butt, Hala Hammond, 143

Cambodia, 493
capitalism: communism and, 479; destruction of, 220; family breakdown and, 432; modern, 49, 96, 99, 100; Negroes and, 257; oppression of, 447; political parties and, 415; sexism and, 448; social responsibility and, 411; unions and, 448; women and, 49, 414–15, 431
Caraway, Hattie W., 323

career(s): artistic, 45–46; for mothers, 342–43; success in, 44; for women, 403
Catt, Carrie Chapman, 141, 143, 145, 147, 148–49, 205, 219; NAWSA and, 227; NLWV and, 227–28
Census Bureau, colored women in, 371
Chafe, William, 285
charities: bourgeois women and, 414; impoverished women and, 406
chattel(s): slavery laws, 291–92; women as men's, 439, 463
Chicago Women's Liberation Union, 350
child abandonment, 249
children: bills for, 296; college statistics for, 61–62; daycare for, 445; education for colored, 381–82; as guardians of health, 129–30; illegitimate, 301; intelligent care of, 115; Maria Montessori and, 23; mother relations with, 343, 432; naming and rearing of, 44–45, 340–41; plantation women and rearing of, 121; support of, 19, 438; teaching skill and joy to, 130; training for college, 53; votes for, 190–91; on wanting, 46; as wards of state, 133–34. See also infants; youths
Christians, early, 110–11
church(es), 33–34, 75; as center of civilization, 462; higher education and, 386
Churchill, Winston, 471
Cieciorka, Bobbi, 454
CIO. See Congress of Industrial Organizations (CIO)
cities: breakdown of social organism in, 106; housekeeping and, 116; jobs in, 404; Social Settlements in, 114
citizens, second class, 484, 486
citizenship: amendment of 1907 law of married women and, 218; rights of women and, 276
City Mothers, 127
civic capacities, opportunities to serve in, 17
civil defense, women volunteers in, 453
civil rights movement, Black national pride and, 231
Civil War, 76, 141, 142, 149; race question and, 157
civilization: ballot as necessity of, 193; centers of, 462; as stronger than nature, 43; warfare and, 68
clan, as economic unit, 419
class(es): abolishing social privilege in, 32–33, 97; dividing of, 106, 419; duties of superior, 113; equality between nations and, 31–32; interdependence of, 25; political parties outlook on, 266; power of ruling, 450, 493; struggle, 365, 415; women in, 447. See also middle class; socialism
Clayton Federal Act, 256
Cleveland, Grover, 183
clothes, 73
co-operative(s): play, 342; use of, 468
Cobden-Sanderson, Anne, 145
Cold War, 350, 490; communism during, 454
collective bargaining, women and, 320
college(s), 114; coeducational, 47, 58; electives chosen by men and women in, 59–61; freedom in social life at, 54; as hotbeds of atheism, 52–53; inferiority of women in, 55–56; interracial, 383–86; physical education in, 52, 57–58; proof of equality between men and women in, 58; protests at, 455, 494; public service after, 62; selection of courses for, 53, 60; specialized women's courses in, 60–61; superficial knowledge in, 53; women outnumbering men in, 60. See also education
colored. See African Americans; Negroes
Colored American Magazine, 143, 148
Colored Women Political League, 257
combat: as physical process, 68; as real business of life, 70–71. See also politics; war; warfare
Commission on Demobilization, 387
committee, legislative, 175–76
Committee for Industrial Equality, Women's, 389, 390
Committee on Open Air Schools, 130
Committee on Social Welfare, 131
communal life, 419–20
communism, 410; capitalism and, 479; common ownership and, 424; and freedom, 238, 423; in Korea, 454; labor movement and, 349–50; women and, 350, 416–25
Communist Manifesto, 433
Communist Party, 408; of the United States, 415
community, beginning of, 475
compulsory service for women, 453, 467–69
conference(s), 197, 242–45, 255–56; spirit of, 117–19
Conger-Kaneko, Josephine, 144, 146
Congress: improvement in activities of, 218–19; lagging bills in both houses of, 218; legislation and, 179–80; women in, 324

Congress of Industrial Organizations (CIO), 349, 472; colored women and, 408–9; and ERA, 334–35
Congressional Union (CU/NWP): conversion to NWP, 231; founding of, 146. *See also* National Woman's Party (NWP/CU)
consciousness: feminism as new, 29; self, 86; social, 89–90; warfare and new world, 67
conservatism, 16, 273, 364; galvanization of, 3
Conservative Party, 204
Constitution, U.S., 3, 163; amending of, 184–85, 202; ERA and, 284–87, 323; Nineteenth Amendment added to, 150; rights of women citizens under, 276, 336; state, 201–2; suffragists and, 237; Susan B. Anthony Amendment and, 183–85
consumer(s), 124; determine production, 122; making demands effective, 122; women as, 83–84, 86, 123; women as producers into, 101. *See also* manufacturers; National Consumer's League
Consumers' League of New York City: principles of, 124; standard of fair house in, 124–25; "White List" of, 123–24, 125, 127
contraceptives, 80n7
Convention, Alice Paul, 240–242
Convention, National Woman's Party, 242–45; colored women at, 255–56; women speaking at, 245
cooking, 72, 73
Cooley, Winnifred Harper, 4
Coolidge, Mary Roberts, 49
corruption, 13; in elections, 200–201, 202; in parties, 231; against suffrage, 200
Cothren, Mrs. Frank, 27
courage, need of, 11
courts, ERA and, 338
Covington, Mary White, 151
Crawford, Remson, 351
Creel, George, 27
crime, of war, 480
culture(s): value of broad, 9; women and different, 90–92
Curie, Madame, 409
Currey, Margery, 227

Daggett, Mabel Potter, 101–2
Darwin, Charles, 96; social Darwinism and, 96; on superiority of men and women, 48
Debs, Eugene V., 346

Declaration of Independence, 163, 319; banner based on, 211; pragmatist, 167; suffragists and, 237
Declaration of Sentiments, 141–42
demobilization, after war, 387–88, 395
democracy: defending, 469; disfranchisement affect on, 252; embarrassment from, 113; extending benefits of, 98; partial view of, 105; standard of life in, 387; triumph of, 205–6; true, 97; and women, 219
Democrat(s), 146; 1968 platform, 488–90; and African American women, 231; blocking suffrage passage by, 179–80; defeat of, 203–4; as enemy, 147; and ERA, 287; vulnerability of, 150; and withholding of support by suffragists, 180–81, 212; women's interests and, 231, 280
demonstration(s): picketing as advanced form of, 208; suffrage, 177; White House, 208–9. *See also* jail; picketing; White House
Dennett, Mary Ware, 229
Department of Defense (DoD), 495–96
Department of Labor, state, 388
Department of Labor, U.S.: Women in Industry Service in, 388; Women's Bureau in, 286, 320, 348, 391–94
Department of Public Improvement, 131
Department of Streets and Alleys, 127
dependents, women as, 259
Depression, Great: changes created by, 232–33; female labor and, 349, 379–80; feminism affected by, 267, 271–72; unions and, 349; World War II affect on, 234
Deputation of Sixty, 255–56
desegregation, military, 502
destiny, 39, 45; control of, 13
Dewey, John, 97, 98
difference v. equality in women's movement, 284–87
disarmament, 489; national, 456; NWP and, 228–29, 242, 246. *See also* pacifism
discrimination: chattel-slavery laws of, 292; in industry, 308, 439; of labor laws, 311; and morality, 17; against Negroes, 418; NWP on, 230; as racial v. gender issue, 230, 347; sex, 502; at white women's parties, 230–31; against women, 280, 301–2, 326–27, 370, 418, 426; against women of color, 230, 250–54, 367; workplace, 234
disease(s): protection from, 155; war as, 461, 477

disfranchisement: affect on democracy, 252; of colored women, 243–44, 250–54; NWP work against, 255; of women, 402. *See also* discrimination
dissolution, of family, 478
District Suffrage Club, 176
Districts, suffrage propaganda in, 177
divorce: absurdity of, 19; equal suffrage and, 188
doctors, women, 473, 474
domestic management, 118–19; maternal origin of, 66–67. *See also* housekeeping
domestic service: colored women in, 377–78; women in, 392; women as models of, 77
dominance: of few over many, 448; of women, 48, 429
Dorr, Rheta Childe, 27, 28, 286
double standard(s): criticism of sexual, 4; of morality, 36–37
Douglass, Frederick, 426
draft, 488; elimination of, 489–90; military, 454, 484–86; resistance, 486, 487, 490; for women, 470; women's exemption from, 486–87. *See also* compulsory service for women; Selective Service System (SSS)
DuBois, W. E. B., 100

Earhart, Amelia, 409
Eastman, Crystal, 227, 229; views on Alice Paul by, 228–29
Eastman, Max, 27
economic independence, 399; abolition of handicaps to, 17; domestic disadvantages with, 77; national endowment of motherhood and, 139; of women, 58–59, 91, 240, 278, 280, 396, 397
economic power, in groups, 398
Economy Act of 1932, Article 213; marital status clause of, 233, 274; nullification of, 275
Economy Act of 1933, 274–75
education, 26; action from, 97–98; application to daily life, 54; collegiate, 9, 47; and colored children, 381–82; differentiation of sexes in, 51; feminism and revolution in, 221; feminists' ideal of, 240; higher, 387; immigrant, 159; problems in, 51; of self, 8; settlements and, 107–8; shallow argument for, 10; voting as stimulus to women's, 155; of women, 339; WSP and civic, 178. *See also* children; colleges; mental powers; schools
Eighteenth Amendment, 298

Eisenhower, Dwight D., 482
Elders, disdain for sex, 81
election(s): boards as bipartisan, 200; fraud and corruption in, 200–201, 202; growth of socialist vote in, 189; race problem in, 185–86; referendum questions for, 200–201; women in, 260
emancipation, 416; African Americans after, 381; economic equality and, 13; independence in, 13–14; joy in women's, 16, 397; misunderstanding of, 15; origin of true, 16; original aim of woman's, 13; shortcomings of, 15; women's struggle for, 236, 249–50; women's tragedy of, 12–16
emergencies, preparedness in, 10
emotion, intelligence and, 83–84, 94
employee(s): humane and considerate behavior toward, 124; medical inspections for, 126–27
employer(s): as virtually helpless, 124; and wage laws, 307; women as, 322
employment: agencies, 380; appointed positions, voting and, 155; bureau, 404, 407–8; discrimination, 347; of men v. women, 276; of women during war, 395. *See also* discrimination; unemployment
enfranchisement of women, 251, 387, 475
Engels, Frederick, 429–30
England, war in, 471
enlisted men, wives of, 499–50, 502
environment, sexes due to difference in, 64
Epstein, Irene, 350
equalitarians, Blanket Amendment by, 273
equality: independence and, 13–14; for Negro women, 257; NWP convention and, 242; for sexes, 295; of wages for women, 318, 329, 434, 441; for women, 232, 239, 245, 247, 258, 259–62, 264, 267–68, 269; difference of women v., 284–88. *See also* amendments
equal pay for equal work, 441
equal right(s), 318, 330; meaning of, 331; socialism and, 188; Wisconsin law of, 284, 290–92; of women, 389; women against, 298–302
Equal Rights Amendment (ERA): argument for, 293–95, 323–29; courts and, 338; in Europe, 286; and Fourteenth Amendment, 335; merits of, 291, 319, 323–29; and Nineteenth Amendment, 291; opponents of, 285, 295–98; partial text of, 331, 334–35; politicians and, 325, 337; violations of, 290–91; Woman's Party

for, 293–95, 323; women against, 298–302, 319, 330–35; World War II affect on, 287. *See also* Wisconsin Equal Rights Law; Women's Charter, The
Equal Rights League, 145
Equal Rights Treaty, 317
ERA. *See* Equal Rights Amendment (ERA)
ethics, 66; superiority and, 14
European: students, 63; woman, 43–44
European War. *See* World War I
evil, 82, 111; control of, 460
evolution: of thought, 40; of women, 6
executives, 472. *See also* businesses
exercises for different sexes, 64
expediency argument, 144
exploitation: capitalism's, 449; of women, 417, 430, 443

factories, workers in, 328. *See also* manufacturers
Fair Employment Practices Act for women, 280
fair house, 124
Fair Labor Standards Act, 349; and ERA, 287, 325, 332
faith in benignity of individual development, 25–26
Faludi, Susan, 233
family: dissolution of, 478; economic disintegration of Puritan-Colonial, 75; ERA and, 331; feudal, 85, 86, 87; as miniature state, 191; Nineteenth Century, 74–75; sacrifice for, 88
farmers' conferences, 120–21
farming, 72–73; war's affect on, 481–82
farm-management, 467–68
Farnham, Dr. Marynia, 428, 429
fascism, 233, 286, 417, 418, 420, 448; profit system and, 418
father-right, 419
Fauntleroy, Mrs. Somerville, 257
fear(s), 11; crippling influence of, 7; intolerance as, 469
federal laws, against women, 294–95. *See also* laws
Federal Suffrage Amendment. *See* amendments
Federal Women's Bureau, 286
"Female Feminists" v. "Human Feminists," 289
Feminine Mystique, The (Friedan), 234, 350
femininity: loss of, 463; women and, 314, 338, 343
feminism: antagonism to, 276–79; antifeminists and, 338; anti-suffragists and, 187–88; birth control and, 240; business and, 396; conservatives v. militants in, 273; as counterculture, 5; cutting across class lines, 220–21; defined, 277, 398; Depression's affect on, 267; difference, 96; as doctrine of self-development, 24; enlistment of men and, 220, 239; intellectual history of, 4; maternalist, 96–97; and motherhood, 289; multiplicity of definitions for, 3, 22–23, 26, 187–88; as new consciousness, 29; object of, 220, 363; origin of, 3, 30; in other countries, 30–31, 272–73; question of, 22–23; removal of restrictions with, 90; revolution in education and, 221; sexual freedom as central to, 4; socialism and, 364; socialist, 349–50, 446–48; suffrage and, 23, 41; wage laws and, 399; war's affect on, 268
feminist(s): clear objectives of, 220; continual altercations among, 17; development of individual and, 23; education and, 240; first mass meeting of, 26; goals of, 341; "Human" v. "Female," 289; masculine, 338; movement, 363–66; pacifism, 452; practical v. theoretical, 306, 310–11; revolutionary, 494; roles, 343–44; sense of freedom, 238–40; socialist, 446; spirit, 249; theory during early years, 4; women, men and, 314
femme covert, 276, 287, 318
Field, Sara Bard, 253
Fifteenth Amendment, 141, 161, 252; colored men and, 254; woman suffrage and, 196, 299–300
Fisher, Katharine, 348
flop houses, women in, 406
foreigners: North threatened by, 157; women, 413. *See also* European, 413
Fourteenth Amendment, 161, 252, 303, 335; colored men and, 254, 336; as mistake, 163
fraternization in military, 501
fraud among political parties, 200, 202
freedom: of choice in occupation, 238–40, 279; and communism, 238, 423; of contract, 310; economic, 396; meaning of, 409–10; spiritual, 25; struggle for, 153, 238–40; technology and, 448; and a woman's soul, 238; of women and birth control, 229–30, 240, 248–50; women's, 250, 325. *See also* independence
Freudian concepts, 428–29
Friedan, Betty, 234, 350
Frost, Susan, 251

Gale, Zona, 284
Gallichan, Mrs. Walter, 21–22
Galsworthy, Mr., 20–21
Gamble, James N., 384
Garland, Marie Tudor, 219
garment industry: life in, 353–60; strike and, 345, 355, 357–61, 402
Garvey, Amy Jacques, 231
Garvey, Marcus, 231
General Education Board, 379
General Federation of Women's Clubs, 281; and ERA, 281, 299
Gilman, Charlotte Perkins, 5, 48–49, 103, 150; on colored woman voter, 251–52; on humanness, 284; recognition of at-home women by, 234
girls: as future mothers, 468; shop, 351–52; training of, 467–69
Girls' Friendly Society, 299, 332
Glasgow, Ellen, 4
God, 52, 464–65
Goldman, Emma, 3–4, 23, 187–88
Good Housekeeping, middlebrow literature and, 5
gossip, 9
government(s), 116; colored women in, 367–73; foreign, 152, 206, 208–9; as government by party, 179–80; high posts in, 472, 473; intelligent suffrage and, 159–60; learning from foreign government, 206; ownership of utilities, 388; people as loss to, 8; picketing of, 208; science of, 66, 69; stupidity as boomerang upon, 212; women in, 232, 258, 260, 262, 281, 282, 323–24, 462, 471; women's war work and, 207. *See also* politics
graduate schools, 62–63
Great Britain, 150, 180, 201, 205; full suffrage in, 206; mobilization of women in, 206; motherhood endowment in, 138, 140; violent suffragists in, 145, 149, 186–87; women outnumbering men in, 42

habits, unhampered growth out of, 15–16
Hale, Beatrice Forbes-Robertson, 28–29
happiness, 110; pursuit of, 45
Harding, Thomas, 259; political appointments by, 260
Harper, Ida Husted, 141
Harper, Mrs. E. Howard, 231
Harriman, Mrs. J. Borden, 453
Hayden, Carl, 287
Haynes, Elizabeth Ross, 347–48

health and safety, worker, 392–93, 445
health insurance, 136
Hepburn, Katharine, 327
"Her Majesty the Shop Girl" (Crawford), 351–52
heroine(s): differences in, 33; popular men's, 5–6
Heterodoxy Club, 5, 50
Higginson, Thomas Wentworth, 278
Hilles, Mrs. Bayard, 147, 183, 210
Hippodrome, strikers meet at, 345, 355–56
history, women's, 38, 49
Hitler, Adolf, 416, 461
Hollingworth, Leta, 50, 94
home: as center of civilization, 462, 477; conditions of, 475–76; destruction of, 478; economics, 467; as organism, 476
home-made goods v. machine made, 410
homemaking. *See* housekeeping
Hooker, Edith Houghton, 287
Hoover, Herbert, 274
Horowitz, Daniel, 350
hospital(s): interracial, 385; segregation of, 385
housekeeping, 71, 72; as an occupation, 238, 243, 259, 301, 340–41; details in, 76–77; equality of men/women and, 221, 239; joy in, 74, 342; women, business and, 239, 304, 308; women's freedom from, 282. *See also* domestic management; domestic service; public housekeeping
Houses, balance of power in both, 219
housewifery, farming as different from, 73–74
housewives, 339–40, 425, 426; career-minded, 339–40; compensation to, 75; institutional support for, 234; prestige of, 341; sentiment as cherished possession of, 196; votes for, 196–97; working class, 411
Howe, Marie Jenney, 5, 27, 28
Hull House, 97, 99, 100, 117; Chicago Arts and Crafts Society at, 115; three trends of, 111. *See also* Social Settlements
"Human Feminists" v. "Female Feminists," 289
humiliation, of women concerning voting, 201–2
hunger, unemployment and, 406, 407
hunger strike, 215; pickets and, 214
Hunton, Addie, 230
Hutchins, Grace, 349–50

ideal(s): of sexes, 22; teaching and, 194; votes for, 168–69
idiot asylums, 95
ignorance, criminality of, 18

ILGWU. *See* International Ladies' Garment Workers' Union (ILGWU)
imagination, cultivation of, 39–40
immigrant(s), 99, 146; education of, 159; as ineffectual consumer, 122–23; voting by, 105, 158–59, 164, 201
income. *See* wages
independence, emancipation and, 13–14. *See also* freedom
Indians, American, 90; voting and, 159; as wards of nation, 201
individuality: modern, 82, 84; social relations implicit in, 25
individuals, women as, 23–24, 25
industrialism: capitalism, poverty and, 49, 96, 99, 100–101; effect on social institutions, 398; knowledge applied to, 115–16; modern, 84–86, 117; motherhood victimized by, 103; Settlements and, 112; slavery to, 136; thriving, 96
industrial revolution, labor and, 430
industry: as center of civilization, 462; colored women in, 373–77, 379; crab, 380; discrimination, 308, 439; exploitation of women, 434–35; reconstruction, 386; strikes in garment, 345, 355, 357–61, 402; unions in, 388–90; war, 328–29; war affect on, 394–95; women in, 320, 393, 434. *See also* manufacturers
Infant Cloak Makers Union of New York, 346
infanticide, women and, 248, 249
infants, prenatal care of, 130–31
inferiority: security in, 429; of women, 48, 50, 90, 247, 260, 319, 412, 426–27, 429; of women workers, 438
inheritance, women's, 268, 272
insults to women, 427
integration, school, 382, 384. *See also* desegregation; segregation
intelligence: brain v., 92–93; men v. women, 93–95
international agreements, influencing final decisions in, 218
International Alliance, nonpartisanship of, 204
International Congress of Women at The Hague, 452, 457, 458
International Ladies' Garment Workers' Union (ILGWU), 345–46
International Woman Suffrage Alliance, 452
intolerance as fear, 469
investing women, 270
Irwin, Inez Haynes, 285

Jackson, Mary E., 347
Jackson State College, 455
jail: as convenient institution, 212; letter on treatment in Occoquan, 213–14; protesters in, 494; strikers in, 358–59, 402, 403; suffragists in, 150, 209; treatment of suffragists in, 212–15; unconditional release from, 212
James, William, 98
Japan, atomic bomb and, 454
Japanese, work and, 45
Jim Crow laws, 408, 412, 480
job(s): city v. farm, 404; classification, 442; government, 368; layoff, 444, 445; men v. women in, 436–37, 440–41; for Negro women, 441; part-time, 342; rate structure, 442–43, 445; seniority, 444; skill rating, 433; training, 321, 443; turnover in, 437–38; war and, 374, 379; women in men's, 444–45. *See also* industry; labor force; occupations
Johnson, Lyndon, 455; Vietnam policy of, 488
Joiners, 273
Jones, B. J., 221–22
Jones, Mary Mother, 348–49, 360
Journal of Home Economics, 315
Judiciary Committee, 180
Junior Municipal League, 129–30
juries, women on, 267, 290, 336
justice, 141, 298; system control by men, 260. *See also* laws

Kearney, Belle, 143
Kelley, Florence, 100–101, 147, 252, 285
Kendall, Ada Davenport, 150; report on Occoquan Prison, 213–14
Kennedy, John F., 487
Kent State University murders, 455, 493
Key, Ellen, 84, 284
Khan, Genghis, 461
Kirchwey, Freda, 228
Kneeland, Louise, 5
knowledge: reorganization of, 113–14; without organization for demand, 123
Komarovsky, Mirra, 288
Koonan, Karen, 454
Korea: communism in, 454; war in, 480–82

labor force: in industrial revolution, 430; married women in, 144; skilled v. unskilled, 379, 412; women as cheap, 431
labor laws, 311, 398; child, 194, 202; constitutionality of, 396; protective, 285–86,

296–97, 300–312, 316–18; trade unions for, 398; for women, 297, 300–301, 302–12, 316, 328, 393
labor movement, 87–88, 390; closeness of women and, 89; communism, socialism and, 349–50
Labor Party, 203
labor standards, 387
La Follette, Belle Case, 228, 229
La Follette, Fola, 28
La Follette, Robert, 229
La Follette's Magazine, 229
Laidlaw, Harriet, 146
laissez-faire capitalist principles, 233
Laly, Lucy, 382
landlords, 128
lawlessness, as cause of war, 477
Lawrence, D. H., 424
law(s): changes to, 297; of chattel-slavery days, 292; compulsory school, 468; discrimination, 301–2; existing bad, 218; lynching, anti-, 252; maternity, 337; minimum wage, 399; misinterpretation of, 298; night-work, 297, 305, 308–9; property, 259–60; protective labor, 296–97, 300–301, 302–12, 316–18, 328; state labor, 312; wage, 300, 309–10, 337; against women, 294–95, 335. *See also* justice
leadership, and women, 6
League of Nations, 218
League of Neutral Nations (League of Peace), 456
League of Voters, name change of, 228. *See also* National League of Women Voters (NLWV)
legislation: New Deal, 349; welfare, 227, 295. *See also* labor laws; laws
legislature(s): Congress and, 179–80; introduction of bill in, 174–76; progressive, 415; state, 173–76, 199, 319, 334; women in, 232, 265
Lenin, Vladimir Ilich, 410–11, 431
Le Roy, Virginia B., 144
lesbians, 495, 498, 499
Le Sueur, Meridel, 349
Lewis, John L., Committee on Industrial Organizations. *See* Congress of Industrial Organizations (CIO)
Liberal Party, 204
liberation movements, repression of, 494
life: as battle, 8; love as perfection of, 189
Lifshitz, Molly, 232
liquor proponents, 199–200
literature: votes and, 189–90; women producing great, 189
living conditions, for colored women, 375–76

Loebinger, Sofia M., 3, 4, 145
Logan, Adella Hunt, 143, 148
love, 81; family, 86; women's services for, 476
Loyal League, 149
Lucretia Mott Equal Rights Amendment. *See* Equal Rights Amendment (ERA)
Lundberg, Ferdinand, 428, 429
Lutz, Alma, 233, 287
lynching law, anti-, 252

Maffett, Minnie L., M.D., 453
magazines, male control of, 260–61. *See also* media attacks
male supremacy, women's dependence and, 233–34
Maley, Anna, 345
Malkiel, Theresa Serber, 345–46
Maloney, Mollie, 327
manufacturer(s): collective pressure on, 101; colored women and, 373–74, 376, 379–80; humane standards used by, 123; legislation for protection from, 156; segregation and, 374, 375; unskilled v. skilled labor, 379, 412; wages, 379; working conditions, 375–76, 379
Margolin, Shirley, 491
Marine Corps Women's reserve, 453
Market Tens, 101; inner workings of, 129
markets, sanitation regulations for, 128–29
marriage, 418; avoiding, 46; bourgeois theory of, 420–21; career v., 82, 421, 422; equal suffrage and bad effect on, 187, 188; mating and childless, 80, 80n7; parental consent for, 80; as unjust partnership, 75; women teachers and, 275; work as substitution for, 83, 429
Marsden, Dora, 23
Martin, Anne, 231–32
Martinez, Sabina, 349
Marx, Karl, 410
masculinity: boys and girls and, 314; goals of society and, 341; men and, 343; roles, 343–44; women and, 338; women's ideal of, 19–20
mass-meetings, Belasco Theatre, 214–15
maternity: benefits, 136–37; laws, 337
matriarchal state: reversion to, 44; system v. privileges of, 90–91
Matthews, Burnita Shelton, 325
maude, 455
McCulloch, Catharine Waugh, 142
McDowell, Mary, 98–99
Mead, Margaret, 49, 286
media attacks, 428

men: aching in heart of, 20; admitted to Socialist party, 188–89; anti-Feminist, 33, 276–78; brotherhood of, 470; defined, 427; in domestic service, 44–45; dominance over women, 48, 429; emotions, intellect and, 83–84, 93–94; feminism of, 239; heroines and, 19–20; hostility towards, 338; housekeeping and, 53, 54, 239; as "human beings," 79n5; ignorant, 200; individualistic expression and "social sense" of, 24; justice system control by, 260; and labor laws, 297, 300–301; lower wages for, 444; masculine v. feminine, 56–57, 314; modern, 85, 86–87; on nurturing women, 46; objection to picketing, 209; occupations of, 75; outnumbered by women, 42; personification of sex and, 79–81; political party control of, 260; protecting power of, 11; ridicule as weapon used by, 212; rights of, 7; as social beings, 424; superiority over women, 64–65, 343, 389, 425; on teaching in women's colleges, 56–57; in traditional roles, 6; vote and African American, 141; wages v. women, 309–10, 329, 375, 434–37, 439, 442, 443–44; women as equal to, 10–11, 285; women manipulating, 227–28, 236; v. women in occupations, 313, 315, 390, 394, 437; women's contempt for, 43; women's freedom and willingness of, 29; World War I, women and, 41–43

men, colored: ballot and, 192; doubt wisdom of suffrage, 193; enfranchised by federal amendment, 201; Fourteenth/Fifteenth Amendment and, 254, 336. *See also* sexes

mental expansion, women and, 39

mental powers: correlation of moral and spiritual natures with, 52; correlation of physical and, 52; destruction of health through, 51, 57; women as incapable of strenuous, 51

Meredith, George, 20

Middle Ages, 85

middle class(es), 47, 71, 87; feminism, political power, and, 30–31; NAWSA and bias toward, 144; occupations of, 71–72; suffrage movement largely, 170; women and, 71

Middleton, George, 26

Milholland, Inez, 5

Milholland, Jean L., 253

militant(s), 170; campaign, 209–12; lack of American, 187; mild, 209; suffragette, 171; suffragist in England, 187, 204–5; White House picketing by, 209–12; women, 42, 273, 279, 485

military: changes in, 497; draft, 454, 484–86; fraternization, 501; lesbians in, 495, 498, 499; panic, 211; recruitment, 495–96; reform, 500–502; spending, 489; training, 497; women in, 452, 455, 473. *See also* armed forces; enlisted men

Millard, Betty, 350

Miller, Frieda, 287

Miller, Nathan L., 261

mind(s): changes taking place in women's, 36; developed faculties of, 9

miner(s): strikes, 400–402; union, 400–401

minimum wage. *See* wages

Mississippi Valley Conference, 142

modern women, 82, 84, 86–88

monarchies, 196

monogamy: experiment of, 19; origin of, 430

Montessori, Maria, 23

moral: armament, 469–70; superiority, 464

morality: black women as superior in, 192; disregard for, 14; double standards of, 36–37; in education, 52; growth of new, 36; intuition and, 83; modern business effect on, 85, 86; politics and, 13, 67; single standard of, 17; women's intuition and, 83; women's v. men's, 187, 465

Mother-Age, 44

motherhood, 73; endowment, 240, 243; and feminism, 289; importance of, 284, 340–41, 343; maternity leave and, 103; primary functions of, 71–72; public/social function of, 103; sacrifice of, 84, 88; virtues of, 9, 476; widows and, 132–36; work v., 84, 102. *See also* children; infants; youths

motherhood endowment, 218, 221; administration of, 140; cost of, 140; objections to, 139; plan for, 138–40; mother-right, 418–19

mother(s): careers for, 342–43; and child relations, 343, 432; girls as future, 468; paycheck for, 103–4; pensions for, 102, 131–32; recognizing value of, 234; Republican/moral, 144; as teachers, 258; as too modest, 138; votes for, 190; wages for, 137–38

Mother's Pension Law, 102

Mott, Lucretia, 279, 325, 425; amendment, 293–95, 327

movement(s): American reform, 6; anti-suffrage, 23, 29, 187; feminist, 26; human evolution and women's, 40–41; life of organized, 197; middle-class, 30; separate feminist, 219–20;

Socialist, 30; stages of, 197; of true
emancipation, 14–15; Woman Suffrage, 33, 193
Muller v. Oregon, 286
Murray, Ella Rush: on Nineteenth Amendment,
253; on rights of African American women, 230
Murrell, Ethel Ernest, 288

NAACP. *See* National Federation of Colored
Women (NAACP)
names, right of women to keep own, 28, 44
Nation, The, 230
National American Woman Suffrage Association
(NAWSA), 141, 142; convention in Atlantic
City, 148, 197–202; "crisis" of, 197–202;
declaration of principals, 152–53; difference
between first and fortieth convention of,
169–70; dissolution of, 227; federal
amendment aimed at by, 199–200; lack of
organization in, 197–98; mental attitude change
in, 198–99, 202; as precursor to NLWV, 227;
switching of priorities of, 149; three most
common charges aimed at, 148; World War I
and, 205–8
National Anti-Suffrage Association, 187
National Association of Colored Women, 195;
Addie Hunton and, 230; formation of, 148;
social reform and, 231
National Association of Women Lawyers, 287
National Committee on the Status of Women,
281, 287
National Consumers League (NCL), 49; aim of,
122, 126; Department of Education, 130;
Department of Housing, 128–29; and ERA,
299, 302, 332; humane treatment of
employees, 125; laws petitioned by, 127;
Market Department of, 128; organization of
state leagues and, 123; principles of, 121–22;
on public housekeeping, 101; sanitary
inspectors and, 127–29. *See also* consumers;
Consumers' League of New York City;
manufacturers; markets; Market Tens
National Council of Catholic Women, 299, 331–32
National Council of Jewish Women, 332
National Federation of Business and Professional
Women's Clubs, 281
National Federation of Colored Women (NAACP),
195, 256
National Federation of Women's Clubs, 287
National Industrial Recovery Act, 415
National Labor Relations: Act, 349; Board, 349

National League of Colored Woman, 195
National League of Women Voters (NLWV):
capitalist system and, 414–15; Equal Rights
Amendment and, 281, 284–87, 299, 302,
330, 332; mission of, 227–28, 237; name
change of, 228; strategy of, 231, 232; as
successor to NAWSA, 227; suffrage convention
and, 235–37
National Organization for Women (NOW), 501
National Progressive Woman Suffrage Union, 145,
170–71
National Service Star Legion, 332
National Suffrage amendment, 179
National Woman's Party (NWP/CU), 103, 146,
149, 217; Advisory Council of, 254; African
American women and, 230, 243–44, 255; and
Alice Paul, 228–29; areas of controversy of,
228; Belle Case La Follette and, 228; birth
control and, 228–29; Black women's voting
rights and, 228; Convention, 242–45; on
disarmament, 246; discrimination and, 230;
against disfranchisement, 255; dissolution of,
252–53; Equal Rights Amendment and, 281,
323; flag/emblem of, 208; membership decline
of, 228; militancy of, 210; mission of, 228,
254, 323; National Advisory Committee of,
251; Nineteenth Amendment in South and,
230; nonpartisan affiliation of, 217; pacifism
and, 229. *See also* Congressional Union
(CU/NWP)
National Woman Suffrage Association (NWSA),
141
National Women's Trade Union League, 311; Equal
Rights Amendment and, 281, 299, 302; on
social and industrial reconstruction, 386–88
National Youth Administration, 386, 468
Naturalization laws, 201
natural law, as unnatural, 40
nature: lessons of, 8; women and, 42–43
Navy, 496, 500; WAVES, 453, 498
NAWSA. *See* National American Woman Suffrage
Association
Nazi: belief in catharsis of war, 465; Hitler Youth
and Labor Corps, 465, 470
Negro(es), 119, 151, 156; abolitionists, 147;
disenfranchisement of, 142, 221; equal rights
for, 257; higher education for, 386; illiteracy of,
186; industrial education of, 157; men, 143,
148; social ostracism of, 105, 257; suffrage,
157, 164, 190, 192, 193; women v. number of

white women, 185–86; women's jobs, 441.
    See also African Americans; men, colored;
    plantation women; women, colored
Negro World, 231
neighborhood(s): businesses, 342; responding to
    needs of, 99
neurotic, women as, 423
New Deal legislation, 349
New Left, 454
Newman, Pauline M., 346
New Position of Women in American Industry, The, 394
New Review, The, 5
newspapers, male control of, 260–61. *See also*
    media attacks
New York City Citizens Committee on Safety, 362
New York Times, The, 5, 150, 221
New York Women's Trade Union League, 232, 265
newspapers, male control of, 260–61. *See also*
    media attacks
night-work: International Labor Organization and,
    336; laws, 297, 305, 308–9, 328
Nineteenth Amendment, 149, 222; African
    American voting rights and, 230, 242, 246,
    250–51; enforcement of, 252, 253, 254;
    enfranchisement of all women through, 251;
    and ERA, 291; National Woman's Party and,
    230; nullification attempts on, 230; prejudice
    and, 252; ratification of, 3, 150; South and,
    230; violation of, 254, 255
Nixon, Richard, 455, 490
North: salvation by South, 157–58; threatened by
    foreigners, 157–58
North American Review, 33
Northeast Federation of Women's Clubs, 147–48
Norton, Mary T., 323–24
novelists: feminine qualities and, 189–90; women
    as, 21
NOW. *See* National Organization for Women
    (NOW)
nuclear weapons, 454, 489; 1963 Test Ban Treaty,
    454, 487
nursery schools, 342
nursing, 73; prenatal care and, 131
NWP/CU. *See* National Woman's Party
    (NWP/CU)

Oatman, Dr. Miriam E., 328
Occoquan Workhouse, 213–14
occupation(s): for colored women, 373–74,
    377–80, 441; freedom of choice in, 238–40,
    279; housekeeping as, 238, 301; middle class,
    71–72; remunerative, 118; for women, 270,
    274, 276, 278, 295, 313, 315, 320, 392, 394;
    women v. men in, 313, 315, 390, 394, 437.
    See also jobs; vocational training
officer(s): ballot for, 155; female, 495
old age, passage into, 9
oppression, 448; of capitalism, 447, 449; of
    sexism, 449; of women, 350, 418, 428, 446,
    449, 486, 494. *See also* sexism
organization(s): bourgeois women's, 413–15;
    NAWSA lack of, 197–98
organized labor. *See* unions
Origin of the Family (Engels), 429
orphanages, 134
overpopulation, birth control and, 229–30, 248
Ovington, Mary White, 346

pacifism, 50, 229, 456; Belle Case and Robert La
    Follette and, 229; feminist, 452; as instrument
    of war, 478; NWP and, 228–29
Pan-American Convention of labor, 403
Pankhurst, Emmeline, 145, 205
parenthood, 80, 87
Park, Clara Cahill, 102–3, 131
Parkhurst, Genevieve, 233
Parsons, Elsie Clews, 49
Parsons, Mrs. James Russell, 263
partisanship, 204; corruption and, 231; kinds of,
    236–37
parties. *See* political parties
part-time jobs, 342
passivity, of women, 20, 22
patronage, political, 216–17
Patterson, Mrs. Robert M., 231
Paul, Alice, 146, 147, 148, 149, 183, 215;
    Convention, 240–42; on Nineteenth
    Amendment, 252; and NWP, 228–29;
    organizing genius of, 210; power of, 228, 247;
    view on disarmament, 229; woman's
    movement and, 242
Peabody, J. S., 384
peace: program for constructive, 456–57; strike
    for, 482–84
Peace Commission Treaties, 456–57
peace societies, 69
Peace Treaty, 387, 398
Pearl Harbor, 453
pensions: for mothers/children, 102; widow's,
    102–3, 132–36

Pentagon, 490, 501
people, as living beings, 477
Perkins, Frances, 5, 27
personal adornment, 73
personal liberty, 154
personal service. *See* domestic service
personality: liberation of, 21; necessary attributes of, 15, 84–85; as primary goal of feminism, 4; relationship, sex and, 79–81, 84
petitions, NAWSA and, 146
Ph.D. degrees. *See* graduate schools
philanthropy, 198; votes for, 195–96
Phillips, Dr. Lena Madesin, 324
physical conditions, 89
Pickens, William, 250
picketing, 409; as advanced form of demonstration, 208–9; Clayton Federal Act and, 256; money raised from, 215; people responsible for White House, 210–11; prison time served from, 212–15; White House, 208–9
Pitts, Rebecca, 350
plantation women, 100, 136; advantages of education to, 120; farmers' conferences and, 120; marital relations of, 121; sexism and, 450; social improvement of, 119–20; standards of morality among, 121. *See also* Negroes
poem, suffrage, 215–16
poets on woman's mental and moral inferiority, 34
political affiliations/principles, 219
political parties: African American women in, 231; capitalism and, 415; class outlook, 266; control by men of, 260; forming separate, 217, 232–33, 261–62; fraud among, 200–201, 202; indignation for, 203; in NLWV, 237; partisan action in, 203, 235–37; platforms of, 217, 337; progressive v. reactionary, 236, 262; reactionary, 236, 262; safeguard of, 200–201; suffrage support for, 204, 227–28; women's manipulation of, 212, 227; women's separate, 232–33, 261–62; working class women and, 414. *See also specific parties*
political power, 30; four lines of attack for, 31; women's use of, 219, 231, 232, 266–67, 268–69
politics, 46; acute situations in, 210; altruistic/selfish interests in, 219; "bossism" in, 105–6; confusion of warfare and, 70; corruption in, 13; definition of, 66; legislative bill introduction through, 174–76; refrain from playing, 219; science of, 69–70; as servant of industry, 402; women's status and, Woman Suffrage Party and, 172–79; women, suffrage and, 167–68, 264, 265; women in, 269. *See also* governments; war
Popular Front, 349
poverty, 96–97, 98, 157; charities and women in, 406
power(s): balance of, 3, 456; of control, 25; correlation of physical and mental, 52; political, 30, 218–19; of professional women, 397, 471; of ruling class, 450; self-sacrifice and, 21; sociological v. biological, 5; teachers and temptation of, 194
Prehistoric history, 44
prejudice: Nineteenth Amendment and, 252; race, 371. *See also* discrimination, segregation
presidents, weakness in armor of, 211
press coverage, suffrage activity and, 145, 175, 177
prison. *See* jail
private profit system, voting and, 220
private property, 420; evolution of, 419
production, women dictates on, 268
Professional and Business Women's Clubs, 324
professions. *See* businesses; occupations
profit system, 423; Communist Party against, 415; fascism and, 418; proponents of, 414
progressive: movement, 433; political parties, 236, 364
Progressive Era, 6, 96, 104
Progressive Party, 454, 481
Progressive Woman, The, 346
Progressives, 189, 203
progressivism, 96, 100
prohibition movement, 200, 202, 203, 220; workingman and, 403
propaganda, disseminating suffrage, 176–78
property: evolution of private, 419; inheritance of, 44; laws, 259–60; Negro owning, 186; private, 420; rights, 267, 272, 330; voting qualification with, 201; warfare over, 67; woman's taxation on, 152; women as men's, 5, 420–21
prostitution: abolition of, 18; caste discrimination and economics of, 80, 81, 83; monogamy and, 430; in Soviet Union, 432; white slavery and, 366
protection(s): black women and, 192; given to women through ballot, 153–54; legal, 154. *See also* labor laws
Protective Legislation (Baker), 304

protests war, 455, 494
psychic: awakening of women, 37–38; conscious unfolding of, 40
psychology, data on women's, 93–95
public housekeeping, 97, 99, 101, 116–17, 126–27, 131–32. *See also* housekeeping
purchasers. *See* consumers
Puritans, innate craving for motherhood and, 15
Putnam, Mabel Raef, 284
Putnam, Mrs. William Lowell, 131
Putnam, Nina Wilcox, 29

race(s), 31, 41; African American women and, 231; Anglo-Saxons and question of, 162; discrimination and, 347; feminism and, 24, 37–38; national suffrage and problem of, 185–86; prejudice, 371; settlements and, 108; unmixed, 192; woman as perpetuator of, 191; women as pile drivers of, 40; women question and precedence over, 25. *See also* men, colored; Negroes; plantation women; slavery, white; women, colored
racism. *See* discrimination; segregation
radicalism, 16, 364, 486
radicals, female student, 454
Rainbow Literature, 176
Randall, Ollie A., 287
rape, 426n1
reactionary political parties, 236, 262
reason, substitution of sentiment for, 197
reconstruction, social and industrial, 386
redistribution, of goods, 449
Rees, Steve, 455
reform, 97, 102, 104; black women and, 192; military, 500–502; NLWV lobbying for, 232; suffrage, 178–79, 194–95; without fight, 211; women and faith in, 220. *See also* military; social movements; Social Settlements
reformer(s): fears of, 16–17; middle-aged, 16
religion: freedom of, 469; inferiority of women and, 427–28; suffrage and, 188
Renaissance, 79
Representatives, women, 324
reproduction, 476; as primary function of women, 475. *See also* birth control
Republican(s), 146, 203, 212; African Americans and, 231, 256–57; and ERA, 287; Neighborhood Association, 263; Woman's, Club of, 253; women's interests and, 231, 280
responsibility, individual, 10

retrogression, and women, 271–72
revolution, 451; socialist feminists for, 446
Revolutionary War, 149; justification of, 163
Richards, Frances, 5
righteousness, 464–65
right(s): a priori, 144; fallacy of a priori, 166; fallacy of abstract, 165; irreconcilability between individual and social, 24; natural, 3, 141, 166; to organize, 27–28; suffrage and three menaces to equal, 186–87; to vote, 3; of women to have children, 282; of women to keep own name, 28; of women under Constitution, 276, 336; women's, as individuals, 7; women's legal, 280–81, 335; women's reasons for women's, 166; women's v. husband's, 154–55, 281, 295; to work, 27–28. *See also* equal rights
Robinson, Mrs. Douglas (Corinne Roosevelt), 263
Rockefeller, John D., Jr., 401–2
Rodman, Henrietta, 26
Roosevelt, Corinne (Mrs. Douglas Robinson), 263
Roosevelt, Eleanor, 453
Roosevelt, Franklin D., 386; War labor Board of World War II, 435n1
rugged feminism. *See* feminism
Rules Committee, 180

sacrifices, 207
Sand, George, 14
San Francisco Civic Center, 252
Sanger, Margaret, 229–30, 247
sanitary inspectors. *See* National Consumers' League (NCL)
Saturday Evening Post, 234
scabs, 401
Schneiderman, Rose, 27–28; Triangle Fire and, 346; women's bloc and, 232
school(s), 107; compulsory law for, 468; nursery, 342; segregation, 381; teacher vote in, 194. *See also* education
Schreiner, Olive, 84, 85
science, women's movement and, 40–41
second class citizens, 484, 485, 486
Sedition Act, 452
segregation: in education, 381; in hospitals, 385; in manufacturing, 374; occupational, 373, 375; during war, 347, 369, 371; of women, 232–33, 435, 444. *See also* desegregation; integration
Selective Service System (SSS), 484. *See also* draft
self, 7–11; independent sense of, 3; loss of,

465–66; oneness with others and, 12; solitude of, 7–11
self-development, 4; feminism as doctrine of, 24
self-employed women, 322
self-expression: arts as supreme form of, 45–46; men and women bent on, 25; right to activity of, 18
self-sacrifice, 207; power and, 21; women subordinated by, 25
Senate, women in, 323
Senatorial District. *See* Woman Suffrage Party (WSP)
Seneca Falls, peaceful political revolution in, 218
sentiment, substitution of reason for, 197
servitude, of women, 419
Settlements. *See* Social Settlements
Severn, Jill, 454
Sex Disqualification Removal Acts, 275
sex(es), 421; animosity between, 12; aristocracy of U.S., 260; as basis of human relations, 35; biological origins of psychological differences between, 48; characteristics of each, 11–12; consciousness, 81; differences between, 286, 344; discrimination, 502; double standard of, 80; equality for, 193, 295, 420; frankness in, 36; liberation of entire, 34–35; mental traits of, 64–66; new ideals of, 22; personification of, 79–81, 79nn5–6; segregation, 79; sociological/biological differences in, 32, 44–45, 48; third, 43–44; unity, 38; weaker, 464
sexism: capitalism and, 448, 449; oppression and, 446–47, 449; slavery and, 450
sexual activity: elders disdain for, 81; evilness/impropriety of, 82, 103; relationship primary to, 81
sexual equality, activism for, 3
sexual liberation, 3
sexual servility, 421
Shakespeare, William, 8
Shaw, Anna Howard, 141, 142, 148, 149, 206
Sheppard-Towner Act/Law, 227, 296
shop girls, 351–52
Short History of Women's Rights, A (Hecker), 425
sisterhood, 447
skilled labor v. unskilled labor, 379, 412
slavery, sexism and, 450
slavery, white, 31; abolition of, 18; low wages and, 366–67
slavery laws, chattel-, 291–92
slaves. *See* Negroes; plantation women

Smith, Ethel M., 285
Smith, Margaret C., 324
social: responsibility, 411; role of women, 339–44; tyranny, 417, 423
social group, women as, 4
social institutions, industrialism effects on, 398
socialism: class struggle and, 365; defined, 346; feminism and, 30–31, 100, 350, 363–66; feminism not essential part of, 31–32; goal/aim of, 32–33, 257, 363, 433; suffrage and, 188–89, 364
socialist feminism: goals, 446–48; ideology, 450–51
Socialist Labor Party, 346
Socialist Party, 352; exploitation and, 257; platform, 364; suffrage and, 415
Socialist Trade and Labor Alliance, 346
Socialists, 148, 203; all suffragists are, 188; equality for women and, 264, 361; sharp division among, 189; strikes and, 359–60; women voting and, 266
Socialist Woman, The, 144
social movement(s): crucial elements in, 4; energizing of, 3; unsatisfied wants/problems expressed in, 89–90. *See also* reform
social reconstruction, 386
social reform, 415; National Association of Colored Women on, 231
social relations: business and separation in, 49–50, 85–86; establishment of, 25; familial, 85; social conscious and, 87
social science, 89, 90
Social Security Act, 325
Social Service, 195
Social Settlement(s): American v. English, 113; application v. research in, 114; Chicago Arts and Crafts Society from, 115; Christianity in, 110–11; definition of, 105, 114; as experiment, 111–12; Hull House, 111; motives for, 98, 105–10; national bureaus and, 115; no social/political agenda in, 98; origination of, 109–10, 113; propaganda for suffrage in, 177; as provisional, 112–13; University Extension movement and, 107
societies: classless, 424–25; contradictions in, 449; feminine and masculine roles in, 341, 343–44; military conception of, 116; as organized, 25; women's oppression in, 449, 494; women's place in, 339–44
solitude: mitigation of, 9; of self, 11; of soul, 7–8

soul(s): and freedom, 238; rights of individual, 7; as true origin of emancipation, 16

South: Anglo-Saxons and, 157–58, 162; and colored women's disfranchisement, 244, 251; first NAWSA convention held in, 143; has bulk of Negro population, 156–57; Nineteenth Amendment and, 230; political supremacy effort of, 157, 161–62; restricted suffrage and, 160–62, 255; and woman's enfranchisement, 157–58, 160–62, 185–86, 221–22

sovereignty, 3, 15

Soviet Union: feminism and, 350; social responsibility and, 411; women's accomplishments in, 431–32; women's independence in, 423

Spengler, Oswald, 416

spirit: feminine, 249; of Internationalism, 457

spiritual, 24, 40; art as, 45–46; in education, 52; expansion, 39; feminism as, 26; force, 22; force in Settlements, 111; freedom, 25; influence of women, 278, 292; superiority of women, 277, 465; woman's movement as, 39

Staël, Maame de, 12–13

standard of living, war erodes, 492

Stanton, Elizabeth Cady, 3, 141, 149, 169, 425; contributions of, 430–31

Stanton, Mrs. Harriet, 252

Starr, Ellen Gate, 97, 99

state(s): against suffrage, 200; constitutional amendments, 201–2, 203; Department of Labor, 388; election laws and Nineteenth Amendment, 255; family as miniature, 191, 477; labor laws, 312; laws against women, 294–95, 326–27; legislature, 173–76, 199, 319; social reform in, 194–95; suffrage, 163–64, 173, 199, 255; voting and Southern, 156–58; and wage laws, 307, 442; Wisconsin, 290–92

Stevens, Doris, 150

Stone, Lucy, 141, 169

Stone, Mrs. J. Austin, 332

street meetings, 176

strike(s), 353, 413, 430; coal miner, 400–402; in garment industry, 345, 355, 357–61, 402; jail and, 358–59, 402, 403; for peace, 454, 482–84, 490; at Triangle factory, 363; violence during, 402–3

students, female radical, 454

submissions, old social doctrines and new, 37

suffrage, 4; African American, 157, 164; amendments, corruption and, 200–201; argument against women, 163–69; convention for, 235–37; corruption against, 200; democrats and blocking of, 180; eccentric theories of feminism and, 12; educated, 160; effects on women, 167–68; equal, 45; feminism and, 23, 96, 103; foreign countries and, 204; and lack of militancy, 187; liquor proponents against, 199–200; mental attitude change in, 198–99, 202; militancy to secure, 205, 209–10; movement and YWCA, 193; national elections and effect on, 180–81; new test for, 167; outside of U.S., 164; overthrow of home with equal, 188; picketing, 208–9; poem, 215–16; politics and women's, 264; propaganda to promote, 176–78; race problem and national, 185–86; social reform and, 194–95; socialism and, 188–89, 364, 415; South and, 156–58, 160–62, 186, 255; standards of domestic life and, 18; state, 163–64, 173–74, 199; states against, 200; support for political party, 204; Swedish Suffrage Association and, 204–5; teacher vote and, 194; triple alliance against, 199–200; women against, 164; women's fight for, 141–51, 163–65; worldwide, 272. *See also* National American Woman Suffrage Association (NAWSA)

suffragette: difference between suffragist and, 171–72; militant, 148, 150

Suffragist, The, 146, 150, 219–21

suffragists, African American, 147

suffragist(s), American, 4, 146; all socialists are, 188–89; and Declaration of Independence, 237; demands of younger, 17–18; difference between suffragette and, 171–72; evolution of, 16; feminist v., 23, 41; imprisonment of, 208; in jail, 212–13; radicalism of young, 16; U.S. Constitution and, 237; use of militant tactics by, 145, 150

suffragists, British, 145, 150

Sunset, 232

Susan B. Anthony Amendment, The, 147; content of, 183–85

Swanson, Gloria, 232

Swarthout, Gladys, 327

sweaters, 122, 123, 125. *See also* consumers; manufacturers

Swedish Suffrage Association, 204

Swerdlow, Amy, 454

Swift, Mary Wood, 143

Taft, Jessie, 49–50
Taft and Hartley, 428
Talbot, Marion, 47
taxation: ballot and, 193; on property, 152; without representation, 163, 490
Taylor, Eleanor, 103–4
teacher(s), 61; married women, 274; votes and, 194; women, 258. *See also* colleges; education
teamwork, women and, 76
technology, freedom and, 448
tenement housing, 115, 116, 128
Terrell, Mary Church, 347
terrorism, 31
Thomas, M. Carey, 47–48, 337
Thompson, Dorothy, 453
Thompson, Maud, 5
thought(s): new, 36; originality of, 65
Toynee Hall, 97
trade union(s): benefits of, 320; ERA and, 330; and freedom of contract, 310; for labor laws, 398; theoretical feminists for, 310–11. *See also* unions
tradition(s): based on past, 49; unhampered growth out of, 15–16
training: of girls, 467–69; in military, 497; of women, 10, 474
Treaty of Peace, 387, 398
"Triangle Fire, The," 346, 361–63
tribe, as political unit, 419
Truman, Harry, 336
truth, seeking of, 24, 25
Truth, Sojourner, 147
Tuttle, Florence, 5–6
tyranny: social, 417, 423; war and, 460

UE. *See* United Electrical, Radio, and Machine Workers of America (UE)
unemployment: hunger and, 406, 407; women and, 404–8
union(s): capitalism and, 448; colored women and, 374, 408–9; excluding women, 388–90, 472; and freedom of contract, 310; garment industry, 346, 357–58; Great Depression and, 349; miner, 400; scabs, 401; and wages, 442; white slavery and, 367. *See also* collective bargaining; *specific unions*; trade unions
United Electrical, Radio, and Machine Workers of America (UE), 433–34
United Negro Improvement Association (UNIA), 231

universities, as center of civilization, 462
unorganized women, 273–74
unskilled labor. *See* manufacturers

values, changing social, 169
Van Kleeck, Mary, 348
Victory Convention, The, 235–37
Vietnam War, 454, 490; call to end, 488–90; Woman Suffrage Party and, 491; women against, 492
violence, 492; as means of vengeance, 460; during protests, 455, 494; during strikes, 402–3. *See also* militants; rape
vocational training, 130
voluntary motherhood. *See* birth control
Voluntary Parenthood League, 229, 243
volunteer armed forces, 495, 501
volunteer work, suffrage and, 178
voter(s): alien or illiterate, 159–60; educated, 158–59; school system rests on, 155; turnout of women, 232, 283; winning of, 217–18
voting, 105; Black women's rights and, 228, 229–30; for children, 190–91; citizenship beyond, 97; colored women and, 190; to end war, 246; as fetish, 16; foreign countries and, 160, 204, 206; housewives and, 196–97; humiliation of women regarding, 201; ideals v., 168–69; immigrants and, 105, 158–59, 160, 164, 201; Indians and, 159; literature and, 189–90; mothers and, 190; old type, 35; for philanthropy, 195–96; property qualification and, 201; Southern states and, 156–58; teachers and, 194; as weapons of politics, 217, 221; women's power in, 229, 263, 265, 266; women's right to, 3, 99, 260, 263, 365, 402; women's turnout, 232; worldwide, 272. *See also* ballots; elections

WAAC. *See* Women's Auxiliary Army Corps (WAAC)
Wage-Earners' Suffrage League, 179
wage(s), 124, 318; for colored women, 374–75, 377–78, 379, 412; laws, 300, 307, 309–10, 335, 337; in manufacturing, 379; men's v. women's, 155–56, 280, 309–10, 329, 375, 412, 434–37, 439, 442, 443–44; minimum laws and feminism, 399; for mothers, 137–39; state laws and, 442; suffrage and, 169–70; unions and, 442; during war, 399; white slavery and, 366–67; for women, 398–99, 434, 435, 439; women's low, 439, 440

Wage Stabilization Board, 435n1
Wagner Act. *See* National Labor Relations Act
war, 66, 458; affect on farming, 481–82; affect on feminism, 268; affect on jobs, 374, 379, 394–95; affect on women, 455, 461, 466, 492; catharsis of, 465; cause of, 460, 461, 462, 477; civilized, 68, 69; compulsory service during, 453; crime of, 480; demobilization after, 387–88, 395; as disease, 461, 477; in England, 471; financing, 268; government jobs during, 368; group aggression and, 49; heroics of, 466; industries and women, 328–29, 394–95, 453; in Korea, 480–82; lawlessness and, 477; masculinity of, 67; obscene naturalness of, 43; occupations of women during, 394, 453; pacifism and, 478; primitive, 67, 68; reconstruction after, 386–87; sacrifices and demands in, 207, 303; segregation during, 347, 371; sociobiological explanation of, 453; tyranny and, 460; voting to end, 246; wages during, 399; waste of, 79; women's affect on, 459, 471; women's exclusion in, 70. *See also* combat; government; politics; Revolutionary War; Vietnam War; World War I; World War II; World War III
warfare, psychological, 473
War Labor Board of World War II, 435n1, 440
War Risk Insurance Bureau, 369
Washington, Booker, 100, 383
Washington, Margaret Murray, 100
WAVES, Navy, 453, 498
wealth, 97, 98; redistribution of, 447
weapons, 211, 221; of mass destruction, 480
welfare legislation, 227, 295
Wells-Barnett, Ida, 143, 147
Wells, Bettina Borrman, 145
Wells, Marguerite M., 330
West, suffrage in, 182
white: poor, 157; supremacy, 161; women's movement, 230. *See also* Anglo-Saxons
White, Thomas H., 385
White Goods Workers Union, 263
White House: banner for, 211; excuses for picketing, 208–9; military zone around, 211
white label, 101, 127
White League of South, 256
white list. *See* Consumers' League of New York City
widows as mothers, 132–36
Widow's Pension Law, 102–3, 133

Williams, Fannie Barrier, 99–100
Wilson, Dagmar, 454
Wilson, Woodrow, 146, 147, 149, 452; jailed suffragists and, 150; women against, 261
Winsor, Mary, 254
Wisconsin Equal Rights Law, 284–85, 290–92; text of, 290
wives, enlisted men's, 499–50, 502. *See also* housewives
Woman and the New Race (Sanger), 229
Woman Citizen, The, 232
Woman's Committee of the Council of National Defense, 149, 206
Woman's Journal, 142
Woman's Movement: Alice Paul in, 242; collapse of, 279; equality v. difference in, 284–87; labor movement and, 87–88, 89; through depression and war, 232, 282; true work of, 22; viewed from many angles, 37–38
Woman's Municipal League of Boston, 102, 127, 129, 131
Woman's Party, National: African American women at, 230–31; creation of, 219–21; for Equal Rights Amendment, 293–95; as nonpartisan, 217–18
Woman's Peace Party, 149; founding of, 452; program for constructive, 456–57
Woman's Republican Club, 253
Woman's Status Bill, 281
Woman Suffrage amendment, 174
Woman Suffrage Party (WSP), 145; activities of, 173–79; aim/structure of, 172; education for civic life and, 178; legislative work of, 174–76; political district plan of, 172–79; political work of, 173–74; reform and, 178–79; Vietnam War and, 491
women, African American, 142, 147; voting rights of, 229–30
women, colored: AFL, CIO and, 408–9; in agriculture, 378–79, 381; B. J. Jones as helper to, 221–22; carrying destiny of two races, 192; clubs of, 195; in domestic service, 377–78; in government, 367–73; in industry, 379–80; living conditions of, 375–76; in manufacturing, 373–74, 376, 379–80; occupations for, 377–80, 441; reform and, 192; segregation of, 374, 375; as superior in moral responsibility, 192; unions and, 374, 408–9; vote and, 190; wages for, 374–75, 377–78, 379, 412. *See also* Negroes; plantation women; sexes

women, defined, 427
Women in Industry Service, 388
Women's Auxiliary Army Corps (WAAC), 453, 472, 474, 496
Women's Bureau: State Department of Labor, 388; in U.S. Department of Labor, 286, 320, 348, 379, 391–94; on women's wages, 399
Women's Charter, 286–87; purpose of, 317–18; text of, 315–316
Women's Committee for Industrial Equality, 389, 390
women's consciousness, 446
women's liberation movement, 454, 492
women's movement: difference v. equality in, 284–87; divided, 446; strategy for, 445–46
Women's Political Union, 183
Women's Rights Convention, 425
Women's Trade Union League (WTUL), 179, 306, 333; founding of, 345; Triangle Fire and, 362; on women in unions, 389
Women Strike for Peace (WSP), 454
work: African Americans and, 347, 370; ballot and, 192–93; brain v. brute, 43; combined with life, 87–88; conditions, 375–76, 379; desire of women to, 417; governmental regulations for, 101; happiness in, 420; Japanese and, 45; marriage v., 49–50, 82–84, 422, 429; maternity leave from, 103; repetition and drudgery of, 74; right to, 27–28; for sake of independence, 46; socially productive, 38; unnatural v. natural, 90, 95; World War I and women at, 206–7. *See also* career; economic independence; employment; labor laws

worker(s): clubs for, 376–77; against ERA, 299–300; health and safety, 392–93, 445; power of, 355
Workhouse, conditions at, 213, 215
working class: capitalism and, 410, 415; drudgery of, 115; empowerment of, 5; freedom, 410; heterogeneous, 450; hostility towards middle class, 30; legislation, 415; in military, 501; organizing of, 106
Working Woman, The, 408
work place discrimination, 234
World War I, 4, 149; affect on women, 41–42, 282; NAWSA and, 205–8; woman question and, 37
World War II: ERA and, 287; Great Depression and, 234; military women in, 453
World War III, 454, 481
WSP. *See* Woman Suffrage Party
WTUL. *See* Women's Trade Union League
Wyatt, Sophia, 454

Young, Rose, 4–5, 26
Young Women's Christian Association. *See* YWCA
youth(s): education as waste to, 108–9; fatal want of, 106; sense of uselessness, 109; solitude of, 8
YWCA, 193–94, 376; employment agencies and, 405; ERA and, 287, 299, 332; factory workers and, 376–77; suffrage movement and, 193; unique characteristics of, 193; women in industry and, 394

Zetkin, Clara, 416
Zigas, Irma, 491

About the Editors

Dawn Keetley is assistant professor of English at Lehigh University and teaches nineteenth-century and twentieth-century U.S. literature, women's studies, and American studies. She is currently working on a book-length project entitled *The Othello Complex: The Invention of Men's Homicidal Jealousy in Nineteenth-Century America* and has published articles on antebellum literature and culture in numerous journals, including *American Quarterly, Emerson Society Quarterly,* and *Legacy: A Journal of Women Writers.*

John Pettegrew teaches modern U.S. history and directs the American studies program at Lehigh University. He is currently completing a book entitled *Brutes in Suits: The De-Evolutionary Origins of American Masculinity*. He also edited and wrote the introduction and a chapter for *A Pragmatist's Progress? Richard Rorty and American Intellectual History*.